LATINOS
in the
UNITED STATES

LATINOS
in the
UNITED STATES

A Historical Bibliography

Albert Camarillo
Editor

ABC-CLIO
Santa Barbara, California
Oxford, England

Library of Congress Cataloging-in-Publication Data

Latinos in the United States.
   (ABC-Clio research guides)
   Includes index.
   1. Hispanic Americans—History—Bibliography.
I. Camarillo, Albert.   II. Series.
Z1361.S7L37   1986   [E184.S75]   016.973'0468   86-26448
ISBN 0-87436-458-2

*This book is Smyth sewn and printed on acid-free paper to
meet library standards* ∞.

ABC-Clio, Inc.
2040 Alameda Padre Serra, Box 4397
Santa Barbara, California 93140-4397

Clio Press Ltd.
55 St. Thomas Street
Oxford, OX1 1JG, England

Manufactured in the United States of America.

ABC-CLIO RESEARCH GUIDES

The ABC-CLIO Research Guides are designed to provide convenient coverage of the recent journal literature on high-interest topics in history and the related social sciences. These annotated bibliographies are prepared by subject specialists and editor/historians from ABC-CLIO's comprehensive data bases.

The unique subject profile index (ABC-SPIndex), that carries both generic and specific index terms, presents a profile of the indexed article, allowing precise and rapid access to the entries.

The titles in this series are prepared to save researchers, students, and librarians the considerable time and expense usually associated with accessing materials manually or through online searching. ABC-CLIO's Research Guides offer unmatched reference to significant scholarly articles on the topics of most current interest to historians and social scientists.

ABC-CLIO RESEARCH GUIDES

The American Electorate

American Family History

American Maritime History

Corporate America

Crime and Punishment

The Democratic and Republican
   Parties

The Dynamic Constitution

Global Terrorism

The Great Depression

The Jewish Experience in America

Latinos in the United States

Nuclear America

Sino-Soviet Conflict

The Third Reich

The Third Reich at War

The United States in East Asia

The Weimar Republic

Women in the Third World

World War II from an American
   Perspective

CONTENTS

LIST OF ABBREVIATIONS viii

INTRODUCTION ix

1. Historiography, Bibliography, and
   an Overview 1
2. Colonization and Settlement,
   up to 1848 27
3. People from Mexico 78
   1848 to 1900 99
   1900 to 1945 117
   1945 to 1985 138
4. People from the Caribbean, Central
   America, and South America 205

   Subject Index 257
   Author Index 327

LIST OF ABBREVIATIONS

A.	Author-prepared Abstract	*Illus.*	Illustrated, Illustration
Acad.	Academy, Academie, Academia	*Inst.*	Institute, Institut-.
Agric.	Agriculture, Agricultural	*Int.*	International, Internacional,
AIA	Abstracts in Anthropology		Internationaal, Internationaux,
Akad.	Akademie		Internazionale
Am.	America, American	*J.*	Journal, Journal-prepared Abstract
Ann.	Annals, Annales, Annual, Annali	*Lib.*	Library, Libraries
Anthrop.	Anthropology, Anthropological	*Mag.*	Magazine
Arch.	Archives	*Mus.*	Museum, Musee, Museo
Archaeol.	Archaeology, Archaeological	*Nac.*	Nacional
Art.	Article	*Natl.*	National, Nationale
Assoc.	Association, Associate	*Naz.*	Nazionale
Biblio.	Bibliography, Bibliographical	*Phil.*	Philosophy, Philosophical
Biog.	Biography, Biographical	*Photo.*	Photograph
Bol.	Boletim, Boletin	*Pol.*	Politics, Political, Politique, Politico
Bull.	Bulletin	*Pr.*	Press
c.	century (in index)	*Pres.*	President
ca.	circa	*Pro.*	Proceedings
Can.	Canada, Canadian, Canadien	*Publ.*	Publishing, Publication
Cent.	Century	*Q.*	Quarterly
Coll.	College	*Rev.*	Review, Revue, Revista, Revised
Com.	Committee	*Riv.*	Rivista
Comm.	Commission	*Res.*	Research
Comp.	Compiler	*RSA*	Romanian Scientific Abstracts
DAI	Dissertation Abstracts	*S.*	Staff-prepared Abstract
	International	*Sci.*	Science, Scientific
Dept.	Department	*Secy.*	Secretary
Dir.	Director, Direktor	*Soc.*	Society, Societe, Sociedad,
Econ.	Economy, Econom-.		Societa
Ed.	Editor, Edition	*Sociol.*	Sociology, Sociological
Educ.	Education, Educational	*Tr.*	Transactions
Geneal.	Genealogy, Genealogical,	*Transl.*	Translator, Translation
	Genealogique	*U.*	University, Universi-.
Grad.	Graduate	*US*	United States
Hist.	History, Hist-.	*Vol.*	Volume
IHE	Indice Historico Espanol	*Y.*	Yearbook

INTRODUCTION

More so than any other period in U.S. history, the 1980s has witnessed an increasing awareness of the nation's second largest ethnic minority—*Latinos*.[1] This awareness is attributable, in part, to the dramatic increase in the Latino population within the United States in recent decades and the corresponding media coverage. While many Americans may think of Latinos as a people who are products of recent immigration—due to the representation in newspapers, magazines, and on television—the fact is that Latinos as a group have long been a part of America's history.

Beginning in the 1970s, a growing number of scholars from various disciplines began to focus their research on Mexican Americans, Puerto Ricans, Cuban Americans, and other Latino peoples in the United States. This process of intellectual rediscovery for groups previously ignored in American history produced a substantial body of scholarship over the past decade and a half. To be sure, many specialized as well as general bibliographies were published on Latino groups, but few provided citations covering all the Hispanic-origin populations in the United States. To fill the need for bibliographic materials that provide coverage for Latinos of different national origins in the United States, ABC-CLIO has published *LATINOS IN THE UNITED STATES: A HISTORICAL BIBLIOGRAPHY*.

This bibliography contains 1382 citations expertly drawn from dozens of volumes of *AMERICA: HISTORY AND LIFE* published between 1973 and 1985. The entries represent a diversity of disciplinary and interdisciplinary studies taken primarily from the humanities and social sciences. The proliferation of research on Latinos in recent years is aptly reflected in the volume of entries published since 1975.

---

1 *Latino* is a term that refers to all Spanish-origin or Hispanic peoples in the United States. Unlike the term *Hispanic*—a label employed by the federal government in the 1970s to encompass all Spanish-origin subgroups—*Latino* has been used for many decades by various national-origin groups from Central and South America and the Spanish-speaking nations of the Caribbean who reside in the United States. The major Latino-origin subgroups include Mexicans, Puerto Ricans, Cubans, and a host of other smaller populations with roots in the Spanish-speaking nations of the Americas. The 1980 U.S. census outlines these groups, their approximate numbers, and the percentage of the total Latino population in the United States as follows: (1) Mexicans—8,858,000 or 61 percent; (2) Puerto Ricans—2,114,000 or 14.5 percent; (3) Cubans—960,000 or 7 percent; and (4) all other Latino nationality groups—2,675,000 or 18 percent.

LATINOS IN THE UNITED STATES is organized by chapters containing entries arranged according to national origin groups. With the exception of Chapter I, which includes general materials on Latinos (historiography, bibliographies, archives and collections, general histories, etc.), chapters II through IV focus on Mexican Americans; Puerto Ricans, Cubans, and other Caribbeans; and Central and South Americans. There is an emphasis in Chapter II on the movement of all Latinos in the borderlands prior to 1848. Not surprisingly, the majority of abstracts relate to Mexicans and Mexican Americans and, to a lesser extent, Puerto Ricans—the two largest U.S. Latino subgroups.

Hundreds of topics are included in this bibliographic collection. On Mexican Americans alone, for example, articles and books address histories of Spanish exploration and settlement of northern New Spain; the cultural and social adaptation of Mexican Americans in the wake of the Mexican War; immigration from Mexico; current employment and population studies; and information on language, education, and health. Contemporary as well as historical studies are well represented. In addition, the entries on Puerto Ricans, Cubans, and other Caribbean Latinos include studies concerning domestic conditions on the islands as well as international relations and diplomacy. The broad scope and diversity of *LATINOS IN THE UNITED STATES* make it a useful resource for students, research scholars, reference librarians, and general readers alike.

ABC-CLIO produces numerous bibliographies on specialized topics, including several on American ethnic minorities. This newest bibliography is a contribution to the enterprise of providing effective reference tools for those readers and researchers interested in the nation's second largest and fastest growing ethnic group.

Stanford University   ALBERT CAMARILLO

1

HISTORIOGRAPHY, BIBLIOGRAPHY, AND AN OVERVIEW

1. Ahlborn, Richard E. THE HISPANIC HORSEMAN: A SAMPLING OF HORSE GEAR FROM THE FRED HARVEY COLLECTION. *Palacio 1983 89(2): 12-21.* The Fred Harvey collection of items from Spanish and Indian culture, now in Albuquerque's Museum of New Mexico, contains Hispanic horsemen's gear.

2. Alcalay, Rina. HISPANIC WOMEN IN THE UNITED STATES: FAMILY AND WORK RELATIONS. *Migration Today 1984 12(3): 13-20.* Discusses the differences among Mexican-American, Puerto Rican, and Cuban-American women in terms of immigration patterns, occupations, and socioeconomic status.

3. Almaráz, Félix D., Jr. THE STATUS OF BORDERLANDS STUDIES: HISTORY. *Soc. Sci. J. 1976 12(3): 9-18.* Traces the historiography of the US-Mexican border, 1812-1975.

4. Apodaca, Maria Linda. THE CHICANA WOMAN: AN HISTORICAL MATERIALIST PERSPECTIVE. *Latin Am. Perspectives 1977 4(1-2): 70-89.* Critiques the treatment of the Chicana by most Chicano historiography and points out the need for a class analysis. Also, traces the important historic roots of the Chicana's subjugation from Aztec society, through Spanish and Mexican feudalism, to the division of labor in the capitalist mode of production. Thesis is complemented by a biographical essay on an immigrant woman.
J. L. Dietz

5. Armitage, Shelley. NEW MEXICO'S LITERARY HERITAGE. *Palacio 1984 90(2): 20-29.* New Mexico's literature reflects its rich Hispanic, Indian, and Anglo cultural traditions.

6. Arora, Shirley L. A CRITICAL BIBLIOGRAPHY OF MEXICAN AMERICAN PROVERBS. *Aztlán 1982 13(1-2): 71-80.* Surveys compilations of Mexican-American proverbs in books and articles, describing them in terms of quantity, sources, quality of translation, and accuracy. Cautions that some studies have attempted English-language equivalencies where meaning is thereby distorted. Some language translations are better than others. Compila-

tions are arranged regionally and include California, New Mexico, Texas, and Mexico, with proverbs ranging from a few dozen to 12,500.   A. Hoffman

7.   Arriaga Weiss, David; Teja Angeles, Ileana de la; and Sainz Chávez, Luis. ESTADOS UNIDOS: CINCO REALIDADES CONTEMPORANEAS (HEMEROGRAFIA) [United States: five present-day realities (survey of periodicals)]. *Rev. Mexicana de Ciencias Pol. y Sociales [Mexico] 1981 27(104-105): 239-256.* Lists 238 titles illustrating periodical material available in the Faculty of Political and Social Sciences of the Universidad Nacional Autónoma de Mexico and covering five topics: Chicanos and educational policy in the United States; US participation in the Afghan and Middle Eastern conflicts; the energy crisis; US international relations; and domestic conflict in the United States.   J. V. Coutinho

8.   Arroyo, Luis Leobardo. NOTES ON PAST, PRESENT AND FUTURE DIRECTIONS OF CHICANO LABOR STUDIES. *Aztlán 1976 6(2): 137-149.* Early studies of Chicano labor were of the impact of Mexican immigrants on the US economy. Paul Taylor and Manuel Gamio pioneered a new approach which enlarged the field. Recent studies view Mexican Americans as active rather than passive agents in labor history. A critique of articles contained in this issue reveals that Chicano labor history is weak in conceptualization and too narrow in scope. 11 notes.   R. Griswold del Castillo

9.   Bannon, John Francis. THE MISSION AS A FRONTIER INSTITUTION: SIXTY YEARS OF INTEREST AND RESEARCH. *Western Hist. Q. 1979 10(3): 303-322.* Herbert Eugene Bolton's 1917 faculty research lecture at the University of California at Berkeley, subsequently printed and reprinted several times, became "a veritable seed piece." Entitled "The Mission as a Frontier Institution in the Spanish American Colonies," it continues to affect the study of the Spanish Borderlands history. Reviews a selection of the historiography of the subject under several headings: geographic areas, missions, missions and protection, missions and civilization/Hispanicization, and scholars other than historians who study missions. Selected biblio.
D. L. Smith

10.   Barrera, Mario. THE STUDY OF POLITICS AND THE CHICANO. *Aztlán 1974 5(1/2): 9-26.* Study of Mexican Americans by non-Chicano scholars points to the need for a redefinition of the study of politics, including theory and methodology.   S

11.   Benjamin, Thomas. RECENT HISTORIOGRAPHY OF THE ORIGINS OF THE MEXICAN WAR. *New Mexico Hist. Rev. 1979 54(3): 169-181.* Surveys the continuing trends and new interpretations since the mid-1960's. Three basic interpretations are discussed, including the Whig thesis, which held that President James K. Polk (1795-1849) was responsible for the war, and the Democratic thesis, which maintained that Mexico was to blame. A third group of studies, which transcends the Whig-Democratic argument, is more evenhanded and significantly improves the quality of Mexican War historiography. A closer look at the origins of the Mexican War is essential to

the study of American expansionism and of Mexican and Hispanic-American politics and national character. 48 notes.   P. L. McLaughlin

12. Bryce-Laporte, Roy S. VISIBILITY OF THE NEW IMMIGRANTS. *Society 1977 14(6): 18-22.* Discusses legal immigration in the United States, 1965-77, including Latin and Caribbean groups as well as those from Indochina; examines provisions of the Immigration Act (1965) and the impact which has been felt, especially in American daily life and popular culture.

13. Cardoso, Lawrence A. ARCHIVAL SOURCES IN MEXICO FOR THE STUDY OF CHICANO HISTORY. *New Scholar 1978 7(1-2): 255-258.* A survey of the documents held in the Historical Archive of the Secretary of Foreign Relations (AHSRE), Mexico City, which cover Chicano history 1900-39, and include reports regarding investigations and protests during strikes, the draft crisis of World War I, the organization of labor unions and affiliations with radical groups, working conditions, and the welfare of expatriates and their families. Also gives information about the use of the archive and lists the five main categories which contain information on Chicano history; Ramo de la Revolución Mexicana, 1910-20; Ramo Flores Magón, 1904-20's; Legajos de Numeración Corrida; Recortes de Periódicos; and Servicios Culturales de la Secretaría de Relaciones Exteriores. Based on the collections held in the Historical Archive of the Secretary of Foreign Relations, Mexico City; 5 notes.   G. L. Neville

14. Chiswick, Barry R. IMMIGRANTS IN THE U.S. LABOR MARKET. *Ann. of the Am. Acad. of Pol. and Social Sci. 1982 (460): 64-72.* Relative to the population, immigration has increased fivefold since the trough of the 1930's, and in recent years the annual legal inflow has been about 2.2 immigrants per year per thousand population. In the past 15 years, Europe and Canada have declined in importance as sources of immigrants, while Asia, Latin America, and the Caribbean have increased in importance. Illegal immigration has also increased. Overall, adult male immigrants earn about the same as the adult male native-born population, but important differences among the foreign born are attributable to duration of residence in the United States, reason for migrating, and country of origin. On arrival, immigrants have low earnings compared with native born, but with increased length of U.S. residence, their earnings rise. Economic migrants reach earnings equality with the native born when they have been in the United States for about 11 to 15 years. Refugees and tied movers have lower earnings than those who move for economic reasons. Illegal aliens from Mexico have labor market characteristics very similar to those of legal immigrants from Mexico.   J

15. Colgan, Susan. AT HOME WITH THE FOLK ART OF NEW MEXICO: A SANCTUARY FOR SANTOS. *Am. Art and Antiques 1979 2(5): 56-63.* Discusses the New Mexican religious folk art of the 17th-19th centuries on display at the *morada* near Taos, New Mexico.

16. Cooney, Rosemary Santana and Ortiz, Vilma. NATIVITY, NATIONAL ORIGIN, AND HISPANIC FEMALE PARTICIPATION IN THE LABOR FORCE. *Social Sci. Q. 1983 64(3): 510-523.* Integration into the work force

by Puerto Rican, Mexican, and Cuban women is more influenced by their place of birth (United States or foreign) than their national origin, and when national origin is an important factor, it has a larger effect on foreign-born women.

17.   Cordasco, Francesco. BILINGUAL AND BICULTURAL EDUCA-TION IN AMERICAN SCHOOLS: A BIBLIOGRAPHY OF SELECTED REFERENCES. *Bull. of Biblio. and Mag. Notes 1978 35(2): 53-72.* Offers an extensive list of publications on bicultural-bilingual education, including references to important journals and documents of special value.

18.   Cordasco, Francesco. BILINGUAL EDUCATION: AN AMERICAN DILEMMA. *Immigration Hist. Newsletter 1978 10(1): 5-8.* Bilingual education must blend with the aspirations of the ethnic groups which it serves in order to be of the greatest value to the community and the country.

19.   Cordasco, Francesco. BILINGUAL EDUCATION IN AMERICAN SCHOOLS: A BIBLIOGRAPHICAL ESSAY. *Immigration Hist. Newsletter 1982 14(1): 1-8.* Bibliographic essay of publications on elementary bilingual education, 1970's, including an alphabetical listing by author of works cited.

20.   Corwin, Arthur F. MEXICAN-AMERICAN HISTORY: AN ASSESS-MENT. *Pacific Hist. R. 1973 42(3): 269-308.* Surveys research in Mexican-American history under the headings "General Histories," "Topical Studies and Present Research Needs," and "The Present State of Mexican-American Ethnic History." Carey McWilliams' *North From Mexico* (Lippincott, 1949) heads the list of general histories as "an inspired synthesis of the Mexican-American heritage." Mexican- American history still lacks the annotated compilations and reference works now available for black history. Reviews works on borderland history and Mexican immigration, noting a lack of research on the Southwest under Mexico, 1821-48, and on the influence of borderland confrontation on the development of race consciousness. There is also a need for "incisive studies in historical demography." Concludes by discussing the current academic split between the "establishment school," which seeks to integrate Mexican-American history into national history, and "La Raza" school, which seeks a more exclusivist history of "The People." 60 notes.   B. L. Fenske

21.   Costas, Orlando E. ECUMENICAL EXPERIENCES OF AN HISPAN-IC BAPTIST. *J. of Ecumenical Studies 1980 17(2): 118-124.* The author describes his experiences in multidenominational Hispanic organizations and in ecumenical organizations such as the National Council of Churches or the World Council of Churches from the perspective of a Hispanic Baptist. His appointment as minister to various multidenominational churches provides an interesting view of local ecumenism.   J. A. Overbeck

22.   Days, Drew S., III. SEEKING A NEW CIVIL RIGHTS CONSENSUS. *Daedalus 1983 112(4): 197-216.* Despite achievements since 1954, discrimination against such groups as blacks, Asians, Hispanics, women, and the disabled

still exists in the United States, and the momentum in the civil rights movement has slowed.

23. DelaIsla, José. THE POLITICS OF REELECTION: SE HABLA ES-PAÑOL. *Aztlán 1976 7(3): 427-451.* Traces the growing power of Hispanic Americans in elections and the appeal of Richard M. Nixon's administration for their support; the policy of revenue sharing meant that federal funds would no longer flow directly to Hispanic groups, so to reduce opposition the administration channeled grants to key Spanish-speaking groups and Republican sympathizers in time to influence the election of 1972.

24. delaTeja Angeles, Ileana. HEMEROGRAFIA CHICANA SOBRE MEDIOS DE COMUNICACION MASIVA [A survey of Chicano periodicals on mass communications media]. *Rev. Mexicana de Ciencias Pol. y Sociales [Mexico] 1981 27(104-105): 257-266.* This list of 99 titles is the first step toward a survey of Chicanos and the mass media, especially of the present situation, possibilities, and prospects of Chicano studies in the field. Based on Chicano and Hispanic publications in the University of California libraries at Berkeley, Los Angeles, and Riverside. J. V. Coutinho

25. Deloria, Vine, Jr. IDENTITY AND CULTURE. *Daedalus 1981 110(2): 13-27.* Traces the current social and economic inequities suffered by blacks, Puerto Ricans, Mexican Americans, and Indians in the United States back to the destruction of their legal rights in the last decade of the 19th century, and suggests that, in spite of gains made in the 20th century, these nonwhite minorities, in their pursuit of traditional American values, are in danger of losing their own historical and cultural identity.

26. Duty, Michael. MAPPING THE SOUTHWEST: EXPLORATION, LEGEND, AND PLAGIARISM. *Am. West. 1981 18(3): 48-54.* A unique blend of history, art, and science, maps picture much more than a geographic area. They reflect a culture at a particular time, the limits of its knowledge, and the extent of its conceptual sophistication. Cartographers filled in blanks on their maps with any information they could get, often secondhand. Myths and misperceptions were often propagated. Sixteenth-century maps tell much of the contemporary illusion and reality about the American Southwest. Later, European sea power competition kept cartographers busy, often freely copying the works of their competitors, errors and all. Increased firsthand observation, improved methods of measuring, and better printing techniques made maps more reliable. Inaccuracies still persist in modern maps, but to a significantly lesser degree. Maps help document the history of varied contributions from numerous cultures in the American Southwest. 5 illus. D. L. Smith

27. Edwards, J. R. CURRENT ISSUES IN BILINGUAL EDUCATION. *Ethnicity 1976 3(1): 70-81.* The administration and goals of bilingual education programs in American public schools during 1968-76 stressed local support and adequate appreciation of individual needs.

28. Ellis, Richard N. HISPANIC AMERICANS AND INDIANS IN NEW MEXICO STATE POLITICS. *New Mexico Hist. Rev. 1978 53(4): 361-364.*

Gives the historical background of the participation of Hispanic Americans and Indians in New Mexico politics from 1846 to 1976.

29. Engstrand, Iris Wilson. LAND GRANT PROBLEMS IN THE SOUTHWEST: THE SPANISH AND MEXICAN HERITAGE. *New Mexico Hist. Rev. 1978 53(4): 317-336.* Discusses the current conflict between Anglos and Hispanic Americans in New Mexico over land grants and land tenure, an issue which has been of importance since Spain's colonization in New Mexico beginning in the 16th century.

30. Ericksen, Charles A. HISPANIC AMERICANS AND THE PRESS. *J. of Intergroup Relations 1981 9(1): 3-16.* Discusses the problems of press perception confronting Hispanic Americans, and discusses six important areas in which the establishment press fails in its responsibility to Hispanics.

31. Espinosa, J. Manuel. SPANISH FOLKLORE IN THE SOUTHWEST: THE PIONEER STUDIES OF AURELIO M. ESPINOSA. *Americas (Acad. of Am. Franciscan Hist.) 1978 35(2): 219-237.* Reviews professional career of Aurelio M. Espinosa (1880-1958), himself of Spanish New Mexican descent, emphasizing his contribution to the preservation and study of his region's Spanish folklore, particularly northern New Mexico. Bibliography of Espinosa's writings on Spanish folklore and dialectology. 4 notes.   D. Bushnell

32. Estrada, Leobardo F. A DEMOGRAPHIC COMPARISON OF THE MEXICAN ORIGIN POPULATION IN THE MIDWEST AND SOUTHWEST. *Aztlán 1976 7(2): 203-234.* Compares data on Spanish-origin populations in the Southwest and Midwest, classified according to specific origin (Mexican, Puerto Rican, Cuban, and other) and according to state. Gives percentage of foreign born and native born, figures for US internal migration, age, education, marital status, employment of wives, income, and type of employment. There is net migration from Texas to the Midwest, where incomes for Spanish-origin persons are much higher, but also net migration from the Midwest to California, despite lower incomes there. New Mexico is singularly unaffected by migration to and from other states, and is also apparently characterized by an unusually widespread unwillingness among Mexican-origin persons to identify themselves as such. Concludes by listing many areas for further research. Based on 1970 US Census; 14 tables, 4 notes.
L. W. Van Wyk

33. Fitzpatrick, Joseph P. THE LATIN AMERICAN CHURCH IN THE UNITED STATES. *Thought 1984 59(233): 244-254.* Part of the rehispanization of North America is the growth of the Hispanic community within the Catholic Church. Surveys the Church's response to these social changes and the resulting cultural conflicts. Describes the institutions developed for the pastoral care of US Spanish-speaking Catholics. 16 notes.   R. Grove

34. Florez, John. HISPANICS IN THE 80'S: RETRENCHMENT OR SELF-RENEWAL? *J. of Intergroup Relations 1981 9(3): 31-34.* Examines the general political attitudes of Hispanic Americans during 1980-81, commenting on the need for a careful reconsideration of the social programs established for

Hispanics in the 1960's and 1970's and on the dangers of complacency for the progress of the Hispanic community.

35. Fragomen, Austin T., Jr. 1976 AMENDMENTS TO IMMIGRATION AND NATIONALITY ACT. *Int. Migration Rev. 1977 11(1): 95-100.* Criticizes the amendments for their strict curtailment of immigration from Mexico and the elimination from labor certification for parents of minor US citizen children.

36. Garcia, Jesus. HISPANIC PERSPECTIVE: TEXTBOOKS AND OTHER CURRICULAR MATERIALS. *Hist. Teacher 1980 14(1): 105-120.* Examines 10 textbooks on American history published in the late 1970's and reviews the coverage of Hispanic Americans since the 1960's. The historical coverage of Hispanic groups in textbooks has changed from omissions and superficial depictions to more balanced and sensitive treatments of minorities and immigrant groups. The author reviews films and other instructional materials dealing with the role of Hispanics in American history. Secondary sources; 2 tables, 23 notes.   S. H. Frank

37. García, Mario T. CHICANO HISTORY: AN ORAL HISTORY APPROACH. *J. of San Diego Hist. 1977 23(1): 46-54.* Reprints four interviews with Mexican Americans as part of a history and cultural project, 1974, and relates these to methods of teaching Chicano history.

38. Gómez-Quiñones, Juan and Arroyo, Luis Leobardo. ON THE STATE OF CHICANO HISTORY: OBSERVATIONS ON ITS DEVELOPMENT, INTERPRETATIONS, AND THEORY, 1970-1974. *Western Hist. Q. 1976 7(2): 155-185.* Discusses the recent development of Chicano history. Interest is increasing among Anglo, Mexican, and foreign scholars, but especially among Mexican Americans. The greatest emphasis is on the present century, particularly in social history, with focus on topical and local subjects. The concepts and methodologies of the modern social sciences are applicable to these efforts. Much remains relatively unexplored in all areas, but especially in pre-20th-century topics. Surveys the recent historiography, documentary publications, and methodological problems of Chicano history. 52 notes.   D. L. Smith

39. Grenier, Gilles. SHIFTS TO ENGLISH AS USUAL LANGUAGE BY AMERICANS OF SPANISH MOTHER TONGUE. *Social Sci. Q. 1984 65(2): 537-550.* Using a probit regression model, determines that age at migration, years since migration, choice of a non-Hispanic marriage partner, and education level are the most significant factors in shifts from Spanish to English.

40. Grijalva, Joshua. THE STORY OF HISPANIC SOUTHERN BAPTISTS. *Baptist Hist. and Heritage 1983 18(1): 40-47.* Recounts the establishment of Southern Baptist churches among Mexican-American and other Hispanic communities since 1839.

41. Griswold del Castillo, Richard. NEW PERSPECTIVES ON THE MEXICAN AND AMERICAN BORDERLANDS. *Latin American Research*

Review 1984 19(1): 199-209. Reviews David J. Weber's *The Mexican Frontier, 1821-1846: The American Southwest under Mexico* (1982), Robert J. Rosenbaum's *Mexicano Resistance in the Southwest: "The Sacred Right of Self-Preservation"* (1981), Arnoldo de León's *The Tejano Community, 1836-1900* (1982), Juan Gómez-Quiñones and David Maciel's *Al Norte del Río Bravo (Pasado Lejano, 1600-1930)* (1981), and David Maciel's *Al Norte del Río Bravo (Pasado Inmediato, 1930-1981)* (1981). These works represent new directions in borderlands scholarship, particularly the study of the influence of the Mexican nation on peoples living north of the Rio Grande and the analysis of daily life among people of Mexican background. They reveal clearly the necessity of genuinely integrated study, going beyond disciplinary and national boundaries. 6 notes.   J. K. Pfabe

42.   Griswold del Castillo, Richard. QUANTITATIVE HISTORY IN THE AMERICAN SOUTHWEST: A SURVEY AND CRITIQUE. *Western Hist. Q. 1984 15(4): 407-426.* Reviews published materials that have used quantitative methods and data as a principal source for investigation of American Southwest subjects. Surveys the main research directions and themes developed by scholars and predicts a steadily increasing output of published scholarship, especially on the social history of pueblos, haciendas, missions, presidios, and ranchos of the far northern frontiers of New Spain and Mexico. Mexican immigration, the development of border cities, and Mexican-American trade and investment relations are prime contemporary subject prospects for quantitative studies. 63 notes.   D. L. Smith

43.   Gritzner, Charles. HISPANIC LOG CONSTRUCTION OF NEW MEXICO. *Palacio 1979-80 85(4): 20-29.* Photographic essay of the log structures of New Mexico's Hispanic Americans, a little-known method, because emphasis has always been on adobe architecture. Structures were photographed during 1960's-70's. Briefly traces the history of New Mexico's log construction since 1756, when it was first documented.

44.   Gutiérrez, Félix. SPANISH-LANGUAGE MEDIA IN AMERICA: BACKGROUND, RESOURCES, HISTORY. *Journalism Hist. 1977 4(2): 34-41, 65-66.* Traces the development of the Spanish-language mass media in America, its present condition, and its contribution to US mass communications.

45.   Guzmán, Ralph C. CHICANO CONTROL OF CHICANO HISTORY: A REVIEW OF SELECTED LITERATURE. *California Hist. Q. 1973 52(2): 170-175.* Long neglected as a topic for historical research, Chicano history has recently attracted attention from scholars. Of interest are recent works by Chicano writers. The studies range in scope from Ernesto Galarza's nostalgic *Barrio Boy* to Rodolfo Acuna's militant *Occupied America.* Matt Meier and Feliciano Rivera have written a carefully balanced history, *The Chicanos.* Other topics are Cesar Chavez' farm workers' movement and police-Chicano confrontations. As more Chicanos are trained in historical methodology and research, they will rewrite Chicano history and focus on Anglo-American institutions through Chicano eyes. Illus., 4 notes.   A. Hoffman

46. Haghe, Howard. WORKING MOTHERS REACH RECORD NUM-BER IN 1984. *Monthly Labor Review 1984 107(12): 31-34.* During 1970-84, the percentage of mothers in the work force increased for women in all categories of marital status and age of children, while black mothers in 1984 were more likely to be employed than white or Hispanic mothers, with Hispanic mothers working least frequently.

47. Hayghe, Howard. MARRIED COUPLES: WORK AND INCOME PATTERNS. *Monthly Labor Rev. 1983 106(12): 26-29.* Differences in work patterns between husbands and wives in white, black, and Hispanic-American families account for differences in their respective family incomes.

48. Herrick, Robert L. CULTURAL ASPECTS OF PLACENAMES: NEW MEXICO. *Names 1983 31(4): 271-287.* Analysis of 13,879 place names in northern New Mexico reveals that Indian, Spanish, and Anglo cultures followed different patterns of adopting, modifying, or replacing existing place names; these patterns are a function of cultural attitudes.

49. Hewlett, Sylvia Ann. COPING WITH ILLEGAL IMMIGRANTS. *Foreign Affairs 1981-82 60(2): 358-378.* Examines the influx of illegal aliens and efforts of the Carter and Reagan administrations to control it; 1977-81.

50. Hill, Robert B. THE POLLS AND ETHNIC MINORITIES. *Ann. of the Am. Acad. of Pol. and Social Sci. 1984 (472): 155-166.* Polls have enhanced significantly the state of knowledge about the nature and degree of change in American public opinion on race relations. They have documented a steady and sharp decline in intolerant racial attitudes among whites over the past 40 years. Nevertheless, opinion polls on ethnic affairs are characterized by some deficiencies. The views of blacks are usually presented for the group as a whole without any breakdown by subgroup. Data on the attitudes of Hispanics, Asians, and Native Americans are sparse or nonexistent. Distinctions between beliefs and values are obscured. Indices of actual intolerant behavior are lacking. Shifts in relationships between prejudice and discrimination are not monitored. The assessment of the impact of factors in the family, community, and wider society on racial attitudes and actions of individuals is inadequate.

J

51. Hirschman, Charles and Wong, Morrison G. SOCIOECONOMIC GAINS OF ASIAN AMERICANS, BLACKS, AND HISPANICS: 1960-1976. *Am. J. of Sociol. 1984 90(3): 584-607.* Analyzes socioeconomic inequality between five minority populations (blacks, Hispanics, Japanese, Chinese, and Filipinos) and the majority population (white non-Hispanics) by age, nativity, residence, education, and other social background attributes.

52. Hoffman, Abraham. CHICANO HISTORY: PROBLEMS AND PO-TENTIALITIES. *J. of Ethnic Studies 1973 1(1): 6-12.* The body of literature on Mexican Americans is meager. Among scholarly studies, ahistorical works by social scientists predominate, while in-depth historical analyses are more rare. In popular literature, there is little of objective merit. Discusses available works in this neglected field and describes some of the primary sources on

which future research should be based, including Spanish-language newspapers such as *La Opinion* and *La Prensa,* land records, and consular reports and other diplomatic documents. 14 notes.   T. W. Smith

53. Hoffman, Abraham. TEXTBOOKS, MEXICAN AMERICANS, AND TWENTIETH-CENTURY AMERICAN HISTORY. *Teaching Hist.: A J. of Methods 1978 3(2): 65-72.* Assesses college textbook inclusion of Mexican-American contributions to recent American History. Textbooks have moved from brief generalities to more substantive material on minorities, but most which claim to speak for the mainstream of American history still lack a national orientation. A few highly publicized Chicano spokesmen have received textbook attention, but such topics as immigration, participation in labor unions, and sheer physical presence dating back to the 17th century still lack adequate textbook treatment. Based on published sources; 26 notes.   J

54. Hoffman, Abraham. AN UNUSUAL MONUMENT: PAUL S. TAYLOR'S *MEXICAN LABOR IN THE UNITED STATES* MONO-GRAPH SERIES. *Pacific Hist. Rev. 1976 45(2): 255-270.* Reviews the series of 11 monographs, produced by Paul S. Taylor of the University of California during 1926-34, on *Mexican Labor in the United States.* The study used every research technique then available and was altogether new in the field. It remains a monument to Taylor's skill, care, and judicious use of materials. With the renewed interest in Chicano history, the series recently was reprinted. 37 notes.   R. V. Ritter

55. Horgan, Paul. ABOUT THE SOUTHWEST: A PANORAMA OF NUEVA GRANADA. *Southwest R. 1974 59(4): 337-362.* Discusses the environment and history of the Southwest, especially the interplay of the Pueblo Indians, the Spaniards, and the American pioneers.   S

56. Hutchison, Ray. MISCOUNTING THE SPANISH ORIGIN POPULA-TION IN THE UNITED STATES: CORRECTIONS TO THE 1970 CEN-SUS AND THEIR IMPLICATIONS. *Int. Migration [Netherlands] 1984 22(2): 73-89.* The 1970 census overcounted persons of Central and South American origin in the United States by nearly 1,000,000 and set back social science research by 10 years. Corrections to the census figures increase the relative size and importance of the Mexican, Cuban, and Puerto Rican groups and show that the Mexican population is far more important in the Midwest than was previously thought. The corrected figures also indicate that the Spanish-origin population is America's fastest-growing minority population. Based on primary sources; 6 tables, 4 notes, ref.   L. J. Klass

57. Jenkins, J. Craig and Perrow, Charles. INSURGENCY OF THE POW-ERLESS: FARM WORKER MOVEMENTS (1946-1972). *Am. Sociol. Rev. 1977 42(2): 249-268.* Drawing on the perspective developed in recent work by Oberschall (1973), Tilly (1975) and Gamson (1975), authors analyze the political process centered around farm worker insurgencies. Comparing the experience of two challenges, they argue that the factors favored in the classical social movement literature fail to account for either the rise or outcome of insurgency. Instead, the important variables pertain to social resources—in this

case, sponsorship by established organizations. Farm workers themselves are powerless; as an excluded group, their demands tend to be systematically ignored. But powerlessness may be overridden if the national political elite is neutralized and members of the polity contribute resources and attack insurgent targets. To test the argument, entries in the *New York Times Annual Index* are content coded and statistically analyzed, demonstrating how the political environment surrounding insurgent efforts alternatively contains them or makes them successful. J

58. John, Vera. LETTER FROM THE SOUTHWEST: ON BILINGUAL-ISM. *Urban R. 1974 7(1): 43-45.* Discusses recent developments in bilingual education in the wake of Title VII of the Elementary and Secondary Education Act and a subsequent "backlash." S

59. Kanellos, Nicolás. FIFTY YEARS OF THEATRE IN THE LATINO COMMUNITIES OF NORTHWEST INDIANA. *Aztlán 1976 7(2): 255-265.* Discusses the development of Latino theater in Gary and East Chicago. By the 1920's, five Latino theater groups were operating in this area, the most prominent being the Cuadro Dramatico del Circulo de Obreros Catholicos "San José," founded to raise funds for construction of a Catholic church and to provide "wholesome recreation" for the community. The Great Depression and its attendant repatriations caused a hiatus in local Latino theater, but beginning in the 1950's, Puerto Rican Baptists made important contributions. The 1960's saw the formation of the Club Aristico Guadalupano, militantly Catholic and anti-Communist, which provided not only drama, but also a broad range of cultural presentations. The Teatro Desengaño del Pueblo, founded by the author in 1972, continues the tradition of these earlier groups, but with a stronger political emphasis. Based largely on contemporary accounts and announcements in the local Latino press; 26 notes. L. W. Van Wyk

60. Kanellos, Nicolás. FOLKLORE IN CHICANO THEATER AND CHI-CANO THEATER AS FOLKLORE. *J. of the Folklore Inst. 1978 15(1): 57-82.* Surveys the role of folklore in Puerto Rican and Mexican-American little theater in the United States. The movement, beginning in 1966, was designed to support the grape boycott. Sociopolitical and propagandistic themes remain dominant; nearly all of the theaters consist of amateurs and the turnover is high. Folklore themes are primarily borrowed from Mexico, including the ever-present figure of death, the singing warm-up, and the incorporation of social and romantic types. Covers the spread and increasing popularity of these theaters, and the movement of increasing numbers of Latin Americans into the general theater. 6 photos, 23 notes. V. L. Human

61. Kelly, María Patricia Fernández. THE U.S.-MEXICO BORDER: RE-CENT PUBLICATIONS AND THE STATE OF CURRENT RESEARCH. *Latin Am. Res. Rev. 1981 16(3): 250-267.* Reviews eight books published between 1971 and 1979. They reveal the problematic situation that characteriz-es the border, an area that could determine the future relationship between the United States and Mexico. 19 notes. J. K. Pfabe

62.   Krivo, Lauren J. HOUSING PRICE INEQUALITIES: A COMPARI-
SON OF ANGLOS, BLACKS, AND SPANISH-ORIGIN POPULATIONS.
Urban Affairs Q. 1982 17(4): 445-462. Blacks and Spanish-origin populations
(Puerto Ricans, Cuban Americans, and Mexican Americans) pay more than
whites for comparable housing in a sample of standard metropolitan statistical
areas in the rental market, but not in the owners' market. Based on 1975 and
1976 Annual Housing Surveys published by the US Bureau of the Census
(1977-78); 6 tables, 4 notes, ref.   J. Powell

63.   Kutsche, Paul; Van Ness, John R.; and Smith, Andrew T. A UNIFIED
APPROACH TO THE ANTHROPOLOGY OF HISPANIC NORTHERN
NEW MEXICO: HISTORICAL ARCHAEOLOGY, ETHNOHISTORY
AND ETHNOGRAPHY. *Hist. Archaeol. 1976 10: 1-16.* Archaeology, ethnohistory, ethnography—three methodologies within the same body of theory—
can be used cooperatively to reconstruct the cultural history of Hispanic
Northern New Mexico. The leads suggested for the investigation of Hispanic
culture are discussed under the interrelated headings of ecology, social
organization, and trade. Other benefits of intensive joint work include distin-
guishing ideal from real culture and testing theories of culture change. The
approach outlined could serve as a model for the investigation of other
historical traditions in the same or other parts of the world.   J

64.   Loeb, Catherine. LA CHICANA: A BIBLIOGRAPHIC SURVEY.
Frontiers 1980 5(2): 59-74. Bibliographic survey of Chicana issues and literature, emphasizing publications from the 1970's.

65.   Long, James E. PRODUCTIVITY, EMPLOYMENT DISCRIMINA-
TION, AND THE RELATIVE ECONOMIC STATUS OF SPANISH ORI-
GIN MALES. *Social Sci. Q. 1977 58(3): 357-373.* Concludes that both
employment discrimination and low productivity have contributed to the
inferior economic status of Spanish origin males compared with white males.
The data also suggest that recent efforts to upgrade their economic status have
not been very successful.   J

66.   Lopez, Adalberto. PUERTO RICANS AND THE LITERATURE OF
PUERTO RICO. *J. of Ethnic Studies 1973 1(2): 56-65.* A bibliographic essay
on the historical, sociological, and political literature on Puerto Rico and the
Puerto Rican community in the United States. Finds that until recently Puerto
Rican studies were scarce and their quality usually discouraging. Following the
experiences of black studies, the literature on Puerto Ricans on the mainland
and on the island is improving in both its coverage and depth.   T. W. Smith

67.   Lucas, Isidro. BILINGUALISM AND HIGHER EDUCATION: AN
OVERVIEW. *Ethnicity 1981 8(3): 305-319.* Hispanic Americans are underrepresented in higher education. Government programs are needed to redress
this imbalance. 2 tables, 25 notes.   T. W. Smith

68.   Martínez, Oscar J. CHICANO ORAL HISTORY: STATUS AND
PROSPECTS. *Aztlán 1978 9: 119-132.* Surveys the present status of Chicano
oral history as a field of scholarly research, and the research opportunities

available, and lists the Chicano holdings of oral history programs in the United States. The use of this methodology has not been adequately exploited by professional historians in the study of Chicano history despite several areas where it might be particularly fruitful. An appendix lists both institutional and individual projects in Chicano oral history with appropriate descriptive information. 8 notes, 2 appendixes.   R. V. Ritter

69.   Massey, Douglas S. HISPANIC RESIDENTIAL SEGREGATION: A COMPARISON OF MEXICANS, CUBANS, AND PUERTO RICANS. *Sociol. and Social Res. 1981 65(3): 311-322.* Measures residential segregation of Mexicans, Cubans, and Puerto Ricans in eight urbanized areas. These Hispanic groups were found to be highly segregated from blacks, and less segregated from non-Hispanic whites. An apparent exception to this generalization was the Puerto Rican population of the northeast, which was less segregated from blacks than from whites. Hispanics also tended to be less concentrated within central cities than blacks. Mexicans, Cubans, and Puerto Ricans also displayed a high degree of segregation between themselves. Socioeconomic status played a major role in the residential pattern of Hispanic Americans.   J/S

70.   Massey, Douglas S. and Mullan, Brendan P. PROCESSES OF HISPANIC AND BLACK SPATIAL ASSIMILATION. *Am. J. of Sociol. 1984 89(4): 836-873.* Blacks are less able than Hispanic Americans to convert status attainment into spatial assimilation and acceptance in new white neighborhoods.

71.   Massey, Douglas S. A RESEARCH NOTE ON RESIDENTIAL SUCCESSION: THE HISPANIC CASE. *Social Forces 1983 61(3): 825-833.* The entry of a minority group into an established white neighborhood sometimes causes white emigration until the neighborhood is totally populated by the minority group—a phenomenon called residential succession. In several Western cities, however, the influx of Hispanics either did not result in residential succession, or the phenomenon was less pronounced than for an influx of blacks. Census data.   D. Powell

72.   Mathes, W. Michael. SOURCES IN MEXICO FOR THE HISTORY OF SPANISH CALIFORNIA. *California History 1982 61(3): 223-226.* Describes the holdings in Mexican archives on materials pertaining to California from 1535 to 1821. The Archivo General de la Nación has published catalogs on some 70 collections ranging from administrative matters to annual reports of the Jesuits. The Archivo Franciscano of the Biblioteca Nacional covers 1683-1821 and contains material on missionary work. Other archives include the Archivo Histórico de Baja California Sur "Pablo Martínez," and the archives at Guadalajara and other Mexican cities. Many of the documents have been microfilmed and can thus be used at the Bancroft Library. Photos.   A. Hoffman

73.   McBane, Margo and Winegarden, Mary. LABOR PAINS: AN ORAL HISTORY OF CALIFORNIA WOMEN FARMWORKERS. *California History 1979 58(2): 179-181.* The California Women Farmworkers Project is

producing a radio program and multimedia slide and tape show relating the contributions of women to California farm labor. More than 70 interviews have been conducted under various oral history projects, with funding from the California Council for the Humanities in Public Policy. The project investigates a topic neglected by historians and public officials. Women comprise more than 40% of the agricultural labor force, yet their efforts remain largely unknown. Questions such as poor union representation, job discrimination, medical care, and problems of working mothers are now being examined. The project focuses on the work of women in fields and packing sheds. Photo.

A. Hoffman

74.   McKay, Roberta V. AMERICANS OF SPANISH ORIGIN IN THE LABOR FORCE: AN UPDATE. *Monthly Labor Rev. 1976 99(9): 3-6.* Analyzes unemployment of workers of Spanish origin and compares these to whites and blacks during the 1974-75 recessions.

75.   McLean, Malcolm D. ARTÍCULOS SOBRE TEXAS, PUBLICADOS EN EL *DIARIO DEL GOBIERNO DE LA REPÚBLICA MEXICANA,* 1836-1845 [Articles on Texas published in the *Diario del Gobierno de la República Mexicana,* 1836-45]. *Humánitas [Mexico] 1979 20: 357-414.* Investigators of Texan history are hampered by the large volume of material and the fact that it is widely scattered; an important source for the period of the Texas Republic (1836-45) is the *Diario del Gobierno de la República Mexicana,* the official journal of the Mexican government; cites the locations of available collections in the United States.

76.   McLean, Malcolm D. OUR SPANISH HERITAGE IN TEXAS. *Humánitas [Mexico] 1976 17: 569-616.* Discusses Spanish contributions to Texas history and culture, and gives sources for the historiography of Spanish Texas.

77.   McWatters, D. Lorne; Chappell, Bruce S.; and Getzler-Eaton, Michael. A NEW GUIDE TO SOURCES OF SPANISH FLORIDA HISTORY. *Florida Hist. Q. 1978 56(4): 495-497.* A National Endowment for the Humanities grant to the P. K. Yonge Library of Florida History, University of Florida, Gainesville, has initiated the preparation of a guide, to be completed by 1980, to the Florida Borderlands collection. The collection, documenting Spain's presence in Florida, contains material in three major divisions: the East Florida Papers from 1784-1821; the John B. Stetson Collection, photostats of documents from various Spanish archives dating from 1518-1819; and the *Papeles Procedentes de Cuba,* records of Spanish colonies in North America until 1821. 2 notes.   P. A. Beaber

78.   McWilliams, Carey. AND THE PEOPLE CAME. *Westways 1976 68(7): 38-49.* Discusses immigration to California, including the variety of ethnic groups in the state and the effect these groups have had on California's character, 1850-1976.

79.   Mohl, Raymond A. CUBANS IN MIAMI: A PRELIMINARY BIBLIOGRAPHY. *Immigration Hist. Newsletter 1984 16(1): 1-10.* Briefly reviews

Cuban immigration into Miami, Florida, and presents a bibliography of works on the topic.

80.   Mohr, Eugene V. FIFTY YEARS OF PUERTO RICAN LITERA-TURE IN ENGLISH—1923-1973, AN ANNOTATED BIBLIOGRAPHY. *R. Interamericana R. [Puerto Rico] 1973 3(3): 290-298.* A selected list of books in English that are a part of modern Puerto Rican literature.

J. A. Lewis

81.   Morales, Cecilio J., Jr. HISPANICS AND OTHER "STRANGERS": IMPLICATIONS OF THE NEW PASTORAL OF THE U.S. CATHOLIC BISHOPS. *Migration Today 1984 12(1): 37-39.* The National Conference of Catholic Bishops, in their 9,000-word pastoral letter "The Hispanic Presence: Challenge and Commitment," singled out the rapidly growing US Hispanic population as a "gifted" people presenting a special challenge to the Church's ability to maintain unity among its diverse followers.

82.   Muñoz, Carlos, Jr. POLITICS AND THE CHICANO: ON THE STA-TUS OF THE LITERATURE. *Aztlán 1974 5(1/2): 1-7.* Examines the pauci-ty of scholarship on the Mexican Americans and their cultural and political experience.   S

83.   Neighbor, Howard D. THE VOTING RIGHTS ACT OLD AND NEW: A FORECAST OF POLITICAL MATURITY. *Natl. Civic Rev. 1983 72(9): 481-488.* The political maturation of blacks and Hispanics under federal protection was the great achievement of the Voting Rights Act as amended through 1975. The act as amended in 1982 furthers the protection of minorities' voting rights against indirect forms of discrimination, such as at-large representation and gerrymandering designed to reduce the political power of minorities.   J/S

84.   Newman, Morris J. A PROFILE OF HISPANICS IN THE U.S. WORK FORCE. *Monthly Labor Rev. 1978 101(12): 3-14.* Focuses on Mexi-cans, Puerto Ricans, Cubans, and internal migration; covers 1973-77.

85.   Oczon, Annabelle M. LAND GRANTS IN NEW MEXICO: A SELEC-TIVE BIBLIOGRAPHY. *New Mexico Hist. Rev. 1982 57(1): 81-87.* Lists bibliographies, guides, books, theses, and essays generally covering land grants in New Mexico.   A. C. Dempsey

86.   Olivas, Michael A. RESEARCH AND THEORY ON HISPANIC EDUCATION: STUDENTS, FINANCE, AND GOVERNANCE. *Aztlán 1983 14(1): 111-146.* Reviews the status of Hispanic education, contending that present studies have failed to deal with the difficulties facing Hispanic Americans at all educational levels. Hispanic students are less likely to complete high school, have not obtained an equitable share of financing for higher education, are slighted by school boards and funded studies, and are in a vicious circle wherein they lack the political voice to gain access to better education. 3 tables, 75 notes, biblio.   A. Hoffman

87.   Olson, James S. THE BIRTH OF A DISCIPLINE: AN ESSAY ON CHICANO HISTORIOGRAPHY. *Social Studies 1974 65(7): 300-302.* Depicts the circumstances of the beginning of Chicano historiography as a new discipline in the 1960's. Chicano culture can now be presented and evaluated objectively. 25 notes.   L. R. Raife

88.   Ortiz, Vilma and Cooney, Rosemary Santana. SEX-ROLE ATTITUDES AND LABOR FORCE PARTICIPATION AMONG YOUNG HISPANIC FEMALES AND NON-HISPANIC WHITE FEMALES. *Social Sci. Q. 1984 65(2): 392-400.* First-generation Hispanic females held significantly more traditional sex-role attitudes than second- or third-generation females or non-Hispanic white females, and first- and second-generation Hispanic females were significantly less likely to participate in the labor force than non-Hispanic white females, but the Hispanic-white difference in labor force participation was due primarily to differences in educational attainment, not differences in traditional sex-role attitudes.

89.   Otheguy, Ricardo. THINKING ABOUT BILINGUAL EDUCATION: A CRITICAL APPRAISAL. *Harvard Educ. Rev. 1982 52(3): 301-314.* Discusses the controversy surrounding bilingual education by examining the role of the government in these programs and the impact of race and ethnicity on education.

90.   Padilla, Felix M. ON THE NATURE OF LATINO ETHNICITY. *Social Sci. Q. 1984 65(2): 651-664.* Latino ethnic identification in Chicago, Illinois, is situational and political, the result of interethnic relations among various Spanish-speaking groups.   J/S

91.   Piore, Michael. THE "ILLEGAL ALIENS" DEBATE MISSES THE BOAT. *Working Papers for a New Soc. 1978 6(2): 60-69.* Asserts that immigration policy should be responsible to the economic conditions in the United States and not to the whims of Congress, 1978.

92.   Portes, Alejandro and Bach, Robert L. IMMIGRANT EARNINGS: CUBAN AND MEXICAN IMMIGRANTS IN THE UNITED STATES. *Int. Migration Rev. 1980 14(3): 315-341.* Studies the applicability of the determinants of earnings for these two groups, interviewed upon arrival in 1973 and then again in 1976, to recent perspectives on income.

93.   Reid, Richard A.; Bartlett, Edward E.; and Kozoll, Richard. THE CHECKERBOARD AREA HEALTH SYSTEM: DELIVERING COMPRE-HENSIVE CARE IN A REMOTE REGION OF NEW MEXICO. *Human Organization 1982 41(2): 147-155.* Analyzes the application of the comprehensive health center concept in a rural area of northwestern New Mexico inhabited by Navajo Indians and Spanish Americans, and describes the region's population and economy during the period 1971-78.

94.   Reimers, Cordelia W. SOURCES OF THE FAMILY INCOME DIF-FERENTIALS AMONG HISPANICS, BLACKS, AND WHITE NON-HISPANICS. *Am. J. of Sociol. 1984 89(4): 889-903.*

95. Reimers, Cordelia. THE WAGE STRUCTURE OF HISPANIC MEN: IMPLICATIONS FOR POLICY. *Social Sci. Q. 1984 65(2): 401-416.* Estimates wage functions (correcting for selectivity bias) for Mexican-American, Puerto Rican, Cuban, Central and South American, "other Spanish," and black and white non-Hispanic men.

96. Richardson, Sister Jonathan. A SELECTED AND ANNOTATED BIBLIOGRAPHY OF THE MEXICAN AMERICANS OF THE SOUTHWEST UNITED STATES. *Am. Benedictine R. 1973 24(2): 145-180.* A bibliography of English language materials published prior to January 1973 and divided into five sections: history of Mexican Americans in the Southwest, current socioeconomic conditions and problems, school and library needs, the Mexican-American civil rights movement, and literary and artistic contributions in the southwest. Contains 180 entries. J. H. Pragman

97. Ríos-Bustamante, Antonio José. A CONTRIBUTION TO THE HISTORIOGRAPHY OF THE GREATER MEXICAN NORTH IN THE EIGHTEENTH CENTURY. *Aztlán 1976 7(3): 347-356.* Examines theoretical approaches to the study of the American Southwest during the Spanish and Mexican periods, evaluating the work of historians such as France V. Scholes.

98. Rock, Rosalind Z. A HISTORY OF LIBRARIES IN NEW MEXICO: SPANISH ORIGINS TO STATEHOOD. *J. of Lib. Hist. 1979 14(3): 253-273.* Traces the development of the Archives of New Mexico, the Territorial Library, and the beginning of public libraries, 1598-1912. During the Spanish and Mexican periods the literate population was small. Coupled with the Church-state conflict which existed through much of the period, lack of public interest hindered the development of a library system. The American territorial government fostered the public library system. Archival, primary, and secondary sources; 76 notes. S

99. Rockett, Ian R. H. ETHNICITY, IMMIGRATION PROCESS AND SHORT-TERM OCCUPATIONAL MOBILITY. *Int. Migration [Netherlands] 1983 21(3): 358-371.* As a result of the 1965 Immigration Act, nonwhite immigration has risen dramatically in the United States, especially from Latin America. Occupational mobility is affected by two dimensions of ethnicity: race and sociocultural distance. The relationship between race and short-term occupational mobility is significant; the class change for blacks and Hispanics is predominately downward although the degree of educational attainment of immigrants is also a factor. When the educational attainment factor is controlled, the occupational mobility performance of Asians more closely resembles that of blacks and Hispanics than whites. Further research on mobility direction should be implemented with more flexible data than those now available. 12 notes, 7 tables, ref. L. Moore

100. Roeder, Beatrice A. HEALTH CARE BELIEFS AND PRACTICES AMONG MEXICAN AMERICANS: A REVIEW OF THE LITERATURE. *Aztlán 1982 13(1-2): 223-256.* Surveys the historical development of research on the medical care beliefs and practices of Mexican Americans. Published studies fall into four categories: works on the historical development and

sources of Mexican folk medicine, pioneering studies (1894-1954), the research of Lyle Saunders and his followers in placing Mexican-American health practices in a cultural context, and research in the 1970's examining socioeconomic factors and criticizing Saunders's approach. Scholars in the field differ regarding the frequency of use of health care facilities by Mexican Americans and how such facilities can better serve Mexican-American needs. Note, ref.

A. Hoffman

101.   Rott, Renate. THE ONCE FORGOTTEN MINORITY: MEXICAN AMERICANS IN THE UNITED STATES: REPORT AND BIBLIOGRA-PHY. *Amerikastudien/Am. Studies [West Germany] 1975 20(2): 320-335.* The Mexican Americans are the second largest minority in the United States. The problems concerning this group of people have been neglected for quite some time, in social reality as well as in literature. It is only during the past ten years that Mexican Americans have become a subject of general national interest, especially in the Southwest, where the majority of them lives. This bibliographical report cannot offer a complete survey of all topics, research problems and literature available; it will focus mainly on the literature of the social sciences. The essay is subdivided as follows: 1. introductory remarks about the social position and the factors contributing to the self-awareness of Mexican Americans; 2. bibliographies; 3. general works (with homage to the work of Carey McWilliams); 4. labor conditions and social movements; 5. history and local history, and 6. some concluding remarks about minorities and the concept of assimilation.   J

102.   Roucek, Joseph S. and de la Quintana Oriol, Juan, transl. INMI-GRANTES DE ORIGEN ESPAÑOL EN LOS ESTADOS UNIDOS [Immi-grants of Spanish origin in the United States]. *Rev. de Política Social [Spain] 1975 (107): 9-28.* The *hispaños,* New Mexican descendants of Spanish conquistadors, live in small communities, preserving Spanish customs and language. Immigration from Spain itself peaked in the second decade of the 20th century, with immigrants settling in large east-coast and some midwestern cities. The Basques became shepherds in the Far West, notably in Nevada and Idaho; their industry is dying now. Spanish contributions to American culture include customs, place names, vocabulary, architecture, agricultural procedures, and aspects of Hispanic law. 30 notes.   J. Tull

103.   Ruiz, Ramón Eduardo and García, Mario T. CONQUEST AND ANNEXATION. *New Scholar 1978 7(1-2): 237-254.* Examines the effects of conquest and annexation by the English colonists and Americans on the Indians, Mexicans, Hawaiians, Eskimos, Virgin Island natives, the inhabitants of Guam and Samoa, Filipinos, and Puerto Ricans, 16th-20th centuries. Details the treatment of the Indians by English colonists and Americans, how diseases were introduced by conquering soldiers and settlers, how the Indians were moved from their native lands to reservations, and how they adapted their lifestyles. Also analyzes the treatment of Mexicans by the Americans after 1821, the annexation of Texas in 1836, and the causes and results of the Mexican War, 1846-48, and shows how the other groups with non-Western cultures adapted. Biblio.   G. L. Neville

104.   Salces, Luis M. SPANISH AMERICANS' SEARCH FOR POLITI-
CAL REPRESENTATION: THE 1975 ALDERMANIC ELECTION IN
CHICAGO. *J. of Pol. and Military Sociol. 1978 6(2): 175-187.* Spanish
Americans' search for political representation in Chicago has not been very
successful. In the 1975 aldermanic election, an unusual event took place when
four Spanish surnamed politicians challenged four incumbent aldermen backed
by Mayor Daley's Democratic Organization. Using official election returns for
each of the precincts included in the four wards, this study attempts to
determine to what extent ethnic solidarity had a greater effect than party
identification on the voting behavior of Spanish Americans. The results of the
analysis using ecological regression indicates that in two of the four wards
under study, Spanish surnamed registrants voted for the Spanish American
candidate, while in another ward they showed a preference for the candidate of
the Democratic organization. Moreover, with only one exception the participation of Spanish Americans had a negligible or negative effect on the election's
turnout. Overall, the findings suggest that in 1975 the presence of a Spanish
American candidate is not sufficient to produce a political mobilization on the
part of the Spanish American collectivity.   J

105.   Santos, Richard. EARNINGS AMONG SPANISH-ORIGIN MALES
IN THE MIDWEST. *Social Sci. J. 1982 19(2): 51-59.* Analyzes the incomes
of Spanish-origin males in Illinois, Indiana, Michigan, Ohio, and Wisconsin,
concluding that they earn approximately one-fifth less than a comparable
group of white males.

106.   Saragoza, Alex M. THE FLORESCENCE OF CHICANO HISTORI-
CAL SCHOLARSHIP. *New Scholar 1982 8(1-2): 483-487.* Albert Camarillo's
*Chicanos in a Changing Society: From Mexican Pueblos to American Barrios
in Santa Barbara and Southern California, 1848-1930* (1979) marks a new
phase in Chicano historiography combining local history with social history's
methodology. 5 notes.   D. K. Pickens

107.   Sehgal, Ellen and Vialet, Joyce. DOCUMENTING THE UNDOCU-
MENTED: DATA, LIKE ALIENS, ARE ELUSIVE. *Monthly Labor Rev.
1980 103(10): 18-21.* Gathering statistics concerning illegal aliens in the United
States, particularly their number and their role in the labor market, is
extremely difficult.

108.   Sena-Rivera, Jaime. VICTIMIZATION: THERAPY AND THE HIS-
PANIC CLIENT. *Migration Today 1981 9(2): 14-18.* Hispanic clients often
suffer from a victimization perspective and therapists can aid clients in
confronting victimization and in developing skills that "may enable the client
to draw upon internal resources when dealing with problems."

109.   Shapiro, David. WAGE DIFFERENTIALS AMONG BLACK, HIS-
PANIC, AND WHITE YOUNG MEN. *Industrial and Labor Relations Rev.
1984 37(4): 570-581.* There is still a significant black-white difference in hourly
wage rates among young men not enrolled in school, but not among students.
Hispanic-white wage differences are not significant among either students or

nonstudents. Longer job tenure contributes to significantly higher wage rates among white nonstudents, but not among black nonstudents.   J

110.   Silvestrini-Pacheco, Blanca and Castro Arroyo, María de los Angeles. SOURCES FOR THE STUDY OF PUERTO RICAN HISTORY: A CHALLENGE TO THE HISTORIAN'S IMAGINATION. *Latin Am. Res. Rev. 1981 16(2): 156-171.* Describes the variety of archival resources in Spain, the United States, and Puerto Rico. Describes research tools available for using archival holdings. 2 tables, 12 notes, 2 appendixes.   J. K. Pfabe

111.   Slesinger, Doris P. and Okada, Yoshitaka. FERTILITY PATTERNS OF HISPANIC MIGRANT FARM WOMEN: TESTING THE EFFECT OF ASSIMILATION. *Rural Sociol. 1984 49(3): 430-440.* Interviews with Hispanic migrant farm women revealed that they have greater numbers of children than other women in the United States. They bear children at younger ages, have greater infant mortality, and use fewer contraceptive techniques. The variable most strongly associated with live births is age; when age is controlled, education is the main predictor. When the effects of both age and education are controlled, bilingual capacity also contributes to explaining births. Education, on the other hand, explains most of the variance in expected number of children.

112.   Spalding, Rose. MEXICAN IMMIGRATION: A HISTORICAL PERSPECTIVE. *Latin Am. Res. Rev. 1983 18(1): 201-209.* Reviews Albert Camarillo's *Chicanos in a Changing Society: From Mexican Pueblos to American Barrios in Santa Barbara and Southern California, 1848-1930* (1979), Mark Reisler's *By the Sweat of Their Brow: Mexican Immigrant Labor in the United States, 1900-1940* (1976), Lawrence A. Cardoso's *Mexican Emigration to the United States, 1897-1931* (1980), Arthur F. Corwin, ed., *Immigrants—and Immigrants: Perspectives on Mexican Labor Migration to the United States* (1978), and George C. Kiser and Martha Woody Kiser, ed., *Mexican Workers in the United States: Historical and Political Perspectives* (1979). Coming after a period of neglect of the study of Mexican immigration, these books enhance our knowledge about factors stimulating emigration and immigration and social standing of Mexicans in the United States. Further research is necessary, particularly on theoretical issues such as the process of *descampesinización* and the structure of political power in the US Southwest. 6 notes.   J. K. Pfabe

113.   Stoddard, Ellwyn R. THE STATUS OF BORDERLANDS STUDIES: AN INTRODUCTION. *Social Sci. J. 1976 12(3): 3-8.* Outlines approaches to problems arising along the US-Mexican border from the Gulf of Mexico to El Paso-Ciudad Juarez in 1952-75.

114.   Stoddard, Ellwyn R. THE STATUS OF BORDERLANDS STUDIES: SOCIOLOGY AND ANTHROPOLOGY. *Social Sci. J. 1976 12(3): 29-54.* Reviews 20th-century contributions to the sociology and anthropology of the US-Mexican border area.

115.   Sweeny, Judith. CHICANA HISTORY: A REVIEW OF THE LITERATURE. Sánchez, Rosaura and Martinez Cruz, Rosa, ed. *Essays on la Mujer*

(Los Angeles, Ca.: Chicano Studies Center Publ., 1977): 99-111. Presents a brief history of Chicanas, or Mexican-American women, from the Colonial period through the 19th century to the contemporary period as a background for a guide to historical and literary works concerning Chicanas. Although a significant contribution has been made to the documentation of the Chicana's history, further research should be made into the social structure of the Southwest, and to date a good synthesis of the Chicana's history is lacking. 8 notes, biblio.   M. T. Wilson

116.   Taylor, James R. THE STATUS OF THE BORDERLANDS STUD-IES: ECONOMICS. *Social Sci. J. 1976 12(3): 69-76.* Reviews contributions of the 1970's to the economics of the US-Mexican border area.

117.   Thernstrom, Abigail M. E PLURIBUS PLURA: CONGRESS AND BILINGUAL EDUCATION. *Public Interest 1980 (60): 3-22.* The history of the Elementary and Secondary Education Act (US, 1968) and the Bilingual Education Act (US, 1967) reveals that, while blacks influenced Congress to support a bill to deal with the educational problems of children deficient in English, this legislation was later used to promote the new ethnicity and cultural pluralism. Federal policy initiatives promoting bilingualism were perhaps unnecessary, given the history of local initiatives in these areas, yet there is no reliable estimate of the number of "limited English speaking ability" children. No data show that bilingual programs are either necessary or helpful. Traces the history of modifications of this legislation and relevant court decisions. Between 1968 and 1978, Hispanics in particular benefited from bicultural education, and even though considerable political opposition had evolved toward the concept, it was entrenched in the social fabric. Nevertheless, bicultural education runs contrary to American tradition.
                                                                                    J. M. Herrick

118.   Thomas, Erwin K. THE OTHER AMERICA: RACE-RELATED NEWS COVERAGE. *J. of Ethnic Studies 1984 11(4): 124-126.* Much of the coverage of race-related news is characterized, in whole or part, by lack of variety; stress on negative events; lack of background material; and emphasis on conflict, injustice, and violence. Black, Indian, Latino, and Chicano news is reported from a white viewpoint, and is reduced to social problems, such as crime, housing, education, and unemployment. Minorities are not "presented as ordinary members who contribute positively to the society." In short, minorities receive significant coverage only when they engage in antisocial behavior, while the contexts in which they live and work are largely ignored. Primary sources; 10 notes.   G. J. Bobango

119.   Tienda, Marta and Neidert, Lisa J. LANGUAGE, EDUCATION, AND THE SOCIOECONOMIC ACHIEVEMENT OF HISPANIC ORIGIN MEN. *Social Sci. Q. 1984 65(2): 519-536.* Retention of the Spanish language generally does not hinder the socioeconomic achievements of Hispanic origin men, provided that they acquire a minimum education (high school) and English proficiency.

120. Tienda, Marta. MARKET CHARACTERISTICS AND HISPANIC EARNINGS: A COMPARISON OF NATIVES AND IMMIGRANTS. *Social Problems 1983 31(1): 59-72.* National origin and birthplace, work experience, education, and English language proficiency affect the employability and earnings of male Hispanic Americans.

121. Tienda, Marta. NATIONALITY AND INCOME ATTAINMENT AMONG NATIVE AND IMMIGRANT HISPANIC MEN IN THE UNITED STATES. *Sociol. Q. 1983 24(2): 253-272.* Data from 1976 indicate that Hispanics earned less than whites, partly due to discrimination, and that the presence of too many other Hispanics in an area diluted earning power.

122. Valverde, Leonard A. and Brown, Frank. EQUAL EDUCATIONAL OPPORTUNITY AND BILINGUAL-BICULTURAL EDUCATION: A SOCIOECONOMIC PERSPECTIVE. *Educ. and Urban Soc. 1978 10(3): 277-294.* Analyzes the expectation that bilingual education, as an intervention strategy, will improve the educational achievement and self-concept of children whose "first language" is not English, and therefore improve their future economic position.

123. Vigil, Maurilio E. HISPANICS GAIN SEATS IN THE 98TH CONGRESS AFTER REAPPORTIONMENT. *Int. Social Sci. Rev. 1984 59(1): 20-30.* The convening of the 98th Congress in January 1983 saw the greatest number of Hispanic congressmen ever in US history. Eleven Hispanics now belong to the Congressional Hispanic Caucus, the coalition of congressmen who represent Hispanic interests. Four new Hispanic congressmen (two from California, one from Texas, and one from New Mexico) were elected in 1982. The congressional reapportionment process, following the release of the 1980 census, resulted in additional congressional seats for these sun-belt states; the electoral process and other circumstances enabled Hispanics to capture four of these seats.   J

124. Wareing, J. THE CHANGING PATTERN OF IMMIGRATION INTO THE UNITED STATES, 1956-1975. *Geography [Great Britain] 1978 63(3): 220-224.* The Immigration and Nationality Act (US, 1965) was a turning point in US immigration laws. By 1968, the quota system of allocating visas was abolished, and replaced with a first-come first-served system, with quotas used only on a hemisphere-wide basis. One unexpected result was to increase the number of illegal aliens entering the United States. Immigrants were required to have jobs waiting for them in the United States, and Latin Americans were restricted by the Western Hemisphere quota. Illegal immigration into the United States, particularly from Mexico, has risen sharply since the passage of the 1965 act, and shows no signs of diminishing. In addition, the 1965 act resulted in increased immigration from southern Europe and Asia. Despite some flaws, the main problems with the 1965 act and US immigration policies in general, are caused by illegal aliens—a problem which, by its nature, cannot be directly affected by legislation. Table, 3 fig.   J. W. Leedom

125. Weber, David J. MEXICO'S FAR NORTHERN FRONTIER, 1821-1854: HISTORIOGRAPHY ASKEW. *Western Hist. Q. 1976 7(3):*

279-293. The historiography of the American Southwest is "notably unbalanced, ethnocentric, and incomplete." Except for studies of explorers, trappers, and traders, there is very little historiography of Mexico's far northern frontier as a whole. There is little interest in themes or historical questions which need a comparative approach. The Mexican period in the American Southwest remains open for historical research, especially by historians who combine linguistic skills, interdisciplinary training, and impartiality. 43 notes.

D. L. Smith

126. Weber, David J. MEXICO'S FAR NORTHERN FRONTIER, 1821-1845: A CRITICAL BIBLIOGRAPHY. *Arizona and the West 1977 19(3): 225-266.* Mexico's far northern frontier was lost to the United States as a consequence of the Mexican War and the Gadsden Purchase. Its historiography is dominated by American historians, and is "unbalanced, ethnocentric, and incomplete." The 157 annotated book and article bibliographic entries are arranged in alphabetical order by states. Emphasizes political, economic, and social history. Excludes edited primary sources, extremely narrow and unusually low-quality works, broad studies whose major focus is elsewhere, institutional histories and biographies prominent at a later date, most encyclopedic state histories, and mining and diplomatic histories. D. L. Smith

127. Weber, Devra. ORAL SOURCES AND THE HISTORY OF MEXICAN WORKERS IN THE UNITED STATES. *Int. Labor and Working Class Hist. 1983 (23): 47-50.* The paucity of written records on Mexican-American laborers and labor relations during the 1920's-30's requires that scholars use oral history approaches to the subject.

128. Welch, Susan and Hibbing, John R. HISPANIC REPRESENTATION IN THE U.S. CONGRESS. *Social Sci. Q. 1984 65(2): 328-335.* Hispanic representatives have a more liberal voting record than their non-Hispanic counterparts, even after controlling for salient party and constituency characteristics; representatives with substantial numbers of Hispanic constituents also vote more liberally than their counterparts.

129. Westfall, Loy Glenn. IMMIGRANTS IN SOCIETY. *Américas (Organization of Am. States) 1982 34(4): 41-45.* Reviews the reasons for the formation of societies by ethnic groups to provide social and medical programs for immigrants during the 19th century; specifically treats those of Spanish or Cuban origin in Florida, some of which still exist.

130. Wilson, William Julius. INNER-CITY DISLOCATIONS. *Society 1983 21(1): 80-86.* Urban social problems for blacks, Hispanics, and other minorities are complex and interrelated, not simply matters of racial discrimination and the "culture of poverty"; public policy hoping to address these problems must deal with fundamental economic and social change.

131. Woods, Richard D. LIBRARIES AND MEXICAN AMERICAN BIBLIOGRAPHY. *Coll. and Res. Lib. 1977 38(1): 32-36.* Mexican-American bibliographies which are prepared as guides to the holdings of one library many times fall short of their potential: These works often do not mention

some of the basic sources; they lack search strategies for the unsophisticated user; their arrangement does not promote accessibility; they attempt to reflect the holdings on several minority groups; and they do not mention standards for inclusion. To remedy these defects, the following article suggests seven criteria to improve Chicano bibliographies and provides five titles of exemplary works in this field.   J

132. Yanez, Elva Kocalis and Kazlauskas, Edward John. THE SPANISH-SPEAKING MENTAL HEALTH RESEARCH CENTER BIBLIOGRAPH-IC DATA BASE. *RQ 1980 19(4): 354-359.* A machine-readable data base of bibliographic information pertaining to the mental health of Hispanics in the United States is described. Topics covered include the history of the system, methods used to obtain citations for the data base, and the development of the computer-based file. There is also a discussion of vocabulary control and the currently available computerized search service.   J

133. Young, Anne McDougall. FEWER STUDENTS IN WORK FORCE AS SCHOOL AGE POPULATION DECLINES. *Monthly Labor Rev. 1984 107(7): 34-37.* Examines reasons for the decline in the student work force, noting differences in employment rates among white, black, and Hispanic youth.

134. Zinn, Maxine Baca. CHICANO FAMILY RESEARCH: CONCEPTU-AL DISTORTIONS AND ALTERNATIVE DIRECTIONS. *J. of Ethnic Studies 1979 7(3): 59-71.* Criticizes social sciences studies of Mexican Americans, particularly studies of the Chicano family which have led to negative stereotyping, and suggests alternative methodologies for examining the role of the Chicano family in acculturation and assimilation; 1970's.

135. Zinn, Maxine Baca. MEXICAN AMERICAN WOMEN IN THE SOCIAL SCIENCES. *Signs: J. of Women in Culture and Soc. 1982 8(2): 259-272.* Recent scholarship on women in general and Mexican-American women in particular has tended to be uniformed concerning gender, and based on narrative rather than analysis. Stereotypes about machismo and female submissiveness have been incorrectly perpetuated. New literature that moves in the direction of a feminist analysis of Mexican-American women includes: Alfredo Mirande and Evangelina Enriques's *La Chicana: The Mexican-American Woman* (1979), Margarita B. Melville's *Twice a Minority: Mexican American Women* (1980), and Adelaida R. DelCastillo's *Mexican Women in the United States: Struggles Past and Present* (1980). 48 notes.
                                                                         S. P. Conner

136. Zucker, Norman L. REFUGEE RESETTLEMENT IN THE UNITED STATES: POLICY AND PROBLEMS. *Ann. of the Am. Acad. of Pol. and Social Sci. 1983 (467): 172-186.* Federal refugee resettlement policies and programs, like admission policy, developed in an ad hoc way. Federal involvement in resettlement started out modestly as aid to Cubans, grew enormously with aid to the Indochinese, and continued to grow even more with a catchall program for Soviet and other refugees. Over the years, the private nonprofit voluntary agencies became institutionalized as the private-

sector link between admissions and local resettlement. The Refugee Act of 1980 was an attempt to design a coherent and comprehensive refugee admission and resettlement policy.   J/S

137. Zunz, Olivier. NEW ASSAULTS ON THE "BREAKDOWN THE-SIS." *Reviews in American History 1984 12(2): 248-252.* Virginia E. Sanchez Korrol's *From Colonia to Community: The History of Puerto Ricans in New York City, 1917-1948* (1983) and Richard Romo's *East Los Angeles: History of a Barrio* (1983) lay the groundwork for future studies on Hispanic-American communities, but neither is an in-depth study of an immigrant group in one specific area.

138. —. [CUBANS AND MEXICANS IN THE UNITED STATES]. *Cuban Studies 1981-82 11-12(2-1): 79-103.*
Pedraza Bailey, Silvia. CUBANS AND MEXICANS IN THE UNITED STATES: THE FUNCTIONS OF POLITICAL AND ECONOMIC MIGRATION, *pp. 79-97.* The common assumption that Cuban immigrants are more successful in the United States than Mexican immigrants because of class origin is only a half-truth. Cuban immigrants have received considerable assistance from the government because they are political exiles while Mexican migrants have been denied this help.
Pérez, Lisandro. COMMENT—CUBANS AND MEXICANS IN THE UNITED STATES, *pp. 99-103.* Bailey points out new facets of Cuban immigration. 2 tables, 47 notes.   J. A. Lewis

139. —. FESTIVALS. *Palacio 1975 81(1): 26-30.* Excerpts from WPA files chronicle Hispanic and Catholic holidays in New Mexico: Las Posadas, La Noche Buena, Los Dias, St. John's Day, and Farmers' Patron Day.

140. —. IMMIGRATION ISSUES IN AN ERA OF UNSANCTIONED MIGRATION: A SYMPOSIUM. *Industrial and Labor Relations Rev. 1980 33(3): 295-314.*
Fogel, Walter. UNITED STATES IMMIGRATION POLICY AND UN-SANCTIONED MIGRANTS, *pp. 295-311.* After providing an introduction to the symposium as a whole, this paper argues that basic changes are needed in this country's immigration policy to cope with the large flow of migrants who have entered the United States illegally in recent years. Fogel attacks the position, described best in Michael J. Piore's recent study, *Birds of Passage,* that most illegal immigrants fill only those jobs that native workers will not take and intend their stay in the United States to be temporary, not permanent. Fogel disputes both of those claims and argues that alternate forms of adjustment to labor shortages are available and preferable. He favors an immigration policy that would make our society less heavily dependent on rapid economic growth and, by reducing the number of migrants permitted to enter this country, would increase the relative wage of low-skilled indigenous workers. He recommends particularly the adoption of a law prohibiting the employment of illegal aliens and levying civil or criminal penalties on employers who violate that law. 47 notes.

Piore, Michael J. COMMENT, *pp. 312-314.* This comment presents a brief response to Fogel's criticism of the author's position on immigration policy. Piore summarizes his recent study, *Birds of Passage,* as arguing in part that most undocumented migration to this country in recent years has been initiated by employers with jobs to fill that native workers shun; that most migrants originally intended their stay to be temporary; and that severe problems resulted when this migration, like many others, failed to remain temporary in nature. The author recommends that public policy should focus less on controlling the supply of foreign labor than on controlling the demand for such labor, through improving the terms and enforcement of minimum wage and similar laws.   J

141.   —. [MIGRANT EDUCATION]. *Explorations in Ethnic Studies 1981 4(1): 50-61.*
Laughlin, Margaret A. AN INVISIBLE MINORITY: AN EXAMINATION OF MIGRANT EDUCATION, *pp. 50-59.* Discusses the special educational disadvantages faced by children of migrant workers in the United States, and describes some attempts to improve the situation.
Stewart, Dennis. CRITIQUE, *pp. 60-61.* Suggests that the problems of the migrant workers are caused not by education but by the economic structure of the nation.

142.   —. THE NEW IMMIGRATION: AN EXCHANGE. *Dissent 1980 27(3): 341-351.*
Graham, Otis L., Jr. ILLEGAL IMMIGRATION AND THE LEFT, *pp. 341-346.* Bases a discussion on stricter limits on immigration on new research regarding the impact of immigration on US population growth and labor market, proposing that, in view of this new evidence of the adverse impact of immigration, restrictionism should appeal more to liberals and radicals.
Piore, Michael. ANOTHER VIEW OF MIGRANT WORKERS, *pp. 347-351.* Graham creates a distorted view of the immigration issue; a nonracist approach to restricted immigration is impossible; and Graham has failed to understand the forces that are governing the migration.

2

COLONIZATION AND SETTLEMENT, UP TO 1848

143. Adams, Eleanor B. FRAY FRANCISCO ATANASIO DOMINGUEZ AND FRAY SILVESTRE VELEZ DE ESCALANTE. *Utah Hist. Q. 1976 44(1): 40-58.* Fray Francisco Atanasio Dominguez (1740-ca 1805), was a commissary visitor and Fray Silvestre Velez de Escalante (ca 1750-80), was a mission friar in New Mexico before their expedition to discover a route from New Mexico to Monterey, California in 1776. Letters and reports on spiritual and economic conditions in New Mexico and the feasibility of the Monterey route reveal both as keen observers, similar in outlook, temperament, and unswerving moral rectitude. Internal and external evidence indicates both were responsible for the expedition diary. Based on primary and secondary sources; 3 illus., 30 notes. J. L. Hazelton

144. Almaráz, Félix D., Jr. CARLOS E. CASTAÑEDA AND *OUR CATHOLIC HERITAGE*: THE INITIAL VOLUMES (1933-1943). *Social Sci. J. 1976 13(2): 27-37.* Studies the background, commitment, and problems encountered by Carlos E. Castañeda in writing *Our Catholic Heritage* on the history of Spanish colonization in Texas.

145. Almaráz, Félix, Jr. ASPECTS OF MEXICAN TEXAS: A FOCAL POINT IN SOUTHWEST HISTORY. *Red River Valley Hist. Rev. 1975 11(3): 363-379.* Examines animosities between Americans who colonized Texas, 1822-36, and the Tejanos, Mexican Texans thrown into the fight between Santa Anna and Americans favoring independence for Texas.

146. Aragón, Janie Louise. THE PEOPLE OF SANTA FÉ IN THE 1790S. *Aztlán 1976 7(3): 391-417.* Examines population growth, economic development, and the ethnic composition of Santa Fe, New Mexico.

147. Arana, Luis Rafael. THE FORT AT MATANZAS INLET. *Escribano 1980 17: 1-32.* The Spanish constructed Fort Matanzas along the Matanzas River at Matanzas Inlet near St. Augustine, Florida, in 1740-41 to protect the area from the British; traces the history of the area, 1565-1821.

148. Archambeau, Ernest R. PANHANDLE BOUNDARY LINES. *Panhandle-Plains Hist. Rev. 1975 48: 64-69.* By terms of the 1819 Adams-Onis Treaty, the United States and Spain agreed on boundaries separating their

western claims, and this agreement remained in force until Texas won its independence in 1836. The Republic of Texas subsequently asserted its rights over the eastern half of present-day New Mexico, along with sections of Colorado, Kansas and Wyoming. Yet Texas was never able to effectively dominate this northwestern area and after 1846 the United States gradually strengthened its claim by virtue of military occupation during the Mexican War. The Compromise of 1850 solved the volatile problem by setting the present boundaries of Texas in return for $10 million in federal bonds paid to the state of Texas. 5 notes.   M. L. Tate

149.   Archer, Christon I. THE MAKING OF SPANISH INDIAN POLICY ON THE NORTHWEST COAST. *New Mexico Hist. Rev. 1977 52(1): 45-69.* During the latter half of the 18th century the Spanish empire in North America expanded. Spain developed a settlement system, the mission-presidio. The Franciscans led the way while the army and navy provided the necessary defense. Although there were occasional periods of peace, the Spanish had to be prepared to cope with Indian attacks at any time. The Spanish were required to withdraw due to the advance of the English across the continent.
                                                          J. H. Krenkel

150.   Archibald, Robert. ACCULTURATION AND ASSIMILATION IN COLONIAL NEW MEXICO. *New Mexico Hist. Rev. 1978 53(3): 205-217.* Much recent scholarship has focused on acculturation and assimilation, which were characteristic of the Spanish conquest of the Americas. 39 notes.
                                                          J. H. Krenkel

151.   Archibald, Robert. THE ECONOMY OF THE ALTA CALIFORNIA MISSION, 1803-1821. *Southern California Q. 1976 58(2): 227-240.* Describes the economic activities of the Alta California missions from the death of Father President Fermín de Lasuén in 1803 until the winning of independence by Mexico in 1821. During this period the Alta California missions were largely self-sufficient and highly successful in a large number of economic endeavors. The missions produced hides, lard, tallow, wine, blankets, mules, saddles, and other products. Faced with mercantile restrictions and inadequate markets for their products, the Franciscan missions actively participated in smuggling operations with foreign ships and traders. The missions also supplied the presidios with food and provisions. The success of the missions aroused jealousy from settlers and helped promote the very end of the mission system through government secularization. The mission Indians who produced many of the products failed to obtain much benefit, and indeed suffered high infant mortality and epidemics caused by European diseases. Outwardly the missions were prosperous during this period; but forces were at work which also spelled their decline. Based on primary and secondary sources; 56 notes.
                                                          A. Hoffman

152.   Archibald, Robert. INDIAN LABOR AT THE CALIFORNIA MISSIONS: SLAVERY OR SALVATION? *J. of San Diego Hist. 1978 24(2): 172-182.* The mission system in California set out to institute social change and transformation of cultural values, often with force which unintentionally resulted in virtual slavery for the Indians; covers 1775-1805.

153. Arthur, Don; Costello, Julia; and Fagan, Brian. A PRELIMINARY ACCOUNT OF MAJOLICA SHERDS FROM THE CHAPEL SITE, ROYAL SPANISH PRESIDIO, SANTA BARBARA, CALIFORNIA. *Kiva 1975 41(2): 207-214.* The Santa Barbara Presidio represents a Spanish occupation in Alta California dating from 1782 to around 1850. Although stratigraphic controls for the recovered Majolica sherds were difficult to maintain due to the urban nature of the site, the collection does represent the decorative styles present at the presidio during the latest period of Spanish colonialism in North America.   J

154. Aschman, Homer. A LATE RECOUNTING OF THE VIZCAINO EXPEDITION AND PLANS FOR THE SETTLEMENT OF CALIFORNIA. *J. of California Anthrop. 1974 1(2): 174-185.* Discusses the explorations in 1602-03 of Sebastian Vizcaíno and the recommendations for settlement made following his travels.   S

155. August, Jack. BALANCE-OF-POWER DIPLOMACY IN NEW MEXICO: GOVERNOR FERNANDO DE LA CONCHA AND THE INDIAN POLICY OF CONCILIATION. *New Mexico Hist. Rev. 1981 56(2): 141-160.* Discusses the successful Indian policy of Don Fernando Simon Ignacio de la Concha (b. 1744), the Spanish governor of New Mexico from 1787 to 1793. Following a long period of warfare with the many tribes in New Mexico, Concha guided the province through a reversal of this policy and into a period of conciliation with the Indians. Concha's use of alliances and balance of power diplomacy consolidated peace with the Indian tribes and effected a decade of prosperity and stability in New Mexico. Based on the Spanish Archives of New Mexico located at the State Records Center and Archives, Santa Fe, New Mexico, and other primary sources; illus., 50 notes.
                                                                            P. L. McLaughlin

156. Ballard, Dave. THE BATTLE OF SAN PASQUAL. *Am. Hist. Illus. 1978 13(1): 4-11, 46-48.* In the summer of 1846, American forces encountered no resistance in taking possession of California, during the Mexican War, but in late September, a revolt broke out among the California rancheros—not in favor of a return to Mexican rule, but in the name of an independent California. In early December, Colonel Stephen Kearny arrived in the area of San Diego after an exhausting march from Fort Leavenworth, Kansas. Informed en route of the initial American success, but ignorant of the revolt, Kearny had left most of his force to garrison New Mexico, and he now requested reinforcements from San Diego. With these, he unsuccessfully attacked a force of Californians under Andres Pico near the village of San Pasqual on December 6. The next day Kearny's men captured a piece of high ground and held out until reinforcements arrived. 9 illus., map.
                                                                            L. W. Van Wyk

157. Barnes, Mark R. HISPANIC PERIOD ARCHAEOLOGY IN THE TUCSON BASIN: AN OVERVIEW. *Kiva 1984 49(3-4): 213-223.* Provides a brief overview of historical events in the Tucson Basin and the events that occurred outside this area that influenced the people of southern Arizona. The Hispanic period may best be understood by reviewing historical records and

associated artifacts in terms of site function, networks of trade and communication, and social interaction among cultural groups. Excavations in Hispanic period sites in the Tucson Basin and Santa Cruz Valley, dating from Eusebio Francisco Kino's expeditions of the 1690's to the withdrawal of Mexican soldiers from the Tucson presidio in 1856 have produced ceramics—Piman, Hispanic, European, Oriental, and American—that give a better understanding of conditions recorded in the historical documents.   J

158.   Beerman, Eric. ANTONIO DE MENDOZA. *Pacific Hist. 1980 24(1): 71-78, (2): 182-191; (3): 295-300.* Part I. Antonio de Mendoza (ca. 1490-21 July 1552), a distinguished diplomat, was the first viceroy of New Spain (Mexico), 1535-49. He established Spanish control over Mexico and sent expeditions into the Pacific Ocean, North America, and Mexico. Under his leadership, too, Juan Rodriguez Cabrillo discovered San Diego Bay in 1552. Mendoza is credited with bringing the printing press to Mexico. Brief biographical sketches of his wife, Catalina de Vargas y Carvajal, two sons, Indigo and Francisco, one daughter, Francisca; his father, mother, and four brothers are included. Archival sources; illus., 2 maps, 14 notes. Part II. During Mendoza's reign, he had to control the conquistadores as they embarked on expeditions of discovery of new lands and wealth. Mendoza wanted credit for discovering the great wealth of the area. In 1540, Pedro de Alvarado, one of Cortez's former lieutenants, finally reached an agreement with Mendoza whereby all expenses and prizes of Alvarado's expedition would be divided equally. Mendoza had a similar agreement with Coronado. In 1541, Alvarado died of wounds suffered while fighting the Indians. Mendoza took over complete ownership of the expedition and named as leader Juan Rodriguez Cabrillo. The ships sailed for Baja California on 27 June 1542 and proceeded to explore the shoreline on their way north. Archival sources; 24 notes. Part III. Discusses Cabrillo's voyage along California. After he died at the Santa Barbara Channel Islands on 3 January 1543, Bartolome Ferrelo took command. After the return to Mexico, Mendoza sent Ferrelo to Peru. Mendoza himself went there in 1551. Archival sources; 9 notes.   G. L. Lake

159.   Beerman, Eric. BRUNO DE HECETA THE FIRST EUROPEAN DISCOVERER OF THE COLUMBIA RIVER. *Pacific Hist. 1979 23(1): 103-115.* The Spanish knew the Columbia River as the Entrada de Heceta, named after the Basque naval officer who first discovered it, Bruno de Heceta y Fontecha (1743-1807). Details the naval career of de Heceta from the time he entered the Spanish coast guard in 1758 until his retirement, a few months before his death. Heceta accidentally discovered the mouth of the Columbia River on 17 August 1775 while on a voyage to shadow Russian vessels that were moving south from Alaska to Spanish-held California. He thought that the estuary was simply a large bay. He was the first European to discover the Columbia River; this was only one of several important events in his life. He retired with the rank of *teniente general* in the Spanish navy; he had worked his way up from the lowest rank. Based on the service record of de Heceta in the Museo Naval, El Viso, Spain, and his diary in the Archivo Historica Nacional, Madrid; 37 notes.   H. M. Parker, Jr.

160. Beerman, Eric. THE VICEROY MARQUIS DE CROIX: A BIO-GRAPHICAL SKETCH. *J. of San Diego Hist. 1979 25(1): 60-67.* A Flemish soldier in the service of Spain, Carlos Francisco de Croix (1699-1786) established the Mission San Diego de Alcalá in 1769 and established and maintained Spanish territorial claims in California.

161. Benes, Ronald J. ANZA AND CONCHA IN NEW MEXICO, 1787-1793: A STUDY IN NEW COLONIAL TECHNIQUES. *J. of the West 1965 4(1): 63-76.* Discusses the military techniques of Governor Juan Bautista de Anza and Don Fernando Simon Ignacio de la Concha of the Spanish royal navy, during their efforts to maintain peace between Spain and American Indians in New Mexico.

162. Benham, Priscilla. DIPLOMATIC CORRESPONDENCE OF THE UNITED STATES CHARGÉS D'AFFAIRES TO THE REPUBLIC OF TEXAS, 1837-1843. *Red River Valley Hist. Rev. 1980 5(1): 37-55.* Discusses the correspondence of Alcée La Branche of Louisiana (1837-40), George H. Flood of Ohio (1840-41), Joseph Eve (1841-43), and William S. Murphy (1843-44) on the issues surrounding the annexation of Texas.

163. Bewley, Fred W., ed. CAPISTRANO—THE JEWEL OF THE MIS-SIONS. *California Historian 1976 22(3): 34-36.* Retraces the history of the building (1776) and development by the Franciscans of Mission San Juan Capistrano, whose architecture is famous in California.

164. Bolton, Herbert Eugene. THE MISSION AS A FRONTIER INSTI-TUTION IN THE SPANISH AMERICAN COLONIES. Weber, David J., ed. *New Spain's Far Northern Frontier: Essays on Spain in the American West, 1540-1821* (Albuquerque: U. of New Mexico Pr., 1979): 49-65. The missionaries of the American Southwest had the responsibilities of converting and acculturating the Indians, and of exploring, colonizing, and defending the frontier during the 16th-18th centuries. Reprinted from the *American Historical Review* 1917 22(1): 42-61.

165. Bowden, Henry Warner. SPANISH MISSIONS, CULTURAL CON-FLICT AND THE PUEBLO REVOLT OF 1680. *Church Hist. 1975 44(2): 217-228.* In 1598 the upper Rio Grande valley was viewed as an outpost of Spanish civilization, providing an opportunity for colonization, mining, and missionary exploits. From the outset, missionary work seemed to do well, but the repressive measures adopted by the missionaries caused a general native uprising. Methodically, the Indians rid themselves of Spanish intrusion by destroying property, especially churches. The author maintains that the revolt occurred because of religious and cultural differences. 34 notes.

M. D. Dibert

166. Bowen, Dorothy Boyd. A BRIEF HISTORY OF SPANISH TEXTILE PRODUCTION IN THE SOUTHWEST. *Palacio 1979 85(2): 20-23.* Chronicles the introduction and adaptation of sheep raising and weaving among the native inhabitants of New Mexico, 1540's-1860's.

167.   Branson, Branley Allan. HISTORY ON THE ROCKS. *Américas 1977 29(1): 10-14.* Discusses rock inscriptions made by Spanish explorers at El Morro National Monument in New Mexico; inscriptions and petroglyphs date from prehistory-1620.

168.   Brasseaux, Carl A. and Chandler, Richard E. THE *BRITAIN* INCIDENT, 1769-1770: ANGLO-HISPANIC TENSIONS IN THE WESTERN GULF. *Southwestern Hist. Q. 1984 87(4): 357-370.* On 5 January 1769, 34 Acadians and 40 German Catholics sailed on the *Britain* from Port Tobacco, Maryland. Bound for New Orleans, under the command of Philip Ford, the ship landed instead on the Matagorda Peninsula of Texas, where it soon was taken into Spanish custody. After many delays, the Spaniards returned the crew and passengers to British territory, where local authorities demanded compensation for the loss of the ship and the detainment of the immigrants. Neither Britain nor Spain, however, wanted their already poor relations to deteriorate further and, by diplomatic finesse, defused a potentially dangerous situation. Based on depositions and other government papers in the Archivo General de la Nación in Mexico City and the Public Records Office in London; 30 notes.   R. D. Hurt

169.   Briggs, Walter. DOMINGUEZ AND ESCALANTE. *Am. West 1976 13(4): 18-31.* Retraces the 29 July 1776-2 January 1777 Dominguez-Escalante expedition. Led by Franciscan friars Francisco Atanasio Dominguez and Silvestre Velez de Escalante, the expedition was to find a route from Santa Fe, New Mexico, to Monterey, California. In its failure, however, the expedition did explore much of the Great Basin and established a first in crossing the Colorado River before returning to Santa Fe. Based on a recently published book; 5 illus.   D. L. Smith

170.   Brumgardt, John R. THE COLONEL'S GADFLY FATHER PEDRO FONT AND THE SECOND ANZA EXPEDITION, 1775-1776. *California Historian 1975 22(2): 23-25.* Comments on Father Pedro Font's descriptions of the second De Anza expedition and his uneven relationship with Juan Bautista de Anza, 1775-76.

171.   Burroughs, Jean M. FROM CORONADO'S CHURROS. *Palacio 1977 83(1): 9-13.* First introduced into the Southwest by Francisco Vásquez de Coronado's exploratory expedition in 1540, sheep played an important role in the economy and were focal points for range wars 1870's-80's.

172.   Campbell, Leon G. THE SPANISH PRESIDIO IN ALTA CALIFORNIA DURING THE MISSION PERIOD 1769-1784. *J. of the West 1977 16(4): 63-77.* Examines presidial development and society in Alta California. Stresses the construction of the 11 missions at the expense of the four presidios which were built at the same time—San Diego (1769), Monterey (1770), San Francisco (1776), and Santa Barbara (1782). Discusses the tensions between the soldiers and the missionaries. 14 illus., 2 maps, 37 notes.   R. Alvis

173. Capen, Dorothy. A WALKING TOUR OF OLD MONTEREY. *Early Am. Life 1979 10(1): 36-37, 61.* Discusses landmarks, sites, and restorations from the Spanish, Mexican and early American periods, 1770-1849.

174. Carlson, Alvar W. SPANISH-AMERICAN ACQUISITION OF CROPLAND WITHIN THE NORTHERN PUEBLO INDIAN GRANTS, NEW MEXICO. *Ethnohist. 1975 22(2): 95-110.* Spanish Americans acquired much of the irrigable cropland within the eight Northern Pueblo Indian Grants of New Mexico's upper Rio Grande Valley during the last half of the 1800's. Most of them received titles to their small long-lot farms after hearings were held by the Pueblo Lands Board, established in 1924. The availability of this irrigable cropland was an important factor in accommodating the growing Spanish-American population which remained concentrated in the upper Rio Grande Valley. Spanish-American ownership of the irrigable cropland changed the agricultural landscape of the Northern Pueblo Indian Grants. J

175. Carrico, Richard L. PORTOLÁ'S 1769 EXPEDITION AND COAST-AL NATIVE VILLAGES OF SAN DIEGO COUNTY. *J. of California Anthrop. 1977 4(1): 30-41.* Discusses Gaspar de Portolá's exploratory trip from San Diego north to Monterey, especially 14 July-22 July and the 14 San Diego-area Indian villages through which the party marched.

176. Champlin, Brad. THE MISSION AT SONOMA. *Pacific Hist. 1978 22(4): 357-360.* Mission San Francisco Solano, northernmost and the last established (1823), is the only one built under Mexican rule. It was founded by a young priest from Mission San Francisco de Asís, Father Jose Altimira, with the cooperation of Governor Luis Arguello. The young padre was succeeded by Padre Buenaventura Fortuni, who brought exceptional organizing ability to its development and growth. Traces its development under successive padres until its secularization in 1834 by order of Mexico City authorities. Illus., 3 notes.
R. V. Ritter

177. Chandler, R. E. FORT ST. GABRIEL AND FORT BUTE: A BOR-DER INCIDENT OF 1768. *Rev. de Louisiane 1979 8(2): 174-185.* Account of a dispute between the English and Spanish in 1768 on the Iberville River in Louisiana where the British built Fort Bute in 1765 and the Spanish built Fort St. Gabriel opposite the British post in 1768, based on correspondence reprinted here between British commandant Thomas Home and Spanish governor of Louisiana Don Antonio de Ulloa, and between Spanish military officer Don Joseph de Onieta and Ulloa.

178. Chandler, R. E. ULLOA AND THE ACADIANS. *Louisiana Hist. 1980 21(1): 87-91.* The rebels who in 1768 ousted colonial Louisiana's first Spanish governor, Don Antonio de Ulloa (1716-95), spread the word that he had treated newly arrived Acadians cruelly in 1766. Some historians have accepted this Black Legend view of Ulloa, but the truth appears to be the reverse. For both poltical and humane reasons, Ulloa assisted the Acadians. A letter to his superior in Spain is translated in full to substantiate this contention. Based on a letter in the Archivo General de Indias, Seville; 7 notes.
D. B. Touchstone

179.   Chavez, Angelico. NUESTRA SEÑORA DE LA MACANA. *New Mexico Hist. Rev. 1959 34(2): 81-97.* The statue of Our Lady of Macana, a smaller copy of a statue in Spain, came to New Mexico in 1598, and is the subject of history and legend, particularly regarding its role in the Indian Rebellion of 1680 in New Mexico.

180.   Chavez, Thomas E. DON MANUEL ALVAREZ (DE LAS ABEL-GAS): MULTI-TALENTED MERCHANT OF NEW MEXICO. *J. of the West 1979 18(1): 22-31.* Manuel Alvarez was a native of Spain who lived in Mexico and Cuba before settling in Santa Fe, New Mexico, in 1824. His application for Mexican citizenship was denied, but as a merchant and fur trader, he developed a reputation for industry and honesty. In 1839, on a visit to Missouri, he was appointed US consul in Santa Fe. His job of representing US citizens to the Mexican government was complicated by the Texas uprising and Texan raids on Mexican commerce on the Santa Fe Trail. Alvarez became a US citizen in 1842, and helped the transition of New Mexico to US rule during the Mexican War. Alvarez is largely an unknown figure despite his local prominence in the development of the Southwest. Primary and secondary sources; 7 photos, 57 notes.   B. S. Porter

181.   Chavez, Thomas Esteban. THE TROUBLE WITH TEXANS: MANUEL ALVAREZ AND THE 1841 "INVASION." *New Mexico Hist. Rev. 1978 53(2): 133-144.* Texas claimed its independence in 1836, but the Mexican government refused to recognize it. Thus, the arrival of a Texan trading expedition into New Mexico in 1841 was perceived as an invasion. Manuel Alvarez, US Consul in New Mexico, made heroic efforts to protect Americans living there and to placate the Mexican government. The US government did nothing in behalf of his consular efforts. 56 notes.
                                                        J. H. Krenkel/G. Fox

182.   Chipman, Donald. THE OÑATE-MOCTEZUMA-ZALDÍVAR FAM-ILIES OF NORTHERN NEW SPAIN. *New Mexico Hist. Rev. 1977 52(4): 297-316.* In the settlement of New Mexico, historians are well acquainted with the work done by the Zaldívar brothers, Juan and Vicente. More research needs to be done on the work of Hernán Cortes and his lieutenants. Genealogical chart, 27 notes.   J. H. Krenkel

183.   Clark, Harry. THEIR PRIDE, THEIR MANNERS, AND THEIR VOICES: SOURCES OF THE TRADITIONAL PORTRAIT OF THE EARLY CALIFORNIANS. *California Hist. Q. 1974 53(1): 71-82.* Assesses conventional picture of Californios in the early 19th century through analysis of four contemporary best-sellers: James Ohio Pattie's (1804-50) *Personal Narrative,* Richard Henry Dana's (1815-82) *Two Years Before the Mast,* Alfred Robinson's *Life in California,* and Edwin Eustace Bryant's (1835-1903) *What I Saw in California.* Each of these works, based on direct observation of the Californios' life style, contained comments on the populace, the arbitrariness of the governor, and characterizations which gave a general image of the Californios as a gracious, leisure class people, maintaining with minimum effort a moribund society lacking in eagerness for enterprise. The attractive features of the California life-style, hospitality, graciousness, and suggestion of a higher

culture fallen on harsh times, became romanticized in the works of Helen Hunt Jackson's (1830-85) *Ramona* and the writings of Gertrude Franklin Atherton (1857-1948). Based on the books by Pattie, Dana, Robinson, and Bryant; illus., note. A. Hoffman

184. Clayton, Lawrence A. THE BORDERLANDS REVISITED. *Latin Am. Res. Rev. 1980 15(3): 261-265.* Reviews José Agustín Balseiro, ed., *The Hispanic Presence in Florida: Yesterday and Today, 1513-1976* (Miami: E. A. Seemann Publ. Inc., 1977), and Eugene Lyon's *The Enterprise of Florida: Pedro Menéndez de Avilés and the Spanish Conquest of 1565-1568* (Gainesville: U. Pr. of Florida, 1976). These books provide a variety of insights into the Spanish presence in Florida. J. K. Pfabe

185. Coomes, Charles S. OUR COUNTRY'S OLDEST PARISH RECORDS. *Escribano 1981 18: 74-83.* Describes the contents of the church records of St. Augustine, Florida, 1594-1763 which were taken by the Spaniards to Cuba in 1763-64, only to be discovered by historians in the 20th century.

186. Corbett, Theodore G. MIGRATION TO A SPANISH FRONTIER IN THE SEVENTEENTH AND EIGHTEENTH CENTURIES: ST. AUGUSTINE. *Hispanic Am. Hist. R. 1974 54(3): 414-430.* Discusses origins and background of the early inhabitants of St. Augustine, Florida in the Spanish colonial period using quantitative methods. A majority of immigrants from the Iberian peninsula were Andalusians, many immigrants came from New Spain, and large concentrations of blacks and mulattoes also inhabited St. Augustine. Most immigrants were "rootless soldiers," as St. Augustine was a presidio town without civic and economic development. Based on church records, documents from the *Archivo General de Indias*, and secondary sources; table, 60 notes. N. J. Street

187. Crosby, Harry. EL CAMINO REAL IN BAJA CALIFORNIA: LORETO TO SAN DIEGO. *J. of San Diego Hist. 1977 23(1): 1-45.* Follows the route (through historic tracts, pictures, and maps) of El Camino Real, the principal road connecting all the missions in Baja California and going up to San Diego in Alta California, 1697-1771.

188. Crosby, Harry W. EL CAMINO REAL IN BAJA CALIFORNIA: A COMMENTARY ON THE PROBLEMS OF THE SERRA ROUTE BY RONALD L. IVES. *J. of San Diego Hist. 1976 22(2): 49-55.* Comments on a previous article by Ronald L. Ives and discusses difficulties in determining and retracing El Camino Real, the route used for overland travel between Loreto in Baja California and San Diego by Father Junipero Serra and other Franciscan missionaries.

189. Cutter, Donald C. THE LEGACY OF THE TREATY OF GUADALUPE HIDALGO. *New Mexico Hist. Rev. 1978 53(4): 305-315.* Discusses the background and importance of the Treaty of Guadalupe Hidalgo, which ended the war between Mexico and the United States in 1848.

190.   Cutter, Donald C. PLANS FOR THE OCCUPATION OF UPPER CALIFORNIA: A NEW LOOK AT THE "DARK AGE" FROM 1602 TO 1769. *J. of San Diego Hist. 1978 24(1): 78-90.* Discusses planned discovery and exploration for the proposed colonization of Upper California, 1602-1769, between the voyage of Sebastian Vizcaino (1602-03) and the overland expedition of Gaspar de Portolá and Father Junípero Serra in 1769 and the actions of José de Gálvez, who was largely responsible for that expedition.

191.   Cutter, Donald C. SPANISH SCIENTIFIC EXPLORATION ALONG THE PACIFIC COAST. Weber, David J., ed. *New Spain's Far Northern Frontier: Essays on Spain in the American West, 1540-1821* (Albuquerque: U. of New Mexico Pr., 1979): 35-47. Notes the Spanish expeditions along the Pacific Coast of the United States and Canada that were instructed to report on the geography, botany, and zoology of the territory explored, 18th century. Reprinted from Robert G. Ferris, ed., *The American West: An Appraisal* (Santa Fe, 1963): 151-160, 243-245.

192.   Daniel, James M., transl. and ed. DIARY OF PEDRO JOSÉ DE LA FUENTE: CAPTAIN OF THE PRESIDIO OF EL PASO DEL NORTE, AUGUST-DECEMBER, 1765. *Southwestern Hist. Q. 1980 83(3): 259-278.* Continued from a previous article in *Southwestern Historical Quarterly* 1956 60: 260-281. The diary of Captain Pedro José de la Fuente (b. 1722), commander of the presidio of El Paso (modern Texas), August-December 1765, discusses the many trade caravans between Santa Fe and lower Mexico, problems with horse-stealing Apache Indians, and an expedition into New Mexico. Map, 44 notes.   J. H. Broussard

193.   Debien, Gabriel and LeGardeur, René, Jr. LES COLONS DE SAINT-DOMINGUE REFUGIES A LA LOUISIANE (1792-1804) [The colonists from Hispaniola sheltered in Louisiana, 1792-1804]. *Louisiana Rev. 1981 10(1): 11-49, (2): 97-141.* Continued from a previous article. Part 2. Focuses on colonists from Hispaniola during 1798-1803. Part 3. Discusses the migration of hundreds of colonists from Hispaniola to New Orleans, providing the names and estimated dates of arrival of some of the refugees.

194.   Debien, Gabriel and LeGardeur, René. LES COLONS DE SAINT-DOMINGUE RÉFUGIÉS À LA LOUISIANE, 1792-1804 [The refuge of Santo Domingo colonists in Louisiana, 1792-1804]. *Louisiana Rev. 1980 9(2): 101-140.* Reviews relations between the Hispaniola and Louisiana colonies before and after France ceded Louisiana to Spain in 1763, and examines four periods of immigration of colonists from Santo Domingo to Louisiana, 1791-1815.

195.   De la Peña, José Enrique. ¡RECUERDA EL ALAMO! *Am. Heritage 1975 26(6): 57-61, 92-97.* De la Peña described the battle at the Alamo which he witnessed. It could have been avoided if Mexican troops had not allowed the Texans to seek refuge there. Also the Alamo was inconsequential and could have been easily bypassed in the march northward. Santa Anna should not have initiated a battle when he had no medical units to care for the wounded. Poor military leadership resulted in excessive Mexican casualties. From the

book *With Santa Anna in Texas: A Personal Narrative of the Revolution,* by José Enrique de la Peña, translated by Carmen Perry (1975). 7 illus.

B. J. Paul

196. Depalo, William A., Jr. THE ESTABLISHMENT OF THE NUEVA VIZCAYA MILITIA DURING THE ADMINISTRATION OF TEODORO DE CROIX 1776-1783. *New Mexico Hist. R. 1973 58(3): 223-249.* During the 18th century Spanish authorities were much concerned about the security of the northern frontier of New Spain. The area was subjected to attacks by the Apaches and there was a fear that the Russians might organize an attack from Alaska. In 1776 Teodoro de Croix, the Commandant General, organized a militia. Croix then turned his attention to the establishment of military settlements. The growing aggressiveness of the United States caused Spain to take more interest in trying to protect Florida after 1789. J. H. Krenkel

197. Devereaux, Linda Ericson. THE MAGEE-GUTIERREZ EXPEDITION. *Texana 1973 11(1): 52-63.* Chronicles the events of the 1811-15 expedition of the Republican Army of the North, a group of American soldiers from Texas, into Mexican territory under the leadership of an American, Augustus W. Magee, and a Mexican, José Bernardo Maxmilliano Gutierrez de Lara, their aid in the attempt to overthrow the Spanish government, and a massacre of Royalists which they carried out in San Antonio in 1813. 20 notes.

198. Dickason, Olive Patricia. EUROPEANS AND AMERINDIANS: SOME COMPARATIVE ASPECTS OF EARLY CONTACT. *Hist. Papers [Canada] 1979: 182-202.* Surveys the dealings of Spain, Portugal, France, England, Sweden, and the Netherlands with Indians of North, Central, and South America from 1493 to 1888. "The Spaniards came as conquerors, but worried whether their actions were justified on moral or legal grounds. They institutionalized Amerindian forced labour... that stopped just short of slavery, yet they thrashed out the question of Amerindian rights on a scale that far surpassed that of any other European nation in the Americas. Both the Portuguese and the French came as traders and stayed. .. to develop plantation economies based on slavery, but in New France the French founded their hegemony on a system of alliances.... The English came to farm, but found they had to conquer in order to stay. The business-like Dutch, minor colonizers in North America and principally interested in trade, made a major impact by legitimizing their intrusion... by means of land purchases.... It was a procedure which came closest to recognizing Amerindian possessory territorial rights." 84 notes. French summary. S

199. Dillon, Merton L. POLK, EXPANSIONISM, AND MORALITY. *R. in Am. Hist. 1974 2(3): 389-394.* David M. Pletcher's *The Diplomacy of Annexation: Texas, Oregon, and the Mexican War* (Columbia: U. of Missouri Pr., 1973) examines the diplomacy of imperialism and James K. Polk in the 1830's and 1840's, and John H. Schroeder's *Mr. Polk's War: American Opposition and Dissent, 1846-1848* (Madison: U. of Wisconsin Pr., 1973) focuses on the inefficacy of congressional and public antiwar sentiment.

200.   Din, Gilbert C. FRANCISCO BOULIGNY'S 1778 PLANS FOR SET-
TLEMENT IN LOUISIANA. *Southern Studies 1977 16(2): 211-224.* In
November 1776, Captain Francisco Bouligny was appointed lieutenant gover-
nor of the province of Louisiana in charge of immigration, commerce, and
Indian relations. Reprints the text of a letter Bouligny sent on 4 August 1778
to the Minister of the Indies in Seville. Bouligny requested discharged Spanish
soldiers and their wives from Malaga to settle in purely Spanish towns in
Louisiana, recommending Ouachita. Loyal Spanish settlers would offset the
French Creoles and prevent either the English or Americans from encroaching.
The letter also provides information on conditions in Louisiana at the time of
the American Revolution. Based on documents in Archivo General de Indias
in Seville and secondary sources; 18 notes.   J. Buschen

201.   Din, Gilbert C. SPAIN'S IMMIGRATION POLICY AND EFFORTS
IN LOUISIANA DURING THE AMERICAN REVOLUTION. *Louisiana
Studies 1975 14(3): 241-257.* Heeding the detailed 1776 report of Captain
Francisco Bouligny, the Spanish government from 1776 to 1783 attempted to
strengthen its colony in Louisiana by attracting immigrants, developing
commerce, and improving military defenses. The man primarily responsible for
implementing the advice of Bouligny, the dictum of the government, and the
report of Intendant Martin Navarro, who in 1780 wrote *Political Reflections
on the Present Condition of the Province of Louisiana,* was Governor Bernardo
de Galvez. But the Spanish efforts were largely unsuccessful, and in 1787-88
Spain adopted a policy of encouraging Anglo-American settlers to come to
Louisiana. Primary and secondary sources; 50 notes.   B. A. Glasrud

202.   Dix, Agnes S. SPANISH WAR DOGS IN NAVAJO ROCK ART AT
CANYON DE CHELLY, ARIZONA. *Kiva 1980 45(4): 279-283.* A Navajo
pictograph at Canyon de Chelly, which portrays Spanish dragoons, a priest and
large dogs, supports the tentative identification of "Spanish greyhound" bones
excavated from Awatovi Pueblo ruins. The pictograph and dog bones suggest
the use of war dogs by conquistadors on the northern frontier of Mexico. Part
of the mural is interpreted to represent a walking dog master, carrying a long
baton, in charge of a pack of two greyhounds and four smaller dogs.   J

203.   Duffy, John. PHARMACY IN FRANCO-SPANISH LOUISIANA.
Bender, George A. and Parascandola, John, ed. *American Pharmacy in the
Colonial and Revolutionary Periods* (Madison, Wisconsin: American Inst. of
the Hist. of Pharmacy, 1977): 15-26. Examines medical availability and the
practice of pharmacy (including the legal aspects of it) during the French
(1717-69), Spanish (1769-1803), and US (1803-52) jurisdictions in Louisiana;
sketches individuals involved.

204.   Dunlay, Thomas W. INDIAN ALLIES IN THE ARMIES OF NEW
SPAIN AND THE UNITED STATES: A COMPARATIVE STUDY. *New
Mexico Hist. Rev. 1981 56(3): 239-258.* Compares the similarities in the use of
Indian military auxiliaries by the armies of Spain and the United States on the
US frontier, 1561-1886. The US Army adopted many of the Spanish practices
in dealing with Indian allies. They integrated Indians into the military force,
armed them, rewarded them, protected them against other Indians, used them

as intelligence agents, and accepted some as defensive buffer zones against other Indians. The US Army in dealing with Indians used methods that the Spanish had previously found necessary and effective. Primary sources; photo, 38 notes.   P. L. McLaughlin

205.   Ebright, Malcolm. MANUEL MARTÍNEZ'S DITCH DISPUTE: A STUDY IN MEXICAN PERIOD CUSTOM AND JUSTICE. *New Mexico Hist. Rev. 1979 54(1): 21-34.* No formal legal system was established in New Mexico by the Spanish or Mexican authorities. This study demonstrates how custom and tradition, illustrated by a water dispute in 1832, involving Manuel Martinez, was used to settle judicial disputes in the absence of written laws. The relationship between the central government in Santa Fe and the local *ayuntamiento* in New Mexico during the Mexican period is clarified. Local officials, usually in office longer than the governors, had acquired substantial autonomy during this period. Based on documents in the Mexican Archives of New Mexico and secondary sources; illus., 38 notes.   P. L. McLaughlin

206.   Ellis, Bruce T. LA GARITA: SANTA FE'S LITTLE SPANISH FORT. *Palacio 1978 84(2): 2-22.* Discusses the adobe Spanish fort, La Garita, whose origins are shrouded in legend, and which crumbled to the ground by 1954.

207.   Elsasser, Albert B., ed. EXPLORATIONS OF HERNANDO ALAR-CÓN IN THE LOWER COLORADO RIVER REGION, 1540. *J. of California and Great Basin Anthrop. 1979 1(1): 8-37.* Reprints the report of Hernando Alarcón, the first Spanish explorer to have encountered Indians in the southeast corner of California in his search for the "Seven Cities of Cíbola."

208.   Elstob, Winston. ON THE TRAIL OF JUAN BAUTISTA DE ANZA. *Am. West 1976 13(4): 16-17, 63.* Describes the reenactment of the August 1775-June 1776 expedition of Juan Bautista de Anza from Mexico to establish a colony in California. The August 1975-June 1976 bicentennial expedition followed Anza's original route and schedule as closely as possible. Illus.
                                                                    D. L. Smith

209.   Espinosa, Gilberto. TOME VS. VALENCIA, 1846. *New Mexico Hist. R. 1973 48(1): 57-92.* The controversy between the villages of Tome and Valencia in the Rio Grande Valley of New Mexico resulted from a dispute over the celebration of Easter Week in 1846. The people of Tome failed to extend to the curate, Father Baca, the usual invitation to conduct the Easter Week services at their church. Offended, the curate announced that the services would be held in his chapel at Valencia. On 22 March 1846, Father Baca and several followers from Valencia appeared in Tome. He claimed that he was confronted in the plaza by a well-armed group of men. What really happened is unknown, but it led to charges and countercharges, and eventually the matter was taken to court.   J. H. Krenkel

210.   Ezell, Paul. THE EXCAVATION PROGRAM AT THE SAN DIEGO PRESIDIO. *J. of San Diego Hist. 1976 22(4): 1-20.* Discusses the archaeologi-

cal excavations of the San Diego Presidio sponsored by the Serra Museum in San Diego, California, 1964-70's, explaining the founding and early history of the mission during 1769-75.

211. Fairbanks, Charles H. FROM MISSIONARY TO MESTIZO: CHANGING CULTURE OF EIGHTEENTH-CENTURY ST. AUGUS-TINE. *Eighteenth-Century Florida and the Caribbean 1976: 88-99.* Two St. Augustine houses recently were excavated. The abundance of Indian ceramics and the study of food remains indicate the gradual absorption of Indians into Spanish society as food providers, craftsmen, or soldiers' wives. The chronic shortage of all supplies also must have stimulated the use of Indian pottery. The increased amount of British ceramics supports this view and indicates the penetrating power of British trade. Seminole artifacts and military equipment were conspicuously lacking. Biblio.   W. R. Hively

212. Faulk, Odie B. THE PRESIDIO: FORTRESS OR FARCE? Weber, David J., ed. *New Spain's Far Northern Frontier: Essays on Spain in the American West, 1540-1821* (Albuquerque: U. of New Mexico Pr., 1979): 67-76. Presidios in the American Southwest could withstand siege but could not prevent Indian incursions into the Spanish domain, 17th-18th centuries. Reprinted from *Journal of the West* 1969 8(1): 22-28.

213. Feather, Adlai, ed. COLONEL DON FERNANDO DE LA CONCHA DIARY, 1788. *New Mexico Hist. Rev. 1959 34(4): 285-304.* Introduction to and excerpts from the diary of the Governor of New Mexico, Colonel Don Fernando de la Concha, describing the circumstances surrounding the 1788 expedition against the Gila and Mimbres Apaches.

214. Ferguson, Catherine C. and Hoover, Robert L. CERAMIC EFFIGIES FROM MISSION SAN ANTONIO. *Masterkey 1983 57(1): 28-33.* Describes several of the fired clay effigies found in the Salinan neophyte dormitories at Mission San Antonio de Padua in California.

215. Fernández, José B. OPPOSING VIEWS OF *LA FLORIDA:* ALVAR NUÑEZ CABEZA DE VACA AND EL INCA GARCILASO DE LA VEGA. *Florida Hist. Q. 1976 55(2): 170-180.* Alvar Nuñez Cabeza de Vaca (ca. 1490-1556) first published his journal *La Relación,* often called *Los naufragios,* in 1542. Using his own experience as a soldier in De Soto's expedition, he wrote an unfavorable description to warn others of the hardships, Indian dangers, and lack of food. Garcilaso de la Vega (1539-1616) never visited Florida, but he wrote a glowing account, *La Florida del Inca,* in 1605 to encourage colonization. Both accounts helped publicize Florida. 31 notes.   P. A. Beaber

216. Fernández-Santamaría, José A. JUAN GINES DE SEPULVEDA ON THE NATURE OF THE AMERICAN INDIANS. *Americas 1975 31(4): 434-451.* The Spanish 16th-century humanist Juan Ginés de Sepúlveda (1490-1573) is often viewed as one who held the American Indians to be "natural slaves," but his thought was more complex. He considered them inferior and justly conquered, if need be; but if they willingly accepted Spanish

rule they could not properly be treated as slaves, and even if they lost their freedom by unjust resistance to Spain they could not be enslaved unconditionally. Based mainly on his published works; 48 notes. D. Bushnell

217. Fernandez-Shaw, Carlos M. QUIXOTES NORTH OF THE RIO GRANDE. *Américas (Organization of Am. States) 1976 28(9): 8-14.* Discusses Spain's cultural colonialism in Florida, Texas, and the Louisiana Territory, 1513-1803.

218. Gapp, Frank W. THE "CAPTURE" OF MONTEREY IN 1842. *US Naval Inst. Pro. 1979 105(3): 46-54.* In 1842, Commodore Thomas ap Catesby Jones was commander of the US Navy's Pacific Squadron. At Callao, Peru, in August 1842, Jones became concerned not only that war between the United States and Mexico was imminent but that Mexico was on the verge of ceding California to Great Britain. Jones knew that the US government was interested in California and would not let that area of the continent go by default. Accordingly, he took two ships to Monterey, California's chief trading post, arriving there on 19 October 1842. Although there was no sign of a British fleet, or any signs of war between the United States and Mexico, Jones landed a force, occupied the fort, and took over the town. Jones was soon convinced that he had made a mistake, so he withdrew his sailors and gave the town back to the Spanish authorities. He remained in Monterey until November, and partied with the town's citizens. Eventually, he returned to his post as squadron commander, knowing he would be recalled for his actions. He became known as the man who captured Monterey four years too soon. Primary and secondary sources; 4 photos, 22 notes. A. N. Garland

219. Garner, Van Hastings. THE DYNAMICS OF CHANGE: NEW MEXICO 1680 TO 1690. *J. of the West 1979 18(1): 4-13.* In 1680 the Pueblo Indians rebelled against Spanish rule, throwing Hispanic settlers into confusion and conflict with their traditional social, political, and economic system which depended on Indian subjugation. The *ecomienda,* a government grant to citizens for military obligations, had given the settlers some political independence from the government. When the Indian uprising forced the Spanish New Mexicans to flee to El Paso, Texas, and the protection of the presidio, the refugees at first resisted the governor's attempts to change their status from citizen-soldiers to farmers. New Mexico's frontier society was adaptive, however, and the settlers eventually accepted their loss of political power in exchange for a new economic support through service at the presidio. Primary and secondary sources; map, 3 tables, 52 notes. B. S. Porter

220. Garner, Van Hastings. SEVENTEENTH CENTURY NEW MEXICO. *J. of Mexican Am. Hist. 1974 4(1): 41-70.* Maintains that a much more complicated set of circumstances existed in New Mexico before the Pueblo Revolt of 1680 than the traditional views of France V. Scholes, *Church and State in New Mexico 1610-1650* (Clair Shores: Scholarly Press, 1971) or Jack D. Forbes, *Apache, Navaho and Spaniard* (Norman: U. of Oklahoma Press, 1963) would indicate. Examines the interrelationship of soldier, governor, Pueblo and Athapascan Indian, and the mission system in New Mexico. Primary and secondary sources; 85 notes. R. T. Fulton

221. Garr, Daniel J. POWER AND PRIORITIES: CHURCH-STATE BOUNDARY DISPUTES IN SPANISH CALIFORNIA. *California History 1978-79 57(4): 364-375.* Traces the conflict between Franciscan missionaries and Spanish efforts to establish civil settlements in Alta California in the late 18th century. Father Junípero Serra opposed establishing the San Jose pueblo in 1777, and Father Fermín de Lasuén protested against the location of Villa de Branciforte 20 years later. The missionaries held that such settlements violated laws guaranteeing the integrity of mission Indian settlements, property, and livestock. Spanish viceroys, however, placed greater priority on the need for civil settlements, increased population of Spanish subjects, and control of territory threatened by encroachment from other countries. To the viceroys and governors, the missionary view unrealistically promoted isolation and perpetual stewardship over the Indians, not true colonization of the province. Primary and secondary sources; illus. (reproductions); 58 notes.

A. Hoffman

222. Garr, Daniel J. A RARE AND DESOLATE LAND: POPULATION AND RACE IN HISPANIC CALIFORNIA. *Western Hist. Q. 1975 6(2): 133-148.* Logistic problems in the remote frontier and the decreasing inclination and resources of Spanish and Mexican colonizers crippled efforts to settle California. In theory, Spanish policy dictated that California should be settled by respectable and industrious soldiers and settlers along with their families. In practice, the only sustained governmental program brought in periodic shipments of convicts and vagabonds from the jails and streets of New Spain. The best Spanish designs were compromised by circumstances beyond their control. Spanish colonization efforts failed to produce any significant effect on California, while an underpopulated and under-financed Mexico virtually abdicated California to the Yankees. 75 notes.

D. L. Smith

223. Garr, Daniel. VILLA DE BRANCIFORTE: INNOVATION AND ADAPTATION ON THE FRONTIER. *Americas (Acad. of Am. Franciscan Hist.) 1978 35(1): 95-109.* Planned as a combination of civilian settlement and military outpost, Villa de Branciforte was the last Spanish colonial town founded in California. In its main features, it was to have continued a "generally successful tradition of frontier endeavor." The first settlers reached the site in 1797. However, because of administrative incompetence and inadequate resources the settlement never lived up to expectations. It disappeared as "an identifiable entity" in 1907. Primary sources; 85 notes.

D. Bushnell

224. Geiger, Maynard. HARMONIOUS NOTES IN SPANISH CALIFORNIA. *Southern California Q. 1975 57(3): 243-250.* Describes the work of Franciscans, especially Fray Narciso Durán, in teaching Indian neophytes to sing and play musical instruments. Durán worked at the San Jose and Santa Barbara missions 1806-46. He devised rules for Indians to follow in playing from musical notation; some of his compositions, which combined singing and playing of instruments, are still performed. Includes a letter from Durán to the College of San Fernando in 1819 requesting that an organ be provided for Mission San Jose. Based on primary and secondary sources; 24 notes.

A. Hoffman

225. Gerster, Patrick and Cords, Nicholas. OLD WORLD UTOPIANISM AND NEW WORLD MYTHOLOGY. *Indiana Social Studies Q. 1975/76 28(3): 95-106.* Cites utopian myths from England, Spain, and France in the 16th to 18th centuries, and their effect on exploration and colonization of the Americas.

226. Getzler, Michael H.; Chappell, Bruce S.; and McWatters, D. Lorne. NEW ACCESS TO THE HISTORY OF SPANISH FLORIDA: THE SPANISH FLORIDA BORDERLANDS PROJECT. *Escribano 1978 15: 49-60.* Describes the holdings of the P. K. Yonge Library in Gainesville, Florida, specifically the John P. Stetson Collection, the East Florida Papers, and the Papeles de Cuba, as they relate to the history of Spanish East Florida, 1565-1821, being studied under the Spanish Florida Borderlands Project.

227. Gilbert, Benjamin F. SPAIN'S PORT OF SAN FRANCISCO, 1755-1822. *J. of the West 1981 20(3): 21-29.* San Francisco Bay long eluded explorers of the California coast, until its discovery by an overland party in 1769. Recognizing the potential of the excellent harbor, Spain sent navigators to chart the bay (1774) and colonists to settle the land (1776). The first foreign ships in the Spanish port came in the 1790's. Prohibitions against foreign commerce were difficult to enforce after 1800 due to the lack of Spanish supply ships and the enticements of manufactured trade goods. Spain's restrictive commercial policies retarded economic development of the port city. After California came under Mexican control (1822), barriers were relaxed and the hide and tallow trade began to flourish. 8 photos, 56 notes.   B. S. Porter

228. Goss, Robert C. THE CHURCHES OF SAN XAVIER, ARIZONA AND CABORCA, SONORA: A COMPARATIVE ANALYSIS. *Kiva 1975 40(3): 165-180.* "Located less than 200 miles apart on opposite sides of the international border separating Arizona and Sonora, Mexico are two mission churches, strikingly similar in appearance, but of undetermined relationship. The churches of San Xavier del Bac, located near Tucson, Arizona, and Nuestra Señora de la Purísima Concepción del Caborca in the town of Caborca, Mexico have been referred to as sister or twin churches. Visually the resemblance between the structure is sufficiently strong to suggest kinship. However, of the many Latin cross plan churches built with crossing domes and twin towers in New Spain, a considerable number probably appeared quite similar without necessarily sharing the same plan, architect, or inspiration. Since little evidence concerning the facts of construction of either the San Xavier or Caborca church has been uncovered, the existing structures themselves must be examined for clues that help explain their similarity. This paper investigates the relationship between the two mission churches by analyzing their historical backgrounds, architectural and sculptural styles, structural dimensions, and the materials and probable techniques used in their construction. A comparison of these elements permits judgments to be made concerning the degree and nature of kinship between the churches."   J

229. Guest, Francis F. AN EXAMINATION OF THE THESIS OF S. F. COOK ON THE FORCED CONVERSION OF INDIANS IN THE CALIFORNIA MISSIONS. *Southern California Q. 1979 61(1): 1-77.* Argues

against the view of scholar Sherburne Friend Cook that Franciscan missionaries during the last half of the mission period forced Indians into the California missions and then forcibly converted them. Cook mistranslated, misread, misunderstood, and omitted important documentation bearing on the problem. In 1943 he formulated a thesis and proceeded to find evidence to support it, resulting in an influential addition to the Black Legend. Cook's thesis is refuted: missionaries did not administer baptism indiscriminately; expeditions which brought back Indians were military rather than religious in nature; often such expeditions visited Christian and non-Christian villages without seizing Indians; Indians captured for horse-stealing were considered prisoners, not candidates for conversion; only a fraction of the California Indians were ever baptized; many Indians working in Hispanic society during and after the mission period never became Christians; and other important points. Primary and secondary sources; 224 notes, 2 appendixes.   A. Hoffman

230. Habig, Marion A., ed.; Leutenegger, Benedict, transl.; and Puelles, José María de Jesús. PUELLES' REPORT OF 1827 ON THE TEXAS-LOUISIANA BOUNDARY. *Louisiana Hist. 1978 19(2): 133-181.* A translation of the "Report to the President of the Mexican Republic on the Boundaries between the Provinces of Texas and Louisiana," prepared by the Franciscan missionary Father José María de Jesús Puelles (1772-1840) in 1827. The original *Informe* was published in Zacatecas in 1828. This report supports Spanish and Mexican claims that the boundary between Texas and Louisiana was the Calcasieu River and Arroyo Hondo, rather than the Sabine River as the United States claimed. Puelles detailed the history of the border region chronologically from 1512 to 1813. He had made a thorough investigation of the question in 1806-07, and prepared this report in response to a request by the Mexican government in 1827. Reproduces his map, which accompanied the report. 180 notes.   R. L. Woodward, Jr.

231. Hale, Duane K. CALIFORNIA'S FIRST MINING FRONTIER AND ITS INFLUENCE ON THE SETTLEMENT OF THAT AREA. *J. of the West 1979 18(1): 14-21.* Mining in California began about 20 years after its settlement by Spanish missionaries. Metals, including gold and silver, were found near Santa Barbara, San Fernando, San Diego, Santa Ana, and San Francisco. The development of mines in California coincided with declining production in Mexico before 1790. After that year, improved technology revived the Mexican mines, and Upper California's mineral resources were neglected and forgotten. During the Mexican period, placer gold was mined near San Luis Obispo and Los Angeles. These discoveries failed to bring large immigration to the frontier because the Hispanic governments were unable to provide adequate supplies or protection. Published primary and secondary sources; 2 illus., map, 54 notes.   B. S. Porter

232. Hale, Duane Kendall. MINERAL EXPLORATION IN THE SPANISH BORDERLANDS, 1513-1846. *J. of the West 1981 20(2): 5-20.* Spanish and Mexican period mineral explorations in the states of Florida, Georgia, the Carolinas, New Mexico, Arizona, Texas, and California were more extensive than historians have generally recognized. Mining also was widely established, following the spread of missions, as shown by Spanish documents and the

discovery of mining remains by 19th-century American miners. Mining development in the borderlands did not match that of the mines in Mexico; shortage of labor was a major problem. Based on US government geological surveys and accounts of Spanish explorations; 5 maps, 5 illus., 146 notes.

B. S. Porter

233.   Hall, E. Boyd. PORTFOLIO OF SPANISH COLONIAL DESIGN. *Palacio 1975 81(2): 1-10.* Discusses folk arts in New Mexico (primarily *santos bultos* and *ex-votos* associated with Catholic iconography), decorative arts, and manuscript production, 16th-17th centuries.

234.   Hall, G. Emlen. JUAN ESTEVAN PINO, "SE LOS COMA": NEW MEXICO LAND SPECULATION IN THE 1820S. *New Mexico Hist. Rev. 1982 57(1): 27-42.* Discusses the influence of politician Juan Estevan Pino as a speculator in New Mexico land. Pino exemplified the growing inclination to regard land as an important asset for its monetary rather than its purely agricultural value. His actions "laid the groundwork" for subsequent land speculation in this area. Based on the US Bureau of Land Management records, Surveyor General's Reports at the State Records Center and Archives, Santa Fe, New Mexico, and other primary sources; map, 40 notes.

A. C. Dempsey

235.   Hammond, George P. THE SEARCH FOR THE FABULOUS IN THE SETTLEMENT OF THE SOUTHWEST. Weber, David J., ed. *New Spain's Far Northern Frontier: Essays on Spain in the American West, 1540-1821* (Albuquerque: U. of New Mexico Pr., 1979): 17-33. Recounts Spanish expeditions of discovery in the American Southwest and the myths that prompted them, such as the story of the Seven Cities of Cibola, 16th-18th centuries. Reprinted from *Utah Historical Quarterly* 1956 24(1): 1-19.

236.   Herring, Patricia Roche. THE SILVER OF EL REAL DE ARIZO-NAC. *Arizona and the West 1978 20(3): 245-258.* An Indian discovery of nuggets of silver ore along an arroyo near Real de Arizonac, a mining district in northern Sonora, precipitated a rush in 1736. It was rumored that the silver was refined and perhaps buried treasure. An official investigation generated a controversy that involved local prospectors, merchants, the viceroy of New Spain, and the crown. A complicated legal system raised insurmountable obstacles to exploitation, but local officials could not carry out the king's orders to collect the controversial silver. Although it was a minor event in the history of New Spain, it left an enduring legacy: it perpetuated the idea of great riches in northern Sonora, and it permanently fastened Arizona as the name of the region. 3 illus., map, 28 notes.

D. L. Smith

237.   Hitsman, J. Mackay. THE TEXAS WAR OF 1835-1836. *Hist. Today [Great Britain] 1960 10(2): 116-123.* Discusses the struggle of Texas to gain independence from Mexico in 1835-36 and the military role of Sam Houston (1793-1863) in achieving it.

238.   Hoffman, Paul E. A NEW VOYAGE OF NORTH AMERICAN DISCOVERY: PEDRO DE SALAZAR'S VISIT TO THE "LAND OF THE

GIANTS." *Florida Hist. Q. 1980 58(4): 415-426.* Captain Pedro de Salazar was perhaps the first Spaniard to explore North America north of Florida. Salazar conducted a slaving raid that touched the North and South Carolina mainland between northern Georgia and Cape Fear between 1514 and 1516. Salazar's raid laid the basis for future Spanish exploration of that coast. Based on Spanish-Indian records (Madrid) and secondary sources; 38 notes.

N. A. Kuntz

239.   Hoffman, Paul E. ST. AUGUSTINE 1580: THE RESEARCH PROJECT. *Escribano 1977 14: 5-19.* Discusses a project involving research into documents, maps, manuscripts, and personal journals to reconstruct daily life in St. Augustine, Florida, in 1580.

240.   Holmes, Jack D. L. EDUCATIONAL OPPORTUNITIES IN SPANISH WEST FLORIDA, 1781-1821. *Florida Hist. Q. 1981 60(1): 77-87.* The legend of Spanish incompetence in terms of educational opportunities does not withstand examination. An analysis of official reports, diaries, and memoirs indicates surprising educational opportunities in West Florida. Based on family letters, military records, and other sources; 46 notes.

N. A. Kuntz

241.   Holmes, Jack D. L. JUAN DE LA VILLEBEUVRE AND SPANISH INDIAN POLICY IN WEST FLORIDA, 1784-1797. *Florida Hist. Q. 1980 58(4): 387-399.* Juan de la Villebeuvre (1732-97) was a crucial figure in the development of Spanish-Choctaw relations. Between 1784 and 1797 he was instrumental in formulating treaties in the Old Southwest that insured Choctaw loyalty to Spain. He represents the best aspect of Spanish-Indian relations. Based on Spanish records (Madrid) and secondary sources; 49 notes.

N. A. Kuntz

242.   Holmes, Jack D. L. A NEW LOOK AT SPANISH LOUISIANA CENSUS ACCOUNTS: THE RECENT HISTORIOGRAPHY OF ANTONIO ACOSTA. *Louisiana Hist. 1980 21(1): 77-86.* Briefly describes the research of a young Spanish demographer-historian, Antonio Acosta Rodríquez, whose careful studies of the censuses of Spanish colonial Louisiana will cause some reassessment of this period in Louisiana history. Cites in full the 74 census reports analyzed in Acosta's PhD dissertation (U. of Seville, 1976). Based on census reports in the Archivo General de Indias, Seville; 80 notes.

D. B. Touchstone

243.   Holmes, Jack D. L. UP THE TOMBIGBEE WITH THE SPANIARDS: JUAN DE LA VILLEBEUVRE AND THE TREATY OF BOUCFOUCA. *Alabama Hist. Q. 1978 40(1-2): 51-61.* Provides the text of the Treaty of Boucfouca (1793), which Lieutenant Colonel Juan de la Villebeuvre concluded between Spain and the Choctaw Indians, who seemed to welcome Spanish protection against American frontiersmen.   S

244.   Hoover, Robert L. AGRICULTURAL ACCULTURATION AT MISSION SAN ANTONIO. *Masterkey 1980 54(4): 142-145.* Archaeological excavations in the 1970's at Mission San Antonio de Padua, California, reveal the complex nature of acculturation among the Salinan Indians between 1771 and

1832, especially in regard to the agricultural practices at the Mission which combined imported crops and technology with native plants and methods.

245.   Hoover, Robert L. A SPANISH *ACEQUIA* AT MISSION SAN ANTONIO. *Masterkey 1982 56(2): 69-72.* Describes the excavations by California Polytechnic State University, San Luis Obispo at Mission San Antonio de Padua in Monterey County, during 1979-81; discoveries included an *acequia* or aqueduct built for the soldiers' barracks in 1776.

246.   Hornbeck, David and Tucey, Mary. ANGLO IMMIGRATION AND THE HISPANIC TOWN: A STUDY OF URBAN CHANGE IN MONTEREY, CALIFORNIA 1835-1850. *Social Sci. J. 1976 13(2): 1-8.* Argues that the effect of Anglo immigration on developing California was not restricted to gold mining areas and that much urban change and expansion took place in Hispanic towns such as Monterey before 1850.

247.   Hornbeck, David. LAND TENURE AND RANCHO EXPANSION IN ALTA CALIFORNIA, 1784-1846. *J. of Hist. Geography 1978 4(4): 371-390.* Popular writers and historians have viewed the rancho as a symbol of the halcyon days of hispanic California and often have overlooked the role of rancho land grants in changing the land tenure system of Alta California during Mexican occupance. This paper views the rancho as an integral part of a land tenure system under which considerable land was granted and examines the patterns of rancho land grants to 1846. The majority of rancho grants were less than six years old at the end of Mexican rule, but they were instrumental in introducing a new land tenure system which imposed a distinct order and design on the Alta California landscape. The land policies of Mexico have been strikingly persistent; rancho boundaries still constitute a prominent part of the modern landscape of California. As a settlement institution, the rancho was more than boundaries delimiting ownership of land, it was the primary means by which resources were distributed, organized and exploited. While the granting of land in Alta California was a distinctive practice, an investigation of how this land system came about and its impact on the land adds to our understanding of tenure practices in general and in particular provides insights into the way in which cultural and economic values are impressed on the land through land ordinances.   J

248.   Hutchinson, C. Alan. GENERAL JOSÉ ANTONIO MEXIA AND HIS TEXAS INTERESTS. *Southwestern Hist. Q. 1978 82(2): 117-142.* Discusses the political and financial interests of General José Antonio Mexia (1800?-39), whose career centered around Mexican Texas. Initial documented activity was in connection with attempted colonization by Louisianians in Mexican Texas under Emperor Iturbide in early 1823. He had a close connection with the Masonic order in Mexico, an influence which was several times of value to him. Mexia married an English girl, Charlotte Walker, who subsequently took a lively interest in Mexican politics. Mexia was connected with General Nicolás Bravo, a lifelong friendship with Father José Maria Alpuche e Infante. José Ignacio Esteva obtained for him a post as a customs official, the foundation of his fortune. Very large investments were made by Mexia in Texas land. He first aided General Antonio López de Santa Anna,

then broke with him. Mexia was executed by Santa Anna in 1839 after an unsuccessful revolt. Archival and secondary material; 3 illus., 55 notes.

J. L. B. Atkinson

249.   Hutchinson, C. Alan. AN OFFICIAL LIST OF THE MEMBERS OF THE HIJAR-PADRES COLONY FOR MEXICAN CALIFORNIA, 1834. *Pacific Hist. R. 1973 42(3): 407-418.* Reprints a list made just before the colonists set sail from San Blas, Mexico, on 3 August 1834 for Alta California, which nearly doubles the number previously thought to have been in the expedition. Lists the 239 passengers alphabetically under each ship, including age, occupation, and familial relationships when known. 7 notes.

B. L. Fenske

250.   Ives, Ronald L. FATHER KINO'S 1697 ENTRADA TO THE CASA GRANDE RUIN IN ARIZONA: A RECONSTRUCTION. *Arizona and the West 1973 15(4): 345-370.* In 1934, historian Herbert Eugene Bolton retraced the 1697 route of Father Eusebio Francisco Kino (Chini) from his mission station at Dolores, Sonora, Mexico, to the prehistoric ruin at Casa Grande, Arizona. Bolton's reconstruction contained many discrepancies. The author used Kino-party diaries, geological maps, aerial photographs, and field expeditions 1968-72, to accurately trace the Kino expedition route. 5 illus., 6 maps, 57 notes.
D. L. Smith

251.   John, Elizabeth A. H. GOOD NEWS AND BAD ON THE MEXICAN FRONTIER: A REVIEW ESSAY. *New Mexico Hist. Rev. 1982 57(3): 289-293.* David J. Weber's *The Mexican Frontier, 1821-1846: The American Southwest Under Mexico* is an excellent treatment of the border and Mexican-American relations in Texas, New Mexico, Arizona, and California. This edition discusses the wide range of problems and growth. The importance of greater understanding is currently necessary. Some research is currently funded by private and federal grants. The work undertaken by the Southwestern Mission Research Center (Arizona State Museum, Tucson) reflects current interest. With grants currently limited, Weber's work will be considered one of the best on Mexican-American border history.   K. E. Gilmont

252.   Johns, Sally Cavell. VIVA LOS CALIFORNIOS: THE BATTLE OF SAN PASQUAL. *J. of San Diego Hist. 1973 19(4): 1-13.*

253.   Johnson, Kenneth M. THE BATTLE OF SAN PASQUAL. *Pacific Hist. 1977 21(4): 368-373.* Describes the 1847 Battle of San Pasqual, the only real battle during the American occupation of California in the Mexican War. General Stephen Watts Kearny used bad judgment, and the battle could have been avoided. Bibliographical note.   G. L. Olson

254.   Jones, Oakah L., Jr. HISPANIC TRADITIONS AND IMPROVISATIONS OF THE FRONTERA SEPTENTRIONAL OF NEW SPAIN. *New Mexico Hist. Rev. 1981 56(4): 333-347.* Discusses some of the social and economic customs of Spanish settlers on the northern frontier of New Spain in the 18th century. Many of the folk practices of the Spanish settlers, although modified by New World circumstances, had their basis in Old World Hispanic

customs. The preservation of Spanish customs and the creation of new folk practices to meet the frontier conditions, help to explain the nature of colonial life and the preservation of traditional Hispanic practices by settlers on the northern frontier. Based on the Spanish Archives of New Mexico, State Records Center and Archives, Santa Fe, and other primary sources; photo, 63 notes. P. L. McLaughlin

255. Jones, Oakah L., Jr. PUEBLO INDIAN AUXILIARIES IN NEW MEXICO, 1763-1821. *New Mexico Hist. Rev. 1962 37(2): 81-109.* Discusses how Spain tried to control the Indians by placing them in settled communities, and using Indians as auxiliary members of the Spanish military, focusing on the Pueblo auxiliaries in New Mexico; 1763-1821.

256. Jones, Oakah L., Jr. SPANISH CIVIL COMMUNITIES AND SETTLERS IN FRONTIER NEW MEXICO, 1790-1810. Coker, William S., ed. *Hispanic-American Essays in Honor of Max Leon Moorhead* (Pensacola, Fla.: Perdido Bay Pr., 1979): 37-60. Examines both the Spanish civil communities and the compositon of their population in New Mexico in the late 18th and early 19th centuries, noting classes, origins, and occupations of these populations. The population grew and dispersed from the Río Grande Valley into the mountains and plains. Society was formally, though not rigidly, stratified. The extended family was the basis of society. Intermarriage among classes was common. Few European-born Spaniards were present. Assimilation of Indians into Spanish society was notable. Farmers, day laborers, and weavers constituted the majority of the population. Based on various *padrones* (census returns of 1790, in the Spanish Archives of New Mexico), and the "Noticia de las Misiones" of Fray Josef Benito Pereyo (1810), in the William G. Ritch Collection of the Huntington Library; map, 5 tables, 48 notes. J. Powell

257. Kells, Robert. THE SPANISH INHERITANCE: THE MEXICAN FORCES OF ALTA CALIFORNIA, 1822-1846. *J. of the West 1981 20(4): 12-19.* The Mexican period of California history is characterized by political instability caused in part by the government's neglect of the remote province. The military force inherited from the ousted Spanish government had long suffered from lack of supplies and pay, a circumstance not improved under Mexican rule, and resulting in a weak defense establishment. In 1842, faced with a severe shortage of troops, Governor Manuel Micheltorena brought about 350 men from Mexico, convicts and other undesirables who contributed nothing to security but who preyed on the civilians they were supposed to protect. After the missions were secularized, the former presidial troops became private armies for their officers, such as Mariano Vallejo, and participated in the bloodless battles fought by rival political factions. 4 photos, 32 notes. B. S. Porter

258. Kelly, Annamaria. EUSEBIO CHINO, PIONEER OF THE AMERICAN SOUTHWEST. *Italian Americana 1977 3(2): 131-144.* A short biography of Italian Jesuit Eusebio Francisco Kino (1645-1711), who under Spanish jurisdiction in the New World was one of the first explorers of the southwestern areas of the United States. M. T. Wilson

259.   Kelsey, Harry. THE CALIFORNIA ARMADA OF JUAN RODRI-
GUEZ CABRILLO. *Southern California Q. 1979 61(4): 313-336.* Traces the
construction and disposition of 13 ships built in the 1530's by Juan Rodríguez
Cabrillo for his friend and commander, Pedro de Alvarado, to explore Pacific
islands and California. Delays occurred with the outbreak of an Indian war in
June 1541, the death of Alvarado, and a major earthquake in Guatemala. After
a year the expeditions were again organized, under the sponsorship of Viceroy
Antonio de Mendoza. Cabrillo received command of three ships for the
exploration of the coast of California, and the fleet sailed in February 1542.
Examines conflicting evidence about the number of ships in the fleet, the
number under Cabrillo's command, and their names. Cabrillo died on the
voyage, his fleet was dispersed, and a report was filed and forgotten in the
Spanish archives. 107 notes.   A. Hoffman

260.   Kessell, John L. A MAN CAUGHT BETWEEN TWO WORLDS:
DIEGO ROMERO, THE PLAINS APACHES, AND THE INQUISITION.
Am. West 1978 15(3): 12-16. The governor of Santa Fe, New Mexico, sent
Capt. Diego Romero (d. 1678) with a packtrain of trade merchandise to the
Plains Apache Indians in Texas. The object of the 1660 expedition was to
obtain prime buffalo hides and tanned skins. Romero's father had been an
honored trader with the Apache so they made him an honorary "captain" also.
The ceremony, a probable "marriage" to an Apache maiden, and his relations
with other Apache women became the basis for a multiple indictment by the
Mexican Inquisition in 1663. His modified sentence included banishment from
New Mexico for ten years. Before the exile terminated he married under an
assumed name. The Inquisition caught up with the "incorrigible backslider"
again and sentenced him to six years in the galleys. He died in a Mexican jail
while waiting for his first galley assignment. Bibliographic note, 2 illus.
D. L. Smith

261.   Kessell, John L. A TALE OF TWO PUEBLOS. *Palacio 1979 85(3):
2-5.* New Mexico's Governor Francisco Antonio Marín del Valle switched
titles on maps for the locations of the abandoned pueblos of Tajique and
Quarai, calling the actual Tajique "Quarai" because the remains of the holy
Franciscan Father Jerónimo de la Llana were discovered in the actual Tajique
in 1759 on the 100th anniversary of his death, even though the actual Quarai
had been listed as his burial place.

262.   Killea, Lucy. THE TRUE ORIGINS OF SPANISH COLONIAL
OFFICIALS AND MISSIONARIES. *J. of San Diego Hist. 1977 23(1): 55-63.*
Castillians were among the first to join in the conquest of New Spain, but
Spaniards from peripheral parts of the Iberian Peninsula were primary in
exploration and settlement of Alta California, 1691-1810.

263.   Kinnaird, Lawrence and Kinnaird, Lucia. SECULARIZATION OF
FOUR NEW MEXICAN MISSIONS. *New Mexico Hist. Rev. 1979 54(1):
35-41.* In 1767 the Spanish government began to tighten its control over the
mission system. Inspection tours of the northern frontier revealed that as the
Spanish population increased, the Indians decreased. Many Indians served by
the Franciscans were *genízaros,* Indians captured as children and reared in

Spanish families. There were not enough Indians in many places to justify maintaining missions at government expense. In July 1767, Viceroy Croix approved the secularization of four of the 28 Franciscan missions in New Mexico. The four missions were at Santa Fe, El Paso, Albuquerque, and Santa Cruz de la Cañada. Based on manuscripts from the Pinart Collection in the Bancroft Library and secondary sources; 2 letters, 6 notes.

P. L. McLaughlin

264. Kinnaird, Lawrence. SPANISH TREATIES WITH INDIAN TRIBES. *Western Hist. Q. 1979 10(1): 39-48.* Spanish Indian policy was to conquer, convert, and civilize. When Spain acquired Louisiana by diplomacy rather than conquest, her officials there realized the old methods would not work in the new territory. Instead, trade and diplomacy were employed reasonably to control the Indians on the Louisiana frontier. Establishing treaty relationships lessened the necessity of military force and provided "a peaceful chapter" in the history of the Spanish borderlands. 23 notes.

D. L. Smith

265. Kraemer, Paul M. NEW MEXICO'S ANCIENT SALT TRADE. *Palacio 1976 82(1): 22-30.* Traces the importance of New Mexico's Estancia Basin saline lakes for the procurement and trade of salt among indigenous peoples, Spanish explorers, and Mexican and American settlers, prehistory-1840's.

266. Lacy, James M. NEW MEXICAN WOMEN IN EARLY AMERICAN WRITINGS. *New Mexico Hist. Rev. 1959 34(1): 41-51.* Reprints excerpts from accounts of American travelers in New Mexico during the first half of the 19th century describing the women there as beautiful and mannered despite living in a rough and barren land.

267. Langellier, John Phillip and Peterson, Katherine Meyers. LANCES AND LEATHER JACKETS: PRESIDIAL FORCES IN SPANISH ALTA CALIFORNIA, 1769-1821. *J. of the West 1981 20(4): 3-11.* Presidial soldiers, and later their families, were the core of early California's European population. Their primary duties were to protect the missions, explore unknown territory, and represent the Spanish government to foreign visitors. For this, the soldiers received a meager pay, which also had to cover the cost of uniforms and equipment. Most soldiers were young, illiterate, of humble birth, and from the northern provinces of Mexico. Despite their poor beginnings, many individuals found military service a means to improve their lot through promotion, civil service appointment, and—the key to social status—acquisition of land. Based on documents in the Bancroft Library, University of California at Berkeley; 8 photos, 50 notes.

B. S. Porter

268. Langum, David J. *CALIFORNIO* WOMEN AND THE IMAGE OF VIRTUE. *Southern California Q. 1977 59(3): 245-250.* Examines the stereotype of *Californio* women as virtuous and chaste. Contemporary observers had conflicting opinions; some endorsed the virtuous view, while others found *Californio* women to have dubious morals. Suggests that the reason for the variety of opinion lies in the level of social class observed by the visitor; thus Richard Henry Dana may have seen lower class women, while William Heath

Davis extolled upper class females. Based on contemporary published works; 14 notes.   A. Hoffman

269.   Langum, David J. CALIFORNIOS AND THE IMAGE OF INDO-LENCE. *Western Hist. Q. 1978 19(2): 181-196.* Almost all Americans who traveled in California before the Mexican War characterized the male Californios as lazy, without personal initiative, and unwilling to work. The conventional causal explanations for these American attitudes of Manifest Destiny, Anglo-Saxon racism, and militant Protestantism are insufficient. Historians have confused correlation with causation. Russian, French, English, German, Swedish, and even Spanish writers expressed similar views of the Californios. This suggests that the American and European attitudes were probably more related to the Industrial Revolution than to the traditionally attributed causal factors. 51 notes.   D. L. Smith

270.   Langum, David J. THE CARING COLONY: ALTA CALIFORNIA'S PARTICIPATION IN SPAIN'S FOREIGN AFFAIRS. *Southern California Q. 1980 62(3): 217-228.* The Spanish province of Alta California was not as isolated from world events as historians have depicted. When Spain fought against England (1779-83), France (1793-95), England (1796-1802), and France (1808-13), the colony raised funds, offered prayers, and made contingency plans in case of invasion. During the Spanish-American Wars of Independence, Alta California experienced a major conspiracy plot and an attack by the forces of Argentine privateer Hippolyte Bouchard. The involvement in the mother country's wars strongly suggests that Californians were far more concerned and far less isolated than heretofore believed. 31 notes.
                                                                      A. Hoffman

271.   Lavender, David. EUSEBIO FRANCISCO KINO: MISSIONARY-EXPLORER OF THE SOUTHWEST. *Am. West 1978 15(3): 4-11.* Eusebio Francisco Kino (d. 1711) was a Jesuit missionary prominent in Spanish expansionism from Sonora, Mexico, into Arizona. As a particular mission enterprise succeeded, the establishment was turned over to secular clergy and the mission properties were divided among the local Indians. The missionaries moved on to begin anew. Kino believed that the inordinately harsh land could be tamed for fruitful uses and that the taming could be accomplished without annihilating the Indians. Adapted from a forthcoming book. 3 illus., map.
                                                                      D. L. Smith

272.   Lecompte, Janet. THE INDEPENDENT WOMEN OF HISPANIC NEW MEXICO, 1821-1846. *Western Hist. Q. 1981 12(1): 17-35.* Geographic-, Indian-, and Spanish mercantilism-induced insularity, and their relations in alternately fighting and trading with their Indian neighbors, account for the distinctive culture which New Mexicans, especially women, developed during the Spanish period, 1598-1821. This underwent significant modifications and changes in the 1821-46 years of the Mexican republic. Foreign visitors, traders, and trappers introduced new skills, attitudes, and materials. Accounts of visitors, although marred by cultural bias and ignorance, and New Mexican alcalde court archives, reveal a clear description of women's legal and social rights. 44 notes.   D. L. Smith

273.   Lecompte, Janet. LA TULES AND THE AMERICANS. *Arizona and the West 1978 20(3): 215-230.* Doña Gertrudis Barceló (1800-50), known as La Tules, the common diminutive for Gertrudis, was a woman of personal charm, business acumen, keen intelligence, and far-flung fame. She owned and ran the most elegant gambling saloon in the New Mexican capital. She was a lady of the highest social standing, a fashion leader, and a close friend and business partner of the governor. Americans, conditioned by a different idea of the place and role of women in society and business were delighted and charmed by this dominant figure in Sante Fe during 1830's-40's; nevertheless, they were careful about being seen with her and associating with her too openly. 2 illus., map, 38 notes.   D. L. Smith

274.   Lecompte, Janet. MANUEL ARMIJO AND THE AMERICANS. *J. of the West 1980 19(3): 51-63.* Manuel Armijo, governor of New Mexico during 1827-29 and 1837-46, was described by contemporary Americans as an assassin and coward for his treatment of captured Texans in 1841, and his flight from General Kearny's army in 1846. In fact, Armijo was a realist who dealt with abusive American trappers and traders and with threats of invasion as well as could be expected. Armijo was an effective administrator who was loyal to the central government, but he lacked adequate financing and military support to protect his territory. Based on the Mexican Archives of New Mexico, State Records Center, Santa Fe; and Manuel Armijo's diary in the Ritch Collection, Henry E. Huntington Library, San Marino, California; 5 photos, 3 maps, 57 notes.   B. S. Porter

275.   Lecompte, Janet. MANUEL ARMIJO'S FAMILY HISTORY. *New Mexico Hist. R. 1973 58(3): 251-258.* Armijo was New Mexico's last Mexican governor. The first biographical sketch of him was written by journalist George Wilkins Kendall and published in the *New Orleans Picayune.*
                                                           J. H. Krenkel

276.   LeRiverend, Julio. PROBLEMAS HISTÓRICOS DE LA CONQUIS-TA DE AMÉRICA: LAS CASAS Y SU TIEMPO [Historical problems of the conquest of America: Las Casas and his times]. *Casa de las Américas [Cuba] 1974 15(85): 4-15.* Discusses the missionary Fray Bartolomé de Las Casas (1474-1566), discussing his writings and their effect on later conquests of America.

277.   Leutenegger, Benedict and Habig, Marion A., ed. REPORT ON THE SAN ANTONIO MISSIONS IN 1792. *Southwestern Hist. Q. 1974 77(4): 487-498.* The five Indian missions established by the Spanish in the San Antonio area were the most successful in Texas. About the 1770's they began to decline because of the decreasing number of Coahuiltecan Indians that remained to be converted and civilized. Reproduces the 1792 report of José Francisco López, father president of the Texas missions, advocating seculariza-tion to recognize the Indians' change from pagan and neophyte to Christian status and to free the missionaries for service elsewhere. 16 notes.
                                                           D. L. Smith

278.   Lummis, Keith. FATHER SERRA'S LAST BAPTISM. *Masterkey 1981 55(4): 147-151.* Using baptismal records, reviews the final days at Mission San Carlo Borromeo of Franciscan missionary to California Junipero Serra in July 1784.

279.   Lyon, Eugene. ST. AUGUSTINE, 1580: THE LIVING COMMUNI-TY. *Escribano 1977 14: 20-33.* Describes the daily life, social organization, and civil-military relations in the town and presidio of St. Augustine, Florida, 1580.

280.   Lyon, Eugene. SPAIN'S SIXTEENTH-CENTURY NORTH AMERI-CAN SETTLEMENT ATTEMPTS: A NEGLECTED ASPECT. *Florida Hist. Q. 1981 59(3): 275-291.* Spanish efforts at settlement in the New World have been culturally stereotyped as exploitive. A study of 16th-century Spanish settlements in Florida reveals an overriding interest in land. The settlement at Santa Elena was the result of land hunger and an effort to duplicate the agricultural interests of Castille. Based on Spanish colonial records and other sources; 51 notes.   N. A. Kuntz

281.   Manucy, Albert. TOWARD RE-CREATION OF 16TH CENTURY ST. AUGUSTINE. *Escribano 1977 14: 1-4.* The St. Augustine Restoration Foundation promotes historical preservation so that past architecture, history, and culture will be available to contemporary history students.

282.   Marchena Fernández, Juan. GUARNICIONES Y POBLACION MI-LITAR EN FLORIDA ORIENTAL, 1700-1820 [Garrisons and military population in East Florida, 1700-1820]. *Rev. de Indias [Spain] 1981 41(163-164): 91-142.* The exigencies of military defense conditioned the admin-istrative, fiscal, and commercial development of the Spanish possessions in America; and in particular East Florida's whole existence as a Spanish province evolved around military considerations. The author makes a quantita-tive study of the Spanish military population there, taking into account the structure of defense, legislation, military hierarchy, geographic and social origins of Florida soldiers, and their years of service. Throughout is stressed the near equation between military population and total population on this frontier. Documentation is from the General Archive of the Indies in Seville, the General Archive of Simancas, and the East Florida Papers in the P. K. Younge Library at Gainesville; 20 tables, graph, 97 notes, 3 charts.
                                                        S. L. Hilton

283.   Mason, Bill. THE GARRISONS OF SAN DIEGO PRESIDIO: 1770-1794. *J. of San Diego Hist. 1978 24(4): 399-424.* Gives data and anecdotes regarding soldiers and employees in San Diego during the Hispanic period, discussing names and activities and their role in the development of the pueblo of Los Angeles.

284.   Mathes, W. Michael. CALIFORNIA'S FIRST EXPLORER: SEBAS-TIÁN VIZCÁINO. *Pacific Hist. 1981 25(3): 8-14.* Explorer and navigator Sebastián Vizcáino (1548-1627) made two voyages to the coast of California. The first in 1596 established a settlement at LaPaz; the second more successful

voyage in 1602 mapped and charted the coast as far north as San Diego. Vizcáino was appointed the first official European ambassador to Japan in 1611 and charted the Japanese coast. 3 maps. H. M. Evans

285. Mathes, W. Michael. FRAY ANTONIO DE LA ASCENSION AND CALIFORNIA, PARADISE ISLE. Dodd, Horace L. and Long, Robert W., ed. *People of the Far West* (Brand Book no. 6; San Diego: Corral of the Westerners, 1979): 3-11. Fray Antonio de la Ascensión's lavish description of California and his belief that it was an island, gained from participating in Sebastian Vizcaíno's voyage of 1602, continued until the 1730's to mislead Spanish explorers who set out from Mexico.

286. Mathes, W. Michael. THE PUERTO DE DON GASPAR: A NOTE ON AN ERRONEOUS CALIFORNIA PLACE-NAME. *J. of San Diego Hist.* *1975 20(4): 30-32.* Claims that the Spanish explorer Sebastian Vizcáino during his California voyage during 1602-03 did not intentionally change Sebastian Rodriguez Cermeno's "Bahia de San Francisco," today's Drake's Bay, to Puerto de Don Gaspar. The name change was based upon an error, later rectified, in Vizcáino's journal of the voyage. S

287. Mathes, W. Michael. SOME REFLECTIONS ON CALIFORNIA, 1776. *J. of San Diego Hist.* *1976 22(4): 48-53.* Discusses the establishing of Dominican and Franciscan missions in California following the expulsion of the Jesuits from Spain, 1768-76, emphasizing the works of Fray Junípero Serra.

288. Matter, Robert Allen. MISSION LIFE IN SEVENTEENTH-CENTU-RY FLORIDA. *Catholic Hist. Rev.* *1981 67(3): 401-420.* Crude facilities, pestilence, martyrdom, and toil by Franciscan friars and Indians in the wilderness mirrors colonial Florida mission life. A shipwrecked English Quaker's favorable account and those of Church inspectors offer interesting comparisons and provide much of our sparse knowledge of this subject. Spanish impotence and church-state dissension contributed to the missions' downfall. Exploitation of Christian Indians engendered native resentment and throttled economic development. The padres, early Indian champions, became principal targets of Indian-abuse charges. Franciscan dedication varied inversely to temporal prosperity. The number baptized, a measure of evangelistic success, left the depth of the converts' faith to the judgment of God.

289. Mawn, Geoffrey P. "*AGRIMENSOR Y ARQUITECTO*": JASPER O'FARRELL'S SURVEYING IN MEXICAN CALIFORNIA. *Southern California Q.* *1974 56(1): 1-12.* An account of the work of Jasper O'Farrell, Alta California's official surveyor, 1844-46. Studies of Mexican land grants have erroneously claimed that no regular surveys were made of California's ranchos. O'Farrell, a native of Ireland who came to California in 1843, was appointed as surveyor by Governor Manuel Micheltorena, and surveyed 21 ranchos in northern and southern Alta California between January 1844 and May 1846. The quality of his surveying is proved by the US Board of Land Commissioners' approval of all of the grants he surveyed. Based on archival materials and published works; 26 notes. A. Hoffman

290. McClure, Charles R. TEXAN-SANTA FE EXPEDITION OF 1841. *New Mexico Hist. R. 1973 48(1): 45-56.* The purpose of the Texan expedition of 1841 was to promote trade with Mexico. It was not very successful, but talk of expansionist expeditions continued.   J. H. Krenkel

291. McDonald, Archie P. COMMENTARY: ANGLO VS. SPANIARD: EARLY CONFLICT. *Military Hist. of Texas and the Southwest 1980 16(1): 23-32.* From the late 1790's until the Adams-Onís Treaty of 1819, American and Spanish relations were less than peaceful and Americans settled in Spanish (later Mexican) Texas.

292. McGinty, Brian. MONTEREY: CAPITAL OF OLD CALIFORNIA. *Early Am. Life 1979 10(1): 32-35.* History of Monterey through the Spanish, Mexican, and early American eras, 1770-1849.

293. McGinty, Brian. PAGEANT OF THE CALIFORNIOS. *Westways 1974 66(12): 26-29, 65.* Highlights the Christmas festivities, especially La Pastorela, of the early Spanish settlers of California.   S

294. Meyer, Larry L. A STATE OF LESS THAN ENCHANTMENT. *Am. West 1975 12(5): 4-9; 60-62.* Although New Mexico seemed a likely place for Spaniards and Juan de Oñate brought countrymen in 1598 who intended to stay in its valleys, New Spain's far-northern colony did not progress beyond subsistence agriculture, cattle and sheep raising, and trade with nomadic Indians. A bishop's inspection tour in 1760 confirmed that New Mexico was "a complete failure financially and a bad investment spiritually." New Mexico was not abandoned. During the years of the American Revolution, exciting and significant history transpired there: Santa Fe was the beginning and terminal place of the famed Domingues-Escalante exploration of the Southwest, and a general Indian War threatened the Spanish outposts along the frontier from Texas to Arizona. Adapted from a forthcoming book. 2 illus., map.
                                                                        D. L. Smith

295. Meyer, Larry L. WAKERS FROM THE DREAM. *Westways 1975 67(8): 14-19, 61.* Discusses Indian-Spanish relations in California in the 1770's.
                                                                                  S

296. Miller, Janice Borton. THE REBELLION IN EAST FLORIDA IN 1795. *Florida Hist. Q. 1978 57(2): 173-186.* A rebellion of Spanish subjects who had originally come from Georgia and South Carolina ended in the fall of 1795 when Spanish authorities under Juan Nepomuceno de Quesada reoccupied San Nicolas. The trial of the rebels ended in 1798. Although the leaders were found guilty, there is no evidence they were ever executed. Based on microfilmed manuscript sources; 59 notes.   P. A. Beaber

297. Miller, Robert Ryal, ed. and trans. NEW MEXICO IN MID-EIGHTEENTH CENTURY: A REPORT BASED ON GOVERNOR VÉLEZ CACHUPÍN'S INSPECTION. *Southwestern Hist. Q. 1975 79(2): 166-181.* Thomas Vélez Cachupín was Spain's governor of New Mexico for two five-year terms (1749-54 and 1762-67). This translated and edited report was

written by him or one of his aides ca. 1754. The report outlines provincial problems, recommends cultivation of friendship and trade with the Comanche Indians to offset French influence, suggests defense improvements in this outpost of empire, provides information on the economy, and suggests ways to improve the effectiveness of the Franciscans' missionary activities. Based on the original 16-page MS in the Real Academia de la Historia in Madrid; 3 tables, 28 notes. C. W. Olson

298. Miranda, Gloria E. GENTE DE RAZÓN MARRIAGE PATTERNS IN SPANISH AND MEXICAN CALIFORNIA: A CASE STUDY OF SANTA BARBARA AND LOS ANGELES. *Southern California Q. 1981 63(1): 1-21.* Traces marriage patterns of Californians in the Spanish and Mexican periods, focusing on the Santa Barbara Mission and Presidio and the Los Angeles pueblo. Women were considered at age 13 to be marriageable, and men by their midteens, although men usually waited until their late 20's before marrying. Men averaged about 10 years older than women at time of marriage. "Cradle marriages," a popular sterotype of the era, were exceptions to the norm. Couples desiring to be married had to obtain parental consent; love matches were more common than arranged marriages. The Catholic Church conducted investigative tribunals about motives for marriage and to insure that no close blood ties existed. Between 1786 and 1848, Santa Barbara missionaries performed 306 marriages. 4 charts, 50 notes. A. Hoffman

299. Moorhead, Max L. THE PRESIDIO SUPPLY PROBLEM OF NEW MEXICO IN THE EIGHTEENTH CENTURY. *New Mexico Hist. Rev. 1961 36(3): 210-229.* Discusses various attempts to compensate the troops serving at the Presidial Company of Santa Fe with enough income to cover their expenses in the remote outpost, and to prosecute the officers who cheated the troops by overcharging and double charging them for supplies; 18th century.

300. Moorhead, Max L. SPANISH DEPORTATION OF HOSTILE APACHES: THE POLICY AND THE PRACTICE. *Arizona and the West 1975 17(3): 205-220.* Official Spanish policy of removing hostile Apache Indians from their homelands in the American Southwest to the remote environs of Mexico City was established by a 1729 regulation which attempted a uniform system for the borderlands. The intention of providing safeguards for the health and welfare of the prisoners was forgotten in practice as the captured Apache suffered "a hideous punishment." They were subjected to forced labor, permanent confinement, private wardship, and domestic service as late as 1809. After 1772, however, many were freed under a prisoner-exchange policy and a general amnesty. 26 notes. D. L. Smith

301. Moses, Robert J. SMALLPOX IMMUNIZATION IN ALTA CALI-FORNIA: A STORY BASED ON JOSÉ ESTRADA'S 1821 POSTSCRIPT. *Southern California Q. 1979 61(2): 125-145.* Discusses vaccination for small-pox emphasizing its use in Alta California. Vaccination against smallpox using cowpox lesions was recognized as safer than inoculation with smallpox lesions. Edward Jenner's pioneering investigations became well known in the late 18th century. England and Russia recognized the efficacy of smallpox vaccination,

and Spain endorsed the practice in her New World colonies. Although smallpox was unknown in Alta California, settlers were aware of its dangers. José Estrada, a paymaster at Monterey, noted in 1821 the vaccination of 54 people by a visiting Russian surgeon. The surgeon came from the Russian war vessel *Kutuzov* which had obtained the vaccine in Peru. The event illustrates the interest in combating smallpox in the work of Jenner and supported by Russia, Spain, and other countries. Primary and secondary sources; 32 notes.

A. Hoffman

302.   Mutunhu, Tendai. ESTEVANICO: AFRICA'S GREATEST EX-PLORER OF THE SOUTH-WEST OF THE UNITED STATES AND THE "DISCOVERER" OF ARIZONA AND NEW MEXICO. *Kenya Hist. Rev. [Kenya] 1975 3(2): 217-233.* Describes the achievements of the Moroccan explorer Esteban, who made a pioneering journey for Spain into what is now Florida, Louisiana, and Texas, and notes his diplomacy with the Indians, 1528-39.

303.   Myres, Sandra L. THE RANCHING FRONTIER: SPANISH INSTI-TUTIONAL BACKGROUNDS OF THE PLAINS CATTLE INDUSTRY. Weber, David J., ed. *New Spain's Far Northern Frontier: Essays on Spain in the American West, 1540-1821* (Albuquerque: U. of New Mexico Pr., 1979): 79-94. The Spanish found the cattle ranch to be the ideal institution to make the American Southwest into a productive area, and Americans adopted their technology and lore, 18th-19th centuries. Reprinted from Harold M. Hollings-worth and Sandra L. Myres, ed., *Essays on the American West* (Austin, 1969): 19-39.

304.   Navarro García, Luis; Gard, Elizabeth and Weber, David J., transl. THE NORTH OF NEW SPAIN AS A POLITICAL PROBLEM IN THE EIGHTEENTH CENTURY. Weber, David J., ed. *New Spain's Far Northern Frontier: Essays on Spain in the American West, 1540-1821* (Albuquerque: U. of New Mexico Pr., 1979): 201-215. Reprinted from *Estudios Americanos.* Focuses on the response of Spanish officials, especially the Marqués de Rubí and José de Gálvez to defend northern Mexico and the American Southwest from the Indians and foreign powers, 1759-88.

305.   Neri, Michael C. NARCISO DURÁN AND THE SECULARIZA-TION OF THE CALIFORNIA MISSIONS. *Americas (Acad. of Am. Fran-ciscan Hist.) 1977 33(3): 411-429.* Spanish-born Franciscan Narciso Durán (1776-1846) was the church official primarily responsible for California Indian missions during the post-independence process of secularization. He did not refuse to cooperate with the secular authorities but repeatedly urged ways to lessen the disruption caused. He particularly was concerned with the situation of the Indians themselves but was not indifferent to the larger welfare of Mexican California. Primary sources; 75 notes.   D. Bushnell

306.   Nofi, Albert A. THE ALAMO: VICTORY IN DEATH: MARCH 6, 1836. *Strategy & Tactics 1981 (86): 41-50.* Details events before, during and after the Battle of the Alamo in 1836 during the Texas War of Independence from Mexico.

307. Nolan, James L. ANGLO-AMERICAN MYOPIA AND CALIFORNIA MISSION ART. *Southern California Q. 1976 58(1): 1-44, (2): 143-204, (3): 261-331.* Part I. California's mission art and liturgical plays have long been misunderstood and misinterpreted by Anglo-American observers. *Los Pastores*, a favorite liturgical play performed in the missions for mission Indian audiences, and mission iconography have been incorrectly identified as to design, characters, and interpretation. Even defenders of mission art, such as Rev. Zephyrin Engelhardt, misinterpreted the religious art of the missionaries. A key misunderstanding concerns the presence of St. Michael in the nativity scene. Anglos have often identified him as St. Gabriel, a reflection of Northern European post-Reformation religious thought rather than a Catholic view. Thus mission art observers view it while lacking a proper frame of reference. Based on primary and secondary sources; photos, 94 notes. Part II. The San Antonio Mission's altar pieces and paintings during the mission's restoration were misinterpreted as to location and meaning. The mission's art is based on the structure of medieval scholasticism which envisioned a geocentric universe and an Apocalyptic world view. This view was taught by Father Junipero Serra in Spain in the early 1740's at the Convent of San Francisco. Books in the Mission San Carlos library also reflect Scotist thought. Thus the Franciscan padres, as typified in the art of Mission San Antonio, attempted to bring their Indian neophytes into a world view based on scholasticism and through that system to Europeanize them. Based on primary and secondary sources, and on art objects and artifacts; illus., photos, 36 notes. Part III. Anglo-American historians of the Spanish missions of California have misunderstood the importance of the visual impact of the iconography of the missions, resulting in reconstruction and restoration of the missions that misidentified saints and moved them about indiscriminately. Mission Santa Barbara is a major example of this cultural myopia. The iconographic system reflects the system found in medieval society from Constantinople to London in an era of general illiteracy when worshipers found the story of genesis and apogenesis imparted visually. The rise of literacy in the wake of the Reformation saw this tradition ended in Protestant societies. The California missions therefore represent the reawakening of a great medieval tradition, the use of a visual language to impart the Catholic faith. Based on primary and secondary sources, photo, 81 notes.

A. Hoffman

308. Oates, Stephen B. LOS DIABLOS TEJANOS: THE TEXAS RANGERS IN THE MEXICAN WAR. *J. of the West 1970 9(4): 487-504.* Records the exploits of the Texas Rangers in the Mexican War (1846-48), and describes a series of encounters between the Rangers and the Mexicans. Their personal courage and reckless daring against the enemy was offset by uncontrollable brawling and unprovoked atrocities perpetrated in the towns and among the people. Their general indisposition to obey orders made them a problem to the US military command. Most studies of the Texas Rangers omit this side of the picture, not yet ready to admit that in war man could strip himself "of all compassion, all diplomacy, and fight with uninhibited fury, as the violent nature of his soul dictated." 49 notes.

R. V. Ritter

309. Oberly, James W. SOURCES AT THE NATIONAL ARCHIVES FOR GENEALOGICAL AND LOCAL HISTORY RESEARCH. *Prologue*

1982 14(1): 25-34. Discusses military bounty land warrants of the Mexican War. The government offered the land warrants as incentives for enlistment in the military to counteract the chronic manpower shortage prior to 1861. The 1847 land warrants took the form of letterpress folios with the front reserved for eligibility information and the inside and back pages reserved for assignments. A study of these warrants locates the geographical origin of the army as primarily from the Mississippi Valley and provides a clear impression of the social background of the soldiers. Based on Record Group 49, National Archives, and newspapers; 5 illus., 3 tables, 22 notes.   M. A. Kascus

310. O'Brien, Rita H. FOUR HUNDRED AND TEN YEARS AGO... *Escribano 1975 12(4): 124-126.* Discusses the St. Augustine, Florida, 1975 commemoration of explorer Pedro Menéndez de Avilés of Spain's landing and discovery of the city in 1565.

311. Olsen, Stanley J. THE DOMESTIC ANIMALS OF SAN XAVIER DEL BAC. *Kiva 1974 39(3/4): 253-256.* "Little is known and even less has been published regarding the kinds of domestic animals that were associated with Colonial Spanish settlements in the Southwest. Recent excavations of the Spanish mission, San Xavier del Bac, near Tucson, have produced domestic animal bones in a large enough quantity to allow for recording and evaluating these early introductions into Arizona."   J

312. O'Neill, Ynez Violé. FATHER SERRA PLANS THE FOUNDING OF MISSION SAN JUAN CAPISTRANO. *California Hist. Q. 1977 56(1): 46-51.* Reproduces a memorandum, written by Father Junípero Serra on 21 August 1775, ordering the establishment of the sixth California mission, Mission San Juan Capistrano. Plans included its staffing with two friars, six soldiers, and six Indians; provisions for food, livestock, necessary equipment and tools; and items for the church and sacristy. Fathers Fermín Lasuén and Gregorio Amurrío began work on the mission in October 1775, but news of an Indian massacre at San Diego caused a year's delay. The mission was officially founded on 1 November 1776. Father Serra conducted the first Mass. A translation of the original document appears in the article. Primary and secondary sources; illus., 31 notes.   A. Hoffman

313. Ortiz, Roxanne Dunbar. THE ROOTS OF RESISTANCE: PUEBLO LAND TENURE AND SPANISH COLONIZATION. *J. of Ethnic Studies 1978 5(4): 33-53.* The social structures of northern New Mexico Indians arose from a hydraulic agriculture economy. Irrigation is the key to the historical process of land use. Spanish conquest and colonization after 1598, with its *encomiendas, repartimientos,* and *haciendas,* introduced slavery and feudalism, disrupted trade patterns and tribal accommodations, and devastated Pueblo land tenure. The great 1680 revolt of Pueblos, Apaches, Navajos, and Hopis produced 12 years of independence, but Diego de Vargas reconquered the region and brought back the Spanish "culture of conquest," a term more apropos than "culture of Spain" to describe colonial society in 17th-century New Mexico. Secondary works; 52 notes.   G. J. Bobango

314.   Page, James K., Jr. REBELLIOUS PUEBLOS OUTWITTED SPAIN THREE CENTURIES AGO. *Smithsonian 1980 11(7): 86-95.* The Spanish moved into the Rio Grande Basin in the 1620's. They enslaved the Pueblo Indians economically and interfered with their religious practices. In August 1680, the Pueblos, incited by a contemporary sorcerer named Po'pay, revolted against their Spanish conquerors. In a short time almost every mission was destroyed and many Spanish settlers and missionaries killed. Survivors retreated to El Paso. When the Pueblo tribes fell again into disunity the Spanish returned. This time they left the native religion and culture alone and remained until early in the 19th century. Based on contemporary Spanish records and Indian oral history; 5 illus.   J. G. Packer

315.   Paredes, Raymund. THE ORIGINS OF ANTI-MEXICAN SENTIMENTS IN THE UNITED STATES. *New Scholar 1977 (6): 139-165.* Anti-Mexican sentiments in colonial America were encouraged by the general Hispanophobia created by the Protestant Reformation. European notions, mainly Spanish, also influenced English images of Mexico. The doctrine of miscegenation, increasingly popular during the 19th century, led back to Hispanophobia. From a special issue, "New Directions In Chicano Scholarship." 79 notes.   D. K. Pickens

316.   Patrick, Elizabeth Nelson. LAND GRANTS DURING THE ADMINISTRATION OF SPANISH COLONIAL GOVERNOR PEDRO FERMÍN DE MENDINUETA. *New Mexico Hist. R. 1976 51(1): 5-18.* New Mexico was perhaps the most stable of the New Spain provinces. Its governor during the 1770's was Colonel Pedro Fermín de Mendinueta. He was not only a soldier of high achievement, but also a good governor. Most of the information of his administration was obtained from *Laws of the Indies* Book IV, Title 12, Law 1. Considerable trouble resulted from poor surveying of the land grants given during his administration. It is impossible to determine the exact number of acres transferred from the public domain to private ownership. There were 3,726,848 acres in conflict concerning who had the right title. 41 notes.
                                                        J. H. Krenkel

317.   Payne, Steven. VILLA DE BRANCIFORTE. *Pacific Hist. 1978 22(4): 403-410.* Viceroy de Branciforte, faced with the fear of British incursion into Alta California, planned Villa de Branciforte as a means of securing and protecting Spanish claims to this area following the establishment of the Nootka Convention of 28 October 1790. It was established on the east side of the San Lorenzo River, opposite Mission Santa Cruz. By combining military capabilities with the basis for an established and increasingly populated community he hoped for a more permanent settlement than the presidios were able to provide. Colonists began arriving on 12 May 1797. The excellent planning failed to produce satisfactory results, largely because of the class of people sent there (largely convicts), and became an embarrassment to the Spanish government. 17 notes.   R. V. Ritter

318.   Pearce, T. M. THE DUKE OF ALBUQUERQUE. *Palacio 1976 82(2): 36-41.* Chronicles events in New Mexico and social disorder, political intrigue

and scandal in Mexico during the administration of Don Francisco Fernández de la Cueva Henríquez, Duque de Albuquerque, Viceroy of Mexico, 1702-11.

319.   Pearson, Fred Lamar, Jr. EARLY ANGLO-SPANISH RIVALRY IN SOUTHEASTERN NORTH AMERICA. *Georgia Hist. Q. 1974 58(Supplement): 157-171.* Spanish interest in the Americas was initiated by Columbus in 1492 and intensified with various explorers in the 1500's. English interest was not important until the late 1500's. The point of competition was in the Southeast where the Spanish used the Indian population to present a hostile front to the English colonization efforts. The Spanish were eventually unsuccessful because of their inability to sustain Indian hostility toward the English. Primary sources; 40 notes.   M. R. Gillam

320.   Pearson, Fred Lamar, Jr. SPANISH-INDIAN RELATIONS IN FLORIDA 1602-1675: SOME ASPECTS OF SELECTED *VISITAS. Florida Hist. Q. 1974 52(3): 261-273.* The *visita* was a Spanish inspection of provincial outposts. The Spanish gathered much information regarding Indians in Florida during various *visitas* conducted during 1602-75. Comments on conduct of the religious orders appeared often. Of special note was the *visita* of 1657 in which an investigation of the Indian insurrection against the Franciscans was carried out. Primary and secondary sources; 49 notes.   J. E. Findling

321.   Phillips, George Harwood. INDIANS AND THE BREAKDOWN OF THE SPANISH MISSION SYSTEM IN CALIFORNIA. *Ethnohistory 1974 21(4): 291-302.* Historians have attributed the collapse of the Spanish mission system in California solely to the activities of land-hungry Mexican officials and aristocrats who cheated the Indian neophytes out of their promised lands when the missions were secularized in the 1830's. As inmates of the mission, a plural institution, the neophytes formed a cultural section that constituted a population majority with distinct burdens and disabilities. Since social identity was ascriptive, there was no way in which they could change their sectional status. The resulting neophyte discontent was largely manifested in a process of continual withdrawal from the missions. Before secularization, however, withdrawal was usually a matter of individual initiative. Afterwards, the neophytes fled from the mission practically en masse, since they had little to fear from their politically emasculated rulers. Their action was a near-unanimous rejection of an oppressive social system, and it clearly exhibits the active role they played in its collapse.   J

322.   Polzer, Charles W. THE DOCUMENTARY RELATIONS OF THE SOUTHWEST. *Hispanic Am. Hist. Rev. 1978 58(3): 460-465.* The Documentary Relations of the Southwest project at the Arizona State Museum is designed ultimately to publish (in Spanish and English) documents dealing with native and Spanish contact in the Southwest (including parts of northern Mexico) in the colonial period. After two years, more than 100,000 documents have been screened; 5,000 of them have been placed in the master index. Biographical and geographical corollary files have been added to overcome variant spellings. 2 notes.   B. D. Johnson

323. Quintana, Frances Leon and Snow, David H. HISTORICAL ARCHE-OLOGY OF THE RITO COLORADO VALLEY, NEW MEXICO. *J. of the West 1980 19(3): 40-50.* Research involving archival, oral history, and archaeological methods has helped locate the sites of ranchos in the Rito Colorado Valley, New Mexico, dating to the 1720's. The earliest dwellings were small and scattered, suited to the needs of livestock raising, but larger homes appeared after 1750. More detailed information on settlement patterns will depend on an opportunity for site excavation. In the meantime, the sites are threatened by suburban development, cultivation, soil erosion, and scavenging for artifacts. Based on Land and Property documents in the Spanish Archives of New Mexico, State Records Center, Santa Fe, and archeological field survey; 8 illus., 12 photos, map, 2 notes.   B. S. Porter

324. Reeve, Frank D. NAVAHO-SPANISH DIPLOMACY, 1770-1790. *New Mexico Hist. Rev. 1960 35(3): 200-235.* The period of Navajo-Spanish diplomacy from 1770 to 1790 was characterized by intra-Indian fighting in New Mexico.

325. Reeve, Frank D. THE NAVAHO-SPANISH PEACE: 1720'S-1770'S. *New Mexico Hist. Rev. 1959 34(1): 9-40.* Traces the period of peace between the Navajos and the Spanish in New Mexico from the 1720's to the 1770's, characterized by Spanish attempts to Christianize the Indians, which lasted until the Indians felt the pressure of Spanish settlement on their land.

326. Reeve, Frank D. NAVAHO-SPANISH WARS 1680-1720. *New Mexico Hist. Rev. 1958 33(3): 204-231.* Traces the successful war for independence by the Navajo Indians against the Spanish in New Mexico with the help of some Apaches and other Indians.

327. Reilly, Stephen Edward. A MARRIAGE OF EXPEDIENCE: THE CALUSA INDIANS AND THEIR RELATIONS WITH PEDRO MENÉN-DEZ DE AVILÉS IN SOUTHWEST FLORIDA, 1566-1569. *Florida Hist. Q. 1981 59(4): 395-421.* Carlos, Calusa Indian chief, manipulated Pedro Menéndez de Avilés, the adelantado of Florida, into marrying Doña Antonia, a sister and wife of the chief. The marriage was to centralize political power for Carlos. The event provides a glimpse into the world of a little known but advanced Indian culture. Based on Spanish memoirs and records and other sources; 87 notes.   N. A. Kuntz

328. Reilly, Tom. A SPANISH-LANGUAGE VOICE OF DISSENT IN ANTEBELLUM NEW ORLEANS. *Louisiana Hist. 1982 23(4): 325-339.* The English-language newspapers of New Orleans, strong supporters of the principle of manifest destiny, received outspoken competition from the Spanish-language paper known successively as *El Hablador, La Patria,* and *La Union.* This newspaper served as the nation's primary source of news about Texas, the Mexican War, and the filibustering expeditions in Latin America, but growing hostility to its pro-Mexican and pro-Spanish line culminated in its offices and equipment being destroyed in a riot after the execution of 50 filibustering Americans in Cuba in August 1851. The Spanish papers rebutted the expansionist views of the English-language papers, served the business and

literary needs of their readership, and often reflected political sentiment in the Spanish community. Based on newspapers and other printed sources; 75 notes.

D. J. Nicholls

329.   Riley, Carroll L. MESOAMERICAN INDIANS IN THE EARLY SOUTHWEST. *Ethnohist. 1974 21(1): 25-36.* Beginning in the late 1530's, numbers of Mesoamerican Indians traveled to the Southwest with various Spanish parties. Some who came in 1540 with the Coronado expedition were still living with Pueblo Indians forty years later. We have the names and places of origin of a few of these Mesoamerican Indians. Their effect on Southwestern Pueblo Indians is difficult to evaluate but they probably helped to reinforce the Mesoamerican flavor of Pueblo culture, and also, inadvertently, to prepare Southwestern Indians for Spanish conquest.   J

330.   Ríos-Bustamante, Antonio José. NEW MEXICO IN THE EIGH-TEENTH CENTURY: LIFE, LABOR AND TRADE IN LA VILLA DE SAN FELIPE DE ALBUQUERQUE, 1706-1790. *Aztlán 1976 7(3): 357-389.* A caste-class system developed in Albuquerque, in which there was consider-able social mobility.

331.   Rivera, Julius. VARIETIES OF AMERICA. *New Scholar 1982 8(1-2): 523-527.* Edmund S. Urbansk's *Hispanic America and Its Civilization: Spanish Americans and Anglo-Americans* (1978) examines the Hispanic-American mentality in empirical and humanistic terms. As Europeans explored the New World, the cartographers created clearer maps. Distinctive American cultures emerged, both Anglo and Hispanic.   D. K. Pickens

332.   Robinson, Willard B. COLONIAL RANCH ARCHITECTURE IN THE SPANISH-MEXICAN TRADITION. *Southwestern Hist. Q. 1979 83(2): 123-150.* The architecture of ranches in the Spanish-Mexican Southwest (specifically, southern Texas) illustrates the use of local building materials and the functional need for defense. Ranch headquarters were usually located on high ground near water, fuel, and shade trees. Many houses were primitive as late as 1900, but the patron usually had at least one great stone house with plaster walls, minimal furniture, and gun loopholes rather than windows. 17 illus., 37 notes.   J. H. Broussard

333.   Robinson, William J. MISSION GUEVAVI: EXCAVATIONS IN THE CONVENTO. *Kiva 1976 42(2): 135-175.* Investigation at an 18th century Jesuit mission near Nogales, Arizona were undertaken in 1964-65 and 1965-66 by the Arizona Archaeological and Historical Society. Nine rooms in the living quarters were fully or partially excavated as well as some outlying structures. Material culture was sparse as the mission had evidently been intentionally stripped upon abandonment about 1773. Architectural remains were not sufficiently diagnostic to determine functions for individual rooms. After abandonment, the mission was re-occupied for local mining activities. Little information was obtained on the location or nature of the Indian village for which the mission was presumably built.   J

334.   Rock, Michael J. ANTON CHICO AND ITS PATENT. *J. of the West 1980 19(3): 86-91.* The Anton Chico grant, some 300,000 acres near Las Vegas, New Mexico, was granted to Manuel Rivera and 36 others on a group petition in 1822. After American annexation, the New Mexico Land and Livestock Company, greedy for the grant's commonlands, manuevered to control the land by purchasing deeds from the heirs of Rivera, the only named grantee. This plot appeared defeated in 1915 when the residents of the town of Anton Chico were declared owners of the Anton Chico grant. The cattle company appealed the decision, and in order to settle the suit, the residents deeded 100,000 acres to attorneys as fees, and deeded 35,000 acres to the cattle company. Based on documents of the New Mexico Land Grants-Surveyor General, State Records Center, Santa Fe; 9 photos, map, 20 notes.

B. S. Porter

335.   Ross, Oliver D. WHEAT GROWING IN NORTHERN NEW SPAIN. *North Dakota Q. 1977 45(3): 61-69.* Examines wheat growing in California and Mexico as sponsored and directed by the Franciscans of the Spanish and Mexican mission system, 1730's-70's; examines economic and agricultural relations between California and Mexico.

336.   Santos, Richard G. JUAN NEPOMUCENO SEGUÍN, ESPÍA TEJANO EN LA COMANDANCIA DEL NORESTE DE MÉXICO [Juan Nepomuceno Seguín, Texan spy in the North-East Mexican Command]. *Humánitas [Mexico] 1976 17: 551-567.* Juan N. Seguín, a Hispanic Texan, went over to the Mexican side during the Texas war of independence, but was actually a spy for the Texans and was decorated by the Texas government and given land.

337.   Scholes, France V. ROYAL TREASURY RECORDS RELATING TO THE PROVINCE OF NEW MEXICO, 1596-1683. *New Mexico Hist. R. 1975 50(1): 5-24, 50(2): 139-164.* Part 1. The Archivo General de Indias in Seville contains more than 38,000 bundles of manuscripts and printed documents relating to the colonial history of Spanish America and the Philippine Islands. Crown income in Spanish America included the royal share of gold and silver production, import and export duties, sales taxes, tribute paid by the Indians of Crown towns, royal monopolies, taxes on the salaries of officials, sales of public offices and the royal share of ecclesiastical indulgences. The periodic ledger accounts of the colonial treasury offices constitute an invaluable source of information for research. 36 notes, appendix. Part 2. Royal Treasury Records indicate that most of the money appropriated with regard to New Mexico was to pay the salaries of soldiers. Nevertheless, there was a steady deterioration during the third quarter of the 17th century in the security and defensive position of the province. The outlay for the defense of the province was larger than the income. 41 notes.

J. H. Krenkel

338.   Schuetz, Mardith. PROFESSIONAL ARTISANS IN THE HISPANIC SOUTHWEST: THE CHURCHES OF SAN ANTONIO, TEXAS. *Americas (Acad. of Am. Franciscan Hist.) 1983 40(1): 17-71.* Skilled masons and other craftsmen were brought from Mexico and Europe to build mission churches in the San Antonio area. Some craftsmen were eventually trained in Texas, as well. San José Mission features a particularly outstanding baroque church, but

other churches also display a high degree of professional workmanship. Based on documents in ecclesiastical and local archives; table, 32 fig., 48 notes.

D. Bushnell

339. Servín, Manuel P. CALIFORNIA'S HISPANIC HERITAGE: A VIEW INTO THE SPANISH MYTH. *J. of San Diego Hist. 1973 19(1): 1-9.* Because Alta California was unattractive to pure-blood Spaniards, Mexican mixed-blood and Hispanicized Indian elements predominated, according to analysis of early expeditions into California and of early settlers. 3 illus., 35 notes.

S. S. Sprague

340. Servin, Manuel P. THE LEGAL BASIS FOR THE ESTABLISH-MENT OF SPANISH COLONIAL SOVEREIGNTY: THE ACT OF POS-SESSION. *New Mexico Hist. Rev. 1978 53(4): 295-303.* Discusses Spain's legal right in establishing colonies in New Mexico and the rest of the New World during 15th-18th centuries.

341. Shay, Anthony. FANDANGOS AND *BAILES:* DANCING AND DANCE EVENTS IN EARLY CALIFORNIA. *Southern California Q. 1982 64(2): 99-113.* Traces the popularity of dancing in California during the Spanish and Mexican periods. Isolated geographically and politically, Californios found dancing an acceptable social outlet for both sexes. There were two types of dance events: *bailes,* formal balls by invitation, and fandangos, which attracted people from all social levels and gained a negative image by the time of US annexation. Many of the traditional dances required hours of practice at home and were performed competitively. Dancing provided entertainment, physical exercise, and opportunities for social interaction and thus were an important element in Hispanic California. 26 notes.

A. Hoffman

342. Silverman, Joseph. CULTURAL BACKGROUNDS OF SPANISH IMPERIALISM AS PRESENTED IN LOPE DE VEGA'S PLAY *SAN DIEGO DE ALCALÁ. J. of San Diego Hist. 1978 24(1): 7-23.* Drawing from Lope de Vega's *San Diego de Alcalá,* a play dramatizing Spanish imperialism in the New World, points out cultural, religious, and social reasons for discovery and exploration and for the colonization of Central and North Americas, 17th-18th centuries.

343. Simmons, Marc. GOVERNOR CUERVO AND THE BEGINNINGS OF ALBUQUERQUE: ANOTHER LOOK. *New Mexico Hist. Rev. 1980 55(3): 188-207.* In 1706, Governor Francisco Cuervo y Valdes (fl. 1700) of New Mexico proclaimed to his sovereign the founding of the villa of Albuquerque according to the Spanish laws governing colonial government. Other evidence, particularly that from an investigation in 1712 into the governor's activities, indicates that Cuervo was not truthful in many of his accounts to the king. It is doubtful the traditional belief that Albuquerque was founded as a lawful Spanish municipality can be upheld. Cuervo, rather than an architect of a new and glorious villa, was in actuality the founder of a collection of farms spread along the Rio Grande. Primary sources; illus., photo, 26 notes.

P. L. McLaughlin

344. Simmons, Marc. SETTLEMENT PATTERNS AND VILLAGE PLANS IN COLONIAL NEW MEXICO. Weber, David J., ed. *New Spain's Far Northern Frontier: Essays on Spain in the American West, 1540-1821* (Albuquerque: U. of New Mexico Pr., 1979): 97-115. New Mexico's settlements were founded in an unorganized manner by people driven by economic motivations, frontier individualism, fatalism about the Indian danger, and the desire to escape the paternal control of church and state; they soon dispersed to live near their fields, 17th century-1810. Reprinted from *Journal of the American West* 1969 8(1): 7-21.

345. Simmons, Marc. SPANISH ATTEMPTS TO OPEN A NEW MEXICO-SONORA ROAD. *Arizona and the West 1975 17(1): 5-20.* In early 17th-century Sonora, after missions were established and mines were discovered, merchants and government officials from New Mexico's capital in Santa Fe attempted to develop trade contacts with Sonora. In 1644, Sonora's governor was recruiting settlers and soldiers in Santa Fe to populate and protect his jurisdiction. Although hampered by the rugged terrain, great distances, and the Apache Indian problem on their common border, and although no direct road was established in the Spanish colonial period, evidence suggests that trade contacts between the two provinces were considerably greater than has been supposed. Vestiges of this trade persisted, even after the Mexican War, into the late 1850's. 6 illus., map, 33 notes. D. L. Smith

346. Sinclair, John L. WORKING MIRACLES. *Westways 1975 67(12): 41-43, 69.* Story of a chapel of the Spanish Catholic Church in Santa Fe, New Mexico, in the 1850's-70's. S

347. Sizelove, Linda. INDIAN ADAPTATION TO THE SPANISH MISSIONS. *Pacific Hist. 1978 22(4): 393-402.* A study of the interaction between the padres of California's Spanish missions and the stone-age Indian population. The shaman with his hold over the people became the center of the attack on the native culture. The missions used the Indians' fondness for pageantry in music and dance in the worship of the Church. Likewise, Indian decorative motifs were painted in the churches. The Indians were trained in trades, crafts, husbandry, and the Spanish language. However, there was a fundamental conflict of cultures, and the Indians did not adjust well to moral codes, the work regimen, mission life with limitations on movement, and a state-administered governmental system. Decimation as a result of white men's diseases increased. The Indians were not able to change life-styles rapidly enough for a genuine cultural assimilation to take place. 28 notes, biblio. R. V. Ritter

348. Smith, Andrew T. THE FOUNDING OF THE SAN ANTONIO DE LAS HUERTAS GRANT. *Social Sci. J. 1976 13(3): 35-43.* History (1765-1891) of the Spanish San Antonio de las Huertas grant in New Mexico between Santa Fe and Las Placitas. One of six articles in this issue on Spanish and Mexican land grants in the Southwest.

349. Smith, Dean. CORONADO: MAGNIFICENT FAILURE. *Am. Hist. Illus. 1976 10(10): 4-9, 43-47.* Francisco Vásquez de Coronado (1510-54)

headed a 336-man Spanish force which initiated the recorded history of the Southwest (from Arizona to Kansas) during his 1540-42 expedition. The "Seven Cities of Cibola," advertised by Fray Marcos de Niza, proved to be villages, and the "golden cities of Quivira," related by "The Turk," turned out to be round grass lodges of the Wichita Indians, but the expedition discovered the Colorado River, the Grand Canyon, the Great Divide, The Staked Plains of Texas, and buffalo on the prairies of Western Oklahoma and Kansas. Primary and secondary sources; 9 illus., map.   D. B. Dodd

350. Snow, Cordelia Thomas. A BRIEF HISTORY OF THE PALACE OF GOVERNORS AND A PRELIMINARY REPORT ON THE 1974 EXCA-VATION. *Palacio 1974 80(3): 6-21.* Chronicles the planning and construction of the Palace of Governors (or Casas Reales, as it was originally known) in Santa Fe, New Mexico, by the Spanish colonial government in 1609-10, its use and reconstruction, 17th-19th centuries, its excavation in 1974, and notable artifacts.

351. Snow, David H. SPANISH AMERICAN POTTERY MANUFAC-TURE IN NEW MEXICO: A CRITICAL REVIEW. *Ethnohistory 1984 31(2): 93-113.* Reviews the claim periodically made for the existence of a Hispanic ceramic tradition in northern New Mexico. The accuracy of that claim is mired in local folklore and anchored more or less firmly in published archaeological speculation. Neither the origin, distribution, nor time depth of such a tradition is known, but references to Spanish-American potterymaking are limited to the 1930's.   J

352. Sperling, David. WEAVERS OF THE RIO GRANDE. *Early Am. Life 1984 15(2): 46-48, 70.* Briefly traces the history and technology of weaving by Spanish and Mexican-American settlers in the Rio Grande Valley of northern New Mexico.

353. Spillman, Trish. NEW LIFE FOR AN HISTORIC CRAFT: RIO GRANDE WEAVING AND DYEING WORKSHOP. *Palacio 1977 83(1): 14-24.* Overview of Spanish and Navajo rug and blanket weaving and native dye production, 19th-20th centuries, precedes description of workshops in both conducted in New Mexico, 1976-77, to sustain this folk art.

354. Stoller, Marianne L. GRANTS OF DESPERATION, LANDS OF SPECULATION: MEXICAN PERIOD LAND GRANTS IN COLORADO. *J. of the West 1980 19(3): 22-39.* The immense size of land grants made to several naturalized citizens of Mexico in the 1830's and 1840's suggests that the granting official, Governor Manuel Armijo, sold out his nation's interests to greedy newcomers. Review of the circumstances, however, indicates Armijo was protecting his frontiers by assigning the land to the only persons economically powerful enough to secure the land through settlement. Far from realizing huge profits from their lands, most of the grantees received little or nothing as their holdings broke up in conflicting claims and confused legal decisions. Based on documents in the Spanish Archives of New Mexico, in the State Records Center, Santa Fe; 11 photos, 3 maps, 54 notes.   B. S. Porter

355. Strout, Clevy Lloyd. THE CORONADO EXPEDITION: FOLLOW-ING THE GEOGRAPHY DESCRIBED IN THE SPANISH JOURNALS. *Great Plains J. 1974 14(1): 2-31.* Studies the Coronado expedition into the American Southwest (1540-42), based upon journals of the participants, especially that of Pedro de Castaneda. The journals provide "descriptions of topography, communication possibilities, climatic characteristics, soil conditions, and travel distances... ." As a linguist, the author uses the nuances of meaning of similar Spanish words to illustrate the varying landscape. Based on documents and secondary sources. 9 illus., 4 maps, 58 notes.   O. H. Zabel

356. Strout, Clevy Lloyd. THE RESETTLEMENT OF SANTA FE, 1695: THE NEWLY FOUND MUSTER ROLL. *New Mexico Hist. Rev. 1978 53(3): 261-270.* Many previously obscure details of the Juan Páez Hurtado expedition of 1695 are brought to light by document number 215, housed in the Thomas Gilcrease Institute of American History and Art in Tulsa, Oklahoma. There are important genealogical and demographic implications of this newly discovered document. Map, 8 notes.   J. H. Krenkel

357. Sunseri, Alvin R. AGRICULTURAL TECHNIQUES IN NEW MEX-ICO AT THE TIME OF THE ANGLO-AMERICAN CONQUEST. *Agric. Hist. 1973 47(4): 329-337.* In the arid region of New Mexico a highly complicated system of dryland irrigation developed as a result of the blending of Pueblo Indian and Mexican-American cultures. Water scarcity necessitated communal effort to assure a reliable supply. *Mayordomos* (ditch chiefs) supervised the construction and maintenance of extensive irrigation systems and with the *cacique* controlled access to available water. In large undertakings such as the construction of an *acequia madre* (mother ditch) landowners had to provide the necessary laborers. Many of the irrigation systems in this area go back to Spanish customs of management. Americans entering the area later, critical of the native subsistence level, introduced "progressive" methods of agriculture though the value of water diminished little. Based on primary and secondary sources; 32 notes.   R. T. Fulton

358. Tapia Méndez, Aureliano. FRAY RAFAEL JOSÉ VERGER Y SUAU TÉCNICO DE MISIONES [Fray Rafael José Verger y Suau, founder of missions]. *Humánitas [Mexico] 1975 16: 449-496.* Discusses the life and career of the second bishop of Nuevo León, Fray Rafael José Verger y Suau (1722-90), focusing on his career establishing missions in New Spain (including the American Southwest) after 1767, but particularly in Nuevo León after 1783.

359. Taylor, William B. LAND AND WATER RIGHTS IN THE VICE-ROYALTY OF NEW SPAIN. *New Mexico Hist. R. 1975 50(3): 189-212.* Material on land and water rights in Spanish America is scattered, making research difficult. The *Recopilación de Leyes de las Indias* is a compilation of laws, but not a complete code. Explains the rights in principle and practice as they applied to the use of water and land in the viceroyalty of New Spain. Distribution of the water was based primarily on prior use, need, and the protection of Indian rights, with demand often exceeding the supply. 53 notes.   J. H. Krenkel

360. Thompson, Mary Tittle. THE SOUTHWEST IN 1776. *Daughters of the Am. Revolution Mag. 1976 110(6): 821-825.* Discusses three 1776 expeditions: the Dominguez Expedition over the Escalante Trail; the de Anza Expedition to establish a colony on San Francisco Bay; and the Garcés Expedition to explore a route from California to the East.

361. Timmons, W. H. THE EL PASO AREA IN THE MEXICAN PERIOD, 1821-1848. *Southwestern Hist. Q. 1980 84(1): 1-28.* From 1821, when Mexico became independent, until 1848, when the Treaty of Guadalupe Hidalgo ended the Mexican War, the El Paso region developed into a major commercial center. Before 1840, commercial development resulted primarily from the influence of American traders: many amassed wealth, married Mexican women, and acquired Mexican citizenship. After 1840, most American traders retained their citizenship and remained single. Neither group favored war between the United States and Mexico, because it would upset business activities. After 1848, the Rio Grande became a dividing line between both countries and the flow of commerce shifted from a north-south to an east-west axis. Based on papers in the Juárez, National, Janos, and Chihuahua Archives and other primary sources; 2 illus., 63 notes. R. D. Hurt

362. Timmons, W. H. THE POPULATION OF THE EL PASO AREA: A CENSUS OF 1784. *New Mexico Hist. Rev. 1977 52(4): 311-316.* Considerable hardship resulted when there was a large influx of Spanish, mestizo, and Indian refugees late in the 17th century. Most of the people in El Paso became farm laborers. The population of El Paso and the nearby settlements in 1784 was 4,091. There were slightly more women than men and more girls than boys. 13 notes. J. H. Krenkel

363. Tjarks, Alicia V. DEMOGRAPHIC, ETHNIC AND OCCUPATIONAL STRUCTURE OF NEW MEXICO, 1790. *Americas (Acad. of Am. Franciscan Hist.) 1978 35(1): 45-88.* The best census of colonial New Mexico, prepared in 1790, showed the slow demographic growth of the province, which was almost wholly vegetative. Spanish and caste towns grew, whereas Indian villages were in decline. About half the population was Spanish, though ethnic definitions were not precise. Outside the primary rural sector, occupations were relatively unimportant and undifferentiated. Primary sources; 16 tables, 64 notes. D. Bushnell

364. Tornero Tinajero, Pablo. ESTUDIO DE LA POBLACION DE PENSACOLA (1784-1820) [A study of the population of Pensacola (1784-1820)]. *Anuario de Estudios Americanos [Spain] 1977 34: 537-561.* Because of Spanish censuses taken in 1784, 1788, 1791, 1802, 1805, 1819, and 1820, it is possible to study the population of Pensacola with some sophistication. These censuses divide the population by race, sex, social and marital status, and religion. Based on sources in the Archive of the Indies; 5 graphs, 11 notes.

J. A. Lewis

365. Tornero Tinajero, Pablo. SOCIEDAD Y POBLACION EN SAN AGUSTIN DE LA FLORIDA (1786) [Society and population in St. Augustine, Florida (1786)]. *Anuario de Estudios Americanos [Spain] 1978 35:*

233-260. The Spanish census for St. Augustine in 1786, two years after the British had returned the colony, is a tool which offers historians an unusual glimpse of life in Florida. 2 graphs, 27 notes, 3 appendixes.   J. A. Lewis

366. Torrez, Robert J. THE *JACAL* IN THE TIERRA AMARILLA. *Palacio 1979 85(2): 14-18.* The *jacal* was a simple form of wooden housing construction used by Indians and Spaniards in New Mexico's Tierra Amarilla, 8th-20th centuries.

367. Tower, John, ed. A NACOGDOCHES RESOLUTION ON THE STORMING OF THE ALAMO. *Southwestern Hist. Q. 1975 78(3): 303-306.* An original "Alamo Document" was presented to John Tower, US Senator from Texas, for placing in the Archives of the Texas State Library by Mrs. John Hubble of Baltimore, Maryland. The document is here printed, bearing the title: "At a Meeting of the Citizens of Nacogdoches on the 26th of March, 1836, the Following Preamble and Resolutions Were Unanimously Adopted, and Ordered to be Published."   R. V. Ritter

368. Treutlein, Theodore E. LOS ANGELES, CALIFORNIA: THE QUESTION OF THE CITY'S ORIGINAL SPANISH NAME. *Southern California Q. 1973 55(1): 1-7.* Traces the origin of the official title given to the pueblo of Los Angeles in instructions written by Commandant Teodoro de Croix on 27 December 1779. Subsequent messages from Croix confirmed that the official title was *el nuevo Pueblo de la Reyna de los Angeles al margen del Río de la Porciúncula* "(the new Pueblo of the Queen of the Angels by the Porciúncula River)." The term *Nuestra Señora de los Angeles de Porciúncula*, frequently cited by writers, may have derived from confusion with a religious holiday celebration in the area by the Portolá expedition. However, the founding of Los Angeles was a civil rather than a religious or military affair. Primary and secondary sources; 21 notes.   A. Hoffman

369. Trudell, Clyde F. AYALA AND THE "SAN CARLOS." *Pacific Hist. 1978 22(4): 371-378.* Juan Manuel de Ayala, originally of Andalucia, Spain, in 1775, was given responsibility for exploring and charting San Francisco Bay. Numerous misadventures developed in connection with the Franciscan responsibility to establish six missions in Alta California under Padre Junípero Serra, who had been appointed Presidente in 1769. Both overland sea routes were developed from Mexico to the area. Ayala, in the San Carlos, spent six weeks in the Bay charting and mapping. There were numerous contacts with the friendly Indians. Many of the well-known features of the Bay were given names, some of which have been perpetuated. Illus.   R. V. Ritter

370. Turner, Justin G. THE FIRST LETTER FROM PALM SPRINGS: THE JOSÉ ROMERO STORY. *Southern California Q. 1974 56(2): 123-134.* In 1823-24 José Romero led several expeditions to locate the Cocomaricopa Trail, an ambiguous route going from San Bernardino through Palm Springs to the Colorado River, as the better-known Anza Trail through Yuma was considered risky because of hostile Indians. Romero enjoyed good relations with the Cahuilla Indians of the Palm Springs region, but his first expedition along the Cocomaricopa Trail stopped just short of success. On this trip,

Romero wrote a letter describing his experiences to the governor of Sonora, the first dispatched from the Palm Springs region. A subsequent trip led by Romero was successful, but the most popular route came to be the one that linked San Diego to Tucson after peace was attained with the Yuma tribe. Romero's letter of 16 January 1824, is in the author's possession.

A. Hoffman

371. Tyler, Daniel. GOVERNOR ARMIJO AND THE TEJANOS. *J. of the West 1973 12(4): 589-599.* Despite personal faults and numerous sociopolitical problems, Governor Manuel Armijo of Mexican New Mexico always managed to keep himself in power. He raged against the marauding Texans and defeated them in battle in 1841. He used the fear of foreign invasion to unite the citizenry, who otherwise were not very fond of him. The threat of a new Texan attack in 1846 made Armijo back off, preferring to protect his personal profits rather than the people. 44 notes.   V. L. Human

372. Tyler, Daniel. MEXICAN INDIAN POLICY IN NEW MEXICO. *New Mexico Hist. Rev. 1980 55(2): 101-120.* Focuses on Mexican policy toward the nomadic Indian tribes during 1821-46 on the northern Mexican frontier, particularly in New Mexico. The essential points of Mexican strategy, which were largely a continuation of Spanish policy, were military campaigns, gift giving, trade regulation, and peace treaties. After 1837, the fear of an American invasion resulted in a more aggressive approach toward the Indians in New Mexico. Because of the turbulence on the northern Borderlands, however, the Indian policy in New Mexico failed to cope with the aggressive Indians and the arrival of the North Americans. Based on the Mexican Archives of New Mexico at the State Records Center and Archives, Santa Fe, New Mexico, and other primary sources; illus., 73 notes.   P. L. McLaughlin

373. Tyler, Daniel. THE MEXICAN TEACHER. *Red River Valley Hist. R. 1974 1(3): 207-221.* Public education faced problems in northern Mexico, and later the southwestern United States, 1821-48, despite the presence of dedicated teachers.   S

374. Tyler, S. Lyman and Taylor, H. Darrel. THE REPORT OF FRAY ALONSO DE POSADA IN RELATION TO QUIVIRA AND TEGUAYO. *New Mexico Hist. Rev. 1958 33(4): 285-314.* Fray Alonso de Posada, a missionary in New Mexico during 1650-60 and Custodian of the *Custodia de la Conversión de San Pablo del Nuevo México* during 1661-65, wrote a report ca. 1686-88 on the northern New Mexican provinces of Quivira and Teguayo for the Spanish Council of the Indies in light of French exploration in the area.

375. Ulibarri, George S. THE CHOUTEAU-DEMUN EXPEDITION TO NEW MEXICO, 1815-17. *New Mexico Hist. Rev. 1961 36(4): 263-273.* Account of the expedition undertaken by Auguste P. Chouteau and Julius Demun, former French citizens from St. Louis, Missouri, to New Mexico in 1815-17 to trade with the Indians, that unfortunately ended with their arrest by Spanish colonial authorities for allegedly not leaving the territory when asked, an incident that was not resolved until 1851 when Chouteau and Demun were awarded their claim for the goods seized by the Spanish.

376. Valle, Rosemary Keupper. THE CESAREAN OPERATION IN ALTA CALIFORNIA DURING THE FRANCISCAN MISSION PERIOD (1769-1833). *Bull. of the Hist. of Medicine 1974 48(2): 265-275.*

377. Van Ness, John R. HISPANIC VILLAGE ORGANIZATION IN NORTHERN NEW MEXICO: CORPORATE COMMUNITY STRUCTURE IN HISTORICAL AND COMPARATIVE PERSPECTIVE. *Colorado Coll. Studies 1979 (15): 21-44.* Describes the corporate features of Hispanic villages in northern New Mexico, tracing corporate community structure in Spain, Latin America, and New Mexico since the 16th century.

378. Vigil, Ralph E. BARTOLOME DE LAS CASAS, JUDGE ALONSO DE ZORITA, AND THE FRANCISCANS: A COLLABORATIVE EFFORT FOR THE SPIRITUAL CONQUEST OF THE BORDERLANDS. *Americas (Acad. of Am. Franciscan Hist.) 1981 38(1): 45-57.* Alonso de Zorita (1512-85) arrived in Mexico in 1556 with a record already established as defender of the Indians. Influenced by the ideas of Bartolomé de Las Casas, and working in collaboration with the Franciscans, he unsuccessfully proposed the peaceful conversion and colonization of New Spain's northern frontier. Based on documents in the Archivo General de Indias and published sources; 52 notes. D. Bushnell

379. Vigil, Ralph H. THE HERITAGE OF THE SPANISH BORDERLANDS. *Red River Valley Hist. Rev. 1975 2(3): 413-420.* Review article on John Francis McDermott's *The Spanish in the Mississippi Valley, 1762-1804* (Urbana: U. of Illinois Pr., 1974), Oakah L. Jones, Jr.'s *The Spanish Borderlands: A First Reader* (Los Angeles: Lorrin L. Morrison, 1974), and Robert S. Weddle's *Wilderness Manhunt: The Spanish Search for La Salle* (Austin: U. of Texas Pr., 1973).

380. Walker, Billy D. COPPER GENESIS: THE EARLY YEARS OF SANTA RITA DEL COBRE. *New Mexico Hist. Rev. 1979 54(1): 5-20.* Describes the discovery and development of the Santa Rita copper mines in southwestern New Mexico. Francisco Manuel de Elguea (d. 1809), a wealthy merchant from Chihuahua, was the first to develop the mines into a profitable venture. Spanish and Mexican mining methods and problems at Santa Rita are discussed, emphasizing the years 1800-25. Includes reports concerning the mines from Zebulon M. Pike (1779-1813) and James O. Pattie (1804-1850?). Photo, 51 notes. P. L. McLaughlin

381. Watkins, T. H. DISCOVERERS OF THE MISSISSIPPI. *Am. West 1974 11(2): 4-11.* The discovery of the Mississippi River "was an accident, the fortuitous by-product of the myth-chasing that drove men with overheated imaginations into adventures that were at once fascinating and monumentally ill-conceived." The Spanish roster includes Piñada (1519), Cabeza de Vaca (1528), and De Soto (1541), who were impelled by the dream of gold. The Northwest Passage myth, the supposed waterway to the riches of Cathay, explains French discovery by Groseilliers (1654), Jolliet and Marquette (1673), and La Salle (1679). Excerpted from a forthcoming book. 7 illus. D. L. Smith

382. Watson, Thomas D. A SCHEME GONE AWRY: BERNARDO DE GALVEZ, GILBERTO ANTONIO DE MAXENT, AND THE SOUTHERN INDIAN TRADE. *Louisiana Hist. 1976 17(1): 5-17.* Bernardo de Galvez, governor of Spanish Louisiana, in 1781 broke the sole remaining British foothold along the Gulf of Mexico. He believed that a successful Indian policy must be based upon trade control. The southern Indian trade, principally with the Five Civilized Tribes, consisted overwhelmingly of deerskins. Following the establishment of peace, a memorial by Maxent, a Louisiana fur trader, to Charles III led to the opening of direct trade among French ports, Louisiana, and West Florida. 26 notes.   E. P. Stickney

383. Weber, David J. EL GOBIERNO TERRITORIAL DE NUEVO MÉXICO: LA EXPOSICIÓN DEL PADRE MARTÍNEZ DEL 1831 [The territorial government of New Mexico: the report of Father Martínez of 1831]. *Hist. Mexicana [Mexico] 1975 25(2): 302-315.* In October 1830 the Presbyterian Antonio José Martínez was elected for a two-year term in the New Mexican government. He believed the territory's government weak and inefficient and reported accordingly in 1831. The report was sent by the government to the national congress where it met little response. The report shows the political situation of New Mexico as being very different from the more central areas of Mexico. Includes a transcript of the report; 21 notes.   S. P. Carr/S

384. Weber, David J. FAILURE OF A FRONTIER INSTITUTION: THE SECULAR CHURCH IN THE BORDERLANDS UNDER INDEPENDENT MEXICO, 1821-1846. *Western Hist. Q. 1981 12(2): 125-143.* Secularization of the Catholic Church in the Mexican-American borderlands began under Spain in the late 18th century. Missions, state supported missionaries, and Indian neophytes as wards of the state, were to be replaced by parishes, parish supported clergy, and taxpaying Indian parishoners. The secular church, Mexico's "wealthiest and most powerful single institution," failed to serve the Southwest frontier effectively or to convert the ailing missions into parishes because of shortage of funds and priests, weakened leadership, the decline of morale and morality of the priesthood, and the increasing spiritual neglect of the settlers. A key institution in extending the northern frontier of New Spain, the church lacked the strength to consolidate its position under an independent Mexico. 60 notes.   D. L. Smith

385. Weber, David J. [THE SPANISH SOUTHWEST]. Weber, David J., ed. *New Spain's Far Northern Frontier: Essays on Spain in the American West, 1540-1821* (Albuquerque: U. of New Mexico Pr., 1979): vii-xix. Overview of the history of the American Southwest during the Spanish occupation, 1540-1821.

386. Weber, David J. AN UNFORGETTABLE DAY: FACUNDO MELGARES ON INDEPENDENCE. *New Mexico Hist. R. 1973 48(1): 27-44.* On 6 January 1822, Santa Fe celebrated New Spain's independence with a ceremony including church services, processions, pageants, firing of guns, and ringing of bells. Governor Melgares described the event for *Gaceta Imperial,* the official government newspaper.   J. H. Krenkel

387. Weber, Francis J. CALIFORNIA'S *CAMINITO REAL. California Hist. Q. 1975 54(1): 63-75.* In addition to Alta California's 21 missions, other *capillas,* or chapels, were established to provide religious services and education at the *presidios* and in outlying regions. Surveys such religious facilities, providing the location, date of founding, type of services provided, and discontinuance or destruction. The facilities fell into four categories: two quasi-missions existing briefly near the Yuma Indians, five *asistencias* (assistant missions serving as branches of fully-developed missions, but without resident priests), four *presidio* chapels; and about 11 *estancias,* or mission ranches. While less well-known than the fully-established missions, *capillas* were an important part of the religious network of Alta California. Primary and secondary sources; 91 notes.   A. Hoffman

388. Weber, Francis J. THE DEATH OF FRAY LUÍS JAYME: TWO HUNDREDTH ANNIVERSARY. *J. of San Diego Hist. 1976 22(1): 41-43.* Discusses the death of Franciscan missionary Luís Jayme, who was killed by Yuman Indians at Mission San Diego de Alcalá in San Diego, California, 1775.

389. Weber, Francis J. THE MISSION GRAPE. *Pacific Hist. 1979 23(3): 1-3.* Describes the introduction of viticulture and wine making at the missions of California, introduced first by Jesuit missionary, Padre Juan Ugarte, about 1697 at Mission San Francisco Xavier in Baja California, and from there carried to other California missions.   R. V. Ritter

390. Wilkinson, S. Kristina and Hardwick, Michael R. LA PURISIMA, A LIVING MUSEUM OF SPANISH COLONIAL HISTORY. *Noticias 1973 9(2): 1-9.* Mission La Purisima Concepcion was founded in 1787, the third of three missions established in the Santa Barbara area. Originally located in the present-day city of Lompoc, it was abandoned after the 1812 earthquake. It was relocated at the site of the present location of the restored La Purisima State Historic Park. Construction of a mission on this second site was under the direction of Padre Mariano Payeras. After his death the mission declined, and after secularization the mission was abandoned. Finally, in 1934 the Catholic Church and the Union Oil Company, which had acquired part of the land in 1905, turned the land over to the county of Santa Barbara. The state and the county bought additional land and restoration of the mission began under the Civilian Conservation Corps. Using as a guide information from the archival collection of the mission, restoration was as accurate as possible. Currently, the mission is administered by the California Department of Parks and Recreation.   K. Butcher

391. Williams, Jack S. A FLINTLOCK MECHANISM FROM MISSION SAN ANTONIO. *Masterkey 1981 55(1): 23-26.* Describes the miguelet flint-lock found in a room of the barracks area of Mission San Antonio de Padua in southern Monterey County, California, associated with soldiers of Northern New Spain in the 18th century.

392. Williams, Margaret Jean McClennan. STORY OF THE SANTA FE TRAIL. *Daughters of the Am. Revolution Mag. 1981 115(5): 420-422.*

Describes the route, landmarks, and history of the Santa Fe Trail from Arrow Rock, Missouri, to the Plaza of Santa Fe, New Mexico; 1806-80.

393.   Wilson, Kax. RIO GRANDE WEAVING: HISPANIC TRADITION IN THE SOUTHWEST. *Am. Art and Antiques 1979 2(6): 92-99.* The wool blankets and rugs woven during the 19th and 20th centuries in the Rio Grande Valley of northern New Mexico represent a combination of the three cultures of the Navajo and Pueblo Indians and Hispanic Americans; provides a brief history of wool and cotton in the area since the 15th century.

394.   Worcester, Donald E. THE SIGNIFICANCE OF THE SPANISH BORDERLANDS TO THE UNITED STATES. *Western Hist. Q. 1976 7(1): 4-18.* The Spanish northward movement from Mexico and the Caribbean is second only to the Anglo-American westward movement in importance in American history. Spanish influence, present from the beginning, is manifested in the present US monetary system, place names, farming and ranching, literature, folklore, political practices, racial blending, legal heritage, and mining techniques. Historians tend to treat the subject as if the Spanish Borderlands history terminated when the Spanish colonial period ended. The Spanish-language culture frontier continues to move steadily northward, however, with projections that the Spanish-speaking population of the United States will exceed the black population in 15 years. Illus., 26 notes.

D. L. Smith

395.   Wroth, William. THE FLOWERING AND DECLINE OF THE NEW MEXICAN *SANTERO:* 1780-1900. Weber, David J., ed. *New Spain's Far Northern Frontier: Essays on Spain in the American West, 1540-1821* (Albuquerque: U. of New Mexico Pr., 1979): 273-282. As the Spanish Franciscans began to leave New Mexico, local artisans began to carve and paint images of saints *(santos)* to fill the void; the folk art flourished until the American occupation when efforts were made to suppress it in order to Americanize and modernize the Catholic Church. Reprinted from Fine Arts Gallery of San Diego, *The Cross and the Sword* (San Diego, 1976).

396.   —. [CALIFORNIOS AND THE IMAGE OF INDOLENCE]. *Western Hist. Q. 1979 10(1): 61-69.*
Weber, David J. HERE RESTS JUAN ESPINOSA: TOWARDS A CLEARER LOOK AT THE IMAGE ON THE "INDOLENT" CALIFORNIOS, *pp. 61-68.* Examines the analysis of indolence of Californios in David J. Langum, "Californios and the Image of Indolence." Finds Langum's religion-nationalism-racism and industrializing explanations leading into "a quagmire on the road to historical explanation." Poses two questions that need answers to put us back "on solid ground." Espinosa is an apocryphal Californio indolent. 23 notes.
Langum, David J. A BRIEF REPLY, *p. 69.* Defends his original position and suggests fallacies in Weber's reasoning.   D. L. Smith

397.   —. DATOS HISTÓRICOS SOBRE LA COLONIZACIÓN ESPAÑOLA DE LA FLORIDA Y YUCATÁN (BEIMENI) [Historical data on Spanish colonization of Florida and Yucatán (Beimeni)]. *Acad. Puertorriqueña*

de la Hist. Bol. [Puerto Rico] 1972 2(8): 237-257. Furnishes data on 16th-century miners, settlers, explorers, and missionaries of Florida and Yucatán, underlining Spanish influence on that area and its settlers' concern for education and evangelization. Based on documents in the General Archive of the Indies. M. C. F. (IHE 91528)

398. —. THE GREAT PUEBLO REVOLT. *Palacio 1980-81 86(4): 10-33.*
Simmons, Marc. THE PUEBLO REVOLT: WHY DID IT HAPPEN?, *pp. 11-15.*
Kessell, John L. ESTEBAN CLEMENTE: PRECURSOR OF THE PUEBLO REVOLT, *pp. 16-17.*
Ortiz, Alfonso. POPAY'S LEADERSHIP: A PUEBLO PERSPECTIVE, *pp. 18-22.*
Warren, Nancy Hunter. IMAGES FROM THE PUEBLO TRICENTEN-NIAL, *pp. 23-26.*
Agoyo, Herman. THE TRICENTENNIAL YEAR IN PUEBLO CON-SCIOUSNESS, *pp. 27-31.*
Chavez, Thomas E. BUT WERE THEY ALL NATIVES?, *p. 32.*
—. A CHRONOLOGY OF THE PUEBLO REVOLT, *p. 33.*
Tensions between the Pueblo Indians and the Spaniards began in 1650 when Pueblos and friendly Apaches planned a revolt because of the religious attitudes of the Franciscan friars and Spanish colonists, which culminated in the successful 1680 revolt, commemorated in 1980 tricentennial celebrations.

399. —. [IMPACT OF SPANISH COLONIZATION ON CALIFORNIA NATIVES]. *J. of San Diego Hist. 1978 24(1): 121-144.*
Heizer, Robert. IMPACT OF COLONIZATION ON THE NATIVE CALIFORNIA SOCIETIES, *pp. 121-139.* The Spanish mission system (1769-1834), basically inflexible and bent on self-perpetuation, resulted in the enslavement and decimation of the Indians (through disease).
Killea, Lucy L. COMMENTARY ON ROBERT HEIZER'S PAPER "IMPACT OF COLONIZATION ON THE NATIVE CALIFORNIA SOCIETIES," *pp. 140-144.* Relates Heizer's conclusions to the native population under the control of the mission at San Diego, 1769-75.

400. —. THE SPANISH LEGACY. *J. of the West 1979 18(1): 89-91.* The Spanish Mission San Xavier del Bac near Tucson, and Mission San Cayetano del Tumacacori, near Tubac, Arizona, are reminders of early mission efforts in southern Arizona. Both missions are now open to the public. 6 photos courtesy of the Arizona Office of Tourism. B. S. Porter

3

PEOPLE FROM MEXICO

401. Aguirre, Adalbérto, Jr. INTELLIGENCE TESTING AND CHICA-NOS: A QUALITY OF LIFE ISSUE. *Social Problems 1979 27(2): 186-195.* Discusses how low performances by Mexican Americans on standard intelligence tests from the 1920's to the 1970's have helped to legitimate an educational ideology equating lower intelligence with Chicanos' inability to function competently within the American educational structure.

402. Alba-Hernández, Francisco. ÉXODO SILENCIOSO: LA EMIGRA-CIÓN DE TRABAJADORES MEXICANOS A ESTADOS UNIDOS [Silent exodus: the emigration of Mexican workers to the United States]. *Foro Int. [Mexico] 1976 17(2): 152-179.* Discusses Mexican immigration to the United States, characteristics of the Mexican immigrants, reasons for their immigration, and future prospects. Based on a 1973 questionaire, primary and secondary sources; 7 tables, 23 notes, biblio.　　　　　　　　　　D. A. Franz

403. Alvarez, Rodolfo. THE PSYCHO-HISTORICAL AND SOCIOECO-NOMIC DEVELOPMENT OF THE CHICANO COMMUNITY IN THE UNITED STATES. *Social Sci. Q. 1973 53(4): 920-942.* "Using an earlier SSQ contribution as his point of departure, ... traces the psycho-historical and socio-economic development of the Chicano community in the United States. 'The Creation Generation,' characterized by economic subjugation and the object of race and ethnic prejudice, appeared in 1848 when the Mexican American people were created as a people by the signing of the Treaty of Guadalupe Hidalgo. By 1900 the majority of Mexican Americans were members of 'The Migrant Generation' who left a lower class status in Mexico to enter a lower caste status in the United States without being aware of it. Starting somewhere around the time of World War II, Alvarez suggests there developed another state of collective consciousness which he terms the 'Mexican American Generation.' This group moved to the cities, experienced some upward mobility and managed to establish their claims as bona fide citizens of the United States in the eyes of only one of the social-psychologically relevant populations: *themselves.* Finally, in the late 1960's, a new consciousness began to make itself felt among the Mexican Americans. An awareness of citizenship in a pluralistic society, self-determination and higher aspirations are among the characteristics of the 'Chicano Generation.' "　　　J

404. Aragón, Janie Louise. THE COFRADÍAS OF NEW MEXICO: A PROPOSAL AND A PERIODIZATION. *Aztlán 1978 9: 101-118.* Proposes

a methodology for studying Los Hermanos Penitentes, a unit for the social organization of villages and towns of the upper Rio Grande Valley, referring to a large group of cofradías, or brotherhoods, often mentioned, though inadequately understood, by scholars. Lines of investigation are suggested, along with a possible periodization: 1770-1830, 1830-55, 1855-80, 1880-1912, 1912-35, and 1935-65, together with possible primary sources. 29 notes, biblio.

R. V. Ritter

405. Armas, Isabel de. CHICANO, UN VOCABLO COLONIZADOR [Chicano, a colonialist word]. *Cuadernos Hispanoamericanos [Spain] 1983 (394): 193-201.* Reviews Tino Villanueva's *Chicanos: Antología Histórica y Literaria* [Chicanos: a historical and literary anthology] and Tomás Calvo Buezas's *Los Más Pobres en el País Más Rico* [The poorest people in the wealthiest of nations]. Chicano sensibility historically is marked by the cultural clash with Anglo-Americans and by the process of assimilation and integration into North American society.

C. Pasadas-Ureña

406. Bach, Robert L. IMMIGRATION PERSPECTIVES: A REVIEW ESSAY. *J. of Int. Affairs 1979 33(2): 339-350.* Reviews Michael J. Piore's *Birds of Passage: Migrant Labor and Industrial Societies* (Cambridge: Cambridge U. Pr., 1979), Mark Reisler's *By the Sweat of Their Brow: Mexican Immigrant Labor in the United States, 1900-1940* (Westport: Greenwood Pr., 1978), *Immigrants—and Immigrants: Perspectives on Mexican Labor Migration to the United States,* Arthur F. Corwin, ed. (Westport: Greenwood Pr., 1978), and *Mexican Workers in the United States: Historical and Political Perspectives,* George C. Kiser and Martha Woody Kiser, ed. (Albuquerque: U. of New Mexico Pr., 1979).

407. Bach, Robert L. MEXICAN IMMIGRATION AND THE AMERICAN STATE. *Int. Migration Rev. 1978 12(4): 536-558.* Discusses illegal aliens during 1867-1977, in reference to the economic needs and strengths of organized labor in the United States.

408. Batchen, Lou Sage. LA CURANDERA. *Palacio 1975 81(1): 20-25.* Originally written as part of a WPA project; describes the home treatment methods of a New Mexico *curandera,* a doctor (commonly in Hispanic and Indian speaking areas) who heals using herbs and adhering to folk medical beliefs; 19th century-1930's.

409. Benavides, E. Ferol. THE SAINTS AMONG THE SAINTS: A STUDY OF CURANDERISMO IN UTAH. *Utah Hist. Q. 1973 41(4): 373-392.* Examines 20th-century curanderismo, Mexican American folk curing, as it is practiced, particularly in Utah. The curandera or practitioner fills aesthetic, psychological, and emotional needs, as well as physical needs. Curanderismo continues partly because the American medical system fails to serve certain subculture peoples. 5 illus.

D. L. Smith

410. Brackenridge, R. Douglas and Garcia-Treto, Francisco O. PRESBYTERIANS AND MEXICAN AMERICANS: FROM PATERNALISM TO PARTNERSHIP. *J. of Presbyterian Hist. 1977 55(2): 160-178.* Traces Presby-

terian efforts to minister to migrant and resident Mexicans in New Mexico, Arizona, California, Colorado, and Texas. Depicts the various efforts in areas of churches, evangelism, education and medical units. The basic weakness of the Presbyterians was their paternalistic approach, manifested in their refusal to relinquish ecclesiastical control over the ethnic churches which were established, or to accept or admit Mexican pastors as equals in their ecclesiastical judicatories. Only in recent years has the concept of partnership emerged, and provisions are being made for Mexican leadership to work with Spanish-speaking people. Based largely on primary sources and the authors' *Iglesia Presbyteriana: A History of Presbyterians and Mexican Americans in the Southwest* (1974); 46 notes.　　　　　　　　　　　　H. M. Parker, Jr.

411. Briggs, Charles L. ST. ISIDORE, HUSBANDMAN: MEDITATIONS ON A CARVED IMAGE FROM CÓRDOVA, N.M. *Palacio 1981 87(1): 33-40.* Wood carvings of Catholic saints have been made by Hispanos in New Mexico since ca. 1690; focuses on an image of Saint Isidore the Husbandman (ca. 1070-1130) carved by George López of Córdova, New Mexico, in 1949.

412. Briggs, Charles L. WHAT IS A MODERN SANTO? *Palacio 1973 49(4): 40-49.* An adjunct to New Mexico's folk art, santos, polychromed wooden figurines depicting saints and holy persons, were created by José Dolores Lopez (1894-1937) and his son George Lopez (1925-73), in Córdova, New Mexico.

413. Bustamante, Jorge A.; with commentary by Krauze, Enrique. LA MIGRACIÓN HACIA LA FRONTERA NORTE Y LOS ESTADOS UNIDOS [Migration to the northern frontier and to the United States]. Frost, Elsa Cecilia; Meyer, Michael C.; and Zoraida Vázquez, Josefina, ed. *El Trabajo y los Trabajadores en la Historia de México* (Mexico City: Colegio de México, 1979): 518-528. Migration in this century in Mexico has been from country to town, from town to the northern frontier, and (largely illegally) to the United States. It has been studied more in the United States than in Mexico. Despite US preoccupation with the problem and operations such as the expulsion in 1954 of over a million Mexicans, pressure from Mexico and the demand for cheap labor in the United States has insured continued illegal emigration, on which few statistics are available. Commentary, pp. 529-532; bibliography.

　　　　　　　　　　　　　　　　　　　　　　　　　　J. P. H. Myers

414. Candelaria, Cordelia. SIX REFERENCE WORKS ON MEXICAN-AMERICAN WOMEN: A REVIEW ESSAY. *Frontiers 1980 5(2): 75-80.* Review essay of *The Chicana: A Comprehensive Bibliographic Study,* edited by Roberto Cabella-Argandoña, Juan Gómez-Quiñones, and Patricia Herrera Durán. (Los Angeles: UCLA Chicano Studies Center, 1975), Martha P. Cotera's *Diosa y Hembra: The History and Heritage of Chicanas in the U.S.* (Austin: Information Systems Development, 1976), *Essays on La Mujer,* edited by Rosaura Sánchez and Rosa Martinez Cruz (Los Angeles: UCLA Chicano Studies Center Publications, 1977), Alfredo Mirandé and Evangelina Enriquez's *La Chicana: The Mexican-American Woman* (Chicago: U. of Chicago Pr., 1979), and *Twice a Minority: Mexican-American Women,* edited by Margarita Melville (St. Louis: C. V. Mosby, 1980).

415. Cardenas, Gilbert. LOS DESARRAIGADOS: CHICANOS IN THE MIDWESTERN REGION OF THE UNITED STATES. *Aztlán 1976 7(2): 153-186.* Focuses on Mexican and Chicano immigration to the Midwest, which began on a large scale in 1919, and on the legal, social, and economic factors affecting it. Before the repartriations of the 1930's, Mexican-origin immigration to the Midwest was mainly from Mexico; today it is mainly from the US Southwest, especially Texas. But in Chicago and Detroit the Mexican immigrant population is still the most distinctive segment of the Mexican population. Discusses illegal immigration, and the problems of migratory agricultural laborers in the Midwest. Concludes with a socioeconomic profile of the region's Spanish-language population based on data from the 1970 US Census. Published and archival sources; 10 tables, 24 notes, 45 ref.   L. W. Van Wyk

416. Cardoso, Lawrence A. PROTESTANT MISSIONARIES AND THE MEXICAN: AN ENVIRONMENTALIST IMAGE OF CULTURAL DIFFERENCES. *New Scholar 1978 7(1-2): 223-236.* Examines the position of Protestant missionaries in Mexico and the southwestern United States, 1867-1930, and considers their belief that Anglo Americans had nothing to fear from Mexicans, and that Mexicans could become upstanding US citizens. They hoped that Mexican development would benefit from the contact brought about by northward migration. Analyzes the aftermath of the 1910 Mexican revolution, including the attention given to morality and justice; the flight of Mexico's lower classes to the United States, 1914-30, and female emancipation in 1917. 27 notes.   G. L. Neville

417. Carlson, Alvar W. CORRALES, NEW MEXICO: TRANSITION IN A SPANISH-AMERICAN COMMUNITY. *Red River Valley Hist. Rev. 1979 4(3): 88-99.* Traces land use, development, and ownership of Corrales, New Mexico, 1710-1970's, concentrating on the period 1930's-70's and the transition from a Hispanic-American pocket to an Anglo suburban community abutting Albuquerque.

418. Carlson, Alvar W. EL RANCHO AND VADITO: SPANISH SETTLEMENTS ON INDIAN LAND GRANTS. *Palacio 1979 85(1): 28-39.* The Spanish American settlements of El Rancho and Vadito which sprang up along the Pojoaque River in present-day New Mexico adjacent to Pueblo Indian settlements in the late 18th century, although illegally standing on Indian land, were allowed to remain by the adjudication of the Pueblo Lands Board, 1913-40's.

419. Cazares, Ralph B.; Murguia, Edward; and Frisbie, W. Parker. MEXICAN AMERICAN INTERMARRIAGE IN A NONMETROPOLITAN CONTEXT. *Social Sci. Q. 1984 65(2): 626-634.* An examination of marriage records for Pecos County, Texas, from 1880 to 1978 shows an overall outmarriage rate of .091 for marriages and .048 for individuals, documenting a considerable social distance which historically has existed between Mexican Americans and Anglo Americans in this region; intermarriage rates are significantly higher after 1970, which may indicate an important diminution of social distance separating Anglos and Mexican Americans in an area where close social contact between the two groups has heretofore been minimal.

420.   Chavira, Ricardo. A CASE STUDY: REPORTING OF MEXICAN EMIGRATION AND DEPORTATION. *Journalism Hist. 1977 4(2): 59-61.* Compares the reporting in two newspapers, one Spanish- and one English-speaking, of the emigration and deportation of Mexicans in the 1930's, 1950's, and 1970's.

421.   Cook, Sherburne F. TYPE OF MARRIAGE CEREMONY AS A CARRYOVER IN ACCULTURATION OF MEXICANS IN THE UNITED STATES. *Ethnohistory 1976 23(1): 45-63.* A study of 4,750 marriages in Santa Clara County, California, which occurred between 1908 and 1968, and all of which involved participants of Mexican descent, demonstrated a carryover from Mexican to American culture. The character used as a test was the tendency of Mexican Americans to seek civil rather than religious officiation at the marriage ceremony. That this tendency is derived from the Mexican cultural complex is shown by the facts that, after excluding divorce, persons of Mexican origin react differently from Portuguese and Italian immigrants, and that intermarriage by Mexicans in this country with members of other ethnic groups drastically reduces the number of civil as compared with religious ceremonies. On the other hand the geography of birth exerts relatively little influence, for the choice of type of marriage ceremony has no association with birth in Mexico or the United States.   J

422.   Cornelius, Wayne A. LA MIGRACIÓN ILEGAL MEXICANA A LOS ESTADOS UNIDOS: CONCLUSIONES DE INVESTIGACIONES RECIENTES, IMPLICACIONES POLÍTICAS Y PRIORIDADES DE IN-VESTIGACIÓN [Illegal Mexican immigration to the United States: conclusions of recent research, political implications, and research priorities]. *Forot Int. [Mexico] 1978 18(3): 399-429.* Examines illegal Mexican aliens in the United States, their impact on both countries, and research needed to obtain data for dealing with the problem. Concludes that little can be done until conditions in Mexico make emigration for employment unattractive. Covers 1930-70's. Based on interviews and secondary sources; notes, biblio.
                                                                        D. A. Franz

423.   Cornelius, Wayne A. MEXICAN MIGRATION TO THE UNITED STATES. *Pro. of the Acad. of Pol. Sci. 1981 34(1): 67-77.* Mexican migration became institutionalized over many decades and generations. Elemental human needs and desires will continue to drive Mexican workers across the border, no matter how harshly US immigration laws are enforced and no matter what hardships must be endured. Covers ca. 1880-1980. 5 notes.
                                                                    T. P. Richardson

424.   Corwin, Arthur F. CAUSES OF MEXICAN EMIGRATION TO THE UNITED STATES. *Perspectives in Am. Hist. 1973 7: 557-635.* Mexicans emigrated to the United States for reasons similar to those for emigrants from other countries—overpopulation at home, a shortage of arable land, and social conditions imposed by the turmoil of domestic politics. But the aspiring Mexican emigrants had one advantage over most European and Oriental emigrants: they were citizens of a country contiguous to the United States. This gave rise to a migratory class which moved in and out of the country

despite the tightening of border controls. During 1901-73, 1.75 million Mexicans were legally admitted for permanent residence in the United States. Estimates place the numbers of those who illegally resided in the United States at closer to four million. 6 tables, 199 notes.   W. A. Wiegand

425. DelCastillo, Adelaida R. STERILIZATION: AN OVERVIEW. Mora, Magdalena and DelCastillo, Adelaida R., ed. *Mexican Women in the United States: Struggles Past and Present* (Los Angeles: U. of California Chicano Studies Res. Center, 1980): 65-70. Discusses the predominantly punitive rationale underlying the advocacy of sterilization in the United States, especially involving Mexican women. The first sterilization bill was passed in the United States in 1907. More recently, legislators, judges, and doctors have advocated and mandated forced sterilization for other than eugenic purposes. The poor and ethnic minorities, by extension, have come to be seen as social misfits and an economic drain on the state. Their sterilization has been advocated even though it violates a number of juridical precedents, laws, and constitutional rights that protect the fundamentals of privacy and procreation. 40 notes.   J. Powell

426. Delgado, James P. JUAN PABLO BERNAL: CALIFORNIA PIO-NEER. *Pacific Hist. 1979 23(3): 50-62.* Discusses Juan Pablo Bernal (1810-78), whose family had come to California in the early period of Spanish rule. Born in San José de Guadalupe, he saw the territory pass to Mexican rule in 1822, his father obtaining a Mexican land grant. Increase in wealth through cattle breeding on his ranch and successful business transactions in Pueblo de San José in addition to his original El Rancho de Santa Teresa made possible his gaining title to El Valle de San José in partnership with others of his family. In 1846 the area fell to its American conquerors. After legal battles to maintain titles with American authorities, and bad business deals, he lost much of his wealth. In 1877, one year before his death, he was interviewed at the request of Hubert Howe Bancroft to get material for his *History of California.* Primary sources; 7 photos, 1 map, 13 notes, biblio.   R. V. Ritter

427. DeMoss, Virginia. DOMÍNGUEZ DOMAIN. *Westways 1981 73(7): 44-46, 69.* Traces the history of the 75,000 acre rancho obtained by Juan José Domínguez in 1784 as a land grant; and discusses subsequent owners and the Domínguez Ranch Adobe, begun in 1825, later given to the Claretian Order, and now a national and state historic site.

428. Dixon, Marlene; Martinez, Elizabeth; and McCaughan, Ed. CHICA-NAS AND MEXICANAS WITHIN A TRANSNATIONAL WORKING CLASS: THEORETICAL PERSPECTIVES. *Rev. (Fernand Braudel Center) 1983 7(1): 109-150.* Looks first at the various processes of colonization and recolonization that have led to the Chicano/Mexicano population as a transnational and exploited sector of the working class. Imperialism's integra-tion of Mexico and the Southwest was a brutal, degrading process, particularly for women and the family. In this context, machismo is not strictly a cultural phenomenon but rather primarily a form of male supremacist ideology serving capital accumulation. Ref.   L. V. Eid

429.   Dworkin, A. Gary and Stephens, Richard C. MEXICAN-AMERICAN ADOLESCENT INHALANT ABUSE: A PROPOSED MODEL. *Youth & Soc. 1980 11(4): 493-506.* Solvents, spray paints, and other inhalants are popular for drug abuse in the barrio. This particular choice is due to cultural tradition in Mexico of inhalant use for medicinal purposes and poverty combined with the cheapness of these drugs. Barrio desire for drugs remains high due to economic, social, and linguistic isolation, combined with a steady influx of new migrants, keeping ties with the old country high. Fig., 4 notes, biblio.   J. H. Sweetland

430.   Ebright, Malcolm. THE EMBUDO GRANT: A CASE STUDY OF JUSTICE AND THE COURT OF PRIVATE LAND CLAIMS. *J. of the West 1980 19(3): 74-85.* In 1725 New Mexico Governor Bustamante conferred the Embudo de Picuris grant to several families of petitioners. In 1786 the heirs of the original petitioners had the deteriorating title papers copied and certified by the local alcalde. The grant claim was submitted for American confirmation in 1863, but the case was delayed for over 30 years. In one of its most unjust decisions, the Court of Private Land Claims rejected the claim in 1898 on the grounds that the alcalde did not have the power to make certified copies of land documents. Based on documents of the New Mexico Land Grants-Surveyor General, State Records Center, Santa Fe; 10 photos, map, 66 notes.
                                                                          B. S. Porter

431.   Ehrlich, Karen Lynn. MINORITIES IN THE CATTLE INDUSTRY: A HISTORIOGRAPHIC ANALYSIS. *J. of NAL Assoc. 1979 4(3-4): 59-63.* Focuses on minorities (blacks, Indians, and Hispanics) in the Anglo-dominated cattle industry in the United States from its beginnings in the 1860's, as seen in the works of many writers and historians, including John Hendrix, Philip Durham, William S. Savage, J. Frank Dobie, and others.

432.   Estrada, Leobardo F.; García, F. Chris; Macías, Reynaldo Flores; and Maldonado, Lionel. CHICANOS IN THE UNITED STATES: A HISTORY OF EXPLOITATION AND RESISTANCE. *Daedalus 1981 110(2): 103-131.* Provides a historical perspective on the Mexican people within the context of the US political economy from the 1830's, and initial military conquests by the United States over Mexico, to the 1970's, and describes the growth of the Chicano movement in America from 1965 to 1980.

433.   Friedlander, Judith. STRUGGLES ON THE RIO PUERCO: ENVI-RONMENTAL STRESS AND ETHNIC CONFLICT IN NORTHERN NEW MEXICO. *Rev. Française d'Études Américaines [France] 1980 5(9): 67-77.* Describes the struggle of Mexican-American farmers for land in the Rio Puerco Valley in northern New Mexico, part of the three-cornered struggle for land between Hispanics, whites, and Indians in that state in the 19th and 20th centuries.

434.   Fulton, Tom. AGRICULTURAL LABOR LEGISLATION IN THE UNITED STATES: A REVIEW OF THE MAJOR NEW DEAL LEGISLA-TION, THE EMERGENCY FARM LABOR SUPPLY PROGRAM, AND THE AGRICULTURAL LABOR RELATIONS ACT OF CALIFORNIA.

J. of NAL Assoc. 1979 4(3-4): 49-58. The above agricultural labor law shows that until recently farmworkers in the United States were not aided by government and did not enjoy a good relationship with American farmers; also gives a brief history of the rights and privileges of land ownership since 17th-century European settlement in North America.

435. Garcia, John A. POLITICAL INTEGRATION OF MEXICAN IM-MIGRANTS: EXPLORATIONS INTO THE NATURALIZATION PRO-CESS. *Int. Migration Rev. 1981 15(4): 608-625.* Discusses the political integration of Mexican immigrants in the United States since 1920, and focuses on the factors leading to nauralization and on the affective and familial ties to Mexico causing a low rate of naturalization among Mexicans.

436. Garcia, Juan R. HISTORY OF CHICANOS IN CHICAGO HEIGHTS. *Aztlán 1976 7(2): 291-306.* A large number of Mexicans and Chicanos came to Chicago Heights during 1910's-20's. They were recruited by the railroads, steel companies, sugar beet concerns; some job-hopped north gradually; and others came and found work on the advice and with the help of relatives. Chicago Heights Mexican nationals were apparently spared during the forced repatriations of the 1930's, but a great many left for economic reasons. World War II and the succeeding prosperity brought a new influx of immigrants, who arrived as agricultural laborers but soon shifted to year-round jobs in other sectors. The present Mexican and Chicano population represents mostly this second group of immigrants and their children. Reviews recent organizational efforts in the local Chicano community. Secondary sources; 55 notes. L. W. Van Wyk

437. García Gómez, Alberto. LOS TRABAJADORES MEXICANOS IN-DOCUMENTADOS [Undocumented Mexican workers]. *Humánitas [Mexico] 1979 20: 447-465.* The problem of undocumented Mexicans in the United States is closely related to Mexico's agrarian problems, which are in turn related to the Indian problem; since the conquest, the Indians have been treated more or less like slaves, and all unrest since 1910 must be understood on that basis. The Burnett law of 1917 created the first restrictions to immigration and, hence, illegal aliens. The "braceros do not fall into this category, since most come in legally" with work contracts. Estimates of illegal Mexicans in the United States range from one to five million. S

438. Gómez-Quiñones, Juan; Krauze, Enrique, commentator. THE ORI-GINS AND DEVELOPMENT OF THE MEXICAN WORKING CLASS IN THE UNITED STATES: LABORERS AND ARTISANS NORTH OF THE RÍO BRAVO, 1600-1900. Frost, Elsa Cecilia; Meyer, Michael C.; and Zoraida Vázquez, Josefina, ed. *El Trabajo y los Trabajadores en la Historia de México* (Mexico City: Colegio de México, 1979): 463-505. Traces the development of the Mexican Far North, the American Southwest, from 1600 to 1900, across the divide produced by the Texas revolution, 1836, and the Mexican War, 1846-48. Far Northern enterprises in mining, textiles, and commercial agricul-ture provide early examples of capitalist development, drawing on Mexico's own resources and population. The 1848 peace cost Mexico half of its territory, three-quarters of its national resources, and over 100,000 people. But the trek

north continued, though industrial development was now large-scale and financed from overseas; and, whatever their origins, Mexican Americans were relegated to the lower stratum of society, forced to defend their culture against a new racism. Commentary on pp. 529-532. Secondary sources; 6 notes.

J. P. H. Myers

439.   Gómez-Quiñónez, Juan. NOTAS PARA UNA INTERPRETACION DE LAS RELACIONES ENTRE LA COMUNIDAD MEXICANA EN LOS ESTADOS UNIDOS Y MEXICO [Notes for an interpretation of the relations between the Mexican community in the United States and Mexico]. *Rev. Mexicana de Ciencias Pol. y Sociales [Mexico] 1981 27(104-105): 153-174.* The politics of the Mexican-American community have had an international dimension owing to the history, geographical situation, cultural ties, demographic growth, and overall economic relations between Mexico and the United States. This dimension can be called pan-Mexican relations. Despite political and economic integration in the United States, contacts with Mexico have been close and influences have been many in socioeconomic as well as political matters.

J. V. Coutinho

440.   Gonzales, Sylvia A. LA CHICANA: GUADALUPE OR MAL-INCHE. Lindsay, Beverly, ed. *Comparative Perspectives of Third World Women: The Impact of Race, Sex and Class* (New York: Praeger, 1980): 229-250. Discusses the introduction of the image of the Mexican woman as Malinche, "the Mexican Eve" who was a traitor and the mistress of Hernando Cortés in Mexico, or as the Virgin de Guadalupe, "the maternal virgin," and how these female ideals affected Mexico's social structure during the colonial period and continue to affect Chicana women today.

441.   González, William H. and Padilla, Genaro M. MONTICELLO, THE HISPANIC CULTURAL GATEWAY TO UTAH. *Utah Hist. Q. 1984 52(1): 9-28.* Monticello, in San Juan County, Utah, settled by Ramon González in 1900, is still a Hispanic cultural center. 5 photos, 12 notes.   S

442.   Griswold del Castillo, Richard. THE DEL VALLE FAMILY AND THE FANTASY HERITAGE. *California Hist. 1980 59(1): 2-15.* Traces the fortunes of the del Valle family from the founding of Rancho San Francisco in 1839 to the death of Reginaldo del Valle in 1938. As upper-class Mexican Californians, the del Valle family survived and prospered through good luck and efficient management as California's population increasingly was dominated by Anglo-Americans after statehood. From 1841 to 1924, in the Santa Clara valley near today's Oxnard and Ventura, the family successfully operated its Rancho Camulos, one of the locales said to be the inspiration for Helen Hunt Jackson's *Ramona.* The family's partial acceptance of the pseudo-Spanish fantasy heritage had some virtues as Mexicanos and new Anglo-American immigrants found that heritage an easy one to adopt. Photos, 46 notes.

A. Hoffman

443.   Hennessy, Alistair. THE RISE OF THE HISPANICS I: CHICANOS. *J. of Latin Am. Studies [Great Britain] 1984 16(1): 171-194.* An overview of Mexican Americans, the Chicano movement, and important scholarship related

to them. Mexican immigration is the key issue in Mexican-American relations. Unlike other immigrants, Mexicans have proved resistant to Americanization, retaining their language and numerous other cultural characteristics. The Chicano movement was part of the broader revolt of the 1960's against the values of establishment America. Chicanos have continually felt a sense of discrimination and from the 1960's they have repeatedly displayed frustration through labor conflict, literary works, and other forms of cultural assertiveness. Scholars have focused on labor problems and, more recently, on immigration. The study of Chicanos and, in particular, Chicano literature should be incorporated into Latin American and American Studies and be made part of an interdisciplinary course of study. 36 notes. Article to be continued.

M. A. Burkholder

444. Klor de Alva, Jorge. GABINO BARREDA AND CHICANO THOUGHT. *Aztlán 1983 14(2): 343-358.* Contrary to the opinions of Mexican philosophers José Vasconcelos and Antonio Caso, Gabino Barreda held moral and philosophical values that are consistent with those of many modern Chicano philosophers. Ironically, the tyrannical government of Porfirio Díaz practiced what Barreda actually opposed, so that today Chicanos mistakenly hold Barreda's views suspect because of a superficial understanding of his philosophy. Barreda's views on medicine, reason instead of force, freedom of thought, education, and love before science are similar to Chicano beliefs and reveal an intellectual parallel between Barreda's positivist philosophy and the thinking of Chicano philosophers today. 20 notes. A. Hoffman

445. Kutsche, Paul and Gallegos, Dennis. COMMUNITY FUNCTIONS OF THE COFRADÍA DE NUESTRO PADRE JESÚS NAZARENO. *Colorado Coll. Studies 1979 (15): 91-98.* Discusses the religious and community purpose and activities of the Penitentes, or Cofradía de Nuestro Padre Jesús Nazareno, and other cofradías in Hispanic villages in New Mexico since the 19th century.

446. Limón, José E. STEREOTYPING AND CHICANO RESISTANCE: AN HISTORICAL DIMENSION. *Aztlán 1973 4(2): 257-270.* Discusses denigrating stereotypes attached to Mexican Americans from the beginning of the 20th century through literature and film and the attacks which Chicano media have made against these stereotypes. S

447. Madrid-Barela, Arturo. TOWARDS AN UNDERSTANDING OF THE CHICANO EXPERIENCE. *Aztlán 1973 4(1): 185-193.* Response to John Womack's "The Chicanos," *New York Review of Books,* 31 August 1972; the proximity of Mexico and the U.S. exploitation and colonization of Chicanos have made Chicano history different from that of other racial minorities. S

448. Majka, Linda C. LABOR MILITANCY AMONG FARM WORKERS AND THE STRATEGY OF PROTEST: 1900-1979. *Social Problems 1981 28(5): 533-547.* Describes the use of Japanese workers and labor militancy during 1900-15, the career of the Industrial Workers of the World during 1913-20, the depression-era militancy of Mexican, Asian and white agricultural

laborers, and the successful organization of the United Farm Workers in the 1960's and 70's, primarily among Chicanos, Mexicans, and Filipinos.

449.   Martinez, Arthur D. THE HISTORICAL DEVELOPMENT OF THE MEXICAN-AMERICAN COMMUNITY OF DODGE CITY, KANSAS. *Int. Social Sci. Rev. 1983 58(3): 159-167.* Examines the economic and social status and the demographic characteristics of the Chicano community; Mexican Americans are experiencing increasing acculturation to the predominantly Anglo culture.   S

450.   Martinez, Arthur D. LOS DE DODGE CITY, KANSAS: A MEXICAN-AMERICAN COMMUNITY AT THE HEARTLAND OF THE UNITED STATES. *Journal of the West 1985 24(2): 88-95.* Discusses the history and current living conditions of the Mexican-American community in Dodge City, Kansas, a town of some 18,000 residents, approximately 1,450 of whom are Mexican Americans. Mexican Americans in Dodge City completed a survey showing most perceive that much racial prejudice persists among Anglo residents of Dodge City, though they add that the situation has continued to improve. While opportunities to advance in education, business, and politics have improved as well, most Mexican Americans feel that they have a long way to go before attaining equality. As a whole, the Mexican-American community of Dodge City is acculturated to Anglo-American life, yet the community is still clearly identifiable, especially in the maintenance of their eastside barrio. Based partly on responses to a questionnaire distributed among Mexican Americans residing in Dodge City, Kansas; 5 notes, biblio.
                                                              B. A. Stenslie

451.   Mayer, Edward H. THE EVOLUTION OF CULTURE AND TRADITION IN UTAH'S MEXICAN-AMERICAN COMMUNITY. *Utah Hist. Q. 1981 49(2): 133-144.* The Utah Mexican-American settlement, originally comprised of settlers from Colorado and New Mexico, began with a series of small farms and ranches. Gradually, Mexican Americans experienced acculturation. They spoke less Spanish at home as they became less identified with Mexico and more identified with the United States. Today, they represent a fragmented community with few cultural ties to Mexico. Photo, 23 notes.
                                                              K. E. Gilmont

452.   Mazón, Mauricio. ILLEGAL ALIEN SURROGATES: A PSYCHO-HISTORICAL INTERPRETATION OF GROUP STEREOTYPING IN TIME OF ECONOMIC STRESS. *Aztlán 1976 6(2): 305-321.* Illegal Mexican immigrants historically have served as scapegoats for the irrational and aggressive impulses of the majority, especially during times of economic depression. Various psychological mechanisms of projection, condensation, reaction formation, and substitution have generated justifications for the oppression of the Mexican immigrant in American society. No one has yet dealt with the problem in a rational way. Based on newspapers, congressional records, and secondary sources; 58 notes.   R. Griswold del Castillo

453.   McWilliams, Perry. THE ALAMO STORY: FROM FACT TO FABLE. *J. of the Folklore Inst. 1978 15(3): 221-233.* Examines the Battle of the

Alamo in 1836 in order to discuss the difference in the interests of the historian whose interest is in historical fact, and the folklorist whose concern is with the fictionalization of an event, and presents several legendary accounts of the Alamo told during the 19th century.

454. Metzgar, Joseph V. THE ATRISCO LAND GRANT, 1692-1977. *New Mexico Hist. Rev. 1977 52(4): 269-296.* The Atrisco grant is unusual, because it is still relatively intact and has been owned continually by the original settlers and their heirs since the 17th century. During the Pueblo Revolt of 1680, Spaniards, mestizos, and their Indian allies temporarily had to leave the area. A decade later the authorities in New Spain launched the reconquest under Don Diego de Vargas. Payment of volunteers was made in land grants of reconquered territory. Map, 63 notes. J. H. Krenkel

455. Metzler, William H. MEXICAN AMERICANS AND THE ACQUIS-ITIVE SYNDROME. *J. of Mexican Am. Hist. 1973 3(1): 1-12.* In Mexico, with an extremely diverse culture, the acquiring of new knowledge and techniques has varied greatly. The stratified culture of the Aztec was merely replaced by the Spanish, and when the Spanish were removed village patrons assumed the autocratic role. Much of this submissive nature has fit all too well into American labor requirements in agricultural areas. Mexican-American organizations in America are now becoming effective in countering this native submissiveness. Secondary sources; 31 notes. R. T. Fulton

456. Meyer, Jean A. LES MIGRATIONS MEXICAINES VERS LES ÉTATS-UNIS AU XXᵉ SIÈCLE [Mexican migrations to the United States in the 20th century]. *Cahiers des Amériques Latines [France] 1975 12: 255-273.* Analyzes the causes and the volume of the phases of Mexican immigration to the United States, 1900-72, which led to the appearance of an ethnic Mexican minority in the United States.

457. Nanez, Alfredo. THE TRANSITION FROM ANGLO TO MEXI-CAN-AMERICAN LEADERSHIP IN THE RIO GRANDE CONFER-ENCE. *Methodist Hist. 1978 16(2): 67-74.* From the appointment of the first missionary to Spanish-speaking people in the Southwest United States in 1874 until 1966 the annual conferences of the Spanish American churches were controlled by the missionaries and agencies of the Methodist Episcopal Church and the Methodist Episcopal Church, South. After continuous struggle the name was established as the Rio Grande Annual Conference and in 1966 the Conference was instructed to serve as the fundamental body of the church in New Mexico and Texas in the same manner as any other conference in the United Methodist Church. 4 notes. H. L. Calkin

458. Narváez, Peter. AFRO-AMERICAN AND MEXICAN STREET SINGERS: AN ETHNOHISTORICAL HYPOTHESIS. *Southern Folklore Q. 1978 42(1): 73-84.* Hypothesizes that Mexican-American culture has influenced Afro-American singers and downhome blues street singers since the early 19th century, when many slaves escaped from their masters and started a colony called Matamoros in Mexico.

459.   Navarro, Armando. THE EVOLUTION OF CHICANO POLITICS. *Aztlán 1974 5(1/2): 57-84.* Analyzes the evolution in Mexican-American politics from the war with Mexico to the present day.   S

460.   Nelson, Kathryn J. EXCERPTS FROM LOS TESTAMENTOS: HISPANIC WOMEN FOLK ARTISTS OF THE SAN LUIS VALLEY, COLORADO: ORAL HISTORY FROM EPPIE ARCHULETA. *Frontiers 1980 5(3): 34-43.* Excerpt from the author's slide and sound program of photographs and oral histories of Eppie Archuleta, a weaver, and Tiva Trujillo, a tapestry embroiderer, of the San Luis Valley in southern Colorado; focuses on Eppie Archuleta's description of her life and work as a weaver; 1922-79.

461.   Nostrand, Richard L. "MEXICAN AMERICAN" AND "CHICANO": EMERGING TERMS FOR A PEOPLE COMING OF AGE. *Pacific Hist. R. 1973 42(3): 389-406.* Discusses Spanish and Mexican colonization of the Southwest and later migratory patterns to provide a basis for a demographic analysis of self-referents among Hispanic settlers. Discusses regional usage of such terms as "Spanish American," "Mexican American," "Latin American," "Mexican," and "Chicano," positing that the current "diffusion of 'Mexican American' and 'Chicano' portends the possible emergence of a strong sense of a common ethnic identity among Hispanos throughout the Southwest." 49 notes.   B. L. Fenske

462.   Ortega-DeSantis, Diana. THE HISPANIC SHEPHERD OF NEW MEXICO'S EASTERN PLAINS. *Palacio 1982 88(1): 12-13.* The lives of traditional Hispanic sheepherder Jesús Cháves and members of his family who worked on the plains of eastern New Mexico were typical of sheepherders.

463.   Ortego, Philip D. FABLES OF IDENTITY: STEREOTYPE AND CARICATURE OF CHICANOS IN STEINBECK'S *TORTILLA FLAT. J. of Ethnic Studies 1973 1(1): 39-43.* John Steinbeck in his 1935 best seller, *Tortilla Flat,* failed to accurately portray Mexican-American life. Steinbeck did not understand the socioeconomic position of Chicanos and the complexity of their culture. Similar shortcomings in ethnic and racial characterizations are cited for F. Scott Fitzgerald's *The Great Gatsby* and William Styron's *The Confessions of Nat Turner.*   T. W. Smith

464.   Padilla, Fernando V. and Ramirez, Carlos B. PATTERNS OF CHICANO REPRESENTATION IN CALIFORNIA, COLORADO, AND NUEVO MÉXICO. *Aztlán 1974 5(1/2): 189-234.*

465.   Paredes, Américo. FOLKLORE, *LO MEXICANO,* AND PROVERBS. *Aztlán 1982 13(1-2): 1-11.* Analyzes proverbs that exemplify Mexican and Mexican-American culture. As a minority in the United States, Mexican Americans find the essence of their culture in folklore, the "unofficial" history and heritage of a minority. *Dichos* (sayings or proverbs) express in a few words the views of a people—their outlook on life, traditions, and values. But, if taken out of context, these sayings can easily be misinterpreted and misunderstood, as has happened with folklorists and social scientists who have studied proverbs. Often the intended meaning of a proverb is the very opposite of what

it states, or it presents advice applicable to a specific circumstance. To study proverbs, one must know the language, the people, and the situation. Secondary sources and fieldwork; 2 notes.   A. Hoffman

466. Paredes, Américo. TEXAS-MEXICAN CANCIONERO: FOLK-SONGS OF THE LOWER BORDER. *Southern Exposure 1982 10(4): 50-57.* The stories and meaning behind the folksongs of the border Mexican-Americans of the Rio Grande Valley.

467. Parra, Ricardo; Rios, Victor; and Gutiérrez, Armando. CHICANO ORGANIZATIONS IN THE MIDWEST: PAST, PRESENT, AND POSSI-BILITIES. *Aztlán 1976 7(2): 235-253.* Midwest Chicano institutions have developed in three successive surges. First, during 1900-40, there arose the Sociedades Mexicanas: fraternal, cultural, and mutual aid organizations. Later came groups of a frankly assimilationist character such as the League of United Latin American Citizens and the American G. I. Forum. Finally, in the 1960's and early 1970's there emerged the Chicano movement, embodied in such groups as La Raza Unida, the Brown Berets, and academically, the Centro de Estudios Chicanos at Notre Dame. Characterizes the second type of organization as "parallel", since these groups mimic similar Anglo groups, while the first and third kinds ("alternative" groups) are genuine expressions of the genius of the Chicano people. 42 notes.   L. W. Van Wyk

468. Pena, Manuel H. FOLKSONG AND SOCIAL CHANGE: TWO CORRIDOS AS INTERPRETIVE SOURCES. *Aztlán 1982 13(1-2): 13-42.* Contrasts two famous Mexican-American corridos (ballads) in the context of their times. "El Corrido de Gregorio Cortez" depicted a heroic Mexican who overcame enormous odds in fighting the injustice done to him, in effect reversing the status of Anglo and Mexican in Texas in 1901. In contrast, "Discriminación a un Martir" portrayed Felix Longoria, a Mexican American killed in World War II, as a martyr when his hometown of Three River, Texas, refused to receive his body in the town funeral home, an incident that galvanized Mexican Americans nationwide. In both corridos, Mexicans were victimized by a vicious Anglo system. Where Cortez fought back on a legendary heroic level, Longoria became famous as a symbol of protest for a minority growing politically aware of its rights. Both types of corrido continue to be popular, and the genre continues to reflect the desire of Chicanos for political and social equality. 44 notes.   A. Hoffman

469. Pierce, Lorraine Esterly. MEXICAN AMERICANS ON ST. PAUL'S LOWER WEST SIDE. *J. of Mexican Am. Hist. 1974 4(1): 1-18.* Replacing Jewish, German and Russian immigrant workers at local factories, Mexican Americans began arriving in St. Paul's lower west side during World War I. During the Depression, Mexican Americans in St. Paul occupied the lowest rung on the economic ladder, settling in the least expensive areas and building a cohesive ethnic community. Renovation of the area into an industrial park in the 1960's forced a massive relocation of the inhabitants, who moved into similar neighborhoods and succeeded in retaining the identity and cohesiveness of St. Paul's Mexican-American community. Primary and secondary material; table, 51 notes.   R. T. Fulton

470.   Pino, Frank, Jr. A CHICANO PERSPECTIVE ON AMERICAN CULTURAL HISTORY. *J. of Popular Culture 1979 13(3): 488-500.* Introductory essay to a section on Mexican-American life. The diverse cultural heritage in the American Southwest is underscored, to emphasize shortcomings in traditional American historiographical perspectives on Mexican-American cultural history.   D. G. Nielson

471.   Pyle, David. THE ETHNOGRAPHIC PHOTOGRAPHY OF W. D. SMITHERS. *Lib. Chronicle of the U. of Texas at Austin 1982 (19): 148-165.* Reproduces and describes the work of photojournalist W. D. Smithers, whose photographic work, although amateurish, was an honest depiction of Mexican-American life in Texas.

472.   Rael, Juan B. and Martinez, Reyes. ARROYO HONDO: PENITENTES, WEDDINGS, WAKES. *Palacio 1975 81(1): 3-19.* Delineates folk beliefs, social customs, and ceremonies associated with Hispanic culture in New Mexico, 16th-20th centuries.

473.   Reyna, José R. NOTES ON TEJANO MUSIC. *Atzlán 1982 13(1-2): 81-94.* Traces the development of Chicano music in Texas, a process which has produced a distinctive style of popular bicultural music. Tejano music falls into two categories: *conjunto,* a musical group consisting of accordion, *bajo sexto* guitar, bass, and drums, which evolved from the Mexican culture for over a century to achieve maturity in the 1940's and 1950's; and *bandas,* larger bands based on the Anglo bands of the Big Band era. Both types have experimented with different instruments (such as organs and six-string guitars) to achieve their distinctive sounds. Many individuals in the groups have gained prominence in the world of professional popular music. Tejano music continues as an identifiable yet flexible musical form firmly grounded in cultural traditions. Based on secondary sources, interviews, and recordings.   A. Hoffman

474.   Robe, Stanley L. A BORDER *CANCIONERO* AND A REGIONAL VIEW OF FOLKSONG. *New Scholar 1977 6: 257-268.* Reviews Americo Paredes's *A Texas-Mexican Cancionero: Folksongs of the Lower Border* (Urbana: U. of Illinois Pr., 1976). The cultural change accelerated by World War II has affected the content and style of border ballads. Traditional folk songs are out of style with the younger generation who increasingly accept Anglo norms in music. Part of the special issue, "New Direction in Chicano Scholarship." 9 notes.   D. K. Pickens

475.   Roberts, Shirley J. MINORITY-GROUP POVERTY IN PHOENIX: A SOCIO-ECONOMIC SURVEY. *J. of Arizona Hist. 1973 14(4): 347-362.* The southern part of Phoenix has always been the residence of the poverty level minority groups, principally Mexican, Indian, black, Chinese, health seekers, and migrant agricultural workers. Anglo-American hostility and indifference have changed toward a sense of responsibility. In the last few decades this change has been manifested in welfare projects and government housing. The combination of poverty and ethnic and racial barriers makes it difficult for these groups to leave this section of the city, with the exception of

the Chinese, who have overcome these difficulties and have dispersed throughout the city. 2 maps, 53 notes.   D. L. Smith

476. Rocard, Marcienne. LE PARADOXE DU MEXICAN-AMÉRICAIN: ÉTRANGER DANS SON PAYS [The paradox of the Mexican-American: stranger in his country]. *Rev. Française d'Études Américaines [France] 1980 5(9): 59-66.* Examines the dilemma of Mexican Americans in the Southwest, both Spanish and Indian, whether newcomers or natives, alienated from both Mexican *and* American culture.

477. Rocco, Raymond. POSITIVISM AND MEXICAN IDENTITY: THEN AND NOW. *Aztlán 1983 14(2): 359-371.* Compares the acceptance of positivist philosophy in late 19th-century Mexico with the neopositivism governing Chicano research in the United States today. Positivist goals for peaceful development of Mexican society were corrupted by the *científicos* under Porfirio Díaz and were used as a rationale for control of the masses by the elite. Modern research incorporates positivism by uncritically accepting science as value-free, but Chicano researchers who accept the positivist belief in scientific enterprise may find themselves restricted by similar elitist assumptions. 11 notes.   A. Hoffman

478. Rodríguez, Jacobo. ALIENATION OF A NEW GENERATION OF CHICANOS. *Aztlán 1973 4(1): 147-154.*

479. Romo, Ricardo. A PERSPECTIVE ON CHICANO HISTORY. *Rev. in Am. Hist. 1976 4(1): 32-37.* Review article prompted by Norris Hundley, Jr., ed., *The Chicano* (Santa Barbara, California: ABC-Clio Pr., 1975).

480. Rothenberg, Irene Fraser. MEXICAN-AMERICAN VIEWS OF U.S. RELATIONS WITH LATIN AMERICA. *J. of Ethnic Studies 1978 6(1): 62-78.* A brief review of Mexican-American political history and political thought reveals a clear ideological thrust toward greater political identification with Latin America. Surveying the orientations and emphases of the "four horsemen," César Chávez, Reies López Tijerina, Rodolfo "Corky" Gonzalez, and José Angel Gutiérrez and their respective forms of "Chicanismo," Rothenberg finds two common themes: a clear trend away from assimilation and toward cultural dualism; and the politicization of this dualism into "cultural nationalism" which postulates a direct unity of interests with Latin America. Combined with this new Pan-American definition of *la raza* is a second dimension focusing on the "Mexican" in the Mexican American and embodied in two powerful political symbols: the mythical Aztec nation of Aztlán, and the Mexican Revolution of 1910. Both are potential rallying themes for combatting the "internal colonialism" experienced by Mexican Americans. Primary and secondary materials; 53 notes.   G. J. Bobango

481. Sanchez, Armand J. and Wagner, Roland M. CONTINUITY AND CHANGE IN THE MAYFAIR BARRIOS OF EAST SAN JOSE. *San José Studies 1979 5(2): 6-20.* Traces the development of the Mayfair barrio area of East San Jose during 1777-1975, noting the degeneration of an integral community into one of social fragmentation, ethnic intermixture, and trans-

cient population, and the concurrent growth in politicization due to the
Chicanismo movement of the 1960's.

482.   Sanchez, Rosaura. CHICANO BILINGUALISM. *New Scholar 1977
6: 209-226.* Four types of bilingualism are used in this article: stable, dynamic,
transitional and vestigial. Economic structure has limited Chicano acculturation. Mexican Americans were a cheap labor force which happened to be
Spanish-speaking. Loyalties to cultural and language roots are not significant.
Given the present socioeconomic-political reality, the movement toward English shall continue unless organized efforts for Spanish language maintenance
are undertaken. Part of the special issue, "New Direction In Chicano
Scholarship." 36 notes.   D. K. Pickens

483.   Santos, Richard G. CHICANOS OF JEWISH DESCENT IN TEXAS.
Western States Jewish Hist. Q. 1983 15(4): 327-333. Spanish-speaking immigrants in Texas have come primarily from the Mexican states that comprised
the old Spanish colony of Nuevo Reyno de León. The colony was settled partly
by people of Sephardic Jewish origin. Despite their isolation from Jewish
cultural centers and their assimilation into the dominant Hispanic culture, they
retained some of their Jewish culture in food items, butchering methods,
myths, and even religion. Reprinted from the *San Antonio Express,* 2 July
1973.   B. S. Porter

484.   Sapiens, Alexander. SPANISH IN CALIFORNIA: A HISTORICAL
PERSPECTIVE. *J. of Communication 1979 29(2): 72-83.* Describes the Spanish language and Spanish speakers of California in relation to the Spanish,
Mexican, and Anglo periods and to educational, legal, immigration, religious,
social, and political issues.

485.   Schement, Jorge Reina and Flores, Ricardo. THE ORIGINS OF
SPANISH-LANGUAGE RADIO: THE CASE OF SAN ANTONIO, TEX-
AS. *Journalism Hist. 1977 4(2): 56-58, 61.* Describes the development of
station KCOR in San Antonio, Texas, and the factors that contributed to the
growth of Spanish-language radio in the United States during 1928-74.

486.   Servín, Manuel P. THE MEXICAN-AMERICAN AWAKENS: AN
INTERPRETATION. *J. of the West 1975 14(4): 121-130.* Synopsis of the
background of Mexican Americans and their heritage of discrimination; centers
on Mexican Americans, 1930-75 and emphasizes evolving political awareness
within the minority group. Biblio.

487.   Silkerstein, Fred B. READINGS ON LA RAZA: THE TWENTIETH
CENTURY. *J. of Intergroup Relations 1974 3(4): 44-47.* Reviews Matt S.
Meier's and Feliciano Rivera's *Readings on La Raza: The Twentieth Century*
(New York: Hill and Wang, 1974).

488.   Slatta, Richard W. CHICANOS IN THE PACIFIC NORTHWEST:
AN HISTORICAL OVERVIEW OF OREGON'S CHICANOS. *Aztlán 1975
6(3): 327-340.* The Spanish speaking population of the Northwest is becoming
more significant numerically and politically. In the 19th century Mexicans

worked as skilled vaqueros or muleteers. In the 20th century the bracero program and Mexican immigration brought large numbers of low wage migrant farm workers. In the last 20 years Chicanos have found employment in nonagricultural areas and they have established a variety of cultural and political organizations, newspapers, radio and television stations, and educational programs. Based on government documents, interviews and newspapers; 38 notes, biblio.   R. Griswold del Castillo

489.   Smith, W. Elwood and Foley, Douglas E. MEXICANO RESISTANCE TO SCHOOLING IN A SOUTH TEXAS COLONY. *Educ. and Urban Soc.* *1978 10(2): 145-176.* Traces the development of Mexican Americans' recognition of their power of resistance against the Anglo power structure in a city in Texas, from the 1930's to 1969, particularly Mexican American resistance in the 1950's and Chicano student activism in the late 1960's.

490.   Snow, David H. RURAL HISPANIC COMMUNITY ORGANIZATION IN NORTHERN NEW MEXICO: AN HISTORICAL PERSPECTIVE. *Colorado Coll. Studies 1979 (15): 45-52.* Provides a history of the community organization among Hispanic villages in northern New Mexico since the 16th and 17th centuries, when Spaniards first settled there.

491.   Soto-Pérez, Héctor. LOS CHICANOS: GENESIS Y EVOLUCIÓN DEL PROBLEMA [The Chicanos: genesis and evolution of the problem]. *Am. Latina [USSR] 1977 (3): 105-120.* Mexico occupies a risky position due to its geographical location next to the United States. Historically Mexico has lost much land to the United States and has been bullied by its northern neighbor in other ways. A major turning point was 1848, because the United States forcibly took nearly half of Mexico's national territory. The Mexicans who were left in the United States have been subject to racial prejudice and economic exploitation since that time. Some Chicano heroes fought back but they were not strong enough to halt the oppression of their people. During the depression the Chicanos suffered more than the general population and many were deported. A new consciousness has awakened in Chicanos in recent years due to increased Mexican nationalism, the Vietnam War, and the awareness of all people in the Third World that they are victims of capitalist exploitation. Based on secondary sources; 13 notes.   J. D. Barnard

492.   Steel, Thomas J. THE SPANISH PASSION PLAY IN NEW MEXICO AND COLORADO. *New Mexico Hist. Rev. 1978 53(3): 239-259.* Spanish passion plays have been performed regularly in New Mexico and Colorado, since the 1830's. Interest in them grew or dwindled depending on the priests' interest. 28 notes.   J. H. Krenkel

493.   Stoddard, Ellwyn R. ILLEGAL MEXICAN LABOR IN THE BORDERLANDS: INSTITUTIONALIZED SUPPORT OF AN UNLAWFUL PRACTICE. *Pacific Sociol. R. 1976 19(2): 175-210.* Analysis of the use of illegal Mexican labor since the 1820's reveals that US social institutions support the practice in Texas and other areas in the Southwest.

494.   Street, Richard Steven. THE ECONOMIST AS HUMANIST: THE CAREER OF PAUL S. TAYLOR. *California History 1979-80 58(4): 350-361.* Discusses Paul S. Taylor, economist emeritus at the University of California, Berkeley. Now age 84, Taylor continues a lengthy career that has included research into Mexican immigration and labor, California farm labor, the Okie migrations, and implementation of the Newlands Act (US, 1902). His work has been characterized by his openness to students, interdisciplinary approach to his studies, and refusal to compromise on issues of integrity. His marriage to photographer Dorothea Lange produced a professional union that yielded the classic study *An American Exodus.* At times neglected over his long career because of the sometime unfashionability of his research, Taylor now sees the relevance of his work vindicated by renewed interest in the rights of farm workers and the efforts to enforce the Reclamation Act. 3 photos, 24 notes.
A. Hoffman

495.   Surace, Samuel J. ACHIEVEMENT, DISCRIMINATION, AND MEXICAN AMERICANS. *Comparative Studies in Soc. and Hist. [Great Britain] 1982 24(2): 315-339.* This nonquantitative study of differences in achievement patterns focuses on discrimination against the Mexican American in both the historical context and the racial context. Contrary to the prevailing pattern, the record of low status attainment of Mexican Americans is unique among national groups in the United States. The role of prejudice has been addressed by many researchers but inadequately analyzed. Yet to be answered are why and how certain group features become focal points of discrimination and how certain groups, like the Japanese Americans, have succeeded despite intense discrimination. 9 notes, biblio.   S. A. Farmerie

496.   Swadesh, Frances Leon. STRUCTURE OF HISPANIC-INDIAN RE-LATIONS IN NEW MEXICO. *Colorado Coll. Studies 1979 (15): 53-61.* Traces relations since the 17th century.

497.   Torres, Luisa; Brandi, Gioia, comp.; and James, Betsy, transl. PALA-BRAS DE UNA VIEJITA: HABLA LUISA TORRES DE GUADALUPI-TA, NEW MEXICO [The words of an old one: Luisa Torres writes of her life in Guadalupita, New Mexico]. *Palacio 1978 84(3): 8-18.* Luisa Torres (b. 1903) discusses beliefs, folk medicine, the Catholic Church, and her remembrances of growing up, 1910's-70's.

498.   Treviño, Jesús Salvador. CHICANO CINEMA. *New Scholar 1982 8(1-2): 167-180.* Surveys the portrayal of Mexicans and Mexican Americans in US films and discusses emerging Chicano films and filmmakers. Includes a 1967-79 Chicano filmography.   S

499.   Vigil, Ralph H. THE WAY WEST: JOHN NICHOLS AND HISTOR-ICAL REALITY. *Journal of the West 1985 24(2): 54-63.* Author John Nichols successfully employs a combination of humor and seriousness to portray the unique character of New Mexico's Spanish-American history and people since the mid 19th century in such works as *If Mountains Die: A New Mexico Memoir* (1979), *The Milagro Beanfield War* (1974), and *The Magic Journey* (1978). The Spanish-American people's ties to their land, their

struggle against corrupt politicians and wealthy land developers, their reverence for life and respect for the aged all come together to form rich and accurate characterizations in Nichols's work. Based on the writings of John Nichols and secondary sources; 10 photos, 47 notes. B. A. Stenslie

500. Villanueva, Tino. SOBRE EL TÉRMINO "CHICANO" [On the term "chicano"]. *Cuadernos Hispanoamericanos [Spain] 1978 112(336): 387-410.* Traces the origins, indigenous influence, semantic development, and diffusion of the term "chicano" and refers to the related "pocho" and "pachucho" in social class differentiation applied to Mexican Americans. The author notes the first documented use of "chicano" in 1911 and cites subsequent references in print, indicating pejorative connotations and subtle shifts in meaning, and comments on the use of the term in legal contexts and in current usage. Secondary sources; 11 notes, biblio. P. J. Taylorson

501. Vollmar, Edward R. *LA REVISTA CATOLICA. Mid-America 1976 58(2): 85-96.* The origin of *La Revista Catolica,* the Spanish-language publication of the Jesuits of the New Mexico-Colorado Mission of the Neapolitan Province, involved New Mexico's first Bishop, J. B. Lamy, who brought the dispersed Neapolitans to the Southwest in 1867. Father Gaspari instigated the immediately successful Las Vegas (New Mexico)-based *Revista,* and it inspired short-lived Protestant counter publications. Succeeding editors and managers, the move to El Paso (Texas), the 1919 dissolution of the mission, and declining subscriptions all influenced *Revista.* Primary and secondary sources; 20 notes. T. H. Wendel

502. Weber, Kenneth R. ECOLOGY, ECONOMY, AND DEMOGRAPHY: SOME PARAMETERS OF SOCIAL CHANGE IN HISPANIC NEW MEXICO. *Social Sci. J. 1980 17(1): 53-64.* Examines the shift from a subsistence economy to involvement in the national cash economy in the Hispanic region of north central New Mexico and its demographic impact.

503. Weigle, Martha. GHOSTLY FLAGELLANTS AND DOÑA SEBASTIANA: TWO LEGENDS OF THE PENITENTE BROTHERHOOD. *Western Folklore 1977 36(2): 135-147.* Examines two important components of the predominantly Hispanic Penitente religious cult of New Mexico and Colorado. Reports on the folklore associated with reported appearances of ghostly skeletal figures during certain rites and also examines the folk art of the carved "death angels" often called Doña Sebastiana. Primary and secondary sources; illus., 29 notes. S. L. Myres

504. Williams, Linda. TYPE AND STEREOTYPE: CHICANO IMAGES IN FILM. *Frontiers 1980 5(2): 14-17.* Discusses stereotypes of Mexican Americans in American films as villians, dope addicts, and sex fiends, focusing on *Let Katie Do It* (1915), *Martyrs of the Alamo* (1915), and Moctezuma Esparsa's *Only Once in a Lifetime* (1978); two films not stereotypical are *Salt of the Earth* (1953) and *Alambrista!* (1978).

505. Wroth, William. NEW HOPE IN HARD TIMES: HISPANIC CRAFTS ARE REVIVED DURING TROUBLED YEARS. *Palacio 1983*

89(2): 22-31. The New Mexican native crafts revival began in 1932, during the Depression, as a recovery measure to create employment and revive the traditional crafts industry, which had largely disappeared following the American arrival in 1846.

506. —. [HISPANO HOMELAND IN NEW MEXICO]. *Ann. of the Assoc. of Am. Geog. 1984 74(1): 157-171.*
Blaut, J. M. and Ríos-Bustamante, Antonio. COMMENTARY ON NOST-
RAND'S "HISPANOS" AND THEIR "HOMELAND," *pp. 157-164.*
Refutes Richard Nostrand's thesis that a distinct Spanish-derived non-
Mexican subculture (Hispanos) existed in New Mexico in 1900.
Nostrand, Richard L. HISPANO CULTURAL DISTINCTIVENESS: A RE-
PLY, *pp. 164-169.*
Simmons, Marc; Chavez, Angelico; Meinig, D. W.; and Hall, Thomas D.
REJOINDERS, *pp. 169-171.* All agree with Richard Nostrand.

507. —. [HISPANOS IN THE SOUTHWEST]. *Ann. of the Assoc. of Am. Geographers 1981 71(2): 280-283.*
Hansen, Niles. THE HISPANO HOMELAND IN 1900, *pp. 280-282.* Cri-
tiques Richard L. Nostrand's article regarding Mexican Americans in the
Southwest.
Nostrand, Richard L. COMMENT IN REPLY, *pp. 282-283.* Responds to
Hansen's objections to the terms "Hispanic-American" and "Hispano"
and the degree of "Hispano" rejection of Mexican culture.

508. —. THE NEW CHICANO URBAN HISTORY: TWO PERSPEC-
TIVES. THREE RECENT BOOKS AND TWO ANALYTICAL AND
BIBLIOGRAPHIC ESSAYS. *Hist. Teacher 1983 16(2): 219-247.*
Lotchin, Roger W. THE NEW CHICANO HISTORY: TWO PERSPEC-
TIVES, *pp. 219-222.* Briefly summarizes three major studies of Mexican
Americans in the Southwest: Albert Camarillo's *Chicanos in a Changing
Society,* which focuses on the Mexican-American experience in Santa
Barbara, California, and other southern California communities during
1848-1930; Richard Griswold del Castillo's *The Los Angeles Barrio,
1850-1890: A Social History,* which argues that Mexican Americans were
progressively pushed out of their position in society by their Anglo
neighbors; and Mario T. Garcia's *Desert Immigrants,* which surveys the
migration and accommodation of Mexicans to El Paso, Texas, from
1880-1920.
Weber, David. THE NEW CHICANO URBAN HISTORY, *pp. 223-229.*
The books by Camarillo, Griswold del Castillo, and Garcia "comprise the
sum of historiography on the Chicano urban experience." Through the use
of new methods and sources, they document generalizations about social
conditions that formerly were only impressionistic, such as widespread
unemployment, lack of social mobility, and segregation. They establish the
city as the "crucible of change in Chicano society and culture," and
establish the importance of the 19th century for understanding the
Chicano Experience in the 20th century. 18 notes.
Lotchin, Roger W. THE NEW CHICANO HISTORY: AN URBAN HISTO-
RY PERSPECTIVE, *pp. 229-247.* Urban history before the 1960's was

mostly biography. This situation was drastically altered by a new emphasis on reform, social science methodology, interdisciplinary research, and topical specialization. Unfortunately, these productive trends have partly obscured the broad picture of urban life. Thus, Camarillo, Griswold del Castillo, and Garcia have underestimated the importance of the urban context, while focusing on race and capitalism as the major factors in the Mexican-American experience. 57 notes.   S

1848 to 1900

509. Agogino, George A. and Ferguson, Bobbie. *CURANDERISMO:* THE FOLK HEALER IN THE SPANISH-SPEAKING COMMUNITY. *Masterkey* 1983 57(3): 101-106. Discusses the importance of *curanderos* in Mexican-American culture and gives a detailed account of the famous Don Pedrito Jaramillo, *curandero* of Los Almos, Texas, who used prayer and very simple cures to heal patients.

510. Aguirre, Yjinio F. ECHOES OF THE CONQUISTADORES: STOCK RAISING IN SPANISH-MEXICAN TIMES. *J. of Arizona Hist. 1975 16(3): 267-286.* Discusses ranching and the ranchers of Arizona, ca. 1853-1910, including information on daily life, branding, and cattle lore on the rancheros. 19 photos, sketch of brands.

511. Arbuckle, H. C., III. DON JOSÉ AND DON PEDRITO. *Southwest R. 1974 59(2): 189-194.* Don José C. Lozano describes a 19th-century South Texas folk healer, Pedrito Jaramillo, and relates stories of some of his cures.
                                                                                                        S

512. Baca, Luis and Baca, Facundo. HISPANIC PIONEER: DON FELIPE BACA BRINGS HIS FAMILY NORTH TO TRINIDAD. *Colorado Heritage 1982 (1): 26-35.* Don Felipe Baca (1829-74) and 12 other Hispano families moved from New Mexico in 1862 to the area of Trinidad, Colorado. He was active in Colorado territorial politics and was a large sheep producer. Two of his sons, Luis (an engineer) and Facundo (a physician) left personal narratives of their father, excerpts from which are included. Also included is a comment in Spanish made "in an Albuquerque Spanish-language newspaper" on Felipe's wife, Maria Gonzales Baca. The Baca adobe house is now a regional museum operated by the Colorado Historical Society. 10 photos.   O. H. Zabel

513. Bailey, David T. and Haulman, Bruce E. ETHNIC DIFFERENCES ON THE SOUTHWESTERN UNITED STATES FRONTIER, 1860. Miller, David Harry and Steffen, Jerome O., ed. *The Frontier: Comparative Studies,* Vol. 1 (Norman: U. of Oklahoma Pr., 1977): 243-257. In Santa Fe (New Mexico) and San Antonio (Texas), occupational discrimination by race prevailed in 1860. Too, Spanish-surnamed individuals were more likely to be illiterate than were Anglos. Hispanic Americans were likelier to marry, and then to have more children, than non-Hispanics. San Antonio was much more Anglicized than was Santa Fe. Based on the census of 1860; 6 tables, biblio.

514. Bailey, David T. and Haulman, Bruce E. PATTERNS OF LAND-HOLDING IN SANTA FE IN 1860 AND 1870. *Social Sci. J. 1976 13(3): 9-19.* One of six articles in this issue on the subject of Spanish and Mexican land grants in the Southwest.

515. Baxter, John O. SALVADOR ARMIJO, CITIZEN OF ALBUQUERQUE, 1823-1879. *New Mexico Hist. Rev. 1978 53(3): 219-237.* Salvador Armijo presided over a meeting in April 1874 to consider the plight of the poor in Albuquerque. As chairman, Armijo made the largest contribution to benefit the poor: 30 sacks of corn, 15 fanegas (about 22.5 bushels) of wheat, two fanegas (three bushels) of beans, and 20 ristras of chili, the total value of which amounted to about $140. Photo, 63 notes.   J. H. Krenkel

516. Bell, Samuel E. and Smallwood, James M. ZONA LIBRE: TRADE & DIPLOMACY ON THE MEXICAN BORDER, 1858-1905. *Arizona and the West 1982 24(2): 119-152.* Mexico established the Zona Libre in 1858 to counteract the highly favorable trade conditions enjoyed by the American towns along the Texas-Tamaulipas border. It was subsequently extended to the Pacific Ocean. The Mexican towns had an unprecedented boom during the Civil War, siphoning European goods to the Confederacy. The trade balance shifted to the American side after the war. American border merchants protested the zone because it encouraged smuggling and it became a sore point in diplomatic relations between the two countries. Mexico, fearful of revolution along the border and disliking American bullying, continued the zone's existence beyond its economic usefulness. Its abolition in 1905 paved the way for improved relations between the two countries. Map, 6 illus., 84 notes.
                                                                        D. L. Smith

517. Blevins, Don. THE FORGOTTEN PEACEMAKER, NICHOLAS TRIST. *Am. Hist. Illus. 1979 14(3): 4-8, 42-47.* Describes the efforts and success of Nicholas Trist in obtaining approval of the Treaty of Guadalupe Hidalgo, ending the Mexican War in 1848.

518. Bloom, John P. NEW MEXICO VIEWED BY ANGLO-AMERICANS, 1846-1849. *New Mexico Hist. Rev. 1959 34(3): 165-198.* Provides excerpts of descriptions of New Mexico by American military men, explorers, merchants, and forty-niners.

519. Butruille, Susan G. THE AMERICAN COWBOY: FROM FRONTIER TO FANTASY. *Westways 1983 75(9): 48-51, 80-81.* The life of open-range cowboys, many of them Indians, Latinos, or blacks, although romanticized, was hard, dangerous, and dull.

520. Cannon, Marian G. PÍO PICO: THE LAST DON. *Westways 1981 73(6): 49-51, 80.* Traces Pío Pico's (1801-94) career from his beginnings in San Diego to his tenure as governor of California under the Mexican government and his role as councilman of Los Angeles after the American takeover in 1847, and discusses his position as a pivotal figure in the rancho period of Californian history.

521. Case, Robert. LA FRONTERA TEXANA Y LOS MOVIMIENTOS DE INSURRECCION EN MEXICO—1850-1900 [The Texan border and rebellions in Mexico: 1850-1900]. *Hist. Mexicana [Mexico] 1981 30(3): 415-452.* After the Treaty of Guadalupe Hidalgo of 1848 established the Rio Grande as the border between Mexico and Texas the 400 kilometers between Eagle Pass and Brownsville became the base of operations for Mexican rebels. They recruited men; purchased arms, ammunitions, and supplies; published antigovernment propaganda; and harassed the northern region of Mexico. A study of their activities and the reaction of both governments gives an idea of the border problems of the two countries, which continued into the present century. Based on primary material in Mexican and US national archives; 108 notes, biblio.   J. V. Coutinho

522. Casillas, Mike. MEXICAN LABOR MILITANCY IN THE U.S.: 1896-1915. *Southwest Econ. and Soc. 1978 4(1): 31-42.* Mexican Americans' militancy in the Southwestern states resulted from desire for economic parity and from perceived social, cultural, and ethnic prejudice.

523. Castillo, Pedro; Krauze, Enrique, commentator. THE MAKING OF THE MEXICAN WORKING CLASS IN THE UNITED STATES: LOS ANGELES, CALIFORNIA: 1820-1920. Frost, Elsa Cecilia; Meyer, Michael C.; and Zoraida Vázquez, Josefina, ed. *El Trabajo y los Trabajadores en la Historia de México* (Mexico City: Colegio de México, 1979): 506-517. From the end of the Mexican War in 1848 to 1880 there was a gradual transition in Los Angeles from a rural to an urban way of life, in which the Mexican Americans sank to the bottom of the social structure: during the quickening of industrial development down to 1920, they remained there as the poorest of the laboring communities, to be Americanized or eradicated according to one's point of view. Their numbers increased after 1920: but apart from living in their own quarters, they showed little coherence as a group, or much interest in labor politics. Commentary on pp. 529-532. Secondary sources; table, 33 notes.
                                                                J. P. H. Myers

524. Christian, Garna L. RIO GRANDE CITY: PRELUDE TO THE BROWNSVILLE RAID. *West Texas Hist. Assoc. Year Book 1981 57: 118-132.* Describes several incidents of violence between Anglo and Hispanic civilians and black soldiers along the Texas-Mexican border during 1899-1900, and focuses on one incident at Rio Grande City in November 1899, when, after discrimination and police harassment black soldiers of Troop D of the 9th Cavalry fired on the town.

525. Cuthbertson, Gilbert M. CATARINO E. GARZA AND THE GARZA WAR. *Texana 1974 12(4): 335-348.* Catarino E. Garza (1858-95) was one of the most colorful journalists in Texas in the latter part of the 19th century; now he is virtually forgotten. Born in Mexico, he came to Texas in the 1880's, where he edited *El Libre Pensador* and later *El Comercio Mexicano.* Both of these newspapers violently attacked the Mexican government under President Diaz. In the early 1890's, he became an active revolutionary against Diaz in Mexico, where he was killed in 1895. Based on primary and secondary sources; 36 notes.   B. D. Ledbetter

526.   deBuys, William. FRACTIONS OF JUSTICE: A LEGAL AND SO-
CIAL HISTORY OF THE LAS TRAMPAS LAND GRANT, NEW MEXI-
CO. *New Mexico Hist. Rev. 1981 56(1): 71-97.* Shady land dealings, long a
practice in New Mexico before the United States took control in 1846, were
continued on an even more unscrupulous level by the Anglos. Using Las
Trampas Grant as an example, the author shows how Anglo speculators
between 1859 and 1914 swindled Hispanic farmers out of their land holdings.
The federal government was responsible for much of the dishonesty and
corruption in land grant crime because of its tardiness in settling grant claims.
Based on Santa Fe District Court Records and Bureau of Land Management
Surveyor General's Reports at the State Records Center and Archives, Santa
Fe, New Mexico, and other primary sources; photo, map, 76 notes.
P. L. McLaughlin

527.   DeLeon, Arnoldo and Stewart, Kenneth L. LOST DREAMS AND
FOUND FORTUNES: MEXICAN AND ANGLO IMMIGRANTS IN
SOUTH TEXAS, 1850-1900. *Western Hist. Q. 1983 14(3): 291-310.* Analysis
of migration into south Texas from Mexico and from the United States and
Europe. Examines the historical forces that determined the destiny of the two
groups in the area that promised an equal start but eventually developed into
inequalities. Mexican impoverishment was the result of historical conditions
rather than any migratory impulse or any difficulty in living in an American
context. 3 tables, 30 notes.   D. L. Smith

528.   DeLeon, Arnoldo and Stewart, Kenneth L. A TALE OF THREE
CITIES: A COMPARATIVE ANALYSIS OF THE SOCIO-ECONOMIC
CONDITIONS OF MEXICAN-AMERICANS IN LOS ANGELES, TUC-
SON, AND SAN ANTONIO, 1850-1900. *Journal of the West 1985 24(2):
64-74.* A quantitative analysis of socioeconomic conditions of Mexican Americans in Los Angeles, Tucson, and San Antonio in the late 19th century shows
that there were significant differences in both the pace and causes of economic
and occupational decline in these cities. To provide an adequate understanding
of these data, further research must explain why such heterogeneity of
socioeconomic opportunity prevailed among Mexican-American communities
in the Southwest. Institutionalized racism is a long-ignored factor in research
considering the plight of Mexican Americans in the Southwest. Socioeconomic
decay has left disastrous effects on the Hispanic psyche and culture in the 20th
century. Based on Census Bureau data, quantitative analysis, and secondary
sources; 7 tables, 4 photos, illus., 23 notes.   B. A. Stenslie

529.   Dobson, John M. DESPERADOES AND DIPLOMACY: THE TER-
RITORY OF ARIZONA V. JESÚS GARCÍA, 1893. *J. of Arizona Hist. 1976
17(2): 137-160.* In July 1893 Mexican citizen Jesús García was arrested for
participating in a saloon brawl in Nogales, Arizona Territory. He escaped and
headed for the international boundaries. Recaptured by an Arizona sheriff,
Garcia claimed he was caught on the Sonora side of the border. The continuing
dispute over the circumstances provoked strained foreign relations for over
three years between Mexico and United States. This minor offense received
undeserved publicity because of a rash of border violations by an assortment of

desperadoes from both countries during the summer of 1893. 2 illus., map, 39 notes.   D. L. Smith

530.   Dysart, Jane. MEXICAN WOMEN IN SAN ANTONIO, 1830-1860: THE ASSIMILATION PROCESS. *Western Hist. Q. 1976 7(4): 365-375.* The Anglo sense of racial and cultural superiority in the Southwest inhibited large-scale marriage with Mexicans. Since Anglo penetration of the Southwest was preponderantly male, intermarriage was almost exclusively between Anglo men and Mexican women. The Anglo male-oriented frontier society limited the wife's function to home management and child care, while the husband made the decisions which affected the family's relationship to society. Using San Antonio, Texas, as a case study, it is found that the few Mexican women who became wives of Anglos lost their distinctive ethnic identity. In many cases their children rejected their Mexican cultural legacy. 45 notes.   D. L. Smith

531.   Ebright, Malcolm. THE SAN JOAQUÍN GRANT: WHO OWNED THE COMMON LANDS? A HISTORICAL-LEGAL PUZZLE. *New Mexico Hist. Rev. 1982 57(1): 5-26.* Traces litigation leading to *Rio Arriba Land and Cattle Company* v. *United States,* a landmark case decided in 1897 by the US Supreme Court, to show how the question of ownership under Spanish law of the common lands of a community land grant was handled. The Supreme Court made its decision lacking all the facts and previous legal authority. Based on US Bureau of Land Management records, Surveyor General's Reports, and other primary sources; illus., map, 74 notes.   A. C. Dempsey

532.   Ellis, Bruce T. FRAUD WITHOUT SCANDAL: THE ROQUE LOVATO GRANT AND GASPAR ORTIZ Y ALARID. *New Mexico Hist. Rev. 1982 57(1): 43-62.* The Roque Lovato Grant claim of 1871 is an example of a fraudulent land grant claim in New Mexico. Chronicles an attempt to acquire land in the public domain, a socially acceptable practice at the time, and provides a biography of the perpetrator. Based on the US Bureau of Land Management, Surveyor General's Reports, records of the Archives of the Archdiocese of Santa Fe, and other primary sources; illus., 40 notes.
                                                                        A. C. Dempsey

533.   Finzsch, Norbert. ANTI-MEXICAN "NATIVISM" IN THE CALIFORNIA GOLD MINES, 1848-1856. *Jahrbuch für Geschichte von Staat, Wirtschaft und Gesellschaft Lateinamerikas [West Germany] 1984 21: 283-302.* Americans in California quickly developed nativist prejudices against foreigners working in the gold fields, whom they claimed were taking what rightfully belonged to Americans. Nativists rejected Chinese and Latins in particular, whom they claimed were uncivilized. Nativists attempted to expel foreigners from the gold fields by discriminatory legislation and vigilante action. The cause of this nativist resentment was the bourgeois get-rich-quick dreams of American gold miners, who therefore preferred individual enterprise. But the shift to large-scale quartz mining required a capitalist group effort that squeezed out the individual miners. Since Chinese and Latins were willing to work as wage laborers in the quartz mining operations, they became the targets of the antiforeign, anticapitalist nativist resentment. Based on California

newspapers, journals, diaries, and secondary sources; 87 notes.

T. Schoonover/S

534. García, Mario T. THE CALIFORNIOS OF SAN DIEGO AND THE POLITICS OF ACCOMMODATION 1846-1860. *Aztlan 1975 6(1): 69-85.* The upper class *ricos* in San Diego hoped to accommodate themselves to the Anglo American conquest after 1848. In the numerical majority and owning most of the property, they were able to gain cultural and social recognition, but they failed to control the political process. By 1860 the Californios were on the decline economically as a result of political disfranchisement, economic depression, and high taxes. Based on US manuscript censuses, tax rolls, and newspapers; 89 notes, biblio.   R. Griswold del Castillo

535. Gil, Carlos B. MIGUEL ANTONIO OTERO, FIRST CHICANO GOVERNOR. *J. of Ethnic Studies 1976 4(3): 95-102.* Examines the three volume autobiography by Miguel Antonio Otero, a rich primary source for American Western social history. Suggests "variations in the patterns of intimidation and exploitation" which traditionally kept Chicanos from full participation in American society. In 1897 Otero became the first "Chicano" governor in the United States and the first native-born governor of New Mexico. His ancestry, although not lacking Hispano names, was heavily Anglo-American as was his education at St. Louis and Notre Dame universities. Yet his life "suggests total identification and commitment to his native homeland," while seeking accommodation in the new Anglo-American order. He was a man of his time, an example of the adaptation which affected frontier areas of the Spanish Empire. Primary and secondary sources; 9 notes.

G. J. Bobango

536. Gonzales, Manuel G. CARLOS I VELASCO. *Journal of Arizona History 1984 25(3): 265-284.* Carlos Velasco (1837-1914) was representative of the Mexican immigrants to Arizona during the 19th century. He was educated, started the successful newspaper *El Fronterizo* in Tucson, founded the Alianza Hispano-Americana in 1894 and contributed to the defense of Mexican rights in Tucson. Based on Arizona Historical Society archives and secondary sources; 3 photos, 93 notes.   G. O. Gagnon

537. Griswold del Castillo, R. HEALTH AND THE MEXICAN AMERI-CANS IN LOS ANGELES, 1850-1887. *J. of Mexican Am. Hist. 1974 4(1): 19-27.* The public health of the Mexican-American community of Los Angeles, 1850-87, was inferior to that of the Anglo-American population, particularly in regard to the care of infants and the treatment of infectious disease. Once a Mexican American had passed through the dangerous years prior to age 21, his chances of surviving were relatively better than the majority of Anglo Americans. Primary and secondary sources; 2 tables, 19 notes.

R. T. Fulton

538. Griswold del Castillo, R. LA FAMILIA CHICANA: SOCIAL CHANGE IN THE CHICANO FAMILY IN LOS ANGELES, 1850-1880. *J. of Ethnic Studies 1975 3(1): 41-58.* Examines the reaction of Mexican Ameri-can families in light of the impact of modernization (urbanization and

industrialization) during the period 1850-80. The pre-modern family is found to be paternalistic and extended. Modernization led to a decline in the proportion of extended families, a rise in the proportion of female headed families, and an increase in common law marriages. Rather than being functional adjustments to industrialization, these are interpreted as dysfunctional since both literacy and social mobility were associated with the declining extended family structure. Based largely on manuscript censuses and other primary sources; 27 notes. T. W. Smith

539. Griswold del Castillo, Richard. CHICANOS' CULTURAL VITALITY UNDER PRESSURE. *Center Mag. 1980 13(4): 47-52.* Mid-19th century barrioization led to Chicano community development and was both a factor and a hindrance in their assimilation to Anglo culture; discussion follows. Primary sources. J. R. Grant

540. Griswold del Castillo, Richard. LITERACY IN SAN ANTONIO, TEXAS, 1850-1860. *Latin Am. Res. Rev. 1980 15(3): 180-185.* The percentage of literate Mexican Americans doubled between 1850 and 1860, although it still lagged far behind Anglo Americans. Census errors and sociocultural differences may explain this. Differences in literacy between the two groups may not have been as great as census data indicate. Based on 19th-century manuscript census returns; 4 tables, 4 notes. J. K. Pfabe

541. Griswold del Castillo, Richard. MYTH AND REALITY: CHICANO ECONOMIC MOBILITY IN LOS ANGELES 1850-1880. *Aztlán 1976 6(2): 151-171.* Contrary to the American myth of success, the Chicano working class in Los Angeles did not experience upward socioeconomic mobility in the late 19th century. Compared to the Anglo population, Chicanos became second-class citizens economically. All classes were reduced in socioeconomic status and persisting residents experienced the same fate. Based on manuscript census returns; 17 notes. A

542. Griswold del Castillo, Richard. A PRELIMINARY COMPARISON OF CHICANO, IMMIGRANT AND NATIVE BORN FAMILY STRUCTURES 1850-1880. *Aztlan 1975 6(1): 87-95.* Compares European immigrants and native born Anglo Americans in Detroit, Michigan, with Mexican Americans in Los Angeles during 1850-80. The urban Chicano family was more drastically affected by economic changes and economic opportunities were more restricted for Chicano household heads. Chicano family structure resembled that of the native born Anglo American. 14 notes. A

543. Griswold del Castillo, Richard. TUCSONENSES AND ANGELENOS: A SOCIO-ECONOMIC STUDY OF TWO MEXICAN-AMERICAN BARRIOS, 1860-1880. *J. of the West 1979 18(1): 58-66.* Tucson, Arizona, and Los Angeles, California, had a common origin in Spain's policy of establishing frontier outposts for defense against Indians and foreign encroachment. A comparative study of the two populations and their progress under US rule, however, shows that the Tucsonenses enjoyed a better socioeconomic status, as measured by occupations distribution and property holdings. The reason for this is primarily the Tucsonenses' numerical superiority to Anglo-Americans,

which enabled traditional Hispanic cultural traditions to endure. US census records and published sources; 5 photos, 4 tables, 19 notes.   B. S. Porter

544.   Harrington, Marie. A LETTER TO LUMMIS. *Masterkey 1983 57(2): 73-75.* Reprints 1924 letters between Joseph Smith of Boston, Massachusetts, and Californian Charles Lummis, in which each recalls fondly his days living among Indians and Mexican Americans in the Southwest during the late 19th century.

545.   Hoffman, Abraham. THE CONTROVERSIAL CAREER OF MAR-TIN AGUIRRE: THE RISE AND FALL OF A CHICANO LAWMAN. *California History 1984 63(4): 293-304, 339-341.* Traces the law enforcement career of Martin Aguirre. A native Californio, Aguirre acquired early fame when he rescued 19 people from the Los Angeles River in a January 1886 rainstorm. He served as sheriff of Los Angeles County, 1888-90, losing a reelection bid in a hotly contested election. His loyalty to the Republican Party won him an appointment as warden of San Quentin Prison in 1899, but his term was marred by accusations of political favoritism and graft. Thereafter he served as a deputy sheriff and bailiff in Los Angeles County until his death in 1929. Illus., 5 photos, 48 notes.   A. Hoffman

546.   Hughes, Charles. THE DECLINE OF THE CALIFORNIOS: THE CASE OF SAN DIEGO, 1846-1856. *J. of San Diego Hist. 1975 21(3): 1-31.* Describes the political and economic demise of native Californians in San Diego County following the War of 1846.   S

547.   Jensen, Carol. CLEOFAS M. JARAMILLO ON MARRIAGE IN TERRITORIAL NORTHERN NEW MEXICO. *New Mexico Hist. Rev. 1983 58(2): 153-171.* Cleofas M. Jaramillo, "a prominent New Mexican citizen," wrote about the marriage procedures of Catholics in the Hispanic villages of northern New Mexico in the late 19th century. Her descriptions, although more folkloric than historic, recorded the interactions of the groom's and bride's families, Bishop Lamy's role, the expectations of high Spanish Catholic society, and other customs typical of the area. Photo, 72 notes.
K. E. Gilmont

548.   Johnson, Susan L. SHARING BED AND BOARD: COHABITA-TION AND CULTURAL DIFFERENCE IN CENTRAL ARIZONA MIN-ING TOWNS. *Frontiers 1984 7(3): 36-42.* The nature and consequences of cohabitation in central Arizona mining towns varied according to the ethnicity of the parties; although traditionally accepted among Mexican Americans, Anglo society disapproved of cohabitation, especially for women, and most Anglo men who cohabited did so with Mexican women, who suffered discrimination because of it.

549.   Jordan, Terry G. THE 1887 CENSUS OF TEXAS' HISPANIC POPU-LATION. *Aztlán 1981 12(2): 271-278.* Describes the 1887 Texas state census, recently rediscovered by the author, in terms of its importance to Mexican-American demography. Long overlooked by scholars, this census provides the only reasonably accurate estimate of Mexicans and Mexican Americans in

Texas prior to 1930. Although the data has some shortcomings, adjustments to the figures are within reason. There were approximately 83,433 Hispanics in Texas in 1887, or 4.14% of the state's population. They were heavily concentrated in the southern part of the state. 2 maps, table, 11 notes.

A. Hoffman

550. Juárez, José Roberto. LA IGLESIA CATÓLICA Y EL CHICANO EN SUD TEXAS, 1836-1911. [The Catholic Church and the Chicano in southern Texas, 1836-1911]. *Aztlán 1973 4(2): 217-255.*

551. Kenner, Charles L. THE GREAT NEW MEXICO CATTLE RAID: 1872. *New Mexico Hist. Rev. 1962 37(4): 243-259.* Provides a description of, and background to, the raid led by John Hittson in 1872 against the Comancheros (Hispanic traders) to restore cattle stolen by Indians: an event which increased racial antagonism between Hispanic New Mexicans and Texas ranchers.

552. Knowlton, Clark S. THE TOWN OF LAS VEGAS COMMUNITY LAND GRANT: AN ANGO-AMERICAN COUP D'ÉTAT. *J. of the West 1980 19(3): 12-21.* In 1835 the Mexican government approved a community grant of land in northern New Mexico to 29 family heads and any new settlers who could be accommodated on arable land. Following American annexation in 1846, lengthy litigation revolved around the interpretation of the community grant. According to Mexican Law, the land belonged collectively to all grant inhabitants; but some Spanish-American heirs argued that the common lands belonged only to the first grantees and their heirs; and American ranchers claimed that the commons were public domain subject to sale and homesteading. The rural inhabitants eventually lost their land to Anglo-American and Spanish-American ranchers and businessmen. Based on documents in the National Archives; 10 photos, 2 maps, 33 notes. B. S. Porter

553. Langum, David J. FROM CONDEMNATION TO PRAISE: SHIFTING PERSPECTIVES ON HISPANIC CALIFORNIA. *California History 1983 61(4): 282-291.* Traces the shift in viewpoint from negative stereotyping of Hispanic Californians as indolent and lazy to an equally stereotypical image of a hospitable, generous, and romantic people swept aside by Yankee conquest. The change may have been due to desire to believe in a romantic past for a foreign land that now is part of the United States. Efforts by writers such as Charles F. Lummis, Mary Austin, and George W. James resulted in an attempt to create a regional identity and an aesthetic reaction to Gilded Age materialism. Photos, 20 notes. A. Hoffman

554. Larson, Robert W. THE WHITE CAPS OF NEW MEXICO: A STUDY OF ETHNIC MILITANCY IN THE SOUTHWEST. *Pacific Hist. R. 1975 44(2): 171-185.* Juan José Herrera organized the White Caps of New Mexico in 1889 as a Hispano vigilante group to save the Hispano communal land grant (Las Vegas Community Grant) from Anglo and corporate ranchers. Their activities dramatized the issue sufficiently that legislative and court action preserved the grant. The White Caps were also responsible for the rapid growth of the Knights of Labor in San Miguel County, New Mexico, during

1889-90. After 1890, Herrera turned to politics, organizing a People's Party which had some success in 1890 and 1892, but was eliminated as a political force in 1894. Based on newspapers, private papers in New Mexico State Records Center and New Mexico Highlands University, published primary sources, interviews and communications with Herrera's descendants, and secondary sources; 50 notes.   W. K. Hobson

555. Ledbetter, Barbara A. BLACK AND MEXICAN SLAVES IN YOUNG COUNTY, TEXAS, 1856-1865. *West Texas Hist. Assoc. Year Book 1980 56: 100-102.* Lists surnames and first names.

556. Lee, Hector H. THE REVERBERANT JOAQUÍN MURIETA IN CALIFORNIA LEGENDRY. *Pacific Hist. 1981 25(3): 38-47.* Reviews the historical and legendary facts surrounding the name of Joaquín Murieta: whether he was a bandit or another Robin Hood will probably never be solved. 7 illus.   H. M. Evans

557. Leon, Arnoldo de. WRESTING A COMPETENCE IN NINE-TEENTH CENTURY TEXAS: THE CASE OF THE CHICANOS. *Red River Valley Hist. Rev. 1979 4(4): 52-64.* Mexican Americans, "having to exist under terms dictated to them by white society, invented, manipulated, and improved upon endurance mechanisms to withstand a society where dependency relegated them to impoverishment."

558. López, Larry. THE FOUNDING OF SAN FRANCISCO ON THE RIO PUERCO: A DOCUMENT. *New Mexico Hist. Rev. 1980 55(1): 71-78.* A party of Hispanic New Mexicans in 1866 colonized San Francisco on the Rio Puerco, a northern tributary of the Rio Grande. The original document of colonization, signed by the settlers and listing the rules and conditions of settlement, is translated and briefly discussed. Primary sources; 18 notes.   P. L. McLaughlin

559. Martinez, Oscar J. ON THE SIZE OF THE CHICANO POPULA-TION: NEW ESTIMATES, 1850-1900. *Aztlan 1975 6(1): 43-67.* Previous estimates of the Chicano population in the 19th-century Southwest were too small, due to errors in the US censuses. After a review of the historical reasons for the undercounting of Mexican Americans, the author arrives at an upper- and lower-range estimate based on rates of natural increase, immigration, and systematic census errors. 43 notes, appendixes.   R. Griswold del Castillo

560. Mawn, Geoffrey P. A LAND-GRANT GUARANTEE: THE TREA-TY OF HIDALGO OR THE PROTOCOL OF QUERÉTARO? *J. of the West 1975 14(4): 49-63.* Considers the validity of both the Treaty of Guada-lupe Hidalgo (1848) and the Protocol of Querétaro (1848) in guaranteeing Spanish and Mexican land grants in the Mexican cession and the state of Texas; traces the work of Nicholas P. Trist as an executive agent. 61 notes.

561. Meyer, Doris L. BANDITRY AND POETRY: VERSES BY TWO OUTLAWS OF OLD LAS VEGAS. *New Mexico Hist. R. 1975 50(4): 277-290.* The two outlaws in New Mexico who were bandits as well as poets

were Vicente Silva and Lorenzo Lopez. Silva was a native New Mexican who settled in Las Vegas in 1875. He established a saloon which was a hideout for outlaws. There is a difference in opinion as to whether there was a connection between the two outlaws. Both Silva and Lopez were involved to some extent in Las Vegas politics. J. H. Krenkel

562. Meyer, Doris L. EARLY MEXICAN-AMERICAN RESPONSES TO NEGATIVE STEREOTYPING. *New Mexico Hist. Rev. 1978 53(1): 75-91.* Most people who visited New Mexico in the early 19th century believed in Anglo-Saxon superiority. They saw Mexicans as inferior people. Anti-Spanish feeling in the United States was a result of prejudices formed by the conflict between Protestant England and Catholic Spain. American authors of the early 19th century did not distinguish between frontier Mexicans and those of the interior whose culture was more developed. 24 notes. J. H. Krenkel

563. Miller, Darlis A. CROSS-CULTURAL MARRIAGES IN THE SOUTHWEST: THE NEW MEXICO EXPERIENCE, 1846-1900. *New Mexico Hist. Rev. 1982 57(4): 335-358.* As the Southwest became more populated by Anglo men, the number of marriages (legal and common-law) among Hispanic women increased. Most of these arrangements were quite suitable. Mexican women assumed their expected domestic roles. Civilian and military intermarriages tended to be restricted to the same socioeconomic classes, although there were a few instances where Mexican men married American women. The general resultant intercultural marriages produced children who married others born from intercultural unions. Photo, 69 notes. K. E. Gilmont

564. Mount, Graeme S. NUEVO MEXICANOS AND THE WAR OF 1898. *New Mexico Hist. Rev. 1983 58(4): 381-396.* Mexican-American reaction in New Mexico to the Spanish-American War was either one of apathy or of support for the American position. Governor Miguel A. Otero vigorously supported the US war effort. Captain Maximiliano Luna fought with American forces and died in the Philippines. While older generations of Mexican-Americans were more supportive of the American effort than were young people, there were no known expressions of Spanish support, either verbally or in publications. Photo, 54 notes. K. E. Gilmont

565. Myres, Sandra L. MEXICAN AMERICANS AND WESTERING ANGLOS: A FEMININE PERSPECTIVE. *New Mexico Hist. Rev. 1982 57(4): 319-333.* As the Southwest became populated by westward-moving Americans, Mexican and Anglo women at first feared and distrusted each other, largely due to exaggerated magazine and newspaper articles. However, as the two cultures mixed, many fears were dispelled as each society found the other to be human and socially beneficial, disproving preconceived stereotypes. Photo, 49 notes. K. E. Gilmont

566. Neri, Michael C. GONZALEZ RUBIO AND CALIFORNIA CATHOLICISM, 1846-1850. *Southern California Q. 1976 58(4): 441-457.* Assesses the work of Father José González Rubio (1804-75), who as governor of the mitre (diocesan administrator) for Upper and Lower California presided

over the shift from Mexican to American law and culture during 1846-50. González Rubio faced such problems as intermarriage of Protestants and Catholics, the need for tithing, and a shortage of qualified priests. He believed the mission lands rightfully belonged to the Indians and that Church possessions would be fairly adjudicated by the United States. At the end of his tenure Californians commissioned a painting of him in appreciation of his efforts on their behalf. It is at Mission Santa Barbara. In a time of uncertainty and transition, González Rubio helped the Catholic Church to survive in California. Primary and secondary sources; 63 notes.   A. Hoffman

567.   Nostrand, Richard L. THE HISPANO HOMELAND IN 1900. *Ann. of the Assoc. of Am. Geographers 1980 70(3): 382-396.* In five southwestern states in 1900, 140,000 Hispanic Americans lived and to varying degrees prospered.

568.   Nostrand, Richard L. MEXICAN AMERICANS CIRCA 1850. *Ann. of the Am. Assoc. of Am. Geographers 1975 65(3): 378-390.* Discusses the demography of Mexican Americans in California and the New Mexico Territory.   S

569.   Oczon, Annabelle M. BILINGUAL AND SPANISH-LANGUAGE NEWSPAPERS IN TERRITORIAL NEW MEXICO. *New Mexico Hist. Rev. 1979 54(1): 45-52.* The importance of bilingual and Spanish-language newspapers in the development of New Mexico has been underestimated. These newspapers and the Spanish-American journalists behind them played a vital role in the social, political, and cultural history of New Mexico during the territorial period. The newspapers helped preserve Hispanic culture and brought the Spanish-American and Anglo-American cultures closer together. 29 notes.   P. L. McLaughlin

570.   Padilla, Fernando V. EARLY CHICANO LEGAL RECOGNITION: 1846-1897. *J. of Popular Culture 1979 13(3): 564-574.* Traces the twisted trail of legal decisions regarding citizenship and naturalization rights of Mexican Americans from the time of the Republic of Texas Constitution to the 1897 *Rodrigues* decision. The major issue in each instance was one of race versus nationality. State and federal court records; 65 notes.   D. G. Nielson

571.   Paredes, Raymund A. THE MEXICAN IMAGE IN AMERICAN TRAVEL LITERATURE, 1831-1869. *New Mexico Hist. Rev. 1977 52(1): 5-13.* Most of the information available to the people of the United States concerning Mexico in the mid-19th century is found in travel accounts written by Americans visiting Mexico. As Mexico became more familiar to the Americans, fewer such accounts were published. One of the best assessments of New Mexico is found in Josiah Gregg, *Commerce on the Prairies* (1844). He is generally complimentary in writing about the people of New Mexico, but he thought the provincial government was corrupt. Other travelers from the United States who wrote about Mexico and Mexicans in the West and Far West included: James Ohio Pattie, Albert Pike, Mary Austin Holley, George Wilkins Kendall, Richard Henry Dana, Alfred Robinson, Walter Colton, Bayard Taylor, John Russell Bartlett, Albert Gilliam, Brantz Mayer, John T.

Hughes, Frank S. Edwards, Captain W. S. Henry, Adolph Wislizenus, Rufus Sage, Samuel Hammett, William Shaler, Thomas J. Farnham, Thomas Davis, William H. Emory, W. W. H. Davis, and J. Ross Browne. J. H. Krenkel

572. Park, Joseph F. THE 1903 "MEXICAN AFFAIR" AT CLIFTON. *J. of Arizona Hist. 1977 18(2): 119-148.* The Arizona Clifton-Morenci copper mining country was virtually isolated and subject to Apache raids. For one reason or another, neither Indian, Anglo-American, nor Chinese labor was sufficient or satisfactory to work the mines. Mexican labor, both alien and domestic, first introduced in 1872, became the predominant labor force. Traces the origin, growth, treatment, and eventual rebellion of the Mexican workers. Even though the Western Federation of Miners could not gain a foothold with them, the Mexicans tied up the entire Clifton-Morenci district with their walkout in 1903. The "Mexican affair" was "the opening gun of a long series" of labor-management skirmishes over the issue of Mexican workers. Extracted from a graduate thesis; 9 illus., 56 notes. D. L. Smith

573. Park, Roberta J. SAN FRANCISCANS AT WORK AND AT PLAY, 1846-1869. *J. of the West 1983 22(1): 44-51.* As San Francisco changed from a Mexican village to a cosmopolitan American city, its citizens' pastimes reflected the cultures of the changing population. The early Hispanic-Indian peoples enjoyed fiestas, fandangos, horse races, bullfights, bearbaiting, and rodeo events. After the gold discovery of 1848, the predominantly American newcomers spent much of their free time drinking and gambling on card games. Ethnic groups brought Chinese New Year, German *Mai-Fest,* and Irish St. Patrick's Day celebrations. As the community became better established, the city acquired the recreational tastes of other American cities for parks, libraries, theaters, and sports arenas. Based on newspaper articles; 5 photos, 34 notes. B. S. Porter

574. Peterson, Richard H. ANTI-MEXICAN NATIVISM IN CALIFOR-NIA, 1848-1853: A STUDY OF CULTURAL CONFLICT. *Southern California Q. 1980 62(4): 309-327.* Discusses why American goldseekers persecuted Mexican prospectors in the first years of the California gold rush. In addition to economic competition and resentment over Mexican success in finding gold, Anglo-Americans held a cultural bias against Mexicans. Their view of California, taken from the writings of such observers as Richard Henry Dana and Alfred Robinson, was that Californians were thriftless, indolent, and inferior people, a mixture of decadent Spanish and lowly Indian. Mexicans had lost the recent war. Protestant Americans held bigoted views of Mexican Catholicism, and thought that God had saved California's gold for American miners. Such attitudes resulted in extreme prejudice, passage of the Foreign Miners' Tax aimed at Mexicans, and efforts to expel Mexican prospectors from the gold fields. Modern attitudes of Americans toward illegal immigrants from Mexico may reflect the earlier economic and cultural prejudice. 84 notes. A. Hoffman

575. Primera, Joe C. LOS HERMANOS TORRES: EARLY SETTLERS OF PECOS COUNTY. *Permian Hist. Ann. 1980 20: 89-96.* Traces the history of the ranches founded by the Torres brothers, Juan (d. 1896), Cesario

(d. 1911), and Bernardo (d. 1882), from 1869 to 1896, in the West Texas area of Pecos County, describing the brothers' contributions to early frontier society as farmers, ranchers, and merchants.

576. Ramirez, Elizabeth C. A HISTORY OF MEXICAN AMERICAN PROFESSIONAL THEATRE IN TEXAS PRIOR TO 1900. *Theatre Survey 1983 24(1-2): 99-116.* The art and music of Mexican Americans in 19th-century Texas was greatly influenced by Mexico and Spain, and theater became a cohesive and unifying force in the Mexican-American community.

577. Richmond, Douglas W. LA GUERRA DE TEXAS SE RENOVA: MEXICAN INSURRECTION AND CARRANCISTA AMBITIONS, 1900-1920. *Aztlán 1980 11(1): 1-32.* Traces efforts by the Mexican government, under the leadership of President Venustiano Carranza, to foment revolt among Mexicans living in Texas. Since 1848, Mexicans, numerically the vast majority of the population of south Texas, had endured discrimination and exploitation. Prompted by American reluctance to give legitimacy to his movement and by anger over Anglo mistreatment of Texas Mexicans, Carranza supported the Plan of San Diego in 1915, an effort designed to recapture Texas for Mexico through a coalition of Mexicans, blacks and Indians. The scheme failed to attract widespread support, but for more than a year Mexican raids over the border resulted in numerous outbreaks of violence and created political turmoil in south Texas. Tensions between Mexico and the United States increased with the Pershing Expedition to chase Francisco Villa in Mexico in 1916, and a point short of war was reached in 1919 as Texas conservatives advocated armed intervention in Mexico. As long as Carranza remained in power, he continued to support revolutionary agitation in Texas. 94 notes.   A. Hoffman

578. Roberts, Virginia C. FRANCISCO GANDARA AND "WAR ON THE GILA." *J. of Arizona Hist. 1983 24(3): 221-236.* Relates the events surrounding a brief interethnic clash in Arizona Territory. The conflict, which began with the disappearance of an Anglo-American, William McFarland, exploded in a gun battle that killed Mexican-American Francisco Gándara and two Anglo-Americans, and ended only after more shootings and army intervention. Newspapers and rumors escalated the violence into an international incident. The violence was exacerbated by the absence of law officials as well as interethnic distrust. Based on Gándara family records and contemporary periodicals; map, 2 photos, 36 notes.   G. O. Gagnon

579. Rock, Michael J. THE CHANGE IN TENURE NEW MEXICO SUPREME COURT DECISIONS HAVE EFFECTED UPON THE COMMON LANDS OF COMMUNITY LAND GRANTS IN NEW MEXICO. *Social Sci. J. 1976 13(3): 53-63.* Covers 1821-90, concentrating on Mexican land grants. One of six articles in this issue on Spanish and Mexican land grants in the Southwest.

580. Ross, Steve. THE BAD MAN OF SOCORRO. *Mankind 1973 4(4): 52-57.* Elfego Baca (1865-1945) held off 80 men during a shootout at Socorro, New Mexico, in 1884.   S

581. Scharf, Thomas L., ed. PAGES FROM THE DIARY OF CAVE JOHNSON COUTS: SAN DIEGO IN THE SPRING AND SUMMER OF 1849. *J. of San Diego Hist. 1976 22(2): 9-19.* Reprints excerpts from Couts' diary and his remembrances of San Diego as an American soldier stationed in California following the War with Mexico.

582. Scurlock, Dan. *PASTORES* OF THE VALLES CALDERA: DOCUMENTING A VANISHING WAY OF LIFE. *Palacio 1982 88(1): 3-11.* Describes the life of sheepherders *(pastores)* in the Valles Caldera of New Mexico.

583. Sheridan, Thomas E. PEACOCK IN THE PARLOR: FRONTIER TUCSON'S MEXICAN ELITE. *Journal of Arizona History 1984 25(3): 245-264.* After the Gadsden Purchase, southern Arizona's social elite remained primarily Mexican American until the coming of the railroad in the 1880's. Describes members of the elite, including Estevan Ochoa, Mariano Samaniego, and Leopoldo Carillo. Based on contemporary newspapers and secondary sources; 4 photos, 75 notes.   G. O. Gagnon

584. Smith, Pamela and Hughey, Kirk. *THE GRINGO AND GREASER. Palacio 1980 86(1): 40-41.* Describes colorful semimonthly English- and Spanish-language newspaper, *The Gringo and Greaser,* put out by editor-publisher Charles L. Kusz in Manzano, New Mexico, from August 1883 to March 1884, and provides examples of Kusz's writing.

585. Standart, M. Colette. THE SONORAN MIGRATION TO CALIFORNIA, 1848-1856: A STUDY IN PREJUDICE. *Southern California Q. 1976 58(3): 333-357.* Describes the movement of Sonorans from Mexico to the California goldfields. The State of Sonora suffered from Indian attacks, economic stagnation, and political quarrels, and the state's proximity to California made the trip a feasible one. Large numbers of Sonorans emigrated despite warnings from the Mexican press and government of exploitation and hardship. Experienced as miners, the Sonorans did relatively well in locating gold, particularly in the southern goldfields in early 1848. As increasing numbers of Sonorans competed with Anglo prospectors, tensions escalated. Jealous of Sonoran mining successes, Anglos imposed a foreign miners' tax, jumped claims, and forced Sonorans out of the goldfields. Some Sonorans reacted to this discrimination by turning to banditry. By 1851 Sonoran emigration had declined, and many returned to Mexico; others remained in California as wage-earning miners or mule drivers. An attempt in 1855 to organize further repatriation met with negative results. Animosity to Sonorans lessened as Anglos directed their prejudices against the Chinese. Primary and secondary sources; 113 notes.   A. Hoffman

586. Steele, Thomas J. THE DEATH CART: ITS PLACE AMONG THE SANTOS OF NEW MEXICO. *Colorado Mag. 1978 55(1): 1-14.* Discusses the appearance of the death cart around 1860, "a constant feature of the Penitente morada" in northern New Mexico and southern Colorado "during the last part of the nineteenth century and first part of the twentieth... " Its surface meanings were: 1)symbol of involuntary death, 2)warning against a

"bad death," and 3)encouragement to live for "a good death in a state of grace... " But there were cultural implications, too, related to the mid-19th century conquest of the area by the United States and the sublimation of Spanish cultural life under the pressure of an alien culture. It also served to emphasize confrontation with personal death, mortification, and the Christian paradox itself. Primary and secondary sources; 6 illus., 20 notes.

O. H. Zabel

587. Steiner, Stan. ON THE TRAIL OF JOAQUIN MURIETA. *Am. West 1981 18(1): 54-57, 66.* When the forty-niners reached the California gold fields, Sonorans were already exploiting the best claims. These "foreigners" were soon subjected to brutal treatment and run off their claims. In response, some of the Mexicans became outlaws. After Joaquin Murieta was beaten and his wife raped and murdered, Murieta bacame leader of a gang of highwaymen. His style and bravado catapulted him into legend. He was credited with simultaneous robberies and murders over hundreds of miles. His band of outlaws were soon called revolutionaries who were bent on ousting the Yankees. The California Rangers collected a reward for Murieta's head; but the Mexican Indians insisted it was the wrong head and that Murieta lived on. He is remembered as a patriot in California barrios and Sonora to this day. Hard evidence and vital statistics are fragmentary at best. 2 illus., biblio.

D. L. Smith

588. Stewart, Kenneth L. and DeLeon, Arnoldo. EDUCATION, LITERACY, AND OCCUPATIONAL STRUCTURE IN WEST TEXAS, 1860-1900. *West Texas Historical Association Yearbook 1984 60: 127-143.* English-speaking West Texans used education to widen career and employment opportunities, whereas Spanish-speaking West Texans found themselves sorted out of the system.

589. Sunseri, Alvin R. SHEEP RICOS AND SHEEP FORTUNES IN THE AFTERMATH OF THE AMERICAN CONQUEST, 1846-1861. *Palacio 1977 83(1): 2-8.* Beginning from Spanish-supplied stock, Hispanic rancheros amassed fortunes in sheep ranching, food production, and textile manufacture in New Mexico, 1846-61.

590. Taylor, Morris F. THE UÑA DE GATO GRANT IN COLFAX COUNTY. *New Mexico Hist. R. 1976 51(2): 121-143.* Colfax County, New Mexico, has had legal problems due to land grants whose owners have had difficulty in proving their ownership. The term Uña de Gato means cat's claw (derived from the black locust bush which abounds south of the Arkansas River). Early in 1874 Manuel A. Otero purchased the Uña de Gato grant from Jesús María Gómez y López for $5,000, paid part in livestock and part in groceries and other things. The sale was immediately contested in the courts. In 1887, Surveyor General George A. Julian accused Senator Stephen W. Dorsey of Arkansas of illegally using the homestead and preemption laws to gain control of the Uña de Gato land. This particular grant was but a small part in a general protest against land grants. Map.

J. H. Krenkel

591. Theisen, Lee Scott. FRANK WARNER ANGEL'S NOTES ON NEW MEXICO TERRITORY, 1878. *Arizona and the West 1976 18(4): 333-370.* In 1878 Frank W. Angel (b. 1845) was sent as a special investigator to New Mexico to study land grant frauds, alleged corruption among federal officials, the death of a British subject, and mounting violence. As part of the briefing for newly appointed Governor Lew Wallace, Angel filled Wallace's address book with terse comments on leading personalities and newspapers in the territory. Angel's comments are printed herein, with annotations and bibliographic information; 3 illus., 8 notes. D. L. Smith

592. Trafzer, Clifford and Trafzer, Daniel. JOSÉ MARÍA REDONDO: A SELF-MADE MAN OF THE SOUTHWEST. *Pacific Hist. 1981 25(3): 54-61.* José María Redondo arrived in California in 1849 to join the gold rush. In addition to mining he was a salesman and ferryman and became a wealthy businessman and rancher. He was elected to the territorial legislature of Arizona. 4 illus. H. M. Evans

593. Trulio, Beverly. ANGLO-AMERICAN ATTITUDES TOWARD NEW MEXICAN WOMEN. *J. of the West 1973 12(2): 229-239.* Diaries and journals of the first half of the 19th century show that Anglo-Americans held the Mexican women of New Mexico in relatively high esteem, admiring them for "their physical attractiveness, alluring dress, and immorality." Yet the women of this period failed to escape the stigma of racial bias. 62 notes.
E. P. Stickney

594. Van Ness, John R. SPANISH AMERICAN VS. ANGLO AMERICAN LAND TENURE AND THE STUDY OF ECONOMIC CHANGE IN NEW MEXICO. *Social Sci. J. 1976 13(3): 45-52.* Examines the social consequences of economic change throughout the territorial period of New Mexico, 1846-91, examining basic differences in the land tenure of Spanish Americans and that of Anglo Americans for both Spanish and Mexican land grants. One of six articles in this issue on Spanish and Mexican land grants in the Southwest.

595. Weber, David J. SCARCE MORE THAN APES: HISTORICAL ROOTS OF ANGLO-AMERICAN STEREOTYPES OF MEXICANS. Weber, David J., ed. *New Spain's Far Northern Frontier: Essays on Spain in the American West, 1540-1821* (Albuquerque: U. of New Mexico Pr., 1979): 293-307. Anglo-Americans in the 19th century stereotyped Mexicans in the American Southwest as being lazy and superstitious, though Mexican women were held in higher regard than the men. Reprinted from Manuel P. Servín, ed., *An Awakened Minority: the Mexican-Americans* (Beverly Hills, Calif., 1974): 18-26.

596. Weiss, Michael. EDUCATION, LITERACY AND THE COMMUNITY OF LOS ANGELES IN 1850. *Southern California Q. 1978 60(2): 117-142.* A quantitative survey of literacy in Los Angeles in 1850. The federal census of 1850 made such an analysis possible because a question was included regarding ability to read and write in English or any other language. Statistical analyses can be made revealing literacy by ethnicity, sex, age, and other

factors. The results show that few women or Indians were literate; Caucasian males were the most literate; and literacy depended greatly on one's status, occupation, wealth, sex, and age. The American concept of public education brought to Los Angeles a much greater opportunity for learning than the pueblo had experienced in the Spanish and Mexican periods. Includes a profile of John R. Evertsen, the deputy census marshal who compiled the census. Based on the 1850 federal census and contemporary and secondary published works; 11 tables, 49 notes.   A. Hoffman

597.   Whelan, Harold A. EDEN IN JURUPA VALLEY: THE STORY OF AGUA MANSA. *Southern California Q. 1973 55(4): 413-429.* An account of the founding of the Agua Mansa community in San Bernardino Valley in 1845. Conceived by ranchers Antonio María Lugo and Juan Bandini as a buffer against hostile Indians, the community was settled by pioneers from New Mexico led by Lorenzo Trujillo. In contrast to other Alta California pueblos, Agua Mansa citizens were not taken from jails, were not gamblers and drunkards, and were known to be hard-working and law-abiding. After California became a state, Agua Mansa and adjacent settlements were formed into the town of San Salvador in San Bernardino County. Agua Mansa's existence suddenly ended in 1862 when the Santa Ana River flooded the area and destroyed the town. Primary and secondary sources; 66 notes.
                                                                          A. Hoffman

598.   White, Robert Rankin. FELIX MARTINEZ: A BORDERLANDS SUCCESS STORY. *Palacio 1981-82 87(4): 12-17.* Hispanic Felix Martinez (1857-1916), born in Taos County, New Mexico, was a mercantilist who became active in real estate and politics; he was elected on the Democratic ticket to the Territorial House of Representatives in 1888, moved to El Paso, Texas, in 1897, and became most well-known for his participation in the development of irrigation in the El Paso Valley and in New Mexico's Mesilla and Rincon valleys.

599.   Williams, James C. CULTURAL TENSION: THE ORIGINS OF AMERICAN SANTA BARBARA. *Southern California Q. 1978 60(4): 349-377.* Traces the evolution of Santa Barbara, California, from Hispanic pueblo to an American-European commercial center. At the time of statehood in 1850 Santa Barbara's population was predominantly Hispanic, its economic base agricultural, its buildings adobe, and its streets unaligned. Within a few years the pueblo dramatically changed; the cattle industry was eliminated by natural disasters in the early 1860's. The laying out of streets in a grid pattern resulted in an American-occupied business center south of *El Pueblo Viejo,* the original community, and the city exercised eminent domain over buildings located on the newly surveyed streets. A variety of businesses, brick homes, and increased immigration brought a cosmopolitan air to the community. By the 1870's the culture of Santa Barbara was transformed from its Hispanic origins to an American-oriented community, with the original *El Pueblo Viejo* section left to Spanish-speaking residents. Primary and secondary sources; 4 maps, 49 notes.   A. Hoffman

600. Wittenburg, Mary Ste. Therese. A CALIFORNIA GIRLHOOD: REMINISCENCES OF ASCENSION SEPULVEDA Y AVILA. *Southern California Q.* 1982 64(2): 133-139. Describes María Ascensión Sepúlveda y Ávila's childhood years and marriage to Thomas Mott in 1861. She descended from two of California's oldest families. Ascensión's family lived in Los Angeles and owned Rancho San Joaquin. She met Mott when she was 15; the courtship observed tradition, and the wedding climaxed a week of festivities. The marriage produced 11 children and marked the transition from a formal Spanish society into the less rigid American society. Based on unpublished memoirs and other primary and secondary sources; photos; 3 notes.
A. Hoffman

601. Yurtinus, John F. IMAGES OF EARLY CALIFORNIA: MORMON BATTALION SOLDIERS' REFLECTIONS DURING THE WAR WITH MEXICO. *Southern California Q.* 1981 63(1): 23-43. During the Mexican War, President James K. Polk called upon Mormons to help defeat Mexican forces in the Southwest. Brigham Young approved of the idea, seeing in it possibilities for establishing Mormon settlements in California at the end of the war. The Mormon Battalion arrived in California early in 1847 and saw little combat, but did interact with the Californios and Indians. Many Mormons kept diaries, and their observations reflect the views of common men as opposed to more literate observers of California life. They viewed the Indians with sympathy, distrusted the Californios, and detested the Missourians who had come to the region. Californio culture often shocked them, but the Mormons viewed Californios as individuals more often than as stereotypes. 83 notes.
A. Hoffman

1900 to 1945

602. Almaguer, Tomás. RACIAL DOMINATION AND CLASS CON-FLICT IN CAPITALIST AGRICULTURE: THE OXNARD SUGAR BEET WORKERS' STRIKE OF 1903. *Labor Hist.* 1984 25(3): 325-350. Japanese and Mexican farm workers in Oxnard, California, organized the Japanese-Mexican Labor Association (JMLA) in February 1903, after the formation of a new farm-labor contracting company by Oxnard bankers and businessmen in 1902 led to the reduction of wages for farm workers thinning the sugar beet fields and to the displacement of Japanese and Mexican farm-labor contractors. A strike in February and March 1903 succeeded in reestablishing the old wage for thinning sugar beets. The JMLA, however, failed to become a permanent labor organization, and conditions for sugar beet workers grew worse in the following years. Based on contemporary newspaper accounts and other primary sources; 62 notes.
L. F. Velicer

603. Almaráz, Félix D., Jr. CARLOS E. CASTAÑEDA'S RENDEZVOUS WITH A LIBRARY: THE LATIN AMERICAN COLLECTION, 1920-27— THE FIRST PHASE. *J. of Lib. Hist.* 1981 16(2): 315-328. Discusses the career of Carlos Eduardo Castañeda. He was born in 1896 in Mexico, and then attended school in Texas. He was regional director of President Franklin D.

Roosevelt's Committee on Fair Employment Practices, librarian of the Benson Latin American Collection at the University of Texas at Austin, and a first-rate historian of the Borderlands. This article discusses the first phase of Castañeda's involvement with the library, which began in 1920 and concluded in 1927, when he assumed responsibility for the Latin American Collection. Personal correspondence; 38 notes.   J. Powell

604.   Almaráz, Félix D., Jr. CARLOS EDUARDO CASTAÑEDA, MEXI-CAN-AMERICAN HISTORIAN: THE FORMATIVE YEARS, 1896-1927. *Pacific Hist. R. 1973 42(3): 319-334.* A biography of Carlos Eduardo Castañeda, Texas historiographer best known for *The Mexican Side of the Texas Revolution and Our Catholic Heritage in Texas, 1519-1936.* "No Mexican American historian in this century has approximated his solid publishing record of twelve books and seventy-eight articles." Born on 11 November 1896 in a small Mexican border town, Castañeda surmounted the difficulties inherent in his ethnic background, financial position, and geographic setting to establish himself as a scholar of the first rank, teacher, and librarian of the Latin American collection of the University of Texas. 42 notes.
                                                              B. L. Fenske

605.   Anders, Evan. BOSS RULE AND CONSTITUENT INTERESTS: SOUTH TEXAS POLITICS DURING THE PROGRESSIVE ERA. *Southwestern Hist. Q. 1981 84(3): 269-292.* From 1882 through 1920, Democratic machine politics prevailed in Cameron County, Texas, under boss James B. Wells. The Wells political machine was astutely sensitive to constituents' needs, particularly those of ranchers, businessmen, and Mexican Americans. After 1905, however, railroad transportation and the development of irrigation lured large numbers of Anglo Americans into the county. These newcomers did not have ties to the political machine and this new majority resented boss-rule, political manipulation, and Mexican American participation in the governmental process. As a result, insurgent influence in local politics, together with Mexican border raids in 1915 and 1916 and growing racial hatred, caused the collapse of the Wells political machine in 1920. Based on the James B. Wells papers and newspapers; 12 illus., 28 notes.   R. D. Hurt

606.   Arroyo, Luis Leobardo. CHICANO PARTICIPATION IN ORGA-NIZED LABOR: THE CIO IN LOS ANGELES 1938-1950. *Aztlán 1976 6(2): 277-313.* During 1938-50 Chicanos were active leaders in the Los Angeles Congress of Industrial Organizations locals and the CIO Council. They worked in close association with community organizations to help solve *Mexicano* problems, among them the Sleepy Lagoon incident and the Zoot Suit Riots. After 1943 Chicano unionists lost an effective voice in the CIO Council but continued to work on the local level. Based on newspapers, oral interviews and labor union proceedings; 101 notes.   R. Griswold del Castillo

607.   Barrera, Mario. CLASS SEGMENTATION AND THE POLITICAL ECONOMY OF THE CHICANO, 1900-1930. *New Scholar 1977 (6): 167-181.* A Marxian interpretation of class segments, the relationship of an individual to the means of production, and ethnic identity. Chicanos were a

subordinated class segment during 1900-30. This article is in the special issue "New Directions In Chicano Scholarship." 48 notes.   D. K. Pickens

608.   Barton, Josef J. LAND, LABOR, AND COMMUNITY IN NUECES: CZECH FARMERS AND MEXICAN LABORERS IN SOUTH TEXAS, 1880-1930. Luebke, Frederick C., ed. *Ethnicity on the Great Plains* (Lincoln: U. of Nebraska Pr., for the Center for Great Plains Studies, 1980): 190-209. Discusses the similarities and contrasts between Czech farmers and Mexican laborers, and the relationships of land and family in Nueces County, Texas, early in the 20th century. Both groups were highly transient, but each was united by bonds of common origin and kinship. Whereas Czechs were linked by generational lines, Mexicans were united by lateral ties among kinfolk. Among the Czechs landownership quickly became the mode, but Mexican tenant farmers were reduced to a migrant, landless rural proletariat. Both groups attempted to use familiar forms as they faced new and altered circumstances. Out of such confrontations emerged ethnic cultures that shaped and sustained their lives. Religion became the bond of community in both groups, as cooperative efforts were transformed into institutions and ritual associations into resources for collective action. Secondary sources; 31 notes.
                                                                        J. Powell

609.   Betten, Neil and Mohl, Raymond A. FROM DISCRIMINATION TO REPATRIATION: MEXICAN LIFE IN GARY, INDIANA, DURING THE GREAT DEPRESSION. *Pacific Hist. R. 1973 42(3): 370-388.* Relates the social, economic, and political discrimination faced by Mexican Americans in the 1920's-30's in Gary, Indiana, culminating in the forced exodus of a large segment of the Mexican population during the early 1930's. The economic tensions generated by the Depression produced a new wave of nativism throughout the United States, and were fostered by anti-ethnic sentiments expressed in the *Saturday Evening Post* aimed particularly at Mexican Americans. "Undoubtedly the Mexican's darker skin, his Catholicism, and the usual problems and vices associated with the poor affected national opinion as well." From 1931 to May 1932 repatriation was voluntary, supported by most local institutions in Gary, including US Steel Co. and the International Institute, an immigrant-oriented welfare agency. However, "after May 1932, when the township trustee's office assumed direction of repatriation, repressive measures were used to force the return of reluctant voyagers." The organized efforts in Gary against Mexicans reflected the xenophobia present throughout American society during the early 1930's. 33 notes.   B. L. Fenske

610.   Blackwelder, Julia Kirk. WOMEN IN THE WORK FORCE: AT-LANTA, NEW ORLEANS, AND SAN ANTONIO, 1930 TO 1940. *J. of Urban Hist. 1978 4(3): 331-358.* By studying women in three ethnically distinct communities (Atlanta—white, New Orleans—black, and San Antonio—Hispanic), compares the work experiences and motivations of different cultural groups of women. Matriarchy does not appear to be the main explanation for black women entering the labor force, and was actually higher among the supposedly close-knit Hispanics. 12 tables, 20 notes.
                                                                        T. W. Smith

611.   Boswell, Terry and Bush, Diane Mitsch. LABOR FORCE COMPOSI-
TION AND UNION ORGANIZING IN THE ARIZONA COPPER IN-
DUSTRY: A COMMENT ON JIMENEZ. *Review (Fernand Braudel Center)
1984 8(1): 133-151.* Comments on "The Political Formation of a Mexican
Working Class in the Arizona Copper Industry, 1870-1917," by Andrés
Jiménez, in *Review (Fernand Braudel Center)* 1981 4(3): 535-569. To attribute
to racist practices the major blame for the decline of unionism and of working-
class politics in Arizona in the late 19th and early 20th centuries is to provide
only an incomplete and sometimes invalid picture. A complete explanation of
the demise of the labor movement in Arizona during this period must include
consideration of racism, of union ideology, of differences between union
organizations, and of direct repression of the labor movement. Ref.

L. V. Eid

612.   Brown, Harold Palmer. ASSIGNMENT: VILLA RAID! *Palacio 1980
86(3): 3-14.* Photographs, with captions and a brief journal commentary
written later by news photographer Harold Palmer Brown of William Randolph Hearst's International Film Service, of the aftermath of Pancho Villa's
raid on Columbus, New Mexico, on 9 March 1916, of members of the Villa
family, and the family of President Venustiano Carranza, taken in El Paso,
Texas.

613.   Cardoso, Lawrence A. LA REPATRIACIÓN DE BRACEROS EN
ÉPOCA DE OBREGÓN: 1920-1923 [The repatriation of laborers in the
epoch of Obregón: 1920-23]. *Hist. Mexicana [Mexico] 1977 26(4): 576-595.* A
grave problem was faced by the Álvaro Obregón administration when 100,000
Mexicans lost their jobs in the United States during the depression following
World War I. The government attempted to help and to avoid a similar event
by discouraging emigration, but the events of the 1930's highlighted the failure
of these plans. Based on Obregón's presidential papers, and American and
Mexican archives; 39 notes.   S. P. Carr

614.   Chacón, Ramón D. THE CHICANO IMMIGRANT PRESS IN LOS
ANGELES: THE CASE OF "EL HERALDO DE MEXICO," 1916-1920.
Journalism Hist. 1977 4(2): 48-50, 62-64. Examines the Spanish-language press
of immigrants after the Mexican Revolution, to seek social, political, and
economic insights into their community.

615.   Ciro, Sepulveda. UNA COLONIA DE OBREROS: EAST CHICAGO,
INDIANA. *Aztlán 1976 7(2): 327-336.* A history of the colonia in the
Indiana Harbor district of East Chicago, from the first large-scale arrival of
Mexicanos (as strikebreakers) in 1919 to the mass deportations of 1932. During
the 1920's, Inland Steel Company of Indiana Harbor was the largest single
employer of Mexicanos in the United States, and the colonia grew up on Block
and Pennsylvania Avenues near the Inland Steel plant. Living conditions here
were extremely bad, while working conditions were hazardous and a worker in
the blast furnaces averaged approximately 60 hours/week. Rivalry for the best
jobs caused some friction within the colonia, but relations with non-Mexicano
neighbors were generally good. Primary (mainly press) and secondary sources;
map, 41 notes.   L. W. Van Wyk

616. Day, Mark. THE PERTINENCE OF THE "SLEEPY LAGOON" CASE. *J. of Mexican Am. Hist. 1974 4(1): 71-98.* Through the use of documents preserved by Carey McWilliams, then chairman of the Citizens Committee for the Defense of Mexican-American Youth, and others, discusses the trial and aftermath (including the eventual acquittal) of 22 Mexican-American youths in Los Angeles in 1942. The "Sleepy Lagoon" trial marked the first time in Los Angeles that organized Mexican Americans were to win a victory in the courts.   R. T. Fulton

617. De Leon, Arnoldo. BLOWOUT 1910 STYLE: A CHICANO SCHOOL BOYCOTT IN WEST TEXAS. *Texana 1974 12(2): 124-140.* In 1910 the San Angelo Board of Education prohibited the integration of Anglos and Mexicans, and the Chicanos organized in an effort to integrate the public schools. They were unsuccessful, but in 1912 the Presbyterian Church established the Mexican Presbyterian Mission School and the Chicanos pulled out of the public schools completely for several years. As time passed, they began to accept the separate school system and drifted back into public schools. Primary and secondary sources; 45 notes.   B. D. Ledbetter

618. Dinwoodie, D. H. DEPORTATION: THE IMMIGRATION SERVICE AND THE CHICANO LABOR MOVEMENT IN THE 1930S. *New Mexico Hist. Rev. 1977 52(3): 193-206.* During the 1930's, Chicanos were the object of much investigation as to whether they had entered the United States illegally. The investigations generally took place when the immigrants organized labor unions. In 1935, Julio Herrera was deported on charges that he had entered the United States illegally. The following year Jesus Pallares was deported, after subversion charges were brought against him. Actually he was deported as a result of his activities in organizing the *Liga Obrera de Habla Español*. Chicanos were encouraged to organize labor unions by the policies of the New Deal, although local authorities were opposed to these policies. 39 notes.   J. H. Krenkel

619. Durón, Clementina. MEXICAN WOMEN AND LABOR CONFLICT IN LOS ANGELES: THE ILGWU DRESSMAKERS' STRIKE OF 1933. *Aztlán 1984 15(1): 145-161.* Describes the International Ladies' Garment Workers' Union-led strike against Los Angeles garment industry employers in 1933. About 75% of the dressmakers were Mexican-American women, laboring for less than $16 a week under harsh conditions. Their grievances came to the attention of the ILGWU in 1933, although the union believed that Mexican women could not be organized. The strike lasted for 26 days. Although the strike ended inconclusively, it demonstrated the willingness of Mexican-American women to organize and offered them an opportunity to develop organizing skills. Based mainly on newspapers and secondary sources; 36 notes.   A. Hoffman

620. Gamboa, Erasmo. MEXICAN MIGRATION INTO WASHINGTON STATE: A HISTORY, 1940-1950. *Pacific Northwest Q. 1981 72(3): 121-131.* Although Mexicans had migrated to the Pacific Northwest during the 19th century, the real turning point came during World War II when the wartime labor shortage necessitated a search for farm workers living outside the region.

Agreements between the United States and Mexico launched the Bracero Program whereby Mexican workers came under contract to work in the fields. Blatant discrimination and broken contractual arrangements hounded those braceros and Chicanos who went to Washington, but many remained there after the official programs had ended and they formed the nucleus of today's Hispanic community in the Yakima Valley. Based on secondary sources and newspapers; 12 photos, 4 tables, 32 notes.   M. L. Tate

621.   Gamio, Manuel. SEÑORA FLORES DE ANDRADE. Mora, Magdalena and DelCastillo, Adelaida R., ed. *Mexican Women in the United States: Struggles Past and Present* (Los Angeles: U. of California Chicano Studies Res. Center, 1980): 189-192. Provides a personal account of the life of Flores de Andrade, a Mexican immigrant who came to El Paso, Texas, in 1906. In 1909 she founded the Daughters of Cuauhtemoc, a women's secret organization allied with the Liberal Party in opposition to the dictatorship of Porfirio Diaz in Mexico. In 1911 she was nearly executed for her activities, but escaped. Reprinted from Manuel Gamio's *The Mexican Immigrant: His Life Story* (1931).   J. Powell

622.   Gamio, Manuel; Galarza, Ernesto; and Castañeda, Carlos E. TRES ESTUDIOS ESPECIALIZADOS ACERCA DE LOS BRACEROS [Three specialized studies concerning the braceros]. *Bol. del Archivo General de la Nación [Mexico] 1980 4(4): 38-52.* Reprints three studies taken from the Manuel Avila Camacho papers in the National Archives of Mexico dealing with the US-Mexico bracero program in 1944. Illus., 2 photos.   J. A. Lewis

623.   García, Juan R. MIDWEST *MEXICANOS* IN THE 1920S: ISSUES, QUESTIONS, AND DIRECTIONS. *Social Sci. J. 1982 19(2): 89-99.* Presents a brief historical overview of Mexicanos in the Midwest during the 1920's, focusing on their entrance into the United States primarily as laborers, relations between Mexicanos and other ethnic groups, the formation of mutual aid societies that served primarily as social groups for Mexicanos, the importance of the Catholic Church, and Mexicano publications.

624.   Garcia, Mario T. AMERICANIZATION AND THE MEXICAN IMMIGRANT, 1880-1930. *J. of Ethnic Studies 1978 6(2): 19-34.* American perceptions of Mexican Americans focused on their preindustrial background which produced cultural habits and values looked upon as retarding progress and unfitted to the patterns of industrial life. Official reports perceived superior tractability, obedience, and strength, but also saw laziness, lack of time sense, drunkenness, and work irregularity. Southwest employers and reformers saw the public schools as the principal institution of Americanization; thus "education" for Mexicans meant primarily vocational and industrial training, along with heavy doses of American notions of sanitation, ethics, and English. Cultural and racial "clash" has not been eliminated, however, for the movement of Mexicans to the United States has never ceased. Primary and secondary writings; 47 notes.   G. J. Bobango

625.   Garcia, Mario T. AMERICANS ALL: THE MEXICAN AMERICAN GENERATION AND THE POLITICS OF WARTIME LOS ANGELES,

1941-45. *Social Sci. Q. 1984 65(2): 278-289.* Examines the rise of Mexican-American political generational leadership in Los Angeles during World War II. The war coincided with the coming of political age of what is termed the Mexican-American Generation. Representing for the most part first generation American-born Mexicans, the Mexican-American Generation stressed integration into American life and pursued the politics of reform in the hope of accomplishing their goals. The war aided this reform movement through the stress on the equality and unity of all Americans. In Los Angeles, the Coordinating Council for Latin-American Youth symbolized this new breed of Americanized Mexican Americans.   J

626. Garcia, Mario T. THE CHICANA IN AMERICAN HISTORY: THE MEXICAN WOMEN OF EL PASO, 1880-1920: A CASE STUDY. *Pacific Hist. Rev. 1980 49(2): 315-337.* Mexican women accompanied their husbands who immigrated into the western United States to work, and the nuclear family prevailed among Chicanos. At El Paso, Texas, Mexican wives did not work outside the home. Because of poverty and exploitation and neglect by landlords and city officials, Mexicans lived in overcrowded and unsanitary conditions. Mexican wives guarded Mexican cultural traditions in the family, thereby retarding American assimilation. Unmarried women who worked outside the home were employed mostly as servants and laundresses, although some were production workers. Their wages were lower than non-Mexican Americans', and Mexican women were involved in major labor strikes in the Southwest. Based on census reports, US Senate documents, contemporary newspapers, and secondary sources; 47 notes.   R. N. Lokken

627. García, Mario T. MEXICAN AMERICANS AND THE POLITICS OF CITIZENSHIP: THE CASE OF EL PASO, 1936. *New Mexico Hist. Rev. 1984 59(2): 187-204.* When El Paso, Texas, city registrar Alex K. Powell and health officer Dr. T. J. McCammont reclassified Mexican Americans as "colored," rather than "white," storms of protest followed. Cleofas Calleros, head of La Federación de Sociedades Latinos-Americanos, Texas congressman Maury Maverick, and others successfully fought to have the ruling rescinded. Photo, 43 notes.   K. E. Gilmont

628. Garcia, Mario T. ON MEXICAN IMMIGRATION, THE UNITED STATES, AND CHICANO HISTORY. *J. of Ethnic Studies 1979 7(1): 80-88.* Review essay of Mark Reisler's *By the Sweat of Their Brow: Mexican Immigrant Labor in the United States, 1900-1940* (Greenwood Pr., 1976).

629. García, Mario T. RACIAL DUALISM IN THE EL PASO LABOR MARKET, 1880-1920. *Aztlán 1976 6(2): 197-217.* Mexicans in El Paso suffered from structural discrimination. They received less pay for the same work as Anglos and did not have opportunities for advancement. Most Mexicans tolerated their subordinate economic position, believing they would soon return to Mexico. Some Mexican *obreros* engaged in strikes and labor organization. Based on US census documents, newspapers, and secondary sources; 61 notes.   R. Griswold del Castillo

630. Garcia, Richard A. CLASS, CONSCIOUSNESS, AND IDEOLOGY: THE MEXICAN COMMUNITY OF SAN ANTONIO, TEXAS: 1930-1940. *Aztlán 1978 9: 23-70.* Analyzes the Mexican-American community of San Antonio, Texas, in a period of turmoil and change, emphasizing ideology and causes. The rise of class differentiation within the Mexican community, of cultural and class consciousness within the different classes, and of corresponding ideologies within each of these classes, and the social and political activities of each class, receive particular attention. Primary sources; 125 notes, biblio.
R. V. Ritter

631. Gonzales, Gilbert C. EDUCATIONAL REFORM AND THE MEXICAN COMMUNITY IN LOS ANGELES. *Southwest Econ. and Soc. 1978 3(3): 24-51.* Examines the curricula of the Los Angeles public schools as it served and affected the Mexican Americans in the community during the 1920's-30's.

632. Gonzalez, Gilbert G. RACISM, EDUCATION AND THE MEXICAN COMMUNITY IN LOS ANGELES, 1920-30. *Societas 1974 4(4): 287-301.* Between 1922 and 1932 published studies of Mexican-American children strongly influenced the education offered them in Los Angeles. On the basis of I.Q. tests and projection of career goals, many Mexican Americans were placed in vocational training for menial jobs or slow-learner tracks.
W. H. Mulligan, Jr.

633. Gonzalez, Gilbert G. SEGREGATION OF MEXICAN CHILDREN IN A SOUTHERN CALIFORNIA CITY: THE LEGACY OF EXPANSIONISM AND THE AMERICAN SOUTHWEST. *Western Historical Quarterly 1985 16(1): 55-76.* Children born in Mexico or in the United States of Mexican parentage were subjected to segregation. The history of its development, maintenance, and dismantling in the Santa Ana, California, public schools is revealed in the records of the city's Board of Education. It was a product of the social and political relations between the Mexican and Anglo communities that developed out of the 19th-century American belief in a manifest destiny. Recent US foreign policy and the Cold War highlighted discrimination in the country and helped reform and democratize minority-nonminority relations. The termination of *de jure* segregation in Santa Ana schools was a consequence of this reform. 70 notes.
D. L. Smith

634. Griswold del Castillo, Richard. THE MEXICAN REVOLUTION AND THE SPANISH-LANGUAGE PRESS IN THE BORDERLANDS. *Journalism Hist. 1977 4(2): 42-47.* Discusses the work of Chicano editors in interpreting the Mexican Revolution and in strengthening the sense of identification with Mexico among US Spanish-speakers in the United States, 1911-17.

635. Gutiérrez, Armando. HISPANICS AND THE SUNBELT. *Dissent 1980 27(4): 492-499.* Provides a history of Mexican Americans, focusing on their rising political power in the Southwest; identifies issues that have captured the attention of Chicanos over the last two decades, such as increased educational and occupational opportunities.

636. Guzmán, Ralph. LA REPATRIACIÓN FORZOSA COMO SOLU-CIÓN POLÍTICA CONCLUYENTE AL PROBLEMA DE LA IMMIGRA-CIÓN ILEGAL: UNA PERSPECTIVA HISTÓRICA [Forced repatriation as the final political solution to illegal immigration: an historical perspective]. *Foro Int. [Mexico] 1978 18(3): 494-513.* Surveys forced repatriation of illegal Mexican laborers by the United States during ca. 1929-56. Based on interviews and on primary and secondary printed sources; fig., 40 notes.   D. A. Franz

637. Harper, James W. THE EL PASO-JUÁREZ CONFERENCE OF 1916. *Arizona and the West 1978 20(3): 231-244.* Pancho Villa violated American territory and took American lives on his raid on Columbus, New Mexico, 9 March 1916. General John J. Pershing was sent into Mexico several days later to capture Villa. Public opinion on both sides of the border polarized and seriously restricted the diplomatic flexibility of both governments. The May 1916 El Paso-Juárez Conference failed to resolve the questions raised by the intrusions, but it temporarily reduced border tension and gave the United States precious time to deal with a crisis that had developed with Germany over submarine warfare. 4 illus., 36 notes.   D. L. Smith

638. Harris, Charles H., III and Sadler, Louis R. THE PLAN OF SAN DIEGO AND THE MEXICAN-UNITED STATES WAR CRISIS OF 1916: A REEXAMINATION. *Hispanic Am. Hist. Rev. 1978 58(3): 381-408.* The Plan of San Diego called for a Mexican-American rebellion and the establishment of an independent republic in the Southwest. Guerrilla raids on Anglos in south Texas followed, February 1915-July 1916. These were fomented by Mexican leader Venustiano Carranza (1859-1920) in a move first to force US recognition of his government and later to force the removal of US troops which had pursued raiders into Mexico. There is no solid evidence of German involvement in the plan. The plan resulted in a legacy of racial tension in south Texas. 100 notes.   B. D. Johnson

639. Harris, Charles H., III and Sadler, Louis R. THE 1911 REYES CONSPIRACY: THE TEXAS SIDE. *Southwestern Hist. Q. 1980 83(4): 325-348.* Views the Mexican Revolution from a Texan perspective. General Bernardo Reyes tried to overthrow Mexican President Francisco I. Madero in 1911 with support from Mexican American politicians in Texas, and the benevolent neutrality of state officials. But when the plot fell apart under pressure from the US government, Texas Governor Oscar B. Colquitt claimed credit. Reyes's associates, Amador Sanchez and Francisco A. Chapa, were defended by leading Texas lawyers and received light sentences and friendly treatment from federal judge Waller T. Burns. Primary sources; 78 notes.   J. H. Broussard

640. Henderson, Peter B. N. MEXICAN REBELS IN THE BORDER-LANDS, 1910-1912. *Red River Valley Hist. R. 1975 2(2): 207-220.* Discusses the activity of Francisco Madero and Bernardo Reyes in organizing political exiles from Mexico in Texas to overthrow the government of Porfirio Diaz.

641. Hendrick, Irving G. EARLY SCHOOLING FOR CHILDREN OF MIGRANT FARMWORKERS IN CALIFORNIA: THE 1920'S. *Aztlán*

1977 8: 11-26. As State Superintendent of Schools, Georgiana Carden worked diligently to enforce legislation funding mandatory elementary education for the children of Mexican-American farmworkers in order to encourage assimilation and guarantee equality of education in California.

642. Hernández Rodríguez, Rogelio. EL PROBLEMA DE LOS BRACE-ROS EN EL PERÍODO DE 1942 A 1946 [The Bracero problem from 1942 to 1946]. *Bol. del Archivo General de la Nacion [Mexico] 1980 4(4): 3-4.* There were two types of Mexican immigration into the United States during the war years of 1942-46, the traditional illegal immigration and that under the bracero program. The latter evolved from official agreements reached between the governments of the United States and Mexico. Note.   J. A. Lewis

643. Hewitt, William L. MEXICAN WORKERS IN WYOMING DURING WORLD WAR II: NECESSITY, DISCRIMINATION AND PROTEST. *Ann. of Wyoming 1982 54(2): 20-33.* World War II created labor problems in the Wyoming sugar beet fields as potential laborers marched off to military service. Farm owners solicited workers among high school students, Japanese Americans from relocation camps, and migratory harvesters from other states, but the numbers remained insufficient. Mexican Americans and Mexican nationals answered the call in 1942, but were confronted with blatant racism and a wage scale lower than that of whites. Despite their stereotype of docility, these people fought against the injustice through legal channels. Hispanic railroad workers especially achieved a level of success in the Fair Employment Practices Committee by challenging union discrimination. Based on Wyoming newspapers and manuscripts in the Western History Research Center at the University of Wyoming; illus., 8 photos, map, 70 notes.
M. L. Tate

644. Hoffman, Abraham. EL CIERRE DE LA PUERTA TRASERA NOR-TEAMERICANA: RESTRECCIÓN DE LA INMIGRACIÓN MEXICANA [The closure of the North American back door: restriction of Mexican immigration]. *Hist. Mexicana [Mexico] 1976 25(3): 302-422.* On the eve of the Depression various groups sought to reduce immigration into the United States. Racists, some unions, and small-scale agriculturalists wished to reduce Mexican immigration, while larger-scale agricultural and industrial concerns needing labor were less hostile. The 1924 Immigration Bill was vigorously enforced and the State Department advised consulates to restrict the issuance of visas; by September 1929 a 30% reduction in visas granted had occurred. Based on State department documents, the press, and memoirs; 39 notes.
S. P. Carr

645. Hoffman, Abraham. THE EL MONTE BERRY PICKERS' STRIKE, 1933: INTERNATIONAL INVOLVEMENT IN A LOCAL LABOR DISPUTE. *J. of the West 1973 12(1): 71-84.* A detailed account of the 1933 berry pickers' strike in El Monte, California, which involved "Mexican laborers, Communist agitators, Japanese employers, Los Angeles Chamber of Commerce and business representatives, and state and federal mediators. .. over issues of wages, hours, and working conditions... . The El Monte strike, however, claimed the distinction of direct involvement by the government of Mexico, in

the form of diplomatic pressure, monetary assistance, and consular interven- tion.... In contrast to the active assistance of the Mexican consuls, the Japanese consul maintained a low profile, probably because of his awareness that excessive publicity would raise questions about Japanese leasing of property in a state that had already endorsed two alien land laws." 44 notes.

D. D. Cameron

646. Hoffman, Abraham. A NOTE ON THE FIELD RESEARCH INTER- VIEWS OF PAUL S. TAYLOR. *Pacific Historian 1976 20(2): 123-131.* During 1927-30 Dr. Paul S. Taylor interviewed more than 1,000 people for the publication, *Mexican Labor in the United States.* Reports on the results of the National Endowment for the Humanities grant which funded the reorganiza- tion and editing of interviews. Based on primary sources; 8 notes.

G. L. Olson

647. Hoffman, Abraham. STIMULUS TO REPATRIATION: THE 1931 FEDERAL DEPORTATION DRIVE AND THE LOS ANGELES MEXI- CAN COMMUNITY. *Pacific Hist. R. 1973 42(2): 205-219.* Studies the main thrust of Secretary of Labor James J. Davis' promise to reduce unemployment at the height of the depression—ousting aliens holding jobs, concentrating on illegal aliens, and curtailing legal entries. Although the campaign did not single out any one ethnic group, Mexicans were most affected. Of these most lived in Southern California, specifically in Los Angeles County. Analyzes the series of developments resulting from the activities of the federal agents which led to a mass exodus of 50,000 to 75,000 people. The fear tactics used by the federal agents had been designed to bring about that deportation and emigration. 43 notes.

R. V. Ritter

648. Jensen, Joan M. "DISFRANCHISEMENT IS A DISGRACE": WOM- EN AND POLITICS IN NEW MEXICO, 1900-1940. *New Mexico Hist. Rev. 1981 56(1): 5-35.* Discusses the movement in New Mexico between 1900 and 1940 for women's political rights and its effect on the state's political history. New Mexico women achieved suffrage later than those in other western states because of insufficient organizational support, a limiting constitutional compro- mise, and opposition from some of the state's congressional representatives. After achieving suffrage in 1920 there was a dramatic increase in political participation by both Anglo and Hispanic women as well as strong mobiliza- tion efforts by the major parties to gain the support of the female voters. Based on the National Woman's Party Papers and the National American Woman's Suffrage Association Papers at the Library of Congress and other primary sources; illus., photo, 3 tables, fig., 49 notes.

P. L. McLaughlin

649. Jensen, Joan M. WOMEN TEACHERS, CLASS, AND ETHNICITY: NEW MEXICO, 1900-1950. *Southwest Econ. and Soc. 1978-79 4(2): 3-13.* Discusses research on the effect of women teachers on perpetuating class and ethnic stratification in New Mexico schools during 1900-50.

650. Kerr, Louise A. CHICANO SETTLEMENTS IN CHICAGO: A BRIEF HISTORY. *J. of Ethnic Studies 1975 2(4): 22-32.* Describes the adaptation to and participation in political, economic, and social life of

Chicago Chicanos in their three major neighborhoods: the Near West Side, Back of the Yards, and South Chicago. Distinctive neighborhood patterns "have at least partially determined the variable development of Chicano identity." The greatest obstacle to the progress has been lack of Chicano unity, especially in the face of the most significant recent problem, large-scale Puerto Rican immigration. This, combined with the antagonisms of Poles and Italians, and domination of housing by the Irish, produced varying degrees of development, parallel but different, in Chicano gains in employment, housing, social organization, interethnic relationships, and parish organization. By the 1960's the growing Black and other "Latino" populations, the closing of the stockyards, and urban renewal produced major internal changes in two of the neighborhoods. Worsened social conditions along with a new dynamism continue to coexist. Primary and secondary sources; 38 notes.

G. J. Bobango

651.   Kiser, George and Silverman, David. MEXICAN REPATRIATION DURING THE GREAT DEPRESSION. *J. of Mexican Am. Hist. 1973 3(1): 139-164.* Presents background to the repatriation of US resident Mexicans during the Great Depression. Discusses interests supporting and opposing repatriation in Mexico and the United States, and the role of the Hoover administration. Describes the departure of Mexicans from Los Angeles and Detroit, and the fate of the repatriates. Primary and secondary sources; 85 notes.   R. T. Fulton

652.   Lamb, Blaine P. THE CONVENIENT VILLAIN: THE EARLY CINEMATIC VIEWS OF THE MEXICAN AMERICAN. *J. of the West 1975 14(4): 75-81.* Discusses racial stereotypes attached to Mexican Americans in American films, 1897-1917. 81 notes.

653.   Leon, Arnoldo de. *LOS TASINQUES* AND THE SHEEP SHEARERS' UNION OF NORTH AMERICA: A STRIKE IN WEST TEXAS, 1934. *West Texas Hist. Assoc. Year Book 1979 55: 3-16.* Chronicles the attempted unionization and unsuccessful strike of Mexican *tasinques* (sheep shearers), and the numerous racial, economic, and political factors which doomed their cause.

654.   Limón, José E. EL PRIMER CONGRESO MEXICANISTA DE 1911: A PRECURSOR TO CONTEMPORARY CHICANOISM. *Aztlán 1974 5(1/2): 85-117.* Reviews the activities of the 14-22 September 1911 El Primer Congreso Mexicanista in Laredo, Texas, as a precursor to present Mexican American political activity.   S

655.   Longoria, Mario D. REVOLUTION, VISIONARY PLAN, AND MARKETPLACE: A SAN ANTONIO INCIDENT. *Aztlán 1981 12(2): 211-226.* Describes the Plan de San Diego, a diversionary part of the Huerta-Orozco scheme to regain control of Mexico in 1915, and the incident that took place in San Antonio, Texas, on 30 August 1915. The Plan de San Diego was an irrendentist scheme to recapture the Mexican soil lost to the United States in the Mexican War. Germany promised assistance, believing that the plan would create enough confusion to distract the United States from the European

war. News of the plan did create considerable agitation along the border, and acts of violence were committed. In San Antonio, 1,000 Mexicans gathered in the marketplace to hear revolutionary rhetoric. Federal authorities arrested 26 men. Orozco's death put an end to the scheme, but the incident was noteworthy because of the possible support Mexicans of South Texas might have given to the Plan de San Diego. Appendix, 43 notes.   A. Hoffman

656.   Lopez, Larry S., ed. SAMPLE PARTIDO CONTRACTS. *New Mexico Hist. Rev. 1977 52(2): 111-116.* Partido contracts provided that work with livestock would be paid for in wool, sheep or cattle. The contracts were short and simple when both parties were Hispanic. When one party was Anglo, the contracts were long and detailed. Provides samples of three contracts. 8 notes.
                                                              J. H. Krenkel

657.   Madrid-Barela, Arturo. POCHOS: THE DIFFERENT AMERICANS, AN INTERPRETIVE ESSAY, PART I. *Aztlán 1976 7(1): 51-64.* Using examples from literature, discusses the traumas of the *Pochos,* Mexican Americans of the Southwest who were rejected by their counterparts, the Chicanos, for attempting to integrate and acculturate into the broader society. At the same time, they were spurned by Anglos, who used "Mexican" almost as an obscenity, 1910's-40's. 16 notes. To be continued.   J. Tull

658.   McBride, James D. THE LIGA PROTECTORA LATINA: A MEXICAN AMERICAN BENEVOLENT SOCIETY IN ARIZONA. *J. of the West 1975 14(4): 82-90.* Discusses the establishment in 1914 of the Liga Protectora Latina, and the work done by this benevolent organization to help Mexican Americans until its demise in 1940. 35 notes.

659.   McCain, Johnny M. TEXAS AND THE MEXICAN LABOR QUESTION, 1942-1947. *Southwestern Hist. Q. 1981 85(1): 45-64.* Since 1920, the annual trek of Mexican workers into the US southwest has caused one of the most persistent and perplexing problems in relations between Mexico and the United States because of the low wages and discrimination against workers. During World War II, Mexico attempted to prohibit its migrant labor force from entering Texas. Mexican policy failed, however, because Texas could not guarantee an end to discrimination, and because migrant workers entered the state illegally. Mexico made no attempt to stop that migration, preferring to have its surplus labor force working while avoiding the responsibility of rectifying discrimination complaints which the illegal migrants levied against Texans. Labor records in the National Archives, newspapers, and secondary sources; 44 notes.   R. D. Hurt

660.   Medeiros, Francine. LA OPINIÓN, A MEXICAN EXILE NEWSPAPER: A CONTENT ANALYSIS OF ITS FIRST YEARS, 1926-1929. *Aztlán 1980 11(1): 65-87.* Analyzes the editorial and news content of the Los Angeles *La Opinión.* Founded in 1926 by Ignacio Lozano as a west coast version of his San Antonio *La Prensa, La Opinión* soon attained financial success and an audience beyond the area of southern California. The editorial perspective of the paper presented several anomalies. Although published in the United States it represented in many ways a Mexican paper in exile, much more concerned

with social, political, and economic problems in Mexico than with concerns of Mexicans in the United States. While urging Mexicans to stand fast against Anglo stereotyping by working hard and excelling in education, it also endorsed repatriation to Mexico as a long-range goal for its readers. Yet its antiassimilationist tone contrasted with its continuing success as a vehicle of information for Mexicans living in the United States. Further research into the editorial development of the paper in succeeding years is needed. 3 tables, chart, 35 notes.   A. Hoffman

661.   Meyer, Doris. FELIPE MAXIMILIANO CHACÓN: A FORGOT-TEN MEXICAN-AMERICAN AUTHOR. *New Scholar 1977 (6): 111-126.* Felipe Maximiliano Chacón was an editor of Spanish newspapers in early 20th-century New Mexico. Analyzes and gives examples of his prose and poetry. Although undistinguished in their literary style, Chacón's writings are significant recreational reading for the masses and have a significant place in Chicano literature. This article is in the special issue, "New Directions In Chicano Scholarship." 9 notes.   D. K. Pickens

662.   Mohl, Raymond A. *THE SATURDAY EVENING POST* AND THE "MEXICAN INVASION." *J. of Mexican Am. Hist. 1973 3(1): 131-138.* World War I and the immigration laws of the 1920's severely restricted the flow of Europeans to the United States, but served to quicken the influx from countries such as Mexico, which were unaffected by the war and the quota system. The American press such as the *Post* and other periodicals, reflecting the intolerance and nativism of the decade, consistently portrayed Mexican immigrants as less desirable than European immigrants. 12 notes.
R. T. Fulton

663.   Monroy, Douglas. AN ESSAY ON UNDERSTANDING THE WORK EXPERIENCE OF MEXICANS IN SOUTHERN CALIFORNIA, 1900-1939. *Aztlán 1981 12(1): 59-74.* During 1900-39 Mexicans were relegated to a secondary low wage sector of the labor force. With social mobility limited, job advancement over seasonal agricultural employment was found not only in skilled work but in jobs that offered a measure of stability. Such employment, however, came at the price of disruption of Mexican families through work schedules, exposure to American customs, and generational conflicts. But the challenges of American urban life also brought Mexican participation in labor unions and the benefits gained through union activities. Theses and dissertations, contemporary and secondary published studies; 24 notes.   A. Hoffman

664.   Monroy, Douglas. LA COSTURA EN LOS ANGELES, 1933-1939: THE ILGWU AND THE POLITICS OF DOMINATION. Mora, Magdalena and DelCastillo, Adelaida R., ed. *Mexican Women in the United States: Struggles Past and Present* (Los Angeles: U. of California Chicano Studies Res. Center, 1980): 171-178. Describes the situation which Mexicanas in Los Angeles confronted in la costura during the Depression, the enthusiastic union organization drives, and the ideology and political philosophy of the International Ladies' Garment Workers' Union as related to the Mexicana rank and file. From this can be seen some negative effects of successful union organizing.

Often another layer of authority, the union leadership, rarely Mexicano or female, burdened Mexicanas. In this case, while making crucial gains in wages and hours, the union did not significantly increase the power and control which rank and file women exercised over their work. Secondary sources; 33 notes. J. Powell

665. Monroy, Douglas. LIKE SWALLOWS AT THE OLD MISSION: MEXICANS AND THE RADICAL POLITICS OF GROWTH IN LOS ANGELES IN THE INTERWAR PERIOD. *Western Hist. Q. 1983 14(4): 435-458.* Examines the business class's view of Mexican Americans in Los Angeles County, California, and their role during the interwar period. The first concern of the local elites was to manipulate the Mexican Americans to fill their labor needs. The seasonality, low wages, and substandard working conditions that prevailed in the competitive and service industries necessitated an exploitable supply of labor. The racially fragmented labor force hindered union organization. Table, 50 notes. D. L. Smith

666. Nelson-Cisneros, Victor B. LA CLASE TRABAJADORA EN TEJAS, 1920-1940 [The working class in Texas, 1920-1940]. *Aztlán 1976 6(2): 239-265.* In Texas Mexican Americans were relegated to the lowest-paid jobs and worked in subhuman conditions. They were unable to organize stable agricultural or industrial unions due to the geographic mobility of membership, failures of leadership, poverty, and the AFL's racist policies. Some short-lived, successful Chicano unions engaged in strikes, among them the Associación de journaleros, U.C.A.P.A.W.A., and the Pecan Shelling Workers of San Antonio. Based on interviews and secondary sources; 125 notes.
R. Griswold del Castillo

667. Nelson-Cisneros, Victor B. UCAPAWA AND CHICANOS IN CALIFORNIA: THE FARM WORKER PERIOD, 1937-1940. *Aztlán 1976 7(3): 453-477.* The United Cannery, Agricultural, Packing and Allied Workers of America (UCAPAWA), began as primarily a farm workers' union before it became mainly concerned with food processing.

668. Nelson-Cisneros, Victor B. UCAPAWA ORGANIZING ACTIVITIES IN TEXAS, 1935-50. *Aztlán 1978 9: 71-84.* A study of the activities of the United Cannery, Agricultural, Packing and Allied Workers of America, which changed its name in 1944 to Food, Tobacco, Agricultural and Allied Workers Union of America (FTA), to include the tobacco workers, as it sought to organize Mexican Americans in Texas, 1937-50. Agricultural and packing shed workers on the one hand, and grain and cotton process workers on the other, are considered. The unions lost influence and membership for reasons which included possible communist infiltration and the deportation of Mexican citizens. Based on primary sources, viz., the union newspaper, labor archives at the University of Texas, Arlington, and other sources. 52 notes.
R. V. Ritter

669. Pace, Anne. MEXICAN REFUGEES IN ARIZONA, 1910-1911. *Arizona and the West 1974 16(1): 5-18.* Hundreds of Mexican citizens, mostly from the state of Sonora, crossed the border into Arizona in 1910-11. Some

were belligerents seeking political asylum while they secured arms and support for the aid of Francisco Madero; some were middle- and upper-class refugees from the war who feared for their financial and physical safety; some were peasants who fled conscription and wanted employment; and some were followers of Porfirio Diaz who fled as the Maderistas triumphed. There were similar activities in Texas, New Mexico, and California. This helps to explain why the revolution broke out and had its initial successes in northern Mexico. 8 illus., 35 notes.   D. L. Smith

670.   Pintó, Alfonso. WHEN HOLLYWOOD SPOKE SPANISH. *Américas 1980 32(10): 3-8.* Discusses Hollywood's Spanish-language films made during the 1930's for Spanish and Latin American audiences; mentions Mexican, Latin American, Portuguese, and Spanish stars who appeared in them.

671.   Redwine, Augustin. LOVELL'S MEXICAN COLONY. *Ann. of Wyoming 1979 51(2): 26-35.* Lovell, Wyoming, experienced a boom in sugar beet production by 1916. Its chief employer, Great Western Sugar Company, searched far and wide for field hands to raise and harvest the beets. The company recruiters found a willing work force among Mexican Americans and Mexican nationals in the western states. The company provided some small housing and oversaw a colony of workers with strict paternalism. Despite discrimination toward the workers, the colony persisted until its demolition in 1954. Based on interviews and published sources; 3 photos, 41 notes.
                                                                         M. L. Tate

672.   Reisler, Mark. ALWAYS THE LABORER, NEVER THE CITIZEN: ANGLO PERCEPTIONS OF THE MEXICAN IMMIGRANT DURING THE 1920S. *Pacific Hist. Rev. 1976 45(2): 231-254.* A systematic study of how Americans viewed Mexican workers in the 1920's. Popular perceptions were translated into public policy, and pressure groups were able to influence federal action on the Mexican immigration issue. Two themes were stressed: "the Mexican's Indian blood would pollute the nation's genetic purity, and his biologically determined degenerate character traits would sap the country's moral fiber and corrupt its institutions." He might be a good laborer, but he could never become a potential citizen. 86 notes.   R. V. Ritter

673.   Reisler, Mark. THE MEXICAN IMMIGRANT IN THE CHICAGO AREA DURING THE 1920'S. *J. of the Illinois State Hist. Soc. 1973 66(2): 144-158.* Mexican immigrants replaced European labor in Chicago as European immigration was restricted after World War I and more single young Mexicans worked their way to Chicago. Illinois had more Mexican immigrants than any state except Texas, California, and Arizona. They worked as track maintenance hands for the railroads and competed with southern blacks as strikebreakers in the steel mills and packinghouses which paid more than the railroads. Mexican labor was played off against workers of other nationalities to prevent the organization of labor unions. Shifting employment patterns, poor health and housing, plus limited English slowed improved conditions for Mexican labor. Most Mexicans hoped to return to Mexico. Based on government reports, social service periodicals, and monographs; 4 illus., 52 notes.
                                                                      A. C. Aimone

674. Richmond, Douglas W. MEXICAN IMMIGRATION AND BORDER STRATEGY DURING THE REVOLUTION, 1910-1920. *New Mexico Hist. Rev. 1982 57(3): 269-288.* Following the defeat of rivals, Venustiano Carranza attempted to solve Mexico's border difficulties with the United States. Negotiating with President Woodrow Wilson and New Mexico and Arizona territorial governments, Carranza sought to alleviate poor working conditions, living arrangements, and American business interests in northern Mexico and among border towns in the United States. Despite rival groups within Mexico and American immigration policies, his open policies had antagonized Americans and reflected his strong support for Mexicans living on both sides of the border. 4 photos, 57 notes.   K. E. Gilmont

675. Romo, Ricardo. RESPONSES TO MEXICAN IMMIGRATION 1910-1930. *Aztlán 1976 6(2): 173-194.* Mexican immigrants to the United States have, since the 1880's, played an important role in developing the economy of the Southwest and Midwest. Without Mexican-American labor, high profits, enabling the expansion of industry, would have been impossible. The Mexican revolution, World War I, and agribusiness recruitment generated a massive movement from Mexico to the United States. Organized labor and restrictionalists opposed this immigration. Based on oral interviews, newspapers, and secondary sources; 91 notes.   R. Griswold del Castillo

676. Romo, Ricardo. WORK AND RESTLESSNESS: OCCUPATIONAL AND SPATIAL MOBILITY AMONG MEXICANOS IN LOS ANGELES, 1918-1928. *Pacific Hist. Rev. 1977 46(2): 157-180.* This quantitative study of Los Angeles Mexicanos during 1918-28 reveals a lower rate of upward occupational mobility and a higher rate of geographical mobility than found by historians of other groups in Los Angeles and other cities. Mexicanos worked primarily in transportation, manufacturing, and agriculture. Low wages, a high cost of living, discrimination, and excessive competition for jobs explain the high geographical mobility. Even second- and third-generation Mexicanos experienced little upward mobility. Based on Los Angeles marriage records and city directories, and on published primary sources; 7 tables, 54 notes.   W. K. Hobson

677. Rosales, Francisco A. and Simon, Daniel T. CHICANO STEEL WORKERS AND UNIONISM IN THE MIDWEST, 1919-1945. *Aztlán 1976 6(2): 267-275.* Chicano and Mexican workers comprised a large portion of the labor force in Chicago (Illinois), Gary (Indiana), and East Chicago (Indiana). Racial discrimination motivated them to actively participate in labor union organization. They played prominent roles in major strikes in the steel industry during the 1930's. Based on newspapers and secondary sources; 27 notes.   R. Griswold del Castillo

678. Rosales, Francisco Arturo. THE REGIONAL ORIGINS OF MEXICANO IMMIGRANTS TO CHICAGO DURING THE 1920'S. *Aztlán 1976 7(2): 187-201.* Of the Mexicano immigrants to the colonias of South Chicago and East Chicago during the 1920's, 68% came from the bajio region in west central Mexico. Their precursors had followed the railroads, for which many of them worked, to the Midwest, and were followed by thousands of immigrants

during the revolution, in 1915. The inhabitants of the bajio were less affected by the injustices and hardships that sparked the revolution than by those it occasioned, and hence were less often moved to join it, more often to flee from it, than other Mexicanos. Many of the immigrants were recruited by US steel manufacturers. Many, too, were Catholic militants in exile. Secondary sources; 2 tables, 41 notes.   L. W. Van Wyk

679.   Ruybalid, M. Keith. MISSION SCHOOL IN THE HOMELAND. *Adventist Heritage 1979 6(1): 41-49.* Discusses the founding of the Spanish-American Seminary near Sandoval, New Mexico, which opened in 1942, from 1928 when the Adventist General Conference Committee agreed to address the needs of Spanish-American children's education in the Southwest, until 1953.

680.   San Miguel, Guadalupe, Jr. THE STRUGGLE AGAINST SEPA-RATE AND UNEQUAL SCHOOLS: MIDDLE CLASS MEXICAN AMER-ICANS AND THE DESEGREGATION CAMPAIGN IN TEXAS, 1929-1957. *Hist. of Educ. Q. 1983 23(3): 343-359.* Educational discrimination against Mexican Americans in Texas was challenged primarily by the ideologically liberal League of United Latin American Citizens and the G.I. Forum. Both organizations were dominated by middle-class Mexican Americans. These organizations established the illegality of discrimination against Mexican-American pupils, encouraged the Mexican community to take advantage of public schools, and maintained the spirit of resistance to discrimination. The liberal political outlook of these organizations, however, prevented them from examining the sources of social inequality and from developing "revolutionary strategies" to eliminate them. Based on the records of the League of Latin American Citizens and the G.I. Forum, and on letters and interviews; 73 notes.
                                                                                J. T. Holton

681.   Shankman, Arnold. THE IMAGE OF MEXICO AND THE MEXI-CAN-AMERICAN IN THE BLACK PRESS, 1890-1935. *J. of Ethnic Studies 1975 3(2): 43-56.* Finds little evidence of a "Third World" brotherhood between black and Mexican Americans in the first third of this century. blacks were angered by certain antiblack actions of the Mexican government, by the economic competition from Mexican labor, and by the ability of Mexicans to stand on the white side of the color line. The failure of various black migration schemes to Mexico and religious conflict also contributed to a feeling of hostility. Based on primary and secondary sources; 56 notes.   T. W. Smith

682.   Sheridan, Thomas E. FROM LUISA ESPINEL TO LALO GUERRE-RO: TUCSON'S MEXICAN MUSICIANS BEFORE WORLD WAR II. *Journal of Arizona History 1984 25(3): 285-300.* Describes the careers of Mexican-American musical entertainers from Tucson who have achieved international fame. Among them were Luisa Espinel, Julia Rebeil, Manuel Montijo, Jr., and Lalo Guerrero. Based on Arizona Historical Society archives; 12 photos, 21 notes.   G. O. Gagnon

683.   Sifuentes, Roberto. APROXIMACIONES AL "CORRIDO DE LOS HERMANOS HERNANDEZ EJECUTADOS EN LA CAMARA DE GAS DE LA PENITENCIARIA DE FLORENCE, ARIZONA EL DIA 6 DE

JULIO DE 1934" [Approaches to the "Corrido de los Hermanos Hernández Ejecutados en la Cámara de Gas de la Penitenciaría de Florence, Arizona, el día 6 de Julio de 1934"]. *Aztlán 1982 13(1-2): 95-109.* Analyzes the content of the ballad of the Hernández brothers by Epifanio Alonso, based on a true incident. Federico and Manuel Hernández were convicted of murdering an old miner in the Arizona desert in 1934. Originally sentenced to die by hanging, the brothers were chosen to be the first to test the state's new gas chamber. The ballad places the Hernández brothers and the state of Arizona in opposition, symbolizing the conflict between the Mexican minority in the United States and Anglo dominance of that minority. Ballad text and secondary sources; 3 notes. A. Hoffman

684. Simon, Daniel T. MEXICAN REPATRIATION IN EAST CHICAGO, INDIANA. *J. of Ethnic Studies 1974 2(2): 11-23.* By the late 1920's East Chicago, Indiana, had a 10% Mexican minority, and Inland Steel in that city was "the largest single employer of Mexican labor" in the United States. White residents resented the Mexicans, who occupied the lowest socioeconomic positions. At least a third of the city's population was on relief by 1932, including half of the Mexicans. Relief agencies began programs of repatriation which involved a degree of coercion. Since Mexicans were the newest and least established immigrant group and had a poor record of seeking citizenship, they were most vulnerable. The local American Legion Post 266 took the leading role in removal, under Russell F. Robinson and Paul E. Kelly. Conditions were created to make it easier for Mexicans to accept repatriation than get relief funds. Specially scheduled nonstop trains took 1,032 Mexicans to Laredo, Texas, from East Chicago. While the people were well-treated generally, the whole movement illustrates the appeal of the simplistic solution for the Depression, the mistake that it could be solved at the local level, and the increased ethnic tensions brought by the 1930's. Based on primary and secondary works; 43 notes. G. J. Bobango

685. Smith, Michael M. BEYOND THE BORDERLANDS: MEXICAN LABOR IN THE CENTRAL PLAINS, 1900-1930. *Great Plains Q. 1981 1(4): 239-251.* A general spatial, occupational and distributional survey of Mexican migrant labor in Oklahoma, Kansas, Nebraska, South Dakota and North Dakota, 1900-30, offering economic reasons for migration; Mexicans today remain an "invisible minority" in the northern and central plains, whose role in the economic development of these plains areas should be incorporated into the history of the region.

686. Taylor, Paul S. MEXICAN WOMEN IN LOS ANGELES INDUSTRY IN 1928. *Aztlán 1980 11(1): 99-131.* Compiled in 1928, this analysis of Mexican women in Los Angeles industry is now published for the first time. Mexican women from upper, middle, and lower class backgrounds were interviewed. Places of employment for most of the 110 women interviewed included clothing and needle trades, packing houses, canneries, laundries, and other places. Mexican women undertook employment primarily because of economic necessity. The women in the family who went to work experienced changes in social attitudes, especially since such employment was contrary to Mexican custom. When young girls went to work, family conflicts often

resulted. Some employers found Mexican women poor workers, while others said they were as good as or better than other nationalities. Distinctions were noted between women born in Mexico and those born in the United States. Primary sources.   A. Hoffman

687.   Tyler, Ronnie C. THE LITTLE PUNITIVE EXPEDITION IN THE BIG BEND. *Southwestern Hist. Q. 1975 78(3): 271-291.* A study of bandit raids in the Big Bend region of Texas and Mexico at the time of the Mexican Revolution. Mexican bandits raided across the border, resulting in a US punitive expedition into Coahuila, Mexico, led by Major George T. Langhorne. The worst raids had been at Glenn Springs and Boquillas, on the same night of 5 May 1916 with 80 bandits participating. Commissioned to track them down, Langhorne crossed into Mexico on 11 May and carried on a very successful campaign, freeing two prisoners, killing and wounding several bandits, capturing five, dispersing the rest, and recapturing most of their booty. Map, 8 photos, 34 notes.   R. V. Ritter

688.   VanOsdol, Scott, photog., and Dickey, Dan W. LA MUSICA NORTE-ÑA: A PHOTOGRAPHIC ESSAY. *Southern Exposure 1983 11(1): 38-41.* Portrays the popularity of Norteña, a blend of 19th-century dances and 20th-century Latin Caribbean rhythms, within the Spanish community of San Antonio, Texas, since the 1930's.

689.   Vigil, Ralph H. REVOLUTION AND CONFUSION: THE PECU-LIAR CASE OF JOSE INES SALAZAR. *New Mexico Hist. Rev. 1978 53(2): 145-170.* Pinpoints the involvement of Jose Ines Salazar in the Mexican revolution and describes his fleeing to Texas, his arrest, and his escape from a New Mexico jail, 1910-18.   J. H. Krenkel

690.   Wollenberg, Charles. *MENDEZ V. WESTMINSTER*: RACE, NA-TIONALITY AND SEGREGATION IN CALIFORNIA SCHOOLS. *California Hist. Q. 1974 53(4): 317-332.* Studies *de jure* segregation in California as it affected Mexican-American children. Though not specified by state law as was the case with other ethnic groups, Mexican-American children were placed in segregated public schools in numerous districts. Justification for this practice came from beliefs that Mexican-American children had poor hygiene habits, could not compete with Anglo children, and that "Mexican" schools could do better for them. In the 1930's and 1940's these views came under attack from educators who held that assimilation could best be achieved through school integration. Mexican-American parents also protested the segregation of their children. In 1945 Gonzalo Mendez and four other Mexican-American fathers brought suit against the Westminster School District and other districts in Orange County on charges of unconstitutional discrimination through segregation. The plaintiffs won the case and were sustained when the districts appealed. While the decision ended *de jure* segregation in California, *de facto* segregation continues to present problems yet to be solved. Based on the court decision, newspapers, and published works; 2 photos, 78 notes.
                                                                    A. Hoffman

691. Zamora, Emilio. SARA ESTELA RAMÍREZ: UNA ROSA ROJA EN EL MOVIMIENTO [Sara Estela Ramírez: a red rose in the movement]. Mora, Magdalena and DelCastillo, Adelaida R., ed. *Mexican Women in the United States: Struggles Past and Present* (Los Angeles: U. of California Chicano Studies Res. Center, 1980): 163-169. Sara Estela Ramírez (1881-1910), a journalist and literary figure in southern Texas, was one of the women leaders in the Partido Liberal Mexicano. Her group was responsible for assuming public roles which persecuted leaders of the party could not undertake. Her writing legitimized the Liberal Party of Mexico and other movements by justifying the application of given moral and ethical considerations. 15 notes, appendix.   J. Powell

692. Zamora, Emilio, Jr. CHICANO SOCIALIST LABOR ACTIVITY IN TEXAS 1900-1920. *Aztlán 1976 6(2): 221-236.* Many Chicano workers in central and south Texas organized and joined socialist labor unions influenced by Mexican and Anglo radicals. In Laredo, due to ethnic conflicts, Mexican Americans did not follow strict socialist trade union principles and engaged in numerous railway strikes. In central and south Texas Chicano organizers worked within the Renter's Union of America and the Land League. They were more concerned with bread and butter issues than the Laredo group. 55 notes.   R. Griswold del Castillo

693. Zelman, Donald L. ALAZAN-APACHE COURTS: A NEW DEAL RESPONSE TO MEXICAN AMERICAN HOUSING CONDITIONS IN SAN ANTONIO. *Southwestern Hist. Q. 1983 87(2): 123-150.* In July 1939, construction began on the first low-income public housing project in San Antonio, Texas. Opened in August 1940 and completed in late 1944, the project was known as the Alazan-Apache Courts. It represented a small but successful effort by the San Antonio Housing Authority, under the leadership of Father Carmelo Tranchese, and the US Housing Authority to provide jobs, promote better health, and improve the standard of living in San Antonio's poverty-stricken west side. Based on federal government records; the Carmelo Tranchese Papers at St. Mary's University, San Antonio; reports of the San Antonio Housing Authority; and local newspapers; 53 notes, 8 photos.   R. D. Hurt

694. —. CONDICIONES SOCIOECONÓMICAS DE LOS BRACEROS [Socioeconomic conditions of the braceros]. *Bol. del Archivo General de la Nación [Mexico] 1980 4(4): 21-33.* Reprints 12 documents from the Manuel Avila Camacho papers in the National Archives of Mexico explaining working conditions and treatment of braceros in the United States, 1942-45. Photo.   J. A. Lewis

695. —. NÚMERO Y DESTINO DE BRACEROS EMPLEADOS POR COMPAÑÍAS FERROCARRILERAS [Number and destination of braceros employed by railroad companies]. *Bol. del Archivo General de la Nación [Mexico] 1980 4(4): 57-59.* Reprints two graphs taken from the Oficinia Documentadora de Braceros papers in the National Archives of Mexico showing distribution and use of braceros working for American railroad companies.   J. A. Lewis

1945 to 1985

696.   Aaron, William S.; Alger, Norman; and Gonzales, Ricardo T. CHICA-NOIZING DRUG ABUSE PROGRAMS. *Human Organization 1974 33(4): 388-390.* Examines drug addicts in a Mexican-American population in Oxnard, California to establish what cultural values could be adapted for use in drug abuse treatment.   S

697.   Aguirre, Adalberto, Jr. LANGUAGE USE IN BILINGUAL MEXICAN AMERICAN HOUSEHOLDS. *Social Sci. Q. 1984 65(2): 565-572.* Language choice is closely associated with a person's sex, a pattern of cross-sex language use is present among siblings, and home language use is closely associated with a parent's country of birth.

698.   Aguirre, Adalberto, Jr. THE SOCIOLINGUISTIC SITUATION OF BILINGUAL CHICANO ADOLESCENTS IN A CALIFORNIA BORDER TOWN. *Aztlán 1979 10: 55-67.* Reports on the social dimensions of bilingualism among Mexican Americans, based on a study of 75 Mexican American adolescents in a California border town. Concludes that bilingual Chicano adolescents maintain a high degree of loyalty to and use of the Spanish language, particularly in a familial context. In addition, Spanish language mass media contribute to the use of Spanish by the Mexican American speech community. Calls for further research into questions such as the association between language loss and social assimilation. 8 notes, biblio.   A. Hoffman

699.   Alba, Francisco. INDUSTRIALIZACIÓN SUSTITUTIVA Y MIGRACIÓN INTERNACIONAL: EL CASO DE MÉXICO [Import substitution industrialization and international migration: the Mexican case]. *Foro Int. [Mexico] 1978 18(3): 464-479.* Migration of Mexican labor to the United States is a function of Mexican imports substitution industrialization, concomitant structural unemployment, and a reflection of the general world trend of labor moving from the periphery to centers of growth. Based on newspaper articles and secondary sources; 31 notes.   D. A. Franz

700.   Alba, Francisco. LA FECUNDIDAD ENTRE LOS MEXICANO-NORTEAMERICANOS EN RELACION A LOS CAMBIANTES PATRONES REPRODUCTIVOS EN MEXICO Y LOS ESTADOS UNIDOS [Fertility of Mexican Americans in relation to changing reproductive patterns in Mexico and the United States]. *Demografía y Econ. [Mexico] 1982 16(2): 236-249.* Compares the characteristics of population growth in Mexico and the United States among the Mexican-American populations; notes trends and parallels in socioeconomic conditions.

701.   Allsup, Carl. EDUCATION IS OUR FREEDOM: THE AMERICAN G.I. FORUM AND THE MEXICAN AMERICAN SCHOOL SEGREGATION IN TEXAS, 1948-1957. *Aztlán 1977 8: 27-50.* The American G.I. Forum, founded in 1948 in Texas and composed of Mexican Americans, sought to encourage the enrollment and educational attainment of elementary and secondary age Mexican- American students and to enforce desegregation

of public schools to improve socioeconomic conditions for Chicanos in that state.

702.   Allsup, Carl. WHO DONE IT? THE THEFT OF MEXICAN-AMER-ICAN HISTORY. *Journal of Popular Culture 1983 17(3): 150-155.* In spite of the contemporary Chicano movement, 19th- and early 20th-century myths and stereotypes about Mexicans and Mexican Americans are perpetuated by movies and television, and the history of many decades of contributions to American culture by them are ignored. 20 notes.   D. G. Nielson

703.   Almaraz, Felix D., Jr. BILINGUAL EDUCATION IN NEW MEXI-CO: HISTORICAL PERSPECTIVE AND CURRENT DEBATE. *New Mexico Hist. Rev. 1978 53(4): 347-360.* Discusses the background to bilingual education in New Mexico, and projects beginning with the Bilingual Education Act (US, 1968).

704.   Althoff, Phillip. THE POLITICAL INTEGRATION OF MEXICAN-AMERICANS AND BLACKS: A NOTE ON A DEVIANT CASE. *Rocky Mountain Social Sci. J. 1973 10(3): 79-84.* A case study of local political integration of Mexican Americans and blacks in Manhattan, Kansas.   S

705.   Angel, Ronald. THE COSTS OF DISABILITY FOR HISPANIC MALES. *Social Sci. Q. 1984 65(2): 426-443.* Though there are significant differences between nationality groups, Hispanics generally suffer greater loss of work and income than do non-Hispanics as the result of disability; among disabled Hispanics, those who have a poor command of the English language suffer an increased loss of earnings and are less successful than non-Hispanics in compensating for such loss through alternative income sources.

706.   Angel, Ronald J. and Cleary, Paul D. THE EFFECTS OF SOCIAL STRUCTURE AND CULTURE ON REPORTED HEALTH. *Social Sci. Q. 1984 65(3): 814-828.* Addresses problems in comparing the health status of individuals of Mexican origin and non-Hispanics; high Mexican cultural identification leads to less reported illness than would be expected once a number of health-related economic and demographic factors are controlled.

707.   Antunes, George and Gaitz, Charles M. ETHNICITY AND PARTIC-IPATION: A STUDY OF MEXICAN-AMERICANS, BLACKS, AND WHITES. *Am. J. of Sociol. 1975 80(5): 1192-1211.* Drawing on the findings of Orum (1966) and Olsen (1970), this study hypothesizes that, because of a process of "compensation" or "ethnic identification," members of disadvantaged ethnic groups have higher levels of social and political participation than persons of the same social class who are members of the dominant social group. Data taken from a community survey only partially support the hypothesis with regard to 11 participation variables. When social class is controlled, black levels of participation generally exceed or equal those of whites; however, levels of participation among Mexican Americans tend to be lower than those of whites. Several explanations which might account for these discrepant findings are discussed.   J

708.   Antunes, George; Gordon, Chad; Gaitz, Charles M.; and Scott, Judith. ETHNICITY, SOCIOECONOMIC STATUS, AND THE ETIOLOGY OF PSYCHOLOGICAL DISTRESS. *Sociol. and Social Res. 1974 58(4): 361-368.* "To identify the mechanisms responsible for the inverse association between social class and psychological distress, we used a research design created by Dohrenwend and Dohrenwend contrasting the distress level of Anglos, Blacks, and Mexican Americans for two levels of socioeconomic status. Our data support a social selection rather than a social stress explanation of this relationship."   J

709.   Aragon de Valdez, Theresa. ORGANIZING AS A POLITICAL TOOL FOR THE CHICANA. *Frontiers 1980 5(2): 7-13.* Chicanas' low socioeconomic status is due to race, sex, and the language barrier; Chicanas can organize for change not necessarily in spite of, but because of, external constraints; 1973-76.

710.   Arce, Carlos H. LANGUAGE SHIFT AMONG CHICANOS: STRATEGIES FOR MEASURING AND ASSESSING DIRECTION AND RATE. *Social Sci. J. 1982 19(2): 121-132.* Studies Mexican-ancestry households in California, New Mexico, Arizona, Texas, Colorado, and the Chicago metropolitan area to determine Chicano language maintenance; "Chicanos are undergoing substantial shift away from Spanish and that very large proportions of the Chicano population retain Spanish and attain balanced bilingualism."

711.   Arce, Carlos H. A RECONSIDERATION OF CHICANO CULTURE AND IDENTITY. *Daedalus 1981 110(2): 177-191.* Describes the gradual achievement of a distinct Chicano identity in the United States during the past two decades, though the economic downturn of the 1970's and early 1980's has threatened to neutralize the modest gains initiated by Chicanos in the 1960's.

712.   Arizpe, Lourdes. THE RURAL EXODUS IN MEXICO AND MEXICAN MIGRATION TO THE UNITED STATES. *Int. Migration Rev. 1981 15(4): 626-649.* Two movements during the 1950's-80's of Mexican workers, that of migrants to the United States and the internal rural-urban migration within Mexico, were previously thought to be related, but were distinct and separate; migrants to the United States were a specific type while those who relocated in Mexican cities were the poor, landless people.

713.   Arora, Shirley L. PROVERBS IN MEXICAN AMERICAN TRADITION. *Aztlán 1982 13(1-2): 43-69.* Reports on research being done in the greater Los Angeles area on Mexican-American proverbs. A representative sampling of the community yielded information on favorite proverbs, how they are passed down to the next generation, their use in teaching and giving advice, and their maintenance through the continuing use of the Spanish language. Some respondents note that loss of fluency in Spanish has caused some loss in proverb maintenance. Also, second- and third-generation Mexican Americans continue the tradition less well than do Mexican-born informants; but older respondents report using proverbs more frequently than when they were younger. Calls for studies in proverb use as an important ethnic and cultural resource. Field research and secondary sources; 19 notes.   A. Hoffman

714. Arreola, Daniel D. MEXICAN AMERICAN EXTERIOR MURALS. *Geog. Rev. 1984 74(4): 409-424.* Chicano mural painting on exterior surfaces emerged in the wake of La Raza militancy during the late 1960's. The murals initially emphasized ethnic and political expression. Themes displaying place and environmental consciousness are beginning to appear in this form of exterior art. The murals are a cultural mirror of group identity for the Mexican-American community. J

715. Arroyo, Laura E. INDUSTRIAL AND OCCUPATIONAL DISTRIBUTION OF CHICANA WORKERS. *Aztlán 1973 4(2): 343-382.*

716. Ashmore, Harry S. BELOW THE BOTTOM LINE. *Virginia Q. Rev. 1983 59(3): 384-398.* Both Reaganomics and the New Federalism of the Reagan administration are unworkable. The latter is not "new," but a return to old "states' rights" federalism. There is growing evidence that such a retreat from federal responsibity is no longer a viable political option. Hard-core poverty is rapidly increasing welfare costs, crime, and destruction of conventional family structure especially among blacks and Hispanics. O. H. Zabel

717. Avila, Lorenzo; Balderrama, Virginia; and Freeman, Hal M. "CHI-CHI" IN PARADISE: HELPING AGENCIES AND THE SPANISH SPEAKING. *Public Welfare 1973 31(2): 40-47.*

718. Baca, Reynaldo and Bryan, Dexter. MEXICAN UNDOCUMENTED WORKERS IN THE BINATIONAL COMMUNITY: A RESEARCH NOTE. *Int. Migration Rev. 1981 15(4): 737-748.* Discusses research on undocumented restaurant workers in Los Angeles who work in the United States and reside in both the United States and in Mexico, including information from a 1979 survey of undocumented workers regarding "citizenship aspirations and residency rights preferences," and "settlement patterns, employment histories, occupational aspirations, and resettlement plans."

719. Baca Zinn, Maxine. POLITICAL FAMILIALISM: TOWARD SEX ROLE EQUALITY IN CHICANO FAMILIES. *Aztlan 1975 6(1): 13-37.* Interprets changes in the Chicano family in light of the family's self-conscious efforts to resist colonial oppression and discrimination. Political familialism is the fusion of cultural and political resistance within the family unit. The family, for Mexican Americans, has come to have a broader meaning than in the past, since it incorporates loyalty to political or cultural organizations. Chicanos have been changing their own values regarding *machismo* and women's roles. 37 notes. R. Griswold del Castillo

720. Baca-Ramirez, Reynaldo and Bryan, Dexter Edward. THE UNDOCUMENTED MEXICAN WORKER: A SOCIAL PROBLEM? *J. of Ethnic Studies 1980 8(1): 55-70.* Undocumented laborers from Mexico form a permanent force in the United States. Immigration has been stimulated by the desire for social mobility. A class structure is emerging with a new middle class of Mexican-American professionals, a brown collar lower middle class, and an underclass of recent undocumented workers. Biblio. S

721.   Bain, Kenneth and Travis, Paul. SOUTH TEXAS POLITICS. *Southern Exposure 1984 12(1): 49-52.* Mexican-American activists used voter registration drives to politically organize the Mexican-American population of South Texas and finally gain political representation in local government.

722.   Barrientos, Guido A., Hosch, Harmon M., Lucker, William G.; and Alvarez, Aldolfo J. WHAT DRIVES MEXICAN ILLEGAL BORDER-CROSSERS INTO THE U.S.? A PSYCHOLOGICAL PERSPECTIVE. *New Scholar 1984 9(1-2): 87-98.* Examines the motives that draw Mexican illegal border-crossers into the United States, based on a survey of illegal aliens held at La Tuna Federal Correction Institute in El Paso, Texas. The Mexicans viewed the United States as an economic resource, and their desire was to have a secure future in Mexico. Note, ref.   S

723.   Batzer, Arild. LA HUELGA, LANDARBEIDEREN OG CESAR CHAVEZ [The strike, farmworkers, and Cesar Chavez]. *Samtiden [Norway] 1970 79(10): 649-662.* Describes Cesar Chavez (founder of the United Farm Workers Union) and the strike by California grape pickers, 1965-70.
                                                                          M. A. Bott

724.   Bean, Frank D. COMPONENTS OF INCOME AND EXPECTED FAMILY SIZE AMONG MEXICAN AMERICANS. *Social Sci. Q. 1973 54(1): 103-116.* "Considering alternative hypotheses relevant to the income-fertility relationship, husband's income is partitioned into two components, each of which bears special salience to alternative hypotheses. The different relations of the components to expected family size among Mexican Americans underscores the notion that social processes of a reference group nature need to be better taken into account in the socioeconomic theory of family formation."
                                                                          J

725.   Bean, Frank D. and Swicegood, Gray. GENERATION, FEMALE EDUCATION AND MEXICAN-AMERICAN FERTILITY. *Social Sci. Q. 1982 63(1): 131-144.* The decrease in Mexican-American fertility is due to the length of exposure to the receiving society (measured by generation) and to rising socioeconomic status (measured by female education); moreover, most Mexican-American women of later generations and greater education manifest even lower cumulative fertility than would be expected considering indicators of these variables separately, which suggests a modified theory of minority group status effects on fertility.

726.   Bean, Frank D.; Cullen, Ruth M.; Stephen, Elizabeth H.; and Swicegood, C. Gray. GENERATIONAL DIFFERENCES IN FERTILITY AMONG MEXICAN AMERICANS: IMPLICATIONS FOR ASSESSING THE EFFECTS OF IMMIGRATION. *Social Sci. Q. 1984 65(2): 573-582.* An examination of the effects of generational status on both current and cumulative fertility for the Mexican-origin population, disaggregated by age group, shows evidence of fertility reduction the longer the familial exposure to life in the United States.

727. Belenchia, Joanne M. COWBOYS AND ALIENS: HOW THE INS OPERATES IN LATINO COMMUNITIES. *Peace and Change 1980 6(3): 10-19.* Provides a brief background of the Immigration and Naturalization Service, focusing on INS operations involving Latinos in the Southwest and Midwest, particularly Illinois, Mexican migrants' destination choice after California and Texas; ca 1973-76.

728. Bensusan, Guy. SOME CURRENT DIRECTIONS IN MEXICAN AMERICAN RELIGIOUS MUSIC. *Latin Am. Res. Rev. 1975 10(2): 186-190.* With Vatican Council II (1962-65), which decreed vernacular Masses, a religious revival began among Mexican Americans, affecting Protestants as well as Catholics and leading many churches to adapt their messages to Mexican-American culture and to translate their hymns and literature into Spanish.

729. Bernal, Ernest M., Jr. ASSESSMENT PROCEDURES FOR CHICANO CHILDREN: THE SAD STATE OF THE ART. *Aztlán 1977 8: 69-81.* Chicano children tend to test lower than most children on intelligence testing due to lack of Mexican American samplings within test development, lack of test wiseness, impractical or useless test results, and use by some educators to fulfill the belief in underachievement.

730. Bernstein, Alan et al. SILICON VALLEY: PARADISE OR PARADOX? Mora, Magdalena and DelCastillo, Adelaida R., ed. *Mexican Women in the United States: Struggles Past and Present* (Los Angeles: U. of California Chicano Studies Res. Center, 1980): 105-112. Santa Clara County, California, in the 1970's has developed into one of the most affluent counties in the nation because of its strong economic base in the electronics industry. High technology products such as satellites, computer memory disks, light emitting diodes, etc., are produced by over 120,000 workers in the 175 major electronics companies alone. While the products are impressive, the working conditions and wages of assemblers and technicians, most of whom are women, leave much to be desired. Often workers are exposed to hazardous chemicals while on the job. Despite these difficulties very few companies have union organizations. The same conditions prevail in the Latin American and Asian branches of these companies. Based on surveys of five electronics plants in Santa Clara County, California; table, 2 charts.   J. Powell

731. Blount, Alma; Gonzalez, Martin; and Petrow, Steven. LOST IN THE STREAM. *Southern Exposure 1980 8(4): 67-76.* Discusses the hardships of migrant laborers, specifically the conditions of Jamaican cane cutters in South Florida with photographs of Mexican American and black farmworkers in Florida; 1980.

732. Borjas, George J. THE EARNINGS OF MALE HISPANIC IMMIGRANTS IN THE UNITED STATES. *Industrial and Labor Relations Rev. 1982 35(3): 343-353.* There are major differences in the rate of economic mobility of the various Hispanic groups. In particular, the rate of economic progress by Cuban immigrants exceeds that of other Hispanic groups, the result in part of the fact that Cuban immigrants have invested more heavily in

US schooling than other Hispanic immigrants arriving in this country at the same time. These findings are consistent with the hypothesis that political refugees are likely to face higher costs of return immigration than do "economic" immigrants, and therefore the former have greater incentives to adapt rapidly to the US labor market.   J

733. Borjas, George J. THE LABOR SUPPLY OF MALE HISPANIC IMMIGRANTS IN THE UNITED STATES. *International Migration Review 1983-84 17(4): 653-671.* Examines the effects of assimilation on the employment probability and labor supply of male Hispanic immigrants to the United States.

734. Borjas, George J. THE SUBSTITUTABILITY OF BLACK, HISPANIC, AND WHITE LABOR. *Econ. Inquiry 1983 21(1): 93-106.* Analyzes labor market competition among blacks, Hispanic Americans, and whites, 1976.

735. Boswell, Thomas D. and Jones, Timothy C. A REGIONALIZATION OF MEXICAN AMERICANS IN THE UNITED STATES. *Geographical Rev. 1980 70(1): 88-98.* The Hispanic population is the second largest and fastest growing minority in the United States. Persons of Mexican origin represent approximately 60 percent of all Hispanic Americans. With increasing numbers and political awareness, "Chicano Power" may become one of the major social movements of the 1980's. The purpose of this investigation is to provide a regionalization of Mexican Americans that is designed to highlight critical socioeconomic and spatial differences in this group. Eleven social and economic indicators for 67 areal units were exposed to a factor analysis of the principal components variety. The resultant factor scores were used in a hierarchical grouping to produce seven types of homogeneous regions of Mexican Americans. The analysis will be useful to both academicians and planners in future research dealing with the results of the 1980 Census of Population. Map, 4 tables, fig., 31 notes.   J

736. Bradshaw, Benjamin S. and Bean, Frank D. TRENDS IN THE FERTILITY OF MEXICAN AMERICANS, 1950-1970. *Social Sci. Q. 1973 53(4): 688-696.* "The data provide little evidence to support the thesis that the fertility levels of the Anglo and Mexican-American populations have substantially converged during the last two decades."   J

737. Bradshaw, Benjamin Spencer. POTENTIAL LABOR FORCE SUPPLY, PLACEMENT, AND MIGRATION OF MEXICAN-AMERICAN AND OTHER MALES IN THE TEXAS-MEXICO BORDER REGION. *Internat. Migration R. 1976 10(1): 29-45.* Discusses the migration and potential labor force supply of Mexican-American males in the Texas-Mexico border region in the 1960's and 70's.

738. Brawner, Marlyn R. MIGRATION AND EDUCATIONAL ACHIEVEMENT OF MEXICAN AMERICANS. *Social Sci. Q. 1973 53(4): 727-737.* "Comparing migrants' children with a same-age, same-sex sample from one of the communities of emigration shows greater scholastic achieve-

ments among the former. With cultural variables held constant, emphasis appears to fall upon the influence of peers, the school system, and the community."   J

739. Briggs, Vernon M., Jr. ILLEGAL ALIENS: THE NEED FOR A MORE RESTRICTIVE BORDER POLICY. *Social Sci. Q. 1975 56(3): 477-484.* Uses what many would regard as conventional economic arguments.
                                                                                   J

740. Briggs, Vernon M., Jr. LA CONFRONTACIÓN DEL CHICANO CON EL IMMIGRANTE MEXICANO [The confrontation between the Chicano and the Mexican immigrant]. *Foro Int. [Mexico] 1978 18(3): 514-521.* Discusses the impact of illegal immigrants in the US southwest on Mexican Americans, within a political and economic context. Secondary sources; 7 notes.   D. A. Franz

741. Brown, Robert L. SOCIAL DISTANCE PERCEPTION AS A FUNC-TION OF MEXICAN-AMERICAN AND OTHER ETHNIC IDENTITY. *Sociol. and Social Res. 1973 57(3): 273-287.* "Slightly modified Bogardus Social Distance Scales were administered to students in sociology classes of a South Texas university. Emphasis was upon comparisons between Other Whites and Mexican Americans. Hypothesizes that Racial Distance Indices would reflect the student's own ethnic group, related ethnic groups and regional subcultural features, were borne out. Additionally, major differences were found to be due to ethnicity rather than social class."   J

742. Bruce-Novoa, Juan. CHICANO LITERATURE: ART, FIRST OF ALL. *Américas (Organization of Am. States) 1980 32(2): 32-36.* Briefly summarizes the messages of Chicano poets, dramatists, and writers, including Thomas Rodolfo Gonzales and Sergio Elizando, 1970's.

743. Bruce-Novoa, Juan. *POCHO* AS LITERATURE. *Aztlán 1976 7(1): 65-77.* Examines literarily José Antonio Villareal's novel, *Pocho,* which has previously been approached solely from a sociological or historical point of view. The novel deals with the migration of a Mexican family to the United States after the Mexican Revolution and its subsequent assimilation into American society. The plot focuses on the son, Richard, his struggle with tradition and God, and his beginnings as a writer. His work turns the emptiness he finds in reality into an affirmation of life. Suggests that *Pocho* itself is the work Richard writes.   J. Tull

744. Bruce-Novoa, Juan. ROUND TABLE ON CHICANO LITERA-TURE. *J. of Ethnic Studies 1975 3(1): 99-103.* Yale University holds monthly discussions on Chicano literature and culture. Presents a partial transcript of a discussion on 24 January 1974 among Philip Ortego, Tino Villanueva, Carlos Morton, and the author. The discussion covers such topics as the genres of Chicano literature, publication difficulties, the Chicano author's social role, and the Chicano-Mexican relationship. 2 notes.   T. W. Smith

745.   Buehler, Marilyn H. VOTER TURNOUT AND POLITICAL EFFI-
CACY AMONG MEXICAN-AMERICANS IN MICHIGAN. *Sociol. Q.*
1977 18(4): 504-517. A description and explanation of the research on levels of
political interest and feelings of political efficacy among Mexican Americans is
presented. The primary concerns are comparing Mexican Americans with
other Americans, determining the effect of the Mexican-American subculture,
and evaluating the usefulness of standard explanations of variations in political
interest and feeling of political efficacy in explaining variations among Mexican
Americans. The research sample included 465 Mexican Americans in Michigan. Contrary to past studies, which have described Mexican Americans as
politically inactive and fatalistic, we found that Mexican Americans did not
differ significantly from other similar Americans in voting turnout and political
efficacy. The Mexican-American subculture did not discourage voting or
encourage a sense of powerlessness. Generally, standard theories were useful in
explaining variations in voting turnout and political efficacy among Mexican
Americans. An additional factor of importance was the perception of the status
of Mexican Americans in society.   J

746.   Bustamante, Jorge A. EL ESPALDA MOJADA, REPORTE DE UN
OBSERVADOR PARTICIPANTE [The wetback: notes of a participating
observer]. *Rev. Mexicana de Ciencia Pol. [Mexico] 1973 19(71): 81-107.*
Though it is considered illegal in the United States, to become a wetback is a
socially accepted means of entering the United States in order to seek work,
and carries no stigma in Mexico.

747.   Bustamante, Jorge A. EMIGRACIÓN INDOCUMENTADA A LOS
ESTADOS UNIDOS [Undocumented emigration to the United States]. *Foro*
Int. [Mexico] 1978 18(3): 430-463. Discusses characteristics of illegal Mexican
laborers in the United States, the status of information about them, and
solutions to the problem they present. Covers 1930-77. Based on interviews,
statistical analysis, and secondary sources; 3 graphs, 6 tables, notes, ref.
                                                                           D. A. Franz

748.   Bustamante, Jorge A. and Cockroft, James D. ONE MORE TIME:
THE "UNDOCUMENTED." *Radical Am. 1981 15(6): 7-15.* Increased unemployment in Mexico, caused by US dominated multinational corporations
and by a growing lack of unskilled labor in parts of the US labor market,
insures a continued presence of the "undocumented." The size of this
population and the costs to the United States are frequently exaggerated by the
press and by organized labor. However, governmental negotiations to structure
the flow of illegal aliens will be mingled with concern for oil concessions and
for a common market arrangement with Mexico. 4 notes, 7 illus.
                                                                           C. M. Hough

749.   Bustamante, Jorge. STRUCTURAL AND IDEOLOGICAL CONDI-
TIONS OF THE MEXICAN UNDOCUMENTED IMMIGRATION TO
THE UNITED STATES. *Am. Behavioral Scientist 1976 19(3): 364-376.*
Examines the social situation of Mexican nationals who enter the United States
illegally, taking a Marxist perspective on social policy and the class structure of
American society.

750. Bustamante, Jorge A. and Martínez, Gerónimo G. UNDOCUMENT-ED IMMIGRATION FROM MEXICO: BEYOND BORDERS BUT WITH-IN SYSTEMS. *J. of Int. Affairs 1979 33(2): 265-284.* Examines statistics derived from the research project Encuesta Nacional de Emigración a la Frontera Norte y a los Estados Unidos, the National Survey on Emigration to the Northern Border and to the United States (ENEFNEU), sponsored by the government of Mexico, and derives profiles of illegal immigrants to the United States.

751. Bustamante, Jorge A. UNDOCUMENTED IMMIGRATION FROM MEXICO: RESEARCH REPORT. *Int. Migration Rev. 1977 11(2): 149-177.* Discusses undocumented immigration of Mexican nationals into the United States from the angle of present research, what is presently known on the subject, how this information has been presented in nine Mexican border cities, past attempts at solving the problem, and methods for future curtailment, 1975-77.

752. Buzan, Bert C. CHICANO COMMUNITY CONTROL, POLITICAL CYNICISM AND THE VALIDITY OF POLITICAL TRUST MEASURES. *Western Pol. Q. 1980 33(1): 108-120.* The central hypothesis of the study is that Chicano community control is associated with high Chicano political cynicism. Political cynicism was operationalized in terms of government and regime-level attitudinal objects and support for unconventional political behavior. Test data were collected [in Texas] in a Chicano-controlled city and in a city with a history of bi-ethnic coalitionism. The "Chicano control/political cynicism" hypothesis was corroborated for regime-level objects and behavioral predispositions but not for government-level objects. The author argues that the historical intervention of the "Watergate affair" between the administration of the two surveys accounts for this unexpected finding. 4 tables, 25 notes, appendix.   J

753. Buzan, Bert C. and Phillips, Diana Buder. INSTITUTIONAL COM-PLETENESS AND CHICANO MILITANCY. *Aztlán 1980 11(1): 33-64.* Examines the relationship of institutional completeness on Chicano militancy, contrasting Chicano attitudes regarding assimilation and retention of Chicano culture. High school students in Crystal City, Texas, and Corpus Christi, Texas, were surveyed for their willingness to participate in political innovation, and the degree of their acceptance of Anglo institutions. In Crystal City, where since 1969 Chicanos have controlled political offices, students indicated a greater sense of political activism for the Chicano community than in Corpus Christi, where the Chicano community is less complete institutionally. Predicts that militant young Chicanos may bring tremendous political pressure on middle-class assimilationists who find it increasingly difficult to fulfill promises made to Chicano communities. 8 tables, 43 notes.   A. Hoffman

754. Cain, Bruce E. and Kiewiet, D. Roderick. ETHNICITY AND ELEC-TORAL CHOICE: MEXICAN AMERICAN VOTING BEHAVIOR IN THE CALIFORNIA 30TH CONGRESSIONAL DISTRICT. *Social Sci. Q. 1984 65(2): 315-327.* The 1982 election in California offers a unique natural experiment in ethnic and racial bloc voting. The race in the predominantly

Hispanic 30th Congressional District matched a well-financed Anglo Republican, John Rousselot, against an incumbent Hispanic, Marty Martinez. On the ballot with Martinez and Rousselot were the successful Republican candidates for governor and US senator, George Deukmejian and Pete Wilson, and the losing Democratic candidates, Tom Bradley (who is black) and Jerry Brown. These variations in the race and ethnicity of the candidates on the ballot in 1982 were used to estimate the impact of ethnic and racial considerations in voting decisions.   J

755. Cardenas, Gilbert. WHO ARE THE MIDWESTERN CHICANOS: IMPLICATIONS FOR CHICANO STUDIES. *Aztlán 1976 7(2): 141-152.* Introduces an issue devoted to Chicanos in the Midwest. Briefly reviews each article presented, and notes that important areas of investigation, e.g. Puerto Ricans in the Midwest and Chicanos in the Great Plains states, remain untouched. Attempts to provide a theoretical framework for understanding the study of the Midwest Chicano experience, which is essential for broadening and clarifying a discipline too closely tied, until recently, to the Southwestern United States. Points the way toward a national geopolitical perspective in Chicano studies. Notes the growth since 1970 of institutions, e.g. the Midwest Council of La Raza, Inc. at the University of Notre Dame, for promoting Midwest Chicano studies. 9 notes.   L. W. Van Wyk

756. Cárdenas de Dwyer, Carlota. CULTURAL REGIONALISM AND CHICANO LITERATURE. *Western Am. Literature 1980 15(3): 187-194.* Discusses how everyday life and ways of life experienced by Mexican Americans of the Southwest have been used by Chicano authors. Selects examples from the writings of Tomas Rivera and Rolando Hinojosa to illustrate this kind of narrative writing. Each of these authors uses the Chicano way of life to fulfill an important narrative purpose. These writers omit the familiar and conventional constraints of a unified narrative form.

M. Genung

757. Carillo, Loretta and Lyson, Thomas A. THE *FOTONOVELA* AS A CULTURAL BRIDGE OF HISPANIC WOMEN IN THE UNITED STATES. *Journal of Popular Culture 1983 17(3): 59-64.* Content analysis of 62 Mexican *fotonovelas* distributed in the United States during 1976-80 reveals distinct and recurring themes that reinforce the traditional Mexican values and norms of lower-class American Hispanic women readers who have not yet assimilated American middle-class values. Table, 9 notes.   D. G. Nielson

758. Carlson, Alvar W. SEASONAL FARM LABOR IN THE SAN LUIS VALLEY. *Ann. of the Assoc. of Am. Geographers 1973 63(1): 97-108.* "Specialty agriculture has been the mainstay of the agricultural economy of the San Luis Valley, Colorado. The dependence of Valley farmers upon thousands of local, intrastate, and interstate seasonal farm laborers is important in understanding the evolution of this agricultural region. Spanish-surname people have been available for farm labor since the early settlement of the Valley."   J

759. Castellanos, Leonard. CHICANO CENTROS, MURALS, AND ART. *Arts in Soc. 1975 12(1): 38-43.* Examines the work of the Mechicano Art Center in East Los Angeles in the 1970's.   S

760. Castillo, Leonel J. DEALING WITH THE UNDOCUMENTED ALIEN: AN INTERIM APPROACH. *Int. Migration Rev. 1978 12(4): 570-577.* Reviews Carter administration attitudes and policy toward illegal aliens, 1977-78.

761. Castro, Rafaela. MEXICAN WOMEN'S SEXUAL JOKES. *Aztlán 1982 13(1-2): 275-293.* Examines sexual jokes told by Mexican and Mexican-American women. Such jokes are enjoyed by women and are shared at work and in social situations. Favorite themes include jokes about nuns and priests, sexual organs, and scatological jokes. Many jokes utilize word play, puns, facial expressions, and hand gestures. Sexual organs are not called by their names but are referred to with alternative names. The jokes fall into the area of folklore, and their study can provide insights into the Mexican experience in the United States. Based on interviews and secondary sources; 35 notes.
A. Hoffman

762. Chande, Roberto Ham and Bustamante, Jorge A. LAS EXPULSIONES DE INDOCUMENTADOS MEXICANOS [The expulsions of undocumented Mexicans]. *Demografía y Econ. [Mexico] 1979 13(2): 185-207.* Presents statistics from US government sources describing undocumented Mexicans deportable from the United States, 1972-77.

763. Chandler, Charles R. VALUE ORIENTATIONS AMONG MEXICAN AMERICANS IN A SOUTHWESTERN CITY. *Sociol. and Social Res. 1974 58(3): 262-271.* "Value orientation questions related to activity, integration with kin, trust, and occupational primacy were asked of a random sample of 300 Mexican-American men and women in an urban setting [Lubbock, Texas]. As hypothesized, 'modern' orientations were expressed by younger respondents with more formal schooling and higher-status occupations. Others, and in fact the majority, gave 'traditional' responses. The results are discussed in relation to other studies and in light of 'modernism' theory."   J

764. Chavez, Cesar. THE CALIFORNIA FARM WORKERS' STRUGGLE. *Black Scholar 1976 7(9): 16-19.* Reprints an article from the *Los Angeles Times,* 8 April 1976. The author, who is president of the United Farm Workers of America, AFL-CIO, discusses the present struggle of the farm workers to obtain an effective farm labor law in California.   B. D. Ledbetter

765. Chavez, Mauro. CARRANZA'S *CHICANISMO: PHILOSOPHICAL FRAGMENTS. J. of Ethnic Studies 1979 7(3): 95-100.* Review essay of Elihu Carranza's *Chicanismo: Philosophical Fragments* (Kendall-Hunt, 1978); covers late 1960's-70's.

766. Cheyney, Arnold B. and Adams, Georgia B. CHILD CARE NEEDS OF MIGRANT CHILDREN. *Contemporary Educ. 1974 45(4): 274-277.*

767.   Cockcroft, Eva. THE STORY OF CHICANO PARK. *Aztlán 1984 15(1): 79-103.* Traces the efforts by residents of the Barrio Logan neighborhood in San Diego, California, to create a people's park beneath the Bay Bridge that was built through the community in the 1960's. In 1970, community activists occupied the land scheduled for a California Highway Patrol substation; since then, not without struggle and negotiation, the acreage for the park has grown. To decorate the park, Chicano artists and nonartists have painted a series of murals on the pillars of the bridge and the freeway offramp. The murals reflect the views of the community on the political changes that have taken place since 1970, moving from community issues to a sense of cultural nationalism and back to local political questions such as the adjacent junkyards. They illustrate the history and culture of the people who have fought for a place of beauty in a stark urban environment. Based on interviews, newspapers and secondary sources; appendix, map, 19 notes.

A. Hoffman

768.   Cohen, Gaynor. ALLIANCE AND CONFLICT AMONG MEXICAN AMERICANS. *Ethnic and Racial Studies [Great Britain] 1982 5(2): 175-195.* Divides the recent history of Mexican Americans into three phases: assimilation and integration (pre-1960's); the civil rights movements of 1960-68, which allied various disadvantaged groups; and the development of a separate Chicano movement during 1968-78, whose goals brought it into conflict with other groups; focuses on the San Jose, California, school district, 1950-79, when issues of bilingual education and school integration brought black and Chicano groups into conflict.

769.   Coltharp, Lurline H. DUAL INFLUENCES ON CHICANO NAMING PRACTICES. *Names 1981 29(4): 297-302.* Studies the preferences of members of the El Paso, Texas, community for naming children to determine the influence of English and Spanish on Mexican Americans.

770.   Comer, John C. CORRELATES OF RECOGNITION AND APPROVAL OF ETHNIC ORGANIZATIONS IN A NON REINFORCING ENVIRONMENT: MEXICAN AMERICANS IN OMAHA, NEBRASKA. *J. of Pol. and Military Sociol. 1980 8(1): 113-120.* Participation of Mexican Americans in ethnic organizations has typically been quite low. This conclusion is based almost exclusively, however, on studies of Mexican Americans in the Southwest. This analysis examines levels of recognition, approval, and membership in a number of Chicano organizations among a sample of Mexican Americans in Omaha, Nebraska. It also explores the relationship between recognition and approval and a number of social characteristics. The study adds to our knowledge by providing data on Mexican Americans outside the Southwest and by examining in a systematic way a number of the explanations frequently offered to account for low levels of group participation.   J

771.   Cooney, Rosemary Santana. CHANGING LABOR FORCE PARTICIPATION OF MEXICAN AMERICAN WIVES: A COMPARISON WITH ANGLOS AND BLACKS. *Social Sci. Q. 1975 56(2): 252-261.* Data on Mexican-American married women, aged 15-54, in the Southwest in 1960 and 1970 and data on comparable Anglo and black females substantiate the

importance of socioeconomic factors for explaining interethnic variations in female labor force participation, but are also consistent with the hypothesis that the importance of familism for the Mexican-American population has declined. J

772. Cornelius, Wayne A. INTERVIEWING UNDOCUMENTED IMMI-GRANTS: METHODOLOGICAL REFLECTIONS BASED ON FIELD-WORK IN MEXICO AND THE U.S. *Int. Migration Rev. 1982 16(2): 378-411.* Discusses whether or not research on undocumented Mexican immi-grants is necessary, what methodology to use, the validity of the interviews, and solutions to other problems such as gaining trust and providing confidenti-ality.

773. Corralejo, Jorge. REPORT ON PROPOSITION 14: FARMWORK-ERS VS. BIG GROWERS, BIG MONEY AND BIG LIES. *Radical Am. 1977 11(2): 74-78.* Proposition 14 on the California ballot in 1976 represented an effort by the United Farmworkers to place into the state constitution the essence of the legislation contained in the California Agriculture Labor Relations Act (1975). Agribusiness campaigned against the proposition and raised the myth of protecting the rights of the yeoman farmer and the individual against the group. The union employed its considerable boycott staff and its liberal-left-clergy coalition of supporters in the unsuccessful fight to enact the proposition. The campaign strengthened the existing law by calling needed attention to it and familiarizing many with its provisions. The struggle also may have pushed the union closer to acting more and more as a traditional trade union. N. Lederer

774. Cota-Cárdenas, Margarita. THE CHICANA IN THE CITY AS SEEN IN HER LITERATURE. *Frontiers 1981 6(1-2): 13-18.* Even the briefest examination of literature about or by contemporary Mexican-American women shows the triple oppression of Chicanas: their oppression as members of a minority group, as females, and as inheritors of a culture that tends to be male-dominated.

775. Coyle, Laurie; Hershatter, Gail; and Honig, Emily. WOMEN AT FARAH: AN UNFINISHED STORY. Mora, Magdalena and DelCastillo, Adelaida R., ed. *Mexican Women in the United States: Struggles Past and Present* (Los Angeles: U. of California Chicano Studies Res. Center, 1980): 117-143. Garment workers at Farah Manufacturing Company in El Paso, Texas, began a strike in May 1972, which was not settled until March 1974. Explores the effect of the strike on the women who initiated and sustained it. The story of the strike includes descriptions of the working conditions, events leading to the strike, the strike itself, the development of the union, and the lives of the strikers as Mexican-American women in the Southwest. The social and economic context in which the strike took place is also presented. Based on interviews with strikers; 8 notes. J. Powell

776. Cuellar, José B. SOCIAL SCIENCE RESEARCH IN THE U.S. MEX-ICAN COMMUNITY: A CASE STUDY. *Aztlán 1981 12(1): 1-21.* Describes how the US Mexican community responded in 1972 to a federally funded

proposal by the University of Southern California to study aspects of aging in different social and cultural contexts. Mexican community representatives objected to a project that failed to include input from the community being studied and failed to employ minority professionals and students on the project staff. Following intense negotiations on the issues, the Mexican community achieved its goal of emphasizing new norms of community control of research. Recommends research methodology that supports a symbiotic relationship between researcher and community, as anything else is exploitative of the community under study. 20 notes.   A. Hoffman

777. Cuthbert, Richard W. and Stevens, Joe B. THE NET ECONOMIC INCENTIVE FOR ILLEGAL MEXICAN MIGRATION: A CASE STUDY. *Int. Migration Rev. 1981 15(3): 543-550.* Studies Mexican farm workers in the Hood River Valley in Oregon during the fall apple harvest to determine the "net earnings differential" between wages earned in the United States and those earned in Mexico; net earnings in the United States were three times those in Mexico, less than usually stated by researchers.

778. Dagodag, W. Tim. SOURCE REGIONS OF COMPOSITION OF ILLEGAL MEXICAN IMMIGRATION TO CALIFORNIA. *Internat. Migration R. 1975 9(4): 499-511.* Discusses economic and labor factors in the illegal immigration of workers from west-central Mexico to California in the 1970's.

779. Davidson, Chandler and Gaitz, Charles M. ETHNIC ATTUTUDES AS A BASIS FOR MINORITY COOPERATION IN A SOUTHWESTERN METROPOLIS. *Social Sci. Q. 1973 53(4): 738-748.* "Using a stratified sample of Anglos, Mexican Americans and blacks in the city of Houston, it was found that Mexican Americans generally were more tolerant of and sympathetic with blacks than were Anglos in matters of equality, civil rights and social interaction. However, consistent with previous findings, Mexican-American attitudes were in several respects closer to those of Anglos than of blacks."
                                                                                         J

780. Davis, Jacaleen. WITCHCRAFT AND SUPERSTITIONS OF TORRANCE COUNTY. *New Mexico Hist. Rev. 1979 54(1): 53-59.* Discusses Spanish legends and beliefs, many of which are present today, concerning witchcraft in Torrance County, New Mexico. The causes and cures of several diseases, including *empacho* or stomach congestion, *suspendido* or suspended colon, and *mal ojo* or the evil eye, are mentioned. The concepts of *curanderos* or healers, *bruja* or witch, and *arbulario* or witch doctor, are also discussed. The people of Torrance County are reluctant to discuss witchcraft, which shows that it still influences them. 26 notes.   P. L. McLaughlin

781. Davison, Victoria F. and Shannon, Lyle W. CHANGE IN THE ECONOMIC ABSORPTION OF A COHORT OF IMMIGRANT MEXICAN AMERICANS AND NEGROES BEFORE 1960 AND 1971. *Int. Migration Rev. 1977 11(2): 190-214.* Examines data from 280 Mexican Americans, 280 blacks, and 413 Anglos in Racine, Wisconsin, discovering that during 1960-71 economic differences between Anglos, Mexicans, and blacks

remained essentially the same in occupation and income measures, while level of living and home conditions were slightly decreased.

782. DeLaGarza, Rodolfo and Vaughan, David. THE POLITICAL SO-CIALIZATION OF CHICANO ELITES: A GENERATIONAL AP-PROACH. *Social Sci. Q. 1984 65(2): 290-307.* Rejects traditional explanations of elite socialization in favor of a generational model to explain the development of contemporary Mexican-American political elites. Further, class is more important than region in explaining the political socialization of Mexican-American leaders. J/S

783. delaGarza, Rodolfo O. "AND THEN THERE WERE SOME...": CHICANOS AS NATIONAL POLITICAL ACTORS, 1967-1980. *Aztlán 1984 15(1): 1-24.* Assesses the successes and limitations of Mexican-American political leaders at the national level during 1967-80. Only five Mexican Americans have been elected to Congress, four to the House and one to the Senate, with little impact for their constituencies. Although many Mexican Americans have been appointed to administrative posts, especially during the Carter years, most have been at middle or junior levels with little impact on policymaking. A number of lobbying organizations have made some impact, but for the most part they are poorly funded, lack contacts, and, because they represent an electorally ineffective minority, are not taken seriously. Progress has been made, but the Mexican-American role in national politics is only beginning. Based on interviews and secondary sources; 2 tables, 34 notes.

A. Hoffman

784. delaPeña Brown, M. H. *UNA TAMALADA:* THE SPECIAL EVENT. *Western Follore 1981 40(1): 64-71.* As women interact and discuss matters of mutual interest appropriate to the occasion, including the making and serving of tamales, they learn from one another and thus increase skills and refine abilities; they express and reinforce values regarding food and food making which might also extend to other realms of life; and they share in a single experience which produces in some a sense of closeness, intimacy, and even unity—which in turn may serve as the justification and inspiration for participating in a similar event in the future. Based on personal experience.

J. Powell

785. DelCastillo, Adelaida R. MEXICAN WOMEN IN ORGANIZATION. Mora, Magdalena and DelCastillo, Adelaida R., ed. *Mexican Women in the United States: Struggles Past and Present* (Los Angeles: U. of California Chicano Studies Res. Center, 1980): 7-16. Provides a general evaluation of women's participation in Southern Californian Chicano student and community organizations from the late 1960's to the mid-1970's. The increase in the number of women in political activities did not change the general nature of their organizational roles, which continued to consist of office, secretarial, and culinary activities. Chicana feminism was an immediate response to the sexism of the movement. It sought solutions outside of the Marxist-Leninist perspective, speaking of the liberation of all women in general, and failing to make the connection between the liberation of a class, an oppressed nationality, and women. By the mid-1970's the acceptance of Marxist concepts by Chicanos

gave a wider social perspective to their aims. Secondary sources; 3 notes.

J. Powell

786. Delgado, Gary. ORGANIZING UNDOCUMENTED WORKERS. *Social Policy 1983 13(4): 26-29.* An account of the struggle of a fledgling coalition of labor organizations to unionize undocumented Hispanic-American workers.

787. DelosSantos, Alfredo G., Jr.; Montemajor, Joaquin; and Solis, Enrique, Jr. CHICANO STUDENTS IN INSTITUTIONS OF HIGHER EDUCA-TION: ACCESS, ATTRITION, AND ACHIEVEMENT. *Aztlán 1983 14(1): 79-110.* Compares enrollment/access, retention/attrition, and completion/achievement data for students at community colleges and universities in California and Texas. Hispanic students have higher attrition rates in Califor-nia than in Texas. Fewer Hispanics than non-Hispanics complete degrees. 14 tables, 10 fig., 3 notes, ref.   A. Hoffman

788. Donahue, Francis. ANATOMY OF CHICANO THEATER. *San José Studies 1977 3(1): 37-48.* Discusses guerrilla theater used by Mexican Ameri-cans to bring about social consciousness and social change; examines the types of dramatic presentations used, and characterizations, 1965-76.

789. Donahue, Francis. THE CHICANO STORY. *Colorado Q. 1973 21(3): 307-316.* Chicanos are the second largest minority group in the United States and total 3% of the population. Most Chicanos live in the Southwest where they receive fewer benefits from the American life-style. Discusses the career of Cesar Chavez (b. 1927) and the establishment of La Raza Unida Party in 1968. The four goals of the Chicano movement are 1) self-identity, 2) pluralistic philosophy of subculture, 3) social protest, and 4) unity within the movement.

B. A. Storey

790. Dowdall, George W. and Flood, Lawrence G. CORRELATES AND CONSEQUENCES OF SOCIOECONOMIC DIFFERENCES AMONG CHICANOS, BLACKS AND ANGLOS IN THE SOUTHWEST: A STUDY OF METROPOLITAN STRUCTURE. *Social Sci. J. 1982 19(2): 25-36.* Based on a study of 32 Southwestern metropolitan areas using data from the 1970 census, discusses how the "size, industrial patterns, and residential segregation" of Chicanos and blacks, "vis-à-vis the Anglo Majority" affect their "education, occupation, and income."

791. Drescher, Tim and Garcia, Rupert. RECENT RAZA MURALS IN THE U.S. *Radical Am. 1978 12(2): 15-31.* The last 10 years have witnessed the creation in many urban and rural Chicano and Latino communities of murals that relate on several levels to community involvement and support. These murals contain various motifs but generally portray in realistic fashion the contemporary plight and the historical oppression of Hispanic peoples. Artistically, the murals draw upon various sources for inspiration, commonly including the earlier work of the Mexican muralists Diego Rivera, Jose Clemente Orozco, and David Alfaro Siqueiros. Many Raza muralists are as

much concerned with obtaining community participation in the creation of their murals as they are in the results of their labors. N. Lederer

792. Eberstein, Isaac W. and Frisbie, W. Parker. DIFFERENCES IN MARITAL STABILITY AMONG MEXICAN AMERICANS, BLACKS AND ANGLOS: 1960 AND 1970. *Social Problems 1976 23(5): 609-621.* The frequency of marital disruption during 1960-70 is lowest among Mexican Americans, followed by Anglos and finally blacks.

793. Eberstein, Isaac W. and Pol, Louis G. MEXICAN-AMERICAN ETHNICITY, SOCIOECONOMIC STATUS, AND INFANT MORTALITY: A COUNTY-LEVEL ANALYSIS. *Social Sci. J. 1982 19(2): 61-71.* A study of Spanish language/Spanish surname persons in Arizona, California, Colorado, New Mexico, and Texas shows that both lower socioeconomic status and lack of prenatal care affect infant mortality.

794. Eiselein, E. B. and Marshall, Wes. MEXICAN-AMERICAN TELEVISION: APPLIED ANTHROPOLOGY AND PUBLIC TELEVISION. *Human Organization 1976 35(2): 147-156.* Project Fiesta, a Spanish-language public television series broadcast in southern Arizona was based on anthropological research.

795. Eribes, Richard A. THE OLDER MEXICAN: THE INVISIBLE ELDERLY. *Aztlán 1979 10: 91-100.* Surveys the problems of aged Mexican Americans. With a lower life expectancy than Anglos, elderly Mexican Americans often do not live long enough to enjoy the Social Security benefits to which they heavily contribute. Undercounted in the 1970 census, elderly Mexican Americans have missed out on programs for senior citizens, and existing programs often are insensitive to the culture of Mexican Americans. 3 tables, charts, 19 notes. A. Hoffman

796. Espinosa, Rubén W.; Fernández, Celestino; and Dornbusch, Sanford M. CHICANO PERCEPTIONS OF HIGH SCHOOL AND CHICANO PERFORMANCE. *Aztlán 1977 8: 133-156.* Attitudinal comparisons among Chicano, black, Anglo, and Asian students in San Francisco, California high schools indicated that Mexican Americans cared about education, saw a close link between education and future occupations, perceived parental belief in education and teacher warmth, and were generally not alienated from school; ascribes low academic achievement to improper preparation in mathematical and reading skills in lower grades; 1974-75.

797. Farge, Emile J. A REVIEW OF FINDINGS FROM "THREE GENERATIONS" OF CHICANO HEALTH CARE BEHAVIOR. *Social Sci. Q. 1977 58(3): 407-411.* Tests the hypotheses summarized by Weaver *(SSQ, 1973)* on a sample of 150 Mexican-American household heads. His findings confirm Weaver's suspicions that most observers wrongly typify this population. J

798. Faught, Jim D. CHICANOS IN A MEDIUM-SIZED CITY: DEMOGRAPHIC AND SOCIOECONOMIC CHARACTERISTICS. *Aztlán 1976 7(2): 307-326.* A study of the Chicano population of South Bend, Indiana,

based on 1974 interviews with 136 respondents. Examines age and occupational structure of the population, education, income, and economic mobility. Finds evidence that the 1970 US Census heavily overrepresents the more highly educated Chicanos, and that it seriously underestimates the number of persons living at very low income levels. Enlightened action to alleviate the chronically tenuous economic position of such persons as many of those surveyed requires first a general agreement on the facts involved. 8 tables, fig., 14 notes.   L. W. Van Wyk

799.   Felice, Lawrence G. MEXICAN AMERICAN SELF-CONCEPT AND EDUCATIONAL ACHIEVEMENT: THE EFFECTS OF ETHNIC ISOLATION AND SOCIOECONOMIC DEPRIVATIONS. *Social Sci. Q. 1973 53(4): 716-726.* "His multiple regression analysis, including eight independent factors, indicates that for Mexican Americans, two factors consistently exercise the largest influence for two measures of educational achievement: self-concept and the racial/ethnic compositional climate of the school."   J

800.   Finger, Bill. VICTORIA SOBRE FARAH. *Southern Exposure 1976 4(1-2): 45-49.* During 1972-74 garment workers, mostly Mexican Americans, successfully struck the Farah Company's El Paso, Texas, Gateway plant in order to join the Amalgamated Clothing Workers Union of America.

801.   Fischer, Nancy A. and Marcum, John P. ETHNIC INTEGRATION, SOCIOECONOMIC STATUS, AND FERTILITY AMONG MEXICAN AMERICANS. *Social Sci. Q. 1984 65(2): 583-593.* Mexican-American couples residing in neighborhoods of Mexican-American concentration have higher fertility than those residing elsewhere, independent of a negative effect of education on fertility.

802.   Flores, Nancy de la Zerda and Hopper, Robert. MEXICAN AMERICANS' EVALUATIONS OF SPOKEN SPANISH AND ENGLISH. *Speech Monographs 1975 42(2): 91-98.* Mexican-American adults listened to samples of standard English, Spanish-accented English, standard Spanish, and Tex-Mex (Texas Spanish). Attitude reactions interacted significantly with the subject's ethnic self-referent, the amount of Spanish spoken, income, level of education, and age. "Standard" dialects were generally preferred to "nonstandard" dialects in both English and Spanish.   J

803.   Ford, Larry R. and Griffin, Ernst. CHICANO PARK: PERSONALIZING AN INSTITUTIONAL LANDSCAPE. *Landscape 1981 25(2): 42-48.* Traces the creation of Chicano Park in 1970 in a section of San Diego known as Barrio Logan, an area that became a Mexican American slum by the 1950's; the park was designated as a historic site by the Historical Site Board of the City of San Diego in 1980.

804.   Fragomen, Austin T., Jr. THE UNDOCUMENTED ALIEN AND HIS AFTERMATH. *Int. Migration Rev. 1977 11(2): 241-243.* Examines the problem of illegal aliens, and Mexicans in particular, in the United States; proposes five points which should be considered in the Carter administration's attack on the problem: amnesty for those already unlawfully in the United

States; prevention of further illegal immigration; laws for social security, income tax, and minimum hourly wage; penalties for employers who would exploit such persons; and viable foreign development programs, 1977.

805. Friedland, William H. and Thomas, Robert J. PARADOXES OF AGRICULTURAL UNIONISM IN CALIFORNIA. *Society 1974 11(4): 54-62.* Analyzes Cesar Chavez' revitalization of the grape and lettuce boycott, and discusses the paradox of Teamsters and United Farm Workers competing for workers' allegiance; one of five articles on "State Politics and Public Interests." S

806. Frisbie, Parker. MILITANCY AMONG MEXICAN AMERICAN HIGH SCHOOL STUDENTS. *Social Sci. Q. 1973 53(4): 865-883.* "Through the use of a standard contingency design and a weighted least squares technique, four variables are shown to be significantly related to militancy among Mexican-American high school students.... finds that perception of Anglo discrimination, frequency of the use of Spanish, and expectancy of success of militancy are positively associated with the expressed willingness to take part in political protest. Also, males are more likely to manifest a militant orientation than females." J

807. Frisbie, Parker. ILLEGAL MIGRATION FROM MEXICO TO THE UNITED STATES: A LONGITUDINAL ANALYSIS. *Internat. Migration R. 1975 9(1): 3-13.* Analyzes illegal migration from Mexico to the United States, 1946-65, focusing on economic causes of migration.

808. Frisbie, W. Parker and Neidert, Lisa. INEQUALITY AND THE RELATIVE SIZE OF MINORITY POPULATIONS: A COMPARATIVE ANALYSIS. *Am. J. of Sociol. 1977 82(5): 1007-1030.* Socioeconomic differentials separating whites and blacks have been shown to correlate positively with the percentage of blacks in a population. However, in multiracial or multiethnic populations, it is necessary to take into account the effects of the relative size of each minority present in nonnegligible numbers. In the research reported here, the relationship between socioeconomic inequality and the proportion of Mexican Americans and blacks in the population of metropolitan areas was decomposed through path-analytic techniques. Analysis of a model incorporating the impact of the size of both minorities indicates that minority income levels are inversely related to minority size and that disparaties between majority and minority size increases. Mexican-American occupational levels vary positively with the percentage of blacks, but black occupational status was found to be virtually unrelated to the proportional representation of Mexican Americans in metropolitan areas. Finally, the positive relationship between minority percentage and inequalities of income and occupation persists net of the effects of a number of plausible alternative explanations. J

809. Frisbie, W. Parker; Bean, Frank D.; and Eberstein, Isaac W. RECENT CHANGES IN MARITAL INSTABILITY AMONG MEXICAN AMERICANS: CONVERGENCE WITH BLACK AND ANGLO TRENDS? *Social Forces 1980 58(4): 1205-1220.* The research reported here employs a type of cohort analysis to compare recent (1960-70) changes in the prevalence of

marital instability among Mexican-American women with those observed among black and Anglo women in the southwestern United States. Analyses of detailed categories of marital status, as well as a summary measure of instability, reveal that women in all three groups recorded increases in marital dissolution. However, differences in the rate of increase by ethnic group, especially among the younger cohorts, suggested an overall pattern of divergence in trend. Some small degree of convergence was detected for a few cohorts, and lessened differentials were more common between blacks and Anglos than between blacks and Mexican Americans. US Censuses, 1960 and 1970; 4 tables, 9 notes, 27 ref.   J

810. Fritsch, Johann. LAGE UND KAMPF DER LANDARBEITER DER USA IN DEN SIEBZIGER JAHREN: ZUR GRÜNDUNG DER UNITED FARM WORKERS UNION [Conditions and struggle of the farm workers in the USA in the seventies: On the founding of the United Farm Workers]. *Zeitschrift für Geschichtswissenschaft [East Germany] 1976 24(12): 1414-1423.* After initial success in organizing farm workers in the 1930's, the farm labor movement fell victim to McCarthyism in subsequent decades. In the 1960's the movement was revived in California, America's leading agricultural state. With the Delano strike in 1965, the United Farm Workers Union became the leading agricultural union in the US, and after defeating a challenge by the reactionary Teamsters' Union, it attained legal recognition of agricultural workers' unions in California. The UFWU has played a leading role in the struggle against racism. Primary and secondary sources; 32 notes.   J. T. Walker

811. Fugita, Stephen S. and O'Brien, David J. ECONOMICS, IDEOLOGY, AND ETHNICITY: THE STRUGGLE BETWEEN THE UNITED FARM WORKERS UNION AND THE NISEI FARMERS LEAGUE. *Social Problems 1977 25(2): 146-156.* Relations between the Mexican American United Farm Workers Union and the Japanese American Nisei Farmers League during 1974-76 in California's San Joaquin Valley were affected by not only economic structural factors but also each group's interpretation of ethnicity.

812. Fugita, Stephen S. A PERCEIVED ETHNIC FACTOR IN CALIFORNIA'S FARM LABOR CONFLICT: THE NISEI FARMER. *Explorations in Ethnic Studies 1978 1(1): 50-72.* Examines the conflict between the Nisei Farmers League and the United Farm Workers Union in California's San Joaquin Valley over agricultural labor, 1971-77.

813. Gándara, Arturo. CHICANOS Y EXTRANJERSO ILEGALES: LA CONJUNCIÓN DE SUS DERECHOS CONSTITUCIONALES FRENTE AL ESTADO NORTEAMERICANO [Chicanos and illegal immigrants: the convergence of their constitutional rights before the North American state]. *Foro Int. [Mexico] 1978 18(3): 480-493.* Surveys the legal impact of the US attempt to contain illegal Mexican immigration on the rights of Mexican Americans, and concludes that the constitutional and civil rights of Mexican Americans have been adversely affected. Based on court cases and secondary sources; 19 notes.   D. A. Franz

814. Garcia, Eugene E. JOINT FACULTY APPOINTMENTS: AN AD-MINISTRATIVE DILEMMA IN CHICANO STUDIES. *Explorations in Ethnic Studies 1979 2(2): 1-8.* Discusses the establishment of the Chicano Studies Department on the University of California's Santa Barbara campus, focusing on the advantages and disadvantages of the "joint position" faculty appointment policy begun in 1975 under which all permanent ladder-rank faculty serve 50% of their time in Chicano Studies and 50% in another academic department.

815. Garcia, F. Chris. ORIENTATIONS OF MEXICAN AMERICAN AND ANGLO CHILDREN TOWARD THE U.S. POLITICAL COMMU-NITY. *Social Sci. Q. 1973 53(4): 814-829.* "This study of more than 1,200 school children in California reveals divergent orientations between Mexican and Anglo students in responses containing references to Mexico." J

816. Garcia, Flaviano Chris. MANITOS AND CHICANOS IN NUEVO MÉXICO POLITICS. *Aztlán 1974 5(1/2): 177-188.* Describes the participation of Manitos (New Mexicans of Mexican-Spanish heritage) and Chicanos (Mexican Americans) in New Mexico's politics. S

817. Garcia, John A. AN ANALYSIS OF CHICANO AND ANGLO ELECTORAL PATTERNS IN SCHOOL BOARD ELECTIONS. *Ethnicity 1979 6(2): 168-183.* More and more Hispanic Americans are seeking elective office. Analyzes Arizona school board elections and finds that ethnic or block voting is common. This may represent either a short-term or an enduring pattern. 6 tables, 39 notes. T. W. Smith

818. Garcia, John A. SELF-IDENTITY AMONG THE MEXICAN-ORI-GIN POPULATION. *Social Sci. Q. 1981 62(1): 88-98.* Uses the Survey of Income and Education (1976) data for Arizona, California, Colorado, New Mexico and Texas. A total of 151,170 households were interviewed. Five ethnic labels were used to determine variation of perception by Mexican-origin people of those labels. Secondary data, literature; 2 tables, 19 notes. M. Mtewa

819. Garcia, Jose Z.; Clark, Cal; and Clark, Janet. POLICY IMPACTS ON CHICANOS AND WOMEN: A STATE CASE STUDY. *Policy Studies J. 1978 7(2): 251-257.* Studies the changes of status of Mexican Americans and women in the New Mexico state government work force during 1971-78.

820. Garcia, Philip and Maldonado, Lionel A. AMERICA'S MEXICANS: A PLEA FOR SPECIFICITY. *Social Sci. J. 1982 19(2): 9-24.* Discusses educational, occupational, income, and generational data to point out the misleading conclusions that are drawn when the Mexican-American population is grouped under the broad Hispanic category in the US Census.

821. Garcia, Philip. DUAL-LANGUAGE CHARACTERISTICS AND EARNINGS: MALE MEXICAN WORKERS IN THE UNITED STATES. *Social Science Research 1984 13(3): 221-235.* A study of income differentials indicates that Mexican immigrants speaking English do not have an economic advantage, that there is a small reward for Mexican Americans who speak

English only, and that Mexican Americans who are Spanish-dominant bilinguals are at a distinct disadvantage.

822.   Garcia, Philip. AN EVALUATION OF UNEMPLOYMENT AND EMPLOYMENT DIFFERENCES BETWEEN MEXICAN AMERICANS AND WHITES: THE SEVENTIES. *Social Sci. J. 1983 20(1): 51-62.* Unemployment rates for Mexican Americans are higher than for Anglos and are more sensitive to changes in the demand for labor.

823.   Garcia, Philip. TRENDS IN THE RELATIVE INCOME POSITION OF MEXICAN-ORIGIN WORKERS IN THE U.S.: THE EARLY SEVENTIES. *Sociol. and Social Res. 1982 66(4): 467-483.* Lower incomes among Mexican Americans are highly related to lower job statuses. Mexican immigrants experience unique obstacles to earnings. Mexican-white differences in annual income widen during the periods of high national employment.   J/S

824.   Garcia-Bahne, Betty. LA CHICANA AND THE CHICANO FAMILY. Sánchez, Rosaura and Martinez Cruz, Rosa, ed. *Essays on la Mujer* (Los Angeles, Ca.: Chicano Studies Center Publ., 1977): 30-47. Emphasizes socioeconomic factors as determinants of family organization rather than describing certain qualities of Mexican Americans' families as being cultural and inherent. Lower incomes mean fewer options, consequently the majority of Chicanas marry young. Women are usually subject to male domination and are expected to cooperate and help to unify the family. Any attempt to assert independence is seen as a threat to the protective role that the family plays for the Chicanos in an otherwise hostile society. "The Chicano family can thus be seen as a vehicle which incorporates those strengthening qualities that are necessary for social units to survive under exploitative conditions and paradoxically embodies those values which mitigate against the development and exercise of self-determination." Table, 14 notes.   M. T. Wilson

825.   Garza, Rodolfo O. de la. DEMYTHOLOGIZING CHICANO-MEXICAN RELATIONS. *Pro. of the Acad. of Pol. Sci. 1981 34(1): 88-96.* Presents a framework for predicting the kinds of relationships that may arise between Chicanos and Mexicans. Identification of types of actors most likely to be involved, their resources, and the issues around which they interact. Because Mexican leaders seem willing to invest substantial sums in educational and cultural relations, Chicanos will continue to be the greatest beneficiary of the developing relationship. Neither Mexico nor the United States will be particularly affected by the continued growth of Chicano-Mexican ties. Covers 1970-80.   T. P. Richardson

826.   Garza, Rudolph O. de la. VOTING PATTERNS IN "BI-CULTURAL EL PASO": A CONTEXTUAL ANALYSIS OF CHICANO VOTING BEHAVIOR. *Aztlán 1974 5(1/2): 235-260.*

827.   Gecas, Viktor. FAMILY AND SOCIAL STRUCTURAL INFLUENCES ON THE CAREER ORIENTATIONS OF RURAL MEXICAN-AMERICAN YOUTH. *Rural Sociol. 1980 45(2): 272-289.* Discusses a study on the effects of the family environment and obstacles from the cultural and

economic situations of rural Mexican-American families on the career orientations of rural Mexican-American youth, based on a survey of migrant and settled rural Mexican-American families in Yakima Valley, Washington, in 1971; concludes that cultural and economic situations affect career orientations as much as family influences do.

828. Gerking, Shelby D. and Mutti, John H. COSTS AND BENEFITS OF ILLEGAL IMMIGRATION: KEY ISSUES FOR GOVERNMENT POLICY. *Social Sci. Q. 1980 61(1): 71-85.* Examines the effects of illegal Mexican immigration on output and income distribution in the southwestern United States. Workers who possess skills similar to illegal alien laborers suffer lower wages when the rate of illegal immigration rises. The effects of increased immigration on the rest of the labor force and the owners of capital, however, are ambiguous. A general equilibrium model highlights the results. Based on Immigration and Naturalization Service data and on secondary works; 2 fig., 19 notes, biblio. L. F. Velicer

829. Goldberg, Robert A. RACIAL CHANGE ON THE SOUTHERN PERIPHERY: THE CASE OF SAN ANTONIO, TEXAS, 1960-1965. *J. of Southern Hist. 1983 49(3): 349-374.* San Antonio's experience with desegregation illustrates what occurred on the Southern periphery as opposed to the desegregation experience in the more publicized Deep South. A small black population, a large Mexican-American minority, the presence of five US military bases, desegregationist religious leadership, and a peace and property Good Government League combined to create an atmosphere ready for change. Since the local black population and the NAACP were largely passive and impotent, desegregation was granted, not won. Texas state officials preferred to retain control of desegregation by doing it "the Texas way." Based upon San Antonio newspapers, city council records, and interviews with San Antonio residents; 85 notes. T. Schoonover

830. Goldman, Shifra M. MEXICAN MURALISM: ITS SOCIAL-EDUCATIVE ROLES IN LATIN AMERICA AND THE UNITED STATES. *Aztlán 1982 13(1-2): 111-133.* Traces the development of Mexican mural art since the 1920's and its influence on Chicano artists in the 1960's and 70's. The first great muralists—Diego Rivera, José Clemente Orozco, and David Alfaro Siqueiros—drew on indigenous themes in the 1920's; they and other artists also paid homage to the mestizo in Mexican history and important figures of the 1910 Revolution. Their work influenced mural artists in many Latin American countries. Since the 1960's, Chicanos have done more than 1,000 murals in California alone, varying greatly in style but united in theme from the experience of living in the United States. The murals have promoted political action, taught the history of the Mexican heritage, and played an important social role in Mexico and the Southwest. Ref. A. Hoffman

831. Gonzales, Sylvia. THE WHITE FEMINIST MOVEMENT: THE CHICANA PERSPECTIVE. *Social Sci. J. 1977 14(2): 69-76.* Discusses the perspective which Chicanas bring to the women's movement, including sources of oppression from both Latin and US cultures; more white women must become sympathetic to Chicana needs.

832. González, Gustavo. SOME CHARACTERISTICS OF THE EN-GLISH USED BY MIGRANT SPANISH-SPEAKING CHILDREN IN TEXAS. *Aztlán 1976 7(1): 27-49.* Discusses the speech of migrant children, with special emphasis on deviations in grammar. Migrant children were interviewed, then their responses were analyzed grammatically for verb forms, subject-verb agreement and negations. Many reflected Spanish usages in their English. Calls for research to help teachers of bilingual programs, 1976.
J. Tull

833. Gonzalez, Rosalinda M. and Fernandez, Raul A. U.S. IMPERIALISM AND MIGRATION: THE EFFECTS ON MEXICAN WOMEN AND FAMILIES. *Rev. of Radical Pol. Econ. 1979 11(4): 112-124.* Illegal Mexican immigration into the United States is a consequence of US imperialism. Having destroyed the economy of Mexico, US capitalists have acted to keep the Mexican people as a reserve force of cheap labor. Especially exploited are women and children, who will labor for less money and are less skilled at demanding their rights. At present, the all-powerful capitalists are striving to shut off illegal immigration on the one hand, in order to prevent having to pay higher wages, and to keep those who have entered in a position of second-class persons without rights for the same purpose. 34 notes.
V. L. Human

834. Gonzalez, Rosalinda Mendez. MEXICAN WOMEN AND FAMI-LIES: RURAL-TO-URBAN, AND INTERNATIONAL MIGRATION. *Southwest Econ. and Soc. 1978-79 4(2): 14-27.* Discusses the labor activities of Mexican women and their families after immigration to the United States from Mexico, specifically the ability of immigrants to fit into the American capitalist system from a rural labor system, 1970's.

835. Graham, Otis L., Jr. THE PROBLEM THAT WILL NOT GO AWAY: ILLEGAL IMMIGRATION. *Center Mag. 1977 10(4): 56-66.* Each year, 60-90 percent of the million illegal immigrants to the United States are Mexicans; examines the causes and implications of this situation.

836. Grandjeat, Yves-Charles. LE THÉÂTRE CHICANO EN MARGE DE *ZOOT-SUIT:* DIXIÈME FESTIVAL TENAZ [The Chicano Theater in connection with *Zoot-Suit:* Tenth Tenaz Festival]. *Rev. Française d'Études Américaines [France] 1980 5(10): 249-254.* Discusses the plays *Zoot-Suit, El Louie, El Quetzal,* and *Angel Death,* shown at the June 1979 festival of Chicano theater in Santa Barbara, California, sponsored by Tenaz (Teatro Nacional de Aztlán).

837. Greenberg, Bradley S. et al. LOCAL NEWSPAPER COVERAGE OF MEXICAN AMERICANS. *Journalism Q. 1983 60(4): 671-676.* Examines the composition and extensiveness of daily newspaper coverage of Mexican Americans in locations with substantial populations of that ethnic group. There is great variability among the newspapers, depending on whether a premium is placed on quantity, representativeness, or content. Primary sources; 4 tables, 9 notes.
A. C. Drysdale

838. Grider, Sylvia Ann. *CON SAFOS*: MEXICAN-AMERICANS, NAMES AND GRAFFITI. *J. of Am. Folklore 1975 88(348): 132-142.* Graffiti in Mexican-American districts in the United States reflect the high value attached to personal names in Mexican culture. The term *con safos* (roughly, "the same to you") is used to protect name graffiti from defacement by suggesting that any slurs added pertain to the vandal alone. The graffiti are intended for people who will recognize the names. Interviews from Dallas, Texas, and secondary sources; 16 illus., 26 notes.   W. D. Piersen

839. Gruhl, John; Welch, Susan; and Spohn, Cassia. WOMEN AS CRIMI-NAL DEFENDANTS: A TEST FOR PATERNALISM. *Western Pol. Q. 1984 37(3): 456-467.* Compares the treatment of about 10,000 white, black, and Hispanic male and female defendants charged with felonies and processed through the Los Angeles County Superior Court, controlling for relevant legal factors and for race. It reveals that courts actually treat black and Hispanic female defendants, but not white female defendants, more leniently than male defendants, and it attributes this to judicial paternalism.   J

840. Gutierrez, Armando and Hirsch, Herbert. THE MILITANT CHAL-LENGE TO THE AMERICAN ETHOS: "CHICANOS" AND "MEXICAN AMERICANS." *Social Sci. Q. 1973 53(4): 830-845.* "Based on a survey of 786 students in grades seven through twelve in Crystal City, Texas. The main purpose is to ascertain whether students who self identify as 'Chicanos' differ in their social and political perceptions from students who self identify as 'Mexican Americans.' [The authors] find that there are no significant differ-ences in perceptions of means to achieve success, but that students who self identify as 'Chicano' tend to have a higher level of political consciousness than students who self identify as 'Mexican Americans.' "   J

841. Gutierrez, Armando G. and Hirsch, Herbert. POLITICAL MATURA-TION AND POLITICAL AWARENESS: THE CASE OF THE CRYSTAL CITY CHICANO. *Aztlán 1974 5(1/2): 295-312.* Examines the case of Crystal City, Texas, where Mexican Americans were elected to a majority of seats on the school board.   S

842. Hall, Grace and Saltzstein, Alan. EQUAL EMPLOYMENT OPPOR-TUNITY FOR MINORITIES IN MUNICIPAL GOVERNMENT. *Social Sci. Q. 1977 57(4): 864-872.* Newly available data from 26 Texas cities reveal unexpectedly complex employment patterns for blacks and Mexican Americans in municipal government. Indices which consider both a minority group's representation and its distribution across salary levels demonstrate that blacks are more disadvantaged than Spanish surnamed individuals. Mexican-Ameri-can employment is related more strongly to the professional and educational characteristics of that population than is the case for blacks. Urbanization has not affected the hiring of both groups equally; black employment potential seems to increase in rapidly growing central cities. Based on Equal Employ-ment Opportunity statistics and secondary sources; 3 tables, 3 notes, biblio.
                     W. R. Hively

843.   Hammerback, John C. and Jensen, Richard J. THE RHETORICAL WORLDS OF CÉSAR CHÁVEZ AND REIES TIJERINA. *Western J. of Speech Communication 1980 44(3): 166-176.* Reies Tijerina, a Chicano political and religious leader in Texas, and Cesar Chavez, a union organizer among California farm laborers, gained political aims for the groups they led through persistent public appearances and development of persuasive rhetorical styles; 1960's-70's.

844.   Hancock, Joel. THE EMERGENCE OF CHICANO POETRY: A SURVEY OF SOURCES, THEMES, AND TECHNIQUES. *Arizona Q. 1973 29(1): 57-73.* A survey of modern Chicano poetry as a reflection of the "Renaissance of the Barrios." Analyzes the work of many Chicano poets and surveys the history of the Chicano literary movement with emphasis on the work of Rodolfo "Corky" Gonzalez, Alurista, Octavio I. Romano-V., and the "prison poets." Discusses several recent anthologies and the major periodicals and journals which publish Chicano poetry. Based on secondary sources; 30 notes.   S. L. Myres

845.   Haro, Carlos M. TRUANT AND LOW-ACHIEVING CHICANO STUDENT PERCEPTIONS IN THE HIGH SCHOOL SYSTEM. *Aztlán 8: 99-131.* Examines academic, socioeconomic, racial (perceived and real), and cultural aspects of truancy among Mexican-American students in high schools in predominantly Chicano institutions in central Los Angeles, California; 1974-75.

846.   Haro, Carlos Manuel. CHICANOS AND HIGHER EDUCATION: A REVIEW OF SELECTED LITERATURE. *Aztlán 1983 14(1): 35-77.* Discusses the obstacles faced by Mexican Americans in pursuing higher education. Despite their growing numbers, Chicanos are underrepresented in American colleges and universities, especially in the more elite institutions. Problems of access, retention, attrition, and funding have been slighted by college administrations who have also given little attention to Chicano Studies programs, hiring Hispanic faculty, and modifying unfair admissions criteria. The Scholastic Aptitude Test and other standardized tests are culturally biased in favor of the majority population. Suggests major revisions in admissions policies to accept Chicano students for professional careers, not by special admissions but through significant reforms in admissions criteria. 4 tables, ref., biblio.
                                                                                A. Hoffman

847.   Haro, Robert P. HOW MEXICAN-AMERICANS VIEW THE LIBRARY. *Wilson Lib. Bull. 1977 44(7): 736-742.* Examines use of libraries (public, school, and college) among Mexican Americans; librarians should be willing to revamp library practice goals and to go into the Chicano community. One of 11 articles in this issue on libraries and the Spanish-speaking.

848.   Hawkes, Glenn R.; Guagnano, Gregory A.; Smith, Jeanne W.; and Forest, M. Kathryn. THE INFLUENCE OF WORK AND NONWORK FACTORS ON JOB SATISFACTION FOR MEXICAN-AMERICAN MALE WORKERS. *Rural Sociol. 1984 49(1): 117-126.* Nonwork factors

such as family life and recreational opportunities are important elements in the level of job satisfaction reported by Mexican-American males in the Southwest.

849.   Hawkes, Glenn R.; Guagnano, Gregory A.; Acredolo, Curt; and Helmick, Sandra A. STATUS INCONSISTENCY AND JOB SATISFACTION: GENERAL POPULATION AND MEXICAN-AMERICAN SUBPOPULATION ANALYSES. *Sociol. and Social Res. 1984 68(3): 378-379.* Occupation, education, and income status levels and inconsistencies between status levels were examined for their influence on job satisfaction in samples from the general population and the Mexican-American subpopulation. Dramatic differences were observed between the two samples in both general status and status inconsistency effects. Strong status inconsistency effects may exist in subpopulations but remain hidden in samples of the general population.   J/S

850.   Hayes-Bautista, David E.; Schinek, Werner O.; and Chapa, Jorge. YOUNG LATINOS IN AN AGING AMERICAN SOCIETY. *Social Policy 1984 15(1): 49-52.* In the representative state of California, the higher Latino birthrate is leading to a stratified population of working younger Latinos supporting the social programs of aged Anglos, and policy decisions now must aim toward economic and educational gains and social cohesion for Latinos and other minorities.

851.   Hernández, José; Estrada, Leo; and Alvírez, David. CENSUS DATA AND THE PROBLEM OF CONCEPTUALLY DEFINING THE MEXICAN AMERICAN POPULATION. *Social Sci. Q. 1973 53(4): 671-687.* "Definitions used by the U. S. Bureau of the Census in the 1970 and previous enumerations are evaluated for effectiveness in measuring the Mexican-American population. Recommendations regarding the use of published data in social science research are drawn, with special emphasis on comparability. Preliminary figures for 1970 are analyzed to illustrate methodological problems and observations are made concerning the improvement of demographic concepts and sources of information."   J

852.   Hernandez, Patrícia. LIVES OF CHICANA ACTIVISTS: THE CHICANO STUDENT MOVEMENT (A CASE STUDY). Mora, Magdalena and DelCastillo, Adelaida R., ed. *Mexican Women in the United States: Struggles Past and Present* (Los Angeles: U. of California Chicano Studies Res. Center, 1980): 17-25. Distinguishes the nature of Chicano student activism and Chicana activism in San Diego via the political orientation and problems encountered by two women leaders at San Diego State College. They began their political careers with the Chicano Student Movement in the late 1960's. Shows the personal effects of politics on their lives during 1968-76. The interviews were taped as the women were questioned concerning family reactions, relationships with friends, time spent in political activity, marriage roles, and motherhood. Biblio.   J. Powell

853.   Herrick, John M. HEALTH CARE: THE DILEMMA OF DELIVERY. *Aztlán 1979 10: 123-127.* Reports on problems of health care facilities and use by poor people, focusing on a study by Isaih C. Lee (1976) on services provided in two neighborhoods in Los Angeles, California. Mexican Ameri-

cans' use of the facilities fell beneath expectations. Suggests that delivery of health care must consider factors such as sociocultural background of potential users, the socioeconomic status of the users, employment of community residents in paraprofessional capacities in health care facilities, and correlation between cultural background and types of medical care offered or sought. Better communications between clinic staff and neighborhood residents is essential. Ref.   A. Hoffman

854.   Hessler, Richard M. CITIZEN PARTICIPATION, SOCIAL ORGA-NIZATION, AND CULTURE: A NEIGHBORHOOD HEALTH CENTER FOR CHICANOS. *Human Organization 1977 36(2): 124-134.* This paper reports on the relationship between the organization of a comprehensive neighborhood health center and the cultural dynamics of several Chicano barrios. The paper focuses on consumer participation in health care decision-making as a way to include cultural factors in the organization of health services. Principles related to social organization and public policy are discussed.   J

855.   Hirsch, Herbert. ETHNIC IDENTITY AND STUDENTS' PERCEP-TIONS OF A COMMUNITY CONTROLLED SCHOOL. *Social Sci. Q. 1974 55(2): 425-438.* "Presents data demonstrating significant differences in Anglo, Chicano, and Mexican-American students' perceptions of the schools as agents of political information transmission, degree of politicization of the schools, and fairness of the schools. ...Finds that controls for sex and grade in school had some impact, but that ethnic self-identity accounted for the greatest amount of variance in the dependent variables."   J

856.   Hirschman, Charles. PRIOR U.S. RESIDENCE AMONG MEXICAN IMMIGRANTS. *Social Forces 1978 56(4): 1179-1203.* From a survey of legal Mexican immigrants to the U.S. in late 1973 and early 1974, over 60 percent of the sample report having previously lived in the United States for some time. This suggests the modal path of legal immigration begins with an illegal stay in the U.S. which often makes possible legal entry. Return-immigrants to the U.S. (legal immigrants with prior U.S. residence) have lower socioeconomic origins, educational attainment, and occupational levels than first-time immigrants. While part of the lower occupational attainment of return-immigrants is due to their poorer social origins and educational attainment, most of it can be attributed to their prior residence in the U.S. This effect is interpreted as a measure of the occupational discrimination that was encountered during their prior residence in the United States.   J

857.   Hoehn, Richard A. THE CHICANO ETHOS: AN ANGLO VIEW. *Lutheran Q. 1976 28(2): 166-172.* The Chicano experience offers important, alternative characteristics which could prove to be attractive additions to the American ethos. The oppression they have suffered provides them with a strong sense of the will-to-be, and their own racial heritage has made racial pluralism for Chicanos a fact of life. Even more important, the Chicano ethos with its strong emphases on family, community, and open expressions of emotion presents important alternative qualities that should be taken into

consideration in the future evolution of the American character. Based on secondary sources; 4 notes.   J. A. Kicklighter

858. Hoffman, Abraham. MEXICAN REPATRIATION: RESEARCH NEEDS AND PERSPECTIVES. *J. of Mexican Am. Hist. 1973 3(1): 165-170.* Although Paul S. Taylor's works on Mexican and Mexican-American migration remains the beginning point for scholars, the time is past due for additional research in Mexican repatriation. Several possibilities for research exist. It is the responsibility of Mexican-American and Chicano historians to encourage and concentrate on the potentiality of this neglected field.
R. T. Fulton

859. Holmes, Malcolm D. and Daudistel, Howard C. ETHNICITY AND JUSTICE IN THE SOUTHWEST: THE SENTENCING OF ANGLO, BLACK, AND MEXICAN ORIGIN DEFENDANTS. *Social Sci. Q. 1984 65(2): 265-277.* Compares severity of case disposition for Anglo, black and Mexican-American burglary and robbery defendants in two metropolitan jurisdictions in the southwestern United States. Both the additive effects of the race variables and their interactions with other determinants of sentence severity were considered. Substantial evidence of discrimination in both additive and interactive models was obtained for one jurisdiction, but the evidence of discrimination was considerably weaker for the other. Jurisdictional differences that may explain this contrast are discussed.   J

860. Holscher, Louis M. TIENE ARTE VALOR AFUERA DEL BARRIO: THE MURALS OF EAST LOS ANGELES AND BOYLE HEIGHTS. *J. of Ethnic Studies 1976 4(3): 43-52.* Discusses the murals painted by young Chicano artists during the late 1960's-70's, their colors, line, depth, and the meaning they hold both for the barrio inhabitant and the non-Chicano. They are newspapers on walls presenting the attitudes, feelings, and life styles of the Chicano community, and can greatly enlighten those unaware of Chicano history and culture. They represent a search for identity, an affirmation of Chicano culture, a concern for poverty and racism, and a joy in brotherhood, in "Chicanismo." They continue the tradition fostered by David Siqueiros and Diego Rivera. 6 illus., map.   G. J. Bobango

861. Holtz, Janicemarie Allard. THE "LOW-RIDERS": PORTRAIT OF A YOUTH SUBCULTURE. *Youth and Soc. 1975 6(4): 495-512.* Describes a mostly Mexican-American subculture in East Los Angeles based on the possession of an elaborately modified and decorated automobile. The subculture emphasizes a media-based image of leisure. Based on 1974 interviews and observations, secondary works; 9 notes, biblio.   J. H. Sweetland

862. Howell, Frances Baseden. A SPLIT LABOR MARKET: MEXICAN FARM WORKERS IN THE SOUTHWEST. *Sociol. Inquiry 1982 52(2): 132-140.* The split-labor-market theory explains importation of foreign contract workers, passage of farm labor legislation, development and implementation of mechanized equipment, expansion of the "runaway shop," and decrease in the number of independent farmers concurrent with an increase in large-scale corporate farms; the farm worker movement, the United Farm Workers

and the Arizona Farm Workers being two of the most familiar examples, also has a major impact.

863. Hurstfield, Jennifer. "INTERNAL" COLONIALISM: WHITE, BLACK AND CHICANO SELF-CONCEPTIONS. *Ethnic and Racial Studies [Great Britain] 1978 1(1): 60-79.* Discusses differences in the self-perceptions of black, white and Chicano adolescents in a Los Angeles junior high school in 1971.

864. Jacobs, Sue-Ellen. "TOP-DOWN PLANNING": ANALYSIS OF OBSTACLES TO COMMUNITY DEVELOPMENT IN AN ECONOMICALLY POOR REGION OF THE SOUTHWESTERN UNITED STATES. *Human Organization 1978 37(3): 246-256.* Sees a lack of communication and cooperation between government agencies and the local Spanish-speaking and Indian peoples in planning a dam and canal system for the Espanola Valley in New Mexico during the 1970's.

865. Jenkins, J. Craig. THE DEMAND FOR IMMIGRANT WORKERS: LABOR SCARCITY OR SOCIAL CONTROL? *Int. Migration Rev. 1978 12(4): 514-535.* Analyzes the economic role of Mexican immigrant workers in the United States since the 1950's, based on the labor scarcity and social control agruments.

866. Jenkins, J. Craig. PUSH/PULL IN ILLEGAL MEXICAN MIGRATION TO THE U.S. *Int. Migration Rev. 1977 11(2): 178-189.* Discusses the "push/pull" hypothesis of immigration of illegal aliens, Mexicans, into the United States, 1948-72; maintains that the "push" of conditions in Mexico, economic development favoring private rather than peasant agricultural development, outweighed the "pull" of economic opportunity in the United States.

867. Jensen, Richard J. AN INTERVIEW WITH JOSÉ ANGEL GUTIÉRREZ. *Western J. of Speech Communication 1980 44(3): 203-213.* Interview with political activist José Angel Gutiérrez centers on the importance of public speaking in the Chicano nationalist movement, Gutiérrez's use of rhetoric, and his personal political aspirations as they affect the La Raza Unida movement, 1979.

868. Jensen, Richard J. and Hammerback, John C. RADICAL NATIONALISM AMONG CHICANOS: THE RHETORIC OF JOSÉ ANGEL GUTIÉRREZ. *Western J. of Speech Communication 1980 44(3): 191-202.* By using rhetorical tactics which created new cultural terms (Chicano, Aztlan, and La Raza Unida), restructuring Chicano reality to recognize the myth of passivity and the actuality of Anglo suppression, and originating threats of violence (which though usually unacted upon, created a symbolic violent aura), José Angel Gutiérrez, a radical nationalist Chicano political activist in Crystal City, Texas, became instrumental in establishing the Chicano nationalist movement; 1969-79.

869. Jones, Lamar B. and Rice, G. Randolph. AGRICULTURAL LABOR IN THE SOUTHWEST: THE POST BRACERO YEARS. *Social Sci. Q. 1980*

61(1): 86-94. Examines the wage and employment effects of excluding temporary Mexican farm workers from the agricultural labor market in Texas, California, New Mexico, and Arizona. Utilizing a simple time trend model, the authors detect no significant improvement in agricultural wages from 1965, the year braceros were excluded, to 1977. The effect of exclusion on employment is inconclusive due to the increasing number of illegal aliens following termination of the Mexican Bracero Program. Based on Department of Agriculture and Department of Labor data; 4 tables, 8 notes, biblio.　　　　L. F. Velicer

870.　Jones, Richard C. CHANNELIZATION OF UNDOCUMENTED MEXICAN MIGRANTS TO THE U.S. *Econ. Geog. 1982 58(2): 156-176.* Based on the work of social geographers, discusses whether the migration of undocumented Mexicans to the United States is beneficial or detrimental, examines the migration in numbers, and focuses on the origins of migrants, their destinations, and flow patterns, particularly what is called "channelization" or "a disproportionately large flow of migrants between a specific origin and a specific destination"; 1975-82.

871.　Jones, Richard C. UNDOCUMENTED MIGRATION FROM MEXICO: SOME GEOGRAPHICAL QUESTIONS. *Ann. of the Assoc. of Am. Geog. 1982 72(1): 77-87.* Liberalization of US immigration enforcement, declining economic conditions in Mexico, and increased Mexican migrant awareness have promoted dispersion in states other than California and Texas.

872.　Kahn, David. CHICANO STREET MURALS: PEOPLE'S ART IN THE EAST LOS ANGELES BARRIO. *Aztlan 1975 6(1): 117-121.* Chicano mural art is a reflection of a social, cultural, and political reality in which Mexican Americans find themselves in the barrio. The murals give a visible identity to those who have been denied recognition. The themes of frustration, despair, hope, and creativity find symbolic expression in this art form. 9 notes.　　　　R. Griswold del Castillo

873.　Kane, Tim D. CHICANO EMPLOYMENT PATTERNS: AN ANALYSIS OF THE EFFECTS OF DECLINING ECONOMIC GROWTH RATES IN CONTEMPORARY AMERICA. *Aztlán 1979 10: 15-29.* Analyzes employment patterns for Chicanos from full employment in 1969 to severe recession in 1975. Real income of Chicano families declined, the recession forced Chicanos into employment with poorer wages and potential, and Chicanos failed to share in expected relative wage increases. Mexican Americans were more adversely affected by the recession than were Anglo workers. 9 tables, 7 notes.　　　　A. Hoffman

874.　Kanellos, Nicolas. CHICANO THEATRE: A POPULAR CULTURE BATTLEGROUND. *J. of Popular Culture 1979 13(3): 541-555.* Overview of the agitation-propaganda role of *El Teatro Chicano,* a recent but already widespread weapon within Mexican American communities to hold the dominant culture at bay. In sketches based on satirically cutting *actos,* often using a mixture of Spanish and English, the Chicano Theater examines everything from TV commercials and stereotypes to the American Dream, in order to enhance Mexican-American identity. Based on the author's experiences as an actor-director in *Teatro;* 4 photos, 9 notes.   D. G. Nielson

875. Keefe, Susan Emley. REAL AND IDEAL EXTENDED FAMILISM AMONG MEXICAN AMERICANS AND ANGLO AMERICANS: ON THE MEANING OF "CLOSE" FAMILY TIES. *Human Organization 1984 43(1): 65-70.* Both Anglo and Mexican Americans value their extended families, but within the Anglo definition, geographic mobility of family members is permitted; both ethnic groups are capable of adapting to urban, industrial society so that differences in achievement should not be attributed to different cultural traits.

876. Kirstein, Peter N. AGRIBUSINESS, LABOR, AND THE WET-BACKS: TRUMAN'S COMMISSION ON MIGRATORY LABOR. *Historian 1978 40(4): 650-667.* Demands for labor by agribusiness and railroad industries in the early 1940's led to the adoption of the bracero program of labor importation from Mexico. By 1950, however, divergent attitudes between organized labor and agribusiness over the use of alien labor and immigration led President Harry S. Truman to appoint a President's Commission on Migratory Labor. Examines the relationship between the problem-plagued bracero program and the Truman commission's investigation of social, economic, health, and educational conditions among migratory workers. Another focus of the study dealt with the extent of illegal migration into the United States and with means to eliminate it. Although the investigation was thorough and significant proposals were advanced, none of the recommendations were adopted. Concludes that "a quarter of a century after the commission's report, virtually nothing has been achieved in ameliorating the plight of domestic and Mexican national migratory labor in America."   M. S. Legan

877. Korman, Frank and Valenzuela, Nicholas. PATTERNS OF MASS MEDIA USE AND ATTITUDES ABOUT MASS MEDIA AMONG SELECTED ANGLO AND CHICANO OPINION LEADERS. *Aztlán 1975 4(2): 335-342.* Compares patterns of mass media use among local opinion leaders among the Chicano and Anglo populations of Austin, Texas.   S

878. Kutz, Jack. THE WHIP AND THE CROSS. *Mankind 1974 4(7): 36-40, 60-61.* Traces can still be found of the extra-legal order of flagellants, Los Hermanos Penitentes del Tercer Order de Franciscanos.   S

879. Laine, Janice E. A LANGUAGE ANALYSIS OF SUCCESSFUL AND NONSUCCESSFUL READERS: COMPARING LINGUISTIC ABILITY IN BLACK, CHICANO, AND ANGLO BOYS. *J. of Black Studies 1978 8(4): 439-451.* A test of 60 seven year-old and 60 10 year-old Black, Chicano, and Anglo boys in Los Angeles revealed that "successful readers are more fluent in both oral and written language than nonsuccessful readers across age, SES [socioeconomic status], and ethnicity." Black students' reading problems are caused by their utilization of "a nonstandard linguistic system," not by any deficiency in language ability. Before starting reading programs, educators "should involve themselves in clarifying the dimensions of language

acquisition and development as related to reading." Primary and secondary sources; 4 tables, 2 graphs, biblio.   R. G. Sherer

880. Lajous, Roberta and Oropeza, María Eugenia. LOS CHICANOS Y LA EDUCACION BILENGÜE [The Chicanos and bilingual education]. *Rev. Mexicana de Ciencias Pol. y Sociales [Mexico] 1981 27(104-105): 137-152.* Describes the special situation of Chicanos in North American society, analyzes the pressure mechanisms which have insured the provision of bilingual education, and examines the obstacles that have kept such education from being generally available to all who seek it. 4 tables, 22 notes.
                                                                    J. V. Coutinho

881. Lamare, James W. THE POLITICAL INTEGRATION OF MEXI-CAN-AMERICAN CHILDREN: A GENERATIONAL ANALYSIS. *Int. Migration Rev. 1982 16(1): 169-188.* While second generation Mexican-American children in El Paso, Texas assimilate and acculturate more than their first generation parents, the following generations experience a "recession in political acculturation and assimilation."

882. Lampe, Philip E. THE ACCULTURATION OF MEXICAN AMERI-CANS IN PUBLIC AND PAROCHIAL SCHOOLS. *Sociol. Analysis 1975 36(1): 57-66.* "The influence of the school system on the acculturation of Mexican-American students was examined in San Antonio, Texas. During the spring of 1973, 383 eighth-grade minority students from nine public and nine parochial schools were given questionnaires to discover the extent to which their feelings, attitudes and values were similar to those of a group of WASP [White Anglo-Saxon Protestant] respondents. The results revealed that the school system attended made a greater difference than did SES [Socio-economic status] or sex. Parochial school respondents were significantly more acculturated than their public school counterparts, and the difference remained even when other variables such as SES, sex, religiosity, aspirational level and ethnic composition of school were controlled."   J

883. Lampe, Philip E. and Andreasen, Vera K. LA ASIMILACION DE LOS MEXICO-NORTEAMERICANOS EN ESCUELAS PRIMERAS [The assimilation of Mexican Americans in primary schools]. *Rev. de Ciencias Sociales [Puerto Rico] 1973 17(3): 339-346.* A study based on questionnaires distributed to students of Mexican descent in the eighth grade of primary schools in San Antonio, Texas. The results indicate differences in assimilation behaviors according to sex, social class of the children's parents, and public vs. parochial schools. Based on questionnaire evaluation and secondary works; table, 12 notes.   F. Pollaczek

884. Lampe, Philip E. TOWARDS AMALGAMATION: INTERETHNIC DATING AMONG BLACKS, MEXICAN AMERICANS AND ANGLOS. *Ethnic Groups 1981 3(2): 97-109.* Ethnically homogenous marriages are favored in the United States. Mate selection is relatively open, however, and is usually accomplished through the dating process. There are some indications that interethnic dating has been on the increase in the United States. College students from the three major ethnic groups, black, Mexican American and

Anglo, were surveyed to determine the extent of such dating. The majority of the 251 students had engaged in interethnic dating with males being significantly more active than females and Mexican Americans than whites or blacks. Those whose friends had dated interethnically were themselves more likely to have done so. Age was not a significant consideration.   J/S

885.   Lampe, Philip E. "VIVA LA RAZA": A POSSIBLE CHICANO DILEMMA. *Social Sci. 1981 56(3): 158-163.* During the 1960's a growing sense of ethnic awareness, cultural pride, and nationalistic spirit among a segment of the Hispanic community came to be identified as the Chicano Movement. The movement is generally seen as a reaction to the economic experiences of assimilative pressures and ethnic rejection. Among the expressed goals of the Chicanos are the preservation of their cultural heritage and a restructuring of the status quo in society. There may, however, be a tension between these goals.   J

886.   Lee, Eun Sul and Roberts, Robert E. ETHNIC FERTILITY DIFFERENTIALS IN THE SOUTHWEST: THE CASE OF MEXICAN AMERICANS REEXAMINED. *Sociol. and Social Res. 1981 65(2): 194-210.* Socioeconomic factors exert different effects on fertility in different ethnic groups and ethnic fertility differentials vary at different stages of child progression. Based on 1970 census data.   J/S

887.   Lemus, Frank C. NATIONAL ROSTER OF SPANISH SURNAMED ELECTED OFFICIALS, 1973. *Aztlán 1974 5(1/2): 313-410.* Lists by state information about elected public officials of Spanish surname.   S

888.   Leonard, Olen E. and Cleland, Courtney B. OCCUPATIONAL CHANGES IN NORTH CENTRAL NEW MEXICO: A RESPONSE TO SOCIAL AND ECONOMIC ALTERATIONS IN A TRADITIONAL AGRICULTURE AREA. *Social Sci. J. 1976 13(2): 95-102.* Observes the increased trend among young farm workers in a sample of North Central New Mexican rural and agricultural villages towards migration or commuting to the cities in an effort to improve social and economic lifestyle, ca. 1930-50.

889.   Levenstein, Harvey. SINDICALISMO NORTEAMERICANO, BRACEROS Y "ESPALDAS MOJADAS" [North American trade unionism, Mexican contract laborers, and wetbacks]. *Hist. Mexicana [Mexico] 1978 28(2): 153-184.* Analyzes the attitude of US trade unions to the issue of imported Mexican labor during 1945-74. North American unions have traditionally regarded Mexico's large population of migrant laborers as a threat to the economic livelihood of their membership. For this reason, the unions were lukewarm to the bracero program which, beginning in 1943, permitted the legal importation of temporary Mexican labor. Official opposition surfaced only in 1950 when a slump in agricultural prices produced widespread unemployment. Reacting to adverse economic conditions, the unions joined with other political sectors to mount a campaign against the Bracero Program. In 1964 their efforts culminated in the termination of the program. Frustrating the objectives of the unions, termination of the contract labor movement brought a flood of illegal aliens. Based on documents in the Archives of Labor

History and Urban Affairs, Wayne State University, Detroit, official minutes, and secondary works; 76 notes. F. J. Shaw, Jr.

890. Limón, José E. AGRINGADO JOKING IN TEXAS MEXICAN SOCIETY: FOLKLORE AND DIFFERENTIAL IDENTITY. *New Scholar 1977 (6): 33-50.* Provides four examples of the verbal behavior of agringados, Texas Mexicans who culturally identify with Anglos. Particularly significant is the language used to define the objects of scorn—the agringados. The jokes indicate a continuing historical conflict which includes class values. Jokes from Chicano sources express group pride and identity. They relate small-group dynamics to resisting social domination and induced cultural change from Anglo institutions. This article is in the special issue on "New Directions In Chicano Scholarship." 34 notes. D. K. Pickens

891. Limón, José E. HISTORY, CHICANO JOKING, AND THE VARI-ETIES OF HIGHER EDUCATION: TRADITION AND PERFORMANCE AS CRITICAL SYMBOLIC ACTION. *J. of the Folklore Inst. 1982 19(2-3): 141-166.* There are two traditional types of the Mexican-American ethnic joke: the "stupid American" joke wherein the Mexican American outwits and makes a fool of the *gringo,* and the self-satirical joke in which the Mexican American is unable to function effectively in the realm of the Anglo. Although traditionally explained as a means to channel and manage hostility, the jokes have a more subtle significance. They provide a basis for attacking Anglo-American dominance of a region where Mexican Americans are dominant in terms of population but subordinate in terms of political, economic, and educational power. The jokes, particularly in the all-male environment of the *carne asada* ("barbecue"), provide an outlet for "open oppositon to the hegemony of the dominant social order." Based on field studies of Chicano male students and secondary sources; 36 notes. C. D. Geist

892. Limón, José E. LEGENDRY, METAFOLKLORE, AND PERFOR-MANCE: A MEXICAN-AMERICAN EXAMPLE. *Western Folklore 1983 42(3): 191-208.* In examining legends, folklorists traditionally concentrate on textual analysis and belief. In contrast, the collective rendition of the legend of the vanishing hitchhiker by Mexican-American women as opposed to men is described in terms of performance and content. The differences in content, performance, and setting provide different meanings for men and women from the same legend. 47 notes. R. E. Goerler

893. Loomis, Charles P. EL CERRITO, NEW MEXICO: A CHANGING VILLAGE. *New Mexico Hist. Rev. 1958 33(1): 53-75.* Discusses the 1956 study of the life and culture of the Spanish-speaking inhabitants of the village of El Cerrito, 30 miles from Las Vegas, New Mexico, 17 years after an original study, focusing on the changes in community communication and interaction, social processes, and values and structural elements, concluding that the exodus of families from El Cerrito in search of work resulted in the loss of 75% of the population and that contact with the outside resulted in major structural and value changes in the village.

894.   Lopez, David E. CHICANO LANGUAGE LOYALTY IN AN UR-
BAN SETTING. *Sociol. and Social Res. 1978 62(2): 267-278.* Previous investigators have concluded that the use of Spanish is stable among Chicanos in the
Southwest. But most Chicanos are bilingual and bilingualism involving socially
dominant and subordinate languages usually signals language shift to the
dominant language. Recent survey data from Los Angeles indicate that in this
urban environment the intragenerational loyalty to and intergenerational
transmission of Spanish among Chicanos is only moderately greater than
ethnic language maintenance among European immigrant groups earlier in this
century. Chicanos who grew up in Mexico continue to use Spanish but second
and especially subsequent generations are shifting to English and not passing
Spanish on to their children. The persistence of Spanish is accounted for by
continuing immigration, a model that fits the Chicano language experience
better than wave immigration, colonialism or ethnic enclave models developed
to describe the experiences of other groups. Loyalty to Spanish in Los Angeles
is related to low educational attainment, but not necessarily to other aspects of
social status. Nor is it clearly related to continuing ethnic social ties, suggesting
that language shift does not necessarily mean a decline in ethnic integration.
J

895.   López, Sonia A. THE ROLE OF THE CHICANA WITHIN THE
STUDENT MOVEMENT. Sánchez, Rosaura and Martinez Cruz, Rosa, ed.
Essays on la Mujer (Los Angeles, Ca.: Chicano Studies Center Publ., 1977):
16-29. Examines the political development of Mexican American women, or
Chicanas, within the Chicano student movement and their role in the
formulation of Chicana groups and organizations throughout the American
Southwest. In 1970 Chicanas first met to discuss specific issues unique to
women, i.e., their subordinate role in movement activities, their oppressed
position within their families, and the Catholic Church's role in their
subjugation. These women met with tremendous resistance from their male
comrades and other Chicanas within the movement. The emphasis of the
Chicana groups was to place Chicanas in the educational system, thereby
providing good role models and classroom courses for other Chicanas.
Although important, these struggles did not include the most oppressed
Chicanas who were working in the fields, factories, and in menial service jobs,
and were not aimed at making radical changes in the socioeconomic system
that exploits the Chicano community in general. Based on documents published by the Chicano movement and other secondary sources; 8 notes.
M. T. Wilson

896.   Loveman, Brian and Hofstetter, C. Richard. AMERICAN PERCEP-
TIONS OF UNDOCUMENTED IMMIGRANTS: POLITICAL IMPLICA-
TIONS. *New Scholar 1984 9(1-2): 111-118.* Surveys San Diego, California
residents on their attitudes toward undocumented migration. Most respondents
see the undocumented immigrants as necessary for agriculture, but they also
believe the workers downgrade living conditions in the United States. The
political implications for cultural diversity and political pluralism are not
encouraging. 8 notes.   D. K. Pickens/S

897. Lovrich, Nicholas P., Jr. and Marenin, Otwin. A COMPARISON OF BLACK AND MEXICAN AMERICAN VOTERS IN DENVER: ASSERTIVE VERSUS ACQUIESCENT POLITICAL ORIENTATIONS AND VOTING BEHAVIOR IN AN URBAN ELECTORATE. *Western Pol. Q. 1976 29(2): 284-294.* The voting behavior and political attitudes of black and Mexican American voters in Denver are analyzed. The major conclusion is that the comparative weakness of Mexican-American political forces, as typified by their failure to win an ethnically salient pair of elections wherein conditions were favorable to them, stems from their comparative weakness of political consciousness. The Denver Urban Observatory attitude survey of 1972, which sampled Mexican American and black citizens in the City Council districts under study, included only citizens who had voted in these 1971 elections. A comparison of responses given by these voter groups to questions re political interest, evaluation of public policy, self-identification (e.g., black vs. Negro, Chicano vs. Spanish American), shows that blacks are much more highly unified and politicized in this urban electorate. An attempt is made to generalize from these Denver findings to the broader area of American ethnic political behavior. J

898. Lovrich, Nicholas P., Jr. DIFFERING PRIORITIES IN AN URBAN ELECTORATE: SERVICE PREFERENCES AMONG ANGLO, BLACK, AND MEXICAN AMERICAN VOTERS. *Social Sci. Q. 1974 55(3): 704-717.* Examines data relating to the satisfaction or dissatisfaction of ethnic groups in Denver, Colorado, with city government services. S

899. Lozano, Anthony Girard. EL ESPAÑOL CHICANO Y LA DIALECTOLOGÍA [Chicano Spanish and the study of dialects]. *Aztlán 1976 7(1): 13-18.* Focuses on the sociolinguistic characteristics and the morphosyntax of the Chicano Spanish language, classifying it as part of a macrodialect spoken in Mexico and the southwestern states. After citing examples of the dialect, the influence of English, and code switching, concludes that morphosyntax is important in dialectical studies for a number of reasons. 6 notes. J. Tull

900. MacGregor-Villarreal, Mary. CELEBRATING *LAS POSADAS* IN LOS ANGELES. *Western Folklore 1980 39(2): 71-105.* Describes four public *posadas* (traditional Hispanic Christmas celebrations in which the journey of Joseph and Mary to Bethlehem is dramatized) in the Los Angeles neighborhoods of San Gabriel Mission, Pico Adobe, Plaza de la Raza, and Olvera Street. The author compares public and home *posadas,* then analyzes the reasons for presenting public *posadas,* the kinds of modifications necessary for a public event, the conceptions of the organizers, and the basis for their success. Based on field research and interviews; 16 photos, 41 notes, glossary.
S. L. Myres

901. Macías, Reynaldo Flores. DEVELOPING A BILINGUAL CULTURALLY-RELEVANT EDUCATIONAL PROGRAM FOR CHICANOS. *Aztlán 1973 4(1): 61-84.*

902. Macias, Reynaldo Flores. OPINIONS OF CHICANO COMMUNITY PARENTS ON CURRICULUM AND LANGUAGE USE IN BILINGUAL PRESCHOOL EDUCATION. *Aztlán 1973 4(2): 315-334.*

903. Macias, Ysidro Ramón. NUESTROS ANTEPASADOS Y EL MOVIMIENTO [Our ancestors and the movement]. *Aztlán 1974 5(1/2): 143-154.* Examines the spiritual basis for the Mexican-American movement.   S

904. Madrid-Barela, Arturo. IN SEARCH OF THE AUTHENTIC PACHUCO: AN INTERPRETATIVE ESSAY. *Aztlán 1973 4(1): 31-60.* Test the validity of various literary interpretations of the Pachuco (Mexican American youth, in California) against the reality of the 1940's.   S

905. Mahood, Wayne. THE PLIGHT OF THE MIGRANT. *Social Educ. 1973 37(8): 751-755.* Discusses migrant laborers and the inherent social and educational problems which plague them.   S

906. Maibaum, Matthew and López, Genevieve. DRUG ABUSE IN THE EAST LOS ANGELES HEALTH DISTRICT. *Aztlán 1981 12(1): 139-155.* A statistical analysis of drug abuse, drug abuse treatment, and drug abuse arrests in Los Angeles County in the 1970's. The data indicate that a serious drug abuse problem exists in the East Los Angeles Health District; but while arrests for drug abuse are higher than in the rest of the county, drug abuse treatment facilities are lacking in the East Los Angeles Health District. 7 tables, 29 notes.   A. Hoffman

907. Marcum, John P. and Bean, Frank D. MINORITY GROUP STATUS AS A FACTOR IN THE RELATIONSHIP BETWEEN MOBILITY AND FERTILITY: THE MEXICAN AMERICAN CASE. *Social Forces 1976 55(1): 135-148.* This paper sets forth contrasting hypotheses about the influence of racial and ethnic group membership on the relationship between mobility and fertility. One may be termed the *minority group status* approach, and the other the *underdevelopment* approach. Both perspectives offer bases for predicting fertility levels that deviate from the level that is roughly the average of the fertility levels typical of the social strata between which mobility has occurred. But the former implies greater fertility deviations the *more* integrated the minority group is into the larger society, whereas the latter suggests greater deviations the *less* integrated the minority group is into the larger society. These ideas are tested using data from a sample of Mexican-American couples, split according to generational distance from Mexico. The results indicate more support for the minority group status than the underdeveloped hypothesis, as revealed by lower than average expected fertility on the part of couples removed at least three generations from Mexico.   J

908. Marin, Christine. RODOLFO "CORKY" GONZALES: THE MEXICAN AMERICAN MOVEMENT SPOKESMAN, 1966-1972. *J. of the West 1975 14(4): 107-120.* Discusses the founding of the Crusade for Justice in Denver, Colorado, by Rodolfo "Corky" Gonzales and the political and social work which was done for Mexican Americans by the organization throughout the west and southwest. 52 notes.

909.   Markides, Kyriakos S. and Cole, Thomas. CHANGE AND CONTI-
NUITY IN MEXICAN AMERICAN RELIGIOUS BEHAVIOR: A
THREE-GENERATION STUDY. *Social Sci. Q. 1984 65(2): 618-625.* Using
data from a three-generation study of Mexican Americans in San Antonio,
Texas, it was found that the overwhelming majority of respondents were
Catholics and that little change in religious affiliation took place from
generation to generation, although older and middle generations attended
church more frequently than the younger generation.

910.   Markides, Kyriakos S. and Hoppe, Sue Keir. MARITAL SATISFAC-
TION IN THREE GENERATIONS OF MEXICAN AMERICANS. *Social
Science Quarterly 1985 66(1): 147-154.* Replicates Gilford and Bengtson's
analysis of marital satisfaction with data from a three-generation study of
Mexican Americans and finds that members of the younger generation have
the highest marital satisfaction.

911.   Martínez, Oscar J. CHICANOS AND THE BORDER CITIES: AN
INTERPRETIVE ESSAY. *Pacific Hist. Rev. 1977 46(1): 85-106.* A distinctive lifestyle syncretizing Anglo-Saxon and Mexican cultures has developed in
border cities along the United States-Mexican border. As a result, border
Chicanos have less ambivalent bicultural social patterns than Chicanos isolated
in enclaves in the US interior. Mexico's border cities have historically served
three major economic functions: as springboards for workers coming to the
United States, as receptacles for economically displaced Mexicans who formerly resided in the United States, and as a locus for cheap labor in assembly
factories. One result of these economic functions has been widespread poverty
in Mexican border cities. Based on documents and on published primary and
secondary sources; 68 notes.   W. K. Hobson

912.   Martinez, Vilma S. ILLEGAL IMMIGRATION AND THE LABOR
FORCE: AN HISTORICAL AND LEGAL VIEW. *Am. Behavioral Scientist
1976 19(3): 335-363.* Discusses illegal immigration into the United States by
Mexican nationals, from a legal standpoint, and also from the perspective of
Mexican Americans, showing the effect of this immigration on the contempo-
rary US labor force.

913.   Massey, Douglas S. and Schnabel, Kathleen. BACKGROUND AND
CHARACTERISTICS OF UNDOCUMENTED HISPANIC MIGRANTS
TO THE U.S. *Migration Today 1983 11(1): 6-13.* Finds that undocumented
Hispanic migrants to the United States are 60% Mexican, male, and usually
between the ages of 15 and 39; also finds that due to the decreasing birthrate in
the United States, immigrants will be needed for the low-skill labor market for
many years.

914.   McCleskey, Clifton and Merrill, Bruce. MEXICAN AMERICAN PO-
LITICAL BEHAVIOR IN TEXAS. *Social Sci. Q. 1973 53(4): 785-798.*
"Compared with Anglos and blacks, Mexican-American political behavior in
Texas is characterized by low rates of participation. However, on such
measures of electoral behavior as party identification, ideological orientation,
and political efficacy and alienation, they generally occupy an intermediate

position between the other two groups. [The authors] present several different types of data including results from a state-wide survey."   J

915. McDowell, John H. SOCIOLINGUISTIC CONTOURS IN THE VERBAL ART OF CHICANO CHILDREN. *Aztlán 1982 13(1-2): 165-193.* Examines the parameters of bilingual speech usage among Chicano children in East Austin, Texas. Identifies speech constructions in children's use of English and Spanish in rhymes, game songs, riddles, and casual switching from one language to another. These children make full use of their bilingual-bicultural heritage as expressed in their speech repertoire, a usage that preserves tradition while adapting to needs of the moment. Based on field research and secondary sources; appendix, ref.   A. Hoffman

916. McLemore, S. Dale. THE ORIGINS OF MEXICAN AMERICAN SUBORDINATION IN TEXAS. *Social Sci. Q. 1973 53(4): 656-670.* "Tests the applicability of Noel's general theory of the origin of ethnic stratification... Finds that the theory offers a parsimonious yet complete explanation of the development of the subordinate status of this group."   J

917. McWilliams, Carey. ONCE A WELL-KEPT SECRET. *Pacific Hist. R. 1973 42(3): 309-318.* "The story of how *North from Mexico* (Boston, 1949) came to be written has a relevance, if somewhat marginal, to the history of Mexican Americans as a minority." The author links the original disinterest in his book, projected as part of "The Peoples of America" series edited by Louis Adamic, with the obscurity at that time of Mexican Americans as a subject of social interest. "By 1968 the position of Mexican Americans had undergone a radical change" due to their emergence on social, economic, and political levels as a viable force in American life, particularly in California. Relates his political involvement in incidents in Los Angeles resulting from unrest in the Mexican-American sector, in particular the Sleepy Lagoon Murder case of 1942 and the Zoot Suit Riots of 1943. The author denies his role as spokesman for ethnic group, but shows how his interest and self-education led him to become involved in the Mexican-American experience. Note.   B. L. Fenske

918. Melville, Margarita B. MEXICAN WOMEN ADAPT TO MIGRATION. *Int. Migration Rev. 1978 12(2): 225-235.* The mental stress experienced by Mexican women in the process of acculturation can be partly attributed to illegal status among nearly 50% of those interviewed during 1977.

919. Metzgar, Joseph V. THE ETHNIC SENSITIVITY OF SPANISH NEW MEXICANS: A SURVEY AND ANALYSIS. *New Mexico Hist. R. 1974 49(1): 49-73.* Most writers on Spanish-speaking New Mexicans have been unsympathetic Anglos. Gives the results of a survey to which 229 persons responded. The questionnaire required mostly multiple-choice answers. Responses indicate that more men than women of Spanish ancestry prefer to be called Chicano. Most people of Spanish ancestry in the United States do not like to be called Mexican. 20 notes.   J. H. Krenkel

920. Metzgar, Joseph V. GUNS AND BUTTER: ALBUQUERQUE HISPANICS, 1940-1975. *New Mexico Hist. Rev. 1981 56(2): 117-139.* Discusses

the effects which World War II and the resulting period of economic growth and urbanization had on the Mexican Americans of Albuquerque, New Mexico. The percentage of Hispanic to Anglo population in Albuquerque dropped considerably between 1940 and 1970 due to the large influx of Anglos. This led to confrontation between the religious and rural oriented Hispanic community and the more secular and urban society of the Anglos. Despite problems with crime, drugs, and poverty, the Hispanic population of Albuquerque made significant advancement in employment, business, education, and income during this period. Primary sources; 2 photos, 2 charts, 53 notes.

P. L. McLaughlin

921. Miller, Lawrence W.; Polinard, Jerry L.; and Wrinkle, Robert D. ATTITUDES TOWARD UNDOCUMENTED WORKERS: THE MEXICAN AMERICAN PERSPECTIVE. *Social Sci. Q. 1984 65(2): 482-494.* Explores Mexican-American attitudes toward undocumented immigration, suggesting significant differences among Mexican Americans of different education, income, and generational levels.

922. Miller, Michael V. CHICANO COMMUNITY CONTROL IN SOUTH TEXAS: PROBLEMS AND PROSPECTS. *J. of Ethnic Studies 1975 3(3): 70-89.* Attempts to assess the political prospects for Chicanismo in South Texas. Poverty, illiteracy, substandard housing, and general economic exploitation have prevented interest-oriented political activity until recent years. Anglo techniques of electoral manipulation and illicit use of poll taxes severely hampered attempts at ethnic power-bloc formation. Other debilitative factors have been strong psychosocial attachments to Mexico by Chicanos, and the cultural trait of *envidia* which weakened any emerging ethnic leadership. Analyzes Crystal City as a "case history of organizational success," with its "revolutions" in 1963 and 1970. The Anglo establishment was ousted by an all Mexican-American slate, which took control of city government and the school system. Reasons for this success centered on catching the Anglo city manager off guard through organized poll tax payments by Chicanos' groups, and the fact that, unlike other South Texas cities, Crystal City had a union organization independent of local economic constraints. Finally *La Raza Unida* under José Gutierrez provided solid leadership. Whether other towns will be as successful, however, is dubious at this time. Primary and secondary sources; 20 notes.

G. J. Bobango

923. Miller, Michael V. and Valdez, Avelardo. IMMIGRATION AND PERCEPTIONS OF ECONOMIC DEPRIVATION AMONG WORKING-CLASS MEXICAN AMERICAN MEN. *Social Sci. Q. 1984 65(2): 455-464.* Mexican immigrants and the less acculturated and assimilated do not perceive themselves as less deprived than other Mexican Americans do; actual income is the primary factor influencing levels of reported economic well-being.

924. Miller, Michael V. MEXICAN AMERICANS, CHICANOS AND OTHERS: ETHNIC SELF-IDENTIFICATION AND SELECTED SOCIAL ATTITUDES OF RURAL TEXAS YOUTH. *Rural Sociol. 1976 41(2): 237-247.*

925. Miller, Michael V. VARIATIONS IN MEXICAN AMERICAN FAMILY LIFE: A REVIEW SYNTHESIS OF EMPIRICAL RESEARCH. *Aztlán 1978 9: 209-231.* Major errors about the family life of Mexican Americans occur, largely because of uncritically accepted assumptions uniformly applied to Mexican Americans. However, social science research has revealed important deviations across Mexican-American families. Results can be synthesized in the following areas: familism, family roles, ritual kinship relations, and intermarriage. Mexican Americans, because of a bondage to family, are not their own worst enemies: rather, stereotypes are not supported by the facts. Family systems vary considerably, conditioned by many factors. 93 notes.   R. V. Ritter

926. Mindiola, Tatcho, Jr. AGE AND INCOME DISCRIMINATION AGAINST MEXICAN AMERICANS AND BLACKS IN TEXAS, 1960 AND 1970. *Social Problems 1979 27(2): 196-208.* Estimates discrimination in income for Mexican Americans and blacks in Texas in 1960 and 1970, showing that younger groups experienced less discrimination and that blacks suffered greater discrimination than Mexican Americans, but, while discrimination against blacks declined, that against Mexicans increased.

927. Mirandé, Alfredo. THE CHICANO AND THE LAW: AN ANALYSIS OF COMMUNITY-POLICE CONFLICT IN AN URBAN BARRIO. *Pacific Sociol. Rev. 1981 24(1): 65-86.* A case study of a southern California barrio in 1975 suggests that a rising crime rate increases support for police power, limiting civil liberties, while fear of police reduces support of police power and increases support for civil guarantees.

928. Mirandé, Alfredo. SOCIOLOGY OF CHICANOS OR CHICANO SOCIOLOGY? A CRITICAL ASSESSMENT OF EMERGENT PARADIGMS. *Pacific Sociol. Rev. 1982 25(4): 495-508.* Examines and critically evaluates Maxine Baca Zinn's article on sociological theory about Chicanos; calls for a new paradigm in the sociology of Mexican Americans that eschews majority perspectives.

929. Mirowsky, John and Ross, Catherine E. LANGUAGE NETWORKS AND SOCIAL STATUS AMONG MEXICAN AMERICANS. *Social Sci. Q. 1984 65(2): 551-564.* Participation by Mexican Americans in Spanish-speaking networks lowers the expected level of socioeconomic status, while higher status decreases the expected level of participation in Spanish-speaking networks.

930. Moles, Jerry A. WHO TILLS THE SOIL? MEXICAN-AMERICAN WORKERS REPLACE THE SMALL FARMER IN CALIFORNIA: AN EXAMPLE FROM COLUSA COUNTY. *Human Organization 1979 38(1): 20-27.* Data collected 1950-69 in Colusa County, California, indicate that small farmers forced out of agriculture by rising costs incommensurate with increased production have been replaced by labor provided by Mexican Americans.

931. Moore, Joan; Vigil, Diego; and Garcia, Robert. RESIDENCE AND TERRITORIALITY IN CHICANO GANGS. *Social Problems 1983 31(2):*

182-194. Members of Chicano youth gangs in Los Angeles, California, often do not reside in their gang's territory.

932. Morrissey, Marietta. ETHNIC STRATIFICATION AND THE STUDY OF THE CHICANOS. *J. of Ethnic Studies 1983 10(4): 71-99.* Three analytical perspectives emerged as prominent in the sociological study of ethnic stratification during the last two decades: internal colonialism, class, and the international world-system and Marxian views. All have influenced Chicano studies. Though an evolution in these perspectives may be implied though not substantiated, still they reflect general trends in American sociological thought. First, group conflict over forms of wealth now rivals ideological conflict in explaining racial inequality. Secondly, theory is shifting away from a single cause hypothesis for racial inequality across historical eras and geographic regions. Finally, movement is now away from discrete units of analysis (the "internal Colony") to broader constructs allowing variations in form. Secondary sources; 12 notes; ref. G. J. Bobango

933. Muñoz, Carlos, Jr. and Barrera, Mario. LA RAZA UNIDA PARTY AND THE CHICANO STUDENT MOVEMENT IN CALIFORNIA. *Social Sci. J. 1982 19(2): 101-119.* Traces the beginnings and rise of La Raza Unida Party, an activist Chicano political organization started in Texas about 1969 by Jose Angel Gutierrez and others, focusing on the party's chapters that were formed beginning in 1970, first in northern California, the role of Chicano students in La Raza Unida, its political activities, and its demise toward the end of 1973 because of internal divisions, the frustration of the 1972 elections, and the decline of general student activism on college campuses.

934. Muñoz, Carlos, Jr. THE POLITICS OF PROTEST AND CHICANO LIBERATION: A CASE STUDY OF REPRESSION AND COOPTATION. *Aztlán 1974 5(1/2): 119-141.* Reviews a case study of Mexican-American political protest involving a 1968 school walk-out staged in East Los Angeles, as an example of the overall failure to institute positive social change. S

935. Murguia, Edward and Frisbie, W. Parker. TRENDS IN MEXICAN AMERICAN INTERMARRIAGE: RECENT FINDINGS IN PERSPECTIVE. *Social Sci. Q. 1977 58(3): 374-389.* [Examines] several areas of the Southwest. Although the secular trend implies slow movement toward higher levels of exogamy, the slope of the trend line varies considerably among areas. The authors suggest that continuing low rates of exogamy in most areas indicate that the Mexican-American population is likely to continue to represent a distinct sociocultural entity for some time to come. J

936. Murray, Douglas L. THE ABOLITION OF *EL CORTITO,* THE SHORT-HANDLED HOE: A CASE STUDY IN SOCIAL CONFLICT AND STATE POLICY IN CALIFORNIA AGRICULTURE. *Social Problems 1982 30(1): 26-39.* Analysis of the 1968-75 conflict over the use of the short-handled hoe by California farm workers, and the 1975 ruling by the state banning the use of the hoe; assesses the efficacy of state legal intervention in resolving such issues.

937.   Naismith, Rachael. THE MOVEABLE LIBRARY: SERVING MI-
GRANT FARM WORKERS. *Wilson Lib. Bull. 1983 57(7): 571-575.* Several
communities in California during the 1970's had some type of "bookmobile"
program for the migrant farmworker, but these valuable services have been
ended or cut since the advent of Proposition 13; details the needs and benefits
of library availability for migrant labor.

938.   Nalven, Joseph. WHO BENEFITS FROM KNOWLEDGE ABOUT
THE HEALTH OF UNDOCUMENTED MEXICANS? *Policy Studies J.
1982 10(3): 556-580.* Discusses the legal context in which health research of
undocumented Mexicans takes place, and brings together the national debate
on undocumented immigration and the maturing research on the health of
Mexican-Americans.

939.   Nash, Irwin. AMERICAN MIGRANT WORKERS: PHOTO ESSAY.
Society 1974 11(3): 47-49. Photo essay on migrant labor in Washington's
Yakima Valley, 1974.   S

940.   Nostrand, Richard L. EL CERRITO REVISITED. *New Mexico Hist.
Rev. 1982 57(2): 109-122.* Analyzes and discusses the changes occurring in a
representative "Hispano" village in New Mexico during 1939-80. Suffering
from a great loss of population, the village may be undergoing a rejuvenation.
Many landowners are active nonresidents, and several nonresidents are becoming residents. Primary sources; 3 photos, 3 maps, 58 notes.   A. C. Dempsey

941.   O'Connor, Karen and Epstein, Lee. A LEGAL VOICE FOR THE
CHICANO COMMUNITY: THE ACTIVITIES OF THE MEXICAN
AMERICAN LEGAL DEFENSE AND EDUCATIONAL FUND, 1968-82.
Social Sci. Q. 1984 65(2): 245-256. Examines the history and activities of the
Mexican American Legal Defense and Education Fund (MALDEF), which
litigates on behalf of Mexican Americans. Examines the litigation activities of
MALDEF between 1968 and 1982, comparing them to the success of other
interest groups in the judicial arena. The factors considered critical to interest
group litigation success are helpful in explaining the evolution of MALDEF.

                                                                                    J/S

942.   Ornstein, Jacob. "RELATIONAL BILINGUALISM"—A NEW AP-
PROACH TO LINGUISTIC-CULTURAL DIVERSITY AND A MEXI-
CAN-AMERICAN CASE STUDY. *Ethnicity 1978 5(2): 148-166.* Discusses a
survey of 301 Anglo and Mexican-American students (5% of the student body)
at the University of Texas-El Paso in 1970-71 and studies based on data from
this survey. Focuses on results of intensive oral and written tests in English
and (Mexican) Spanish proficiency administered to a subsample of 30 bilinguals. An introduction reviews the concept of "relational bilingualism", first
suggested by the author in 1973, which emphasizes bilingual status in its
relation to other societal variables. The conclusion points up some interesting
findings: e.g., that linguistic loyalty and belief in a particular language's
importance bear no apparent relation to actual linguistic performance. 4 tables,
3 notes, 35 ref.   L. W. Van Wyk

943. Ortega, Adolfo. FORJANDO UNA VOZ POLÍTICA EN LA POESÍA CHICANA [Creating a political voice in Chicano poetry]. *Ábside [Mexico] 1978 42(2): 99-115.* Traces the development of the Chicano movement from the 1965 farmworkers' strike in Delano, California, and examines the movement's impact on the poetry of Rodolfo González, Alurista (pseud. of Alberto Baltazar Urista Heredia), Luis Omar Salinas, Sergio Elizondo, and Richard García.

944. Ortiz, Florá Ida. BILINGUAL EDUCATION PROGRAM PRACTICES AND THEIR EFFECTS UPON STUDENTS' PERFORMANCE AND SELF-IDENTITY. *Aztlán 8: 157-174.* ESEA Title VII Bilingual Education Act goals of improving language abilities and self-image among Mexican-American students are being accomplished through the employment of instructional aides working with classroom teachers to coordinate instruction, curriculum, and classroom activities and improve children's social development; 1975-77.

945. Ortiz, Isidro D. CHICANO URBAN POLITICS AND THE POLITICS OF REFORM IN THE SEVENTIES. *Western Political Quarterly 1984 37(4): 564-577.* Describes and accounts for the emergence of the United Neighborhoods Organization in the nation's largest barrio, East Los Angeles, California, and delineates its significance. The organization has made possible the achievement of important socioeconomic and political gains; it has not contributed to the transformation of the power relationship between the residents of the barrio and the institutional sponsor of the organization, the Catholic Archdiocese of Los Angeles. Nevertheless, the emergence of the organization through institutional sponsorship suggests that the prospects for the emergence of vehicles for the improvement of the status of the residents of the barrios are not dim.   J/S

946. Pachon, Harry P. and Moore, Joan W. MEXICAN AMERICANS. *Ann. of the Am. Acad. of Pol. and Social Sci. 1981 (454): 111-124.* Mexican Americans defy census classification and color differentiation, departing sharply from the characteristics of either European immigrants or black Americans. Such factors as settlement patterns, sharp discrimination and segregation, a historical lack of political opportunities, and depressed economic circumstances have made Mexican Americans one of the most distinctive groups in America today.   J/S

947. Padilla, Fernando V. SOCIALIZATION OF CHICANO JUDGES AND ATTORNEYS. *Aztlán 1974 5(1/2): 261-294.* Traces the socialization patterns of Mexican-American members of the bar and judiciary through family background, ethnicity, religion, education, age, and occupation as they occur in the Southwest.   S

948. Peñalosa, Fernando. SOCIOLINGUISTIC THEORY AND THE CHICANO COMMUNITY. *Aztlan 1975 6(1): 1-11.* Reviews current linguistic studies dealing with Chicano bilingualism and shows that sociolinguistic theory has been neglected. Language usage has political implications since it often controls other people's behavior. An articulation of community norms regard-

ing dialect usage is needed, as well as an attempt to influence the monolithic concepts of bilingual education aqencies. 31 notes.   R. Griswold del Castillo

949.   Penley, Larry E.; Gould, Sam; and DeLaVina, Lynda Y. THE COMPARATIVE SALARY POSITION OF MEXICAN AMERICAN COLLEGE GRADUATES IN BUSINESS. *Social Sci. Q. 1984 65(2): 444-454.* Mexican-American graduates of colleges of business administration receive lower salaries than their white non-Hispanic counterparts, but the differences are attributed primarily to variation in regional income, the lower socioeconomic background of Mexican Americans, and academic success in college; Mexican Americans earn an adjusted income comparable to their white non-Hispanic counterparts.

950.   Perez, Arturo P. POESIA CHICANA [Chicano poetry]. *Cuadernos Hispanoamericanos [Spain] 1977 109(325): 123-131.* Discusses the poetry of Mexican Americans, which, though maintaining affinities with Mexican culture is an ethnically unique cultural entity. More than any other literary genre, Chicano poetry expresses the social, economic, and political conditions of the people that produce it. The tone of protest in most Chicano poetry is usually expressed through the collective voice of the oppressed peoples. The poetry forms a part of the general trend in the social evolution of the United States; its message of liberation coincides with that of other marginal and exploited minorities. Based on several examples of Chicano poetry.   S

951.   Pérez, José G. A BIG STEP FORWARD FOR THE RAZA UNIDA PARTIES. *Internat. Socialist R. 1973 34(1): 14-17, 39.* The Raza Unida Party in Texas, 1972-73.   S

952.   Pino, Frank. CHICANO POETRY: A POPULAR MANIFESTO. *J. of Popular Culture 1973 6(4): 718-730.* The current poetry of Mexican Americans represents a minority, bilingual popular culture, often draws on American labor experiences, and identifies with other oppressed people.   S

953.   Portales, Marco A. ANGLO VILLAINS AND CHICANO WRITERS. *J. of Ethnic Studies 1981 9(3): 78-82.* Reviews Saul Sanchez's *Hay Plesha Lichens Tu Di Flac* (Editorial Justa Publications, 1977), an unusual work both for this publishing house and the field of Chicano literature. The Anglo as outright villain figures repeatedly in Chicano writing, but seldom centrally: the Anglo is ordinarily secondary both in presence and character both to Chicanos themselves and their own consciousness. Sanchez, however, reveals the deeper, gut-level response to Anglo culture intimated in the works of most Chicano writers, and, in certain passages and internal monologues, his narrator is virtually consumed by anger.   G. J. Bobango

954.   Portes, Alejandro. ILLEGAL IMMIGRATION AND THE INTERNATIONAL SYSTEM: LESSONS FROM RECENT LEGAL MEXICAN IMMIGRANTS TO THE UNITED STATES. *Social Problems 1979 26(4): 425-438.* Data from case studies of illegal Mexican immigrants conducted during 1972-73 indicate that not all came from backward areas; several came from urbanized areas with comparatively high levels of education and headed

for US cities and urban occupations, thus supporting the idea that such immigration is an outgrowth of the accelerating contradictions effected by capitalist development in Mexico and in other nations on the US periphery.

955. Portes, Alejandro. LABOR FUNCTIONS OF ILLEGAL ALIENS. *Society 1977 14(6): 31-37.* General examination of the subject of illegal aliens, especially those entering across the border from Mexico; examines political and economic impact as well as the effect which the aliens have on the unskilled labor market, 1970's.

956. Portes, Alejandro and Bach, Robert L. LEGALIZING UNAUTHO-RIZED IMMIGRANTS AND ITS CONSEQUENCES. *Int. Migration [Netherlands] 1983 21(3): 415-417.* Studies 822 Mexican immigrants to the United States and finds that unemployment was less than the national average. Employment was almost exclusively in unskilled and semi-skilled jobs, in company with other Hispanics, and largely in the southwestern United States. Although members of the study group were eligible for welfare, their low unemployment rate indicated a preference for low-paid work over welfare.

D. Powell

957. Portes, Alejandro. TOWARD A STRUCTURAL ANALYSIS OF ILLEGAL (UNDOCUMENTED) IMMIGRATION. *Int. Migration Rev. 1978 12(4): 469-484.* Introduces a special issue on illegal aliens.

958. Poston, Dudley L., Jr. and Alvírez, David. ON THE COST OF BEING A MEXICAN AMERICAN WORKER. *Social Sci. Q. 1973 33(4): 697-709.* "Compares the incomes of Anglos with those of Mexican Americans among full-time male workers in the southwestern United States in 1960.... more than half of the difference in average income relates to occupational and educational differences, but a substantial residual remains which is interpreted as resulting from minority status."

J

959. Pullenza de Ortiz, Patricia. CHICANO CHILDREN AND INTELLI-GENCE. *Aztlán 1979 10: 69-83.* Discusses the limitations of standardized intelligence tests in meeting the special needs of minority children. IQ tests have failed to consider such factors as language, culture, socialization, aspiration, and experiences of minority children that differ from standardized norms. Even nonlanguage and so-called culture-free tests exhibit biases, often inadvertently. Educators heavily rely on such tests to measure learning ability; as a result, Chicano children disproportionately repeat grades, are placed in low ability tracks, or are put into programs for the mentally retarded. Calls for improvements in testing instruments that consider the language and cultural background of Chicano children to more accurately assess their academic abilities. Published studies; 25 notes, biblio.

A. Hoffman

960. Ramos, Reyes. A CASE IN POINT: AN ETHNOMETHODOLOGI-CAL STUDY OF A POOR MEXICAN AMERICAN FAMILY. *Social Sci. Q. 1973 53(4): 905-919.* "Treats the practical activities and circumstances of the family and of the helping institutions with which they have contact as topics for empirical inquiry.... Uses the trouble that the family and helping

institutions generate for each other to illustrate how their members manage their daily lives and produce social reality for themselves."   J

961.   Raymond, Richard D. and Sesnowitz, Michael. LABOR MARKET DISCRIMINATION AGAINST MEXICAN AMERICAN COLLEGE GRADUATES. *Southern Econ. J. 1983 49(4): 1122-1136.* Surveying the 1975 wages of Mexican-American graduates from the Pan American University, Rio Grande Valley, Texas, 1966-74, finds that there is more discrimination in the private than in the public sector (though real wages were higher), and that discrimination takes the form of lower salary increments, rather than lower starting salaries.

962.   Reich, Alice H. SPANISH AMERICAN VILLAGE CULTURE: BARRIER TO ASSIMILATION OR INTEGRATIVE FORCE? *Colorado Coll. Studies 1979 (15): 107-113.* Addresses the question of whether or not Hispanic village culture, especially in New Mexico, inhibits or enhances assimilation into Anglo culture, since the 1960's.

963.   Reichert, Josh and Massey, Douglas S. PATTERNS OF U.S. MIGRA- TION FROM A MEXICAN SENDING COMMUNITY: A COMPARISON OF LEGAL AND ILLEGAL MIGRANTS. *Int. Migration Rev. 1979 13(4): 599-623.* Analyzes the differences between legal and illegal Mexican migration to the United States by the migrant population of a mestizo town in Michoacán, Mexico, 1977-78.

964.   Reichert, Joshua S. THE MIGRANT SYNDROME: SEASONAL U.S. WAGE LABOR AND RURAL DEVELOPMENT IN CENTRAL MEXI- CO. *Human Organization 1981 40(1): 56-66.* A 1977-78 field investigation of Guadalupe, a rural Mexican community, suggests that seasonal US migration provides temporary relief from rural poverty, finances public works projects, and prevents permanent emigration to urban areas; on the other hand, migration perpetuates the conditions of underdevelopment, underemployment, and unequal distribution of resources that made migration necessary in the first place.

965.   Reubens, Edwin P. ALIENS, JOBS, AND IMMIGRATION POLICY. *Public Interest 1978 (51): 113-134.* Concerning the economic importance of aliens to the United States and their home countries, new information is available from official reports and commissioned studies, journalistic accounts, and the author's own field trips to the southern and western borders of the United States, Mexico, and other countries. An industrial and occupational breakdown of alien workers shows only a limited area of competition with Americans, although the presence of these aliens probably does hinder unionization. Aliens do not figure importantly in the rendering of public services, nor do they add a large increment to the US population. Few countries consider the migration of professionals to the United States a serious problem because they have a surplus of these individuals. The big problem with which the present system is unable to cope concerns illegal entrants. Following an evaluation of several public policy proposals to deal with this difficulty, including that of the Carter Administration, recommends an informal legitimi-

zation of aliens now here, with tighter border controls and a flexible program for authorizing temporary work. Table. S. Harrow

966. Riddell, Adaljiza Sosa and Aguallo, Robert, Jr. A CASE OF CHICANO POLITICS: PARLIER, CALIFORNIA. *Aztlán 1978 9: 1-22.* A study of the events leading to the Chicano takeover of local government in Parlier, California, a complete turnabout from total Anglo to total Chicano control, with an analysis of the event's significance for Chicano activists and politics. Parlier represents a model for future Chicano politics, as well as a case study which, though not unique in its setting, is unique in its politics. Covers 1971-73. Primary sources; 64 notes. R. V. Ritter

967. Riddell, Adaljiza Sosa. CHICANAS AND EL MOVIMIENTO. *Aztlán 1974 5(1/2): 155-165.* Examines the concept of machismo, and the action of the Catholic Church in the context of American society; discusses how these affect the involvement of Chicanas in the Mexican-American movement during the 1970's. S

968. Rocco, Raymond A. A CRITICAL PERSPECTIVE ON THE STUDY OF CHICANO POLITICS. *Western Pol. Q. 1977 30(4): 558-573.* Focusing on the notion of structural domination, devises a framework for criticism of Chicano politics and political thought, pointing out basic theoretical weaknesses and unreflective and uncritical biases toward dominant ideology, 1960's-70's.

969. Rocco, Raymond A. THE ROLE OF POWER AND AUTHENTICITY IN THE CHICANO MOVEMENT: SOME REFLECTIONS. *Aztlán 1974 5(1/2): 167-176.* Examines the role of power in social movements and reform in general and the delicacy with which such power should be wielded. S

970. Rochin, Refugio I. ECONOMIC DEPRIVATION OF CHICANOS— CONTINUING NEGLECT IN THE SEVENTIES. *Aztlán 1973 4(1): 85-102.*

971. Rogers, Richard G. INFANT MORTALITY AMONG NEW MEXICAN HISPANICS, ANGLOS, AND INDIANS. *Social Sci. Q. 1984 65(3): 876-884.* Compares New-Mexican Hispanics, Anglos, and Indians through endogenous, exogenous, and total aggregate infant mortality rates; Hispanic and Anglo rates are equivalent, while Indian exogenous and total aggregate infant mortality rates are statistically higher.

972. Romero, Leo M. THE QUEST FOR EDUCATIONAL OPPORTUNITY: ACCESS TO LEGAL AND MEDICAL EDUCATION IN NEW MEXICO. *New Mexico Hist. Rev. 1978 53(4): 337-346.* Statistics show that Mexican Americans and Native Americans are underrepresented in law schools and medical schools in New Mexico.

973. Romo, Harriet. THE MEXICAN ORIGIN POPULATION'S DIFFERING PERCEPTIONS OF THEIR CHILDREN'S SCHOOLING. *Social Sci. Q. 1984 65(2): 635-650.* Chicanos and undocumented immigrants have differing perceptions of children's school experiences: recent immigrants value

education but have low expectations of schooling, while Chicanos have higher expectations for children but express more alienation and awareness of discrimination.

974. Rosen, Gerald. THE CHICANO MOVEMENT AND THE POLITI-CIZATION OF CULTURE. *Ethnicity 1974 1(3): 279-294.* Interviews Chicano leaders in Los Angeles in 1968-69 regarding their self-identification, attitudes toward the new movement, and various types of persons in the Mexican American community. They rejected Anglo imposed names, stressed their Indian ancestry and the concept of *la raza*, criticized those seeking the approval of the dominant society as *Tio Tacos*, and discussed the different terms for Anglos and their meanings. The rise of *chicanismo* has symbolized the quest for autonomy and in-group cohesiveness. Biblio.   E. Barkan

975. Rosen, Gerald. THE DEVELOPMENT OF THE CHICANO MOVE-MENT IN LOS ANGELES FROM 1967 TO 1969. *Aztlán 1973 4(1): 155-183.*

976. Rothenberg, Irene Fraser. CHICANOS, THE PANAMA CANAL ISSUES AND THE REAGAN CAMPAIGN: REFLECTIONS FROM 1976 AND PROJECTIONS FOR 1980. *J. of Ethnic Studies 1980 7(4): 37-49.* Mexican Americans, like many US ethnic groups before them, are beginning to see themselves as a domestic lobby for policies favoring the homeland, as evidenced by the unanimity and intensity of the Mexican-American and Spanish-language press opposition to Ronald Reagan's Panama Canal treaties position in the spring of 1976. Content analysis of all available issues of 12 newspapers published between 1 April and 8 June 1976 showed them to be bitterly against Reagan. Any efforts by the ex-governor to revive the issue against the Carter administration in 1980 is certain to provoke a dramatic Chicano response. This group indeed has a better reason than most minorities to look beyond US boundaries in seeking an ethnic identity, living as it does in "conquered Mexico." Contemporary ethnic press, secondary works; 36 notes.
G. J. Bobango

977. Roucek, Joseph S. LOS PROBLEMAS DE LOS INMIGRANTES MEJICANOS EN LOS ESTADOS UNIDOS [Problems of Mexican immigrants in the United States]. *R. de Pol. Social [Spain] 1974 (103): 85-99.* Discusses the impact of the population explosion on illegal Mexican immigration into the United States since the 1950's, especially in southern California and in Texas, focusing on "Operation Wetback" and its effect on legal and illegal immigration; also notes the exploitation of Mexican workers by lawyers.

978. Sabagh, Georges. FERTILITY EXPECTATIONS AND BEHAVIOR AMONG MEXICAN AMERICANS IN LOS ANGELES, 1973-82. *Social Sci. Q. 1984 65(2): 594-608.* A 1982 follow-up survey of Mexican-American women initially interviewed in Los Angeles in 1973 showed: that the women have a higher aggregate and individual inconsistency between fertility expectations and behavior; that expectations were more predictive of the behavior of women reared in the United States than of those reared in Mexico; and that

except for duration of marriage, these expectations had more predictive power than a number of demographic and socioeconomic variables.

979. Sabagh, Georges and Lopez, David. RELIGIOSITY AND FERTILITY: THE CASE OF CHICANAS. *Social Forces 1980 59(2): 431-439.* Data from a probability sample of 1,129 Mexican-American women married to Chicanos and interviewed in Los Angeles, California, in 1973 were used to analyze the effects of religious norms on the fertility of Catholic women 35-44 years old in the sample. If religiosity is a measure of adherence to the norms of the Catholic Church, then these norms do have a net impact on the fertility of Chicanas reared in the United States but not on the fertility of those brought up in Mexico. Characteristics of the country of upbringing have to be taken into account in any analyses of the effects of religious norms on the reproductive behavior of Catholics.   J/S

980. Salazar, Jaime G. and Espinosa, Judith M. A SOCIODEMOGRAPHIC PROFILE OF HISPANIC PHYSICIANS IN THREE UNITED STATES METROPOLITAN AREAS. *Aztlán 1979 10: 111-122.* Surveys Hispanic physicians in San Diego (California), San Antonio (Texas), and Denver (Colorado). Only 3.66% of US physicians are Hispanic; in the three cities surveyed, only 2.64% were Hispanic (180 of 6,824). Of the 180 physicians, 101 were interviewed. It was found that 73% were foreign-born; 55% received their medical education in foreign countries. Also surveyed were obstacles in gaining admission to medical school, percent of clientele that is Hispanic, manner of payment to the physicians, and patient obstacles in obtaining medical care. Concludes that a US medical education is almost impossible to Hispanic Americans. Calls for a nationwide survey of Hispanic physicians and greater documentation of Hispanic health care needs. Census data and published studies; 12 notes.   A. Hoffman

981. San Miguel, Guadalupe, Jr. MEXICAN AMERICAN ORGANIZATIONS AND THE CHANGING POLITICS OF SCHOOL DESEGREGATION IN TEXAS, 1945 to 1980. *Social Sci. Q. 1982 63(4): 701-715.* The League of United Latin American Citizens and the American G.I. Forum played the dominant roles in seeking school integration in the 1960's, when the Mexican American Legal Defense and Education Fund became the leading pressure group and litigation became the major tactic; since the late 1970's, there has been less interest in desegregation and more concern with such issues as bilingual education.

982. Sánchez, Rosaura. THE CHICANA LABOR FORCE. Sánchez, Rosaura and Martinez Cruz, Rosa, ed. *Essays on la Mujer* (Los Angeles, Ca.: Chicano Studies Center Publ., 1977): 3-15. Emphasizes the importance of class differences among women when considering the interests and aims of Mexican Americans. The shift from rural areas to an urban environment in this century has changed important social characteristics of the Chicano family. Women are more likely to work outside the home and make contacts outside the family unit, but they are also freer to be exploited by employers. The majority of the 40% of Chicanas who are employed work in clerical jobs, as operatives, or in service occupations, and their average annual income was $2,682 in 1974 (the

average income for white women was $6,770 that same year). The upward social mobility and the higher education of some Chicanas cannot erase their largely working class backgrounds and it is essential that these women "recognize the low economic status of the majority of Chicano women and identify with their struggle rather than with middle class feminist aspirations." Bureau of Census reports, newspaper articles, and secondary sources; 5 tables.

M. T. Wilson

983.   Sánchez, Rosaura. LA GRAMÁTICA TRANSFORMACIONAL Y EL ESTUDIO DEL ESPAÑOL CHICANO [Transformational grammar and the study of Chicano Spanish]. *Aztlán 1976 7(1): 7-12.* Describes transformational linguistics and its possible application to Chicano Spanish language. Chicano speakers understand passively a great many more nuances of formal Spanish than they do actively. They also use different means of expressing the same thought in different contexts. A transformational grammar might serve to explain these phenomena and others in Chicano Spanish. 3 notes.   J. Tull

984.   Sánchez, Rosaura. SYMPOSIUM ON LINGUISTICS AND THE CHICANO. *Aztlán 1976 7(1): 1-5.* Introduces the symposium by discussing language and educational issues in need of further research. The Chicano population in the Southwest is still bilingual, an oral rather than a literate bilingualism. English dominates, but it is interesting to speculate whether bilingual schooling will affect the situation, leading to full bilingualism for all. Calls for continued and broader implementation of bilingual education and support of research.   J. Tull

985.   Sassen-Koob, Saskia. NON-DOMINANT ETHNIC POPULATIONS AS PARTS OF TOTAL SOCIETY: CHICANOS IN THE U.S. *Aztlán 1973 4(1): 103-121.*

986.   Schlein, Lisa. LOS ANGELES GARMENT DISTRICT SEWS A CLOAK OF SHAME. Mora, Magdalena and DelCastillo, Adelaida R., ed. *Mexican Women in the United States: Struggles Past and Present* (Los Angeles: U. of California Chicano Studies Res. Center, 1980): 113-116. Focuses on the exploitation of workers, the majority of which are Spanish-speaking women. Labor code violations, dispersion of production processes, and runaway shops enhance their exploitability and frustrate efforts to organize them.

J. Powell

987.   Schlossman, Steven. SELF-EVIDENT REMEDY? GEORGE I. SANCHEZ, SEGREGATION, AND ENDURING DILEMMAS IN BILINGUAL EDUCATION. *Teachers Coll. Record 1983 84(4): 871-907.* The research and writings of Hispanic educator George I. Sanchez both exposed and helped change the segregated system in the Southwest, which relegated Hispanics to inferior schools and prevented their assimilation into the dominant Anglo culture. Unlike many of his contemporaries, Sanchez maintained that academic problems associated with bilingualism were a result of and not a justification for segregation. Although increased immigration and new linguistic research later forced Sanchez to concede the need for occasional recourse to bilingual education, he never accepted it as more than a temporary and

potentially harmful expedient. Based on archives of Sanchez material at the University of Texas in Austin and the Rockefeller Archive Center, New York; 75 notes. E. C. Bailey, Jr.

988. Schmidt, Aurora. REFUGEES AND IMMIGRANTS: IN CONFLICT WITH THE AMERICAN POOR? *Migration Today 1981 9(4-5): 17-21.* Discusses the competition of refugees and immigrants for low-wage jobs, social services, and health services; the negative impact of undocumented Mexican immigrants in certain sectors exists but is exaggerated, and in social services the negative impact is negligible.

989. Schoen, Robert; Nelson, Verne E.; and Collins, Marion. INTERMAR-RIAGE AMONG SPANISH SURNAMED CALIFORNIANS, 1962-1974. *Int. Migration Rev. 1978 12(3): 359-369.* Discusses Mexican Americans.

990. Schoen, Robert and Nelson, Verne E. MORTALITY BY CAUSE AMONG SPANISH SURNAMED CALIFORNIANS, 1969-71. *Social Sci. Q. 1981 62(2): 259-274.* Examines mortality by age, sex, and cause of death for Spanish-surnamed whites and other whites and blacks in California; compares the causes of death among Spanish-surnamed whites with those among other whites and blacks.

991. Sedano, Michael Victor. CHICANISMO: A RHETORICAL ANALY-SIS OF THEMES AND IMAGES OF SELECTED POETRY FROM THE CHICANO MOVEMENT. *Western J. of Speech Communication 1980 44(3): 177-190.* Examines themes of the Chicano movement, the barrio, the Anglo world, and Chicanismo extant in Chicano poetry, 1969-79.

992. Segade, Gustavo V. IDENTITY AND POWER: AN ESSAY ON THE POLITICS OF CULTURE AND THE CULTURE OF POLITICS IN CHICANO THOUGHT. *Aztlán 1978 9: 85-100.* An analysis of developments within Chicano thought, and divergence within the group. First developed a sense of identity beneficial in seeking political power that might, in turn, legitimate economic and political aspirations. Some Mexican Americans, however, rejected the cultural approach to liberation for the Marxist. Implemented in the Mexican American Studies program at San Diego State University, the Marxist orientation yielded little, and several Marxist faculty members had to resign. The dialectical relationship between identity and power had come to expression. 11 notes; readings. R. V. Ritter

993. Shannon, Lyle W. and McKim, Judith L. ATTITUDES TOWARD EDUCATION AND THE ABSORPTION OF IMMIGRANT MEXICAN-AMERICANS AND NEGROES IN RACINE. *Educ. and Urban Soc. 1974 6(4): 333-354.*

994. Shannon, Lyle W. FALSE ASSUMPTIONS ABOUT THE DETER-MINANTS OF MEXICAN-AMERICAN AND NEGRO ECONOMIC AB-SORPTION. *Sociol. Q. 1975 16(1): 3-15.* "It generally is believed that with age and time in the urban industrial community, differences between rural-reared and urban-reared persons decline or disappear. This longitudinal study

of 973 families (280 Mexican Americans, 280 blacks and 413 Anglos) in Racine, Wisconsin, finds little significant change (1960-1971) in the relative position of Mexican Americans and blacks on occupational level, income, and level of living, even though controls for age, education, urban work experience, time in the community, and other pertinent variables are introduced. These findings suggest that the community is organized in such a way as to facilitate better the economic absorption of its Anglo immigrants than blacks from the South or Mexican Americans from Southwest, in spite of the fact that numerous programs were introduced in the United States during the 1960's, with the purpose of aiding the less fortunate in our society. Race/ethnicity remains the most powerful determinant of a family's position in the community."   J

995.   Shannon, Lyle W. and McKim, Judith L. MEXICAN AMERICAN, NEGRO, AND ANGLO IMPROVEMENT IN LABOR FORCE STATUS BETWEEN 1960 AND 1970 IN A MIDWESTERN COMMUNITY. *Social Sci. Q. 1974 55(1): 91-111.* "Compares survey and census data on income, occupation and employment status [in Racine, Wisconsin]."   J

996.   Shearer, Derek. FOR THE UFW, A BAD DAY AT THE POLLS: BUT DOES IT MATTER? *Working Papers for a New Soc. 1977 4(4): 12-13.* Discusses Cesar Chavez and the United Farm Workers Union's loss of the Proposition 14 (1976) initiative in California. Considers corporate agriculture's opposition (1975-76) to the measure that would have compelled growers to allow union organizers in their fields.

997.   Simoniello, Katalina. ON INVESTIGATING THE ATTITUDES TO-WARDS ACHIEVEMENT AND SUCCESS IN EIGHT PROFESSIONAL U.S. MEXICAN WOMEN. *Aztlán 1981 12(1): 121-137.* Interviews eight professional US Mexican women with education, law, and politics. They indicated family support for their education with some reluctance for continuing that support in higher education, family concern over neglect of home in favor of career, and experiences of sexism and racism. The women felt the need to excel both in their professional and family roles. Despite conventional views of Chicana women as passive, this small sample demonstrates that Mexican women are capable of overcoming the multiple discrimination of sex and ethnicity. 56 notes.   A. Hoffman

998.   Simson, Eve. CHICANO STREET MURALS. *J. of Popular Culture 1976 10(3): 642-652.* Discusses the sociocultural significance of Los Angeles Chicano street murals, assessing them as assertions of ethnicity and artistic expressions.

999.   Slatta, Richard W. CHICANOS IN THE PACIFIC NORTHWEST: A DEMOGRAPHIC AND SOCIOECONOMIC PORTRAIT. *Pacific Northwest Q. 1979 70(4): 155-162.* Recent census data for Oregon and Washington indicate that the Chicano population is comparatively young, urban, mobile, and composed of relatively large families. Despite evidence of educational, occupational, and economic disadvantages, Chicanos of the Pacific Northwest enjoy substantially higher levels of employment, education, and income than

do their counterparts elsewhere in the nation. Based on census data; map, 8 tables, 27 notes. M. L. Tate

1000. Slatta, Richard W. and Atkinson, Maxine P. THE "SPANISH ORI-GIN" POPULATION OF OREGON AND WASHINGTON: A DEMO-GRAPHIC PROFILE, 1980. *Pacific Northwest Quarterly 1984 75(3): 108-116.* Interprets patterns of change in the Hispanic population of Oregon and Washington between the 1970 and 1980 censuses. Statistics demonstrate that the Hispanic population remained relatively youthful, more heavily male than the general population, economically weaker than the majority population, slightly more urbanized, less successful with schooling, and consisted of larger family units than other groups. Other evidence also indicated an increasing political sophistication and activism. Based on census data; 9 tables, 31 notes. M. L. Tate

1001. Smardz, Zofia J. THE GREAT ILLEGAL ALIEN DEBATE. *Worldview 1976 19(5): 15-20.* Discusses the dearth of reliable statistics on the growing number of illegal aliens in the United States in the last decade, and the traumatic effects of the Immigration and Naturalization Service policies on aliens trying to avoid detection.

1002. Snipp, C. Matthew and Tienda, Marta. MEXICAN AMERICAN OCCUPATIONAL MOBILITY. *Social Sci. Q. 1984 65(2): 364-380.* Mexican Americans are prone to suffer downward mobility relative to their fathers' status, but upward and downward shifts are more evenly distributed for other kinds of mobility.

1003. Snipp, C. Matthew and Tienda, Marta. NEW PERSPECTIVES OF CHICANO INTERGENERATIONAL OCCUPATIONAL MOBILITY. *Social Sci. J. 1982 19(2): 37-49.* "Examines the intergenerational occupational mobility of Chicanos" focusing on "circulation mobility, that is, the net upward or downward movement among an array of occupations, as distinct from structural mobility, that movement which arises from the changing array of positions that result from demographic transformations and historically unique events"; the study's results indicate that social policy should be directed at improving long-term rather than market-entry mobility.

1004. Solís, Faustina. COMMENTARY ON THE CHICANA AND HEALTH SERVICES. Sánchez, Rosaura and Martinez Cruz, Rosa, ed. *Essays on la Mujer* (Los Angeles, Ca.: Chicano Studies Center Publ., 1977): 82-90. Criticizes present health care policies in California for failing to realize the needs and values of those to whom the services are directed, in this case the Mexican Americans. The Chicana mother is generally responsible for health care within her family. However, if state and local services are not easily accessible, including bilingual services, childcare, and transportation, she may not be able to utilize even free services. Women may be reluctant to acknowledge their own failing health because of a tendency to put their needs last and because their dignity prevents them from undergoing a physical examination and revealing the family's medical history. Changes must be directed to the needs of the Chicano community as defined by that community.

Early outreach programs aimed at the young Chicana in high school should be initiated to encourage her participation in health careers.   M. T. Wilson

1005. Stevens, A. Jay. THE ACQUISITION OF PARTICIPATORY NORMS: THE CASE OF JAPANESE AND MEXICAN AMERICAN CHILDREN IN A SUBURBAN ENVIRONMENT. *Western Pol. Q. 1975 28(2): 281-295.* This paper describes variations found among Japanese American, Chicano, and Anglo children on measures of political efficacy, civic duty, and personal competence. The observed variations are explained in terms of cultural patterns transmitted by the family. Japanese-American children manifest the most idealized orientations, while the Mexican-American children's orientations do not encourage political participation. Controls for socioeconomic status, political interest, and the children's perception of how easily laws may be changed are introduced. Socioeconomic status has the greatest effect upon the orientations of the Japanese-American children; political interest primarily differentiates the orientations manifest by the Mexican-American children; and the children's perception of the ease with which laws may be changed affects only the Anglo children. Socioeconomic status and political interest encourage positive participatory orientations, but the Anglo children who feel it is easy to change the laws manifest considerably more negative orientations toward political participation than the children from the other groups studied.   J

1006. Stoddard, Ellwyn R. THE ADJUSTMENT OF MEXICAN AMERICAN BARRIO FAMILIES TO FORCED HOUSING RELOCATION. *Social Sci. Q. 1973 53(4): 749-759.* "Self-evaluations of adjustment success were compared with ten spatial and social factors. A serendipitous discovery was that more crucial to barrio happiness than extended or nuclear family relationships was the mini-neighborhood social unit (an intimate visiting clique of five to seven families)."   J

1007. Stoddard, Ellwyn R. A CONCEPTUAL ANALYSIS OF THE "ALIEN INVASION": INSTITUTIONALIZED SUPPORT OF ILLEGAL MEXICAN ALIENS IN THE U.S. *Internat. Migration R. 1976 10(2): 157-189.* Discusses economic factors in patterns of immigration of illegal aliens from Mexico in the 1960's and 70's, including the role of quota systems and the Bracero Program.

1008. Sullivan, Teresa A.; Gillespie, Francis P.; Hout, Michael; and Rogers, Richard G. ALTERNATIVE ESTIMATES OF MEXICAN AMERICAN MORTALITY IN TEXAS, 1980. *Social Sci. Q. 1984 65(2): 609-617.* Compares variability among four alternative sets of life expectancy estimates for Mexican Americans, Anglos, and blacks, and shows that, depending upon the definition used, Mexican Americans have either higher life expectancies than Anglos or lower ones.

1009. Tafolla, Carmen. CHICANO WRITING: BEYOND BEGINNINGS. *Southern Exposure 1981 9(2): 49-52.* Describes the development of Chicano literature in the United States since 1976, the cultural context from which it rises, its depiction of white oppression, and its rise to international recognition following the awarding of the Latin American literary prize, the *Premio Casa de las Américas,* in 1976 to Rolando Hinojosa for his novel, *Klail City y sus Alrededores.*

1010. Tan, Alexis S. EVALUATION OF NEWSPAPERS AND TELEVISION BY BLACKS AND MEXICAN-AMERICANS. *Journalism Q. 1978 55(4): 673-681.* Surveys attitudes toward portrayals of ethnic groups by newspapers and television among 176 adult blacks and 190 adult Mexican Americans in Lubbock, Texas, in March 1976. Blacks more critical of the media tend to have had more years of education, to be younger, and to identify more closely with their ethnic group than do those less critical. Among Mexican Americans, however, education did not seem to be a factor influencing a negative opinion, although younger age and closer ethnic identification did. 6 tables, 19 notes.   R. P. Sindermann, Jr.

1011. Taylor, Patricia A. and Shields, Susan Walker. MEXICAN AMERICANS AND EMPLOYMENT INEQUALITY IN THE FEDERAL CIVIL SERVICE. *Social Sci. Q. 1984 65(2): 381-391.* Analyzes salary inequality between Mexican Americans and Anglos and examines the possible reasons for such inequality; organizational as well as individual characteristics affect salary, but effects are different for Anglos as compared to Mexican Americans.

1012. Temply-Trujillo, Rita E. CONCEPTIONS OF THE CHICANO FAMILY. *Smith Coll. Studies in Social Work 1974 45(1): 1-20.* Reviews a range of formulations about the Chicano family drawn from a sample of social science literature (1968-74), and criticizes the stereotyped conception of ideal family models used as criteria for study of Mexican Americans.   S

1013. Teske, Raymond H. C., Jr. and Nelson, Bardin H. AN ANALYSIS OF DIFFERENTIAL ASSIMILATION RATES AMONG MIDDLE-CLASS MEXICAN AMERICANS. *Sociol. Q. 1976 17(2): 218-235.* The investigation focused on the identification of variables which might help explain differential assimilation rates among middle-class Mexican Americans. The data were collected from a random probability sample of 151 middle-class Mexican Americans residing in Waco, Austin. McAllen, and Lubbock, Texas. Three Likert-type scales designed to measure various components of the assimilation process were developed out of items abstracted from standardized interview schedules. The multiple correlation technique was used to identify independent variables which contributed significantly to a regression model for explaining variation in scores on each of the three scales. The findings suggested that early socialization patterns incorporating a discontinuous status sequence and a lack of reinforcement as Mexican-American increase the probability that the individual will assimilate into the broader American cultural system.

1014. Teske, Raymond H. C., Jr. and Nelson, Bardin H. MIDDLE CLASS MEXICAN AMERICANS AND POLITICAL POWER POTENTIAL: A DILEMMA. *J. of Pol. and Military Sociol. 1976 4(1): 107-119.* This paper reports findings concerning the political orientations of a sample of middle-class Mexican Americans and their membership in political organizations. The data were collected from a random probability sample of middle-class Mexican Americans in four urban communities in Texas. In brief, the investigation found limited evidence of membership in, or moral support for, Mexican-American political organizations. Subsequently, the dilemma which these findings suggest for Mexican American political power is discussed.   J

1015.   Tienda, Marta. FAMILISM AND STRUCTURAL ASSIMILATION OF MEXICAN IMMIGRANTS IN THE UNITED STATES. *Int. Migration Rev. 1980 14(3): 383-408.* Assesses the connections between geographic mobility, kinship ties, and social status among a sample of 820 people who were interviewed upon entry in 1973-74 and were reinterviewed three years later.

1016.   Tienda, Marta. SEX, ETHNICITY AND CHICANO STATUS ATTAINMENT. *Int. Migration Rev. 1982 16(2): 435-473.* Discusses the "process of status attainment" for US citizens of Mexican ancestry; examines the factors of sex, language capability, education and Mexican ethnicity as determinants of socioeconomic achievement.

1017.   Torres, Esteban E. NEW SPIRIT IN THE BARRIOS. *Cry California 1973 8(4): 9-12.* Discusses a new spirit of political awareness in the Mexican-American barrios of East Los Angeles and elsewhere in California during the 1970's.   S

1018.   Trotter, Robert T., II. *GRETA* AND *AZARCON:* A STUDY OF EPISODIC LEAD POISONING FROM A FOLK REMEDY. *Human Organization 1985 44(1): 64-72.* Discusses the use in communities in Texas, New Mexico, and Arizona of *greta* and *azarcon,* lead-containing home remedies that Mexican Americans use to cure the intestinal ailment *empacho.*

1019.   Turner, Kay F. MEXICAN AMERICAN HOME ALTARS: TOWARDS THEIR INTERPRETATION. *Aztlán 1982 13(1-2): 309-326.* Reports on the research being done on Mexican-American home altars in Austin, Texas. Home altars are made mainly by Catholic women and constitute a folk art. Although generally similar, each one represents a personal and creative source of religious experience. The home altar enables its maker to express her faith in the vitality of the family and to attain grace through art. Based on field research and secondary studies; 4 notes, biblio.   A. Hoffman

1020.   Turner, Ralph H. and Kiecolt, K. Jill. RESPONSES TO UNCERTAINTY AND RISK: MEXICAN AMERICAN, BLACK, AND ANGLO BELIEFS ABOUT THE MANAGEABILITY OF THE FUTURE. *Social Sci. Q. 1984 65(2): 665-679.* Compares Mexican Americans, blacks, and Anglos on three dimensions of response to risk and uncertainty over earthquakes: fatalism, orientation toward science, and time perspective.

1021.   Urrutia, Liliana. AN OFFSPRING OF DISCONTENT: THE ASOCIACION NACIONAL MEXICO-AMERICANA, 1949-1954. *Aztlán 1984 15(1): 177-184.* Describes the efforts of the Asociación Nacional México-Americana (ANMA) to obtain justice and protection for Mexican Americans. Formed in 1949, ANMA soon had chapters in Arizona, New Mexico,

California, Colorado, and Texas, numbering 4,000 members in over 30 locals by 1950. ANMA enjoyed the support of the Congress of Industrial Organizations, and it defended the rights of Mexican Americans harassed by police, especially in Los Angeles. Eventually the red-baiting pressures of the McCarthy era put an end to ANMA, as it was accused of Communist sympathies. Nevertheless, ANMA played an important part in countering the oppression of Mexican Americans and supporting their rights. Based on interviews, newspapers, and secondary sources; 47 notes.   A. Hoffman

1022. Valdés, Guadalupe. LANGUAGE ATTITUDES AND THEIR RE-FLECTION IN CHICANO THEATRE: AN EXPLORATORY STUDY. *New Scholar 1982 8(1-2): 181-200.* Chicano theater, neither intellectual nor artistic in intent, is aimed at ordinary people. The characters and their language, therefore, must be realistic. Examines the use of English and Spanish in selected excerpts. 40 notes.   D. K. Pickens

1023. Valdes-Fallis, Guadalupe. SPANISH AND THE MEXICAN AMER-ICANS. *Colorado Q. 1974 22(4): 483-493.* Contests the view of many Mexican Americans that they speak "low" Spanish. Indeed, Spanish in the Americas is characterized by many dialects just as Spanish in Spain has been characterized by several dialects. The term Spanish is incorrect. The proper term is Castellano, which refers to one dialect of the Spanish language. The speaking of Castellano varies among social classes.   B. A. Storey

1024. Valdez, Avelardo. RECENT INCREASES IN INTERMARRIAGE BY MEXICAN AMERICAN MALES: BEXAR COUNTY, TEXAS, FROM 1971 TO 1980. *Social Sci. Q. 1983 64(1): 136-144.* Discusses a study which indicates more Mexican-American men, as opposed to women, in the San Antonio area of Texas are marrying outside of their group.

1025. Valencia, Richard R. THE SCHOOL CLOSURE ISSUE AND THE CHICANO COMMUNITY: A FOLLOW-UP STUDY OF THE *ANGELES* CASE. *Urban Rev. 1984 16(3): 145-163.* Presents a follow-up of a lawsuit in which three predominantly Chicano elementary schools, located in Santa Barbara, California, were closed due to a decline in the district's enrollment. About 600 Mexican-American children were dispersed to five area Anglo schools. The plaintiffs in the case claimed that an excessive burden was placed on minority groups because of the closures. Examines adverse effects of the school closures, including psychological maladjustment, academic decline, parental involvement decline, and adverse community impact. The closures have placed a tremendous burden on those of low socioeconomic status and will increase social problems and failure in school for the affected children.
      R. J. Wechman

1026. Valencia, Richard R. THE SCHOOL CLOSURE ISSUE AND THE CHICANO COMMUNITY. *Urban Rev. 1980 12(1): 5-21.* Discusses a school trial case in Santa Barbara, California, and its relation to urban schooling in California, especially concerning Mexican Americans. Studies declining enrollments because of population decline, declining enrollments because of white flight to private and other public schools, and fiscal crisis in the public schools.

Concludes that the poor and ethnic minority communities such as Mexican Americans will be forced to carry the exclusive burden of school closures. Also concludes that the decision "means the limited gains Chicanos have made in equalizing education have been virtually wiped out, perhaps never to be recovered."   R. J. Wechman

1027.   Vázquez, Mario F. THE ELECTION DAY IMMIGRATION RAID AT LILLI DIAMOND ORIGINALS AND THE RESPONSE OF THE ILGWU. Mora, Magdalena and DelCastillo, Adelaida R., ed. *Mexican Women in the United States: Struggles Past and Present* (Los Angeles: U. of California Chicano Studies Res. Center, 1980): 145-148. Documents the conflict between management and labor at the Lilli Diamond Originals garment plant in Los Angeles, California. On 26 October 1976, the Western States Region Organizing Department of the International Ladies' Garment Workers' Union was informed that workers at the plant wanted to unionize. On election day, 14 January 1977, immigration officials arrested some of the strike supporters who were illegal aliens.   J. Powell

1028.   Velez-I., Carlos G. SE ME ACABÓ LA CANCIÓN: AN ETHNOGRAPHY OF NON-CONSENTING STERILIZATIONS AMONG MEXICAN WOMEN IN LOS ANGELES. Mora, Magdalena and DelCastillo, Adelaida R., ed. *Mexican Women in the United States: Struggles Past and Present* (Los Angeles: U. of California Chicano Studies Res. Center, 1980): 71-91. Analyzes the involuntary sterilization of 10 Mexican women. Sterilizations result in the total disruption of the victim's social and psychological well-being. Mainly secondary sources; 17 notes, biblio.   J. Powell

1029.   Verdugo, Naomi Turner and Verdugo, Richard R. EARNINGS DIFFERENTIALS AMONG MEXICAN AMERICAN, BLACK, AND WHITE MALE WORKERS. *Social Sci. Q. 1984 65(2): 417-425.* Human capital and structural items are important components of earnings differentials among the three groups and account for most of the white-Mexican American and white-black earnings gap; Mexican Americans and blacks have different labor market experiences as reflected in their earnings profiles; and blacks face somewhat stiffer forms of discrimination in the labor market relative to Mexican Americans, though both groups face considerable discrimination relative to white males.

1030.   Vigil, James Diego and Long, John M. UNIDIRECTIONAL OR NATIVIST ACCULTURATION: CHICANO PATHS TO SCHOOL ACHIEVEMENT. *Human Organization 1981 40(3): 273-277.* Utilizes selected data from a 1976 study of student subjects from two Los Angeles-area high schools, one in a barrio and the other in a working-class suburban tract home area.

1031.   Vigil, Maurilio E. THE ELECTION OF TONEY ANAYA AS GOVERNOR OF NEW MEXICO: ITS IMPLICATIONS FOR HISPANICS. *J. of Ethnic Studies 1984 12(2): 81-98.* Toney Anaya's election as New Mexico's fourth Hispanic governor on November 2, 1982 was due to his combination of charisma and his record of public service as a reformist-activist attorney general, as contrasted with the "good ole boy" demeanor of his opponents. Most importantly, his liberal positions on jobs, education, and social programs, along with union support, enabled him to carry the Hispanic counties in the north and center of the state. Evaluation of past elections shows that Anaya fulfilled the major conditions for a Hispanic candidate to win: he was a Democrat, running in a crowded primary race; he appealed not only to the Hispanic north but to metropolitan Bernalillo County; and he had an Anglo running mate. Based on newspapers and other sources; 2 tables, 20 notes.

G. J. Bobango

1032. Vigil, Maurilio E. JERRY APODACA AND THE 1974 GUBERNA-TORIAL ELECTION IN NEW MEXICO: AN ANALYSIS. *Aztlán 1978 9: 133-150.* A statistical analysis of the 1974 election that gave Jerry Apodaca the governorship of New Mexico and launched him on a career as the most promising Mexican-American politician in the country. The study shows that the ethnic factor helped cause the eclipse of the Anglo candidate. Certain circumstances are favorable for a Mexican American: membership in the Democratic Party, appealing to Democrats in the predominantly Anglo counties, and popularity among Hispanics in the counties where they predominate. 2 tables, 30 notes.

R. V. Ritter

1033. Villarreal, Roberto E. and Kelly, Philip. MEXICAN AMERICANS AS PARTICIPANTS IN UNITED STATES-MEXICO RELATIONS. *Int. Studies Notes 1982 9(4): 1-6.* Since 1970, greater political participation by Mexican Americans and heightened interest in Chicano politics by the government of Mexico have increased the active role of Chicanos in international affairs.

1034. Wagner, Michael K. THE ALIENATION OF AMERICAN LABOR: THE NATIONAL LABOR RELATIONS ACT AND THE REGULATION OF ILLEGAL ALIENS. *New York U. J. of Int. Law and Pol. 1981 13(4): 961-991.* Examines issues raised by the National Labor Relations Board's treatment of undocumented aliens by: 1) examining the case law precedents *NLRB* v. *Sure-Tan, Inc.* (US, 1978) and *NLRB* v. *Apollo Tire Co.* (US, 1979); 2) recounting the development of immigration law and its underlying purposes; 3) reviewing the purposes of the NLRA and its intended coverage; and 4) considering the standards of the judicial review and applying them to the decisions rendered in the *Sure-Tan* and *Apollo Tire* cases.

1035. Waldman, Elizabeth. PROFILE OF THE CHICANA: A STATISTI-CAL FACT SHEET. Mora, Magdalena and DelCastillo, Adelaida R., ed. *Mexican Women in the United States: Struggles Past and Present* (Los Angeles: U. of California Chicano Studies Res. Center, 1980): 195-204. Provides information of the number, marital status, education, employment status, median earnings, and family status of Mexican-American women in the United States in 1975. Based on US Bureau of the Census records; 8 tables.

J. Powell

1036. Warren, Nancy. "LA FUNCION": VILLAGE FIESTAS IN NORTHERN NEW MEXICO. *Palacio 1978 84(2): 23-29.* A photographic essay of "La Funcion del Santo," yearly fiestas held to honor New Mexican villages' patron saints, 1970's.

1037. Weaver, Jerry L. HEALTH CARE COSTS AS A POLITICAL ISSUE: COMPARATIVE RESPONSES OF CHICANOS AND ANGLOS. *Social Sci. Q. 1973 53(4): 846-854.* "Based on information gathered from a sample of 484 Orange County, California residents. The data suggest that the economic burden of health care is a focal concern of a sizable portion of the Chicano community. Compared with Anglos, there was significantly more support for four health cost reduction schemes, even after controls were introduced.... speculates that concern about rising health care costs offers a focus for widespread political mobilization among Chicanos."   J

1038. Weaver, Jerry L. MEXICAN AMERICAN HEALTH CARE BE-HAVIOR: A CRITICAL REVIEW OF THE LITERATURE. *Social Sci. Q. 1973 54(1): 85-102.* "Notes that many scholars report the prevalence of a health care subculture thought to be responsible for general poor health and resistance to scientific medicine... Criticizes the bases for this assumption and notes recent work which challenges the accuracy and validity of the subculture stereotype."   J

1039. Weber, Kenneth R. RURAL HISPANIC VILLAGE VIABILITY FROM AN ECONOMIC AND HISTORIC PERSPECTIVE. *Colorado Coll. Studies 1979 (15): 79-89.* Discusses the decrease in the viability of rural Hispanic villages in New Mexico during the mid-20th century, due to a cash economy, as compared to their subsistence economy during the 18th century.

1040. Welch, Susan; Karnig, Albert K.; and Eribes, Richard A. CHANGES IN HISPANIC LOCAL PUBLIC EMPLOYMENT IN THE SOUTHWEST. *Western Pol. Q. 1983 36(4): 660-673.* Looks at changes in the levels and status of Hispanic municipal employment, focusing on differences in male and female employment, employment as professionals and managers, and employment in police and fire departments. Hispanic municipal employment is highly related to the proportion of the community that is Hispanic, but largely unrelated to the income status and political representation of the Hispanic community.
     J

1041. Welch, Susan; Gruhl, John; and Spohn, Cassia. DISMISSAL, CON-VICTION, AND INCARCERATION OF HISPANIC DEFENDANTS: A COMPARISON WITH ANGLOS AND BLACKS. *Social Sci. Q. 1984 65(2): 257-264.* Examines the dismissal, conviction, and incarceration rates for about 10,000 male defendants in Los Angeles during the late 1970's and compares these rates for Hispanic, Anglo, and black defendants. On controlling for legal and extralegal factors and after using multivariate analysis, little difference in the treatment of these defendants is found.   J

1042. Welch, Susan. IDENTITY WITH THE ETHNIC POLITICAL COMMUNITY AND POLITICAL BEHAVIOR: A RESEARCH NOTE ON SOME MEXICAN AMERICANS. *Ethnicity 1977 4(3): 216-225.* Surveys of attitudes of Mexican Americans in Omaha, Nebraska, link ethnic group identification with political partisanship and participation. Actual voter registration was closely aligned with level of education achieved, but support of protest movements and tendencies toward voting Democratic were both associated with strong ethnic identity. Conceptions of identification with political community add to comprehension of differential participation among Mexican Americans. G. A. Hewlett

1043. Welch, Susan; Comer, John; and Steinman, Michael. POLITICAL PARTICIPATION AMONG MEXICAN AMERICANS: AN EXPLORATORY EXAMINATION. *Social Sci. Q. 1973 53(4): 799-813.* "[The authors] find levels of political activity in a sample of Nebraska Mexican Americans lower, in general, than in national samples of U.S. residents, but at about the same level for more passive kinds of political participation.... attitudinal variables explain more variation in participation among Mexican Americans than do socioeconomic ones." J

1044. Wells, Miriam J. OLDTIMERS AND NEWCOMERS: THE ROLE OF CONTEXT IN MEXICAN ASSIMILATION. *Aztlán 1980 11(2): 271-295.* Examines the context of Mexican-American assimilation in Riverside, Wisconsin, where the dominant community is privately segmented along the lines of ethnic European origin. Mexicans seeking acceptance must divest themselves of cultural and social ties with other Mexicans, yet this gives no assurance of assimilation by the dominant community. Problems also exist in the public sector as negative stereotyping makes it difficult for Mexicans to obtain public services. However, some dominant community members have provided services and employment to Mexicans when doing so was to their own advantage. The difficulty of assimilation for Mexican Americans is compounded by the apparent homogeneity of the dominant community which continues to maintain its own internal differences. 9 notes, biblio.
A. Hoffman

1045. Williams, Herma B. and Williams, Eric. SOME ASPECTS OF CHILDREARING PRACTICES IN THREE MINORITY SUBCULTURES IN THE UNITED STATES. *J. of Negro Educ. 1979 48(3): 408-418.* Minority groups seek to socialize their children into the values of the larger culture, but they also instill other values belonging to their particular ethnic subculture. This paper focuses on the values and child-rearing practices of Mexican Americans, Indians, and blacks. Each group stresses different values in child-rearing, and these in turn are often in conflict with the values promoted in the schools these children must attend. Secondary sources; 22 notes. J. Powell

1046. Williams, J. Allen, Jr.; Babchuk, Nicholas; and Johnson, David R. VOLUNTARY ASSOCIATIONS AND MINORITY STATUS: A COMPARATIVE ANALYSIS OF ANGLO, BLACK, AND MEXICAN AMERICANS. *Am. Sociol. Rev. 1973 38(5): 637-646.* Focuses on the voluntary associations of Anglo, Black, and Mexican Americans in Austin, Texas. A sample of 380 respondents provided the data. An information interview was used; trained interviewers coming from the same ethnic background as the respondent were employed. Ethnicity proved to be an important variable in predicting social participation, with blacks having the highest and Mexican

Americans having the lowest participation rate. Using multiple classification analysis, a number of structural variables were introduced as controls; and these variables, particularly education, were found to be responsible for the difference between Anglo and Mexican Americans. Blacks continued to have significantly higher rates of participation in voluntary associations after controlling on other variables. Both isolation and cultural inhibition theories can be found in previous literature to account for low participation rates among people having a subordinate status, and compensatory and ethnic community theories have been used to account for high rates of affiliation among these same groups. The findings from this study tend to cast doubt on isolation and cultural inhibition theories and to support compensatory and ethnic community theories.   J

1047.   Williams, P. M. and Reilly, S. J. THE 1980 US ELECTION AND AFTER. *Pol. Studies [Great Britain] 1982 30(3): 371-392.* Analyzes the political importance of the 1980 election in the United States and estimates the impact of, and possible reactions to, the rapid shift of population, wealth, and political influence toward the west and south. The election was a heavy defeat, not only for Jimmy Carter, but also for the Democratic Party, but it was not a positive mandate for conservatism. The Democratic Party needs to regain the intellectual initiative it lost and to extend its popularity in the increasingly powerful sunbelt states. Mexican Americans form a large, neglected, and strategically placed group which the Democrats should attract, although this may prove harder than some Democratic optimists suspect. Secondary sources; 2 tables, 65 notes.   G. L. Neville

1048.   Wrinkle, Robert D. and Miller, Lawrence W. A NOTE ON MEXI-CAN AMERICAN VOTER REGISTRATION AND TURNOUT. *Social Sci. Q. 1984 65(2): 308-314.* Examines the relationship between voter registra-tion and turnout among Mexican Americans. Despite earlier speculation that Mexican Americans registered to vote and participated in the primary but not in the general election, the study of a heavily Mexican-American south Texas county reveals that Mexican-American precincts did not have lower (or higher) rates of turnout than did Anglo precincts.   J/S

1049.   Ybarra-Frausto, Tomás. THE CHICANO MOVEMENT AND THE EMERGENCE OF A CHICANO POETIC CONSCIOUSNESS. *New Schol-ar 1977 (6): 81-110.* Chicano poetic consciousness has 19th-century origins, but the focus is on the post-1945 period. From its inception, this poetic consciousness has moved between betterment and liberation. Language, the revitalization of Chicano speech, has played a major role in this poetic development, moving toward cultural nationalism. Newspapers and presses—first Spanish-language and then Chicano—are the creative forces. Finally, this Chicano enterprise has now gone beyond cultural nationalism to a more consciously critical view of American capitalism. From a special issue, "New Directions In Chicano Scholarship." 55 notes.   D. K. Pickens

1050.   Zavella, Patricia. THE IMPACT OF "SUN BELT INDUSTRIAL-IZATION" ON CHICANAS. *Frontiers 1984 8(1): 21-27.* Young Mexican-American working mothers in Albuquerque, New Mexico, entered the job market because of their families' need for a second income, not because of weakening traditional sex roles. S

1051. Zinn, Maxine Baca. EMPLOYMENT AND EDUCATION OF MEX-ICAN-AMERICAN WOMEN: THE INTERPLAY OF MODERNITY AND ETHNICITY IN EIGHT FAMILIES. *Harvard Educ. Rev. 1980 50(1): 47-62.* Examines and compares the role of outside employment and education on conjugal power and ethnicity in Mexican-American women from eight families, 1970's.

1052. Zucker, Martin. WALLS OF BARRIO ARE BROUGHT TO LIFE BY STREET GANG ART. *Smithsonian 1978 9(7): 105-111.* Discusses the recent mural paintings in East Los Angeles which "plead for the traditional values of family, religion and education, and an end to violence, and for preservation of culture, history, hope." Artists such as Manuel Cruz and Judy Baca, following the traditions of Orozco, Rivera, and Siqueiros, have attempted to rehabilitate neighborhoods and provide jobs for young Mexican Americans from the violent barrio gangs in Los Angeles. Although these projects do not solve the street gang problem, participating in mural painting at least provides "one positive experience in a life that is largely negative." 8 illus.

S. R. Quéripel

1053. —. [THE EDUCATION OF RICHARD RODRIGUEZ]. *Change 1982 14(7): 32-42, 48-53.*
Rodriguez, Richard. THE EDUCATION OF RICHARD RODRIGUEZ, *pp. 32-35, 48-53.* Rodriguez's autobiographical statement on the education of a Mexican American in the 1950's and 60's; affirmative action and bilingual education "obscure or devalue the true function" of education, preventing the private person from becoming the public person who can succeed in the public world.
Bell, Michael Davitt. FITTING INTO A TRADITION OF AUTOBIOGRA-PHY, *pp. 36-39.*
Chall, Jeanne. RICH AND SHARP MEMORIES OF READING, *pp. 36, 39-40.*
Willie, Charles V. FIRST LEARNING UNCHALLENGED AND UN-TESTED, *pp. 37, 40-41.*
Olivas, Michael A. PAINFUL TO WRITE, PAINFUL TO READ, *pp. 37, 42.*

1054. —. [ETHNIC IDENTITY AND THE CHICANO NOVEL]. *Explorations in Ethnic Studies 1981 4(2): 14-25.*
Rodriguez, Joe D. GOD'S SILENCE AND THE SHRILL OF ETHNICITY IN THE CHICANO NOVEL, *pp. 14-21.* Explores the problem of Chicano identity in three novels: José Antonia Villareal's *Pocho*, Oscar Zeta Acosta's *Autobiography of a Brown Buffalo,* and Tomás Rivera's *Y No Se Lo Tragó La Tierra.*
Nakadate, Neil. CRITIQUE, *pp. 22-23.* Amplifies Rodriguez's discussion of the conflict between individual and group identity, especially the need of the individual to break away from the group.

Howell, Gladys David. CRITIQUE, *pp. 24-25.* Expands on Rodriguez's insight that in the Chicano community religion is a source of passivity which inhibits formation of an aggressive ethnic identity.

1055.   —. [GAYS IN CHICANO PROSE FICTION]. *Explorations in Ethnic Studies 1981 4(2): 41-55.*
Reinhardt, Karl J. THE IMAGE OF GAYS IN CHICANO PROSE FICTION, *pp. 41-50.* Presents a survey of Chicano literature with homosexual references.
Jamison, W. Thomas. CRITIQUE, *pp. 51-52.* Suggests that a lack of tolerance toward homosexuals is not unique to Chicanos, and indicates areas for further research, especially homosexuality in other cultures.
Bentley, Sara. CRITIQUE, *pp. 52-53.* Provides a summary of Reinhardt's paper.
González, LaVerne. CRITIQUE, *pp. 53-55.* Discusses the homosexual taboo in Chicano culture and literature and indicates areas of further research.

1056.   —. [ILLEGAL IMMIGRATION]. *Center Mag. 1979 12(3): 54-64.*
Graham, Otis L., Jr. ILLEGAL IMMIGRATION AND THE NEW RESTRICTIONISM, *pp. 54-64.* Discusses the magnitude of the problems and frustrations surrounding the issue of illegal immigration of Mexicans in the 1970's.
Villalpando, Vic. MR. GRAHAM'S LOYALTY TEST FOR CHICANOS, *pp. 63-64.* Criticizes Graham's perspective on the issue.

1057.   —. MEXICAN AMERICANS. Sowell, Thomas, ed. *Essays and Data on American Ethnic Groups* (Washington, D. C.: Urban Inst. Pr., 1978): 374-375. Statistics on Mexican Americans' family income distribution; family income distribution by age of family head; occupational distribution; and educational distribution by age. From the US Bureau of the Census, *Current Population Reports,* Series P-20, Nos. 213, 224; 4 tables.   K. A. Talley

1058.   —. REPORT ON THE STATUS OF CHICANOS IN THE PROFESSION, 1974, WESTERN STATES. *Western Pol. Q. 1975 28(4): 739-743.* In 1970 the American Political Science Association published a report on Mexican Americans in the profession and accused political science departments of being out of touch with America's second largest minority. A report to analyze the current situation in 13 western states discovered a large difference between the proportion of Chicanos in political science departments and the percentage in the states' populations. Not all colleges offered courses in Chicano Studies and there was no correlation between course offerings and the size of the Chicano population involved in the department. Although schools perceived a need for Chicano courses, students, and faculty, they were at a loss as to how to recruit them. On the surface universities appeared interested in change, but changing department policies is perceived as a threat to academic standards. Aggressive policies are advocated by professional associations and Chicano scholars to break down exclusionary policies. Based on a report prepared by the committee on the status of Chicanos of the WPSA; 2 figs., 2 notes.   K. McElroy

4

PEOPLE FROM THE CARIBBEAN, CENTRAL AMERICA, AND SOUTH AMERICA

1059. Aguirre, B. E. THE MARITAL STABILITY OF CUBANS IN THE UNITED STATES. *Ethnicity 1981 8(4): 387-405.* Cuban marriages in the United States are quite modern. The institutional marriage model does not accurately predict marital behavior. The model of democratic, companionship marriage is more applicable than stereotypes of male-dominated, Latin marriages. One of the consequences of the modernity of Cuban marriages in the United States is a relatively high divorce rate. Table, 2 fig., 7 notes, biblio.
T. W. Smith

1060. Aguirre, B. E.; Schwirian, Kent P.; and La Greca, Anthony J. THE RESIDENTIAL PATTERNING OF LATIN AMERICAN AND OTHER ETHNIC POPULATIONS IN METROPOLITAN MIAMI. *Latin Am. Res. Rev. 1980 15(2): 35-63.* Residential patterns of groups in Miami generally correspond to nine patterns identified in earlier studies of ethnic groups in terms of centralization, segregation, and dissimilarity. Cubans and Puerto Ricans are more centralized than groups resident there longer. Patterns of segregation and dissimilarity are essentially the same in city and fringe areas. Ethnic self-selectivity is a greater influence on these patterns than enforced constraint. Based on 1970 census tract data; map, 5 tables, 8 notes, biblio.
J. K. Pfabe

1061. Aguirre, Benigno E. ETHNIC NEWSPAPERS AND POLITICS: *DIARIO LAS AMERICAS* AND THE WATERGATE AFFAIR. *Ethnic Groups 1979 2(2): 155-166.* The ethnic perspective and background of the Cuban exiles who operate and are served by the *Diario Las Americas* in Miami influenced the paper's handling of the Watergate scandal. The ethnic paper's coverage was less critical than local nonethnic papers and was greatly influenced by its conspiratorial view of history and anti-Communist orientation. 10 notes, ref.
T. W. Smith

1062. Ahearn, Frederick L. PUERTO RICANS AND MENTAL HEALTH: SOME SOCIO-CULTURAL CONSIDERATIONS. *Urban and Social Change Rev. 1979 12(2): 4-9.* Discusses Puerto Rico since its discovery in 1493, and the social problems faced by Puerto Rican immigrants to the

United States, linking these problems to mental illness among Puerto Ricans until 1978.

1063. Albuquerque, Klaus de; Mader, Paul D.; and Stinner, William F. MODERNIZATION, DELAYED MARRIAGE AND FERTILITY IN PUERTO RICO: 1950-1970. *Social and Econ. Studies [Jamaica] 1976 25(1): 55-65.* Census data is used to test the relationship between urbanization, industrialization, education, and fertility. The expected decline in fertility with an increase in urbanization and industrialization was not found, and increased female education was negatively related to delayed marriage. Fig., 3 tables, 4 notes, 35 references.   E. S. Johnson

1064. Andic, Fuat M. and Mann, Arthur J. SECULAR TENDENCIES IN THE EQUALITY OF EARNINGS IN PUERTO RICO. *R. of Social Econ. 1976 34(1): 13-32.* Analyzes changes in distribution of earnings by the civilian labor force of Puerto Rico during 1949-69, focusing on long-term tendencies for earning distribution in a period of rapid economic growth.

1065. Andic, Suphan and Choudhury, Parimal. DIRECT SUBSIDIES AND INCOME REDISTRIBUTION: THE FOOD STAMP PROGRAM IN PUERTO RICO. *Rev. of Social Econ. 1977 35(1): 95-114.* Uses 1969 income data to examine the food stamp program and assess its income redistribution effects in Puerto Rico since 1974.

1066. Angle, John. MAINLAND CONTROL OF MANUFACTURING AND REWARD FOR BILINGUALISM IN PUERTO RICO. *Am. Sociol. R. 1976 41(2): 289-307.* The literature on language group relations in the economy of Quebec Province suggests that more French Canadians are bilingual than English Canadians because many businesses use English and are owned or operated by English Canadians. Bilingual French Canadians are rewarded, on the average, by placement into better occupations. The hypothesis is made that a similar reward exists for bilingualism in English in the Spanish mother tongue labor force in Puerto Rico. The 1970 Census of Population in Puerto Rico provides data for a test of this hypothesis in which the reward is demonstrated. It is also hypothesized that it is mainland American ownership of businesses which accounts for this reward. This hypothesis is tested on the labor force in manufacturing. It is not confirmed.
                                                                                    J

1067. Aponte, Juan B. THE LASH OF INFLATION ON A DEVELOPING ECONOMY: PUERTO RICO, A CASE STUDY. *Ann. of the Am. Acad. of Pol. and Social Sci. 1981 (456): 132-153.* Considers the relationships among Puerto Rico's unique sociopolitical conditions, the economic achievements attained, and the social changes experienced throughout the years of relative economic stability from World War II to 1973. Examines the 1974 inflationary period and the recession that followed, from which the island is not fully recovered, as well as the inflationary trend that has prevailed since 1978, and the difficulties that the economy is now experiencing.   J/S

1068.   Ardura, Ernesto. JOSÉ MARTÍ: LATIN AMERICA'S U.S. CORRE-SPONDENT. *Américas (Organization of Am. States) 1980 32(11-12): 38-42.* Having been exiled from Spain because of his revolutionary activities against the colonial regime in his home Cuba, writer-patriot José Martí (1853-95) came to New York City where he wrote hundreds of articles and essays on life in the United States for Latin American newspapers.

1069.   Arrivi, Francisco. EL ANTIGUO SAN JUAN Y EL TEATRO TAPIA [Old San Juan and the Tapia Theater]. *R. del Inst. de Cultura Puertorriqueña [Puerto Rico] 1969 12(45): 40-44.* Historical résumé of theatrical life in Puerto Rico from the 16th century to the present, and of the Tapia Theater.   B. T. (IHE 80495)

1070.   Arroyo, Gilberto. EL SISTEMA DE INSCRIPCIÓN ELECTORAL DE PUERTO RICO: ADAPTACIÓN DEL SISTEMA CANADIENSE DE ENUMERACIÓN DE ELECTORES [The Puerto Rican voter registration system: An adaptation of the Canadian form of listing voters]. *Rev. Interamericana [Puerto Rico] 1977 7(1): 21-29.* In order to combat political apathy, Puerto Rico enacted in 1974 the Canadian form of voter registration, in which state employees go door-to-door to enroll voters. Although the results have been mildly disappointing, more Puerto Ricans than ever before have the right to cast their ballot on election day. Based on primary and secondary sources; table, 23 notes.   J. A. Lewis

1071.   Ashton, Guy T. MIGRATION AND THE PUERTO RICAN SUPPORT SYSTEM. *Revista/Review Interamericana [Puerto Rico] 1982 12(2): 228-242.* Puerto Rican migration to the US mainland takes place within the context of the extended family structure. 7 notes, biblio.   J. A. Lewis

1072.   Ashton, Guy T. THE RETURN AND RE-RETURN OF LONG-TERM PUERTO RICAN MIGRANTS: A SELECTIVE RURAL-URBAN SAMPLE. *Revista/Review Interamericana [Puerto Rico] 1980 10(1): 27-45.* A sizeable percentage of long-term return migrants to Puerto Rico encounter cultural and economic hardships in adjusting to life again on the island. A significant number of these returnees migrate back to the mainland, although often to different areas than where they had lived before. 3 tables, biblio.
                                                                      J. A. Lewis

1073.   Attinasi, John J. LANGUAGE ATTITUDES AND WORKING CLASS IDEOLOGY IN A PUERTO RICAN BARRIO OF NEW YORK. *Ethnic Groups 1983 5(1-2): 55-78.* Two groups of Puerto Ricans studied exhibit strong loyalties to both the Spanish language and Puerto Rican culture. The lack of a rigorous ideology defending Spanish and the culture against bilingualism with English is not a negative characteristic, but a pragmatic reaction to a bilingual social situation. An "interpenetrating bilingualism" constitutes the first element of a bilingual working class consciousness in which positive attitudes reflect a recognition of change on the part of the working class, but a refusal to give up a distinctly Puerto Rican identity.   J/S

1074.   Azicri, Max. CULTURAL AND POLITICAL CHANGE AMONG CUBAN-AMERICANS (1958-1982). *Revista/Review Interamericana [Puerto Rico] 1982 12(2): 200-220.* The Cuban-American community has turned progressively toward dealing with the problems of life in the United States and toward accepting the victory of the revolution in Cuba. Table, 27 notes.

J. A. Lewis

1075.   Bach, Robert L. CARIBBEAN MIGRATION: CAUSES AND CONSEQUENCES. *Migration Today 1982 10(5): 6-13.* Migration from the West Indies is the result of several factors: recruitment by labor and government employers, escape from violence or coercion, family reunification, and a migrant ideology among the people; focuses on the 1970's.

1076.   Bach, Robert L. THE NEW CUBAN EXODUS: POLITICAL AND ECONOMIC MOTIVATIONS. *Caribbean Rev. 1982 11(1): 22-25, 58-60.* Provides statistics showing that the Cuban refugees from Mariel who arrived by boat in 1980 in south Florida were not largely criminals or undesirables but were laborers and professionals, 74% of whom had held jobs for most of their adult lives; discusses the debate over whether the refugees came to the United States for economic or political reasons.

1077.   Bach, Robert L. THE NEW CUBAN IMMIGRANTS: THEIR BACKGROUND AND PROSPECTS. *Monthly Labor Rev. 1980 103(10): 39-46.* Describes Cuban immigrants who arrived in Miami, Florida, from the sealift in 1980; the early arrivals in general had above-average (for Cuba) education and job skills, and although many refugees were ex-offenders, many had been political prisoners; compares the 1980 arrivals with a group that entered the United States in 1973-74.

1078.   Batista, Gustavo. FELIPE GUTIÉRREZ Y SU ACADEMIA DE MÚSICA DE PUERTO RICO [Felipe Gutiérrez and His Musical Academy of Puerto Rico]. *Revista/Review Interamericana [Puerto Rico] 1978-79 8(4): 640-645.* Felipe Gutiérrez y Espinosa founded the first music school on the island in 1871. So successful was this academy that the conservatory became a permanent institution in the music history of the island. 15 notes.

J. A. Lewis

1079.   Beauchamp, José J. LA NOVELA PUERTORRIQUEÑA: UNA ESTRUCTURA DE RESISTENCIA, RUPTURA Y RECUPERACIÓN [The Puerto Rican novel: resistance, rupture and recovery]. *Casa de las Américas [Cuba] 1981 21(124): 67-82.* Examines the development of the Puerto Rican novel within the literary and sociological context of Puerto Rico. Puerto Rican fiction is a search for national affirmation and cultural resistance to alien and inauthentic values imposed by US domination. This does not exclude the fact that it represents a vision of the world that is linked to particular classes or collective entities. 16 notes.

J. V. Coutinho

1080.   Belcher, John C.; Crader, Kelly W.; and Vasquez-Calcarrada, Pablo B. DETERMINANTS OF LEVEL OF LIVING IN RURAL PUERTO RICO. *Rural Sociol. 1973 38(2): 187-195.* Assesses determinants of the standard of living in Puerto Rico, 1960-72, concluding that social rather than economic factors are of greater importance.

1081. Bender, Lynn Darrell. THE CUBAN EXILES: AN ANALYTICAL SKETCH. *J. of Latin Am. Studies [Great Britain] 1973 5(2): 271-278.* A demographic breakdown based on occupation and age of the approximately 510,000 Cubans who have left Cuba since 1959. Mostly settled in Puerto Rico and the continental United States, 350,000 of these Cubans live in the greater Miami area, making it the second largest Cuban city. Although politically disunited, the Cuban exiles in general and their organizations are anti-Castro. Yet many Cubans approve of Castro's reforms, and share his hopes for a "fully sovereign and fully independent Cuba." Based on newspaper accounts, US government reports, and secondary sources; 24 notes. K. M. Bailor

1082. Benjamin, Jules R. THE NEW DEAL, CUBA, AND THE RISE OF A GLOBAL FOREIGN ECONOMIC POLICY. *Business Hist. Rev. 1977 51(1): 57-78.* Revises the conventional thesis that isolationism characterized early New Deal foreign policy. US involvement in Cuba increased during this period, and this helped to establish precedents for the global outlook of American policy in the 1940's and beyond. The new policy was especially visible in the use of the Reconstruction Finance Corporation and the Export-Import Bank to promote American interests. Based on State Department and other US governmental records; 39 notes. C. J. Pusateri

1083. Bergad, Laird W. AGRARIAN HISTORY OF PUERTO RICO, 1870-1930. *Latin Am. Res. Rev. 1978 13(3): 63-94.* US control of Puerto Rico after 1899 significantly changed the economy. A prospering coffee industry was replaced by a large-scale, US-dominated sugar industry. The tobacco industry grew due to stimulus from the United States. Important socioeconomic changes resulted—proletarianization of labor, dependence on US consumption patterns, greater outside control of capital, retarded development of an internal consuming market, and considerable social dislocation. Extensive research is needed for thorough understanding of changes which occurred. Based on economic statistics, census records, and secondary sources; 108 notes. J. K. Pfabe

1084. Berrocal, Luciano. FORCE DE DOMINATION ET DE RÉSIS-TANCE SOCIALE: L'ÉDUCATION À PUERTO RICO [Dominating force and social resistance: education in Puerto Rico]. *Cultures et Développement [Belgium] 1980 12(3-4): 563-590.* Covers 1940-77.

1085. Berrocal, Luciano. À LA RECHERCHE DE L'ÉTAT-NATION: GENÈSE DE L'ÉTAT À PORTO RICO [In search of the nation-state: genesis of the state in Puerto Rico]. *Rev. de l'Inst. de Sociologie [Belgium] 1981 (1-2): 377-396.* Examines the role of the state in Puerto Rico and other dependent societies in relation to different social classes and to the production process, focusing on Puerto Rico's quest to become a state, the origins of its colonial state, the birth of the neocolonial state or the nationalization of dependency, and its transformation into a welfare state; 1930-50.

1086.   Bhana, Surendra. PUERTO RICO AND THE TRUMAN ADMIN-
ISTRATION, 1945-47: SELF-GOVERNMENT "LITTLE BY LITTLE."
Prologue 1973 5(3): 155-165. Describes the politics and policy of gradualism in
securing the appointment of a native Puerto Rican governor and the passage of
an act permitting Puerto Ricans to elect their governor during the Truman
administration, 1945-47. Primary and secondary sources; photo, 39 notes.
R. W. Tissing, Jr.

1087.   Birkner, Michael. THE "FOXARDO AFFAIR" REVISITED: POR-
TER, PIRATES AND THE PROBLEM OF CIVILIAN AUTHORITY IN
THE EARLY REPUBLIC. *Am. Neptune 1982 42(3): 165-178.* David Porter
commanded the West Indies Squadron under orders allowing landings on
uninhabited foreign shores when in pursuit of pirates. In November 1824,
Porter led 200 men ashore at Foxardo, Puerto Rico, where he spiked several
guns and forced an apology from town officials for their treatment of one of his
lieutenants. Porter was recalled because his action was an act of war, could be
viewed as a repetition of Andrew Jackson's 1818 foray into Florida, and
threatened the Monroe Doctrine principle of noninterference. Porter's actions
also threatened the military command process and his publication of a
pamphlet led to an additional charge of insubordination. President John
Quincy Adams and Navy Secretary Samuel Southard acted correctly, if not
generously, toward Porter who had only himself to blame. Based mainly on
Southard's papers in the Princeton University Library and other sources; 35
notes.   J. C. Bradford

1088.   Blades, Rubén; Parker, Robert A., interviewer. THE VISION OF
RUBEN BLADES. *Américas (Organization of American States) 1985 37(2):
15-19.* Interviews the popular Panamanian-born musician Rubén Blades—now
living in New York City—whose *salsa* music explores the feelings of the Latin
American city dweller.

1089.   Blaut, James. ARE PUERTO RICANS A NATIONAL MINORITY?
Monthly Rev. 1977 29(1): 35-55. Examines whether Puerto Ricans in the
United States are a national minority ("an ethnic group is a national minority
if it does not possess the defining attributes of a nation...") or a colonial
minority (a forced-migrant community created by imperialism).

1090.   Bonilla, Frank and Campos, Ricardo. A WEALTH OF POOR:
PUERTO RICANS IN THE NEW ECONOMIC ORDER. *Daedalus 1981
110(2): 133-176.* Describes US colonialism and capitalist expansion in Puerto
Rico since 1900, migration of Puerto Ricans to the United States, which has
increased dramatically since 1950, and their consistently low place in the
American economic scene.

1091.   Booth, Karen Marshall. THE DOMESTIC AND FOREIGN MIS-
SIONARY PAPERS: THE PUERTO RICO PAPERS, 1870-1952. *Hist. Mag.
of the Protestant Episcopal Church 1973 42(3): 341-344.* A brief account of
Episcopalian missionary activity in Puerto Rico and a mention of the
documents from the missionary work which are housed in the archives of the
Church Historical Society in Austin, Texas.

1092.   Boswell, Thomas D. INTERNAL MIGRATION IN PUERTO RICO PRIOR TO ECONOMIC DEVELOPMENT. *Social and Econ. Studies [Jamaica] 1978 27(4): 434-463.* Uses data from a special census in 1935 and the regular census in 1940 to identify the cause of internal migration in Puerto Rico. Multiregression models reveal that economic factors explain most of the observed in and out migration. Such models cannot include such factors as family movement and specialized training. 5 maps, 6 tables, 30 notes, 42 ref.
E. S. Johnson

1093.   Bradford, William Penn. PUERTO RICAN SPIRITISM: CONTRASTS IN THE SACRED AND THE PROFANE. *Caribbean Q. [Jamaica] 1978 24(3-4): 48-55.* Describes Puerto Rican spiritism, "an organized religious cult which adheres to Christian beliefs and bases its authenticity on Biblical passages." Notes the effects of spiritism, which also incorporates African religious practice, on mental disorders and economic, social, and political affairs. Based on the author's personal experience and secondary sources.
R. L. Woodward, Jr.

1094.   Bras, Juan Mari. PUERTO RICO: FORTALEZA IMPERIALISTA EN EL CARIBE [Puerto Rico: Imperialist fortress in the Caribbean]. *Casa de las Américas [Cuba] 1973 14(80): 64-71.* Puerto Rico is an imperialist outpost, breaking Latin American solidarity and becoming itself the victim of imperialist development which does not benefit its own people but serves the aims of the United States.

1095.   Bras, Juan Mari. THE STRUGGLE FOR PUERTO RICAN INDEPENDENCE. *Black Scholar 1976 8(3): 18-26.* Focuses on the period 1960-76.

1096.   Briski, Norman; Lenoir, Claudia Kaiser, interviewer. ENTRETIEN: NORMAN BRISKI [Interview with Norman Briski]. *Cahiers du Monde Hispanique et Luso-Brésilien [France] 1983 (40): 149-156.* An interview with Norman Briski, who speaks of problems of exile, of living in New York City, and of Latin-American theater in the United States generally and New York in particular. The Latin-American community in New York has specific identity problems, since it is uprooted from native culture and not yet assimilated or assimilable into Anglo-American culture. As an Argentine, Briski has special problems with black Latin culture as well.
D. R. Stevenson

1097.   Bruno, Melania and Gaston, Mauricio. LATINOS FOR MEL KING: SOME REFLECTIONS. *Radical America 1983-84 17-18(6-1): 67-79.* Latinos represented 10% of Boston's population at the time of the 1983 mayoral election, their numbers having risen rapidly since the 1950's. Boston's Latinos are more recent arrivals and comprise a smaller proportion of the population than do Latinos in many major cities. In his campaign for mayor, Mel King won a high percentage of the Latino vote (70% in the primary and 66% in the general election) despite various challenges. 5 illus., 2 notes.   C. M. Hough

1098.   Bruyn, Severyn T. PUERTO RICO: SELF-DETERMINATION IN AN INTERDEPENDENT WORLD. *Peace and Change 1976 4(1): 50-59.* Discusses Puerto Rico's struggle to gain political and economic self-determination from US neocolonialism and multinational corporations' foreign investments from the 1950's-70's; considers the significance of the Puerto Rican labor movement.

1099.   Bryce-Laporte, Roy Simón. NEW YORK CITY AND THE NEW CARIBBEAN IMMIGRATION: A CONTEXTUAL STATEMENT. *Int. Migration Rev. 1979 13(2): 214-234.* Focuses on the distinctive features of Caribbean migration from 1965 to 1979, noting that the period coincides with financial problems in New York City, a situation which has engendered considerable anti-migrant sentiment, and the public at large often does not differentiate between native-born Blacks with long histories of residency in the continental U.S. and newly arrived Caribbean Blacks.

1100.   Bulger, Peggy A. LITTLE HAVANA: FOLK TRADITIONS OF AN IMMIGRANT ENCLAVE. *Kentucky Folklore Record 1983 29(1-2): 15-23.* Social customs such as the Afro-Catholic religion of Santeria, the debutante's Fiesta de Quinze, and voodoo thrive in Miami's "Little Havana," the home of Cuban refugees and, outside Havana, the largest Cuban community.

1101.   Burke, Fred G. BILINGUALISM/BICULTURALISM IN AMERICAN EDUCATION: AN ADVENTURE IN WONDERLAND. *Ann. of the Am. Acad. of Pol. and Social Sci. 1981 (454): 164-177.* With Hispanic population increasing rapidly non-Hispanic Americans—both white and black—have reasons to view bilingual education as part of a larger thrust aimed at giving Hispanics increased visibility and political influence. A brief case study of the New Jersey experience with Puerto Ricans and Cubans demonstrates the growth of Hispanics in numbers and sophistication.   J/S

1102.   Burn, Henry Pelham. TWO FACES OF DEVELOPMENT: PUERTO RICO. *Vista 1973 9(3): 30-34.* Discusses the role of the United States in Puerto Rico's economic development and industrialization in the 1960's and 70's.

1103.   Cabranes, José A. PUERTO RICO: OUT OF THE COLONIAL CLOSET. *Foreign Policy 1978-79 (33): 66-91.* The desire for change in Puerto Rico's essentially colonial status is near-universal among that island's population. Advocates of modification in commonwealth status, of independence, and of statehood disagree on the direction of change, but all concur that some form of decolonization must come. Extensive violence in Puerto Rico and the United States is the likely alternative. US policymakers must give serious attention to the future of the US-Puerto Rico relationship, and must include representatives of all major elements of island opinion in their planning. Table, 2 notes.

T. L. Powers

1104.   Cafferty, Pastora San Juan. PUERTO RICAN RETURN MIGRATION: ITS IMPLICATIONS FOR BILINGUAL EDUCATION. *Ethnicity 1975 2(1): 52-65.* Due to the bilingual nature of Puerto Rico, public schools should be made bilingual to promote educational achievement and biculturality, 1970's.

1105. Calderón Cruz, Angel. THE INTERNATIONAL RELATIONS OF THE COMMONWEALTH OF PUERTO RICO. *Rev. Interamericana [Puerto Rico] 1975 5(2): 207-224.* Puerto Rico needs to expand its modest efforts at foreign relations with Latin America and the Caribbean rather than rely on the State Department. The economic and political benefits promise to make the effort worthwhile. Primary and secondary sources; 19 notes.

J. A. Lewis

1106. Calderón Cruz, Angel. THE PUERTO RICAN STATUS QUES-TION: A COMMENTARY. *Rev. Interamericana [Puerto Rico] 1976 6(1): 18-22.* Critiques three papers given at the Second Annual Conference of the Caribbean Studies Association. Sees no immediate resolution of the political status question surrounding Puerto Rico for the rest of the 20th century.

J. A. Lewis

1107. Campos, Ricardo and Bonilla, Frank. BOOTSTRAPS AND ENTER-PRISE ZONES: THE UNDERSIDE OF LATE CAPITALISM IN PUERTO RICO AND THE UNITED STATES. *Rev. (Fernand Braudel Center) 1982 5(4): 556-590.* Following World War II, Operation Bootstrap was successful in eliminating economic poverty in Puerto Rico. Due to billions of dollars invested by US firms, Puerto Rico's growth rate was 6% for the 1950's, 5% for the 1960's, and 4% for the 1970's. On the surface, Puerto Rico can boast of one of the most affluent economies in Latin America. It is an economy, however, heavily dependent on US investment and upon imports and exports. In 1976, despite an expanding economy, unemployment was 34%, and a growing number are dependent on welfare programs. Traditional agriculture has been largely supplanted by agribusiness, and the island must now import 80% of its food. In short, the economy of Puerto Rico has been absorbed into the United States economic system without increasing Puerto Rican control over any significant portion of local economic activity. Secondary sources; 53 notes, ref.

J. Powell

1108. Campos, Ricardo and Bonilla, Frank. INDUSTRIALIZATION AND MIGRATION: SOME EFFECTS ON THE PUERTO RICAN WORKING CLASS. *Latin Am. Perspectives 1976 3(3): 66-108.* Analyzes the dynamics of change in the class structure that have accompanied the rapid monopolization and capitalization of the Puerto Rican economy by US capital. Provides a theoretical explanation for Puerto Rico's employment problems and attempts to compensate via welfare payments. Also deals with Puerto Rican migration to the United States, in which Puerto Ricans provide a cheap and easily exploitable labor force. Shows the historical development of the movement of Puerto Ricans between the island and the mainland and the political conse-quences of migration. Tables.

J. L. Dietz

1109. Casal, Lourdes and Hernández, Andrés R. CUBANS IN THE U.S.: A SURVEY OF THE LITERATURE. *Cuban Studies 1975 5(2): 25-52.* Cuban exiles make up the third largest Spanish-speaking group in the United States and a growing body of literature has emerged about Cubans since 1960. Except to a few experts, unfortunately, much of this literature is unknown in the scholarly world and needs wider dissemination. 99 notes, biblio.

J. A. Lewis

1110. Chesnutis, Diane L. THE ECONOMIC DEVELOPMENT OF PUERTO RICO 1950-1974. *Towson State J. of Internat. Affairs 1975 9(2): 60-75.* Despite some great problems Puerto Rico has a healthy economy with steady growth.   S

1111. Chrisman, Robert. THE CASE FOR THE INDEPENDENCE OF PUERTO RICO. *Black Scholar 1977 9(2): 47-54.* Text of a speech to the UN Committee on Decolonization, 16 August 1977.   B. D. Ledbetter

1112. Cintrón, Celia F. LA DINAMICA DE LA MIGRACION DE REGRESO A PUERTO RICO [The dynamics of return migration to Puerto Rico]. *Revista/Review Interamericana [Puerto Rico] 1980-81 10(4): 534-548.* Personal and family reasons constitute the most important causes for the return of Puerto Ricans from the United States. These migrants are always torn between the realities of their life and their aspirations. Note.

J. A. Lewis

1113. Cintrón García, Arturo. GRACIELA PALAU DE NEMES Y UN PREMIO NOBEL [Graciela Palau de Nemes and a Nobel Prize]. *Horizontes [Puerto Rico] 1983 27(53): 71-75.* In connection with Graciela Palau's *Inicios de Zenobia y Juan Ramón Jiménez en América* (1982) prints memoirs about the Cuban-born author's successful efforts from Ponce, Puerto Rico, supported by the University of Maryland where Spanish author Juan Ramón Jiménez had taught, to nominate Jiménez for the Nobel Prize, which he received in 1956.

J. V. Coutinho

1114. Clark, Thomas R. THE IMPERIAL PERSPECTIVE: MAINLAND ADMINISTRATOR'S VIEWS OF THE PUERTO RICAN ECONOMY, 1898-1941. *R. Interamericana [Puerto Rico] 1974/75 4(4): 505-517.* Revised version of a paper presented to the Pacific Coast Branch of the American Historical Association in Seattle on 27 August 1974. Although concerned, American administrators had no program to improve Puerto Rico's economy before 1941. Nevertheless, the island's governors recognized the major economic problems early and debated most of the present-day remedies used in Puerto Rico. Based on primary and secondary sources; 60 notes.

J. A. Lewis

1115. Clark, Truman R. "EDUCATING THE NATIVES IN SELF-GOVERNMENT": PUERTO RICO AND THE UNITED STATES, 1900-1933. *Pacific Hist. R. 1973 42(2): 220-233.* Examines the proposition that the US policy in Puerto Rican administration was toward "educating the natives in self-government." The United States blamed the low level of self-government in Puerto Rico on demonstrations of incompetence. The fault really lay in US steadfast refusal to let the Puerto Ricans assume responsible governmental roles in such areas as finances, public education, law and order, and long range status. This left it tempting and easy for native populations to see politics as simply contests for the spoils of patronage. 43 notes.   R. V. Ritter

1116. Clemens, Walter C., Jr. THE FIGHT OVER STATUS: NEW DECISION ON PUERTO RICO. *Worldview 1976 19(11): 22-26.* Traces the status of Puerto Rico as an American possession since 1900 and the fortunes of groups favoring statehood, independence, and the status quo.

1117. Cohen, Steve Martin and Kapsis, Robert E. PARTICIPATION OF BLACKS, PUERTO RICANS AND WHITES IN VOLUNTARY ASSOCIATIONS: A TEST OF CURRENT THEORIES. *Social Forces 1978 56(4): 1053-1071.* To interpret the relatively high rates of voluntary organization participation among blacks, theorists have developed deprivation and normative explanations. Both interpretations suggest that oppressed minority groups will develop group coherence and salience to their members. However, unlike the deprivation argument, the normative conception does not view the development of activist norms as an inevitable outcome of this process. By examining the organizational behavior of Puerto Ricans, blacks, and whites in New York City, we test several key postulates from each interpretation. None of the postulates is consistently supported. Most damaging to both arguments is that black ethnic identifiers do not exhibit higher participatory rates than their more assimilated peers. That lower-class black women manifest an unusually active pattern of organizational membership as compared with their male counterparts is shown also to be incompatible with both the deprivation and normative conceptions. Further inquiries into the mechanisms which predispose a particular subgroup within a minority population to be more involved in voluntary organizations than another are recommended.　　J

1118. Cooney, Rosemary Santana and Warren, Alice E. Colón. DECLINING FEMALE PARTICIPATION AMONG PUERTO RICAN NEW YORKERS: A COMPARISON WITH NATIVE WHITE NONSPANISH NEW YORKERS. *Ethnicity 1979 6(3): 281-297.* Every cultural and racial group identified by the census except Puerto Ricans have increased women's participation in the New York labor force during the 1960's. Comparison with white women indicates that education is the major reason for this anomaly. Puerto Ricans are not as well educated as are other groups. Consequently though the number of jobs has increased the number of jobs requiring higher levels of education have increased more rapidly, reducing the opportunities for Puerto Ricans. Puerto Rican women who have acquired better educations move from the city. Based on US censuses; biblio.　　S

1119. Cooney, Rosemary Santana and Min, Kyonghee. DEMOGRAPHIC CHARACTERISTICS AFFECTING LIVING ARRANGEMENTS AMONG YOUNG CURRENTLY UNMARRIED PUERTO RICAN, NON-SPANISH BLACK, AND NON-SPANISH WHITE MOTHERS. *Ethnicity 1981 8(2): 107-120.* Young Puerto Rican single mothers are most likely to head their own households, followed by non-Spanish blacks, and then non-Spanish whites. Number of children, migration status, and education are the best predictors of the ethnic differences. 3 tables, 5 notes, biblio, appendix.
　　T. W. Smith

1120. Cooney, Rosemary Santana; Rogler, Lloyd H.; and Schroder, Edna. PUERTO RICAN FERTILITY: AN EXAMINATION OF SOCIAL CHAR-

ACTERISTICS, ASSIMILATION, AND MINORITY STATUS VARI-ABLES. *Social Forces 1981 59(4): 1094-1113.* Examines the 1969 Goldscheider-Uhlenberg theory of minority group fertility by making a direct assessment of the importance of assimilation and minority status. The influence of assimilation on the fertility behavior of both generations is mediated through social conditions. Minority status insecurity, however, significantly adds to explained variance in the fertility behavior of the younger generation.   J/S

1121. Cooney, Rosemary Santana and Contreras, Maria Alina. RESI-DENCE PATTERNS OF SOCIAL REGISTER CUBANS: A STUDY OF MIAMI, SAN JUAN, AND NEW YORK SMSAS. *Cuban Studies 1978 8(2): 33-50.* The Social Register that was started in Havana before the revolution of 1959 has been continued by Cuban exiles. This list provides a useful tool to study the exile community and measure change. Cubans who migrated to Puerto Rico have maintained a much higher degree of class segregation than those living in the continental United States. Primary and secondary sources; 5 tables, 11 notes, biblio.   J. Lewis

1122. Copeland, Earl, Jr. SAINTS AND SAINTMAKERS OF PUERTO RICO. *Américas (Organization of Am. States) 1975 27(4): 38-47.* Discusses woodcarving in Puerto Rico since 1750, especially the making of santos (carved images of saints); today it is a nearly lost folk art.

1123. Copeland, Ronald. THE CUBAN BOATLIFT OF 1980: STRATE-GIES IN FEDERAL CRISIS MANAGEMENT. *Ann. of the Am. Acad. of Pol. and Social Sci. 1983 (467): 138-150.* The Cuban boatlift of 1980 was a political liability for the Jimmy Carter administration in Florida, and seemed to underscore nationally the administration's image of poor executive leader-ship. It occurred when Carter was beset by the mission to rescue the American hostages in Iran, Secretary of State Cyrus Vance's resignation, and domestic political problems. While it was a surprise to the American public and to most policymakers in Washington, the Cuban boatlift had been forecast by intelli-gence agencies three months prior to the arrival of the first boats. It exemplified the federal government's lack of control over the arrival of large numbers of asylum seekers uninvited and without immigration clearances. However, the federal government missed opportunities to prevent or control the crisis.   J/S

1124. Corrada, Baltasar. PUERTO RICO WILL BENEFIT. *Foreign Policy 1982 (47): 126-128.* With modifications to the Carribean Basin Initiative to protect Puerto Rican industries like rum and tuna fishing, Puerto Rico will benefit from the effects of general economic prosperity in the Carribean Basin.
     M. K. Jones

1125. Cruz, Ramón A. CENTROS DE SERVICIOS EDUCATIVOS: UNA ALTERNATIVA PROMETEDORA [Centers for Educational Services: A promising alternative]. *Rev. Interamericana [Puerto Rico] 1977 7(1): 135-138.* Traditional methods of dealing with Puerto Ricans' high rate of school dropouts have been ineffective. One promising alternative, however, has been Centers for Educational Services. These centers are formed around a library and a core of educational materials. The students teach themselves at their own rate and teachers are employed only for guidance. These centers have shown considerable promise so far.   J. A. Lewis

1126. Cruz Báez, Angel David. "NUEVA ERA AGRÍCOLA" O SÍN-DROME DE DETERIORO AGRÍCOLA: EL COMPORTAMIENTO DE LA AGRICULTURA EN PUERTO RICO EN LOS ÚLTIMOS AÑOS ["A new era in agriculture" of a process of agricultural deterioration: the practice of agriculture in Puerto Rico in recent years]. *Rev. de Ciencias Sociales [Puerto Rico] 1974 18(3-4): 9-39.* Industrialization, based on the importation of capital, raw materials, and technology, and oriented toward foreign markets, is not solving the economic problems of Puerto Rico, which needs efficient and scientific agriculture serving local interests.

1127. Cypess, Sandra Messinger. WOMEN DRAMATISTS OF PUERTO RICO. *Revista/Review Interamericana [Puerto Rico] 1979 9(1): 24-41.* Critics often overlook female playwrights in Puerto Rico, but they have been numerous and important historically. Indeed, the first truly Puerto Rican play, *Los Deudos Rivales,* was written by a woman, Carmen Hernández de Araujo (1846). In spite of some successes, however, most female playwrights have faced so many obstacles in their work that few pen more than one play, preferring to labor in other literary forms. 61 notes.   J. A. Lewis

1128. Darragh, Shaun M. THE PUERTO RICAN MILITARY FORCES. *Military Rev. 1979 58(8): 46-53.* Outlines the structure of the Puerto Rican National Guard. The P.R.N.G. is an anomaly in the sense that it fulfills a state function in a territory that is not a state. The role of the P.R.N.G. needs to be reevaluated in the light of the fact that Puerto Rico is moving towards more autonomy from the United States. 4 illus.   C. Hopkins

1129. Daubon, Ramon and Robinson, Warren C. CHANGES IN CON-SUMPTION PATTERNS DURING ECONOMIC DEVELOPMENT: PUERTO RICO 1940-1970. *Social and Econ. Studies [Jamaica] 1975 24(4): 420-432.* Census data is used to trace the changes in consumer expenditures between 1940 and 1970. Finds a decline in the elasticity for essential goods and an increase in elasticity for durable and luxury items. 7 tables, 7 notes, biblio.
E. S. Johnson

1130. Davis, Lisa E. REVISTA DE LAS ANTILLAS: EL MODERNISMO COMO RESISTENCIA CULTURAL EN PUERTO RICO [Review of the Antilles: Modernism as cultural resistance in Puerto Rico]. *Casa de las Américas [Cuba] 1977 18(105): 54-59.* Reviews the *Revista de las Antillas,* published during 1913-14. It served as the voice of the first generation of Puerto Ricans under US domination, who desired to awaken the national consciousness. The contributors represented all schools of thought but their main purpose was to enlighten readers in art, philosophy, persons, and events of universal significance. The founders of the review belonged to either the Union Party of Puerto Rico that sought more political autonomy for the island or the separatist Party of Independence. Primary sources; 19 notes.
H. J. Miller

1131.   Denis, Manuel Maldonado. THE POLITICAL SITUATION IN PUERTO RICO. *Massachusetts R. 1974 15(1/2): 221-233.* Discusses the effects of US imperialism on the social structure and economic development of Puerto Rico.   S

1132.   Díaz Soler, Luis M. RELACIONES RACIALES EN PUERTO RICO [Racial relations in Puerto Rico]. *R. Interamericana R. [Puerto Rico] 1973 3(1): 61-72.* Unlike the United States and other nations of the New World, racial prejudice barely exists in Puerto Rico. What prejudice does exist stems primarily from social, rather than racial, tensions. This happy state of affairs owes its existence to the limited role that slavery played in Puerto Rico, and to the traditional willingness of all races to intermarry.   J. A. Lewis

1133.   Díaz-Briquets, Sergio. CUBAN-OWNED BUSINESSES IN THE UNITED STATES. *Cuban Studies 1984 14(2): 57-64.* The Census Bureau has published a great deal of information on minority-owned businesses in the United States. Unfortunately, few scholars interested in Cuban activities have utilized this material. Based on the 1977 *Survey of Minority-Owned Business Enterprises;* 4 tables, 3 notes.   J. A. Lewis

1134.   Díaz-Royo, Antonio T. MANEUVERS AND TRANSFORMA-TIONS IN ETHNOBIOGRAPHIES OF PUERTO RICAN MIGRANTS. *Int. J. of Oral Hist. 1983 4(1): 19-28.* The mediation that immigrants make between the need for personal disclosure in interviews and their cultural restrictions against such intimacy is similar to adjustments that immigrants make between their old values and new environment.

1135.   Dietz, James. THE PUERTO RICAN POLITICAL ECONOMY. *Latin Am. Perspectives 1976 3(3): 3-16.* Introduces the journal issue "Puerto Rico: Class Struggle and National Liberation." Provides an overview of the colonial history of Puerto Rico from 1898 to the present and a political-economic analysis of the economic structure, class structure, working class, effects of migration, and proposals for change. Also introduces and summarizes the other contributions to the issue. Tables.   J. L. Dietz

1136.   Dietz, James L. IMPERIALISM AND PUERTO RICO. *Monthly Rev. 1979 30(4): 18-28.* Discusses the effect of "monopoly-based capitalism" on the Puerto Rican political economy since the 1940's.

1137.   Dietz, James L. IMPERIALISM AND UNDERDEVELOPMENT: A THEORETICAL PERSPECTIVE AND A CASE STUDY OF PUERTO RICO. *Rev. of Radical Pol. Econ. 1979 11(4): 16-32.* Neither capitalistic nor Marxist theories of underdevelopment adequately explain its persistence in the Third World. The problem is that capitalism consists of a series of stages, and what is true at one stage is not true at another. The present stage in Puerto Rico features a revolutionizing of the means of production, but maintenance of feudal or precapitalistic forms of production. Thus, the imperialist capitalists benefit from the changes while the native, exploited peoples do not. Future revolutionists should be aware that Puerto Rico and other developing nations are caught in this web of capitalist dependency. 3 tables, 2 fig., 12 notes, ref.

V. L. Human

1138. Dietz, James L. RECENT RESEARCH ON PUERTO RICO. *Latin Am. Perspectives 1981 8(1): 79-87.* Brief review of 13 studies published during 1979-80 in Spanish and English about Puerto Rico in the 19th and 20th centuries. Ref.

J. F. Vivian

1139. Dilla Alfonso, Haroldo and Gómez Martínez, Julián. JOSÉ DE DIEGO: UNA ETAPA DEL INDEPENDENTISMO PUERTORRIQUEÑO [José de Diego: a stage in the movement for Puerto Rican independence]. *Santiago [Cuba] 1979 (36): 9-36.* Traces the political career of José de Diego (1867-1918) in the context of the debate between the advocates of the annexation of Puerto Rico to the United States and the defenders of its Hispanic culture. The independence movement in Puerto Rico in the early part of the century was a reaction of the middle classes to US penetration. 41 notes.

J. V. Coutinho

1140. Domínguez, Virginia R. SPANISH-SPEAKING CARIBBEANS IN NEW YORK: "THE MIDDLE RACE." *R. Interamericana R. [Puerto Rico] 1973 3(2): 135-142.* Although American society traditionally classifies its races as either black or white, such racial distinctions produce bewildering complications among Spanish-speaking communities in New York City. These communities bring their own racial prejudices and perceptions with them from the West Indies and are forced to live in a larger society which maintains different criteria. The result is behavior that often is unpredictable by either native American or West Indian standards. Based on research in Washington Heights, N.Y.

J. A. Lewis

1141. Dower, Catherine. PUERTO RICAN MUSICAL CULTURE FOLLOWING THE SPANISH AMERICAN WAR, 1898-1910. *Revista/Review Interamericana [Puerto Rico] 1978-79 8(4): 620-628.* Musical activity in Puerto Rico did not decline after the Spanish-American War. In many ways, the Hispanic musical heritage on the island continued. It was enriched by new traditions from the United States. Presented as a paper at the Sociedad Musical de Puerto Rico, 24 April 1976, in Rio Grande, Puerto Rico. 29 notes.

J. A. Lewis

1142. Duggal, Ved P. INDUSTRIALIZATION OF PUERTO RICO TILL 1970. *Horizontes [Puerto Rico] 1975 19(37): 93-113.* Traces the development of industrialization in Puerto Rico during 1940-70. Comments on the US interest in the process, the effects of industrialization on employment and income, dependence on US capital, and the quality of industrialization. Stresses the need for the encouragement of local enterprise so that the country does not continue to be subject to the vagaries of foreign trade and investment patterns. Primary and secondary sources; 3 tables, 54 notes, appendix.

P. J. Taylorson

1143. Duggal, Ved P. POVERTY IN PUERTO RICO. *Horizontes [Puerto Rico] 1979 23(45): 53-68.* In 1970, 60% of Puerto Rican families had income below official poverty limits.

1144. Duncan, Ronald J. *THE PEOPLE OF PUERTO RICO* AND THE "CULTURING SYSTEM" CONCEPT. *Revista/Review Interamericana [Puerto Rico] 1978 8(1): 59-64.* Anthropology has moved far beyond the methodology and ideology present in Julian H. Steward, ed., *The People of Puerto Rico: A Study in Social Anthropology* (Urbana: U. of Illinois Pr., 1956). Steward's outdated view of culture needs to be revised to make work such as his relevant. Secondary sources; 17 notes.   J. A. Lewis

1145. Estevez, Guillermo A. RESETTLING THE CUBAN REFUGEES IN NEW JERSEY. *Migration Today 1983 11(4-5): 27-33.* The Caribbean Relief Program of the International Rescue Committee has assisted in the settlement of 124,000 Cuban refugees since 1959, and played a major role in sponsoring Cuban settlement in New Jersey following the 1980 Cuban boat lift.

1146. Farley, Ena L. PUERTO RICO: ORDEALS OF AN AMERICAN DEPENDENCY DURING WORLD WAR II. *Rev. Interamericana [Puerto Rico] 1976 6(2): 202-210.* Although World War II often has been viewed as a time of prosperity for Puerto Rico, there was another side to the war years. The island suffered greatly from food shortages in 1942, and, throughout the war, had a very high rural unemployment rate. Primary and secondary sources; 34 notes.   J. A. Lewis

1147. Fenyo, Mario D. PUERTO RICAN NATIONALISM: "A MODER-ATE REVOLUTION." *Can. Rev. of Studies in Nationalism [Canada] 1973 1(1): 120-125.* Puerto Rico is one of the few areas where nationalism has not enjoyed a great vogue. The word nationalism evokes horrors among the assimilationist majority, and consequently the Nationalist Party remains only a splinter group. Cultural nationalism, even chauvinism, does exist; but since most Puerto Ricans, especially the nouveau riche bourgeoisie and the lower middle classes, attribute their limited economic success to the American presence, they are adopting the ritual, symbolism, and culture of the colonial power. 11 notes.   T. Spira

1148. Fernandez, Gaston A. THE FREEDOM FLOTILLA: A LEGITIMA-CY CRISIS OF CUBAN SOCIALISM? *J. of Interamerican Studies and World Affairs 1982 24(2): 183-209.* The present Cuban regime is experiencing a legitimacy problem among urban youth, unskilled laborers, and ex-prisoners. Support remains strong among prerevolutionary landless peasants, the rural poor, and the older generation. The regime's present problem is partly related to Cuba's prerevolutionary links to the world economy. Expectations and attitudes of urban workers have been shaped by an urban past that created a certain standard of living in Havana and other large Cuban cities. Castro's revolutionary image is less effective than concrete economic gains in winning support in the urban areas. Profiles the refugees who fled to the United States. Based on interviews with 1980 "Freedom Flotilla" emigrants, printed primary materials; 2 notes, 4 tables, appendix, ref.   T. D. Schoonover

1149. Fernández Cintrón, Celia and Rivera Quintero, Marcia. BASES DE LA SOCIEDAD SEXISTA EN PUERTO RICO [The foundations of sexist society in Puerto Rico]. *R. Interamericana [Puerto Rico] 1974 4(2): 239-245.* Puerto Rican females currently occupy a position subordinate to males. The family and schools pass on traditional values concerning women to each generation, but male-dominated economic, religious, and political institutions also play a role in perpetuating sex discrimination. Only direct action by Puerto Rican women can change this situation.   J. A. Lewis

1150. Fitzpatrick, Joseph P. and Parker, Lourdes Travieso. HISPANIC-AMERICANS IN THE EASTERN UNITED STATES. *Ann. of the Am. Acad. of Pol. and Social Sci. 1981 (454): 98-110.* The largest concentration of Hispanics, mainly Puerto Ricans, in the East is found in the New York City area. Cubans predominate in the Dade County area of Florida, with large numbers also in New York City and in the northern New Jersey area. Newcomers from Santo Domingo and Central and South America are found in New York City and other large eastern cities.   J/S

1151. Flores, Juan; Attinasi, John; and Pedraza, Pedro, Jr. *LA CARRETA MADE A U-TURN:* PUERTO RICAN LANGUAGE AND CULTURE IN THE UNITED STATES. *Daedalus 1981 110(2): 193-217.* Describes acculturation of Puerto Ricans in the United States, focusing on Tato Laviera's *La Carreta Made a U-Turn* (1979), a bilingual volume of poetry which illustrates current thinking by Puerto Ricans about ethnicity, cultural identity and the assimilation process.

1152. Foner, Nancy and Napoli, Richard. JAMAICAN AND BLACK-AMERICAN MIGRANT FARM WORKERS: A COMPARATIVE ANALYSIS. *Social Problems 1978 25(5):491-503.* Comparative study of Jamaican and black migrant farm workers in a New York state camp based on data from the 1960's-70's. The Jamaicans are more productive and save most of their earnings because to them their wages have more value and they perceive more opportunity for social mobility. The impact of race greatly affected blacks and caused low productivity. Foreign seasonal farm laborers are likely to be industrious on US farms. Primary and secondary sources; 9 notes; refs.
                    A. M. Osur

1153. Foner, Nancy. WEST INDIANS IN NEW YORK CITY AND LONDON: A COMPARATIVE ANALYSIS. *Int. Migration Rev. 1979 13(2): 284-297.* While thousands of West Indians have come to the United States since the beginning of the century, they have been admitted to Britain in large numbers only since the 1950's. West Indians in New York City have taken advantage of their relatively high economic and professional status and the availability of a large business and professional clientele among American blacks to achieve a social status that has not been achieved by West Indians in Britain or by American blacks.

1154. Fradd, Sandra. CUBANS TO CUBAN AMERICANS: ASSIMILATION IN THE UNITED STATES. *Migration Today 1983 11(4-5): 34-42.* There are significant demographic, cultural, and motivational differences between the Cuban immigrant population in the United States and other immigrant ethnic groups; such differences have been compounded by the nature of the successive outpourings of refugees from Cuba since the revolution in 1959.

1155.   Galvin, Miles. THE EARLY DEVELOPMENT OF THE ORGA-NIZED LABOR MOVEMENT IN PUERTO RICO. *Latin Am. Perspectives 1976 3(3): 17-35.* Analyzes the role of the American Federation of Labor in the early Puerto Rican labor movement. Emphasizes the importance of both Samuel Gompers and Santiago Iglesias Pantín on the changing thrust and militancy of unions and offers an explanation for the early conservatism of early unionization. The intellectual opportunism and reformist politics of both Gompers and Iglesias—as the sole paid union organizer on the island—were extremely important in diverting the thrust of the unions away from radical positions.   J. L. Dietz

1156.   García-Passalacqua, Juan M. *YO QUIERO UN PUEBLO:* A BRIEF HISTORY OF THE PUERTO RICAN MASSES. *Revista/Rev. Interamericana [Puerto Rico] 1981 11(1): 4-24.* The key to Puerto Rican history is understanding the split between the island's elite and its masses. Secondary sources; 30 notes.   J. A. Lewis

1157.   Garrison, Vivian and Weiss, Carol I. DOMINICAN FAMILY NET-WORKS AND UNITED STATES IMMIGRATION POLICY: A CASE STUDY. *Int. Migration Rev. 1979 13(2): 264-283.* Studies the migration methods of a Dominican family which came to the United States during 1962 and 1976 and concludes that the family felt forced to use questionable or illegal means to remain united because its definition of "family" differs from the US Immigration and Naturalization Service's definition of "immediate family."

1158.   Gautier Mayoral, Carmen. APUNTES SOBRE LA REPRESION ACTUAL EN PUERTO RICO [Notes on the present repression in Puerto Rico]. *Casa de las Américas [Cuba] 1980 21(123): 26-38.* Points to four areas in which Puerto Rico has been exploited by the United States in recent years: 1) active intervention by intelligence agencies against the Puerto Rican liberation movement, 2) use of Puerto Rico as a base for repressive operations in the Caribbean, 3) appropriation of Puerto Rican territorial waters which may contain oil and ferromanganese deposits, 4) the referendum announced for 1981 with no guarantees of the requisite conditions for genuine free self-determination. Based on US Senate reports and other sources; 53 notes.   P. J. Durell

1159.   Gecas, Viktor; Thomas, Darwin L.; and Weigert, Andrew J. SOCIAL IDENTITIES IN ANGLO AND LATIN ADOLESCENTS. *Social Forces 1973 51(4): 477-484.* Social identities, conceptualized as self-designations and measured by the TST, were examined for samples of high school adolescents in three societies: the United States, Puerto Rico, and Mexico. Four identities were explored in terms of salience, frequency, and valence: gender, religion, family, and peer. For both males and females in Latin and Anglo cultures gender emerged as the most prominent identity. Religious IDs were more frequent for Catholic adolescents. The strongest cultural difference was found with respect to negative religious IDs: these were significantly more frequent for Anglo adolescents. Positive gender and family IDs were more frequent for Latin adolescents, while peer IDs were slightly more common self-designations for Anglos. These tendencies were generally in the expected direction. Social and cultural differences between these Anglo and Latin societies were considered as explanations for variations in adolescent identity structures.   J

1160. Gelpi Barrios, Juan. PERSONALIDAD JURÍDICA DE LA IGLE-SIA EN PUERTO RICO [Juridical personality of the Catholic Church in Puerto Rico]. *Rev. Española de Derecho Canónico [Spain] 1977 33(95-96): 395-415.* Until 1863, when the "congregational corporation" was defined in the United States, the difference in Church and State relations between the United States and Europe consisted in the American notion of trusteeship. Under trusteeship the Catholic Church had opposed denial of its legal status and the undermining of its religious mission, gratefully confirming the new status in the Third Plenary Council in Baltimore, 1884. In Puerto Rico, the 1898 Treaty of Paris concluding the Spanish-American War assured the continued application of the 1851 concordat between Spain and the Holy See to the Church in Puerto Rico. This juridical status of the Church in Puerto Rico was approved by the US Supreme Court in 1908.   R. D. Rodríguez

1161. George, Philip Brandt. REAFFIRMATION OF IDENTITY: A LA-TINO CASE IN EAST CHICAGO. *Indiana Folklore 1977 10(2): 139-148.* The author's folklore project in urbanized East Chicago, Indiana, 1976, among Cuban Americans and Puerto Ricans, which included assessment of ethnic oral tradition, found that rather than being detrimental to folklore culture, urban areas often strengthened folk beliefs and were responsible for affirmation of ethnicity.

1162. Gil, Rosa Maria. ISSUES IN THE DELIVERY OF MENTAL HEALTH SERVICES TO CUBAN ENTRANTS. *Migration Today 1983 11(4-5): 43-48.* Many of the Cuban refugees in the 1980 boat lift were expelled not for ideological reasons but because of "undesirable characteristics" associated with psychopathology.

1163. Gilder, George. MIAMI'S CUBAN MIRACLE. *Reason 1984 16(6): 21-28.* Cites examples of Cuban immigrants to Miami who have achieved financial success to support the thesis that personal trauma can be a prime ingredient in the rapid and successful rise of a business entrepreneur; for these immigrants, the United States is still the land of opportunity.

1164. Godoy, Gustavo J. JOSÉ ALEJANDRO HUAU: A CUBAN PATRI-OT IN JACKSONVILLE POLITICS. *Florida Hist. Q. 1975 54(2): 196-206.* A naturalized American citizen, José Alejandro Huah (1836-1905) was a successful Jacksonville businessman who involved himself in city politics and became a spokesman for the city's Cuban community. In the 1890's he became increasingly involved in the Cuban freedom movement. He raised money, organized supplies and equipment for expeditions to Cuba, and sponsored Florida appearances of José Martí, a leader in the Cuban freedom movement. Huau spent most of his fortune in the cause of Cuban freedom from Spain and before his death saw the establishment of the Republic of Cuba in 1902. Based on primary and secondary sources; 35 notes.   P. A. Beaber

1165. Gonzalez, Isabel L. THE CUBANS—FROM POLITICAL EXILE TO U.S. CITIZEN. *INS Reporter 1976-77 25(3): 43-46.* Traces Cuban migration to the United States from 1959, when Fidel Castro seized power, to 1973, and examines the difficulty the exiles had in assimilating into American society, although their desire as a group is high as reflected in the number who have become permanent residents and/or United States citizens as of 1976.

1166. González Díaz, Emilio. LA LUCHA DE LAS CLASES Y LA POLITICA EN EL PUERTO RICO DE LA DECADA 40: EL ASCENSO DEL PPD [Class struggle and politics in Puerto Rico in the 1930's: the rise of the Popular Democratic Party (PPD)]. *Rev. de Ciencias Sociales [Puerto Rico] 1980 22(1-2): 35-69.* The weakness and disintegration of the classes socially dominant and of the labor sector during the 1930's strengthened the Popular Democratic Party. The misfortune of the sugar plantation industries, population growth, presentation of the working population as a mass and not as a social class, and the incapacity of traditional classes to put up with the socioeconomic situation contributed to this disintegration as it also made possible a policy for masses and not for a social class. The rise of the PPD corresponded with the development of a new leading class based not on economic and social power in relation with the means of production but on the control of the state apparatus. This process was achieved primarily with the incorporation of North American industrial capital, which finally culminated in the creation of the Commonwealth of Puerto Rico.   J/S

1167. González Díaz, Emilio. LAS BASES PARA EL CONSENSO POLITICO EN LA COLONIA: EL PROBLEMA DE LA DEMOCRACIA EN PUERTO RICO [Bases for political consensus in the colony: the problem of democracy in Puerto Rico]. *Casa de las Américas [Cuba] 1980 21(123): 39-49.* Questions the validity of the basic tenets of colonial ideology which imposes democracy from outside. The principal changes in the development of the economic bases of political accord have occurred in three phases: 1)development and industrialization, 1950-65, 2)crisis and transition, 1965-74, 3)dependence on direct transferences, 1974-79. Three social classes create the conditions for the continuance of colonial domination. Alternative economies capable of generating long-term political consensus do not exist. Based on Junta de Planificación documents and other sources; 3 tables, 13 notes.
                                                                    P. J. Durell

1168. Gray, Lois S. THE JOBS PUERTO RICANS HOLD IN NEW YORK CITY. *Monthly Labor R. 1975 98(10): 12-16.* Examines white- and blue-collar occupations of Puerto Ricans in New York City in 1970 and the high rate of unemployment Puerto Ricans experienced that year.   S

1169. Guendelman, Sylvia R. SOUTH AMERICAN REFUGEES: STRESSES INVOLVED IN RELOCATING IN THE SAN FRANCISCO BAY AREA. *Migration Today 1981 9(2): 19-25.* Recommends that sponsoring agencies seek to resettle refugees in communities open to accepting them and having cultural backgrounds similar to those of the refugees and argues that from 'a social welfare standpoint, delivery of services seems to be most efficient when centralized under one program."

1170. Guerra, Carmen and Venegas, Hernán. LOS TABAQUEROS DE CAYO HUESO: UN HOMENAJE A JOSE MARTI [The tobacco workers of Key West: a tribute to José Martí]. *Islas [Cuba] 1983 (75): 47-75.* In 1891, the Cuban immigrant workers in the E. H. Gato tobacco factory, Key West, Florida, presented José Martí with an album containing words of appreciation and their signatures, which are reproduced here.

1171. Gurak, Douglas T. and Kritz, Mary M. DOMINICAN AND CO-LOMBIAN WOMEN IN NEW YORK CITY: HOUSEHOLD STRUCTURE AND EMPLOYMENT PATTERNS. *Migration Today 1982 10(3-4): 14-21.* Analyzes the social and economic situation of Dominican- and Colombian-American women in New York City.

1172. Hector, Bruce J. PUERTO RICO: COLONY OR COMMON-WEALTH. *New York U. J. of Internat. Law and Pol. 1973 6(1): 115-137.* Examines the Puerto Rican, U.S., and U.N. positions on Puerto Rico's status in international law. Based on primary and secondary sources; 123 notes.
M. L. Frey

1173. Heine, Jorge. A PEOPLE APART. *Wilson Q. 1980 4(2): 119-131.* Traces Puerto Rico's history from 1493, when Columbus stopped there on his second voyage, to present-day debates over the pro-statehood autonomy issue.

1174. Henríquez Ureña, Camila. LA PEREGRINACIÓN DE EUGENIO MARÍA DE HOSTOS, [The journey of Eugenio María de Hostos]. *Casa de las Américas [Cuba] 1974 14(82): 6-17.* Discusses the life and career of Eugenio María de Hostos (1839-1903), Puerto Rican hero of independence, particularly emphasizing his travels and his ideas.

1175. Herbstein, Judith. THE POLITICIZATION OF PUERTO RICAN ETHNICITY IN NEW YORK: 1955-1975. *Ethnic Groups 1983 5(1-2): 31-54.* Analyzes the relationship between social policy and Puerto Rican ethnicity in New York City. Social policy directed toward poor and disadvantaged populations that are in the process of being incorporated into a segmented labor market has stimulated the emergence of ethnic groups, as evident in the growth of ethnic organizations and the development of leadership elites among Puerto Ricans. The emergence and development of an ethnic group is an organizational response to the power structure. The dialectic between official policy and "grass-roots" adaptive mechanisms underlies the emergence of ethnic groups among disadvantaged ethnic populations.   J/S

1176. Hernández, José. LA MIGRACIÓN PUERTORRIQUEÑA COMO FACTOR DEMOGRÁFICO: SOLUCIÓN Y PROBLEMA [Puerto Rican migration as a demographic factor: solution and problem]. *R. Interamericana [Puerto Rico] 1974/75 4(4): 526-534.* The demographic history of Puerto Rico is very complex and often misunderstood. In spite of myths to the contrary, the birthrate on the island is only one percent. The large increase in population over the last decade has come from mainland Puerto Ricans returning home. These new migrants present serious problems for the island, such as employment and reverse discrimination against *Neorricanos*. Based on primary and secondary sources; 3 charts, 6 notes.   J. A. Lewis

1177.   Hernández Novás, Raúl. LUIS PALÉS MATOS: POETA ANTILLA-NO [Luis Palés Matos: Puerto Rican poet]. *Casa de las Américas [Cuba] 1975 15(89): 28-37.* Discusses the life and work of the Puerto Rican poet Luis Palés Matos (1898-1959), focusing largely on his place in Latin American letters as the first major Latin American poet to write about the common black population.

1178.   Hernández-Colón, Rafael. PUERTO RICO: PARTNER OR VICTIM? *Foreign Policy 1982 (47): 123-125.* Unless the United States acts to remedy some of the measures in the Carribean Basin Initiative that are very harmful to Puerto Rico, the Puerto Rican economy will suffer.
                                                                    M. K. Jones

1179.   Hostos, Adolfo de and Lloréns, Washington. UN DIÁLOGO [A Dialogue]. *R. Interamericana R. [Puerto Rico] 1974 3(4): 329-339.* Adolfo de Hostos (b. 1887), one of Puerto Rico's foremost anthropologists and historians, discusses his life's work. Hostos attributes much of his success to the influence of his father, Eugenio María de Hostos (1839-1903). He also gives his opinion on the need for Puerto Ricans to learn a second language and the desirability of the present political status for the island. Based on interview; biblio.
                                                                    J. A. Lewis

1180.   Hoyt, Garry. PUERTO RICO: A CHRONICLE OF AMERICAN CARELESSNESS. *Caribbean Rev. 1979 8(2): 9-14.* The United States' habit of throwing money at Puerto Rico's problems since 1898 but otherwise neglecting the island's difficulties has resulted in the creation of a colony which exploits its colonists by costing the US taxpayers three billion dollars per year, and only thoughtful concern and guidance from the United States can aid Puerto Rico in choosing its future course, whether it be the current Commonwealth arrangement, statehood, or independence.

1181.   Jackson, Peter. A TRANSACTIONAL APPROACH TO PUERTO RICAN CULTURE. *Revista/Review Interamericana [Puerto Rico] 1981 11(1): 53-68.* A transactional view of Puerto Rican culture avoids the negativism of conventional views toward Puerto Rico and does not attempt to make comparisons with North American values. Secondary sources; biblio.
                                                                    J. A. Lewis

1182.   Jaffe, A. J. and Cullen, Ruth M. FERTILITY OF THE PUERTO RICAN ORIGIN POPULATION—MAINLAND UNITED STATES AND PUERTO RICO: 1970. *Internat. Migration R. 1975 9(2): 193-209.* Demonstrates that the apparent higher fertility of Puerto Rican women, both in Puerto Rico and on the mainland, is due to age structure and socioeconomic status.

1183. Jenness, Doug. PUERTO RICANS IN THE US. *Internat. Socialist R. 1974 35(11): 16-21.* An account of the exploitation of Puerto Ricans in America.   S

1184. Jennings, James. EXAMINING AMERICAN COLONIALISM IN PUERTO RICO: THREE APPROACHES. *Social Sci. J. 1983 20(1): 81-87.* Reviews Barry B. Levine's *Benjy Lopez* (1980), Sakari Sariola's *Puerto Rican Dilemma* (1979), and *Labor Migration under Capitalism: The Puerto Rican Experience* (1979) by the History Task Force of the Centro de Estudios Puertoriqueños, all of which consider Puerto Rico's relationship, especially its economic dependence, with the United States since 1898.

1185. Johnson, Roberta Ann. THE "FAILURE" OF INDEPENDENCE IN PUERTO RICO. *Civilisations [Belgium] 1975 25(3/4): 232-250.* The failure of Puerto Rico to gain independence from 1940 to the present is a complicated matter. Belief in independence, when linked to violence and communism, was a liability. Colonialism implanted in Puerto Rico feelings of inferiority and powerlessness, and a sense of resignation. In addition politics were characterized by personalism instead of a tradition of national ideology. 93 notes.   H. L. Calkin

1186. Johnson, Roberta Ann. AN INTERVIEW WITH LUIS MUÑOZ MARÍN. *Revista/Review Interamericana [Puerto Rico] 1979 9(2): 188-198.* Muñoz Marín always felt that economic and social issues were more important than questions dealing with political independence. As a result, he gave the issue of independence secondary attention while governor of Puerto Rico (1948-64). Based on an interview conducted on 4 January 1978; photo, 38 notes.   J. A. Lewis

1187. Johnson, Roberta A. THE 1967 PUERTO RICAN PLEBISCITE: THE PEOPLE DECIDE. *R. Interamericana R. [Puerto Rico] 1975 5(1): 27-46.* The most important problem facing Puerto Rico is whether it will seek independence, statehood, or commonwealth status. The 1967 plebiscite on this issue decided in favor of a commonwealth, but that election encouraged the other points of view also. Based on primary and secondary sources; 113 notes.
                                                                              J. A. Lewis

1188. Korrol, Virginia Sánchez. ON THE OTHER SIDE OF THE OCEAN: THE WORK EXPERIENCES OF EARLY PUERTO RICAN MIGRANT WOMEN. *Caribbean Rev. 1979 8(1): 22-28.* Examines the employment history of Puerto Rican women in New York from the 1920's to the 1940's and finds that piece work, child care, the taking-in of lodgers and employment in the garment, tobacco, and candy-making industries were the chief areas of employment for the vast majority of both married and unmarried working women of Puerto Rican origin.

1189. Koss, Joan D. THERAPEUTIC ASPECTS OF PUERTO RICAN CULT PRACTICES. *Psychiatry 1975 38(2): 160-171.* Studies the social process in Puerto Rican spiritualist cult practices and examines the relationship between patterns of cult social organization and the cult execution of culturally patterned psychotherapeutic processes for committed adherents.   S

1190.   Lega, Leonor I. THE 1980 CUBAN REFUGEES: SOME OF THEIR INITIAL ATTITUDES TOWARD THEIR FUTURE IN A NEW SOCI-ETY. *Migration Today 1983 11(4-5): 23-26.* A sampling of the 125,000 Cuban refugees who entered the United States shows that they had positive attitudes toward their future in a new country.

1191.   Leich, Marian Nash. CONTEMPORARY PRACTICE OF THE UNITED STATES RELATING TO INTERNATIONAL LAW. *Am. J. of Int. Law 1983 77(4): 875-877.* Examines US interpretation of international law on the issue of deporting Cuban refugees who are ineligible to remain in the United States, and on the problem of obtaining information on the fate of persons who hijack airplanes to Cuba.

1192.   Levine, Barry B. SOURCES OF ETHNIC IDENTITY FOR LATIN FLORIDA. *Caribbean Rev. 1979 8(1): 30-33.* Reviews the means of ethnic support and reinforcement available to Latin immigrants to Florida since 1979 (press, radio, television, churches, etc.) and concludes that, while cultural changes are occurring, ethnic identity is being maintained.

1193.   Lidin, Harold. PUERTO RICO'S 1980 ELECTIONS: THE VOTERS SEEK THE CENTER. *Caribbean Rev. 1981 10(2): 28-31.* Discusses the reelection of Carlos Romero Barceló as governor of Puerto Rico against Rafael Hernández of the Popular Democratic Party in the 1980 elections, especially the stalemate in government which led to Barceló's narrow victory.

1194.   Linares, Francisco Watlington. EL RETO DEL DESEMPLEO Y LA POLÍTICA DE DISTRIBUCIÓN DE TIERRAS EN PUERTO RICO [The unemployment rate and the land distribution policy in Puerto Rico]. *Rev. de Ciencias Sociales [Puerto Rico] 1975 19(4): 371-392.* Unemployment in Puerto Rico is growing steadily as existing job markets disintegrate or become irrelevant. General economic decline in the U.S. has reversed emigration, a traditional safety valve which conceals the political constraints to real develop-ment. The lid is being screwed on by, among other things, a solidly institutionalized commitment to the ideology of the status quo that most surely cuts across party lines. One of the few options still open for creating meaningful work and subsistence is rural resettlement. As on the continent, a back to the land movement has been under way for some time, albeit in the face of formidable obstacles imposed by the Planning Board and the Depart-ment of Agriculture. A generation of federally enforced dependency on the land use standards of agricultural capitalism has made most of the Puerto Rican countryside an improductive wasteland, the population an alien or at best marginal presence in urban enclaves. The recent history of the govern-ment's agricultural land distribution program provides a compendium of the contradictions that keep farming from making a significant contribution to the generation of employment and income. A suppressed child of the compromised agrarian reform movement of the 1940's, its survival as a form of social aid to remaining backwater rural poor clashes increasingly with the newer priority of homesteading displaced urbanites. Whether the residential land invasions of the early 70's will be reenacted with an agrarian script probably hinges on the fate of the food stamp program. Meanwhile a fine political warhorse is going for the asking.   J

1195. London, Clement B. G. ON AFRO-AMERICAN AND AFRO-CARIBBEAN COOPERATION. *J. of Ethnic Studies 1980 8(3): 142-147.* Discusses the balkanization and insularity of the Caribbean region, where most of the islands provide the incentive for migration, and sketches the stereotypes held by white Americans toward Caribbean immigrants, views which make the issue of assimilation in the United States problematic both for Hispanophone and Anglophone Caribbean peoples, who are associated with American blacks by most Americans. Arguing that "a dynamic unity must be forged between Afro-Americans and Afro-Caribbeans ... out of the common circumstances of history, slavery, and ethnic identity," the author sees "cultural differences" (such as the intense commitment of the Caribbean migrants to the Protestant work-success ethic) as the basis of most obstacles affecting such a goal. The new Caribbean Council in Washington, D.C., is a positive sign for the future. 8 notes.   G. J. Bobango

1196. López, Adalberto. VITO MARCANTONIO: AN ITALIAN-AMERI-CAN'S DEFENSE OF PUERTO RICO AND PUERTO RICANS. *Caribbean Rev. 1979 8(1): 16-21.* Recounts the political career of Vito Marcantonio (1902-54), Congressman from East Harlem, emphasizing those events that related to the radical Republican's interest in the well-being of his own Puerto Rican constituents in New York as well as to his support of independence for Puerto Rico.

1197. López Yustos, Alfonso. RESUMEN DE LA HISTORIA DE LA RELIGIÓN EN LAS ESCUELAS PÚBLICAS DE PUERTO RICO [Summary of the history of religion in the public schools of Puerto Rico]. *Revista/ Review Interamericana [Puerto Rico] 1979 9(3): 368-399.* Whether religion should be taught in public schools in Puerto Rico has been a controversial topic since the island was taken over by the United States in 1898. For the most part, the religious issue has followed the same pattern that it did in the rest of the United States. 58 notes.   J. A. Lewis

1198. Maldonado, Edwin. CONTRACT LABOR AND THE ORIGINS OF PUERTO RICAN COMMUNITIES IN THE UNITED STATES. *Int. Migration Rev. 1979 13(1): 103-121.* Describes the rise of Puerto Rican communities in the United States before, during, and after World War II as a result of the need for cheap agricultural and industrial labor.

1199. Maldonado, Rita. EDUCATION, INCOME DISTRIBUTION AND ECONOMIC GROWTH IN PUERTO RICO. *R. of Social Econ. 1976 34(1): 1-12.* Investigates the income distribution of Puerto Rico since 1950, in an attempt to establish whether expansion of educational opportunities can modify income inequality during periods of economic growth.

1200. Maldonado, Rita M. THE ECONOMIC COSTS AND BENEFITS OF PUERTO RICO'S POLITICAL ALTERNATIVES. *Southern Econ. J. 1974 41(2): 267-282.* Analyzes the probable economic impact on Puerto Rico of independence, statehood, or continued commonwealth status.   S

1201. Maldonado, Rita M. LA DISTRIBUCIÓN DEL INGRESO Y EL DESARROLLO ECONÓMICO EN PUERTO RICO [The distribution of income and economic development in Puerto Rico]. *Rev. de Ciencias Sociales [Puerto Rico] 1974 18(1-2): 125-144.* The economic savings brought about by US provision of defense and related services should be devoted to ending chronic unemployment and redressing past disparities in the national income.

1202. Maldonado, Rita M. WHY PUERTO RICANS MIGRATED TO THE UNITED STATES IN 1947-73. *Monthly Labor Rev. 1976 99(9): 7-18.* Explains immigration from Puerto Rico to the United States during 1947-73 in terms of economic opportunity and shows how noneconomic variables played a more important role after 1960.

1203. Maldonado-Denis, Manuel. HACIA UNA INTERPRETACIÓN MARXISTA DE LA HISTORIA DE PUERTO RICO [Toward a Marxist interpretation of Puerto Rican history]. *Casa de las Américas [Cuba] 1974 15(86): 16-35.* Discusses the history of Puerto Rico since the 19th century; examines a Marxist approach and attempts to determine whether such an approach applies to Puerto Rican history.

1204. Maldonado-Denis, Manuel. HACIA UNA INTERPRETACIÓN SO-CIOHISTÓRICA DE LA EMIGRACIÓN PUERTORRIQUEÑA [A sociohistorical interpretation of Puerto Rican emigration]. *Casa de las Américas [Cuba] 1976 16(94): 76-91.* Analyzes Puerto Rican emigration to the United States 1945-70, concentrating on emigration as part of a broader picture of the colonial status of Puerto Rico and the relationship of third world countries to industrialized nations rather than on individual experiences of emigrants. Capitalist interests demand surplus cheap labor and do not foster economic independence of a colony or third world nation. Capitalist investments in the colony in the long run tend to be capital-oriented rather than labor-oriented, thus causing more unemployment and emigration. The petrochemical industry in Puerto Rico is a case in point. The post-World War II government in Puerto Rico seeks to solve the problem by pushing emigration and birth control rather than by working for economic independence of the island. Based on Puerto Rican government reports and secondary works; 27 notes.   H. J. Miller

1205. Maldonado-Denis, Manuel. PROSPECTS FOR LATIN AMERICAN NATIONALISM: THE CASE OF PUERTO RICO. *Latin Am. Perspectives 1976 3(3): 36-45.* Analyzes the character of Puerto Rican nationalism and its roots in the early nationalist movement led by Betances. Criticizes Albizu Campos and the Nationalist Party for attempting to achieve their goals in isolation from the world struggle against imperialism. Contrasts Puerto Rican nationalism with Latin American nationalism in general. The inability of Puerto Rican nationalism to achieve national liberation is a reflection of the weak national bourgeoisie. Also analyzes the success of the PPD in light of the above analysis. J. L. Dietz

1206. Maldonado-Denis, Manuel. REFLEXIONES EN TORNO A UN MITO: LA "DOCILIDAD" DEL PUERTORRIQUEÑO [Thoughts on a myth: the "docility" of the Puerto Ricans]. *Casa de las Américas [Cuba] 1980 21(123): 131-135.* Contests the thesis of René Marqués's "El Puertorriqueño Dócil," *Cuadernos Americanos* [Mexico] 1962 21(1): 145, which regards docility and submissiveness as deep-rooted features of the national Puerto Rican character, a view expressed also in writings by Brau, Coll y Toste, and Pedreira. This interpretation of the historical development of a people is not based on sufficient historical and sociological evidence, as demonstrated by the resistance of Taino Indians to the Spanish invaders, frequent insurrections by slaves, opposition to the modes of capitalist production by the working classes, and, in more recent years, student activism. 3 notes. P. J. Durell

1207. Mann, Arthur J. PUBLIC EXPENDITURE PATTERNS IN THE DOMINICAN REPUBLIC AND PUERTO RICO 1930-1970. *Social and Econ. Studies [Jamaica] 1975 24(1): 47-82.* Provides data on the growth of public expenditures in the Dominican Republic and Puerto Rico and attempts to identify the reasons for the growth of the public sector. The surplus earned during World War II and increased public acceptance are important reasons for the growth. Finds many similarities in the public spending of the two countries. 6 tables, 24 notes, 29 refs., 3 data appendixes. E. S. Johnson

1208. Marazzi, Rosa. EL IMPACTO DE LA IMMIGRACIÓN A PUERTO RICO 1800 A 1830: ANÁLISIS ESTADÍSTICO [The impact of immigration to Puerto Rico from 1800 to 1830: statistic analysis]. *Rev. de Ciencias Sociales [Puerto Rico] 1974 18(1-2): 1-42.* The number of immigrants during 1800-30 was greater than previously estimated; immigration significantly affected the increase in population in Puerto Rico in that period.

1209. Márquez, Rosa Luisa. CUARENTA AÑOS DESPUÉS DE "LO QUE PODRÍA SER UN TEATRO PUERTORRIQUEÑO" (1939-1979) [Forty years after "What Could Be the Theater in Puerto Rico" (1939-79)]. *Revista/ Review Interamericana [Puerto Rico] 1979 9(2): 300-306.* In spite of the search for a truly nationalistic theater, the stage in Puerto Rico has not been able to establish itself with the public on the island. Secondary sources; 7 notes. J. A. Lewis

1210. Marrero, J. Edward. EL IMPACTO DE LA REVOLUCIÓN AMERICANA EN EL DESARROLLO DE PUERTO RICO, 1776-1854 [The impact of the American Revolution upon the development of Puerto Rico, 1776-1854]. *Rev. Interamericana [Puerto Rico] 1975-76 5(4): 609-623.* Although the ideas of the American Revolution were not ignored in Puerto Rico, the principal effect of the revolution was economic. Puerto Rico began a flourishing trade with the United States in 1775 that never stopped. Secondary sources; 18 notes. J. A. Lewis

1211. Martínez, Iris. EL TEATRO EN PUERTO RICO, ARMA DE SOBREVIVENCIA DE NUESTRA CULTURA [The theater in Puerto Rico, a weapon for the survival of our culture]. *Casa de las Américas [Cuba] 1980 21(123): 126-130.* The Institute of Puerto Rican Culture was established in 1955 in order to conserve, develop and promote Puerto Rican cultural values: it initiated the theater festival in 1958 and the international theater festival in 1966 and has sponsored many theatrical, balletic and musical events. In the face of recent legislation inimicable to indigenous culture and threatening the continued existence of the institute, a committee has been formed for the defense of Puerto Rican culture. Based partly on Manuel Maldonado-Denis, "El colonialismo, la cultura y la creacion intelectual"; 3 notes.   P. J. Durell

1212. Martínez, Rubén Berríos. INDEPENDENCE FOR PUERTO RICO: THE ONLY SOLUTION. *Foreign Affairs 1977 55(3): 561-583.* Calls for Puerto Rican independence. Statehood and commonwealth status are but continuations of colonialism in new dress. Puerto Rico has been irreparably exploited; the declining economy is kept going only by massive infusions of federal aid. Independence movements are growing rapidly; recent voting trends which purport to show otherwise have been misinterpreted. Puerto Rico represents a huge drain on the American treasury and the American people. Assimilation is impossible; few people even speak English. 14 notes.
                                          V. L. Human

1213. Mass, Bonnie. PUERTO RICO: A CASE STUDY OF POPULA-TION CONTROL. *Latin Am. Perspectives 1977 4(4): 66-82.* Mass steriliza-tion of women in Puerto Rico since the 1930's originated from eugenic thought and the desire to control population size, reduce problems of unemployment, and control the size and composition of the labor force.

1214. Massey, Douglas S. and Schnabel, Kathleen M. RECENT TRENDS IN HISPANIC IMMIGRATION TO THE UNITED STATES. *International Migration Review 1983 17(2): 212-244.* Provides demographic data on immi-grants from Latin America to the United States, showing points of origin and destination and providing information on the sex, age, educational background, and professions of immigrants.

1215. Mathews, Thomas. PDP PP = A*PA*THY: THE END OF THE POPULAR PARTY. *Caribbean Rev. 1980 9(3): 9-11.* Both the tremendous turnout for the funeral of Luis Muñoz Marín, founder of the Popular Democratic Party (PDP) and the Commonwealth of Puerto Rico, and the large turnout for the primary elections, encouraged the PCP, but the lack of direction in its pro-Commonwealth platform may cause the party to lose the next election to the prostatehood New Progressive Party (NPP).

1216. McCabe, Marsha. PORTRAITS FROM THE PUERTO RICAN COMMUNITY. *Spinner: People and Culture in Southeastern Massachusetts 1982 2: 6-19.* Members of the Puerto Rican community of New Bedford, Massachusetts, recount their personal histories and current situations; they mention immigration, jobs, housing, their neighborhood, and their minority status.

1217. McCoy, Terry L. A PRIMER FOR US POLICY ON CARIBBEAN EMIGRATION. *Caribbean Rev. 1979 8(1): 10-15.* Examines US immigration policies from 1924 to the present and concludes that current laws and quotas, especially as they affect the Western hemisphere and therefore the countries of the Caribbean, encourage illegal immigration and exacerbate US relations with Latin America and the Caribbean.

1218. Mead, Margaret and Thompson, Bill. PROBLEMS OF PUERTO RICAN CULTURAL IDENTITY. *R. Interamericana R. [Puerto Rico] 1975 5(1): 5-10.* The problems of cultural identity among Puerto Ricans are to a great extent insoluble. The diaspora of Puerto Ricans split the island's soul, and the limited economic potential of Puerto Rico makes it a society dependent upon the outside world. Based on an interview of Margaret Mead by Bill Thompson. J. A. Lewis

1219. Megenney, William W. THE BLACK PUERTO RICANS: AN ANALYSIS OF RACIAL ATTITUDES. *Phylon 1974 35(1): 83-93.* Studies some facets of racial attitudes among the blacks of Puerto Rico. Racial mixture is the first facet concerning the feelings of equality experienced by Puerto Rican blacks. Black slaves "whitened" themselves by miscegenation; thus, the number of mulattoes increased while the number of whites and blacks diminished. The mulattoes "could not reject that part of themselves that came originally from Africa." Blacks who live outside the two black areas enjoy full racial and social acceptance by whites. 34 notes. E. P. Stickney

1220. Méndez, José Luis. LA LUCHA CULTURAL EN PUERTO RICO [The cultural struggle in Puerto Rico]. *Casa de las Américas [Cuba] 1980 21(123): 50-61.* Demonstrates the systematic process of economic exploitation, cultural aggression, ideological control and political manipulation undertaken by the United States in Puerto Rico since 1898. Attention is directed to the Nationalist Party campaigns for independence since the 1930's and counter-measures taken by the authorities, control of workers by US unions as a cornerstone of the new industrialization policy from the 1940's, the human rights violations and political machinations of the pro-American New Progressive Party government elected in 1968 and 1976, and the work of the Committee for the Defense of Puerto Rican Culture opposing legislation designed to erode cultural identity. Based on Oficina de Puerto Rico documents and other sources; 21 notes. P. J. Durell

1221. Meyn, M. and Rodríguez, J. EL APARATO MILITAR NORTEAMERICANO EN PUERTO RICO [The North American military machine in Puerto Rico]. *Casa de las Américas [Cuba] 1980 21(123): 7-25.* Indicates the changes in the military role of Puerto Rico since the Spanish-American War, covering the following aspects: US colonial expansion and naval power; US intervention in the Caribbean, 1898-1933; the Jones law and large-scale recruitment; remilitarization of the colonial regime during the depression and expansion in World War II; the military role of Puerto Rico in the Cold War; and, in recent years, expenditure, installations, bases and the repressive force of the National Guard. 5 tables, 12 notes. P. J. Durell

1222. Mingo, John J. CAPITAL IMPORTATION AND SECTORAL DE-VELOPMENT: A MODEL APPLIED TO POSTWAR PUERTO RICO. *Am. Econ. R. 1974 64(3): 273-290.* Analyzes the performance of an open and dual developing economy from a sectoral point of view. Postwar Puerto Rico is the subject; a two-sector open growth mathematical model is utilized. The commonwealth imports and exports at perfectly fluid world prices, and borrows at going world interest rates. The model demonstrates a reallocation of labor toward the more productive industrial sector. Foreign investment is thus stimulated and higher wages result. Emigration eliminated actual growth of the labor force. 2 tables, 4 figs., 19 notes, biblio.   V. L. Human

1223. Mintz, Sidney. THE ROLE OF PUERTO RICO IN MODERN SOCIAL SCIENCE. *Revista/Review Interamericana [Puerto Rico] 1978 8(1): 5-16.* Julian H. Stewart, ed., *The People of Puerto Rico: A Study in Social Anthropology* (Urbana: U. of Illinois Pr., 1956) was one of the first works that turned the attention of anthropologists to the Caribbean. It also was a pioneering work in turning the attention of anthropologists to the problems of large underdeveloped areas in the world. Presented as a paper at the Inter-American University Conference on *The People of Puerto Rico*, 10-12 March 1977. Secondary sources; 36 notes.   J. A. Lewis

1224. Mohr, Eugene V. PIRI THOMAS: AUTHOR AND PERSONA. *Caribbean Studies [Puerto Rico] 1980 20(2): 61-74.* Reviews the literary career of Piri Thomas. His works, three of which are autobiographical, offer vivid views of the United States from the viewpoint of a Puerto Rican black, and are especially valuable for their description of life in prison. Biblio.

R. L. Woodward, Jr.

1225. Monk, Janice J. and Alexander, Charles S. MODERNIZATION AND RURAL POPULATION MOVEMENTS: WESTERN PUERTO RICO. *J. of Interamerican Studies and World Affairs 1979 21(4): 523-550.* Geographic studies of modernization focus on urban areas rather than rural studies, and they tend to be either micro or macro without integrating the two levels of research. A large amount of movement within the rural areas has been overlooked. Moreover, these movements reflect markedly altered rural life patterns; for example, settlement tends to move linearly along the main transit routes rather than into villages. This is particularly true of western Puerto Rico where new rural dwellers have access to electricity, water, good transportation, education, and social welfare services. In a sense they have become urbanized, but retain strong preferences for rural living. Some consequences of social significance include the decline of agriculture, high unemployment, and abandonment of land away from the main and secondary roads. Printed primary and secondary sources; 3 tables, 6 fig., 12 notes, ref.

T. D. Schoonover

1226. Morales, Waltraud Queiser. IN SEARCH OF NATIONAL IDENTI-TY: CUBAN AND PUERTO RICAN MIGRATION—A REVIEW ARTI-CLE. *Revista/Review Interamericana [Puerto Rico] 1980-81 10(4): 567-574.* Reviews the History Task Force's *Labor Migration Under Capitalism, the Puerto Rican Experience* (1979), Roberta Ann Johnson's *Puerto Rico, Com-*

monwealth or Colony? (1980), and Grupo Areíto's *Contra Viento y marea, joven Cubanos hablan desde su Exilio en Estados Unidos* (1978), which show that Puerto Rican and Cuban migration to the United States is very similar to that of all new groups entering that country.   J. A. Lewis

1227. Morfi, Angelina. EL TEATRO EN PUERTO RICO EN EL PRIMER TERCIO DEL SIGLO XX [Puerto Rican theater in the first third of the 20th century]. *Revista/Review Interamericana [Puerto Rico] 1979 9(2): 255-299.* Although of uneven quality, Puerto Rican theater was very active in the early 20th century. Puerto Rican theater made a clean break during this period with the Castilian themes that had dominated its stage in the 19th century. Printed sources; 38 notes.   J. A. Lewis

1228. Mosher, W. D. THE THEORY OF CHANGE AND RESPONSE: AN APPLICATION TO PUERTO RICO, 1940 TO 1970. *Population Studies [Great Britain] 1980 34(1): 45-58.* Examines responses to fertility rates, migration, and emigration among Puerto Ricans, based on the Theory of Change and Response.

1229. Mount, Graeme S. PRESBYTERIANISM IN PUERTO RICO: FORMATIVE YEARS, 1899-1914. *J. of Presbyterian Hist. 1977 55(3): 241-254.* The fruits of the Presbyterian Puerto Rico mission appear to be the most numerous of any of that church's undertaking. Article offers suggestions to account for this. For one thing, when the Presbyterians came to Puerto Rico following the Spanish-American War they came with the prestige of being representatives of a liberating power. The fact that they limited their endeavors to the western third of the island in their missionary undertaking meant the conservation of resources and efforts. Further, the Catholic Church in Puerto Rico at that time was in a very weakened condition. Presbyterians capitalized on the poor educational opportunities and developed outstanding schools to correct these deficiencies. It was in education that they made their greatest contributions. Finally, Presbyterian success resulted because natives were trained for the ministry, thus creating an indigenous church leadership. Primary and secondary sources; illus., 3 tables, 63 notes.   H. M. Parker, Jr.

1230. Moynihan, Daniel Patrick. PATTERNS OF ETHNIC SUCCESSION: BLACKS AND HISPANICS IN NEW YORK CITY. *Pol. Sci. Q. 1979 94(1): 1-14.* Reviews the gains achieved by blacks and Hispanics in New York City over the past decade and relates those gains to general patterns of ethnic succession.   J

1231. Nasatir, Abraham P. CHILEANS IN CALIFORNIA DURING THE GOLD RUSH AND THE ESTABLISHMENT OF THE CHILEAN CONSULATE. *California Hist. Q. 1974 53(1): 52-70.* Chileans were among the first to respond to the news of the discovery of gold in California in 1848. Chile's strategic location and merchant fleet permitted thousands of Chileans to make the trip to the gold fields with relative ease, and Chile was an important supplier of food and provisions in the early years of the gold rush. While some Chileans made fortunes from these activities, most encountered prejudice and hostility. Concerned about acts of violence, desertion of sailors, and complaints from destitute gold-seekers, the Chilean government appointed a consul in San Francisco to represent the interests of Chile, but the government offered no salary, and a succession of consuls complained of an overburden of work. Chilean miners, more skilled in extracting gold from quartz than Anglo prospectors, protested against the foreign miners' tax, laws against employment of aliens, and mob actions. Consuls attempted to deal with these complaints, and such consuls as Chilean-born Samuel Price and Pedro Cueto made personal sacrifices in trying to accomplish their tasks. When law was restored to California and Chile's provisioning of gold-seekers declined, the government placed less importance on a San Francisco consulate. Based on research in Chile's Archivo Nacional; illus., photos, 10 notes.   A. Hoffman

1232. Neggers, Gladys. CLARA LAIR Y JULIA DE BURGOS: REMINISCENCIAS DE EVARISTO RIBERA CHEVREMONT Y JORGE FONT SALDAÑA [Clara Lair and Julia de Burgos: Reminiscences of Evaristo Ribera Chevremont and Jorge Font Saldaña]. *R. Interamericana [Puerto Rico] 1974 4(2): 258-263.* The lives and personalities of Puerto Rico's most prominent poetesses of the 20th century, Clara Lair (1895-1973) and Julia de Burgos (1914-53), are explored through the memories of friends. Based on personal interviews; 4 notes, biblio.   J. A. Lewis

1233. Nichols, Nick. CASTRO'S REVENGE. *Washington Monthly 1982 14(1): 39-42.* The indiscriminate acceptance of thousands of Cuban undesirables as legitimate refugees in 1980 has damaged the United States and the hopes of all anti-Castro Cubans.

1234. Nobel, Barry and McDivitt, Marilyn. ENGLISH TEACHING AND BILINGUAL EDUCATION IN PUERTO RICO. *Rev. Interamericana [Puerto Rico] 1978 8(2): 309-315.* Present methods of teaching English (English as a Second Language) in Puerto Rico fail because they seldom motivate students. More successful programs on the island might be had if the methods of English as a Foreign Language or bilingual education were used. Whatever methods are used, only students who volunteer to study English should be employed. Biblio.   J. Lewis

1235. Oliveira, Annette. DOÑA FELA: THE GREAT LADY OF PUERTO RICAN POLITICS. *Américas (Organization of Am. States) 1981 33(1): 49-53.* Sketches the career of Felisa Rincón, who became one of Puerto Rico's most endearing, popular, and powerful political leaders and San Juan's first woman mayor.

1236. Overman, Charles T. RISE AND FALL OF THE *HENRIETTA*: 1827-1918. *R. Interamericana [Puerto Rico] 1974/75 4(4): 493-504.* Traces the genealogical and economic history of *Henrietta*, a substantial sugar plantation in 19th-century Puerto Rico. The daughter of Samuel Morse, American inventor of the telegraph, spent part of her married life there. The abolition of slavery in 1873 caused the plantation to become unprofitable, and eventually it was divided. Based on primary and secondary sources; 4 tables, 18 notes.   J. A. Lewis

1237. Page, J. Bryan. THE CHILDREN OF EXILE: RELATIONSHIPS BETWEEN THE ACCULTURATION PROCESS AND DRUG USE AMONG CUBAN YOUTH. *Youth & Soc. 1980 11(4): 431-447.* Immigrant males from Cuba, more than any other ethnic or racial youth group, show a high level of drug abuse. They favor marijuana, quaaludes, and cocaine. This use is based in Cuban cultural patterns, especially those emphasizing alertness and macho strength. Based on the records of the Dade County (Florida) Comprehensive Drug Program files, secondary sources; 3 tables, biblio.

J. H. Sweetland

1238. Pantojas García, Emilio. ESTRATEGIAS DE DESARROLLO Y CONTRADICCIONES IDEOLÓGICAS EN PUERTO RICO: 1940-1978 [Development strategies and ideological contradictions in Puerto Rico, 1940-78]. *Rev. de Ciencias Sociales [Puerto Rico] 1979 21(1-2): 73-119.* Analyzes Puerto Rican strategies of development conceived as class projects and contradictions generated with their implementation and their manifestation in the class struggle. Political changes before and after implementation of particular development strategies, political struggles, and social forces that emerged are analyzed. Covers: 1) 1940-47: reformist period, 2) 1947-63: period of capital importation, and 3) 1963-78: period of monopolistic intensive capital.

J/S

1239. Pantojas García, Emilio. LA IGLESIA PROTESTANTE Y LA AMERICANIZACIÓN DE PUERTO RICO: 1898-1917 [The Protestant church and the Americanization of Puerto Rico: 1898-1917]. *Rev. de Ciencias Sociales [Puerto Rico] 1974 18(1-2): 97-122.* After US entry to Puerto Rico in 1898, US Protestant missionaries tried deliberately to justify US economic, political, and military exploitation; they called the process "regeneration" and spread their ideas through their control of church, education, and press.

1240. Pedraza-Bailey, Silvia. CUBA'S EXILES: PORTRAIT OF A REFUGEE MIGRATION. *International Migration Review 1985 19(1): 4-34.* The changing phases of the Cuban revolutionary government over two decades determined the kind of political refugees who emigrated from Cuba to the United States, from those who left Cuba after industrial nationalization in 1960 to the large numbers of workers and prisoners who left for both political and economic reasons in 1980.

1241. Percal, Raul Moncarz. THE GOLDEN CAGE: CUBANS IN MIAMI. *Int. Migration [Netherlands] 1978 16(3-4): 160-173.* Evidence indicates that mobility of Cuban Americans in Miami has been minimal. "In terms of educational mobility... the loss of human capital has been very significant." Short-term measures of geographic mobility out of Florida through the Cuban Refugee Center and returning to Florida were very ineffective. The high rate of neutralization among Cubans since 1970 "may enhance their political leverage to economic and political power, but the political power would have come late to the original waves of refugees." As far as income mobility is concerned the study shows that the great percentage of Cuban women in the labor force makes the family income sufficient to own their own homes. 8 tables, 23 notes, biblio.

E. P. Stickney

1242. Pérez, Louis A., Jr. CUBANS IN TAMPA: FROM EXILES TO IMMIGRANTS, 1892-1901. *Florida Hist. Q. 1978 57(2): 129-140.* Cuban cigarworkers in Tampa supported the Cuban independence cause in the 1880's and 1890's. The end of the war in 1898 marked a major shift in the cigarworkers' energies. Most reconciled themselves to permanent residence in the United States. Based mainly on secondary sources; 34 notes.

P. A. Beaber

1243. Pérez, Louis A., Jr. REMINISCENCES OF A *LECTOR*: CUBAN CIGAR WORKERS IN TAMPA. *Florida Hist. Q. 1975 53(4): 443-449.* Describes from personal experience the *lector*'s (reader's) function and influence among the Cuban illiterate workers in a Tampa cigar factory. "A highly developed proletarian consciousness and a long tradition of trade union militancy accompanied the Cuban tobacco workers to the United States." They embraced a variety of radical ideologies. The *lector* often served as a disseminator of the proletarian tradition, as well as a broad variety of written materials. Conflicts arose between the workers and factory owners over the *lector*'s pay and pro-labor materials. 13 notes.

R. V. Ritter

1244. Perez de Jesús, Manuel. EL DESARROLLO ECONÓMICO, LA SOBREPOBLACIÓN Y LA DESIGUALDAD EN PUERTO RICO [Economic development, overpopulation, and inequality in Puerto Rico]. *Rev. de Ciencias Sociales [Puerto Rico] 1973 17(2): 166-213.* Reviews Puerto Rico's spectacular development after 1940. However, the problem of overpopulation is negating economic improvement of the masses. The political taboo of promoting birth control in a solidly Catholic country adds to the severity of the situation. Documents the continuing high unemployment in spite of rapidly progressing industrialization and mass emigration to the continental United States. Based on official statistical data and secondary works; 4 tables, 66 notes.

F. Pollaczek

1245. Petrovich, Janice. DEPENDENCIA, ESTRATIFICACION SOCIAL Y LA EXPANSION DE LA EDUCACION POSTSECUNDARIA EN PUERTO RICO [Dependence, social stratification, and the expansion of postsecondary education in Puerto Rico]. *Rev. de Ciencias Sociales [Puerto Rico] 1979 21(3-4): 411-437.* Educational expansion in Puerto Rico is occurring in the midst of a prolonged fiscal crisis and a scarcity of jobs that have led to a lack of financial resources for a large proportion of the population. The more rapid growth of the private sector has expanded rapidly. Its higher tuition is increasingly subsidized by student aid from the federal government, an example of Puerto Rican dependence on the United States. Greater numbers of Puerto Ricans have been able to meet their aspiration for higher education but economic development plans within a situation of dependency have failed to furnish jobs for an increasingly educated work force. The rapid expansion of private institutions has depended excessively on federally-subsidized tuition. As more postsecondary education has been made available, the educational system has apparently become increasingly stratified with regard to social origins of students.

J/S

1246. Pilditch, Charles. A BRIEF HISTORY OF THEATER IN PUERTO RICO. *Revista/Review Interamericana [Puerto Rico] 1979 9(1): 5-8.* Theater existed in Puerto Rico during most of the colonial period, but not until the late 19th century did it become important. Only after 1930 did the Puerto Rican stage take on a uniquely national character. J. A. Lewis

1247. Poiarkova, N. T. ALBISU CAMPOS: NATSIONALNII GEROI PUERTO RICO [Albizu Campos: national hero of Puerto Rico]. *Novaia i Noveishaia Istoriia [USSR] 1972 (6): 130-141.* Discusses the life of Albizu Campos (1891-1965), the leader of Puerto Rico's struggle for independence. Considers his childhood, the influence the American occupation and colonization had on him, his education at the University of Vermont, his national service, his studies at the university after the war, the formation of the Nationalist Party in 1922, the development of his political ideas, and his return to his native land in 1921. Also examines his entry into the Nationalist Party in 1924, the development of the nationalist movement in the 1930's, the demonstration of March 1937, Campos's imprisonment, his release in 1947, his continued activity and imprisonment, and his influence on his fellow countrymen. Spanish and American secondary sources; 17 notes. L. Smith

1248. Portes, Alejandro; Clark, Juan M.; and Bach, Robert L. THE NEW WAVE: A STATISTICAL PROFILE OF RECENT CUBAN EXILES TO THE U.S. *Cuban Studies 1977 7(1): 1-32.* Cuban immigrants to the United States 1973-74 reflect some of the traditional patterns of immigration from that island. They tend to be white and from Havana, and to go into exile for political or economic reasons. On the other hand, these latest immigrants differ from their predecessors in being older, having a lower level of education, and in planning to remain permanently in the United States. Primary and secondary sources; 11 tables, 2 notes, biblio. J. A. Lewis

1249. Portes, Alejandro and Mozo, Rafael. THE POLITICAL ADAPTATION PROCESS OF CUBANS AND OTHER ETHNIC MINORITIES IN THE UNITED STATES: A PRELIMINARY ANALYSIS. *International Migration Review 1985 19(1): 35-63.* Compares patterns of naturalization, voting behavior, and political orientation of Cuban immigrants with members of other US ethnic groups as a means of comparing the political integration of political refugees with that of other immigrants.

1250. Portes, Alejandro. THE RISE OF ETHNICITY: DETERMINANTS OF ETHNIC PERCEPTIONS AMONG CUBAN EXILES IN MIAMI. *Am. Sociol. Rev. 1984 49(3): 383-397.* Traces the evolution of perceptions of social distance and discrimination by the host society among members of a recently arrived foreign minority. Determinants of these perceptions suggested by three alternative hypotheses in this area are reviewed and their effects compared empirically. The data come from a longitudinal study of adult male Cuban exiles interviewed at the time of arrival in the United States and again three and six years later. Results suggest a significant rise in perceptions of social distance and discrimination from low initial levels and a consistent association of such perceptions with variables suggested by the ethnic resilience perspective. In particular, findings from a series of logistic regressions converge with recent events in southern Florida to demonstrate the significance of interethnic contact and competition in the development of ethnic awareness. Theoretical implications of these results and their bearing on the analysis of differences between labor immigrants and political refugees are discussed.   J

1251. Poyo, Gerald E. CUBAN PATRIOTS IN KEY WEST, 1878-1886: GUARDIANS AT THE SEPARATIST IDEAL. *Florida Hist. Q. 1982 61(1): 20-36.* Key West played an important role in the continuous effort to liberate Cuba from Spanish rule after the Zanjón Pact of 1878. Dedicated rebels continued sacrifices to further the goal of freedom despite economic deprivation and political demoralization. But a recession curtailed cigar production and divided the Cuban community. Resurgence occurred during the late 1880's, and with it came the birth of a new revolutionary center at Tampa Bay. Based on documents from the Archivo Nacional, Havana, Cuba, newspapers, and other primary sources; 41 notes.   N. A. Kuntz

1252. Poyo, Gerald E. KEY WEST AND THE CUBAN TEN YEARS WAR. *Florida Hist. Q. 1979 57(3): 289-307.* Cuban exiles after 1850 located in New Orleans, New York, and Key West. The community at Key West, despite personal conflicts, jealousies, class antagonisms, and tactical disagreements, retained the drive for Cuban independence. The Ten Years' War (1868-78) was the first step toward Cuba's political separation from Spain in 1898. Primary and secondary sources; 2 photos, 62 notes.   N. A. Kuntz

1253. Pozzetta, George E. ¡ALERTA TABAQUEROS! TAMPA'S STRIKING CIGARWORKERS. *Tampa Bay Hist. 1981 3(2): 19-30.* The 1910 general strike in Tampa, Florida was led by thousands of Cuban, Italian, and Spanish immigrants who worked in the community's single major industry, the manufacture of cigars; 1901-11.

1254. Provenzo, Eugene F., Jr. and García, Concepción. EXILED TEACHERS AND THE CUBAN REVOLUTION. *Cuban Studies 1983 13(1): 1-15.* Nearly half of Cuba's teachers left Cuba after Castro's seizure of power, and many of them settled in Florida. In most cases, the emigrant teachers left Cuba because of ideological differences with the government. Based on interviews with exiled teachers in Florida; table, 16 notes.
                      J. A. Lewis

1255. Quintero Rivera, Angel G. [LA CLASE OBRERA Y EL PROCESO POLÍTICO EN PUERTO RICO] [The working class and the political process in Puerto Rico].
LA CLASE OBRERA Y EL PROCESO POLÍTICO EN PUERTO RICO [The working class and the political process in Puerto Rico]. *Rev. de Ciencias Sociales [Puerto Rico] 1974 18(1-2): 145-198.* Part I. Examines the emergence of capitalism as the main mode of production in Puerto Rico since the 19th century.
EL CAPITALISMO Y EL PROLETARIADO RURAL [Capitalism and the rural proletariat]. *Rev. de Ciencias Sociales [Puerto Rico] 1974 18(3-4): 61-107.* Part II. Examines the growth of a rural proletariat as part of the

development of the capitalist sugar cane plantation economy in Puerto Rico.

EL PARTIDO SOCIALISTA Y LA LUCHA POLÍTICA TRIANGULAR DE LAS PRIMERAS DECADAS BAJO LA DOMINACIÓN NORTEAMERICANA [The Socialist Party and the triangular political struggle of the first decades of US domination]. *Rev. de Ciencias Sociales [Puerto Rico] 1975 19(1): 47-100.* Part III. Analyzes the political emergence of the working class and its effect on the political process in Puerto Rico during 1898-1920.

LA CLASE OBRERA Y EL PROCESO POLÍTICO EN PUERTO RICO [The working class and the political process in Puerto Rico]. *Rev. de Ciencias Sociales [Puerto Rico] 1975 19(3): 261-300.* Part IV(1). The previous articles of this series have analyzed the transformation of a seignorial hacienda economy to a capitalist plantation economy, and its impact on the class structure and politics. Particularly, they have examined the proletarianization process that engendered a strong and growing working-class Socialist party, whose threat to hierarchical society by 1924 had become the axis of the political process in Puerto Rico. The fourth article aims to examine the fading away of the working-class menace in the following 25 years. This is the first part of the fourth article, which focusses on the impact on working-class politics of the contradictory development of dependent capitalism. This one was propelled and dominated by imperialism, with all its implications on the fluctuations of the trade-exchange terms, and the relocation of investment (in terms of the market of capitals of the metropolitan economy). This influence had to do also with the instability of the relative relationship between the factors of production and, implicitly, in the development of the productive forces. Especial importance is given to the concatenation of forms of the relative surplus-population which capitalist accumulation engendered, and the paralization in the proletarianization process that it implied, with the growth of unemployment and sporadic unstable "miscellaneous" employment. The transformation in the composition of employment weakened the labor movement, both in the concrete trade-unionist struggle and in the more general ideologico-cultural sphere, as the certainty in the inevitable socialist victory of a growing proletariat began to crumble. This lead the labor movement to a political Coalition with the anti-national bourgeoisie against the still-ruling Party of hacendados, searching material betterment through participation in government. This political practice weakened even more the working-class ideology and its former menace.

LA CLASE OBRERA Y EL PROCESO POLÍTICO EN PUERTO RICO [The working class and the political process in Puerto Rico]. *Rev. de Ciencias Sociales [Puerto Rico] 1976 20(1): 3-48.* Part IV(2). This last article of the series: "La lucha obrera y el proceso político en Puerto Rico" establishes the guidelines for a new approach to the study of the structural transformations to which the Puertorrican society has been subjected. The hindrances to the development of an industrial proletariat in Puerto Rico must be considered for the study and re-making of the Puertorrican working class. For the analysis of the process of industrial growth in Puerto Rico it must be borne in mind that previous to industrialization the beginnings of a capitalist production system had already been founded and thus the bases of a traditional society had been broken. In spite of this fact and even though a strong industrial growth had taken place, a proletariat such as that of the beginning of the 20's is not developed. At the time being this rural working class showed the traits characteristic of a "democratic and socialist" culture. But due to the political and cultural changes that prevailed it experienced a process of disintegration which made it give its support to populism. This populist ideology will thus bring to an end the socioeconomic plantation formation and the class politics. Finally, it will prepare the way for a dependent industrial capitalism replacing in this manner the formation of rural capitalism.   S/J

1256.   Quintero-Rivera, A. G. PUERTO RICAN NATIONAL DEVELOP-MENT: CLASS & NATION IN A COLONIAL CONTEXT. *Marxist Perspectives 1980 3(1): 10-30.* Focuses on the social processes (antiabsolutism, class antagonism, colonialism, capitalism, and the disintegration of the working class) since 1830 that led to the national identity crisis of the 1930's.

1257.   Ramirez, Rafael. RITUALES POLITICOS EN PUERTO RICO [Political rituals in Puerto Rico]. *Rev. de Ciencias Sociales [Puerto Rico] 1973 17(3): 309-324.* The survival and transformation of more primitive tribal rituals are observed by the author in today's political life of Puerto Rico. Takes the 1968 election campaign as an example. Details specific traditional styles in party conventions and electoral campaigns. Based on personal observations, secondary works, and a bibliographic annex.   F. Pollaczek

1258.   Ramírez, Rafael L. NATIONAL CULTURE IN PUERTO RICO. *Latin Am. Perspectives 1976 3(3): 109-116.* Reviews the major approaches to analyzing Puerto Rican culture and analyzes their weaknesses. The traditional approaches are the culturalist, the nationalist, and the modernizer views. The failure of each of these approaches to culture results from their neglect of: 1) Puerto Rico's class structure, 2) its African heritage, and 3) the importance of Puerto Ricans on the mainland.   J. L. Dietz

1259.   Ramírez, Rafael L. PUERTO RICO. *Latin Am. Res. Rev. 1980 15(3): 256-260.* A review article based on six books on Puerto Rico, which deal with such diverse topics as labor, politics, the national character, and delinquency.
                                                                              J. K. Pfabe

1260.   Ramírez, Rafael L. TREINTA AÑOS DE ANTROPOLOGÍA EN PUERTO RICO [Thirty years of anthropology in Puerto Rico]. *Revista/ Review Interamericana [Puerto Rico] 1978 8(1): 37-49.* Although most North American social science research on Puerto Rico has been worthless, Julian H. Steward, ed., *The People of Puerto Rico: A Study in Social Anthropology* (Urbana: U. of Illinois Pr., 1956), has been an exception. It is a part of a tradition of criticizing the power structure in Puerto Rico that most anthropologists on the island believe is necessary. Secondary sources; 56 notes.
                                                                              J. A. Lewis

1261.   Ranis, Peter. PUERTO RICO: SEVEN DECADES OF AMERI-CANIZATION. *Latin Am. Res. Rev. 1980 15(3): 246-255.* Reviews Surendra Bhana's *The United States and the Development of the Puerto Rican Status Question, 1936-1968* (Lawrence: U. Pr. of Kansas, 1975), Truman Clark's *Puerto Rico and the United States, 1917-1933* (Pittsburgh, Pa.: U. of Pittsburgh Pr., 1975), and Thomas Matthews's *Puerto Rican Politics and the New Deal* (New York: Da Capo Pr., 1976). These books can be considered North American defenses of liberal, incremental change which has led to a form of "associated exploitation" in Puerto Rico.   J. K. Pfabe

1262.   Rindfuss, Ronald R. FERTILITY AND MIGRATION: THE CASE OF PUERTO RICO. *Internat. Migration R. 1976 10(2): 191-203.* Discusses the relationship (1965-70) between childbirth, fertility and migration in Puerto Ricans and in Puerto Ricans who have migrated to the US mainland, using US Census statistics.

1263.   Robles, Rafaela R.; Martinez, Ruth E.; and Moscoso, Margarita R. PREDICTORS OF ADOLESCENT DRUG BEHAVIOR: THE CASE OF PUERTO RICO. *Youth & Soc. 1980 11(4): 415-430.* Drug use among youths in Puerto Rico surprisingly resembles patterns in the United States. Parental control has little effect on the decision to use drugs, while peer group pressure has major effects. In general, the heaviest drug use is by males in private high schools. Girls tend to be heavier users of cigarettes and alcohol. Based on a stratified random sample of Puerto Rican high school students in 1975-76, and on other works; 10 tables, biblio.   J. H. Sweetland

1264.   Rodriguez, Clara. A COST-BENEFIT ANALYSIS OF SUBJECTIVE FACTORS AFFECTING ASSIMILATION: PUERTO RICANS. *Ethnicity 1975 2(1): 66-80.* Assesses Puerto Rican attitudes about assimilation into mainstream American society, assessing costs in terms of cultural identity, ghettoization, social mobility, and ethnic pride during 1975.

1265.   Rodriguez, Clara. PUERTO RICANS AND THE MELTING POT: A REVIEW ESSAY. *J. of Ethnic Studies 1974 1(4): 89-98.* Challenges Glazer and Moynihan's analysis of New York's Puerto Rican community in *Beyond the Melting Pot* (Cambridge: M.I.T. Press, 1972) for overlooking economic and other structural factors, for an assimilationist bias, and for a lack of experience and knowledge about the Puerto Rican community. Based on personal experiences and published sources; 17 notes.   T. W. Smith

1266.   Rodriguez, Clara. PUERTO RICANS: BETWEEN BLACK AND WHITE. *New York Affairs 1974 1(4): 92-101.* "A Puerto Rican looks at the differences between United States and Puerto Rican racial perceptions and at what these differences mean to the future of Puerto Rican identity."   J

1267.   Rodriguez, Clara E. PRISMS OF RACE AND CLASS. *J. of Ethnic Studies 1984 12(2): 99-120* Reviews Thomas Sowell's *Ethnic America* (1981), which examines the unique experiences of American ethnic groups, emphasizing those of the Puerto Ricans. 9 notes, ref.   S

1268. Rogg, Eleanor and Homberg, Joan J. THE ASSIMILATION OF CUBANS IN THE UNITED STATES. *Migration Today 1983 11(4-5): 8-11.* Scholars are still engaged in studying the experiences of the first three waves of postrevolutionary Cuban exiles now living in the United States and constituting the third largest Hispanic group in the country.

1269. Rogler, Lloyd H. THE CHANGING ROLE OF A POLITICAL BOSS IN A PUERTO RICAN MIGRANT COMMUNITY. *Am. Sociol. R. 1974 39(1): 57-67.* "Observations in a field study of a Puerto Rican migrant community [in the continental United States] and historical data covering almost four decades are used to discuss the emergence of political bossism in an ethnic community and the social forces sustaining it, the ascent of politically independent ethnic organizations in the face of an established apparent functional alternative (the boss's unofficial political system), the viability of such organizations, and their relationship to the role of the political boss. It is found that a developing modern political machine converts a grassroot centralized ethnic leadership into the role of the political boss. The Puerto Ricans' incentive to form politically independent organizations arises from the evolution of their ethnic identity, as the host society comes increasingly to favor such selected groups and as the boss system ceases to be able to contain or channel inwardly the thrust of assimilation. As Puerto Rican activism changes to fit the prevailing ethos of urban life, the boss's role is disrupted by new organizational pressures." 																		J

1270. Rogler, Lloyd H.; Cooney, Rosemary Santana; and Ortiz, Vilma. INTERGENERATIONAL CHANGE IN ETHNIC IDENTITY IN THE PUERTO RICAN FAMILY. *Int. Migration Rev. 1980 14(2): 193-214.* Derived from a New York City survey of 1976-78, notes that education and age at arrival are significant factors upon ethnicity and that these same factors in children are related to changes in ethnicity in the family.

1271. Rogler, Lloyd H. A PRELIMINARY REPORT ON HELP PATTERNS, THE FAMILY, AND MENTAL HEALTH: PUERTO RICANS IN THE UNITED STATES. *Int. Migration Rev. 1978 12(2): 248-259.* Examines patterns of community and personal support among Puerto Ricans in New York City, which aid in acculturation and accommodation to detrimental economic and social situations, 1950's-70's. Biblio.

1272. Roseberry, William. HISTORICAL MATERIALISM AND *THE PEOPLE OF PUERTO RICO. Revista/Review Interamericana [Puerto Rico] 1978 8(1): 26-36.* Some of the contributors to Julian H. Steward, ed., *The People of Puerto Rico: A Study in Social Anthropology* (Urbana: U. of Illinois Pr., 1956) felt that the basic problem of their work was placing Puerto Rico in a broader economic context, a perspective that Marxist anthropologists also seek. Yet *The People of Puerto Rico* did not quite take its evidence to a logical conclusion, and, as such, is flawed. Secondary sources; 37 notes.

																	J. A. Lewis

1273. Roseman, Marina. THE NEW RICAN VILLAGE: TAKING CONTROL OF THE IMAGE-MAKING MACHINERY. *New York Folklore*

1980 6(1-2): 45-54. Interviews and the author's observation of musical events and organizational meetings of the New Rican Village, a cultural arts center in New York City indicate how the Puerto-Rican artists at the New Rican Village, who are primarily musicians, transmit image-making to their audience; briefly traces the origins of the New Rican Village to the political activism of the Young Lords during the 1960's.

1274. Rosenberg, Terry J. and Lake, Robert W. TOWARD A REVISED MODEL OF RESIDENTIAL SEGREGATION AND SUCCESSION: PUERTO RICANS IN NEW YORK, 1960-1970. *Am. J. of Sociol. 1976 81(5): 1142-1150.* Generally accepted models of ethnic assimilation outline a pattern of decreasing residential segregation associated with increasing similarity to native whites. Similar models for the black population posit continuing residential concentration combined with rapid turnover and succession. Our analysis of data on recent settlement patterns of Puerto Ricans in New York City indicates that this group is conforming to neither type of previously accepted model. Competition between the Puerto Rican minority and the larger, more economically advantaged black minority, a new set of public housing opportunities, and the return migration of successful Puerto Ricans are factors that were not considered in previously developed models. A new model of residential segregation and succession must incorporate these realities of contemporary urbanization.   J

1275. Rosenberg, Terry Jean. SUBURBAN BARRIO. *Society 1981 18(2): 79-83.* A photographic essay, with brief commentary, of life in the Puerto Rican barrio of Long Island, New York, in 1981.

1276. Rosenwaike, Ira. MORTALITY AMONG THE PUERTO RICAN BORN IN NEW YORK CITY. *Social Sci. Q. 1983 64(2): 375-385.* Compares rates and causes of death among native Puerto Ricans living in New York City to mortality among non-Puerto Ricans.

1277. Routté Gómez, Eneid. THE AGONY OF PUERTO RICAN ART. *Caribbean Rev. 1980 9(3): 16-18.* Discusses Puerto Rican art and political status during and after the governorship (1948-64) of Luis Muñoz Marín (d. 1980), focusing on the Institute of Puerto Rican Culture (founded in 1955) and the founding of a rival culture ministry by Governor Carlos Romero Barceló in 1980.

1278. Safa, Helen I. LA PARTICIPACIÓN DIFERENCIAL DE MUJERES EMIGRANTES DE AMÉRICA LATINA EN LA FUERZA DE TRABAJO DE LOS ESTADOS UNIDOS [The participation differential of Latin American emigrant women in the US labor force]. *Demografía y Economía [Mexico] 1978 12(1): 113-128.* Discusses the impact of women of Latin American origin in the labor market in New York City, 1970's.

1279. Safa, Helen Icken. CLASS CONSCIOUSNESS AMONG WORKING CLASS WOMEN IN LATIN AMERICA: A CASE STUDY IN PUERTO RICO. *Pol. and Soc. 1975 5(3): 377-394.* Working class women in Puerto Rico (and Latin America in general) may have achieved the first step toward class consciousness (the cognitive stage), but there is little hope for further progress because of assigned female roles. Extrapolating from studies conducted of shantytown families in San Juan, Puerto Rico, in 1959 and 1969, finds that sexual subordination (Marianismo) is the major stumbling block Latin American women must overcome. Traditional Marxist analysis, which sees women as members of a secondary labor force, also must be revised, and the subordinate family and occupational roles of working class women recognized before further progress can be made. Based on primary and secondary sources; 38 notes. D. G. Nielson

1280. Sánchez-Korrol, Virginia E. BETWEEN TWO WORLDS: EDUCATED PUERTO RICAN MIGRANT WOMEN. *Caribbean Rev. 1983 12(3): 26-29.* Educated women in Puerto Rican immigrant communities quickly established themselves in professional careers and as community and cultural leaders.

1281. Santiago, Jaime. ONE STEP FORWARD. *Wilson Q. 1980 4(2): 132-140.* Discusses Puerto Rico's economy from the boom during World War II, when the island's main business was agriculture, to the current reliance on federal subsidies from the mainland.

1282. Sassen-Koob, Saskia. FORMAL AND INFORMAL ASSOCIATIONS: DOMINICANS AND COLOMBIANS IN NEW YORK. *Int. Migration Rev. 1979 13(2): 314-332.* Examines Dominican and Colombian social organizations in New York City from approximately 1972 to 1976 and concludes that the greater incidence of voluntary associations in the Dominican community and their less instrumental character is rooted in the nature of the gap between place of origin and the receiving society, a gap which is much larger in the case of the Dominican than the Colombian community.

1283. Scanlan, John and Loescher, Gilburt. U.S. FOREIGN POLICY, 1959-80: IMPACT ON REFUGEE FLOW FROM CUBA. *Ann. of the Am. Acad. of Pol. and Social Sci. 1983 (467): 116-137.* Migration from Cuba to the United States has been strongly affected by foreign policy. During the 1959-62 migration wave, particularly prior to the failure of the Bay of Pigs invasion, Cubans were welcomed as temporary exiles likely to topple Castro and return home. The second major migration wave began in 1965, in the midst of a campaign for systematically isolating and economically depriving Cuba and its citizens. When thousands of those citizens left Cuba, primarily to improve their economic circumstances and rejoin family members, they were welcomed as refugees because of the symbolic value of their rejection of Latin America's only Communist state. The third migration wave occurred in 1980, after a decade of detente and gradually improving relations. It served no clear foreign policy ends and was perceived as helping Cuba rid itself of undesirables. Consequently those arriving received little public support. J/S

1284. Schwartz, Francis. THE BUREAUCRACY OF MUSIC IN PUERTO RICO. *Caribbean Rev. 1980 9(3): 19-21.* The newly created Administration for the Development of Art and Culture (ADAC) in Puerto Rico, sponsored by the pro-statehood New Progressive Party, has caused tension among Puerto

Rico's artists and musicians, particularly the musicians who have split over this cultural legislation.

1285. Sharma, M. Dutta and Sharma, P. L. ALTERNATIVE ESTIMA-TORS AND PREDICTIVE POWER OF ALTERNATIVE ESTIMATORS: AN ECONOMETRIC MODEL OF PUERTO RICO. *R. of Econ. and Statistics 1973 55(3): 381-385.*

1286. Silvestrini dePacheco, Blanca. LA VIOLENCIA CRIMINAL EN PUERTO RICO, DE 1940 A 1973: ¿CAMBIO EN EL TIEMPO? [Criminal violence in Puerto Rico from 1940 to 1973: a new phenomenon?]. *Rev. Interamericana [Puerto Rico] 1978 8(1): 65-84.* Part II. Continued from a previous article. Crime in Puerto Rico has increased in the decades since 1940, but the most significant increase is not the number of criminal acts; it is the fact that a much higher percentage of the victims of criminal activities do not know personally their aggressors. Crime has become impersonal. 6 tables, 6 graphs, 41 notes. J. Lewis

1287. Souza, Blase Camacho. TRABAJO Y TRISTEZA—"WORK AND SORROW": THE PUERTO RICANS OF HAWAII 1900-1902. *Hawaiian Journal of History 1984 18: 156-173.* Hawaii and Puerto Rico, both annexed by the United States in 1898, soon became aware of their complementary problems—the overpopulation of Puerto Rico and the need for workers in Hawaii. Migration began in 1900, and the Roman Catholic, Spanish-speaking Puerto Ricans found work, as well as unanticipated economic and cultural problems. 3 illus., 38 notes. M. M. Vance

1288. Stella, Tomás. CERRO MARAVILLA: INJUSTICE IN PUERTO RICO. *Caribbean Rev. 1980 9(3): 12-15, 44-45.* Details the Watergate-like scandal in Puerto Rico over whether police murdered two young independentistas in 1978 at the mountain, Cerro Maravilla (the name given to the case), and whether Puerto Rico's governor, Carlos Romero Barceló, and federal officials are involved in a coverup, which could embarrass President Jimmy Carter and hurt the statehood movement in the plebiscite on US-Puerto Rican relations.

1289. Stinner, William F. and Mader, Paul D. METROPOLITAN DOMI-NANCE AND FERTILITY CHANGE IN PUERTO RICO 1950-1970. *Social and Econ. Studies [Jamaica] 1975 24(4): 433-444.* Relates change in fertility by municipo to distance from and degree of connectivity to a metropolitan center. Finds that a real decline in the closer, better-connected municipos occurred earlier than in the more remote ones, but that by 1970 the fertility patterns were similar. 4 tables, 5 notes, biblio. E. S. Johnson

1290. Szymanski, Albert. THE GROWING ROLE OF SPANISH SPEAK-ING WORKERS IN THE U.S. ECONOMY. *Aztlán 1978 9: 177-208.* Examines and sustains the Marxist theory that capitalism's need of an exploitable group of laborers to do dirty work causes the oppression of national minorities. A new wave of predominantly Latin American immigrants is entering the market with this function, thereby displacing the blacks, who, in turn, are advancing economically and socially. Based primarily on statistics provided by the US Census; 20 tables, 9 notes, biblio. R. V. Ritter

1291. Tanzer, Michael. THE STATE AND THE OIL INDUSTRY IN TODAY'S WORLD: SOME LESSONS FOR PUERTO RICO. *Monthly Rev. 1978 29(10): 1-14.* Preliminary surveys during the 1970's indicated that significant oil deposits may exist off northern Puerto Rico, and that it would benefit the island to finance the exploration and reap the benefits.

1292. Thomas, Piri. A BICENTENNIAL WITHOUT A PUERTO RICAN COLONY. *Crisis 1975 82(10): 407-410.* The United States maintains an iron grip over Puerto Rico and independence is becoming the rallying point for a revolution. Puerto Rico has no control over its natural resources as US interests negotiate to strip mine the copper and build a super port, turning Puerto Rico into a giant gasoline station. The United States cannot celebrate its Bicentennial with an untroubled conscience while it holds sway over Puerto Rico. A. G. Belles

1293. Toro, Rafael de Jesús. UN LIBRO RECIENTE SOBRE LA HISTO-RIA DEL PROBLEMA DEL STATUS POLÍTICO DE PUERTO RICO: COMENTARIOS [A recent book on the history of the Puerto Rican status question: comments]. *Rev. de Ciencias Sociales [Puerto Rico] 1976 20(1): 123-135.* Review article prompted by Surendra Bhana's *The United States and the Development of the Puerto Rican Status Question, 1936-1968* (U. Pr. of Kansas, 1975), which includes a detailed outline of events that resulted in the establishment of the associated free state in 1950-52 and subsequent important developments (the 1953 United Nations resolution, the Fernos-Murray Bill, the Status Commission, the 1967 plebiscite and economic factors).
P. J. Taylorson

1294. Trabold, Robert. PASTORAL STRATEGIES IN THE IMMI-GRANT WORK. *Migration Today 1981 9(4-5): 40-48.* Describes the role of the immigrant parish church, particularly St. Ignatius Parish in the Crown Heights section of Brooklyn, in addressing the cultures of its parishioners and its help in the acculturation process; focuses on St. Ignatius Parish's work with Caribbean immigrants after World War II and with Haitian immigrants beginning in 1968.

1295. Ugalde, Antonio; Bean, Frank D. and Cárdenas, Gilbert. INTERNA-TIONAL MIGRATION FROM THE DOMINICAN REPUBLIC: FIND-INGS FROM A NATIONAL SURVEY. *Int. Migration Rev. 1979 13(2): 235-254.* Studies immigration from the Dominican Republic to the United States from 1965 to 1976 and concludes that migration is primarily a middle class urban phenomenon, economic reasons are the predominant motivation for emigrating, migrants tend to leave the Dominican Republic in the most productive period of their lives, return migration is very common, and international net migration does not seem to be increasing.

1296. Vázquez, José L. LA DINÁMICA POBLACIONAL Y EL FUTURO DE PUERTO RICO [Population Dynamics and the Future of Puerto Rico].

R. Interamericana R. [Puerto Rico] 1974 4(1): 22-27. Puerto Rico suffers from two demographic problems: a high birth rate and a shift of population from the countryside to the cities. Both conditions can be reversed, but if they are not, the island faces a grave future. Secondary sources; note.   J. A. Lewis

1297. Vázquez Calzada, José L. and Morales del Valle, Zoraida. CARAC-TERISTICAS DE LA POBLACION EXTRANJERA RESIDENTE EN PUERTO RICO [Characteristics of the foreign population living in Puerto Rico]. *Rev. de Ciencias Sociales [Puerto Rico] 1979 21(3-4): 245-287.* Continued from a previous article. Non-Puerto Ricans have differentiated characteristics from Puerto Ricans. The foreign group represents a relatively old population with predominance of males in productive ages. It has larger families. This population exhibits a higher proportion of persons enrolled in schools and a higher male and female participation in economic activities. They are better educated and hold better jobs.   J/S

1298. Vázquez Calzada, José L. and Morales del Valle, Zoraida. POBLA-CION DE ASCENDENCIA PUERTORRIQUENA NACIDA EN EL EX-TERIOR [The population of Puerto Rican descent born on the US mainland]. *Rev. de Ciencias Sociales [Puerto Rico] 1980 22(1-2): 1-33.* After the Second World War, Puerto Ricans emigrated massively to the United States, reducing to 34% the population of the island. During 1955-70 approximately 150,000 returned to Puerto Rico. This returned population has had a notable effect on the school system regarding language values and customs. The majority of these immigrants are young people who still depend on their parents. In 1970 the group represented 5% of Puerto Rico's population. In elementary school, it represented more than 9% of the total enrollment. The level of unemployment for returnees is much higher than it is for the rest of the islanders.   J/S

1299. Velázquez, René. JULIAN H. STEWARD'S PERSPECTIVE ON PUERTO RICO. *Revista/Review Interamericana [Puerto Rico] 1978 8(1): 50-58.* Although important in its time, Julian H. Steward, ed., *The People of Puerto Rico: A Study in Social Anthropology* (Urbana: U. of Illinois Pr., 1956) is seriously dated and of little value now. Moreover, it was seriously flawed because it failed to emphasize properly the role of US imperialism on that island. Secondary sources; 51 notes.   J. A. Lewis.

1300. Waldinger, Roger. IMMIGRANT ENTERPRISE IN THE NEW YORK GARMENT INDUSTRY. *Social Problems 1984 32(1): 60-71.* Hispanic immigrants are revitalizing New York City's ailing garment industry by opening small, and largely unseen, factories; analyzes the economic environment that has given rise to this immigrant entrepreneurship, and the business organization and industrial relations of the enterprises themselves.

1301. Walter, John C. and Ansheles, Jill Louise. THE ROLE OF THE CARIBBEAN IMMIGRANT IN THE HARLEM RENAISSANCE. *Afro-Americans in New York Life and Hist. 1977 1(1): 49-66.* Discusses political influences on the Harlem Renaissance, Marcus Garvey and Hubert Harrison, introduction of the Communist Party (begun with Caribbean immigrants Cyril

Briggs and Otto Huiswoud), and the literature introduced by immigrants Eric Walroud and Claude McKay, 1930's.

1302. Weisskoff, Richard and Wolff, Edward. LINKAGES AND LEAK-AGES: INDUSTRIAL TRACKING IN AN ENCLAVE ECONOMY. *Econ. Development and Cultural Change 1977 25(4): 607-628.* Analyzes structural changes during the industrialization of Puerto Rico to understand "the apparent success which that growing economy had had in the simultaneous creation of both *linkages* between local sectors and *leakages* from those sectors to the world economy, in the creation of new industries and the displacement of others." Reviews recent literature on the economy of Puerto Rico during 1948-63 and provides a mathematical analysis of the data. The overall orientation of the Puerto Rican economy is to transact business abroad and the economy is integrated with diminished reliance on imports. Based on published sources; 2 illus., 4 tables, 33 notes.   J. W. Thacker, Jr.

1303. Wells, Henry. DEVELOPMENT PROBLEMS IN THE 1970S IN PUERTO RICO. *Rev. Interamericana [Puerto Rico] 1977 7(2): 169-192.* Puerto Rico's economic gains during the 1940's-60's have slowed considerably. Reasons include the disappearance of many attractions that brought mainland business to the island and the substantial population growth since 1970. The question of political status (statehood or independence) also has played a role in economic development. Primary and secondary sources; 3 tables, 44 notes.
                                                                J. A. Lewis

1304. Wessman, James W. THE DEMOGRAPHIC STRUCTURE OF SLAVERY IN PUERTO RICO: SOME ASPECTS OF AGRARIAN CAPI-TALISM IN THE LATE NINETEENTH CENTURY. *J. of Latin Am. Studies [Great Britain] 1980 12(2): 271-289.* The slave population of San Germán had an unusual age and sex structure as a result of a dwindling slave trade and manumission policies. Individuals controlled over half the slaves, but familial groups were also important. The 20 principal slave-holding families and groups owned over 60% of the slaves. Smaller holdings were losing a greater proportion of their slaves than the larger holdings. By 1900, had trends present in 1872 continued, the Puerto Rican slave population would have been reduced to nothing, being replaced by a population of free black laborers. Document from the municipal archives of San Germán, Puerto Rico; 2 tables, 2 fig., 34 notes.   M. A. Burkholder

1305. Wessman, James W. DIVISION OF LABOUR, CAPITAL ACCU-MULATION AND COMMODITY EXCHANGE ON A PUERTO RICAN SUGAR CANE HACIENDA. *Social and Econ. Studies [Jamaica] 1978 27(4): 464-480.* Marxist economic theory and manuscript bookkeepers' records from the hacienda San Francisco in southwest Puerto Rico are used to analyze the economic structure of a premodern agricultural operation. The hacienda not only produced a commodity for export, but also functioned as a local multipurpose economic unit, subject to the vagaries of supply and demand. 10 notes, 18 ref.   E. S. Johnson

1306. Wessman, James W. THE SUGAR CANE HACIENDA IN THE AGRARIAN STRUCTURE OF SOUTHWESTERN PUERTO RICO IN 1902. *Rev. Interamericana [Puerto Rico] 1978 8(1): 99-115.* At the beginning of the 20th century, the agrarian structure of southwestern Puerto Rico was changing from the family-style hacienda system to that of the corporate sugar mills. This was a change from one form of capitalism to another, not a transition from feudalism or semifeudalism to capitalism as often suggested. Based primarily on information from José Ferreras Pagán's *Biografía de las riquezas de Puerto Rico: riqueza azucarera* (San Juan, 1902); map, 7 tables, 18 notes.   J. A. Lewis

1307. Westfall, L. Glenn. CIGAR LABEL ART: PORTRAITS OF TAMPA'S PAST. *Tampa Bay Hist. 1984 6(1): 5-15.* Tampa's cigar industry began with Cuba's revolt against Spain, which occasioned the emigration of thousands of Cubans to Florida, and which coincided with technological advances in the printing industry that revolutionized the cigar industry's advertising; illustrates and discusses examples of Tampa cigar advertising labels, many of which feature Florida, Cuban, and Spanish themes.

1308. Wilson, Kenneth L. and Martin, W. Allen. ETHNIC ENCLAVES: A COMPARISON OF THE CUBAN AND BLACK ECONOMIES IN MIAMI. *Am. J. of Sociol. 1982 88(1): 135-160.* Compares the economic structure of the Cuban and black communities in Miami, Florida, during the 1920's-80, focusing on Cuban-owned and black-owned businesses; Cubans are successful while the blacks are not.

1309. Winsberg, Morton D. ETHNIC COMPETITION FOR RESIDENTIAL SPACE IN MIAMI, FLORIDA, 1970-80. *Am. J. of Econ. and Sociol. 1983 42(3): 305-314.* The Hispanic population of Miami had a phenomenal rate of growth while the black population also grew rapidly. The non-Hispanic white population numerically declined. The Hispanic population of the city has been highly successful in improving its economic well-being and has been able to penetrate deeply into non-Hispanic white neighborhoods throughout the city. Blacks have not been able to increase their economic well-being as greatly and their expansion has been confined largely to neighborhoods adjacent to older black neighborhoods. Non-Hispanic white neighborhoods shrank considerably in area.   J/S

1310. Winsberg, Morton D. HOUSING SEGREGATION OF A PREDOMINANTLY MIDDLE CLASS POPULATION: RESIDENTIAL PATTERNS DEVELOPED BY THE CUBAN IMMIGRATION INTO MIAMI, 1950-74. *Am. J. of Econ. and Scoiol. 1979 38(4): 403-418.* Latin Americans, principally Cubans, have entered Miami in large numbers since 1950. Although most who arrive have both urban and middle class backgrounds, which greatly facilitate their economic assimilation within the city, they have come in such large numbers that they are not becoming residentially assimilated with the non-Latin population. Instead, through invasion and succession they are creating their own ethnic ghettoes, a fact which is proven in this study through use of the location quotient and indexes of dissimilarity. Miami's black population has always been isolated from both the Latin and non-Latin white populations. The city's major ethnic and family-cycle groups, however, have steadily become more isolated from the Latins since 1950. Furthermore, following the departure of these groups from neighborhoods invaded by Latins, they have relocated throughout the city in a way so that they are becoming increasingly more isolated from each other. 2 maps, 3 tables, 14 notes.   J

1311. Wolf, Eric R. REMARKS ON *THE PEOPLE OF PUERTO RICO. Revista/Review Interamericana [Puerto Rico] 1978 8(1): 17-25.* Julian H. Stewart, ed., *The People of Puerto Rico: A Study in Social Anthropology* (Urbana: U. of Illinois Pr., 1956) studied combinations of capital and labor on that island. It pioneered certain conceptual and methodological approaches that are only now bearing fruit. Secondary sources; 25 notes.   J. A. Lewis

1312. Wolff, Edward N. THE RATE OF SURPLUS VALUE IN PUERTO RICO. *J. of Pol. Econ. 1975 83(5): 935-949.* Puerto Rico's transformation from a preindustrial to an industrialized economy in the period 1948-63 provides an opportunity to measure the impact of technological change on several basic parameters in a Marxian economic framework. The rate of surplus value (estimated using the Morishima-Seton transformation) remains relatively stable at 0.97 in 1948 and 0.93 in 1963, while the organic composition falls from 2.75 to 2.09. The stability in the rate of surplus value results from a 63 percent average fall in labor values counterbalanced by a 143 percent rise in labor's consumption. The rate of surplus value, when adjusted for trade flows, jumps to 1.31 in 1948 and 1.18 in 1963, due to Puerto Rico's large balance-of-trade deficit and the relative import intensity of labor's consumption.   J

1313. Zapata, Carlos R. SITUACIÓN ECONÓMICA DE PUERTO RICO DURANTE EL GOBIERNO DE COALICION (ENERO 1933-ENERO 1941) [The economic situation of Puerto Rico during the coalition government: January 1933-January 1941]. *Horizontes [Puerto Rico] 1980 23(46): 47-64, 24(47): 49-75.* Part 1. Describes the political and economic situation of the island from the Jones Act of 1917 to 1933, noting the effects of American imperialism. The economic system did not make for a stable society or economy. Low subsistence wages barely allowed minimal conditions of existence. Coffee, sugar, and tobacco plantations were subject to the fluctuations of the weather and the buyer's market. A 62% population increase resulted in a series of social problems. Part 2. The effects of natural calamities and the economic depression changed the situation of the masses from deplorable to critical. The previous influx of capital into the sugar industry as well as construction and real estate vanished almost completely. The measures introduced by the New Deal failed, but the information obtained and the errors committed served as bases for future work.   J. V. Coutinho

1314. Zendegui, Guillermo de. CELEBRATING A HERITAGE. *Américas (Organization of Am. States) 1979 31(2): 13-15.* Describes the visible presence of Latin American culture and tradition in Miami, Florida, and the surrounding area in Dade County since recent immigration of large numbers of Cubans to Florida and increased trade with Latin America in the 1970's.

1315. —. THE ECONOMIC IMPORTANCE OF PUERTO RICO FOR THE UNITED STATES. *Latin Am. Perspectives 1976 3(3): 46-65.* This report from the Puerto Rican Socialist Party, translated by Scott Lubeck, analyzes Puerto Rico's crucial role in the US economy. Over 40 percent of all US direct investments is in Puerto Rico and 10 percent of the worldwide profits come from there. Puerto Rico is the fifth largest customer of US goods in the world and is the largest in per capita terms. Tables, charts.

J. L. Dietz

1316. —. [FLOTILLA ENTRANTS]. *Cuban Studies 1982 12(2): 81-85, 87-91.*
Peterson, Mark F. THE FLOTILLA ENTRANTS: SOCIAL PSYCHOLOGI-CAL PERSPECTIVES ON THEIR EMPLOYMENT, *pp. 81-85.*
Gamarra, Eduardo A. THE CONTINUING DILEMMA OF THE FREE-DOM FLOTILLA ENTRANTS, *pp. 87-91.*
Responds to R. L. Bach, J. B. Bach, and T. Triplett's "The Flotilla 'Entrants': Latest and Most Controversial." Discusses the Mariel immigrants' changes of integrating into the American job market. Based on interviews with Cuban refugees; 14 notes, table, biblio. J. A. Lewis

1317. —. [THE FLOTILLA IMMIGRANTS]. *Cuban Studies 1981-82 11-12(2-1): 29-54.*
Bach, Robert L., Bach, Jennifer B., and Triplett, Timothy. THE FLOTILLA "ENTRANTS": LATEST AND MOST CONTROVERSIAL, *pp. 29-48.* Despite popular reports to the contrary, most of the Mariel immigrants who left Cuba in 1980 for the United States came from the same background as earlier groups of Cuban immigrants.
Fernandez, Gaston A. COMMENT—THE FLOTILLA ENTRANTS: ARE THEY DIFFERENT?, *pp. 49-54.* Fernandez's own research supports the conclusion that the Mariel immigrants in 1980 were very similar in origin to earlier Cuban immigrants. The popular press judged the entire group from the small group of criminals and social deviants that also came in this exodus from Cuba. 7 tables, 21 notes. J. A. Lewis

1318. —. [INCORPORATION OF CUBAN EXILES]. *Cuban Studies 1981-82 11-12(2-1): 1-28.*
Portes, Alejandro; Clark, Juan M.; and López, Manuel M. SIX YEARS LATER, THE PROCESS OF INCORPORATION OF CUBAN EX-ILES IN THE UNITED STATES: 1973-1979, *pp. 1-24.* A six-year study of Cuban immigrants in Miami indicates that general assimilation has not taken place at a very fast rate because of the existence of a Cuban enclave that shelters its inhabitants from the outside world.
Rogg, Eleanor Meyer. COMMENT—SIX YEARS LATER, THE PROCESS OF INCORPORATION OF CUBAN EXILES IN THE UNITED STATES: 1973-1979, *pp. 25-28.* It is necessary to compare studies of Cuban immigration with recent studies of other immigrant groups in the United States—something Portes, Clark, and Lopez fail to do. 6 tables, 6 notes, biblio. J. A. Lewis

1319. —. [THE INFLUENCE OF ENGLISH IN PUERTO RICAN SPANISH]. *Rev. Interamericana Rev. [Puerto Rico] 1975 5(3): 347-358.*
Lipsky, John M. THE LANGUAGE BATTLE IN PUERTO RICO, *pp. 347-354.* A critique of two recent studies on Puerto Rican Spanish: Paulino Pérez Sala's *Interferncia lingüistica del inglés en el español hablado en Puerto Rico* (Hato Rey, Inter American U. Pr., 1971), and Arnaud Castel's "L'effritement de la langue et de la culture espagnoles à Porto-Rico," (Dissertation, U. de Paris-Sorbonne, 1974). The author questions whether the methodology of either of these two works has successfully measured the influence of English upon the island's language. 7 notes.
Castel, Arnaud. REPLY TO LIPSKI, *pp. 354-355.*
Pérez Sala, Paulino. RÉPLICA A LIPSKI, *pp. 355-358.*   J. A. Lewis

1320. —. THE MARIEL FLOTILLA AGAIN. *Cuban Studies 1984 14(1): 49-56.*
Fernández, Gastón A. CONFLICTING INTERPRETATIONS OF THE FREEDOM FLOTILLA ENTRANTS, *pp. 49-51.* An earlier study by Eduardo A. Gamarra, "Comment: The Continuing Dilemma of the Freedom Flotilla Entrants," in *Cuban Studies,* 12(2): 87-91, overemphasized the adjustment problems of the Mariel immigrants of 1980. Most already have or shortly will adjust to American life successfully. 15 notes.
Gamarra, Eduardo A. REPLY TO GASTON A. FERNANDEZ, *pp. 53-56.* Although most Mariel immigrants will integrate into American society, this process has been slow and complicated by racial difficulties. 8 notes.
                                                                J. A. Lewis

1321. —. THE MIGRANTS. *Wilson Q. 1980 4(2): 141-146.* Examines the makeup of immigrants to the United States from Puerto Rico between 1909 and 1977, finding that the migration, which was at its height in the 1950's, has dwindled, and that the number of migrants returning to the island has steadily increased and taxed Puerto Rico's economy.

1322. —. [POLITICS OF EXILE]. *Cuban Studies 1981-82 11-12(2-1): 55-78.*
Azicri, Max. THE POLITICS OF EXILE: TRENDS AND DYNAMICS OF POLITICAL CHANGE AMONG CUBAN AMERICANS, *pp. 55-73.* The Cuban community in the United States has gone through four distinct political stages in its relations with its mother country. At present, the predominant sentiment among Cuban Americans toward Castro's Cuba closely reflects the conservative mood of President Reagan's administration.
Baloyra, Enrique A. COMMENT—MAKING WAVES: A VIEW OF THE CUBAN COMMUNITY IN THE U.S., *pp. 75-78.* Azicri adds nothing new to the scholarship on the politics of the Cuban community in the United States. Table, 32 notes.   J. A. Lewis

1323. —. [PUERTO RICAN CULTURAL IDENTITY]. *Rev. Interamericana [Puerto Rico] 1975 5(2): 170-196.*

Fernández, Frank et al. COMMENTS ON DR. MEAD'S INTERVIEW, *pp. 170-181.*

Laguerre, Enrique A. SOBRE LA IDENTIDAD CULTURAL PUERTOR-RIQUEÑA [Concerning Puerto Rican cultural identity], *pp. 182-187.*

Babín, María Teresa. ALGUNAS OBSERVACIONES SOBRE LA INTREVISTA A MARGARET MEAD [Some observations on the Margaret Mead interview], *pp. 188-189.*

Newman, Katherine D. ON BEING AN AMERICAN IN PUERTO RICO, *pp. 190-196.*

Comments on an earlier interview printed in *Rev. Interamericana* 5(1): 1975 which is translated in this issue, pp. 163-169. Most of the commentators do not question Dr. Mead's credentials as an anthropologist, but they do not believe she is very knowledgeable about the island. Some of the problems that Puerto Ricans face outside their country are encountered by Americans in Puerto Rico.   J. A. Lewis

1324.   —. [PUERTO RICAN INDEPENDENCE]. *Caribbean Rev. 1979 8(2): 15-21, 56-59.*

Berríos Martínez, Rubén. INDEPENDENCE FOR PUERTO RICO: THE ONLY SOLUTION, *pp. 15-21, 56-59.*

Benítez, Jaime. A RESPONSE TO BERRÍOS, *p. 21.*

While it is possible to argue from historical, political, and economic factors going back to 1898 that independence for Puerto Rico is the only way in which the island will gain control over its own destiny, the fact remains that since 1956 the people have shown little eagerness (8% at most) for independence, apparently believing that the present Commonwealth status (Estado Libre Asociado) offers Puerto Rico more stability and prosperity than any of the other choices now available.

1325.   —. PUERTO RICANS. Sowell, Thomas, ed. *Essays and Data on American Ethnic Groups* (Washington, D.C.: Urban Inst. Pr., 1978): 380-397. Statistics on Puerto Ricans' personal income by age, education, and sex; personal earnings by occupation, education, and sex; family income distribution by number of income earners per family; family income by age, education, and sex of family head; family earnings by number of income earners, education, and sex of family head; and fertility rates by woman's education and family income. From 1970 US Census Public Use Sample and *Current Population Reports,* Series P-20, Nos. 213, 244; 5 tables.   K. A. Talley

SUBJECT INDEX

In ABC-CLIO's Subject Profile Index (ABC-SPIndex), each index entry is a complete profile of the abstract and consists of one or more subject, geographic, and biographic terms followed by the dates covered in the article. The index terms are rotated so the complete subject profile is cited under each of the terms. No particular relationship between any two terms in the profile is implied; terms within the profile are listed in alphabetical order following the first term. Cities, towns, and countries are listed following their respective states or provinces; e.g., Ohio (Columbus). Terms beginning with an arabic numeral are listed after the letter Z. Cross-references in the form of *See* and *See also* references are provided. In the chronological designation, "c" stands for "century"; i.e., "19c" means "19th century."

The last number, in italics, in each individual index profile refers to the entry number in the book.

A

Academic achievement. Acculturation. California (Los Angeles). High schools. 1975-76. *1030*
—. Attitudes. California (San Francisco). High schools. 1974-75. *796*
Acadians. Colonial Government. Letters. Louisiana. Refugees. Spain. Ulloa, Antonio de. 1766-68. *178*
Acculturation. Academic achievement. California (Los Angeles). High schools. 1975-76. *1030*
—. Attitudes. Cuba. Cubans. Revolution. 1958-82. *1074*
—. Bilingualism. Economic Conditions. 1848-1977. *482*
—. California (Santa Clara County). Marriage. Rites and Ceremonies. 1908-68. *421*
—. Children. Political integration. Texas (El Paso). 1978. *881*
—. Church Schools. Public Schools. Texas (San Antonio). 1973. *882*
—. Cubans. Drug abuse. Immigration. Social Customs. Values. Youth. 1950-80. *1237*
—. Economic Conditions. Hawaii. Immigrants. Puerto Ricans. 1900-02. *1287*
—. Family. Mental illness. New York City. Puerto Ricans. Social Organization. 1950's-70's. *1271*
—. Immigrants. Interviews. Puerto Ricans. 1982. *1134*
—. Immigration. Labor. Literature. 1830-1983. *443*
—. Kansas (Dodge City). 20c. *449*
—. Laviera, Tato (*La Carreta Made a U-Turn*). Poetry. Puerto Ricans. 1979-80. *1151*
—. Pocho (term). Social Status. Southwest. 1910's-40's. *657*
—. Stress. Women. Workers, undocumented. 1977. *918*
—. Utah. 1910-80. *451*
Acosta, Oscar Zeta (*Autobiography of a Brown Buffalo*). Ethnicity. Novels. Rivera, Tomás (*Y No Se Lo Tragó La Tierra*). Villareal, José Antonia (*Pocho*). 1970-79. *1054*
Acosta Rodríquez, Antonio. Census. Colonial Government. Historiography. Louisiana. Spain. 1763-1803. 1976-80. *242*

Administration for the Development of Art and Culture. Bureaucracies. Legislation. Musicians. New Progressive Party. Puerto Rico. 1980. *1284*
Adolescence. Bilingualism. Border towns. California. English language. Spanish language. 1970-79. *698*
—. Blacks. California (Los Angeles). Self-concept. Whites. 1971. *863*
Adolescents. Identity. Mexico. Puerto Rico. USA. 1970's. *1159*
Adventists. Education. Missions and Missionaries. New Mexico (Sandoval). Spanish-American Seminary. 1928-53. *679*
Advertising. Art. Cigars. Cubans. Florida (Tampa). 1868-1930's. *1307*
Age. Blacks. Discrimination. Income. Texas. 1960-70. *926*
—. Economic conditions. Fertility. Puerto Rico. Social Status. Women. 1970. *1182*
—. Education. Ethnicity. Family. New York City. Puerto Ricans. 1958-79. *1270*
Aged. California. Social Policy. Whites. 1978-82. *850*
—. Public Policy. 1970-79. *795*
Agricultural Industry. California. Elections. Labor Unions and Organizations. Proposition 14 (1976). United Farm Workers Union. 1976. *773*
Agricultural Labor. *See also* Migrant labor.
—. Aliens, illegal. Attitudes. Bracero Program. Labor Unions and Organizations. Mexico. 1943-74. *889*
—. Aliens, Illegal. Economic opportunity. Immigration. "Push/pull" hypothesis. 1948-72. *866*
—. Beets. Great Western Sugar Company. Housing. Wyoming (Lovell). 1916-54. *671*
—. Berry pickers. California (El Monte). Foreign Relations. Japan. Mexico. Strikes. 1933. *645*
—. Bracero Program. Employment. Southwest. Wages. 1954-77. *869*
—. California. Chavez, Cesar. Strikes. United Farm Workers Union. 1965-70. *723*
—. California. Government regulation. Hoes. 1968-75. *936*
—. California. Labor law. 1965-76. *764*

—. California. United Cannery, Agricultural, Packing and Allied Workers of America. 1937-40. *667*

—. California. United Farm Workers Union. 1960's-76. *810*

—. California (Colusa County). Farms. 1950-69. *930*

—. California (Oxnard). Japanese-Mexican Labor Association. Strikes. Sugar beets. Wages. 1902-03. *602*

—. California (San Joaquin Valley). Japanese. Nisei Farmers League. United Farm Workers Union. 1971-77. *812*

—. California, University of, Berkeley. Economics. Newlands Act (US, 1902). Taylor, Paul S. 1895-1980. *494*

—. California Women Farmworkers Project. Oral history. Women. 1870's-1970's. *73*

—. Indians. Population. Spain. Texas (El Paso). 1680-1784. *362*

—. Labor Unions and Organizations. 1900-79. *448*

—. Migration, Internal. New Mexico (North Central). Social Change. 1930-50. *888*

—. Southwest. 1971-81. *862*

Agricultural Labor Relations Act (California, 1975). California. Emergency Farm Labor Supply Program. Labor law. New Deal. ca 1930-79. *434*

Agricultural Production. Haciendas. Mills. Puerto Rico, southwestern. Sugar. 1902. *1306*

Agricultural Technology and Research. Assimilation. California. Indians. Mission San Antonio de Padua. Salinan Indians. 1771-1832. 1976-79. *244*

Agriculture. Boycotts. California. Chavez, Cesar. Grapes. International Brotherhood of Teamsters. Labor Unions and Organizations. Lettuce. United Farm Workers Union. 1962-74. *805*

—. Bracero program. Mexico. President's Commission on Migratory Labor. Truman, Harry S. Workers, undocumented. 1950. *876*

—. California. Chavez, Cesar. Elections. Proposition 14 (1976). United Farm Workers Union. 1975-76. *996*

—. Documents. Economic Conditions. Migrant Labor. Social Conditions. Working conditions. 1942-45. *694*

—. Economic Conditions. Industrialization. Puerto Rico. 1960's-70's. *1126*

—. Economic Conditions. Puerto Rico. Social Organization. 1870-1930. *1083*

—. Indians. Irrigation. Mexican Americans. New Mexico. Pueblo Indians. 19c. *357*

Aguirre, Martin. California (Los Angeles County). Law enforcement. 1880's-1929. *545*

Airplanes. Cuba. Deportation. Hijacking. International law. Refugees. 1983. *1191*

Alabama. Bouchfouca, Treaty of. Choctaw Indians. Indian-White Relations. Spain. Villebeuvre, Juan de la. 1793. *243*

Alamo (battle). DelaPeña, José Enrique. Personal Narratives. Santa Anna, Antonio Lopez de. Texas. 1836. *195*

—. Historians. Legends. 19c. *453*

—. Mexico. Texas. 1836. *306*

—. Texas (Nacogdoches). 1836. 1975. *367*

Alarcón, Hernando. California. Colorado River. Discovery and Exploration. Indians. 1540. *207*

Alazan-Apache Courts. Public housing. Texas (San Antonio). 1930-44. *693*

Albuquerque, Duke of (Francisco Fernández de la Cueva Henríquez). Colonial Government. Mexico. New Mexico. Politics. Social Problems. 1702-11. *318*

Alienation. Southwest. 20c. *476*

Aliens. Immigration. Labor. Public policy. 1970's. *965*

Aliens, illegal. *See also* Workers, undocumented.

—. Agricultural Labor. Attitudes. Bracero Program. Labor Unions and Organizations. Mexico. 1943-74. *889*

—. Agricultural Labor. Economic opportunity. Immigration. "Push/pull" hypothesis. 1948-72. *866*

—. Attitudes. Social Psychology. 1984. *722*

—. Bracero Program. Immigration. Mexico. Quota systems. 1960's-70's. *1007*

—. Carter, Jimmy. Federal Policy. Immigration. 1977-78. *760*

—. Carter, Jimmy. Reagan, Ronald. 1977-81. *49*

—. Civil rights. Constitutional Law. 1970-77. *813*

—. Congress. Economic conditions. Immigration. Public Policy. 1978. *91*

—. Economic Conditions. Mexico. USA. 1946-65. *807*

—. Economic Conditions. Stereotypes. 1930-76. *452*

—. Federal Policy. Immigration and Nationality Act (US, 1965). 1956-75. *124*

—. Immigration. Labor. Population. 1970-80. *142*

—. Immigration. Mexico. Statistics. 1978-79. *750*

—. Interviews. Methodology. 1975-81. *772*

—. Labor. Statistics. 1968-80. *107*

—. Labor Unions and Organizations. 1980-83. *786*

—. Mexico. Research. 1930-76. *422*

—. Mexico. Workers, undocumented. 1930-77. *747*

—. Migrant Labor. Oregon (Hood River Valley). Wages. 1978. *777*

—. Research. 1975-77. *751*

Alvarado, Pedro de. Cabrillo, Juan Rodríguez. Colonial Government. Discovery and Exploration. Mendoza, Antonio de. New Spain. Printing press. 1515-52. *158*

Alvarez, Manuel. Commerce. Consular service. Mexico. New Mexico (Santa Fe). 1818-47. *180*

—. Diplomacy. Mexico. New Mexico. Texas. Trading expeditions. 1841. *181*

Amalgamated Clothing Workers Union of America. Farah Manufacturing Company. Garment industry. Strikes. Texas (El Paso). 1972-74. *800*

American dream. Blacks. Identity. Indians. 1890-1980. *25*

American Federation of Labor. Gompers, Samuel. Iglesias Pantín, Santiago. Labor Unions and Organizations. Puerto Rico. 1897-1920's. *1155*

American G.I. Forum. League of United Latin American Citizens. Mexican American Legal Defense and Education Fund. Pressure Groups. School integration. Texas. 1945-80. *981*

—. Public schools. School Integration. Texas. 1948-57. *701*

American history. Colleges and Universities. History Teaching. Mexican Americans. Textbooks. 20c. *53*

—. Textbooks. 1975-80. *36*

American Political Science Association. Colleges and Universities. Political science. Western states. 1970-74. *1058*

American Revolution. Bouligny, Francisco. Letters. Louisiana. Settlement. Spain. 1776-78. *200*

—. International Trade. Puerto Rico. 1775-1854. *1210*

Americanization. Bhana, Surendra. Clark, Truman. Development. Matthews, Thomas. Politics. Puerto Rico (review article). 1917-76. *1261*

—. California (Santa Barbara). Social Change. Urbanization. 1850-70's. *599*

—. Employment. Immigration. Industry. Public schools. 1880-1930. *624*

—. Missions and Missionaries. Protestant Churches. Puerto Rico. 1898-1917. *1239*

Americas (North and South). Colonization. Discovery and Exploration. Europe. Myths and Symbols. Utopianism. 16c-18c. *225*

—. Colonization. Discovery and exploration. Spain. Vega, Lope de *(San Diego de Alcalá).* 17c-18c. *342*

—. Discovery and Exploration. LasCasas, Bartolomé de. Settlement. 16c-17c. *276*

—. Europeans. Indian-White Relations. 1493-1888. *198*

—. Indians. Sepúlveda, Juan Ginés de. Slavery. Spain. ca 1550. *216*

Anaya, Toney. Elections. New Mexico. 1968-82. *1031*

Andrade, Flores de. Immigration. Liberal Party. Mexico. Personal narratives. Revolutionary Movements. Texas (El Paso). 1890-1911. *621*

Anecdotes. Baca, Father. Easter Week. Frontier and Pioneer Life. New Mexico (Tome, Valencia). Rites and Ceremonies. 1846. *209*

Angel, Frank W. Corruption. New Mexico. Violence. Wallace, Lew. 1878. *591*

Angeles et al. v. Santa Barbara School District et al. (California, 1981). California (Santa Barbara). Children. Public Schools (closures). 1981-83. *1025*

Anglo (character). Literature. Sanchez, Saul (review article). Villains. 1970's. *953*

Anglos. *See* Whites.

Animals, domestic. Arizona. Excavations. Mission San Xavier del Bac. 17c-19c. 1974. *311*

Annexation. Diplomacy. Eve, Joseph. Flood, George H. LaBranche, Alcée. Letters. Murphy, William S. Texas. 1837-43. *162*

—. Minorities. 16c-20c. *103*

Anthropologists. Hostos, Adolfo de (interview). Puerto Rico. 1974. *1179*

Anthropology. Borderlands studies. Mexico. Sociology. Southwest. 20c. *114*

—. Ecology. Methodology. New Mexico (northern). Social organization. Trade. 17c-20c. *63*

—. Puerto Rico. Steward, Julian H. *(People of Puerto Rico).* 1956-77. *1223*

Anthropology, applied. Arizona, southern. Project Fiesta. Television, public. 1976. *794*

Anthropology, Cultural. Economic Conditions. Methodology. Puerto Rico. Steward, Julian H. *(People of Puerto Rico).* 1956-77. *1311*

—. Economic Development. Methodology. Puerto Rico. Steward, Julian H. *(People of Puerto Rico).* 1956-77. *1272*

—. Ideology. Methodology. Puerto Rico. Steward, Julian H. *(People of Puerto Rico).* 1956-77. *1144*

—. Imperialism. Puerto Rico. Steward, Julian H. *(People of Puerto Rico).* 1956-77. *1299*

—. Power structure. Puerto Rico. Steward, Julian H. *(People of Puerto Rico).* 1956-77. *1260*

Anti-Mexican sentiments. British North America. Hispanophobia. 17c-19c. *315*

Antiwar sentiment. Expansionism. Mexican War (review article). Pletcher, David M. Polk, James K. Schroeder, John H. 1830's-40's. *199*

Anton Chico grant. Land grants. New Mexico Land and Livestock Company. Rivera, Manuel. Trials. 1822-1915. *334*

Antonia (Indian). Calusa Indians. Carlos (chief). Florida. Indian-White Relations. Marriage. Menéndez de Avilés, Pedro. Politics. 1566-69. *327*

Anza, Juan Bautista de. Bicentennial Celebrations. California. Discovery and Exploration. Mexico. Reenactments. 1775-76. 1975-76. *208*

—. Colonial Government. Concha, Fernando Simon Ignacio de la. Indians. Military Strategy. New Mexico. Spain. 1787-93. *161*

Apache Indians. Indians. Mexico (Mexico City). Removals, forced. Southwest. Spain. 1729-1809. *300*

Apache Indians (Gila, Mimbres). Concha, Fernando Simon Ignacio de la. Diaries. Indian Wars. 1788. *213*

Apodaca, Jerry. Democratic Party. Elections (gubernatorial). New Mexico. Race Relations. 1974. *1032*

Apportionment. Congress. Political Power. 1980-83. *123*

Aqueducts. California Polytechnic State University, San Luis Obispo. Excavations. Mission San Antonio de Padua. Spanish. 1776. 1979-81. *245*

Architecture. Arizona (Tucson). Churches. Mexico (Sonora; Caborca). Mission Nuestra Señora de la Purísima Concepción del Caborca. Mission San Xavier del Bac. 1975. *228*

—. Artisans. Churches. Missions and Missionaries. Texas (San Antonio). 18c. *338*

—. California. Franciscans. Mission San Juan Capistrano. 1776-1976. *163*

—. Housing. Indians. *Jacal* (style). New Mexico (Tierra Amarilla). Spaniards. Wood. 8c-20c. *366*

—. Log structures. New Mexico. 1756-1970's. *43*

—. Ranching. Texas, southern. 1750-1900. *332*

Archival Catalogs and Inventories. California. Mexico. 1535-1821. *72*

—. Historical Archive of the Secretary of Foreign Relations. Mexico (Mexico City). 1900-39. *13*

Archives. Puerto Rico. Spain. 1500-1975. *110*

Archivo General de Indias. Colonial Government. Military Finance. New Mexico. Spain (Seville). Treasury. 1596-1683. *337*

Archuleta, Eppie. Colorado (San Luis Valley). Folk art. Personal Narratives. Women. 1922-79. *460*

Areíto, Grupo. Cubans. History Task Force. Immigration. Johnson, Roberta Ann. Puerto Ricans. 1960's-70's. *1226*

Aristocracy. Colonial Government. New Mexico. New Spain. Settlement. 16c. *182*

Arizona. Animals, domestic. Excavations. Mission San Xavier del Bac. 17c-19c. 1974. *311*

—. Ballads. Capital Punishment. "Corrido de los Hermanos" (ballad). Hernández, Federico. Hernández, Manuel. 1934. *683*

—. Benevolent organizations. Liga Protectora Latina. 1914-40. *658*

—. Business. California. Redondo, José María. Territorial Government. 1849-78. *592*

—. Cattle raising. Ranching. 1853-1910. *510*

—. Copper industry. Labor Unions and Organizations. Politics. Racism. Working Class. 1900-20. *611*

—. Elections. School boards. Voting and Voting Behavior. 1972-74. *817*

—. Gándara, Francisco. McFarland, William. Race Relations. Violence. Whites. 1872-73. *578*

—. Immigration. Mexican Revolution. Refugees. 1910-11. *669*

—. Indians. Jesuits. Kino, Eusebio Francisco. Missions and Missionaries. Spain. 1680's-1711. *271*

—. New Spain (Sonora; Real de Arizonac). Silver. 1736. *236*

Arizona (Canyon de Chelly). Bones. Dogs. Indian Wars. Navajo Indians. Pictographs. Spain. 1750-1863. *202*

Arizona (Casa Grande). Bolton, Herbert Eugene. Explorers. Kino, Eusebio Francisco. 1697. 1934. 1968-72. *250*

Arizona, central. Cohabitation. Mining towns. Whites. 1863-73. *548*

Arizona (Clifton-Morenci area). Copper Mines and Mining. Mexico. Migrant Labor. Strikes. 1872-1903. *572*

Arizona (Nogales). Borders. Foreign relations. García, Jesús. Mexico (Sonora). 1893-96. *529*

—. Excavations. Jesuits. Mission Guevavi. 18c. 1964-66. *333*

Arizona (Phoenix). Poverty. Public Welfare. 1870-1973. *475*

Arizona, southern. Anthropology, applied. Project Fiesta. Television, public. 1976. *794*

—. Mission San Cayetano del Tumacacori. Mission San Xavier del Bac. Spain. 18c. 1979. *400*

Arizona State Museum. Documentary Relations of the Southwest project. Indians. Mexico, northern. Southwest. Spain. 16c-1810. 1975-78. *322*

Arizona (Tucson). Architecture. Churches. Mexico (Sonora; Caborca). Mission Nuestra Señora de la Purísima Concepción del Caborca. Mission San Xavier del Bac. 1975. *228*

—. California (Los Angeles). Economic conditions. Racism. Social Conditions. Texas (San Antonio). 1850-1900. *528*

—. California (Los Angeles). Occupations. Property. Social Customs. 1775-1880. *543*

—. Dancers. Musicians. Popular Culture. 1892-1982. *682*

—. Editors and Editing. *El Fronterizo*. Elites. Velasco, Carlos. 1865-1914. *536*

—. Elites. 1850-80. *583*

Arizona (Tucson Basin). Ceramics. Excavations. Settlement. 1690's-1856. *157*

Armies. Bounties. Land warrants. Mexican War. 1800-61. *309*

—. California. Colonial Government. Mexico. 1822-46. *257*

—. California (Los Angeles, San Diego). Mexico. Presidios. Spain. 1770-94. *283*

—. Indians. Spain. 1561-1886. *204*

Armijo, Manuel. Colorado. Land grants. 1823-1900. *354*

—. Government. New Mexico. 1827-46. *274*

—. Kendall, George Wilkins. New Mexico. 1842-44. *275*

—. Mexico. New Mexico. Provincial Government. Texas. 1827-46. *371*

Armijo, Salvador. Charities. New Mexico (Albuquerque). Poor. 1874. *515*

Art. Advertising. Cigars. Cubans. Florida (Tampa). 1868-1930's. *1307*

—. Bibliographies. Civil Rights. Literature. Mexican Americans. Southwest. 1936-73. *96*

—. California. Catholic Church. Cultural myopia (Anglo-American). Missions and Missionaries. Scholasticism. 1740's-1976. *307*

—. California (East Los Angeles). Mechicano Art Center. Murals. 1970's. *759*

—. California (East Los Angeles). Murals. Social Conditions. 1970-75. *872*

—. California (East Los Angeles). Murals. Values. 1978. *1052*

—. California (Los Angeles). Ethnicity. Murals. 1970's. *998*

—. Culture. Ethnicity. Murals. 1960's-80. *714*

—. Culture. Institute of Puerto Rican Culture. Muñoz Marín, Luis. Puerto Rico. Romero Barceló, Carlos. 1948-55. *1277*

Artisans. Architecture. Churches. Missions and Missionaries. Texas (San Antonio). 18c. *338*

Artists. California (East Los Angeles, Boyle Heights). Murals. 1965-75. *860*

—. Minorities in Politics. Murals. 1970's. *791*

Arts. New Rican Village. New York City. Puerto Ricans. 1960's-78. *1273*

—. Performing arts. Texas. 19c. *576*

Arts and Crafts. Depressions. New Mexico. 1846-1930's. *505*

Ascensión, Antonio de la. California. Discovery and Exploration. Mexico. Vizcaíno, Sebastian. Voyages. 1590-1737. *285*

Asians. Blacks. Education. Ethnicity. Immigrants. Occupational mobility. 1965-70. *99*

Asociación Nacional México-Americana. Civil Rights. Pressure Groups. 1949-54. *1021*

Assimilation. Agricultural Technology and Research. California. Indians. Mission San Antonio de Padua. Salinan Indians. 1771-1832. 1976-79. *244*

—. Attitudes. Bilingualism. New York City. Puerto Ricans. Working class. 1979. *1073*

—. Attitudes. Puerto Ricans. 1975. *1264*

—. Barrios. Community development. 1848-80. *539*

—. Bilingual education. Blacks. California (San Jose). Race Relations. School integration. 1950-79. *768*

—. Blacks. Immigration. West Indies. 1898-1979. *1195*

—. Blacks. Residential segregation. Social Status. Whites. 1960-70. *70*

—. California (Los Angeles). Exiles. Lozano, Ignacio. Newspapers. *Opinión*. 1926-29. *660*

—. Cubans. 1959-83. *1154*

—. Cubans. Ethnicity. Exiles. 1959-76. *1165*

—. Cubans. Exiles. Federal Policy. Mexicans. 1959-81. *138*

—. Cubans. Exiles. Florida (Miami). 1973-79. *1318*

—. Cubans. Refugees. 1980-83. *1320*

—. Cubans. Refugees. Research. 1959-83. *1268*

—. Elementary Education. Texas (San Antonio). 1973. *883*

—. Ethnic identity. Intermarriage. Texas (San Antonio). Women. 1830-60. *530*

—. Ethnicity. Institutions. Political activism. Students. Texas (Corpus Christi, Crystal City). 1969-80. *753*

—. Family. Geographic mobility. Immigrants. Social status. 1890-1977. *1015*

—. Fertility. Puerto Ricans. Social Status. 1969-77. *1120*

—. Glazer, Nathan. Moynihan, Daniel P. New York. Puerto Ricans (review article). 20c. *1265*

—. Immigrants. Labor. Men. 1960's-76. *733*

—. Jews. Mexico (Nuevo Reyno de León). Texas. 16c-20c. *483*

—. Literature. Social Customs. Villareal, José Antonio *(Pocho)*. 1959-76. *743*

—. Middle Classes. Socialization. Texas. 1976. *1013*

—. Models. New York City. Puerto Ricans. Segregation, residential. 1960-70. *1274*

—. New Mexico. Social Customs. Villages. 1960's-79. *962*

—. New Mexico. Spain. 16c-19c. 1970's. *150*

—. Social Mobility. 1945-80. *946*

—. Wisconsin (Riverside). 1973-75. *1044*

Assimilation (review article). Calvo Buezas, Tomás. Villanueva, Tino. 19c-20c. *405*

Athapascan Indians. Indians. Indian-White Relations. Missions and Missionaries. New Mexico. Pueblo Indians. 1600-80. *220*

Atrisco grant. Land grants. New Mexico. New Spain. Pueblo Revolt (1680). 1680-1977. *454*

Attitudes. Academic achievement. California (San Francisco). High schools. 1974-75. *796*

—. Acculturation. Cuba. Cubans. Revolution. 1958-82. *1074*

—. Agricultural Labor. Aliens, illegal. Bracero Program. Labor Unions and Organizations. Mexico. 1943-74. *889*

—. Aliens, illegal. Social Psychology. 1984. *722*

—. Assimilation. Bilingualism. New York City. Puerto Ricans. Working class. 1979. *1073*

—. Assimilation. Puerto Ricans. 1975. *1264*

—. Barrios. California, southern. Civil Rights. Police. Social Conditions. 1975. *927*

—. Bilingual Education. Children. Curricula. Parents. 1960's-70's. *902*

—. Blacks. Earthquakes. Whites. 1977. *1020*

—. Blacks. Education. Immigration. Wisconsin (Racine). 1974. *993*

—. Blacks. Newspapers. Television. Texas (Lubbock). 1976. *1010*

—. Blacks. Puerto Rico. 1950's-70's. *1219*
—. California (Los Angeles). Fertility. Women. 1973-82. *978*
—. California (Los Angeles). High schools. Truancy. 1974-75. *845*
—. California (San Diego). Migration. Workers, undocumented. 1984. *896*
—. Californios. Europeans. Travel accounts. 1780's-1840's. *269*
—. Californios. Europeans. Travel accounts. 1780's-1840's. *396*
—. Children. Public Schools. 1981. *973*
—. Community Schools. Ethnic identity. Students. 1974. *855*
—. Cubans. Refugees. 1980. *1190*
—. Cubans. Refugees. Working Conditions. 1970-81. *1148*
—. Diaries. Discrimination. New Mexico. Women. 1840's-50's. *593*
—. Discrimination. Family. Personal narratives. Professions. Success. Women. 1980. *997*
—. Employment. Sex roles. Whites. Women. Youth. 1979. *88*
—. English language. Popular Culture. Spanish language. Theater. 1970's. *1022*
—. Films. 1908-79. *498*
—. Generations. Marriage. 1981-82. *910*
—. Identity. New Mexico. -1974. *919*
—. Language (dialects). 1975. *802*
—. Minorities. Texas (Houston). -1973. *779*
—. Mothers. New Mexico (Albuquerque). Sex roles. Women. 1960-83. *1050*
—. New Mexico. Spanish-American War. 1898-1900. *564*
—. Workers, undocumented. 1980-82. *921*
Authors. Autobiographies. Blacks. New York City. Prisons. Puerto Ricans. Thomas, Piri. 1950-80. *1224*
—. Daily Life. Steinbeck, John. 20c. *463*
—. Jiménez, Juan Ramón. Memoirs. Nobel Prize. Palau de Nemes, Graciela. Puerto Rico (Ponce). Spain. 1930's-56. *1113*
—. Literature. 1974. *744*
—. New Mexico. Nichols, John. Social Conditions. Spaniards. 1841-1979. *499*
—. New Mexico. Racism. Stereotypes. 19c. *562*
Autobiographies. Authors. Blacks. New York City. Prisons. Puerto Ricans. Thomas, Piri. 1950-80. *1224*
Autonomy. National Guard. Puerto Rico. 1898-1978. *1128*
Ayala, Juan Manuel de. California (San Francisco Bay). Discovery and Exploration. Franciscans. Indians. Spain. 1775. *369*

B

Baca, Elfego. Law Enforcement. New Mexico (Socorro). 1865-1919. *580*
Baca, Father. Anecdotes. Easter Week. Frontier and Pioneer Life. New Mexico (Tome, Valencia). Rites and Ceremonies. 1846. *209*
Baca, Felipe. Colorado (Trinidad). Personal narratives. 1862-74. *512*
Ballads. Arizona. Capital Punishment. "Corrido de los Hermanos" (ballad). Hernández, Federico. Hernández, Manuel. 1934. *683*
—. "Corrido de Gregorio Cortez" (ballad). "Discriminación a un Martir" (ballad). Political Protest. Social change. Texas (Three River). 20c. *468*
Balseiro, José Agustín. Florida (review article). Lyon, Eugene. Menéndez de Avilés, Pedro. Spain. 1513-1977. *184*
Bandits. Big Bend region. Langhorne, George T. Mexico (Coahuila). Punitive expeditions. Texas (Glenn Springs, Boquillas). 1915-16. *687*

Baptists. Costas, Orlando E. Ecumenism. Personal narratives. 1980. *21*
Baptists (Southern). 1839-1970's. *40*
Barceló, Carlos Romero. Elections (gubernatorial). Government. Hernández, Rafael. Puerto Rico. 1980. *1193*
Barceló, Gertrudis. Business. Elites. Gambling. New Mexico (Santa Fe). Women. 1830's-40's. *273*
Barreda, Gabino. Mexico. Philosophy. Positivism. Values. 1860's-1982. *444*
Barrios. Assimilation. Community development. 1848-80. *539*
—. Attitudes. California, southern. Civil Rights. Police. Social Conditions. 1975. *927*
—. California (East Los Angeles). Community Participation in Politics. 1970-73. *1017*
—. Family. Housing. Relocation, forced. -1973. *1006*
—. New York (Long Island). Photographic essays. Puerto Ricans. Suburbs. 1981. *1275*
Beets. Agricultural Labor. Great Western Sugar Company. Housing. Wyoming (Lovell). 1916-54. *671*
Behavior. Bilingualism. Politics. 1970-75. *948*
—. Cultural heritage. Mexico. 16c-20c. *455*
—. Drugs. High schools. Puerto Rico. Youth. 1970-80. *1263*
—. Generations. Religion. Texas (San Antonio). 1981-82. *909*
—. Medical care. Stereotypes. 1940's-70's. *797*
Benevolent organizations. Arizona. Liga Protectora Latina. 1914-40. *658*
Bernal, Juan Pablo. Business. California. Cattle Raising. Land disputes. Wealth. 1822-78. *426*
Berry pickers. Agricultural Labor. California (El Monte). Foreign Relations. Japan. Mexico. Strikes. 1933. *645*
Bhana, Surendra. Americanization. Clark, Truman. Development. Matthews, Thomas. Politics. Puerto Rico (review article). 1917-76. *1261*
Bhana, Surendra (review article). Political Systems. Puerto Rico. 1936-68. 1975. *1293*
Bibliographies. Art. Civil Rights. Literature. Mexican Americans. Southwest. 1936-73. *96*
—. Bilingual education. Elementary Education. 1970's. *19*
—. Bilingual education. Language. 20c. *17*
—. Cubans. Florida (Miami). Immigration. 20c. *79*
—. Dialects. Espinosa, Aurelio M. Folklore. New Mexico, northern. Spain. 1907-54. *31*
—. *Diario del Gobierno de la República Mexicana.* Periodicals. Texas. 1836-45. *75*
—. Educational policy. Energy crisis. Foreign Relations. Middle East. National Autonomous University of Mexico (Faculty of Political and Social Sciences). Periodicals. Social Conditions. 1970-81. *7*
—. English Language. Literature. Puerto Rico. 1923-73. *80*
—. History. Literature. Mexican Americans. Women. 1519-1976. *115*
—. Information storage and retrieval systems. Mental Health Research Center. 1971-79. *132*
—. Land grants. New Mexico. 1851-1981. *85*
—. Libraries. Mexican Americans. 1960's-70's. *131*
—. Mass media. Mexican Americans. Periodicals. 1970's. *24*
—. Mexican Americans. Social sciences. 20c. *101*
—. Mexican Americans. Women. 1970-80. *64*
—. Mexico. Southwest. 1821-45. *126*
—. Proverbs. 1913-80. *6*
—. Puerto Ricans. 20c. *66*
—. Spain. Texas. 16c-20c. *76*
Bibliographies (review article). Meier, Matt S. Rivera, Feliciano. 1974. *487*

Bicentennial Celebrations. Anza, Juan Bautista de. California. Discovery and Exploration. Mexico. Reenactments. 1775-76. 1975-76. *208*
Biculturalism. Bilingual education. Cubans. New Jersey. Puerto Ricans. 19c-20c. *1101*
Big Bend region. Bandits. Langhorne, George T. Mexico (Coahuila). Punitive expeditions. Texas (Glenn Springs, Boquillas). 1915-16. *687*
Bilingual education. 1970's. *122*
—. 1970's. *880*
—. Assimilation. Blacks. California (San Jose). Race Relations. School integration. 1950-79. *768*
—. Attitudes. Children. Curricula. Parents. 1960's-70's. *902*
—. Bibliographies. Elementary Education. 1970's. *19*
—. Bibliographies. Language. 20c. *17*
—. Biculturalism. Cubans. New Jersey. Puerto Ricans. 19c-20c. *1101*
—. California (Los Angeles County). 1968-73. *901*
—. Elementary and Secondary Education Act (US, 1969; Title VII). Federal Aid to Education. 1973. *58*
—. English language. Puerto Rico. Teaching. 1978. *1234*
—. Ethnic groups. 1978. *18*
—. Ethnicity. Government. Race. 1974-81. *89*
—. New Mexico. Spanish language. 1968-78. *703*
—. Public schools. 1968-76. *27*
—. Public schools. Puerto Rico. 1970's. *1104*
—. Sanchez, George I. Segregation. Southwest. 1930-70. *987*
—. Self-image. Students. 1975-77. *944*
—. Southwest. 1976. *984*
Bilingual Education Act (US, 1967). Congress. Elementary and Secondary Education Act (US, 1968). 1960-80. *117*
Bilingualism. Acculturation. Economic Conditions. 1848-1977. *482*
—. Adolescence. Border towns. California. English language. Spanish language. 1970-79. *698*
—. Assimilation. Attitudes. New York City. Puerto Ricans. Working class. 1979. *1073*
—. Behavior. Politics. 1970-75. *948*
—. Children. Speech. Texas (Austin; East Austin). 1974-80. *915*
—. Higher education. 1967-80. *67*
—. Immigrants. Income. Language. 1975. *821*
—. Linguistics. Social Conditions. 1970-78. *942*
—. New Mexico. Newspapers. Spanish (language). 1834-1917. *569*
—. Occupations. Puerto Rico. 1970. *1066*
Birth Rate. Census. Migration. Puerto Rico. 1965-70. *1262*
—. Demography. Puerto Rico. 1974. *1296*
Blacks. Adolescence. California (Los Angeles). Self-concept. Whites. 1971. *863*
—. Age. Discrimination. Income. Texas. 1960-70. *926*
—. American dream. Identity. Indians. 1890-1980. *25*
—. Asians. Education. Ethnicity. Immigrants. Occupational mobility. 1965-70. *99*
—. Assimilation. Bilingual education. California (San Jose). Race Relations. School integration. 1950-79. *768*
—. Assimilation. Immigration. West Indies. 1898-1979. *1195*
—. Assimilation. Residential segregation. Social Status. Whites. 1960-70. *70*
—. Attitudes. Earthquakes. Whites. 1977. *1020*
—. Attitudes. Education. Immigration. Wisconsin (Racine). 1974. *993*
—. Attitudes. Newspapers. Television. Texas (Lubbock). 1976. *1010*
—. Attitudes. Puerto Rico. 1950's-70's. *1219*
—. Authors. Autobiographies. New York City. Prisons. Puerto Ricans. Thomas, Piri. 1950-80. *1224*
—. Business. Cubans. Economic structure. Florida (Miami). 1920's-80. *1308*
—. California. Mortality. Whites. 1969-71. *990*
—. California (Los Angeles). Crime and Criminals. Judicial Administration. Whites. 1977-80. *1041*
—. California (Los Angeles). Language. Reading. Whites. 1970's. *879*
—. California (Los Angeles County). Courts. Men. Sentencing. Whites. Women. 1977-80. *839*
—. Carranza, Venustiano. Indians. Mexico. Rebellions. Texas. Villa, Francisco. 1848-1920. *577*
—. Cattle Raising. Historiography. Indians. ca 1865-1979. *431*
—. Child-rearing. Indians. Values. 1979. *1045*
—. Chinese Americans. Economic Conditions. Filipinos. Japanese. Social Status. 1960-76. *51*
—. City government. Colorado (Denver). Public Opinion. Whites. 1974. *898*
—. City Government. Employment. Texas. Urbanization. 1973. *842*
—. City Life. Economic Conditions. Social Organization. 1960-71. *994*
—. Civil-Military Relations. Discrimination. Race Relations. Texas (Rio Grande City). Violence. Whites. 1899-1900. *524*
—. Colorado (Denver). Political attitudes. Voting and Voting Behavior. 1971. *897*
—. Competition. Labor. Whites. 1976. *734*
—. Cowboys. Daily Life. Indians. Western States. 1860's-90's. *519*
—. Crime and Criminals. Discrimination. Sentencing. Southwest. Whites. 1976-77. *859*
—. Cubans. Discrimination, Housing. Metropolitan Areas. Mexicans. Prices. Puerto Ricans. Whites. 1975-76. *8*
—. Dating. Race Relations. Whites. 1978-79. *884*
—. Demography. Households. Mothers, single. Puerto Ricans. Whites. 1970. *1119*
—. Discovery and Exploration. Esteban. Florida. South Central and Gulf States. Spain. 1528-39. *302*
—. Discrimination, Employment. Men. Wages. Whites. 1980-81. *1029*
—. Divorce. Whites. 1960-70. *809*
—. Economic Conditions. Immigration. New York City. Public Opinion. West Indies. 1965-79. *1099*
—. Economic conditions. Whites. Wisconsin (Racine). 1960-71. *781*
—. Economic status. Ethnicity. Social Classes. Stress. Whites. 1974. *708*
—. Employment. Family. Income. Sex roles. Whites. 1982-83. *47*
—. Employment. Marriage. Mothers. Whites. Women. 1970-84. *46*
—. Employment. Population. Race. Students. Whites. Youth. 1967-83. *133*
—. Employment. Southwest. Whites. Women. 1950-70. *771*
—. England (London). Immigration. New York City. Social status. West Indians. 20c. *1153*
—. Ethnic Groups. New York City. Social Change. 1960's-70's. *1230*
—. Ethnic groups. Political participation. Whites. 1966-75. *707*
—. Farms. Jamaicans. Migrant Labor. New York. Social mobility. 1960's-70's. *1152*
—. Florida. Jamaicans. Migrant labor. 1980. *731*
—. Florida (Miami). Neighborhoods. Population. Residential patterns. Whites. 1970-80. *1309*
—. Income. Metropolitan areas. Occupations. 1970. *808*
—. Income. Whites. 1976. *94*

—. Interpersonal Relations. Marriage. Whites. 1960-70. *792*
—. Kansas (Manhattan). Political integration. 1971. *704*
—. Labor. Whites. Wisconsin (Racine). 1960-70. *995*
—. Measurements. Mortality. Texas. Whites. 1980. *1008*
—. Men. Wages. Whites. 1979. *109*
—. Metropolitan areas. Social Classes. Southwest. Whites. 1970. *790*
—. Mexico. Press, black. Race Relations. 1890-1935. *681*
—. New York City. Puerto Ricans. Voluntary associations. Whites. 1963-78. *1117*
—. Palés Matos, Luis. Poets. Puerto Rico. ca 1915-59. *1177*
—. Political Participation. Voting Rights Act (US, 1965; amended 1982). 1965-83. *83*
—. Texas (Austin). Voluntary associations. Whites. 1969-70. *1046*
—. Wages. Whites. 1976. *95*
Blades, Rubén (interview). City life. Latin Americans. Music. Panama. Salsa. 1974-84. *1088*
Blankets. Dye. Indians. Navajo Indians. New Mexico. Rugs. Spaniards. Weaving. 19c-1977. *353*
Blues. Folk Songs. Fugitive Slaves. Matamoros (colony). Music. 19c-1940's. *458*
Bolton, Herbert Eugene. Arizona (Casa Grande). Explorers. Kino, Eusebio Francisco. 1697. 1934. 1968-72. *250*
—. Borderlands studies. Catholic Church. Colonization. Historiography. Missions and Missionaries. Spain. 1917-79. *9*
Bones. Arizona (Canyon de Chelly). Dogs. Indian Wars. Navajo Indians. Pictographs. Spain. 1750-1863. *202*
Border policy. Economic Conditions. Mexico. Workers, undocumented. 1952-75. *739*
Border towns. Adolescence. Bilingualism. California. English language. Spanish language. 1970-79. *698*
Borderlands. Colonies. Documents. Florida, University of, Gainesville. P. K. Yonge Library of Florida History (guide). Spain. ca 1518-1821. *77*
—. Diplomacy. Mexico. Trade. 1858-1905. *516*
—. Social customs. Southeastern States. Southwest. Spain. 1565-1976. *394*
Borderlands (review article). Jones, Oakah L., Jr. McDermott, John Francis. Mississippi Valley. Southwest. Spain. Weddle, Robert S. 1762-1804. 1973-74. *379*
—. Mexican Americans. Mexico. Social Conditions. ca 1600-1981. *41*
Borderlands studies. Anthropology. Mexico. Sociology. Southwest. 20c. *114*
—. Bolton, Herbert Eugene. Catholic Church. Colonization. Historiography. Missions and Missionaries. Spain. 1917-79. *9*
—. Economic Conditions. Mexico. Southwest. 1970's. *116*
—. Mexico. Southwest. 1952-75. *113*
Borders. Arizona (Nogales). Foreign relations. García, Jesús. Mexico (Sonora). 1893-96. *529*
—. Cities. Daily Life. Poverty. Social Conditions. 1945-77. *911*
—. Compromise of 1850. Spain. Texas Panhandle. 1819-50. *148*
—. Folk Songs (review article). Mexico. Paredes, Americo. Texas. 16c-20c. *474*
—. Foreign Relations (review article). Historiography. Mexico. Southwest. 20c. *61*
—. Frontier and Pioneer Life. Mexico. Race Relations. Southwest (review article). Weber, David J. 1821-46. *251*

—. Historiography. Mexico. 1812-1975. *3*
—. Louisiana. Mexico. Puelles, José María de Jesús. Texas. 1512-1813. 1827-28. *230*
—. Mexico. Rebellions. Texas (Brownsville, Eagle Pass area). 1850-1900. *521*
Bossism. Political Leadership. Puerto Ricans. 1935-73. *1269*
Boucfouca, Treaty of. Alabama. Choctaw Indians. Indian-White Relations. Spain. Villebeuvre, Juan de la. 1793. *243*
Bouligny, Francisco. American Revolution. Letters. Louisiana. Settlement. Spain. 1776-78. *200*
Bouligny, Francisco (report). Gálvez, Bernardo de. Immigration policy. Louisiana. Navarro, Martin *(Political Reflections)*. Spain. 1776-83. *201*
Boundaries. *See* Borders.
Bounties. Armies. Land warrants. Mexican War. 1800-61. *309*
Boycotts. Agriculture. California. Chavez, Cesar. Grapes. International Brotherhood of Teamsters. Labor Unions and Organizations. Lettuce. United Farm Workers Union. 1962-74. *805*
—. Presbyterian Church. Public schools. Segregation. Texas (San Angelo). 1910-15. *617*
Bracero Program. Agricultural Labor. Aliens, illegal. Attitudes. Labor Unions and Organizations. Mexico. 1943-74. *889*
—. Agricultural labor. Employment. Southwest. Wages. 1954-77. *869*
—. Agriculture. Mexico. President's Commission on Migratory Labor. Truman, Harry S. Workers, undocumented. 1950. *876*
—. Aliens, illegal. Immigration. Mexico. Quota systems. 1960's-70's. *1007*
—. Documents. Employment. Railroads. 1945. *695*
—. Documents. Mexico. 1944. *622*
—. Foreign Relations. Immigration. Mexico. 1942-46. *642*
—. Migration. Washington. 1940-50. *620*
Briski, Norman (interview). Exiles. Latin Americans. New York City. Theater. 1970's-82. *1096*
Britain (vessel). Confiscations. Foreign Relations. Great Britain. Spain. Texas (Matagorda Peninsula). 1769-70. *168*
British Columbia. Columbia River. Discovery and Exploration. Heceta y Fontecha, Bruno de. Pacific Northwest. Spain. 1775. *159*
British North America. Anti-Mexican sentiments. Hispanophobia. 17c-19c. *315*
Brown, Harold Palmer. Carranza family. Memoirs. Mexico. New Mexico (Columbus; attack). Photographs. Villa, Pancho. 1916. *612*
Bureaucracies. Administration for the Development of Art and Culture. Legislation. Musicians. New Progressive Party. Puerto Rico. 1980. *1284*
Burgos, Julia de. Font Saldaña, Jorge. Lair, Clara. Personal Narratives. Poets. Puerto Rico. Ribera Chevremont, Evaristo. 20c. *1232*
Business. Arizona. California. Redondo, José María. Territorial Government. 1849-78. *592*
—. Barceló, Gertrudis. Elites. Gambling. New Mexico (Santa Fe). Women. 1830's-40's. *273*
—. Bernal, Juan Pablo. California. Cattle Raising. Land disputes. Wealth. 1822-78. *426*
—. Blacks. Cubans. Economic structure. Florida (Miami). 1920's-80. *1308*
—. Cubans. Entrepreneurs. Florida (Miami). Immigrants. 1960-84. *1163*
—. Cubans. Ownership. 1977. *1133*
Business Education. College graduates. Wages. Whites. 1972-80. *949*

C

Cabeza de Vaca, Alvar Nuñez *(La Relación)*.
Florida. Garcilaso de la Vega, "el Inca" *(La
Florida del Inca)*. 1500-1616. *215*
Cabrillo, Juan Rodríguez. Alvarado, Pedro de.
Colonial Government. Discovery and
Exploration. Mendoza, Antonio de. New Spain.
Printing press. 1515-52. *158*
—. California. Discovery and Exploration.
Shipbuilding. 1532-42. *259*
Cahuilla Indians. California (Palm Springs region).
Cocomaricopa Trail. Indians. Letters. Overland
Journeys to the Pacific. Romero, José. ca
1823-24. *370*
California. Adolescence. Bilingualism. Border towns.
English language. Spanish language. 1970-79.
698
—. Aged. Social Policy. Whites. 1978-82. *850*
—. Agricultural Industry. Elections. Labor Unions
and Organizations. Proposition 14 (1976).
United Farm Workers Union. 1976. *773*
—. Agricultural Labor. Chavez, Cesar. Strikes.
United Farm Workers Union. 1965-70. *723*
—. Agricultural Labor. Government regulation.
Hoes. 1968-75. *936*
—. Agricultural Labor. Labor law. 1965-76. *764*
—. Agricultural Labor. United Cannery,
Agricultural, Packing and Allied Workers of
America. 1937-40. *667*
—. Agricultural Labor. United Farm Workers
Union. 1960's-76. *810*
—. Agricultural Labor Relations Act (California,
1975). Emergency Farm Labor Supply
Program. Labor law. New Deal. ca 1930-79.
434
—. Agricultural Technology and Research.
Assimilation. Indians. Mission San Antonio de
Padua. Salinan Indians. 1771-1832. 1976-79.
244
—. Agriculture. Boycotts. Chavez, Cesar. Grapes.
International Brotherhood of Teamsters. Labor
Unions and Organizations. Lettuce. United
Farm Workers Union. 1962-74. *805*
—. Agriculture. Chavez, Cesar. Elections.
Proposition 14 (1976). United Farm Workers
Union. 1975-76. *996*
—. Alarcón, Hernando. Colorado River. Discovery
and Exploration. Indians. 1540. *207*
—. Anza, Juan Bautista de. Bicentennial
Celebrations. Discovery and Exploration.
Mexico. Reenactments. 1775-76. 1975-76. *208*
—. Architecture. Franciscans. Mission San Juan
Capistrano. 1776-1976. *163*
—. Archival Catalogs and Inventories. Mexico.
1535-1821. *72*
—. Arizona. Business. Redondo, José María.
Territorial Government. 1849-78. *592*
—. Armies. Colonial Government. Mexico.
1822-46. *257*
—. Art. Catholic Church. Cultural myopia (Anglo-
American). Missions and Missionaries.
Scholasticism. 1740's-1976. *307*
—. Ascensión, Antonio de la. Discovery and
Exploration. Mexico. Vizcaíno, Sebastian.
Voyages. 1590-1737. *285*
—. Bernal, Juan Pablo. Business. Cattle Raising.
Land disputes. Wealth. 1822-78. *426*
—. Blacks. Mortality. Whites. 1969-71. *990*
—. Cabrillo, Juan Rodríguez. Discovery and
Exploration. Shipbuilding. 1532-42. *259*
—. Discovery and Exploration. Vizcáino, Sebastián.
1596-1627. *284*
—. Camarillo, Albert. Cities. Garcia, Mario T.
Griswold del Castillo, Richard. Social Change
(review article). Texas. 1848-1982. *508*
—. Catholic Church. Chapels. Indians. Yuma
Indians. ca 1769-1840. *387*

—. Catholic Church. Economic conditions. Indians.
Missions and Missionaries. 1803-21. *151*
—. Catholic Church. González Rubio, José.
Missions and Missionaries. 1846-50. *566*
—. Catholic Church. Indians. Labor. Missions and
Missionaries. 1775-1805. *152*
—. Catholic Church. Indian-White Relations.
Missions and Missionaries. 1770's-1820's. *347*
—. Catholic Church. Mission San Juan Capistrano.
Serra, Junípero. 1775-76. *312*
—. Cesarean operations. Franciscans. Medicine
(practice of). Missions and Missionaries.
1769-1833. *376*
—. Chavez, Cesar. Political activism. Rhetoric.
Texas. Tijerina, Reies. 1960's-70's. *843*
—. Children. Political Attitudes. Whites. -1973.
815
—. Chileans. Consuls. Gold rushes. 1848-60. *1231*
—. Christmas. Social Customs. Spanish settlers. ca
1840-61. *293*
—. Church and State. Colonization. Indians. Spain.
1775-1800. *221*
—. Colleges and Universities. La Raza Unida
Party. Student activism. 1969-73. *933*
—. Colleges and Universities. San Diego State
College. Student activism. Women. 1968-76.
852
—. Colonial Government. Discovery and
Exploration. Missions and Missionaries.
Settlement. Spain. 1691-1810. *262*
—. Colonial Government. Foreign Policy. Spain.
War. 1779-1818. *270*
—. Colonists. Hijar-Padres colony. Mexico (San
Blas). 1834. *249*
—. Colonization. Discovery and exploration.
Mexico. Spain. 1602-1769. *190*
—. Colonization. Mexico. Population. Spain.
1760's-1840's. *222*
—. Colorado. New Mexico. Political representation.
State Politics. ca 1850-1974. *464*
—. Conversion thesis. Cook, Sherburne Friend.
Franciscans. Indians. Missions and Missionaries.
ca 1790-1820's. 1943. *229*
—. Cultural identity. Marxism. Political power.
San Diego State University. 1965-74. *992*
—. Daily Life. Diaries. Mexican War. Mormon
Battalion. Social Customs. 1846-55. *601*
—. Dance. Social Customs. 1820's-50's. *341*
—. DeAnza expedition, 2d. Explorers. Font,
Pedro. 1775-76. *170*
—. delValle family. Rancho Camulos. Upper
Classes. 1839-1938. *442*
—. Demography. New Mexico. ca 1850. *568*
—. Discovery and Exploration. Settlement.
Vizcaíno, Sebastian. 1602-32. *154*
—. Discrimination. Gold Rushes. Mexico (Sonora).
Migration. 1848-56. *585*
—. Dominicans. Franciscans. Jesuits. Missions and
Missionaries. Serra, Junípero. 1768-76. *287*
—. Durán, Narciso. Franciscans. Indians. Missions
and Missionaries. Music. 1806-46. *224*
—. Durán, Narciso. Franciscans. Indians. Missions
and Missionaries. Secularization. 1826-46. *305*
—. Economic Conditions. Immigration, illegal.
Labor. Mexico, west-central. 1970's. *778*
—. Effigies. Mission San Antonio de Padua.
Pottery. 18c-19c. *214*
—. Ethnic groups. Immigration. 1850-1976. *78*
—. Excavations. Majolica pottery sherds. Santa
Barbara Presidio, Chapel. Spain. 1782-1850. *153*
—. Excavations. Missions and Missionaries.
Presidios. San Diego Presidio. Serra Museum.
1769-75. 1964-70's. *210*
—. Franciscans. Mexico. Missions and
Missionaries. Southwest. Wheat growing.
1730's-70's. *335*
—. Franciscans. Mission San Carlo Borromeo.
Serra, Junípero. 1784. *278*

—. Gold Mines and Mining. Industrialization. Nativism. 1845-70. *533*
—. Gold Rushes. Murieta, Joaquín. Outlaws. ca 1848-53. *587*
—. Gold Rushes. Nativism. 1848-53. *574*
—. Higher education. Students. Texas. 1970's. *787*
—. Immigration. Mexico. Mineral resources. Settlement. 1683-1848. *231*
—. Indians. Mexico. Missions and Missionaries. 1830's. *321*
—. Indian-White Relations. Spain. 1770's. *295*
—. Intermarriage. 1962-74. *989*
—. Kearny, Stephen Watts. Mexican War. San Pasqual (battle). 1846. *156*
—. Kearny, Stephen Watts. Mexican War. San Pasqual (battle). 1847. *253*
—. Land grants. O'Farrell, Jasper. Surveying. 1844-46. *289*
—. Land tenure. Mexico. Ranches. 1784-1846. *247*
—. Leadership. Pico, Pío. 1801-94. *520*
—. Legends. Murieta, Joaquín. Outlaws. 1850's. *556*
—. Libraries. Migrant Labor. 1970-80. *937*
—. Literature. Pachuco (term). Youth. 1940's-1960's. *904*
—. Literature. Stereotypes. 1850-1900. *553*
—. Medical care. Women. 1977. *1004*
—. Mexican War. San Pasqual (battle). 1846-47. *252*
—. Mission La Purísima Concepción. Restorations. 1787-1973. *390*
—. Missions and Missionaries. Presidios. 1769-84. *172*
—. Missions and Missionaries. Viticulture. 1697-1858. *389*
—. Murals. 1920's-80. *830*
—. Settlement. 1769-96. *339*
—. Soldiers. 1769-1821. *267*
—. Spanish language. 18c-1979. *484*
California (Colusa County). Agricultural Labor. Farms. 1950-69. *930*
California (Compton). Domínguez, Juan José. Domínguez Ranch Adobe. 1784-1981. *427*
California (Drake's Bay). Discovery and Exploration. Toponymy. Viscáino, Sebastian. 1602-03. *286*
California (East Los Angeles). Art. Mechicano Art Center. Murals. 1970's. *759*
—. Art. Murals. Social Conditions. 1970-75. *872*
—. Art. Murals. Values. 1978. *1052*
—. Barrios. Community Participation in Politics. 1970-73. *1017*
—. Catholic Church. Economic Conditions. Reform. Social Conditions. United Neighborhoods Organization. 1960's-80. *945*
—. Ethnic Groups. Political protest. Social Change. 1968-74. *934*
—. Immigrants (review article). New York City. Romo, Richard. Sanchez Korrol, Virginia E. 20c. *137*
—. Leisure. Low-riders (automobiles). Social Customs. Youth. 1970's. *861*
California (East Los Angeles, Boyle Heights). Artists. Murals. 1965-75. *860*
California (East San Jose; Mayfair district). Social Change. 1777-1975. *481*
California (El Monte). Agricultural Labor. Berry pickers. Foreign Relations. Japan. Mexico. Strikes. 1933. *645*
California (Los Angeles). Academic achievement. Acculturation. High schools. 1975-76. *1030*
—. Adolescence. Blacks. Self-concept. Whites. 1971. *863*
California (Tucson). Economic conditions. Racism. Social Conditions. Texas (San Antonio). 1850-1900. *528*
—. Arizona (Tucson). Occupations. Property. Social Customs. 1775-1880. *543*

—. Art. Ethnicity. Murals. 1970's. *998*
—. Assimilation. Exiles. Lozano, Ignacio. Newspapers. *Opinión*. 1926-29. *660*
—. Attitudes. Fertility. Women. 1973-82. *978*
—. Attitudes. High schools. Truancy. 1974-75. *845*
—. Blacks. Crime and Criminals. Judicial Administration. Whites. 1977-80. *1041*
—. Blacks. Language. Reading. Whites. 1970's. *879*
—. Catholic Church. Christmas. Neighborhoods. Posadas (celebrations). Rites and Ceremonies. 1975-80. *900*
—. Catholic Church. Fertility. Religiosity. Women. 1973. *979*
—. Census. Education. Literacy. Quantitative Methods. 1850. *596*
—. Chicano movement. Interviews. Political Socialization. 1960's. *974*
—. Citizens Committee for the Defense of Mexican-American Youth. "Sleepy Lagoon" trial. Trials. 1942-44. *616*
—. Congress of Industrial Organizations. Labor Unions and Organizations. 1938-50. *606*
—. Croix, Teodoro de. Toponymy. 1769-82. *368*
—. Curricula. Educational reform. Public schools. 1920's-30's. *631*
—. Daily Life. Mott, Thomas. Sepúlveda y Ávila, María Ascensión. 1844-61. *600*
—. Economic mobility. 1850-80. *541*
—. Education. Racism. 1920-32. *632*
—. Employment. Industry. Interviews. Women. 1928. *686*
—. Europe. Family. Immigrants. Michigan (Detroit). Whites. 1850-80. *542*
—. Family. Modernization. Social change. 1850-80. *538*
—. Gangs. Residential patterns. Youth. 1980-83. *931*
—. Garment Industry. International Ladies' Garment Workers' Union. Strikes. Women. 1933. *619*
—. Garment Industry. Women. Working Conditions. 1970-79. *986*
—. Geographic Mobility. Occupational mobility. 1918-28. *676*
—. *Heraldo de Mexico*. Immigrants. Newspapers. Press. 1916-20. *614*
—. Immigration and Naturalization Service. Industrial Relations. International Ladies' Garment Workers' Union. Lilli Diamond Originals. Raids. 1976-77. *1027*
—. Infant mortality. Public health. 1850-87. *537*
—. International Ladies' Garment Workers' Union. Women. Working Conditions. 1933-39. *664*
—. Labor. Workers, Undocumented. 1979. *718*
—. McWilliams, Carey. Personal narratives. Race Relations. 1940's-60's. *917*
—. Medical care. Neighborhoods. Poor. 1970-79. *853*
—. Political Leadership. World War II. 1941-45. *625*
—. Spanish language. 1960's-70's. *894*
—. Sterilization. Women. 1970-78. *1028*
—. United Mexican American Students. Youth Movements. 1967-69. *975*
—. Working class. 1820-1920. *523*
California (Los Angeles area). Proverbs. Tradition. 1970's. *713*
California (Los Angeles County). Aguirre, Martin. Law enforcement. 1880's-1929. *545*
—. Bilingual Education. 1968-73. *901*
—. Blacks. Courts. Men. Sentencing. Whites. Women. 1977-80. *839*
—. Congressional Districts (30th). Ethnicity. Political candidates. Race. Voting and Voting Behavior. 1982. *754*
—. Davis, James J. Deportation. Depressions. Unemployment. 1931. *647*

—. Drug abuse. Law Enforcement. Rehabilitation. Statistics. 1969-79. *906*
—. Labor. 1920's-30's. *665*
California (Los Angeles; Hollywood). Films. Spanish language. 1930-39. *670*
California (Los Angeles, San Diego). Armies. Mexico. Presidios. Spain. 1770-94. *283*
California (Los Angeles, Santa Barbara). Catholic Church. Marriage. Mission Santa Barbara. Social Customs. 1786-1848. *298*
California (Monterey). Discovery and Exploration. Dominguez, Francisco Atanasio. Escalante, Silvestre Velez de. New Mexico. 1765-1805. *143*
—. Discovery and Exploration. Dominguez, Francisco Atanasio. Escalante, Silvestre Velez de. New Mexico (Santa Fe). 1776-77. *169*
—. Estrada, José. Europe. Jenner, Edward. Smallpox. Vaccination. 18c-1821. *301*
—. Great Britain. Jones, Thomas ap Catesby. Mexico. Military Occupation. Navies. 1842. *218*
—. Historical Sites and Parks. Landmarks. Mexico. Spain. 1770-1849. *173*
—. Mexico. Spain. 1770-1849. *292*
—. Migration, Internal. Urban change. 1835-50. *246*
California (Monterey County). Firearms. Flintlocks. Mission San Antonio de Padua. 18c. *391*
California (Orange County). Medical Care (costs). Whites. -1973. *1037*
—. *Mendez v. Westminster* (California, 1946). Public schools. Segregation (*de jure, de facto*). 1850-1970's. *690*
California (Oxnard). Agricultural Labor. Japanese-Mexican Labor Association. Strikes. Sugar beets. Wages. 1902-03. *602*
—. Drug abuse programs. 1972-73. *696*
California (Palm Springs region). Cahuilla Indians. Cocomaricopa Trail. Indians. Letters. Overland Journeys to the Pacific. Romero, José. ca 1823-24. *370*
California (Parlier). Local government. Models. Politics. 1971-73. *966*
California Polytechnic State University, San Luis Obispo. Aqueducts. Excavations. Mission San Antonio de Padua. Spanish. 1776. 1979-81. *245*
California (San Bernardino Valley; Agua Mansa). Pioneers. 1845-62. *597*
California (San Diego). Attitudes. Migration. Workers, undocumented. 1984. *896*
—. Californios. Political power. Upper Classes. 1846-60. *534*
—. Camino Real. Mexico (Baja California). Missions and Missionaries. 1697-1771. *187*
—. Camino Real. Mexico (Loreto). Serra Route. Trails. 1762-1975. *188*
—. Colonial Government. Croix, Carlos Francisco de. Mexico. Mission San Diego de Alcalá. Spain. 1760's-86. *160*
—. Colonization. Indians. Missions and Missionaries. Spain. 1769-1834. *399*
—. Colorado (Denver). Medical Education. Physicians. Texas (San Antonio). 1970-79. *980*
—. Couts, Cave Johnson. Diaries. 1849. *581*
—. Franciscans. Jayme, Luís (death). Mission San Diego de Alcalá. Yuman Indians. 1775. *388*
California (San Diego area). Discovery and Exploration. Indians. Portolá, Gaspar de. South Carolina. 1769. *175*
California (San Diego; Barrio Logan). Chicano Park. Historical Sites and Parks. 1968-80. *803*
—. Community Participation in Politics. Murals. Parks. 1969-84. *767*
California (San Diego County). Californians, native. Social Change. 1846-56. *546*
California (San Francisco). Academic achievement. Attitudes. High schools. 1974-75. *796*
—. Commerce. Spain. 1755-1822. *227*

—. Recreation. Social Change. 1846-69. *573*
California (San Francisco Bay). Ayala, Juan Manuel de. Discovery and Exploration. Franciscans. Indians. Spain. 1775. *369*
California (San Francisco Bay area). Public Welfare. Refugees. Resettlement. South Americans. 1973-79. *1169*
California (San Joaquin Valley). Agricultural labor. Japanese. Nisei Farmers League. United Farm Workers Union. 1971-77. *812*
—. Japanese. Labor Disputes. Nisei Farmers League. United Farm Workers Union. 1974-76. *811*
California (San Jose). Assimilation. Bilingual education. Blacks. Race Relations. School integration. 1950-79. *768*
California (Santa Ana). Public schools. Segregation. 1913-48. *633*
California (Santa Barbara). Americanization. Social Change. Urbanization. 1850-70's. *599*
—. *Angeles et al. v. Santa Barbara School District et al.* (California, 1981). Children. Public Schools (closures). 1981-83. *1025*
—. Public Schools (closures). 1970's. *1026*
—. Teatro Nacional de Aztlán. Theater. 1979. *836*
California (Santa Clara County). Acculturation. Marriage. Rites and Ceremonies. 1908-68. *421*
—. Electronics industry. Women. Working conditions. 1970-79. *730*
California (Sonoma). Catholic Church. Indians. Mission San Francisco Solano. 1823-34. *176*
California, southern. Attitudes. Barrios. Civil Rights. Police. Social Conditions. 1975. *927*
—. Cities. Employment. 1900-39. *663*
—. Immigration. Mexico. "Operation Wetback". Texas. 1950-74. *977*
—. Political Activism. Women. 1960-79. *785*
California, University of, Berkeley. Agricultural Labor. Economics. Newlands Act (US, 1902). Taylor, Paul S. 1895-1980. *494*
California, University of, Santa Barbara. Chicano Studies Department. 1975-79. *814*
California (Villa de Branciforte). Colonization. Spain. 1790's-1907. *223*
—. Colonization. Spain. ca 1790-1821. *317*
California Women Farmworkers Project. Agricultural Labor. Oral history. Women. 1870's-1970's. *73*
Californians, native. California (San Diego County). Social Change. 1846-56. *546*
Californios. Attitudes. Europeans. Travel accounts. 1780's-1840's. *269*
—. Attitudes. Europeans. Travel accounts. 1780's-1840's. *396*
—. California (San Diego). Political power. Upper Classes. 1846-60. *534*
—. Social Classes. Virtue. Women. 1830-46. *268*
—. Social Customs. ca 1826-46. *183*
Calleros, Cleofas. Federación de Sociedades Latinos-Americanos. Maverick, Maury. McCammont, T. J. Powell, Alex K. Race Relations. Texas (El Paso). 1936. *627*
Calusa Indians. Antonia (Indian). Carlos (chief). Florida. Indian-White Relations. Marriage. Menéndez de Avilés, Pedro. Politics. 1566-69. *327*
Calvo Buezas, Tomás. Assimilation (review article). Villanueva, Tino. 19c-20c. *405*
Camarillo, Albert. California. Cities. Garcia, Mario T. Griswold del Castillo, Richard. Social Change (review article). Texas. 1848-1982. *508*
—. Cardoso, Lawrence A. Immigration. Mexican Americans (review article). Reisler, Mark. ca 1848-1970. *112*
—. Historiography. Mexican Americans (review article). 1848-1930. *106*

Camino Real. California (San Diego). Mexico (Baja California). Missions and Missionaries. 1697-1771. *187*
—. California (San Diego). Mexico (Loreto). Serra Route. Trails. 1762-1975. *188*
Campos, Albizu. Independence Movements. Puerto Rico. 1910-65. *1247*
—. Nationalism. Puerto Rico. 20c. *1205*
Canada. Pacific Coast. Scientific Expeditions. Spain. USA. 18c. *191*
—. Political participation. Puerto Rico. Voter registration. 1974-77. *1070*
Capital. Commodity exchange. Economic structure. Plantations. Puerto Rico, southwestern. Sugar cane. 1911. *1305*
—. Economic Development. Labor. Models. Puerto Rico. 1945-70. *1222*
Capital Punishment. Arizona. Ballads. "Corrido de los Hermanos" (ballad). Hernández, Federico. Hernández, Manuel. 1934. *683*
Capitalism. Children. Labor. Mexico. Women. Workers, undocumented. ca 1950-79. *833*
—. Developing nations. Production. Puerto Rico. ca 1940-79. *1137*
—. Economic Structure. Immigration. Labor. Latin Americans. Minorities. ca 1950-70. *1290*
—. Emigration. Puerto Rico. 1945-70. *1204*
—. Plantations. Puerto Rico. Socialist Party. Sugar. Working Class. 19c-1976. *1255*
—. Puerto Rico. 1940's-70's. *1136*
—. Racism. 1845-1977. *491*
Carden, Georgiana. Compulsory Education. Elementary education. Migrant Labor. 1920's. *641*
Cardoso, Lawrence A. Camarillo, Albert. Immigration. Mexican Americans (review article). Reisler, Mark. ca 1848-1970. *112*
Caribbean Studies Association (conference papers). Political status. Puerto Rico. 1976. *1106*
Carlos (chief). Antonia (Indian). Calusa Indians. Florida. Indian-White Relations. Marriage. Menéndez de Avilés, Pedro. Politics. 1566-69. *327*
Carranza, Elihu (review article). 1960's-70's. *765*
Carranza family. Brown, Harold Palmer. Memoirs. Mexico. New Mexico (Columbus; attack). Photographs. Villa, Pancho. 1916. *612*
Carranza, Venustiano. Blacks. Indians. Mexico. Rebellions. Texas. Villa, Francisco. 1848-1920. *577*
—. Foreign Relations. Immigration. Mexico. 1910-20. *674*
—. Foreign Relations. Mexico. Plan de San Diego. Race relations. Texas, south. 1915-16. *638*
Carter, Jimmy. Aliens, illegal. Federal Policy. Immigration. 1977-78. *760*
—. Aliens, illegal. Reagan, Ronald. 1977-81. *49*
—. Cerro Maravilla scandal. Murder. Puerto Rico. Revolutionary Movements. Romero Barceló, Carlos. Statehood. 1978-80. *1288*
—. Cubans. Federal Policy. Immigration. Political Leadership. 1980. *1123*
—. Workers, undocumented. 1977. *804*
Castañeda, Carlos Eduardo. Colleges and Universities. Historiography. Librarians. Texas, University of, Austin (Benson Latin American Collection). 1920-27. *603*
—. Colonization. Historiography. Spain. Texas. 1693-1731. 1933-43. *144*
—. Historians. Texas. 1896-1927. *604*
Catholic Church. *See also* Franciscans; Missions and Missionaries.
—. Art. California. Cultural myopia (Anglo-American). Missions and Missionaries. Scholasticism. 1740's-1976. *307*
—. Bolton, Herbert Eugene. Borderlands studies. Colonization. Historiography. Missions and Missionaries. Spain. 1917-79. *9*

—. California. Chapels. Indians. Yuma Indians. ca 1769-1840. *387*
—. California. Economic conditions. Indians. Missions and Missionaries. 1803-21. *151*
—. California. González Rubio, José. Missions and Missionaries. 1846-50. *566*
—. California. Indians. Labor. Missions and Missionaries. 1775-1805. *152*
—. California. Indian-White Relations. Missions and Missionaries. 1770's-1820's. *347*
—. California. Mission San Juan Capistrano. Serra, Junípero. 1775-76. *312*
—. California (East Los Angeles). Economic Conditions. Reform. Social Conditions. United Neighborhoods Organization. 1960's-80. *945*
—. California (Los Angeles). Christmas. Neighborhoods. Posadas (celebrations). Rites and Ceremonies. 1975-80. *900*
—. California (Los Angeles). Fertility. Religiosity. Women. 1973. *979*
—. California (Los Angeles, Santa Barbara). Marriage. Mission Santa Barbara. Social Customs. 1786-1848. *298*
—. California (Sonoma). Indians. Mission San Francisco Solano. 1823-34. *176*
—. Chapels. New Mexico (Santa Fe). 1850's-70's. *346*
—. Charities. Immigration. New York City (Brooklyn; St. Ignatius Parish). 1945-81. *1294*
—. Church and State. Law. Puerto Rico. ca 1863-1908. *1160*
—. Clergy. Southwest. 1821-46. *384*
—. Coahuiltecan Indians. Indians. Missions and Missionaries. Texas (San Antonio). 1792. *277*
—. Colorado. New Mexico. Passion plays. Spain. 1830's-1978. *492*
—. Colorado, southern. Death Carts. New Mexico, northern. Penitentes. 1860-90's. *586*
—. Design. Folk art. Iconography. Manuscripts. New Mexico. 16c-17c. *233*
—. Ethnic Groups. Machismo (concept). Mexican Americans. Social Customs. Women. 1970's. *967*
—. Feast days. New Mexico. 20c. *139*
—. Fiestas. New Mexico. Rites and Ceremonies. Saints, patron. Villages. 1970's. *1036*
—. Flagellants. New Mexico. Penitentes. 13c-20c. *878*
—. Folk art. Home altars. Texas (Austin). 1970's. *1019*
—. Folk art. New Mexico. Santos. 1780-1900. *395*
—. Folk medicine. New Mexico (Guadalupita). Social Customs. Torres, Luisa. 1910's-70's. *497*
—. Frontier and Pioneer Life. Missions and Missionaries. Southwest. Spain. 16c-18c. *164*
—. Indiana (East Chicago, Gary). Theater. 1920-76. *59*
—. Isidore the Husbandman, Saint. Lopez, George. New Mexico (Córdova). Statues. Wood carving. ca 1070-1130. ca 1690-1980. *411*
—. Jaramillo, Cleofas M. Marriage. New Mexico, northern. Social Customs. 1880-98. *547*
—. Jesuits. *Revista Catolica*. Southwest. 1875-1962. *501*
—. Mexico (Nuevo León). Missions and Missionaries. Southwest. Verger y Suau, Rafael José. 1767-80's. *358*
—. Music, religious. 1962-75. *728*
—. National Conference of Catholic Bishops ("Hispanic Presence: Challenge and Commitment"). 1984. *81*
—. New Mexico. Penitentes. Social Customs. Villages. 19c-1978. *445*
—. Social change. 1960's-82. *33*
—. Texas, southern. 1836-1911. *550*
Cattle raising. Arizona. Ranching. 1853-1910. *510*
—. Bernal, Juan Pablo. Business. California. Land disputes. Wealth. 1822-78. *426*

—. Blacks. Historiography. Indians. ca 1865-1979. *431*
—. Frontier and Pioneer Life. Ranches. Southwest. Spain. 18c-19c. *303*
Cattle Rustling. Comancheros. Hittson, John. Indians. New Mexico. Ranchers. 1872-73. *551*
Census. Acosta Rodríquez, Antonio. Colonial Government. Historiography. Louisiana. Spain. 1763-1803. 1976-80. *242*
—. Birth Rate. Migration. Puerto Rico. 1965-70. *1262*
—. California (Los Angeles). Education. Literacy. Quantitative Methods. 1850. *596*
—. Florida (Pensacola). Spain. 1784-1820. *364*
—. Florida (St. Augustine). Population. 1786. *365*
—. Methodology. Population. Southwest. 1848-1900. *559*
—. Population. 1970-78. *820*
—. Population. Quantitative Methods. 1960-70. *56*
—. Population (definition). 1970-73. *851*
Centers for Educational Services. Education, Experimental Methods. Puerto Rico. 1973-77. *1125*
Centro de Estudios Puertoriqueños (History Task Force). Economic relations. Levine, Barry B. Puerto Rico (review article). Sariola, Sakari. 1898-1970's. *1184*
Ceramics. Arizona (Tucson Basin). Excavations. Settlement. 1690's-1856. *157*
Cerro Maravilla scandal. Carter, Jimmy. Murder. Puerto Rico. Revolutionary Movements. Romero Barceló, Carlos. Statehood. 1978-80. *1288*
Cesarean operations. California. Franciscans. Medicine (practice of). Missions and Missionaries. 1769-1833. *376*
Chacón, Felipe Maximiliano. Literature. New Mexico. Newspapers. 1873-1922. *661*
Change and Response, Theory of. Emigration. Fertility. Migration, Internal. Puerto Rico. 1940's-70. *1228*
Chapels. California. Catholic Church. Indians. Yuma Indians. ca 1769-1840. *387*
—. Catholic Church. New Mexico (Santa Fe). 1850's-70's. *346*
Charities. Armijo, Salvador. New Mexico (Albuquerque). Poor. 1874. *515*
—. Catholic Church. Immigration. New York City (Brooklyn; St. Ignatius Parish). 1945-81. *1294*
Cháves, Jesús (family). Daily life. New Mexico, eastern. Sheepherders. 1850's-1930's. *462*
Chavez, Cesar. Agricultural Labor. California. Strikes. United Farm Workers Union. 1965-70. *723*
—. Agriculture. Boycotts. California. Grapes. International Brotherhood of Teamsters. Labor Unions and Organizations. Lettuce. United Farm Workers Union. 1962-74. *805*
—. Agriculture. California. Elections. Proposition 14 (1976). United Farm Workers Union. 1975-76. *996*
—. California. Political activism. Rhetoric. Texas. Tijerina, Reies. 1960's-70's. *843*
—. La Raza Unida Party. 1968-73. *789*
Chicano movement. California (Los Angeles). Interviews. Political Socialization. 1960's. *974*
Chicano Park. California (San Diego; Barrio Logan). Historical Sites and Parks. 1968-80. *803*
Chicano Studies Department. California, University of, Santa Barbara. 1975-79. *814*
"Chicano" (term). Social Classes. 1911-78. *500*
Child Welfare. Migrant Labor. 1969-74. *766*
Child-rearing. Blacks. Indians. Values. 1979. *1045*
Children. Acculturation. Political integration. Texas (El Paso). 1978. *881*

—. *Angeles et al.* v. *Santa Barbara School District et al.* (California, 1981). California (Santa Barbara). Public Schools (closures). 1981-83. *1025*
—. Attitudes. Bilingual Education. Curricula. Parents. 1960's-70's. *902*
—. Attitudes. Public Schools. 1981. *973*
—. Bilingualism. Speech. Texas (Austin; East Austin). 1974-80. *915*
—. California. Political Attitudes. Whites. -1973. *815*
—. Capitalism. Labor. Mexico. Women. Workers, undocumented. ca 1950-79. *833*
—. English language. Grammar. Texas. 1976. *832*
—. IQ tests. 1970's. *729*
—. IQ tests. 1970-79. *959*
—. Japanese. Political participation. Whites. 1970's. *1005*
Chileans. California. Consuls. Gold rushes. 1848-60. *1231*
Chinese Americans. Blacks. Economic Conditions. Filipinos. Japanese. Social Status. 1960-76. *51*
Choctaw Indians. Alabama. Boucfouca, Treaty of. Indian-White Relations. Spain. Villebeuvre, Juan de la. 1793. *243*
—. Indian-White Relations. Old Southwest. Spain. Treaties. Villebeuvre, Juan de la. 1784-97. *241*
Chouteau, Auguste P. Demun, Julius. Indian-White Relations. Law. New Mexico. Trade. 1815-51. *375*
Chrisman, Robert. Independence. Puerto Rico. 1977. *1111*
Christmas. California. Social Customs. Spanish settlers. ca 1840-61. *293*
—. California (Los Angeles). Catholic Church. Neighborhoods. Posadas (celebrations). Rites and Ceremonies. 1975-80. *900*
Church and State. California. Colonization. Indians. Spain. 1775-1800. *221*
—. Catholic Church. Law. Puerto Rico. ca 1863-1908. *1160*
Church records. Cuba. Florida (St. Augustine). 1594-1763. 20c. *185*
Church Schools. Acculturation. Public Schools. Texas (San Antonio). 1973. *882*
Churches. Architecture. Arizona (Tucson). Mexico (Sonora; Caborca). Mission Nuestra Señora de la Purísima Concepción del Caborca. Mission San Xavier del Bac. 1975. *228*
—. Architecture. Artisans. Missions and Missionaries. Texas (San Antonio). 18c. *338*
Cigar industry. Cuba. Florida (Tampa). General strikes. Spain. 1901-11. *1253*
—. Cubans. Florida (Tampa). Independence Movements. Labor. 1892-1901. *1242*
Cigars. Advertising. Art. Cubans. Florida (Tampa). 1868-1930's. *1307*
CIO. *See* Congress of Industrial Organizations.
Cities. Borders. Daily Life. Poverty. Social Conditions. 1945-77. *911*
—. California. Camarillo, Albert. Garcia, Mario T. Griswold del Castillo, Richard. Social Change (review article). Texas. 1848-1982. *508*
—. California, southern. Employment. 1900-39. *663*
—. California. Mexicans. Puerto Ricans. Residential segregation. 1950's-70's. *69*
—. Decisionmaking. Health centers. Neighborhoods. 1969-70. *854*
—. Literature. Women. 1970's. *774*
—. Neighborhoods. Race Relations. Western States. White flight. 1960's. *71*
—. Public policy. Social problems. 1960's-83. *130*
Citizens Committee for the Defense of Mexican-American Youth. California (Los Angeles). "Sleepy Lagoon" trial. Trials. 1942-44. *616*
Citizenship. Courts. Nationality. Race. 1846-97. *570*
City government. Blacks. Colorado (Denver). Public Opinion. Whites. 1974. *898*

—. Blacks. Employment. Texas. Urbanization. 1973. *842*
City Life. Blacks. Economic Conditions. Social Organization. 1960-71. *994*
—. Blades, Rubén (interview). Latin Americans. Music. Panama. Salsa. 1974-84. *1088*
—. Cubans. Ethnicity. Folklore. Indiana (East Chicago). Puerto Ricans. 1976. *1161*
City politics. Cubans. Florida (Jacksonville). Huah, José Alejandro. Independence Movements. Martí, José. 1836-1905. *1164*
—. Illinois (Chicago). Political representation. Spaniards. Voting and Voting Behavior. 1975. *104*
Civil rights. Aliens, illegal. Constitutional Law. 1970-77. *813*
—. Art. Bibliographies. Literature. Mexican Americans. Southwest. 1936-73. *96*
—. Asociación Nacional México-Americana. Pressure Groups. 1949-54. *1021*
—. Attitudes. Barrios. California, southern. Police. Social Conditions. 1975. *927*
—. Labor Unions and Organizations. North Central States. Social Organizations. 1900-76. *467*
Civil rights movement. Minorities. 1954-83. *22*
Civil Service. Inequality. Wages. Whites. 1977. *1011*
Civil-Military Relations. Blacks. Discrimination. Race Relations. Texas (Rio Grande City). Violence. Whites. 1899-1900. *524*
—. Daily life. Florida (St. Augustine). Social organization. Spain. 1580. *279*
—. Foxardo (battle). Insubordination. Navies. Porter, David. Puerto Rico. 1823-25. *1087*
Clark, Truman. Americanization. Bhana, Surendra. Development. Matthews, Thomas. Politics. Puerto Rico (review article). 1917-76. *1261*
Class consciousness. Ideology. Social Change. Texas (San Antonio). 1930-40. *630*
—. Latin America. Puerto Rico. Women. Working Class. 1959-75. *1279*
Class struggle. Development. Ideology. Political change. Puerto Rico. 1940-78. *1238*
—. Politics. Popular Democratic Party. Puerto Rico. 1930's. *1166*
Clergy. Catholic Church. Southwest. 1821-46. *384*
Coahuiltecan Indians. Catholic Church. Indians. Missions and Missionaries. Texas (San Antonio). 1792. *277*
Coalition Government. Economic Conditions. Puerto Rico. 1917-33. *1313*
Cocomaricopa Trail. Cahuilla Indians. California (Palm Springs region). Indians. Letters. Overland Journeys to the Pacific. Romero, José. ca 1823-24. *370*
Cofradías (brotherhoods). New Mexico. Penitentes. Rio Grande Valley. ca 1770-1970. *404*
Cohabitation. Arizona, central. Mining towns. Whites. 1863-73. *548*
College graduates. Business Education. Wages. Whites. 1972-80. *949*
—. Discrimination. Wages. 1966-74. *961*
Colleges and Universities. American history. History Teaching. Mexican Americans. Textbooks. 20c. *53*
—. American Political Science Association. Political science. Western states. 1970-74. *1058*
—. California. La Raza Unida Party. Student activism. 1969-73. *933*
—. California. San Diego State College. Student activism. Women. 1968-76. *852*
—. Castañeda, Carlos Eduardo. Historiography. Librarians. Texas, University of, Austin (Benson Latin American Collection). 1920-27. *603*
—. Discrimination. 1950's-80's. *846*

—. Ethnicity. Racial Distance Indices. Students. Texas (south). 1973. *741*
Colombians. Dominicans. Employment. Family. Immigrants. New York City. Women. 1981. *1171*
—. Dominicans. New York City. Social organizations. ca 1972-76. *1282*
Colonial Government. Acadians. Letters. Louisiana. Refugees. Spain. Ulloa, Antonio de. 1766-68. *178*
—. Acosta Rodríquez, Antonio. Census. Historiography. Louisiana. Spain. 1763-1803. 1976-80. *242*
—. Albuquerque, Duke of (Francisco Fernández de la Cueva Henríquez). Mexico. New Mexico. Politics. Social Problems. 1702-11. *318*
—. Alvarado, Pedro de. Cabrillo, Juan Rodríguez. Discovery and Exploration. Mendoza, Antonio de. New Spain. Printing press. 1515-52. *158*
—. Anza, Juan Bautista de. Concha, Fernando Simon Ignacio de la. Indians. Military Strategy. New Mexico. Spain. 1787-93. *161*
—. Archivo General de Indias. Military Finance. New Mexico. Spain (Seville). Treasury. 1596-1683. *337*
—. Aristocracy. New Mexico. New Spain. Settlement. 16c. *182*
—. Armies. California. Mexico. 1822-46. *257*
—. California. Discovery and Exploration. Missions and Missionaries. Settlement. Spain. 1691-1810. *262*
—. California. Foreign Policy. Spain. War. 1779-1818. *270*
—. California (San Diego). Croix, Carlos Francisco de. Mexico. Mission San Diego de Alcalá. Spain. 1760's-86. *160*
—. Concha, Fernando Simon Ignacio de la. Indian-White Relations. New Mexico. Spain. 1787-93. *155*
—. Croix, Teodoro de. Militia. New Spain (Nueva Vizcaya). 1776-83. *196*
—. Cuervo y Valdes, Francisco. New Mexico (Albuquerque). Spain. 1706-12. *343*
—. Documents. New Mexico. Spain. Vélez Cachupín, Thomas. ca 1754. *297*
—. Frontier and Pioneer Life. Indian Wars. New Mexico. Pueblo Indians. Spain. Texas (El Paso). 1680-90. *219*
—. Land grants. Mendinueta, Pedro Fermín de. New Mexico. Spain. 1767-79. *316*
Colonialism. Culture. Florida. Louisiana Territory. Spain. Texas. 1513-1803. *217*
—. Democracy. Puerto Rico. 1950-80. *1167*
—. Economic Conditions. Independence movements. Puerto Rico. 1898-1977. *1212*
—. Economic Structure. Migration. Puerto Ricans. 1900-80. *1090*
Colonies. Borderlands. Documents. Florida, University of, Gainesville. P. K. Yonge Library of Florida History (guide). Spain. ca 1518-1821. *77*
—. Florida (St. Augustine). Migration. Quantitative methods. Spain. 1600-1800. *186*
—. Hispaniola. Immigration. Louisiana. 1792-1804. *194*
Colonists. California. Hijar-Padres colony. Mexico (San Blas). 1834. *249*
Colonization. Americas (North and South). Discovery and Exploration. Europe. Myths and Symbols. Utopianism. 16c-18c. *225*
—. Americas (North and South). Discovery and exploration. Spain. Vega, Lope de (San Diego de Alcalá). 17c-18c. *342*
—. Land tenure. New Mexico. Spain. Whites. 16c-1974. *29*
—. Bolton, Herbert Eugene. Borderlands studies. Catholic Church. Historiography. Missions and Missionaries. Spain. 1917-79. *9*

—. California. Church and State. Indians. Spain. 1775-1800. *221*

—. California. Discovery and exploration. Mexico. Spain. 1602-1769. *190*

—. California. Mexico. Population. Spain. 1760's-1840's. *222*

—. California (San Diego). Indians. Missions and Missionaries. Spain. 1769-1834. *399*

—. California (Villa de Branciforte). Spain. 1790's-1907. *223*

—. California (Villa de Branciforte). Spain. ca 1790-1821. *317*

—. Castañeda, Carlos Eduardo. Historiography. Spain. Texas. 1693-1731. 1933-43. *144*

—. DeZorita, Alonso. Franciscans. Indians. Missions and Missionaries. Southwest. 1545-85. *378*

—. Discovery and Exploration. Great Britain. Indian-White Relations. Southeastern States. Spain. 1565-1685. *319*

—. Exploitation. Minorities. Womack, John. 1841-1973. *447*

—. Florida. Mexico (Yucatán). Spain. 16c. *397*

—. Indians. Land tenure. New Mexico. Social Organization. Spain. 1546-1692. *313*

—. Indians. New Spain. Policymaking. Settlement. Spain. 1750-1800. *149*

—. Latin America. Law. New Mexico. Spain. 15c-18c. *340*

—. Mexico. Muster rolls. New Mexico (Santa Fe). Páez Hurtado, Juan. 1695. 1978. *356*

—. New Mexico (Rio Puerco). San Francisco (colony). 1866. *558*

Colorado. Armijo, Manuel. Land grants. 1823-1900. *354*

—. California. New Mexico. Political representation. State Politics. ca 1850-1974. *464*

—. Catholic Church. New Mexico. Passion plays. Spain. 1830's-1978. *492*

—. Folk art. New Mexico. Penitentes. 19c-20c. *503*

Colorado (Denver). Blacks. City government. Public Opinion. Whites. 1974. *898*

—. Blacks. Political attitudes. Voting and Voting Behavior. 1971. *897*

—. California (San Diego). Medical Education. Physicians. Texas (San Antonio). 1970-79. *980*

Colorado River. Alarcón, Hernando. California. Discovery and Exploration. Indians. 1540. *207*

Colorado (San Luis Valley). Archuleta, Eppie. Folk art. Personal Narratives. Women. 1922-79. *460*

—. Migrant Labor. 1973. *758*

Colorado, southern. Catholic Church. Death Carts. New Mexico, northern. Penitentes. 1860-90's. *586*

Colorado (Trinidad). Baca, Felipe. Personal narratives. 1862-74. *512*

Columbia River. British Columbia. Discovery and Exploration. Heceta y Fontecha, Bruno de. Pacific Northwest. Spain. 1775. *159*

Comancheros. Cattle Rustling. Hittson, John. Indians. New Mexico. Ranchers. 1872-73. *551*

Commemorations. Explorers. Florida (St. Augustine). Menéndez de Avilés, Pedro. Spain. 1565. 1975. *310*

Commerce. Alvarez, Manuel. Consular service. Mexico. New Mexico (Santa Fe). 1818-47. *180*

—. California (San Francisco). Spain. 1755-1822. *227*

—. Mexican War. Rio Grande. Texas (El Paso). 1821-48. *361*

Commodity exchange. Capital. Economic structure. Plantations. Puerto Rico, southwestern. Sugar cane. 1911. *1305*

Commons. Land grants. Law. New Mexico. San Joaquín Grant. 1806-97. *531*

Communist Party. Harlem Renaissance. Immigrants. Literature. New York City. West Indians. 1930's. *1301*

Community. Minnesota (St. Paul, lower west side). 1914-65. *469*

Community control. Elections. Texas (Crystal City). 1910-75. *922*

—. Political Attitudes. Texas. 1971-77. *752*

Community development. Assimilation. Barrios. 1848-80. *539*

Community Participation in Politics. Barrios. California (East Los Angeles). 1970-73. *1017*

—. California (San Diego; Barrio Logan). Murals. Parks. 1969-84. *767*

—. Economic Development. Government. Indians. New Mexico (Espanola Valley). Water Supply. 1970's. *864*

Community Schools. Attitudes. Ethnic identity. Students. 1974. *855*

Competition. Blacks. Labor. Whites. 1976. *734*

Compromise of 1850. Borders. Spain. Texas Panhandle. 1819-50. *148*

Compulsory Education. Carden, Georgiana. Elementary education. Migrant Labor. 1920's. *641*

Con safos (term). Graffiti. Names, personal. 1967-75. *838*

Concha, Fernando Simon Ignacio de la. Anza, Juan Bautista de. Colonial Government. Indians. Military Strategy. New Mexico. Spain. 1787-93. *161*

—. Apache Indians (Gila, Mimbres). Diaries. Indian Wars. 1788. *213*

—. Colonial Government. Indian-White Relations. New Mexico. Spain. 1787-93. *155*

Confiscations. *Britain* (vessel). Foreign Relations. Great Britain. Spain. Texas (Matagorda Peninsula). 1769-70. *168*

Conflict. Cubans. Ethnicity. Florida (Miami). 1972-79. *1250*

Congress. Aliens, illegal. Economic conditions. Immigration. Public Policy. 1978. *91*

—. Apportionment. Political Power. 1980-83. *123*

—. Bilingual Education Act (US, 1967). Elementary and Secondary Education Act (US, 1968). 1960-80. *117*

—. Political representation. Roll-call voting. 1972-80. *128*

Congress of Industrial Organizations. California (Los Angeles). Labor Unions and Organizations. 1938-50. *606*

Congressional Districts (30th). California (Los Angeles County). Ethnicity. Political candidates. Race. Voting and Voting Behavior. 1982. *754*

Conservatism. Democratic Party. Elections. Political Attitudes. 1980. *1047*

Conspiracy. Foreign Relations. Mexico. Revolutionary Movements. Reyes, Bernardo. State Politics. Texas. Trials. 1911-12. *639*

Constitutional Law. Aliens, illegal. Civil rights. 1970-77. *813*

Consular service. Alvarez, Manuel. Commerce. Mexico. New Mexico (Santa Fe). 1818-47. *180*

Consuls. California. Chileans. Gold rushes. 1848-60. *1231*

Consumerism. Economic development. Puerto Rico. 1940-70. *1129*

Contracts, partido. Employment. Livestock. New Mexico. 1905-11. *656*

Conversion thesis. California. Cook, Sherburne Friend. Franciscans. Indians. Missions and Missionaries. ca 1790-1820's. 1943. *229*

Cook, Sherburne Friend. California. Conversion thesis. Franciscans. Indians. Missions and Missionaries. ca 1790-1820's. 1943. *229*

Copper industry. Arizona. Labor Unions and Organizations. Politics. Racism. Working Class. 1900-20. *611*

Copper Mines and Mining. Arizona (Clifton-Morenci area). Mexico. Migrant Labor. Strikes. 1872-1903. *572*
—. New Mexico (Santa Rita del Cobre). 1800-25. *380*
Coronado expedition. Diaries. Explorers. Southwest. Spain. 1540-42. *355*
Coronado, Francisco Vásquez de. Discovery and Exploration. Southwest. 1540-42. *349*
—. Explorers. Range wars. Sheep Raising. Southwest. 1540-1880's. *171*
"Corrido de Gregorio Cortez" (ballad). Ballads. "Discriminación a un Martir" (ballad). Political Protest. Social change. Texas (Three River). 20c. *468*
"Corrido de los Hermanos" (ballad). Arizona. Ballads. Capital Punishment. Hernández, Federico. Hernández, Manuel. 1934. *683*
Corruption. Angel, Frank W. New Mexico. Violence. Wallace, Lew. 1878. *591*
Costas, Orlando E. Baptists. Ecumenism. Personal narratives. 1980. *21*
Country Life. Economic Conditions. Family. Occupations. Social Organization. Washington (Yakima Valley). 1971. *827*
Court of Private Land Claims. Embudo de Picuris grant. Land grants. New Mexico. 1725-1898. *430*
Courts. Blacks. California (Los Angeles County). Men. Sentencing. Whites. Women. 1977-80. *839*
—. Citizenship. Nationality. Race. 1846-97. *570*
—. Interest groups. Mexican American Legal Defense and Education Fund. 1968-82. *941*
Couts, Cave Johnson. California (San Diego). Diaries. 1849. *581*
Cowboys. Blacks. Daily Life. Indians. Western States. 1860's-90's. *519*
Crime and Criminals. Blacks. California (Los Angeles). Judicial Administration. Whites. 1977-80. *1041*
—. Blacks. Discrimination. Sentencing. Southwest. Whites. 1976-77. *859*
Croix, Carlos Francisco de. California (San Diego). Colonial Government. Mexico. Mission San Diego de Alcalá. Spain. 1760's-86. *160*
Croix, Teodoro de. California (Los Angeles). Toponymy. 1769-82. *368*
—. Colonial Government. Militia. New Spain (Nueva Vizcaya). 1776-83. *196*
Crusade for Justice. Gonzales, Rodolfo "Corky". Southwest. 1966-72. *908*
Cuba. Acculturation. Attitudes. Cubans. Revolution. 1958-82. *1074*
—. Airplanes. Deportation. Hijacking. International law. Refugees. 1983. *1191*
—. Church records. Florida (St. Augustine). 1594-1763. 20c. *185*
—. Cigar industry. Florida (Tampa). General strikes. Spain. 1901-11. *1253*
—. Cubans. Politics. 1959-81. *1322*
—. Economic Conditions. Political Change. Refugees. 1960-82. *1240*
—. Economic policy. Foreign policy. 1933-34. *1082*
—. Exiles. Florida. Teachers. 1959-70. *1254*
—. Exiles. Florida (Key West). Human Relations. Independence Movements. Ten Years' War. 1868-78. *1252*
—. Florida (Dade County; Miami). Immigration. International Trade. Latin America. Social Customs. 1970's. *1314*
—. Foreign policy. Immigration. 1959-80. *1283*
Cuba (Mariel). Refugees. 1959-81. *1317*
Cubans. Acculturation. Attitudes. Cuba. Revolution. 1958-82. *1074*
—. Acculturation. Drug abuse. Immigration. Social Customs. Values. Youth. 1950-80. *1237*
—. Advertising. Art. Cigars. Florida (Tampa). 1868-1930's. *1307*

—. Areíto, Grupo. History Task Force. Immigration. Johnson, Roberta Ann. Puerto Ricans. 1960's-70's. *1226*
—. Assimilation. 1959-83. *1154*
—. Assimilation. Ethnicity. Exiles. 1959-76. *1165*
—. Assimilation. Exiles. Federal Policy. Mexicans. 1959-81. *138*
—. Assimilation. Exiles. Florida (Miami). 1973-79. *1318*
—. Assimilation. Refugees. 1980-83. *1320*
—. Assimilation. Refugees. Research. 1959-83. *1268*
—. Attitudes. Refugees. 1980. *1190*
—. Attitudes. Refugees. Working Conditions. 1970-81. *1148*
—. Bibliographies. Florida (Miami). Immigration. 20c. *79*
—. Biculturalism. Bilingual education. New Jersey. Puerto Ricans. 19c-20c. *1101*
—. Blacks. Business. Economic structure. Florida (Miami). 1920's-80. *1308*
—. Blacks. Discrimination, Housing. Metropolitan Areas. Mexicans. Prices. Puerto Ricans. Whites. 1975-76. *62*
—. Business. Entrepreneurs. Florida (Miami). Immigrants. 1960-84. *1163*
—. Business. Ownership. 1977. *1133*
—. Carter, Jimmy. Federal Policy. Immigration. Political Leadership. 1980. *1123*
—. Cigar industry. Florida (Tampa). Independence Movements. Labor. 1892-1901. *1242*
—. Cities. Mexicans. Puerto Ricans. Residential segregation. 1950's-70's. *69*
—. City Life. Ethnicity. Folklore. Indiana (East Chicago). Puerto Ricans. 1976. *1161*
—. City politics. Florida (Jacksonville). Huah, José Alejandro. Independence Movements. Martí, José. 1836-1905. *1164*
—. Conflict. Ethnicity. Florida (Miami). 1972-79. *1250*
—. Cuba. Politics. 1959-81. *1322*
—. Deportation. Mental Illness. Refugees. 1980-83. *1162*
—. *Diario Las Americas.* Florida (Miami). Journalism. Politics and Media. Watergate scandal. 1970's. *1061*
—. Economic Conditions. Florida. Politics. Refugees. 1980-81. *1076*
—. Education. Florida (Miami). Geographic mobility. Income. Political power. 1959-78. *1241*
—. Education. Occupations. Political Imprisonment. Refugees. 1973-80. *1077*
—. Employment. Refugees. Social Problems. 1982. *1316*
—. Exiles. 1960-75. *1109*
—. Exiles. Latin America. Martí, José. New York City. Reporters and Reporting. 1880-95. *1068*
—. Exiles. Puerto Rico. 1959-73. *1081*
—. Exiles. Social Classes. 1959-70. *1248*
—. Florida (Key West). Labor. Martí, José. Tobacco Industry. 1891. *1170*
—. Florida (Key West). Revolutionary Movements. Spain. 1878-86. *1251*
—. Florida (Miami). Housing. Middle Classes. Segregation. 1950-74. *1310*
—. Florida (Miami). New York City. Puerto Rico (San Juan). Social Classes. 1950-77. *1121*
—. Florida (Miami). Puerto Ricans. Residential patterns. 1970's. *1060*
—. Florida (Miami; Little Havana). Social customs. 1959-80's. *1100*
—. Florida (Tampa). Labor Disputes. *Lector* (reader). Perez, Louis A., Jr. Personal narratives. Tobacco industry. ca 1925-35. *1243*
—. Foreign Relations. Refugees. 1980-82. *1233*
—. Immigrants. Income. Mexicans. 1973-76. *92*

—. International Rescue Committee (Caribbean Relief Program). New Jersey. Refugees. Settlement. 1959-83. *1145*
—. Marriage. 1957-74. *1059*
—. Mexicans. Migration, internal. North Central States. Puerto Ricans. Social Conditions. Southwest. 1970. *32*
—. Naturalization. Political Participation. Refugees. Voting and Voting Behavior. 1959-84. *1249*
Cuervo y Valdes, Francisco. Colonial government. New Mexico (Albuquerque). Spain. 1706-12. *343*
Cult practices. Psychotherapeutic processes. Puerto Rico. Social organization. 1975. *1189*
Cultural heritage. Behavior. Mexico. 16c-20c. *455*
Cultural identity. California. Marxism. Political power. San Diego State University. 1965-74. *992*
—. Economic conditions. Emigration. Mead, Margaret (interview). Puerto Rico. 1974. *1218*
Cultural myopia (Anglo-American). Art. California. Catholic Church. Missions and Missionaries. Scholasticism. 1740's-1976. *307*
Cultural relations. 1970-80. *825*
Culture. Art. Ethnicity. Murals. 1960's-80. *714*
—. Art. Institute of Puerto Rican Culture. Muñoz Marín, Luis. Puerto Rico. Romero Barceló, Carlos. 1948-55. *1277*
—. Colonialism. Florida. Louisiana Territory. Spain. Texas. 1513-1803. *217*
—. Institute of Puerto Rican Culture. Puerto Rico. Theater. 1955-80. *1211*
—. Literature. New Mexico. 1610-1983. *5*
—. National Characteristics. Puerto Rico. Social Organization. 1930's-70's. *1258*
—. Southwest. 1900. 1980. *507*
Curanderismo. Folk Medicine. Utah. 20c. *409*
Curricula. Attitudes. Bilingual Education. Children. Parents. 1960's-70's. *902*
—. California (Los Angeles). Educational reform. Public schools. 1920's-30's. *631*
Czech Americans. Family. Labor. Land. Social Organization. Texas (Nueces County). 1880-1930. *608*

D

Daily Life. Authors. Steinbeck, John. 20c. *463*
—. Blacks. Cowboys. Indians. Western States. 1860's-90's. *519*
—. Borders. Cities. Poverty. Social Conditions. 1945-77. *911*
—. California. Diaries. Mexican War. Mormon Battalion. Social Customs. 1846-55. *601*
—. California (Los Angeles). Mott, Thomas. Sepúlveda y Ávila, María Ascensión. 1844-61. *600*
—. Cháves, Jesús (family). New Mexico, eastern. Sheepherders. 1850's-1930's. *462*
—. Civil-military relations. Florida (St. Augustine). Social organization. Spain. 1580. *279*
—. Florida (St. Augustine). Research. Spain. 1580. 1970's. *239*
—. Hinojosa, Rolando. Literature. Rivera, Tomás. Social Customs. Southwest. 1980. *756*
—. Immigrants. Latin Americans. Popular culture. West Indians. 1965-77. *12*
—. Indians. Letters. Lummis, Charles. Smith, Joseph. Southwest. 1880's-1924. *544*
—. Labor. New Mexico (Albuquerque). Social mobility. Trade. 1706-90. *330*
—. New Mexico (Valles Caldera). Sheepherders. ca 1875-1941. *582*
—. Photography, Journalistic. Smithers, W. D. Texas. 1910-60's. *471*
Dance. California. Social Customs. 1820's-50's. *341*

Dancers. Arizona (Tucson). Musicians. Popular Culture. 1892-1982. *682*
Dating. Blacks. Race Relations. Whites. 1978-79. *884*
Davis, James J. California (Los Angeles County). Deportation. Depressions. Unemployment. 1931. *647*
DeAnza expedition, 2d. California. Explorers. Font, Pedro. 1775-76. *170*
Death Carts. Catholic Church. Colorado, southern. New Mexico, northern. Penitentes. 1860-90's. *586*
Decisionmaking. Cities. Health centers. Neighborhoods. 1969-70. *854*
Defense Policy. Indian Wars. Mexico, northern. Southwest. Spain. 1759-88. *304*
DelaPeña, José Enrique. Alamo (battle). Personal Narratives. Santa Anna, Antonio Lopez de. Texas. 1836. *195*
DelCastillo, Adelaida R. Enriquez, Evangelina. Melville, Margarita B. Mexican Americans. Mirande, Alfredo. Research. Women (review article). 19c-20c. *135*
delValle family. California. Rancho Camulos. Upper Classes. 1839-1938. *442*
Democracy. Colonialism. Puerto Rico. 1950-80. *1167*
Democratic Party. Apodaca, Jerry. Elections (gubernatorial). New Mexico. Race Relations. 1974. *1032*
—. Conservatism. Elections. Political Attitudes. 1980. *1047*
Demography. *See also* Population.
—. Birth rate. Puerto Rico. 1974. *1296*
—. Blacks. Households. Mothers, single. Puerto Ricans. Whites. 1970. *1119*
—. California. New Mexico. ca 1850. *568*
—. Ecology. Economic Conditions. New Mexico (north central). Social change. 1770-1970. *502*
—. Fertility. 1970-80. *700*
—. Migration. Puerto Rico. Social Problems. 1960-75. *1176*
Demun, Julius. Chouteau, Auguste P. Indian-White Relations. Law. New Mexico. Trade. 1815-51. *375*
Deportation. Airplanes. Cuba. Hijacking. International law. Refugees. 1983. *1191*
—. California (Los Angeles County). Davis, James J. Depressions. Unemployment. 1931. *647*
—. Cubans. Mental Illness. Refugees. 1980-83. *1162*
—. Emigration. Newspapers. Reporters and Reporting. 1930-76. *420*
—. Immigrants. Labor Unions and Organizations. New Deal. 1930's. *618*
—. Labor. Mexico. Migration. 1920-75. *413*
—. Statistics. Workers, undocumented. 1972-77. *762*
Depressions. Arts and Crafts. New Mexico. 1846-1930's. *505*
—. California (Los Angeles County). Davis, James J. Deportation. Unemployment. 1931. *647*
—. Discrimination. Indiana (Gary). Nativism. Repatriation. 1920's-30's. *609*
—. Indiana (East Chicago). Repatriation. 1919-33. *684*
—. Mexico. Migrant Labor. Obregón, Álvaro. Repatriation. 1920-23. *613*
Desegregation. Texas (San Antonio). 1960-65. *829*
Design. Catholic Church. Folk art. Iconography. Manuscripts. New Mexico. 16c-17c. *233*
Developing nations. Capitalism. Production. Puerto Rico. ca 1940-79. *1137*
Development. Americanization. Bhana, Surendra. Clark, Truman. Matthews, Thomas. Politics. Puerto Rico (review article). 1917-76. *1261*
—. Class struggle. Ideology. Political change. Puerto Rico. 1940-78. *1238*

DeZorita, Alonso. Colonization. Franciscans. Indians. Missions and Missionaries. Southwest. 1545-85. *378*

Dialects. Bibliographies. Espinosa, Aurelio M. Folklore. New Mexico, northern. Spain. 1907-54. *31*

—. Southwest. Spanish language. 1976. *899*

—. Spanish language. 1974. *1023*

Diaries. Apache Indians (Gila, Mimbres). Concha, Fernando Simon Ignacio de la. Indian Wars. 1788. *213*

—. Attitudes. Discrimination. New Mexico. Women. 1840's-50's. *593*

—. California. Daily Life. Mexican War. Mormon Battalion. Social Customs. 1846-55. *601*

—. California (San Diego). Couts, Cave Johnson. 1849. *581*

—. Coronado expedition. Explorers. Southwest. Spain. 1540-42. *355*

—. Fuente, Pedro José de la. Indian Wars. Mexico (Chihuahua, Sonora). Military. New Mexico. Texas (El Paso). 1765. *192*

Diario del Gobierno de la República Mexicana. Bibliographies. Periodicals. Texas. 1836-45. *75*

Diario Las Americas. Cubans. Florida (Miami). Journalism. Politics and Media. Watergate scandal. 1970's. *1061*

Diego, José de. Independence Movements. Middle classes. Puerto Rico. 1867-1918. *1139*

Diplomacy. Alvarez, Manuel. Mexico. New Mexico. Texas. Trading expeditions. 1841. *181*

—. Annexation. Eve, Joseph. Flood, George H. LaBranche, Alcée. Letters. Murphy, William S. Texas. 1837-43. *162*

—. Borderlands. Mexico. Trade. 1858-1905. *516*

—. Guadalupe Hidalgo, Treaty of. Mexican War. Trist, Nicholas P. 1848. *517*

—. Indians. Navajo Indians. New Mexico. Spain. 1770-90. *324*

Disability. Employment. English language. Men. Wages. 1976. *705*

Discovery and Exploration. Alarcón, Hernando. California. Colorado River. Indians. 1540. *207*

—. Alvarado, Pedro de. Cabrillo, Juan Rodríguez. Colonial Government. Mendoza, Antonio de. New Spain. Printing press. 1515-52. *158*

—. Americas (North and South). Colonization. Europe. Myths and Symbols. Utopianism. 16c-18c. *225*

—. Americas (North and South). Colonization. Spain. Vega, Lope de *(San Diego de Alcalá).* 17c-18c. *342*

—. Americas (North and South). LasCasas, Bartolomé de. Settlement. 16c-17c. *276*

—. Anza, Juan Bautista de. Bicentennial Celebrations. California. Mexico. Reenactments. 1775-76. 1975-76. *208*

—. Ascensión, Antonio de la. California. Mexico. Vizcaíno, Sebastian. Voyages. 1590-1737. *285*

—. Ayala, Juan Manuel de. California (San Francisco Bay). Franciscans. Indians. Spain. 1775. *369*

—. Blacks. Esteban. Florida. South Central and Gulf States. Spain. 1528-39. *302*

—. British Columbia. Columbia River. Heceta y Fontecha, Bruno de. Pacific Northwest. Spain. 1775. *159*

—. Cabrillo, Juan Rodríguez. California. Shipbuilding. 1532-42. *259*

—. California. Vizcaíno, Sebastián. 1596-1627. *284*

—. California. Colonial Government. Missions and Missionaries. Settlement. Spain. 1691-1810. *262*

—. California. Colonization. Mexico. Spain. 1602-1769. *190*

—. California. Settlement. Vizcaíno, Sebastian. 1602-32. *154*

—. California (Drake's Bay). Toponymy. Viscáino, Sebastian. 1602-03. *286*

—. California (Monterey). Dominguez, Francisco Atanasio. Escalante, Silvestre Velez de. New Mexico. 1765-1805. *143*

—. California (Monterey). Dominguez, Francisco Atanasio. Escalante, Silvestre Velez de. New Mexico (Santa Fe). 1776-77. *169*

—. California (San Diego area). Indians. Portolá, Gaspar de. South Carolina. 1769. *175*

—. Colonization. Great Britain. Indian-White Relations. Southeastern States. Spain. 1565-1685. *319*

—. Coronado, Francisco Vásquez de. Southwest. 1540-42. *349*

—. El Morro National Monument. New Mexico. Rock inscriptions. Spain. Prehistory-1620. *167*

—. Ethnicity. National Characteristics. Social Customs (review article). Urbansk, Edmund S. 17c-18c. *331*

—. Georgia. North Carolina. Salazar, Pedro de. Slave raids. South Carolina. Spain. 1514-16. *238*

—. Jesuits. Kino, Eusebio Francisco. Southwest. 1645-1711. *258*

—. Myths and Symbols. Settlement. Southwest. Spain. 16c-18c. *235*

—. Southwest. 1776. *360*

"Discriminación a un Martir" (ballad). Ballads. "Corrido de Gregorio Cortez" (ballad). Political Protest. Social change. Texas (Three River). 20c. *468*

Discrimination. 1907-73. *478*

—. Age. Blacks. Income. Texas. 1960-70. *926*

—. Attitudes. Diaries. New Mexico. Women. 1840's-50's. *593*

—. Attitudes. Family. Personal narratives. Professions. Success. Women. 1980. *997*

—. Blacks. Civil-Military Relations. Race Relations. Texas (Rio Grande City). Violence. Whites. 1899-1900. *524*

—. Blacks. Crime and Criminals. Sentencing. Southwest. Whites. 1976-77. *859*

—. California. Gold Rushes. Mexico (Sonora). Migration. 1848-56. *585*

—. College graduates. Wages. 1966-74. *961*

—. Colleges and universities. 1950's-80's. *846*

—. Depressions. Indiana (Gary). Nativism. Repatriation. 1920's-30's. *609*

—. Education. 1970's-82. *86*

—. Ethnic Groups. Kansas (Dodge City). Public Opinion. 1900-84. *450*

—. Humor. Social Customs. 1966-75. *891*

—. Income. Men. Whites. 1976. *121*

—. Labor Unions and Organizations. North Central States. Steel workers. 1919-45. *677*

—. Labor Unions and Organizations. Texas (El Paso). 1880-1920. *629*

—. Political consciousness. 1930-75. *486*

—. Political familialism. Sex roles. 1970-75. *719*

—. Social Status. 1845-1980. *495*

Discrimination, Employment. Blacks. Men. Wages. Whites. 1980-81. *1029*

—. Economic Conditions. Men. Productivity. 1960's-70's. *65*

—. Family. New Mexico (Santa Fe). Texas (San Antonio). 1860. *513*

—. Immigration. Residence, prior. 1973-74. *856*

—. Political Protest. World War II. Wyoming. 1941-45. *643*

—. Women. Working class. 1973-76. *982*

Discrimination, Housing. Blacks. Cubans. Metropolitan Areas. Mexicans. Prices. Puerto Ricans. Whites. 1975-76. *62*

Divorce. Blacks. Whites. 1960-70. *809*

Documentary Relations of the Southwest project. Arizona State Museum. Indians. Mexico, northern. Southwest. Spain. 16c-1810. 1975-78. *322*

Documents. Agriculture. Economic Conditions. Migrant Labor. Social Conditions. Working conditions. 1942-45. *694*

—. Borderlands. Colonies. Florida, University of, Gainesville. P. K. Yonge Library of Florida History (guide). Spain. ca 1518-1821. *77*

—. Bracero Program. Employment. Railroads. 1945. *695*

—. Bracero program. Mexico. 1944. *622*

—. Colonial Government. New Mexico. Spain. Vélez Cachupín, Thomas. ca 1754. *297*

—. Episcopal Church, Protestant. Missions and Missionaries. Puerto Rico. 1870-1952. *1091*

Dogs. Arizona (Canyon de Chelly). Bones. Indian Wars. Navajo Indians. Pictographs. Spain. 1750-1863. *202*

Dominguez, Francisco Atanasio. California (Monterey). Discovery and Exploration. Escalante, Silvestre Velez de. New Mexico. 1765-1805. *143*

—. California (Monterey). Discovery and Exploration. Escalante, Silvestre Velez de. New Mexico (Santa Fe). 1776-77. *169*

Domínguez, Juan José. California (Compton). Domínguez Ranch Adobe. 1784-1981. *427*

Domínguez Ranch Adobe. California (Compton). Domínguez, Juan José. 1784-1981. *427*

Dominican Republic. Immigration. 1965-76. *1295*

—. Public expenditures. Puerto Rico. 1930-70. *1207*

Dominicans. California. Franciscans. Jesuits. Missions and Missionaries. Serra, Junípero. 1768-76. *287*

—. Colombians. Employment. Family. Immigrants. New York City. Women. 1981. *1171*

—. Colombians. New York City. Social organizations. ca 1972-76. *1282*

—. Family. Immigration. 1962-76. *1157*

Dramatists. Puerto Rico. Women. 19c-1979. *1127*

Drug abuse. Acculturation. Cubans. Immigration. Social Customs. Values. Youth. 1950-80. *1237*

—. California (Los Angeles County). Law Enforcement. Rehabilitation. Statistics. 1969-79. *906*

—. Economic Conditions. Immigration. Inhalants. Social Conditions. Youth. 1930-80. *429*

Drug abuse programs. California (Oxnard). 1972-73. *696*

Drugs. Behavior. High schools. Puerto Rico. Youth. 1970-80. *1263*

Durán, Narciso. California. Franciscans. Indians. Missions and Missionaries. Music. 1806-46. *224*

—. California. Franciscans. Indians. Missions and Missionaries. Secularization. 1826-46. *305*

Dye. Blankets. Indians. Navajo Indians. New Mexico. Rugs. Spaniards. Weaving. 19c-1977. *353*

E

Earthquakes. Attitudes. Blacks. Whites. 1977. *1020*

Easter Week. Anecdotes. Baca, Father. Frontier and Pioneer Life. New Mexico (Tome, Valencia). Rites and Ceremonies. 1846. *209*

Ecology. Anthropology. Methodology. New Mexico (northern). Social organization. Trade. 17c-20c. *63*

—. Demography. Economic Conditions. New Mexico (north central). Social change. 1770-1970. *502*

Econometrics. Models. Puerto Rico. 1948-64. *1285*

Economic Conditions. Acculturation. Bilingualism. 1848-1977. *482*

—. Acculturation. Hawaii. Immigrants. Puerto Ricans. 1900-02. *1287*

—. Age. Fertility. Puerto Rico. Social Status. Women. 1970. *1182*

—. Agriculture. Documents. Migrant Labor. Social Conditions. Working conditions. 1942-45. *694*

—. Agriculture. Industrialization. Puerto Rico. 1960's-70's. *1126*

—. Agriculture. Puerto Rico. Social Organization. 1870-1930. *1083*

—. Aliens, illegal. Congress. Immigration. Public Policy. 1978. *91*

—. Aliens (illegal). Mexico. USA. 1946-65. *807*

—. Aliens (illegal). Stereotypes. 1930-76. *452*

—. Anthropology, Cultural. Methodology. Puerto Rico. Steward, Julian H. *(People of Puerto Rico).* 1956-77. *1311*

—. Arizona (Tucson). California (Los Angeles). Racism. Social Conditions. Texas (San Antonio). 1850-1900. *528*

—. Blacks. Chinese Americans. Filipinos. Japanese. Social Status. 1960-76. *51*

—. Blacks. City Life. Social Organization. 1960-71. *994*

—. Blacks. Immigration. New York City. Public Opinion. West Indies. 1965-79. *1099*

—. Blacks. Whites. Wisconsin (Racine). 1960-71. *781*

—. Border policy. Mexico. Workers, undocumented. 1952-75. *739*

—. Borderlands studies. Mexico. Southwest. 1970's. *116*

—. California. Catholic Church. Indians. Missions and Missionaries. 1803-21. *151*

—. California. Immigration, illegal. Labor. Mexico, west-central. 1970's. *778*

—. California (East Los Angeles). Catholic Church. Reform. Social Conditions. United Neighborhoods Organization. 1960's-80. *945*

—. Coalition Government. Puerto Rico. 1917-33. *1313*

—. Colonialism. Independence movements. Puerto Rico. 1898-1977. *1212*

—. Country Life. Family. Occupations. Social Organization. Washington (Yakima Valley). 1971. *827*

—. Cuba. Political Change. Refugees. 1960-82. *1240*

—. Cubans. Florida. Politics. Refugees. 1980-81. *1076*

—. Cultural identity. Emigration. Mead, Margaret (interview). Puerto Rico. 1974. *1218*

—. Demography. Ecology. New Mexico (north central). Social change. 1770-1970. *502*

—. Discrimination, employment. Men. Productivity. 1960's-70's. *65*

—. Drug abuse. Immigration. Inhalants. Social Conditions. Youth. 1930-80. *429*

—. Federal Aid to Education. Neocolonialism. Puerto Rico. Social Classes. 1970's. *1245*

—. Federal Government. Puerto Rico. 1898-1941. *1114*

—. Federal Policy. New Federalism. Reagan, Ronald. Social Problems. 1980-83. *716*

—. Foreign Policy. Puerto Rico. 1982. *1178*

—. Government. Puerto Rico. Social classes. 1930-50. *1085*

—. Health services. Indians. Navajo Indians. New Mexico, northwestern. Population. Rural areas. Spaniards. 1971-78. *93*

—. Historiography. Labor. Mexican Americans. 1850-1976. *8*

—. Identity. Southwest. 1900. *567*

—. Immigration. Labor. Mexico. Social control. 1950's-70's. *865*

—. Independence. Interviews. Muñoz Marín, Luis. Political issues. Puerto Rico. Social Conditions. 1948-64. *1186*

—. Land tenure. New Mexico. Social Organization. Spaniards. Whites. 1846-91. *594*

—. Mexico. Workers, undocumented. 1972-73. *954*

—. Migration, internal. Models. Puerto Rico. 1935-40. *1092*
—. Pacific Northwest. 1960-79. *999*
—. Politics. Puerto Rico. 1975. *1292*
—. Politics. Southwest. Workers, undocumented. 1975-78. *740*
—. Puerto Rico. 1946-81. *1107*
—. Puerto Rico. Rural Settlements. Social Organization. Standard of living. 1960-72. *1080*
—. Social Organization. 1971-81. *932*
Economic Development. Anthropology, Cultural. Methodology. Puerto Rico. Steward, Julian H. *(People of Puerto Rico)*. 1956-77. *1272*
—. Capital. Labor. Models. Puerto Rico. 1945-70. *1222*
—. Community Participation in Politics. Government. Indians. New Mexico (Espanola Valley). Water Supply. 1970's. *864*
—. Consumerism. Puerto Rico. 1940-70. *1129*
—. Ethnic Groups. New Mexico (Santa Fe). Population. 1790-99. *146*
—. Immigration. 1910-30. *675*
—. Imperialism. Political conditions. Puerto Rico. Social organization. 1900-72. *1131*
—. Income. Puerto Rico. Unemployment. 1959-70. *1201*
—. Industrialization. Puerto Rico. 1960's-70's. *1102*
—. Mexico (Guadalupe). Migrant Labor. 1977-78. *964*
—. Midwest. Migrant Labor. 1900-30. *685*
—. Political status. Population growth. Puerto Rico. 1940-76. *1303*
—. Population. Puerto Rico. Unemployment. 1940's-70's. *1244*
—. Puerto Rico. 1940-81. *1281*
—. Puerto Rico. 1950-74. *1110*
—. Southwest. Working class. 1603-1900. *438*
Economic growth. Education. Income distribution. Puerto Rico. 1950-76. *1199*
—. Employment. 1969-75. *873*
—. New Mexico (Albuquerque). Urbanization. World War II. 1940-75. *920*
Economic Integration. Industrialization. International Trade. Puerto Rico. 1948-63. *1302*
Economic mobility. California (Los Angeles). 1850-80. *541*
Economic opportunity. Agricultural Labor. Aliens, Illegal. Immigration. "Push/pull" hypothesis. 1948-72. *866*
—. Immigration. Puerto Rico. 1947-73. *1202*
Economic policy. Cuba. Foreign policy. 1933-34. *1082*
Economic relations. Centro de Estudios Puertorriqueños (History Task Force). Levine, Barry B. Puerto Rico (review article). Sariola, Sakari. 1898-1970's. *1184*
Economic status. Blacks. Ethnicity. Social Classes. Stress. Whites. 1974. *708*
Economic structure. Blacks. Business. Cubans. Florida (Miami). 1920's-80. *1308*
—. Capital. Commodity exchange. Plantations. Puerto Rico, southwestern. Sugar cane. 1911. *1305*
—. Capitalism. Immigration. Labor. Latin Americans. Minorities. ca 1950-70. *1290*
—. Colonialism. Migration. Puerto Ricans. 1900-80. *1090*
—. Education. Migrant Labor. 1970-80. *141*
—. New Mexico. Villages. 18c-1978. *1039*
—. Political status. Puerto Rico. 1949-72. *1200*
Economics. Agricultural Labor. California, University of, Berkeley. Newlands Act (US, 1902). Taylor, Paul S. 1895-1980. *494*
—. Investments. Puerto Rico. USA. 1970's. *1315*
Ecumenism. Baptists. Costas, Orlando E. Personal narratives. 1980. *21*

Editors and Editing. Arizona (Tucson). *El Fronterizo*. Elites. Velasco, Carlos. 1865-1914. *536*
—. Press. Revolution. Southwest. 1911-17. *634*
Education. *See also* Bilingual Education, Compulsory Education, and Elementary Education, etc.
—. Adventists. Missions and Missionaries. New Mexico (Sandoval). Spanish-American Seminary. 1928-53. *679*
—. Age. Ethnicity. Family. New York City. Puerto Ricans. 1958-79. *1270*
—. Asians. Blacks. Ethnicity. Immigrants. Occupational mobility. 1965-70. *99*
—. Attitudes. Blacks. Immigration. Wisconsin (Racine). 1974. *993*
—. California (Los Angeles). Census. Literacy. Quantitative Methods. 1850. *596*
—. California (Los Angeles). Racism. 1920-32. *632*
—. Cubans. Florida (Miami). Geographic mobility. Income. Political power. 1959-78. *1241*
—. Cubans. Occupations. Political Imprisonment. Refugees. 1973-80. *1077*
—. Discrimination. 1970's-82. *86*
—. Economic growth. Income distribution. Puerto Rico. 1950-76. *1199*
—. Economic structure. Migrant Labor. 1970-80. *141*
—. Employment. Ethnicity. Family. Women. 1970's. *1051*
—. Employment. New York. Puerto Ricans. Women. 1960's. *1118*
—. Employment. Texas, West. Whites. 1860-1900. *588*
—. Family. Fertility. Income. Occupations. Puerto Ricans. 1969-70. *1325*
—. Family. Income. Occupations. 1969-70. *1057*
—. Fertility. Generations. Women. 1976. *725*
—. Immigration. Puerto Rico. Unemployment. 1955-70. *1298*
—. Income. Indiana (South Bend). Population. Social Mobility. 1970-74. *798*
—. Labor. Political power. Southwest. 1848-1980. *635*
—. Language. Men. Social Status. 1975-76. *119*
—. Migrant labor. Social Problems. 1973. *905*
—. Personal narratives. Rodriguez, Richard. 1950's-60's. *1053*
—. Puerto Rico. 1940-77. *1084*
—. West Florida. 1781-1821. *240*
Education, Experimental Methods. Centers for Educational Services. Puerto Rico. 1973-77. *1125*
Educational achievement. Migration. -1973. *738*
—. Self-perception. -1973. *799*
Educational policy. Bibliographies. Energy crisis. Foreign Relations. Middle East. National Autonomous University of Mexico (Faculty of Political and Social Sciences). Periodicals. Social Conditions. 1970-81. *7*
Educational reform. California (Los Angeles). Curricula. Public schools. 1920's-30's. *631*
Educational Tests and Measurements. Stereotypes. 1920-76. *401*
Effigies. California. Mission San Antonio de Padua. Pottery. 18c-19c. *214*
El Fronterizo. Arizona (Tucson). Editors and Editing. Elites. Velasco, Carlos. 1865-1914. *536*
El Morro National Monument. Discovery and Exploration. New Mexico. Rock inscriptions. Spain. Prehistory-1620. *167*
El Paso-Juárez Conference. Foreign Relations. Mexico. Punitive expeditions. Villa, Pancho. 1916. *637*
Elections. Agricultural Industry. California. Labor Unions and Organizations. Proposition 14 (1976). United Farm Workers Union. 1976. *773*

—. Agriculture. California. Chavez, Cesar. Proposition 14 (1976). United Farm Workers Union. 1975-76. *996*

—. Anaya, Toney. New Mexico. 1968-82. *1031*

—. Arizona. School boards. Voting and Voting Behavior. 1972-74. *817*

—. Community control. Texas (Crystal City). 1910-75. *922*

—. Conservatism. Democratic Party. Political Attitudes. 1980. *1047*

—. Funerals. Muñoz Marín, Luis. New Progressive Party. Popular Democratic Party. Puerto Rico. 1980. *1215*

—. Political Conventions. Puerto Rico. Rites and Ceremonies. 1968. *1257*

Elections (gubernatorial). Apodaca, Jerry. Democratic Party. New Mexico. Race Relations. 1974. *1032*

—. Barceló, Carlos Romero. Government. Hernández, Rafael. Puerto Rico. 1980. *1193*

Elections (mayoral). King, Mel. Massachusetts (Boston). 1983. *1097*

Electronics industry. California (Santa Clara County). Women. Working conditions. 1970-79. *730*

Elementary and Secondary Education Act (US, 1968). Bilingual Education Act (US, 1967). Congress. 1960-80. *117*

Elementary and Secondary Education Act (US, 1969; Title VII). Bilingual education. Federal Aid to Education. 1973. *58*

Elementary Education. Assimilation. Texas (San Antonio). 1973. *883*

—. Bibliographies. Bilingual education. 1970's. *19*

—. Carden, Georgiana. Compulsory Education. Migrant Labor. 1920's. *641*

Elites. Arizona (Tucson). 1850-80. *583*

—. Arizona (Tucson). Editors and Editing. *El Fronterizo.* Velasco, Carlos. 1865-1914. *536*

—. Barceló, Gertrudis. Business. Gambling. New Mexico (Santa Fe). Women. 1830's-40's. *273*

—. Migrant labor. Political conditions. 1946-72. *57*

—. Political socialization. 1978-80. *782*

Elizando, Sergio. Gonzales, Thomas Rodolfo. Literature. 1970's. *742*

Embudo de Picuris grant. Court of Private Land Claims. Land grants. New Mexico. 1725-1898. *430*

Emergency Farm Labor Supply Program. Agricultural Labor Relations Act (California, 1975). California. Labor law. New Deal. ca 1930-79. *434*

Emigration. Capitalism. Puerto Rico. 1945-70. *1204*

—. Change and Response, Theory of. Fertility. Migration, Internal. Puerto Rico. 1940's-70. *1228*

—. Cultural identity. Economic conditions. Mead, Margaret (interview). Puerto Rico. 1974. *1218*

—. Deportation. Newspapers. Reporters and Reporting. 1930-76. *420*

—. Family. Puerto Ricans. Social Organization. 1970-82. *1071*

—. Mexico. 1900-70. *424*

Employment. Agricultural labor. Bracero Program. Southwest. Wages. 1954-77. *869*

—. Americanization. Immigration. Industry. Public schools. 1880-1930. *624*

—. Attitudes. Sex roles. Whites. Women. Youth. 1979. *88*

—. Blacks. City Government. Texas. Urbanization. 1973. *842*

—. Blacks. Family. Income. Sex roles. Whites. 1982-83. *47*

—. Blacks. Marriage. Mothers. Whites. Women. 1970-84. *46*

—. Blacks. Population. Race. Students. Whites. Youth. 1967-83. *133*

—. Blacks. Southwest. Whites. Women. 1950-70. *771*

—. Bracero Program. Documents. Railroads. 1945. *695*

—. California (Los Angeles). Industry. Interviews. Women. 1928. *686*

—. California, southern. Cities. 1900-39. *663*

—. Colombians. Dominicans. Family. Immigrants. New York City. Women. 1981. *1171*

—. Contracts, partido. Livestock. New Mexico. 1905-11. *656*

—. Cubans. Refugees. Social Problems. 1982. *1316*

—. Disability. English language. Men. Wages. 1976. *705*

—. Economic growth. 1969-75. *873*

—. Education. Ethnicity. Family. Women. 1970's. *1051*

—. Education. New York. Puerto Ricans. Women. 1960's. *1118*

—. Education. Texas, West. Whites. 1860-1900. *588*

—. Illinois (Chicago Heights). Politics. Social Conditions. 1910-76. *436*

—. Immigrants. 1973-79. *956*

—. Immigrants. 1976-78. *120*

—. Immigration. Oregon. 1900-70. *488*

—. Latin Americans. New York City. Women. 1970's. *1278*

—. New York. Puerto Ricans. Women. 1920's-40's. *1188*

—. Social services. Workers, undocumented. 1975-79. *988*

—. Women. 1969-74. *715*

—. Women. 1970-82. *16*

Energy crisis. Bibliographies. Educational policy. Foreign Relations. Middle East. National Autonomous University of Mexico (Faculty of Political and Social Sciences). Periodicals. Social Conditions. 1970-81. *7*

England (London). Blacks. Immigration. New York City. Social status. West Indians. 20c. *1153*

English language. *See also* Bilingualism.

—. Adolescence. Bilingualism. Border towns. California. Spanish language. 1970-79. *698*

—. Attitudes. Popular Culture. Spanish language. Theater. 1970's. *1022*

—. Bibliographies. Literature. Puerto Rico. 1923-73. *80*

—. Bilingual education. Puerto Rico. Teaching. 1978. *1234*

—. Children. Grammar. Texas. 1976. *832*

—. Disability. Employment. Men. Wages. 1976. *705*

—. Family. Sex. Spanish language. 1970's. *697*

—. Illinois (Chicago). Southwest. Spanish language. 1979. *710*

—. Names (personal). Spanish language. Texas (El Paso). 1981. *769*

—. Social Change. 1976. *39*

Enriquez, Evangelina. DelCastillo, Adelaida R. Melville, Margarita B. Mexican Americans. Mirande, Alfredo. Research. Women (review article). 19c-20c. *135*

Entrepreneurs. Business. Cubans. Florida (Miami). Immigrants. 1960-84. *1163*

—. Garment industry. Immigrants. New York City. 1981-82. *1300*

Episcopal Church, Protestant. Documents. Missions and Missionaries. Puerto Rico. 1870-1952. *1091*

Equal opportunity. New Mexico. Public Employees. State government. Women. 1971-78. *819*

Escalante, Silvestre Velez de. California (Monterey). Discovery and Exploration. Dominguez, Francisco Atanasio. New Mexico. 1765-1805. *143*

—. California (Monterey). Discovery and Exploration. Dominguez, Francisco Atanasio. New Mexico (Santa Fe). 1776-77. *169*

Espinosa, Aurelio M. Bibliographies. Dialects. Folklore. New Mexico, northern. Spain. 1907-54. *31*

Esteban. Blacks. Discovery and Exploration. Florida. South Central and Gulf States. Spain. 1528-39. *302*

Estrada, José. California (Monterey). Europe. Jenner, Edward. Smallpox. Vaccination. 18c-1821. *301*

Ethnic groups. Bilingual education. 1978. *18*
—. Blacks. New York City. Social Change. 1960's-70's. *1230*
—. Blacks. Political participation. Whites. 1966-75. *707*
—. California. Immigration. 1850-1976. *78*
—. California (East Los Angeles). Political protest. Social Change. 1968-74. *934*
—. Catholic Church. Machismo (concept). Mexican Americans. Social Customs. Women. 1970's. *967*
—. Discrimination. Kansas (Dodge City). Public Opinion. 1900-84. *450*
—. Economic development. New Mexico (Santa Fe). Population. 1790-99. *146*
—. Georgia (Atlanta). Labor. Louisiana (New Orleans). Texas (San Antonio). Women. 1930-40. *610*
—. Gurvitch, Georges. 1973. *985*
—. New Mexico. Occupations. Population. Social Organization. 1790. *363*
—. Population. Puerto Rico. 1940-70. *1297*

Ethnic Groups (review article). Puerto Ricans. Sowell, Thomas. 1898-1983. *1267*

Ethnic identity. Assimilation. Intermarriage. Texas (San Antonio). Women. 1830-60. *530*
—. Attitudes. Community Schools. Students. 1974. *855*
—. Nebraska (Omaha). Political participation. 1970's. *1042*

Ethnicity. 1960-81. *711*
—. 1973-76. *818*
—. Acosta, Oscar Zeta *(Autobiography of a Brown Buffalo)*. Novels. Rivera, Tomás *(Y No Se Lo Tragó La Tierra)*. Villareal, José Antonia *(Pocho)*. 1970-79. *1054*
—. Age. Education. Family. New York City. Puerto Ricans. 1958-79. *1270*
—. Art. California (Los Angeles). Murals. 1970's. *998*
—. Art. Culture. Murals. 1960's-80. *714*
—. Asians. Blacks. Education. Immigrants. Occupational mobility. 1965-70. *99*
—. Assimilation. Cubans. Exiles. 1959-76. *1165*
—. Assimilation. Institutions. Political activism. Students. Texas (Corpus Christi, Crystal City). 1969-80. *753*
—. Bilingual education. Government. Race. 1974-81. *89*
—. Blacks. Economic status. Social Classes. Stress. Whites. 1974. *708*
—. California (Los Angeles County). Congressional Districts (30th). Political candidates. Race. Voting and Voting Behavior. 1982. *754*
—. City Life. Cubans. Folklore. Indiana (East Chicago). Puerto Ricans. 1976. *1161*
—. Colleges and Universities. Racial Distance Indices. Students. Texas (south). 1973. *741*
—. Conflict. Cubans. Florida (Miami). 1972-79. *1250*
—. Discovery and Exploration. National Characteristics. Social Customs (review article). Urbanski, Edmund S. 17c-18c. *331*
—. Education. Employment. Family. Women. 1970's. *1051*
—. Family. Social Organization. Whites. 1983. *875*
—. Fertility. Residential patterns. 1969. *801*
—. Florida. Identity. Immigration. Latin America. 1979. *1192*

—. Health. Social Organization. ca 1979. *706*
—. Herrera, Juan José. Land grants. Militancy. New Mexico (Las Vegas). Vigilantes. White Caps. 1887-94. *554*
—. Illinois (Chicago). ca 1980. *90*
—. Men. Social Classes. Women. 1979. *1016*
—. New Mexico. Social Classes. Teachers. Women. 1900-50. *649*
—. New York City. Politicization. Puerto Ricans. Social policy. 1955-75. *1175*
—. Popular culture. Social Conditions. *Teatro Chicano*. Theater. 1965-79. *874*
—. Social Reform. 1960-80. *885*

Europe. Americas (North and South). Colonization. Discovery and Exploration. Myths and Symbols. Utopianism. 16c-18c. *225*
—. California (Los Angeles). Family. Immigrants. Michigan (Detroit). Whites. 1850-80. *542*
—. California (Monterey). Estrada, José. Jenner, Edward. Smallpox. Vaccination. 18c-1821. *301*

Europeans. Americas (North and South). Indian-White Relations. 1493-1888. *198*
—. Attitudes. Californios. Travel accounts. 1780's-1840's. *269*
—. Attitudes. Californios. Travel accounts. 1780's-1840's. *396*

Eve, Joseph. Annexation. Diplomacy. Flood, George H. LaBranche, Alcée. Letters. Murphy, William S. Texas. 1837-43. *162*

Excavations. Animals, domestic. Arizona. Mission San Xavier del Bac. 17c-19c. 1974. *311*
—. Aqueducts. California Polytechnic State University, San Luis Obispo. Mission San Antonio de Padua. Spanish. 1776. 1979-81. *245*
—. Arizona (Nogales). Jesuits. Mission Guevavi. 18c. 1964-66. *333*
—. Arizona (Tucson Basin). Ceramics. Settlement. 1690's-1856. *157*
—. California. Majolica pottery sherds. Santa Barbara Presidio, Chapel. Spain. 1782-1850. *153*
—. California. Missions and Missionaries. Presidios. San Diego Presidio. Serra Museum. 1769-75. 1964-70's. *210*
—. New Mexico (Rito Colorado Valley). Ranches. 1720-1846. *323*
—. New Mexico (Santa Fe). Palace of Governors. 1609-1974. *350*

Exiles. Assimilation. California (Los Angeles). Lozano, Ignacio. Newspapers. *Opinión*. 1926-29. *660*
—. Assimilation. Cubans. Ethnicity. 1959-76. *1165*
—. Assimilation. Cubans. Federal Policy. Mexicans. 1959-81. *138*
—. Assimilation. Cubans. Florida (Miami). 1973-79. *1318*
—. Briski, Norman (interview). Latin Americans. New York City. Theater. 1970's-82. *1096*
—. Cuba. Florida. Teachers. 1959-70. *1254*
—. Cuba. Florida (Key West). Human Relations. Independence Movements. Ten Years' War. 1868-78. *1252*
—. Cubans. 1960-75. *1109*
—. Cubans. Latin America. Martí, José. New York City. Reporters and Reporting. 1880-95. *1068*
—. Cubans. Puerto Rico. 1959-73. *1081*
—. Cubans. Social Classes. 1959-74. *1248*
—. Liberal Party. Mexico. Propaganda. Texas. Women. 1898-1910. *691*

Expansionism. Antiwar sentiment. Mexican War (review article). Pletcher, David M. Polk, James K. Schroeder, John H. 1830's-40's. *199*

Exploitation. Colonization. Minorities. Womack, John. 1841-1973. *447*

Explorers. Arizona (Casa Grande). Bolton, Herbert Eugene. Kino, Eusebio Francisco. 1697. 1934. 1968-72. *250*

—. California. DeAnza expedition, 2d. Font, Pedro. 1775-76. *170*
—. Commemorations. Florida (St. Augustine). Menéndez de Avilés, Pedro. Spain. 1565. 1975. *310*
—. Coronado expedition. Diaries. Southwest. Spain. 1540-42. *355*
—. Coronado, Francisco Vásquez de. Range wars. Sheep Raising. Southwest. 1540-1880's. *171*
—. Golden Cities myth. Mississippi River. Northwest Passage myth. 1519-1679. *381*

F

Family. Acculturation. Mental illness. New York City. Puerto Ricans. Social Organization. 1950's-70's. *1271*
—. Age. Education. Ethnicity. New York City. Puerto Ricans. 1958-79. *1270*
—. Assimilation. Geographic mobility. Immigrants. Social status. 1890-1977. *1015*
—. Attitudes. Discrimination. Personal narratives. Professions. Success. Women. 1980. *997*
—. Barrios. Housing. Relocation, forced. -1973. *1006*
—. Blacks. Employment. Income. Sex roles. Whites. 1982-83. *47*
—. California (Los Angeles). Europe. Immigrants. Michigan (Detroit). Whites. 1850-80. *542*
—. California (Los Angeles). Modernization. Social change. 1850-80. *538*
—. Colombians. Dominicans. Employment. Immigrants. New York City. Women. 1981. *1171*
—. Country Life. Economic Conditions. Occupations. Social Organization. Washington (Yakima Valley). 1971. *827*
—. Czech Americans. Labor. Land. Social Organization. Texas (Nueces County). 1880-1930. *608*
—. Discrimination, Employment. New Mexico (Santa Fe). Texas (San Antonio). 1860. *513*
—. Dominicans. Immigration. 1962-76. *1157*
—. Education. Employment. Ethnicity. Women. 1970's. *1051*
—. Education. Fertility. Income. Occupations. Puerto Ricans. 1969-70. *1325*
—. Education. Income. Occupations. 1969-70. *1057*
—. Emigration. Puerto Ricans. Social Organization. 1970-82. *1071*
—. English language. Sex. Spanish language. 1970's. *697*
—. Ethnicity. Social Organization. Whites. 1983. *875*
—. Immigration. Occupations. Social Classes. Women. 20c. *2*
—. Income. -1973. *724*
—. Methodology. Mexican Americans. Social sciences. 1970's. *134*
—. Models. Stereotypes. 1968-74. *1012*
—. Poor. Social Work. -1973. *960*
—. Research. ca 1970-75. *925*
—. Women. 1977. *824*
Farah Manufacturing Company. Amalgamated Clothing Workers Union of America. Garment industry. Strikes. Texas (El Paso). 1972-74. *800*
—. Strikes. Texas (El Paso). Women. 1972-74. *775*
Farmers. Indians. Land (disputes). New Mexico (Rio Puerco Valley). Whites. 19c-20c. *433*
Farms. Agricultural Labor. California (Colusa County). 1950-69. *930*
—. Blacks. Jamaicans. Migrant Labor. New York. Social mobility. 1960's-70's. *1152*
Feast days. Catholic Church. New Mexico. 20c. *139*

Federación de Sociedades Latinos-Americanos. Calleros, Cleofas. Maverick, Maury. McCammont, T. J. Powell, Alex K. Race Relations. Texas (El Paso). 1936. *627*
Federal Aid to Education. Bilingual education. Elementary and Secondary Education Act (US, 1969; Title VII). 1973. *58*
—. Economic Conditions. Neocolonialism. Puerto Rico. Social Classes. 1970's. *1245*
Federal Government. Economic conditions. Puerto Rico. 1898-1941. *1114*
—. Land grants. New Mexico (Las Trampas Grant). Swindles. 1859-1914. *526*
Federal Policy. Aliens, illegal. Carter, Jimmy. Immigration. 1977-78. *760*
—. Aliens, illegal. Immigration and Nationality Act (US, 1965). 1956-75. *124*
—. Assimilation. Cubans. Exiles. Mexicans. 1959-81. *138*
—. Carter, Jimmy. Cubans. Immigration. Political Leadership. 1980. *1123*
—. Economic Conditions. New Federalism. Reagan, Ronald. Social Problems. 1980-83. *716*
—. Foreign Relations. Immigration. Latin America. West Indies. 1924-79. *1217*
—. Immigration. Labor. Racism. 1920's. *672*
—. Immigration and Naturalization Service. Workers, undocumented. 1966-76. *1001*
—. Puerto Rico. 1898-1979. *1180*
—. Puerto Rico. Self-government. Truman, Harry S. 1945-47. *1086*
—. Refugees. Resettlement. 1960-82. *136*
Feminism. 1960's-70's. *831*
Fertility. Age. Economic conditions. Puerto Rico. Social Status. Women. 1970. *1182*
—. Assimilation. Puerto Ricans. Social Status. 1969-77. *1120*
—. Attitudes. California (Los Angeles). Women. 1973-82. *978*
—. California (Los Angeles). Catholic Church. Religiosity. Women. 1973. *979*
—. Change and Response, Theory of. Emigration. Migration, Internal. Puerto Rico. 1940's-70. *1228*
—. Demography. 1970-80. *700*
—. Education. Family. Income. Occupations. Puerto Ricans. 1969-70. *1325*
—. Education. Generations. Women. 1976. *725*
—. Ethnicity. Residential patterns. 1969. *801*
—. Generations. 1970. *726*
—. Integration. Social Mobility. 1969. *907*
—. Marriage. Modernization. Puerto Rico. 1950-70. *1063*
—. Metropolitan areas. Puerto Rico. 1950-70. *1289*
—. Migrant Labor. Women. 1978. *111*
—. Southwest. 1970. *886*
—. Whites. 1950-70. *736*
Fiction. Homosexuality. 1970-80. *1055*
Fiestas. Catholic Church. New Mexico. Rites and Ceremonies. Saints, patron. Villages. 1970's. *1036*
Filibustering. *La Union*. Latin America. Louisiana (New Orleans). Newspapers. 1846-51. *328*
Filipinos. Blacks. Chinese Americans. Economic Conditions. Japanese. Social Status. 1960-76. *51*
Films. Attitudes. 1908-79. *498*
—. California (Los Angeles; Hollywood). Spanish language. 1930-39. *670*
—. Literature. Mass Media. Stereotypes. 20c. *446*
—. Racism. Stereotypes. 1897-1917. *652*
—. Stereotypes. 1915-78. *504*
—. Stereotypes. Television. 1960's-70's. *702*
Firearms. California (Monterey County). Flintlocks. Mission San Antonio de Padua. 18c. *391*
Five Civilized Tribes. Fur Trade. Gálvez, Bernardo de. Indians. Louisiana. Maxent, Gilberto Antonio de. Spain. 1749-84. *382*

Flagellants. Catholic Church. New Mexico. Penitentes. 13c-20c. *878*

Flintlocks. California (Monterey County). Firearms. Mission San Antonio de Padua. 18c. *391*

Flood, George H. Annexation. Diplomacy. Eve, Joseph. LaBranche, Alcée. Letters. Murphy, William S. Texas. 1837-43. *162*

Florida. Antonia (Indian). Calusa Indians. Carlos (chief). Indian-White Relations. Marriage. Menéndez de Avilés, Pedro. Politics. 1566-69. *327*

—. Blacks. Discovery and Exploration. Esteban. South Central and Gulf States. Spain. 1528-39. *302*

—. Blacks. Jamaicans. Migrant labor. 1980. *731*

—. Cabeza de Vaca, Alvar Nuñez *(La Relación)*. Garcilaso de la Vega, "el Inca" *(La Florida del Inca)*. 1500-1616. *215*

—. Colonialism. Culture. Louisiana Territory. Spain. Texas. 1513-1803. *217*

—. Colonization. Mexico (Yucatán). Spain. 16c. *397*

—. Cuba. Exiles. Teachers. 1959-70. *1254*

—. Cubans. Economic Conditions. Politics. Refugees. 1980-81. *1076*

—. Ethnicity. Identity. Immigration. Latin America. 1979. *1192*

—. Fort Matanzas. Spain. 1565-1821. *147*

—. Franciscans. Indian-White Relations. 17c. *288*

—. Immigrants. Medical care. Voluntary Associations. 19c-20c. *129*

—. Indian-White Relations. Spain. *Visitas* (provincial tours). 1602-75. *320*

—. Land. Santa Elena (colony). Settlement. Spain. 1560-87. *280*

—. Military. Population. 1700-1820. *282*

—. Preservation. St. Augustine Restoration Foundation. 1977. *281*

—. Rebellions. Spain. Trials. 1795-98. *296*

Florida (Dade County). New York City. 1960-80. *1150*

Florida (Dade County; Miami). Cuba. Immigration. International Trade. Latin America. Social Customs. 1970's. *1314*

Florida (Gainesville). P. K. Yonge Library of Florida History. Spain. Spanish Florida Borderlands Project. 1565-1821. 1977-78. *226*

Florida (Jacksonville). City politics. Cubans. Huah, José Alejandro. Independence Movements. Martí, José. 1836-1905. *1164*

Florida (Key West). Cuba. Exiles. Human Relations. Independence Movements. Ten Years' War. 1868-78. *1252*

—. Cubans. Labor. Martí, José. Tobacco Industry. 1891. *1170*

—. Cubans. Revolutionary Movements. Spain. 1878-86. *1251*

Florida (Miami). Assimilation. Cubans. Exiles. 1973-79. *1318*

—. Bibliographies. Cubans. Immigration. 20c. *79*

—. Blacks. Business. Cubans. Economic structure. 1920's-80. *1308*

—. Blacks. Neighborhoods. Population. Residential patterns. Whites. 1970-80. *1309*

—. Business. Cubans. Entrepreneurs. Immigrants. 1960-84. *1163*

—. Conflict. Cubans. Ethnicity. 1972-79. *1250*

—. Cubans. *Diario Las Americas*. Journalism. Politics and Media. Watergate scandal. 1970's. *1061*

—. Cubans. Education. Geographic mobility. Income. Political power. 1959-78. *1241*

—. Cubans. Housing. Middle Classes. Segregation. 1950-74. *1310*

—. Cubans. New York City. Puerto Rico (San Juan). Social Classes. 1950-77. *1121*

—. Cubans. Puerto Ricans. Residential patterns. 1970's. *1060*

Florida (Miami; Little Havana). Cubans. Social customs. 1959-80's. *1100*

Florida (Pensacola). Census. Spain. 1784-1820. *364*

Florida (review article). Balseiro, José Agustín. Lyon, Eugene. Menéndez de Avilés, Pedro. Spain. 1513-1977. *184*

Florida (St. Augustine). Census. Population. 1786. *365*

—. Church records. Cuba. 1594-1763. 20c. *185*

—. Civil-military relations. Daily life. Social organization. Spain. 1580. *279*

—. Colonies. Migration. Quantitative methods. Spain. 1600-1800. *186*

—. Commemorations. Explorers. Menéndez de Avilés, Pedro. Spain. 1565. 1975. *310*

—. Daily life. Research. Spain. 1580. 1970's. *239*

—. Great Britain. Indians. Social Customs. Spain. Trade. 1700-83. *211*

Florida (Tampa). Advertising. Art. Cigars. Cubans. 1868-1930's. *1307*

—. Cigar industry. Cuba. General strikes. Spain. 1901-11. *1253*

—. Cigar industry. Cubans. Independence Movements. Labor. 1892-1901. *1242*

—. Cubans. Labor Disputes. *Lector* (reader). Perez, Louis A., Jr. Personal narratives. Tobacco industry. ca 1925-35. *1243*

Florida, University of, Gainesville. Borderlands. Colonies. Documents. P. K. Yonge Library of Florida History (guide). Spain. ca 1518-1821. *77*

Folk art. Archuleta, Eppie. Colorado (San Luis Valley). Personal Narratives. Women. 1922-79. *460*

—. Catholic Church. Design. Iconography. Manuscripts. New Mexico. 16c-17c. *233*

—. Catholic Church. Home altars. Texas (Austin). 1970's. *1019*

—. Catholic Church. New Mexico. Santos. 1780-1900. *395*

—. Colorado. New Mexico. Penitentes. 19c-20c. *503*

—. Lopez, George. Lopez, José Dolores. New Mexico (Córdova). Santos. 20c. *412*

—. New Mexico. Santos. 17c-19c. *15*

Folk medicine. Catholic Church. New Mexico (Guadalupita). Social Customs. Torres, Luisa. 1910's-70's. *497*

—. Curanderismo. Utah. 20c. *409*

—. Historiography. Medical care. Mexican Americans. 1894-20c. *100*

—. Indians. New Mexico. 19c-1930's. *408*

—. Jaramillo, Pedrito. Lozano, José C. Texas (south). 19c. *511*

—. Jaramillo, Pedrito. Texas (Los Almos). 1881-1907. *509*

—. Lead poisoning. Southwest. 1983. *1018*

Folk Songs. Blues. Fugitive Slaves. Matamoros (colony). Music. 19c-1940's. *458*

—. Rio Grande Valley. Texas. 1860-1982. *466*

Folk Songs (review article). Borders. Mexico. Paredes, Americo. Texas. 16c-20c. *474*

Folklore. Bibliographies. Dialects. Espinosa, Aurelio M. New Mexico, northern. Spain. 1907-54. *31*

—. City Life. Cubans. Ethnicity. Indiana (East Chicago). Puerto Ricans. 1976. *1161*

—. Humor. Jokes. Sex. Women. 1970's. *761*

—. Men. Vanishing hitchhiker (theme). Women. 1977. *892*

—. Mexicans. Puerto Ricans. Theater. 1966-77. *60*

—. New Mexico. Penitentes. Rites and Ceremonies. Social customs. 16c-20c. *472*

—. Proverbs. Spanish language. 20c. *465*

Font, Pedro. California. DeAnza expedition, 2d. Explorers. 1775-76. *170*

Font Saldaña, Jorge. Burgos, Julia de. Lair, Clara. Personal Narratives. Poets. Puerto Rico. Ribera Chevremont, Evaristo. 20c. *1232*

Food Industry. New Mexico. Ranches. Sheep Raising. Textile Industry. 1846-61. *589*
—. Social Customs. Values. Women. 1980. *784*
Food shortages. Puerto Rico. Unemployment. World War II. 1940-45. *1146*
Food stamp program. Income redistribution. Puerto Rico. 1974-75. *1065*
Foreign Policy. California. Colonial Government. Spain. War. 1779-1818. *270*
—. Cuba. Economic policy. 1933-34. *1082*
—. Cuba. Immigration. 1959-80. *1283*
—. Economic Conditions. Puerto Rico. 1982. *1178*
—. Industry. Puerto Rico. 1982. *1124*
—. Political Participation. Puerto Rico. Self-government. 1900-33. *1115*
—. Political Systems. Public Opinion. Puerto Rico. 1970's. *1103*
Foreign Relations. Agricultural Labor. Berry pickers. California (El Monte). Japan. Mexico. Strikes. 1933. *645*
—. Arizona (Nogales). Borders. García, Jesús. Mexico (Sonora). 1893-96. *529*
—. Bibliographies. Educational policy. Energy crisis. Middle East. National Autonomous University of Mexico (Faculty of Political and Social Sciences). Periodicals. Social Conditions. 1970-81. *7*
—. Bracero program. Immigration. Mexico. 1942-46. *642*
—. *Britain* (vessel). Confiscations. Great Britain. Spain. Texas (Matagorda Peninsula). 1769-70. *168*
—. Carranza, Venustiano. Immigration. Mexico. 1910-20. *674*
—. Carranza, Venustiano. Mexico. Plan de San Diego. Race relations. Texas, south. 1915-16. *638*
—. Conspiracy. Mexico. Revolutionary Movements. Reyes, Bernardo. State Politics. Texas. Trials. 1911-12. *639*
—. Cubans. Refugees. 1980-82. *1233*
—. El Paso-Juárez Conference. Mexico. Punitive expeditions. Villa, Pancho. 1916. *637*
—. Federal Policy. Immigration. Latin America. West Indies. 1924-79. *1217*
—. Geopolitics. 1848-1981. *439*
—. Latin America. Puerto Rico. West Indies. 1975. *1105*
—. Mexico. Migrant labor. Texas. 1942-47. *659*
—. Political participation. 1970-82. *1033*
—. Settlement. Spain. Texas. Westward Movement. ca 1796-1819. *291*
Foreign Relations (review article). Borders. Historiography. Mexico. Southwest. 20c. *61*
Fort Bute. Fort St. Gabriel. Great Britain. Louisiana. Military Occupation. Spain. 1768. *177*
Fort Matanzas. Florida. Spain. 1565-1821. *147*
Fort St. Gabriel. Fort Bute. Great Britain. Louisiana. Military Occupation. Spain. 1768. *177*
Fotonovelas. Literature. Values. Women. Working Class. 1976-80. *757*
Foxardo (battle). Civil-Military Relations. Insubordination. Navies. Porter, David. Puerto Rico. 1823-25. *1087*
France. Louisiana. Medicine (practice of). Pharmacy. Spain. 1717-1852. *203*
Franciscans. Architecture. California. Mission San Juan Capistrano. 1776-1976. *163*
—. Ayala, Juan Manuel de. California (San Francisco Bay). Discovery and Exploration. Indians. Spain. 1775. *369*
—. California. Cesarean operations. Medicine (practice of). Missions and Missionaries. 1769-1833. *376*

—. California. Conversion thesis. Cook, Sherburne Friend. Indians. Missions and Missionaries. ca 1790-1820's. 1943. *229*
—. California. Dominicans. Jesuits. Missions and Missionaries. Serra, Junípero. 1768-76. *287*
—. California. Durán, Narciso. Indians. Missions and Missionaries. Music. 1806-46. *224*
—. California. Durán, Narciso. Indians. Missions and Missionaries. Secularization. 1826-46. *305*
—. California. Mexico. Missions and Missionaries. Southwest. Wheat growing. 1730's-70's. *335*
—. California. Mission San Carlo Borromeo. Serra, Junípero. 1784. *278*
—. California (San Diego). Jayme, Luís (death). Mission San Diego de Alcalá. Yuman Indians. 1775. *388*
—. Colonization. DeZorita, Alonso. Indians. Missions and Missionaries. Southwest. 1545-85. *378*
—. Florida. Indian-White Relations. 17c. *288*
—. Indians. Indian-White Relations. Leadership. New Mexico. Pueblo Indians. Rebellions. 1650-80. 1980. *398*
Frontier and Pioneer Life. Anecdotes. Baca, Father. Easter Week. New Mexico (Tome, Valencia). Rites and Ceremonies. 1846. *209*
—. Borders. Mexico. Race Relations. Southwest (review article). Weber, David J. 1821-46. *251*
—. Catholic Church. Missions and Missionaries. Southwest. Spain. 16c-18c. *164*
—. Cattle Raising. Ranches. Southwest. Spain. 18c-19c. *303*
—. Colonial Government. Indian Wars. New Mexico. Pueblo Indians. Spain. Texas (El Paso). 1680-90. *219*
—. New Mexico. New Spain. 1598-1781. *294*
—. New Mexico. Settlement. 17c-1810. *344*
—. Social Customs. Southwest. Spaniards. 18c. *254*
—. Texas (Pecos County). Torres brothers. 1869-96. *575*
Fuente, Pedro José de la. Diaries. Indian Wars. Mexico (Chihuahua, Sonora). Military. New Mexico. Texas (El Paso). 1765. *192*
Fugitive Slaves. Blues. Folk Songs. Matamoros (colony). Music. 19c-1940's. *458*
Funerals. Elections. Muñoz Marín, Luis. New Progressive Party. Popular Democratic Party. Puerto Rico. 1980. *1215*
Fur Trade. Five Civilized Tribes. Gálvez, Bernardo de. Indians. Louisiana. Maxent, Gilberto Antonio de. Spain. 1749-84. *382*

G

Gálvez, Bernardo de. Bouligny, Francisco (report). Immigration policy. Louisiana. Navarro, Martin *(Political Reflections)*. Spain. 1776-83. *201*
—. Five Civilized Tribes. Fur Trade. Indians. Louisiana. Maxent, Gilberto Antonio de. Spain. 1749-84. *382*
Gambling. Barceló, Gertrudis. Business. Elites. New Mexico (Santa Fe). Women. 1830's-40's. *273*
Gándara, Francisco. Arizona. McFarland, William. Race Relations. Violence. Whites. 1872-73. *578*
Gangs. California (Los Angeles). Residential patterns. Youth. 1980-83. *931*
García, Jesús. Arizona (Nogales). Borders. Foreign relations. Mexico (Sonora). 1893-96. *529*
Garcia, Mario T. California. Camarillo, Albert. Cities. Griswold del Castillo, Richard. Social Change (review article). Texas. 1848-1982. *508*
Garcilaso de la Vega, "el Inca" *(La Florida del Inca)*. Cabeza de Vaca, Alvar Nuñez *(La Relación)*. Florida. 1500-1616. *215*
Garita (fort). Military Camps and Forts. New Mexico (Santa Fe). Spain. 19c-1954. *206*

Garment industry. Amalgamated Clothing Workers Union of America. Farah Manufacturing Company. Strikes. Texas (El Paso). 1972-74. *800*

—. California (Los Angeles). International Ladies' Garment Workers' Union. Strikes. Women. 1933. *619*

—. California (Los Angeles). Women. Working Conditions. 1970-79. *986*

—. Entrepreneurs. Immigrants. New York City. 1981-82. *1300*

Garza, Catarino E. Mexico. Newspapers. Texas. 1880-95. *525*

General strikes. Cigar industry. Cuba. Florida (Tampa). Spain. 1901-11. *1253*

Generations. Attitudes. Marriage. 1981-82. *910*

—. Behavior. Religion. Texas (San Antonio). 1981-82. *909*

—. Education. Fertility. Women. 1976. *725*

—. Fertility. 1970. *726*

—. Occupational mobility. 1979. *1002*

—. Occupational Mobility. Social Mobility. 1979. *1003*

Geographic mobility. Assimilation. Family. Immigrants. Social status. 1890-1977. *1015*

—. California (Los Angeles). Occupational mobility. 1918-28. *676*

—. Cubans. Education. Florida (Miami). Income. Political power. 1959-78. *1241*

—. Workers, undocumented. 1978-79. *871*

Geopolitics. Foreign Relations. 1848-1981. *439*

—. North Central States. Social Sciences. 1970-76. *755*

Georgia. Discovery and Exploration. North Carolina. Salazar, Pedro de. Slave raids. South Carolina. Spain. 1514-16. *238*

Georgia (Atlanta). Ethnic Groups. Labor. Louisiana (New Orleans). Texas (San Antonio). Women. 1930-40. *610*

Glazer, Nathan. Assimilation. Moynihan, Daniel P. New York. Puerto Ricans (review article). 20c. *1265*

Gold Mines and Mining. California. Industrialization. Nativism. 1845-70. *533*

Gold rushes. California. Chileans. Consuls. 1848-60. *1231*

—. California. Discrimination. Mexico (Sonora). Migration. 1848-56. *585*

—. California. Murieta, Joaquín. Outlaws. ca 1848-53. *587*

—. California. Nativism. 1848-53. *574*

Golden Cities myth. Explorers. Mississippi River. Northwest Passage myth. 1519-1679. *381*

Gompers, Samuel. American Federation of Labor. Iglesias Pantín, Santiago. Labor Unions and Organizations. Puerto Rico. 1897-1920's. *1155*

Gonzales, Rodolfo "Corky". Crusade for Justice. Southwest. 1966-72. *908*

Gonzales, Thomas Rodolfo. Elizando, Sergio. Literature. 1970's. *742*

González, Ramon. Utah (San Juan County; Monticello). 20c. *441*

González Rubio, José. California. Catholic Church. Missions and Missionaries. 1846-50. *566*

Government. Armijo, Manuel. New Mexico. 1827-46. *274*

—. Barceló, Carlos Romero. Elections (gubernatorial). Hernández, Rafael. Puerto Rico. 1980. *1193*

—. Bilingual education. Ethnicity. Race. 1974-81. *89*

—. Community Participation in Politics. Economic Development. Indians. New Mexico (Espanola Valley). Water Supply. 1970's. *864*

—. Economic Conditions. Puerto Rico. Social classes. 1930-50. *1085*

—. Minorities in Politics. Names (personal). Spanish language. 1973. *887*

Government regulation. Agricultural Labor. California. Hoes. 1968-75. *936*

Graffiti. Con *safos* (term). Names, personal. 1967-75. *838*

Grammar. Children. English language. Texas. 1976. *832*

—. Linguistics. Spanish language. 1976. *983*

Grants. Nixon, Richard M. Political Campaigns (presidential). Revenue sharing. 1960-72. *23*

Grapes. Agriculture. Boycotts. California. Chavez, Cesar. International Brotherhood of Teamsters. Labor Unions and Organizations. Lettuce. United Farm Workers Union. 1962-74. *805*

Great Britain. *Britain* (vessel). Confiscations. Foreign Relations. Spain. Texas (Matagorda Peninsula). 1769-70. *168*

—. California (Monterey). Jones, Thomas ap Catesby. Mexico. Military Occupation. Navies. 1842. *218*

—. Colonization. Discovery and Exploration. Indian-White Relations. Southeastern States. Spain. 1565-1685. *319*

—. Florida (St. Augustine). Indians. Social Customs. Spain. Trade. 1700-83. *211*

—. Fort Bute. Fort St. Gabriel. Louisiana. Military Occupation. Spain. 1768. *177*

Great Western Sugar Company. Agricultural Labor. Beets. Housing. Wyoming (Lovell). 1916-54. *671*

Gringo and Greaser. Kusz, Charles L. New Mexico (Manzano). Newspapers. 1883-84. *584*

Griswold del Castillo, Richard. California. Camarillo, Albert. Cities. Garcia, Mario T. Social Change (review article). Texas. 1848-1982. *508*

Guadalupe Hidalgo, Treaty of. Diplomacy. Mexican War. Trist, Nicholas P. 1848. *517*

—. Land grants. Protocol of Querétaro. Texas. Trist, Nicholas P. 1847-48. *560*

—. Mexican War. 1846-48. *189*

Gurvitch, Georges. Ethnic groups. 1973. *985*

Gutierrez de Lara, José Bernardo Maxmilliano. Independence Movements. Magee, Augustus W. Mexico. Republican Army of the North. Texas (San Antonio). 1811-15. *197*

Gutierrez, José Angel. Political activism. Radicals and Radicalism. Rhetoric. Self-Determination. Texas (Crystal City). 1969-79. *868*

—. Political activism. Rhetoric. Self-Determination. 1979. *867*

Gutiérrez y Espinosa, Felipe. Musical Academy of Puerto Rico. Puerto Rico. 1871-1900. *1078*

H

Haciendas. Agricultural Production. Mills. Puerto Rico, southwestern. Sugar. 1902. *1306*

Harlem Renaissance. Communist Party. Immigrants. Literature. New York City. West Indians. 1930's. *1301*

Hawaii. Acculturation. Economic Conditions. Immigrants. Puerto Ricans. 1900-02. *1287*

Health. Ethnicity. Social Organization. ca 1979. *706*

—. Public Policy. Workers, undocumented. 1975-82. *938*

Health Care. See also Medical Care.

—. Stereotypes. -1973. *1038*

Health centers. Cities. Decisionmaking. Neighborhoods. 1969-70. *854*

Health services. Economic Conditions. Indians. Navajo Indians. New Mexico, northwestern. Population. Rural areas. Spaniards. 1971-78. *93*

Heceta y Fontecha, Bruno de. British Columbia. Columbia River. Discovery and Exploration. Pacific Northwest. Spain. 1775. *159*

Henrietta (plantation). Puerto Rico. Sugar plantation. 1827-1918. *1236*
Heraldo De Mexico. California (Los Angeles). Immigrants. Newspapers. Press. 1916-20. *614*
Hernández, Federico. Arizona. Ballads. Capital Punishment. "Corrido de los Hermanos" (ballad). Hernández, Manuel. 1934. *683*
Hernández, Manuel. Arizona. Ballads. Capital Punishment. "Corrido de los Hermanos" (ballad). Hernández, Federico. 1934. *683*
Hernández, Rafael. Barceló, Carlos Romero. Elections (gubernatorial). Government. Puerto Rico. 1980. *1193*
Herrera, Juan José. Ethnicity. Land grants. Militancy. New Mexico (Las Vegas). Vigilantes. White Caps. 1887-94. *554*
Hidalgo. *See* Guadalupe Hidalgo, Treaty of.
High schools. Academic achievement. Acculturation. California (Los Angeles). 1975-76. *1030*
—. Academic achievement. Attitudes. California (San Francisco). 1974-75. *796*
—. Attitudes. California (Los Angeles). Truancy. 1974-75. *845*
—. Behavior. Drugs. Puerto Rico. Youth. 1970-80. *1263*
—. Militancy. Students. -1973. *806*
Higher education. Bilingualism. 1967-80. *67*
—. California. Students. Texas. 1970's. *787*
Hijacking. Airplanes. Cuba. Deportation. International law. Refugees. 1983. *1191*
Hijar-Padres colony. California. Colonists. Mexico (San Blas). 1834. *249*
Hinojosa, Rolando. Daily Life. Literature. Rivera, Tomás. Social Customs. Southwest. 1980. *756*
—. Literature. 1976-80. *1009*
Hispaniola. Colonies. Immigration. Louisiana. 1792-1804. *194*
—. Louisiana (New Orleans). Refugees. 1792-1804. *193*
Hispanophobia. Anti-Mexican sentiments. British North America. 17c-19c. *315*
Historians. Alamo (battle). Legends. 19c. *453*
—. Castañeda, Carlos Eduardo. Texas. 1896-1927. *604*
Historical Archive of the Secretary of Foreign Relations. Archival Catalogs and Inventories. Mexico (Mexico City). 1900-39. *13*
Historical Sites and Parks. California (Monterey). Landmarks. Mexico. Spain. 1770-1849. *173*
—. California (San Diego; Barrio Logan). Chicano Park. 1968-80. *803*
Historiography. Acosta Rodríquez, Antonio. Census. Colonial Government. Louisiana. Spain. 1763-1803. 1976-80. *242*
—. Blacks. Cattle Raising. Indians. ca 1865-1979. *431*
—. Bolton, Herbert Eugene. Borderlands studies. Catholic Church. Colonization. Missions and Missionaries. Spain. 1917-79. *9*
—. Borders. Foreign Relations (review article). Mexico. Southwest. 20c. *61*
—. Borders. Mexico. 1812-1975. *3*
—. Camarillo, Albert. Mexican Americans (review article). 1848-1930. *106*
—. Castañeda, Carlos Eduardo. Colleges and Universities. Librarians. Texas, University of, Austin (Benson Latin American Collection). 1920-27. *603*
—. Castañeda, Carlos Eduardo. Colonization. Spain. Texas. 1693-1731. 1933-43. *144*
—. Economic Conditions. Labor. Mexican Americans. 1850-1976. *8*
—. Folk medicine. Medical care. Mexican Americans. 1894-20c. *100*
—. Labor. Mexican Americans. Oral history. 1920's-30's. *127*
—. Marxism. Puerto Rico. 19c-20c. *1203*

—. Methodology. Mexican Americans. 1970-74. *38*
—. Mexican Americans. 1960's. *87*
—. Mexican Americans. 1970's. *45*
—. Mexican Americans. 19c-20c. *20*
—. Mexican Americans. Research. 19c-20c. *52*
—. Mexican Americans. Social Classes. Women. 17c-20c. *4*
—. Mexican War. 1846-48. 1960's-79. *11*
—. Mexico. Southwest. 1821-54. *125*
—. Quantitative methods. Research. Southwest. Prehistory-20c. *42*
—. Scholes, France V. Southwest. 16c-20c. *97*
—. Social history. Southwest. 20c. *470*
History. Bibliographies. Literature. Mexican Americans. Women. 1519-1976. *115*
History Task Force. Areíto, Grupo. Cubans. Immigration. Johnson, Roberta Ann. Puerto Ricans. 1960's-70's. *1226*
History Teaching. American history. Colleges and Universities. Mexican Americans. Textbooks. 20c. *7*
—. Interviews. Mexican Americans. Oral history. 1974. *37*
Hittson, John. Cattle Rustling. Comancheros. Indians. New Mexico. Ranchers. 1872-73. *551*
Hoes. Agricultural Labor. California. Government regulation. 1968-75. *936*
Home altars. Catholic Church. Folk art. Texas (Austin). 1970's. *1019*
Homosexuality. Fiction. 1970-80. *1055*
Hoover, Herbert C. Repatriation. 1930's. *651*
Horses. Museum of New Mexico (Fred Harvey Collection). Museums. Southwest. Stable gear. 18c-20c. *1*
Hostos, Adolfo de (interview). Anthropologists. Puerto Rico. 1974. *1179*
Hostos, Eugenio María de. Independence Movements. Puerto Rico. ca 1860-1903. *1174*
House of Representatives. Marcantonio, Vito. New York. Puerto Ricans. Republican Party. 20c. *1196*
Households. Blacks. Demography. Mothers, single. Puerto Ricans. Whites. 1970. *1119*
Housing. Agricultural Labor. Beets. Great Western Sugar Company. Wyoming (Lovell). 1916-54. *671*
—. Architecture. Indians. *Jacal* (style). New Mexico (Tierra Amarilla). Spaniards. Wood. 8c-20c. *366*
—. Barrios. Family. Relocation, forced. -1973. *1006*
—. Cubans. Florida (Miami). Middle Classes. Segregation. 1950-74. *1310*
Houston, Sam. Mexico. Military. Revolution. Texas. 1835-36. *237*
Huah, José Alejandro. City politics. Cubans. Florida (Jacksonville). Independence Movements. Martí, José. 1836-1905. *1164*
Human Relations. Cuba. Exiles. Florida (Key West). Independence Movements. Ten Years' War. 1868-78. *1252*
Humor. Discrimination. Social Customs. 1966-75. *891*
—. Folklore. Jokes. Sex. Women. 1970's. *761*
Hundley, Norris, Jr. (review article). 18c-1975. *479*

I

Iconography. Catholic Church. Design. Folk art. Manuscripts. New Mexico. 16c-17c. *233*
Identity. Adolescents. Mexico. Puerto Rico. USA. 1970's. *1159*
—. American dream. Blacks. Indians. 1890-1980. *25*
—. Attitudes. New Mexico. -1974. *919*
—. Economic Conditions. Southwest. 1900. *567*

—. Ethnicity. Florida. Immigration. Latin America. 1979. *1192*
—. Jokes. Social Change. Texas. Whites. 1970's. *890*
—. New York. Puerto Ricans. -1974. *1266*
—. Politics. Puerto Rico. Social Customs. 1898-1980. *1220*
—. Rural areas. Social conditions. Texas. Youth. 1976. *924*
—. Southwest. 1598-1970's. *461*
Ideology. Anthropology, Cultural. Methodology. Puerto Rico. Steward, Julian H. *(People of Puerto Rico).* 1956-77. *1144*
—. Class consciousness. Social Change. Texas (San Antonio). 1930-40. *630*
—. Class struggle. Development. Political change. Puerto Rico. 1940-78. *1238*
—. Mexico. Philosophy. Positivism. Science. Social control. 1850-1984. *477*
—. Minorities in Politics. 1960's-70's. *968*
Iglesias Pantín, Santiago. American Federation of Labor. Gompers, Samuel. Labor Unions and Organizations. Puerto Rico. 1897-1920's. *1155*
Illinois. Immigration and Naturalization Service. ca 1970-76. *727*
Illinois (Chicago). City Politics. Political representation. Spaniards. Voting and Voting Behavior. 1975. *104*
—. English language. Southwest. Spanish language. 1979. *710*
—. Ethnicity. ca 1980. *90*
—. Immigration. Social Conditions. 1910's-20's. *678*
—. Labor. 1908-30. *673*
—. Puerto Ricans. Residential patterns. Social conditions. 1920-70. *650*
Illinois (Chicago Heights). Employment. Politics. Social Conditions. 1910-76. *436*
Immigrants. Acculturation. Economic Conditions. Hawaii. Puerto Ricans. 1900-02. *1287*
—. Acculturation. Interviews. Puerto Ricans. 1982. *1134*
—. Asians. Blacks. Education. Ethnicity. Occupational mobility. 1965-70. *99*
—. Assimilation. Family. Geographic mobility. Social status. 1890-1977. *1015*
—. Assimilation. Labor. Men. 1960's-76. *733*
—. Bilingualism. Income. Language. 1975. *821*
—. Business. Cubans. Entrepreneurs. Florida (Miami). 1960-84. *1163*
—. California (Los Angeles). Europe. Family. Michigan (Detroit). Whites. 1850-80. *542*
—. California (Los Angeles). *Heraldo De Mexico.* Newspapers. Press. 1916-20. *614*
—. Colombians. Dominicans. Employment. Family. New York City. Women. 1981. *1171*
—. Communist Party. Harlem Renaissance. Literature. New York City. West Indians. 1930's. *1301*
—. Cubans. Income. Mexicans. 1973-76. *92*
—. Daily life. Latin Americans. Popular culture. West Indians. 1965-77. *12*
—. Deportation. Labor Unions and Organizations. New Deal. 1930's. *618*
—. Employment. 1973-79. *956*
—. Employment. 1976-78. *120*
—. Entrepreneurs. Garment industry. New York City. 1981-82. *1300*
—. Florida. Medical care. Voluntary Associations. 19c-20c. *129*
—. Income. Men. Poverty. Self-perception. Working Class. 1978-79. *923*
—. Labor. 1960's-82. *14*
—. Labor. Workers, Undocumented. 1970's. *913*
—. Leadership. Puerto Ricans. Women. 1910-45. *1280*

Immigrants (review article). California (East Los Angeles). New York City. Romo, Richard. Sanchez Korrol, Virginia E. 20c. *137*
Immigration. 1900-72. *456*
—. Acculturation. Cubans. Drug abuse. Social Customs. Values. Youth. 1950-80. *1237*
—. Acculturation. Labor. Literature. 1830-1983. *443*
—. Agricultural Labor. Aliens, Illegal. Economic opportunity. "Push/pull" hypothesis. 1948-72. *866*
—. Aliens. Labor. Public policy. 1970's. *965*
—. Aliens, illegal. Bracero Program. Mexico. Quota systems. 1960's-70's. *1007*
—. Aliens, illegal. Carter, Jimmy. Federal Policy. 1977-78. *760*
—. Aliens, illegal. Congress. Economic conditions. Public Policy. 1978. *91*
—. Aliens, illegal. Labor. Population. 1970-80. *142*
—. Aliens, illegal. Mexico. Statistics. 1978-79. *750*
—. Americanization. Employment. Industry. Public schools. 1880-1930. *624*
—. Andrade, Flores de. Liberal Party. Mexico. Personal narratives. Revolutionary Movements. Texas (El Paso). 1890-1911. *621*
—. Areíto, Grupo. Cubans. History Task Force. Johnson, Roberta Ann. Puerto Ricans. 1960's-70's. *1226*
—. Arizona. Mexican Revolution. Refugees. 1910-11. *669*
—. Assimilation. Blacks. West Indies. 1898-1979. *1195*
—. Attitudes. Blacks. Education. Wisconsin (Racine). 1974. *993*
—. Bibliographies. Cubans. Florida (Miami). 20c. *79*
—. Blacks. Economic Conditions. New York City. Public Opinion. West Indies. 1965-79. *1099*
—. Blacks. England (London). New York City. Social status. West Indians. 20c. *1153*
—. Bracero program. Foreign Relations. Mexico. 1942-46. *642*
—. California. Ethnic groups. 1850-1976. *78*
—. California. Mexico. Mineral resources. Settlement. 1683-1848. *231*
—. California, southern. Mexico. "Operation Wetback". Texas. 1950-74. *977*
—. Camarillo, Albert. Cardoso, Lawrence A. Mexican Americans (review article). Reisler, Mark. ca 1848-1970. *112*
—. Capitalism. Economic Structure. Labor. Latin Americans. Minorities. ca 1950-70. *1290*
—. Carranza, Venustiano. Foreign Relations. Mexico. 1910-20. *674*
—. Carter, Jimmy. Cubans. Federal Policy. Political Leadership. 1980. *1123*
—. Catholic Church. Charities. New York City (Brooklyn; St. Ignatius Parish). 1945-81. *1294*
—. Colonies. Hispaniola. Louisiana. 1792-1804. *194*
—. Cuba. Florida (Dade County; Miami). International Trade. Latin America. Social Customs. 1970's. *1314*
—. Cuba. Foreign policy. 1959-80. *1283*
—. Discrimination, Employment. Residence, prior. 1973-74. *856*
—. Dominican Republic. 1965-76. *1295*
—. Dominicans. Family. 1962-76. *1157*
—. Drug abuse. Economic Conditions. Inhalants. Social Conditions. Youth. 1930-80. *429*
—. Economic Conditions. Labor. Mexico. Social control. 1950's-70's. *865*
—. Economic Development. 1910-30. *675*
—. Economic opportunity. Puerto Rico. 1947-73. *1202*
—. Education. Puerto Rico. Unemployment. 1955-70. *1298*
—. Employment. Oregon. 1900-70. *488*

—. Ethnicity. Florida. Identity. Latin America. 1979. *1192*

—. Family. Occupations. Social Classes. Women. 20c. *2*

—. Federal Policy. Foreign Relations. Latin America. West Indies. 1924-79. *1217*

—. Federal Policy. Labor. Racism. 1920's. *672*

—. Illinois (Chicago). Social Conditions. 1910's-20's. *678*

—. Income. Labor. Southwest. Workers, undocumented. 1960-80. *828*

—. Indiana (East Chicago; Indiana Harbor). Inland Steel Company. Michigan, Lake. Social Conditions. 1919-32. *615*

—. Labor. Mexico. Women. 1970's. *834*

—. Labor. Public policy. Workers, undocumented. 1950's-70's. *140*

—. Labor. Reisler, Mark (review article). 1900-40. 1976. *628*

—. Labor. USA. 1909-76. *402*

—. Latin Americans. 1960-78. *1214*

—. Law Enforcement. Mexico. 1924-29. *644*

—. Mental illness. Puerto Ricans. Social problems. 1493-1978. *1062*

—. Migrant Labor. 1900-79. *406*

—. Migrant labor. 1950's-80. *712*

—. Migrant Labor. North Central States. Social Conditions. 1919-76. *415*

—. Nativism. Periodicals. *Saturday Evening Post.* 1914-33. *662*

—. Naturalization. 1920-79. *435*

—. Population. Puerto Rico. 1800-30. *1208*

—. Public Policy. Workers, undocumented. 1970's. *835*

—. Puerto Rico. 1909-77. *1321*

—. Spain. 17c-1975. *102*

—. West Indies. 1970's. *1075*

—. Workers, undocumented. 1970's. *1056*

—. Workers, undocumented. 1975-82. *870*

Immigration and Nationality Act (US, 1965). Aliens, illegal. Federal Policy. 1956-75. *124*

Immigration and Nationality Act (US, 1965; amended, 1976). Mexico. USA. 1976. *35*

Immigration and Naturalization Service. California (Los Angeles). Industrial Relations. International Ladies' Garment Workers' Union. Lilli Diamond Originals. Raids. 1976-77. *1027*

—. Federal Policy. Workers, undocumented. 1966-76. *1001*

—. Illinois. ca 1970-76. *727*

Immigration, illegal. California. Economic Conditions. Labor. Mexico, west-central. 1970's. *778*

—. Labor. Law. 1976. *912*

—. Labor. Southwest. Texas. 1821-1975. *493*

—. Marxism. Social policy. 1976. *749*

Immigration policy. Bouligny, Francisco (report). Gálvez, Bernardo de. Louisiana. Navarro, Martin *(Political Reflections).* Spain. 1776-83. *201*

Imperialism. Anthropology, Cultural. Puerto Rico. Stewart, Julian H. *(People of Puerto Rico).* 1956-77. *1299*

—. Economic development. Political conditions. Puerto Rico. Social organization. 1900-72. *1131*

—. Mexico. Migration. Sex Discrimination. Southwest. Women. Working class. 1850-1982. *428*

—. Puerto Rico. 20c. *1094*

Imports. Industrialization. Migrant Labor. 1940-77. *699*

Income. 1970's. *823*

—. Age. Blacks. Discrimination. Texas. 1960-70. *926*

—. Bilingualism. Immigrants. Language. 1975. *821*

—. Blacks. Employment. Family. Sex roles. Whites. 1982-83. *47*

—. Blacks. Metropolitan areas. Occupations. 1970. *808*

—. Blacks. Whites. 1976. *94*

—. Cubans. Education. Florida (Miami). Geographic mobility. Political power. 1959-78. *1241*

—. Cubans. Immigrants. Mexicans. 1973-76. *92*

—. Discrimination. Men. Whites. 1976. *121*

—. Economic development. Puerto Rico. Unemployment. 1959-70. *1201*

—. Education. Family. Fertility. Occupations. Puerto Ricans. 1969-70. *1325*

—. Education. Family. Occupations. 1969-70. *1057*

—. Education. Indiana (South Bend). Population. Social Mobility. 1970-74. *798*

—. Family. -1973. *724*

—. Immigrants. Men. Poverty. Self-perception. Working Class. 1978-79. *923*

—. Immigration. Labor. Southwest. Workers, undocumented. 1960-80. *828*

—. Men. 1975-78. *732*

—. North Central States. 1970. *105*

—. Whites. 1960. *958*

Income distribution. Economic growth. Education. Puerto Rico. 1950-76. *1199*

—. Labor. Puerto Rico. 1949-69. *1064*

Income redistribution. Food stamp program. Puerto Rico. 1974-75. *1065*

Independence. Chrisman, Robert. Puerto Rico. 1977. *1111*

—. Economic Conditions. Interviews. Muñoz Marín, Luis. Political issues. Puerto Rico. Social Conditions. 1948-64. *1186*

—. Melgares, Facundo. New Mexico (Santa Fe). New Spain. 1822. *386*

—. Puerto Rico. 1940-75. *1185*

Independence Movements. Campos, Albizu. Puerto Rico. 1910-65. *1247*

—. Cigar industry. Cubans. Florida (Tampa). Labor. 1892-1901. *1242*

—. City politics. Cubans. Florida (Jacksonville). Huah, José Alejandro. Martí, José. 1836-1905. *1164*

—. Colonialism. Economic Conditions. Puerto Rico. 1898-1977. *1212*

—. Cuba. Exiles. Florida (Key West). Human Relations. Ten Years' War. 1868-78. *1252*

—. Diego, José de. Middle classes. Puerto Rico. 1867-1918. *1139*

—. Gutierrez de Lara, José Bernardo Maxmilliano. Magee, Augustus W. Mexico. Republican Army of the North. Texas (San Antonio). 1811-15. *197*

—. Hostos, Eugenio María de. Puerto Rico. ca 1860-1903. *1174*

—. Puerto Rico. 1898-1979. *1324*

—. Puerto Rico. 1960-76. *1095*

—. Race Relations. Tejanos. Texas. Whites. 1822-36. *145*

Independence, War of. Mexico. Military Intelligence. Seguín, Juan Nepomuceno. Texas. 1830's-40's. *336*

Indian Wars. Apache Indians (Gila, Mimbres). Concha, Fernando Simon Ignacio de la. Diaries. 1788. *213*

—. Arizona (Canyon de Chelly). Bones. Dogs. Navajo Indians. Pictographs. Spain. 1750-1863. *202*

—. Colonial Government. Frontier and Pioneer Life. New Mexico. Pueblo Indians. Spain. Texas (El Paso). 1680-90. *219*

—. Defense Policy. Mexico, northern. Southwest. Spain. 1759-88. *304*

—. Diaries. Fuente, Pedro José de la. Mexico (Chihuahua, Sonora). Military. New Mexico. Texas (El Paso). 1765. *192*

—. Mexico. New Mexico. Trade regulation. Treaties. 1821-46. *372*

—. Missions and Missionaries. Pueblo Indians. Southwest. Spain. 1680. *314*
—. Navajo Indians. New Mexico. Spain. 1680-1720. *326*
—. New Mexico. Our Lady of Macana (statue). Statues. 1598-1957. *179*
—. Presidios. Southwest. Spain. 17c-18c. *212*
Indiana (East Chicago). City Life. Cubans. Ethnicity. Folklore. Puerto Ricans. 1976. *1161*
—. Depressions. Repatriation. 1919-33. *684*
Indiana (East Chicago, Gary). Catholic Church. Theater. 1920-76. *59*
Indiana (East Chicago; Indiana Harbor). Immigration. Inland Steel Company. Michigan, Lake. Social Conditions. 1919-32. *615*
Indiana (Gary). Depressions. Discrimination. Nativism. Repatriation. 1920's-30's. *609*
Indiana (South Bend). Education. Income. Population. Social Mobility. 1970-74. *798*
Indians. Agricultural Labor. Population. Spain. Texas (El Paso). 1680-1784. *362*
—. Agricultural Technology and Research. Assimilation. California. Mission San Antonio de Padua. Salinan Indians. 1771-1832. 1976-79. *244*
—. Agriculture. Irrigation. Mexican Americans. New Mexico. Pueblo Indians. 19c. *405*
—. Alarcón, Hernando. California. Colorado River. Discovery and Exploration. 1540. *207*
—. American dream. Blacks. Identity. 1890-1980. *25*
—. Americas (North and South). Sepúlveda, Juan Ginés de. Slavery. Spain. ca 1550. *216*
—. Anza, Juan Bautista de. Colonial Government. Concha, Fernando Simon Ignacio de la. Military Strategy. New Mexico. Spain. 1787-93. *161*
—. Apache Indians. Mexico (Mexico City). Removals, forced. Southwest. Spain. 1729-1809. *300*
—. Architecture. Housing. *Jacal* (style). New Mexico (Tierra Amarilla). Spaniards. Wood. 8c-20c. *366*
—. Arizona. Jesuits. Kino, Eusebio Francisco. Missions and Missionaries. Spain. 1680's-1711. *271*
—. Arizona State Museum. Documentary Relations of the Southwest project. Mexico, northern. Southwest. Spain. 16c-1810. 1975-78. *322*
—. Armies. Spain. 1561-1886. *204*
—. Athapascan Indians. Indian-White Relations. Missions and Missionaries. New Mexico. Pueblo Indians. 1600-80. *220*
—. Ayala, Juan Manuel de. California (San Francisco Bay). Discovery and Exploration. Franciscans. Spain. 1775. *369*
—. Blacks. Carranza, Venustiano. Mexico. Rebellions. Texas. Villa, Francisco. 1848-1920. *577*
—. Blacks. Cattle Raising. Historiography. ca 1865-1979. *431*
—. Blacks. Child-rearing. Values. 1979. *1045*
—. Blacks. Cowboys. Daily Life. Western States. 1860's-90's. *519*
—. Blankets. Dye. Navajo Indians. New Mexico. Rugs. Spaniards. Weaving. 19c-1977. *353*
—. Cahuilla Indians. California (Palm Springs region). Cocomaricopa Trail. Letters. Overland Journeys to the Pacific. Romero, José. ca 1823-24. *370*
—. California. Catholic Church. Chapels. Yuma Indians. ca 1769-1840. *387*
—. California. Catholic Church. Economic conditions. Missions and Missionaries. 1803-21. *151*
—. California. Catholic Church. Labor. Missions and Missionaries. 1775-1805. *152*
—. California. Church and State. Colonization. Spain. 1775-1800. *221*
—. California. Conversion thesis. Cook, Sherburne Friend. Franciscans. Missions and Missionaries. ca 1790-1820's. 1943. *229*
—. California. Durán, Narciso. Franciscans. Missions and Missionaries. Music. 1806-46. *224*
—. California. Durán, Narciso. Franciscans. Missions and Missionaries. Secularization. 1826-46. *305*
—. California. Mexico. Missions and Missionaries. 1830's. *321*
—. California (San Diego). Colonization. Missions and Missionaries. Spain. 1769-1834. *399*
—. California (San Diego area). Discovery and Exploration. Portolá, Gaspar de. South Carolina. 1769. *175*
—. California (Sonoma). Catholic Church. Mission San Francisco Solano. 1823-34. *176*
—. Catholic Church. Coahuiltecan Indians. Missions and Missionaries. Texas (San Antonio). 1792. *277*
—. Cattle Rustling. Comancheros. Hittson, John. New Mexico. Ranchers. 1872-73. *551*
—. Colonization. DeZorita, Alonso. Franciscans. Missions and Missionaries. Southwest. 1545-85. *378*
—. Colonization. Land tenure. New Mexico. Social Organization. Spain. 1546-1692. *313*
—. Colonization. New Spain. Policymaking. Settlement. Spain. 1750-1800. *149*
—. Community Participation in Politics. Economic Development. Government. New Mexico (Espanola Valley). Water Supply. 1970's. *864*
—. Daily Life. Letters. Lummis, Charles. Smith, Joseph. Southwest. 1880's-1924. *544*
—. Diplomacy. Navajo Indians. New Mexico. Spain. 1770-90. *324*
—. Economic Conditions. Health services. Navajo Indians. New Mexico, northwestern. Population. Rural areas. Spaniards. 1971-78. *93*
—. Farmers. Land (disputes). New Mexico (Rio Puerco Valley). Whites. 19c-20c. *433*
—. Five Civilized Tribes. Fur Trade. Gálvez, Bernardo de. Louisiana. Maxent, Gilberto Antonio de. Spain. 1749-84. *382*
—. Florida (St. Augustine). Great Britain. Social Customs. Spain. Trade. 1700-83. *211*
—. Folk Medicine. New Mexico. 19c-1930's. *408*
—. Franciscans. Indian-White Relations. Leadership. New Mexico. Pueblo Indians. Rebellions. 1650-80. 1980. *398*
—. Infants. Mortality. New Mexico. Whites. 1974-77. *971*
—. Land. New Spain. Southwest. Water rights. 1535-1810. *359*
—. Legal Education. Medical education. New Mexico. 1960's-76. *972*
—. Mexico. New Mexico (Estancia Basin). Salt. Spain. Trade. Prehistory-1840's. *265*
—. Military. Pueblo Indians. Social control. Spain. 1763-1821. *255*
—. Missions and Missionaries. New Mexico. Secularization. Spain. 1767. *263*
—. Navajo Indians. New Mexico, northern. Pueblo Indians. Rio Grande Valley. Weaving. 15c-1979. *393*
—. New Mexico. Political Participation. State politics. 1846-1976. *28*
—. New Mexico. Sheep raising. Weaving. Woolen Industry. 1540's-1860's. *166*
—. New Mexico. Toponymy. Whites. ca 1550-1982. *48*
Indian-White Relations. Alabama. Boucfouca, Treaty of. Choctaw Indians. Spain. Villebeuvre, Juan de la. 1793. *243*
—. Americas (North and South). Europeans. 1493-1888. *198*

—. Antonia (Indian). Calusa Indians. Carlos (chief). Florida. Marriage. Menéndez de Avilés, Pedro. Politics. 1566-69. *327*
—. Athapascan Indians. Indians. Missions and Missionaries. New Mexico. Pueblo Indians. 1600-80. *220*
—. California. Catholic Church. Missions and Missionaries. 1770's-1820's. *347*
—. California. Spain. 1770's. *295*
—. Choctaw Indians. Old Southwest. Spain. Treaties. Villebeuvre, Juan de la. 1784-97. *241*
—. Chouteau, Auguste P. Demun, Julius. Law. New Mexico. Trade. 1815-51. *375*
—. Colonial Government. Concha, Fernando Simon Ignacio de la. New Mexico. Spain. 1787-93. *155*
—. Colonization. Discovery and Exploration. Great Britain. Southeastern States. Spain. 1565-1685. *319*
—. Florida. Franciscans. 17c. *288*
—. Florida. Spain. *Visitas* (provincial tours). 1602-75. *320*
—. Franciscans. Indians. Leadership. New Mexico. Pueblo Indians. Rebellions. 1650-80. 1980. *398*
—. Inquisition. Marriage. New Mexico. Plains Apache Indians. Romero, Diego. 1660-78. *260*
—. Land Tenure. New Mexico (El Rancho, Vadito). Pueblo Indians. Settlement. 17c-1970. *418*
—. Louisiana. Spain. Treaties. 1770-93. *264*
—. Mesoamerican Indians. Pueblo Indians. Southwest. Spain. 1530-98. *329*
—. Missions and Missionaries. Pueblo Revolt (1680). Southwest. Spain. 1590-1680. *165*
—. Navajo Indians. New Mexico. Peace. Spain. 1720-79. *325*
—. New Mexico. 17c-1978. *496*
—. Pioneers. Pueblo Indians. Southwest. Spaniards. 1492-1974. *55*
Industrial Relations. California (Los Angeles). Immigration and Naturalization Service. International Ladies' Garment Workers' Union. Lilli Diamond Originals. Raids. 1976-77. *1027*
Industrialization. Agriculture. Economic Conditions. Puerto Rico. 1960's-70's. *1126*
—. California. Gold Mines and Mining. Nativism. 1845-70. *533*
—. Economic development. Puerto Rico. 1960's-70's. *1102*
—. Economic Integration. International Trade. Puerto Rico. 1948-63. *1302*
—. Imports. Migrant Labor. 1940-77. *699*
—. Migration. Politics. Puerto Rico. Working class. 1870's-1970's. *1108*
—. Puerto Rico. 1940-70. *1142*
—. Puerto Rico. Surplus value. 1948-63. *1312*
Industry. Americanization. Employment. Immigration. Public schools. 1880-1930. *624*
—. California (Los Angeles). Employment. Interviews. Women. 1928. *686*
—. Foreign Policy. Puerto Rico. 1982. *1124*
Inequality. Civil Service. Wages. Whites. 1977. *1011*
Infant mortality. California (Los Angeles). Public health. 1850-87. *537*
Infants. Indians. Mortality. New Mexico. Whites. 1974-77. *971*
—. Mortality. Prenatal care. Social Classes. Southwest. 1970. *793*
Inflation. Puerto Rico. 1945-80. *1067*
Information storage and retrieval systems. Bibliographies. Mental Health Research Center. 1971-79. *132*
Inhalants. Drug abuse. Economic Conditions. Immigration. Social Conditions. Youth. 1930-80. *429*

Inland Steel Company. Immigration. Indiana (East Chicago; Indiana Harbor). Michigan, Lake. Social Conditions. 1919-32. *615*
Inquisition. Indian-White Relations. Marriage. New Mexico. Plains Apache Indians. Romero, Diego. 1660-78. *260*
Institute of Puerto Rican Culture. Art. Culture. Muñoz Marín, Luis. Puerto Rico. Romero Barceló, Carlos. 1948-55. *1277*
—. Culture. Puerto Rico. Theater. 1955-80. *1211*
Institutions. Assimilation. Ethnicity. Political activism. Students. Texas (Corpus Christi, Crystal City). 1969-80. *753*
Insubordination. Civil-Military Relations. Foxardo (battle). Navies. Porter, David. Puerto Rico. 1823-25. *1087*
Integration. Fertility. Social Mobility. 1969. *907*
Interest groups. Courts. Mexican American Legal Defense and Education Fund. 1968-82. *941*
Intergovernmental Relations. Law. Martinez, Manuel. Mexico. New Mexico. Water. 1832. *205*
Intermarriage. Assimilation. Ethnic identity. Texas (San Antonio). Women. 1830-60. *530*
—. California. 1962-74. *989*
—. Men. Texas (San Antonio area). 1971-80. *1024*
—. New Mexico. Whites. 1846-1900. *563*
—. Southwest. 20c. *935*
International Brotherhood of Teamsters. Agriculture. Boycotts. California. Chavez, Cesar. Grapes. Labor Unions and Organizations. Lettuce. United Farm Workers Union. 1962-74. *805*
International Ladies' Garment Workers' Union. California (Los Angeles). Garment Industry. Strikes. Women. 1933. *619*
—. California (Los Angeles). Immigration and Naturalization Service. Industrial Relations. Lilli Diamond Originals. Raids. 1976-77. *1027*
—. California (Los Angeles). Women. Working Conditions. 1933-39. *664*
International law. Airplanes. Cuba. Deportation. Hijacking. Refugees. 1983. *1191*
—. Puerto Rico. UN. 1950-73. *1172*
International Rescue Committee (Caribbean Relief Program). Cubans. New Jersey. Refugees. Settlement. 1959-83. *1145*
International Trade. American Revolution. Puerto Rico. 1775-1854. *1210*
—. Cuba. Florida (Dade County; Miami). Immigration. Latin America. Social Customs. 1970's. *1314*
—. Economic Integration. Industrialization. Puerto Rico. 1948-63. *1302*
Interpersonal Relations. Blacks. Marriage. Whites. 1960-70. *792*
Interviews. Acculturation. Immigrants. Puerto Ricans. 1982. *1134*
—. Aliens, illegal. Methodology. 1975-81. *772*
—. California (Los Angeles). Chicano movement. Political Socialization. 1960's. *974*
—. California (Los Angeles). Employment. Industry. Women. 1928. *686*
—. Economic Conditions. Independence. Muñoz Marín, Luis. Political issues. Puerto Rico. Social Conditions. 1948-64. *1186*
—. History Teaching. Mexican Americans. Oral history. 1974. *37*
—. Labor. *Mexican Labor in the United States* (study). National Endowment for the Humanities. Research. Taylor, Paul S. 1927-30. *646*
Investments. Economics. Puerto Rico. USA. 1970's. *1315*
—. Land. Mexia, José Antonio. Mexico. Politics. Texas. 1823-39. *248*
IQ tests. Children. 1970's. *729*
—. Children. 1970-79. *959*

Irrigation. Agriculture. Indians. Mexican Americans. New Mexico. Pueblo Indians. 19c. *357*
—. Martinez, Felix. New Mexico. Politics. Texas. 1877-1916. *598*
Isidore the Husbandman, Saint. Catholic Church. Lopez, George. New Mexico (Córdova). Statues. Wood carving. ca 1070-1130. ca 1690-1980. *411*

J

Jacal (style). Architecture. Housing. Indians. New Mexico (Tierra Amarilla). Spaniards. Wood. 8c-20c. *366*
Jamaicans. Blacks. Farms. Migrant Labor. New York. Social mobility. 1960's-70's. *1152*
—. Blacks. Florida. Migrant labor. 1980. *731*
Japan. Agricultural Labor. Berry pickers. California (El Monte). Foreign Relations. Mexico. Strikes. 1933. *645*
Japanese. Agricultural labor. California (San Joaquin Valley). Nisei Farmers League. United Farm Workers Union. 1971-77. *812*
—. Blacks. Chinese Americans. Economic Conditions. Filipinos. Social Status. 1960-76. *51*
—. California (San Joaquin Valley). Labor Disputes. Nisei Farmers League. United Farm Workers Union. 1974-76. *811*
—. Children. Political participation. Whites. 1970's. *1005*
Japanese-Mexican Labor Association. Agricultural Labor. California (Oxnard). Strikes. Sugar beets. Wages. 1902-03. *602*
Jaramillo, Cleofas M. Catholic Church. Marriage. New Mexico, northern. Social Customs. 1880-98. *547*
Jaramillo, Pedrito. Folk medicine. Lozano, José C. Texas (south). 19c. *511*
—. Folk Medicine. Texas (Los Almos). 1881-1907. *509*
Jayme, Luís (death). California (San Diego). Franciscans. Mission San Diego de Alcalá. Yuman Indians. 1775. *388*
Jenner, Edward. California (Monterey). Estrada, José. Europe. Smallpox. Vaccination. 18c-1821. *301*
Jesuits. Arizona. Indians. Kino, Eusebio Francisco. Missions and Missionaries. Spain. 1680's-1711. *271*
—. Arizona (Nogales). Excavations. Mission Guevavi. 18c. 1964-66. *333*
—. California. Dominicans. Franciscans. Missions and Missionaries. Serra, Junípero. 1768-76. *287*
—. Catholic Church. *Revista Catolica*. Southwest. 1875-1962. *501*
—. Discovery and Exploration. Kino, Eusebio Francisco. Southwest. 1645-1711. *258*
Jews. Assimilation. Mexico (Nuevo Reyno de León). Texas. 16c-20c. *483*
Jiménez, Juan Ramón. Authors. Memoirs. Nobel Prize. Palau de Nemes, Graciela. Puerto Rico (Ponce). Spain. 1930's-56. *1113*
Job satisfaction. Men. Southwest. 1980. *848*
—. Social Status. 1970's. *849*
Johnson, Roberta Ann. Areíto, Grupo. Cubans. History Task Force. Immigration. Puerto Ricans. 1960's-70's. *1226*
Jokes. Folklore. Humor. Sex. Women. 1970's. *761*
—. Identity. Social Change. Texas. Whites. 1970's. *890*
Jones, Oakah L., Jr. Borderlands (review article). McDermott, John Francis. Mississippi Valley. Southwest. Spain. Weddle, Robert S. 1762-1804. 1973-74. *379*

Jones, Thomas ap Catesby. California (Monterey). Great Britain. Mexico. Military Occupation. Navies. 1842. *218*
Journalism. Cubans. *Diario Las Americas*. Florida (Miami). Politics and Media. Watergate scandal. 1970's. *1061*
Judges. Lawyers. Socialization. Southwest. 1945-74. *947*
Judicial Administration. Blacks. California (Los Angeles). Crime and Criminals. Whites. 1977-80. *1041*

K

Kansas (Dodge City). Acculturation. 20c. *449*
—. Discrimination. Ethnic Groups. Public Opinion. 1900-84. *450*
Kansas (Manhattan). Blacks. Political integration. 1971. *704*
KCOR, station. Radio. Spanish language. Texas (San Antonio). 1928-74. *485*
Kearny, Stephen Watts. California. Mexican War. San Pasqual (battle). 1846. *156*
—. California. Mexican War. San Pasqual (battle). 1847. *253*
Kendall, George Wilkins. Armijo, Manuel. New Mexico. 1842-44. *275*
King, Mel. Elections (mayoral). Massachusetts (Boston). 1983. *1097*
Kino, Eusebio Francisco. Arizona. Indians. Jesuits. Missions and Missionaries. Spain. 1680's-1711. *271*
—. Arizona (Casa Grande). Bolton, Herbert Eugene. Explorers. 1697. 1934. 1968-72. *250*
—. Discovery and Exploration. Jesuits. Southwest. 1645-1711. *258*
Kusz, Charles L. *Gringo and Greaser*. New Mexico (Manzano). Newspapers. 1883-84. *584*

L

La Raza Unida Party. California. Colleges and Universities. Student activism. 1969-73. *933*
—. Chavez, Cesar. 1968-73. *789*
La Union. Filibustering. Latin America. Louisiana (New Orleans). Newspapers. 1846-51. *328*
Labor. Acculturation. Immigration. Literature. 1830-1983. *443*
—. Aliens. Immigration. Public policy. 1970's. *965*
—. Aliens, illegal. Immigration. Population. 1970-80. *142*
—. Aliens, illegal. Statistics. 1968-80. *107*
—. Assimilation. Immigrants. Men. 1960's-76. *733*
—. Blacks. Competition. Whites. 1976. *734*
—. Blacks. Whites. Wisconsin (Racine). 1960-70. *995*
—. California. Catholic Church. Indians. Missions and Missionaries. 1775-1850. *152*
—. California. Economic Conditions. Immigration, illegal. Mexico, west-central. 1970's. *778*
—. California (Los Angeles). Workers, Undocumented. 1979. *718*
—. California (Los Angeles County). 1920's-30's. *665*
—. Capital. Economic Development. Models. Puerto Rico. 1945-70. *1222*
—. Capitalism. Children. Mexico. Women. Workers, undocumented. ca 1950-79. *833*
—. Capitalism. Economic Structure. Immigration. Latin Americans. Minorities. ca 1950-70. *1290*
—. Cigar industry. Cubans. Florida (Tampa). Independence Movements. 1892-1901. *1242*
—. Cubans. Florida (Key West). Martí, José. Tobacco Industry. 1891. *1170*
—. Czech Americans. Family. Land. Social Organization. Texas (Nueces County). 1880-1930. *608*

—. Daily Life. New Mexico (Albuquerque). Social mobility. Trade. 1706-90. *330*
—. Deportation. Mexico. Migration. 1920-75. *413*
—. Economic Conditions. Historiography. Mexican Americans. 1850-1976. *8*
—. Economic Conditions. Immigration. Mexico. Social control. 1950's-70's. *865*
—. Education. Political power. Southwest. 1848-1980. *635*
—. Ethnic Groups. Georgia (Atlanta). Louisiana (New Orleans). Texas (San Antonio). Women. 1930-40. *610*
—. Federal Policy. Immigration. Racism. 1920's. *672*
—. Historiography. Mexican Americans. Oral history. 1920's-30's. *127*
—. Illinois (Chicago). 1908-30. *673*
—. Immigrants. 1960's-82. *14*
—. Immigrants. Workers, Undocumented. 1970's. *913*
—. Immigration. Income. Southwest. Workers, undocumented. 1960-80. *828*
—. Immigration. Mexico. Women. 1970's. *834*
—. Immigration. Public policy. Workers, undocumented. 1950's-70's. *140*
—. Immigration. Reisler, Mark (review article). 1900-40. 1976. *628*
—. Immigration. USA. 1909-76. *402*
—. Immigration, illegal. Law. 1976. *912*
—. Immigration (illegal). Southwest. Texas. 1821-1975. *493*
—. Income distribution. Puerto Rico. 1949-69. *1064*
—. Interviews. *Mexican Labor in the United States* (study). National Endowment for the Humanities. Research. Taylor, Paul S. 1927-30. *646*
—. *Mexican Labor in the United States* (study). Research. Taylor, Paul S. 1926-34. *54*
—. Mexico. Migration. Texas. 1960's-70's. *737*
—. Mexico. USA. Workers, undocumented. 1970's. *955*
—. Mexico. Workers, undocumented. 1973. *746*
—. Migration, internal. 1973-77. *84*
—. Mines. South. Southwest. 1513-1846. *232*
—. National Labor Relations Board. *NLRB v. Apollo Tire Co.* (US, 1979). *NLRB v. Sure-Tan, Inc.* (US, 1978). Workers, undocumented. 1978-79. *1034*
—. Poetry. Popular culture. 1967-73. *952*
—. Puerto Ricans. 1942-51. *1198*
—. Social mobility. Workers, Undocumented. 1970-80. *720*
—. Southwest. 1896-1915. *522*
—. Workers, undocumented. 20c. *748*
Labor Disputes. California (San Joaquin Valley). Japanese. Nisei Farmers League. United Farm Workers Union. 1974-76. *811*
—. Cubans. Florida (Tampa). *Lector* (reader). Perez, Louis A., Jr. Personal narratives. Tobacco industry. ca 1925-35. *1243*
Labor law. Agricultural Labor. California. 1965-76. *764*
—. Agricultural Labor Relations Act (California, 1975). California. Emergency Farm Labor Supply Program. New Deal. ca 1930-79. *434*
Labor movement. Multinational corporations. Neocolonialism. Puerto Rico. Self-determination. 1950's-70's. *1098*
Labor Unions and Organizations. Agricultural Industry. California. Elections. Proposition 14 (1976). United Farm Workers Union. 1976. *773*
—. Agricultural labor. 1900-79. *448*
—. Agricultural Labor. Aliens, illegal. Attitudes. Bracero Program. Mexico. 1943-74. *889*

—. Agriculture. Boycotts. California. Chavez, Cesar. Grapes. International Brotherhood of Teamsters. Lettuce. United Farm Workers Union. 1962-74. *805*
—. Aliens (illegal). 1980-83. *786*
—. American Federation of Labor. Gompers, Samuel. Iglesias Pantín, Santiago. Puerto Rico. 1897-1920's. *1155*
—. Arizona. Copper industry. Politics. Racism. Working Class. 1900-20. *611*
—. California (Los Angeles). Congress of Industrial Organizations. 1938-50. *606*
—. Civil Rights. North Central States. Social Organizations. 1900-76. *467*
—. Deportation. Immigrants. New Deal. 1930's. *618*
—. Discrimination. North Central States. Steel workers. 1919-45. *677*
—. Discrimination. Texas (El Paso). 1880-1920. *629*
—. Mexico. Workers, Undocumented. 1867-1977. *407*
—. Socialism. Texas. 1900-20. *692*
—. Strikes. Texas. 1920-40. *666*
—. Texas. United Cannery, Agricultural, Packing and Allied Workers of America. 1935-50. *668*
LaBranche, Alcée. Annexation. Diplomacy. Eve, Joseph. Flood, George H. Letters. Murphy, William S. Texas. 1837-43. *162*
Lair, Clara. Burgos, Julia de. Font Saldaña, Jorge. Personal Narratives. Poets. Puerto Rico. Ribera Chevremont, Evaristo. 20c. *1232*
Lancastrian system. Mexico, northern. Public Schools. Southwest. 1821-48. *373*
Land. *See also* Property.
—. Czech Americans. Family. Labor. Social Organization. Texas (Nueces County). 1880-1930. *608*
—. Florida. Santa Elena (colony). Settlement. Spain. 1560-87. *280*
—. Indians. New Spain. Southwest. Water rights. 1535-1810. *359*
—. Investments. Mexia, José Antonio. Mexico. Politics. Texas. 1823-39. *248*
—. New Mexico. Pino, Juan Estevan. Speculation. 1820-30. *234*
Land disputes. Bernal, Juan Pablo. Business. California. Cattle Raising. Wealth. 1822-78. *426*
—. Farmers. Indians. New Mexico (Rio Puerco Valley). Whites. 19c-20c. *433*
Land distribution. Puerto Rico. Unemployment. 1970's. *1194*
Land grants. Anton Chico grant. New Mexico Land and Livestock Company. Rivera, Manuel. Trials. 1822-1915. *334*
—. Armijo, Manuel. Colorado. 1823-1900. *354*
—. Atrisco grant. New Mexico. New Spain. Pueblo Revolt (1680). 1680-1977. *454*
—. Bibliographies. New Mexico. 1851-1981. *85*
—. California. O'Farrell, Jasper. Surveying. 1844-46. *289*
—. Colonial Government. Mendinueta, Pedro Fermín de. New Mexico. Spain. 1767-79. *316*
—. Commons. Law. New Mexico. San Joaquín Grant. 1806-97. *531*
—. Court of Private Land Claims. Embudo de Picuris grant. New Mexico. 1725-1898. *430*
—. Ethnicity. Herrera, Juan José. Militancy. New Mexico (Las Vegas). Vigilantes. White Caps. 1887-94. *554*
—. Federal government. New Mexico (Las Trampas Grant). Swindles. 1859-1914. *526*
—. Guadalupe Hidalgo, Treaty of. Protocol of Querétaro. Texas. Trist, Nicholas P. 1847-48. *560*
—. Law. New Mexico (Las Vegas). 1835-1902. *552*
—. Mexico. New Mexico. San Antonio de las Huertas grant. Spain. 1765-1891. *348*

—. New Mexico. Ortiz y Alarid, Gasper. Roque Lovato Grant. 1785-1894. *532*

—. New Mexico. Supreme Court (decisions). 1821-90. *579*

—. New Mexico (Colfax County, Uña de Gato grant). 1870's. *590*

Land Tenure. California. Mexico. Ranches. 1784-1846. *247*

—. Colonization. Indians. New Mexico. Social Organization. Spain. 1546-1692. *313*

—.m Colonization. New Mexico. Spain. Whites. 16c-1974. *29*

—. Economic Conditions. New Mexico. Social Organization. Spaniards. Whites. 1846-91. *594*

—. Indian-White Relations. New Mexico (El Rancho, Vadito). Pueblo Indians. Settlement. 17c-1970. *418*

Land warrants. Armies. Bounties. Mexican War. 1800-61. *309*

Landholding. New Mexico (Santa Fe). 1860-70. *514*

Landmarks. California (Monterey). Historical Sites and Parks. Mexico. Spain. 1770-1849. *173*

—. Santa Fe Trail. 1806-80. *392*

Landownership. New Mexico (Rio Grande Valley). Pueblo Indian Grants, Northern. Spaniards. ca 1500's-1970's. *174*

Langhorne, George T. Bandits. Big Bend region. Mexico (Coahuila). Punitive expeditions. Texas (Glenn Springs, Boquillas). 1915-16. *687*

Language. Bibliographies. Bilingual education. 20c. *17*

—. Bilingualism. Immigrants. Income. 1975. *821*

—. Blacks. California (Los Angeles). Reading. Whites. 1970's. *879*

—. Education. Men. Social Status. 1975-76. *119*

—. Puerto Rico. 1975. *1319*

Language (dialects). Attitudes. 1975. *802*

LasCasas, Bartolomé de. Americas (North and South). Discovery and Exploration. Settlement. 16c-17c. *276*

Latin America. Class consciousness. Puerto Rico. Women. Working Class. 1959-75. *1279*

—. Colonization. Law. New Mexico. Spain. 15c-18c. *340*

—. Cuba. Florida (Dade County; Miami). Immigration. International Trade. Social Customs. 1970's. *1314*

—. Cubans. Exiles. Martí, José. New York City. Reporters and Reporting. 1880-95. *1068*

—. Ethnicity. Florida. Identity. Immigration. 1979. *1192*

—. Federal Policy. Foreign Relations. Immigration. West Indies. 1924-79. *1217*

—. Filibustering. *La Union*. Louisiana (New Orleans). Newspapers. 1846-51. *328*

—. Foreign relations. Puerto Rico. West Indies. 1975. *1105*

—. Nationalism. Political Attitudes. Social Customs. 1848-1976. *480*

—. New Mexico, northern. Social Organization. Spain. Villages. 16c-20c. *377*

Latin Americans. Blades, Rubén (interview). City life. Music. Panama. Salsa. 1974-84. *1088*

—. Briski, Norman (interview). Exiles. New York City. Theater. 1970's-82. *1096*

—. Capitalism. Economic Structure. Immigration. Labor. Minorities. ca 1950-70. *1290*

—. Daily life. Immigrants. Popular culture. West Indies. 1965-77. *12*

—. Employment. New York City. Women. 1970's. *1278*

—. Immigration. 1960-78. *1214*

Laviera, Tato *(La Carreta Made a U-Turn)*. Acculturation. Poetry. Puerto Ricans. 1979-80. *1151*

Law. Catholic Church. Church and State. Puerto Rico. ca 1863-1908. *1160*

—. Chouteau, Auguste P. Demun, Julius. Indian-White Relations. New Mexico. Trade. 1815-51. *375*

—. Colonization. Latin America. New Mexico. Spain. 15c-18c. *340*

—. Commons. Land grants. New Mexico. San Joaquín Grant. 1806-97. *531*

—. Immigration, illegal. Labor. 1976. *912*

—. Intergovernmental Relations. Martinez, Manuel. Mexico. New Mexico. Water. 1832. *205*

—. Land grants. New Mexico (Las Vegas). 1835-1902. *552*

—. New Mexico. Social Status. Women. 1821-46. *272*

Law enforcement. Aguirre, Martin. California (Los Angeles County). 1880's-1929. *545*

—. Baca, Elfego. New Mexico (Socorro). 1865-1919. *580*

—. California (Los Angeles County). Drug abuse. Rehabilitation. Statistics. 1969-79. *906*

—. Immigration. Mexico. 1924-29. *644*

Lawyers. Judges. Socialization. Southwest. 1945-74. *947*

Lead poisoning. Folk Medicine. Southwest. 1983. *1018*

Leadership. California. Pico, Pío. 1801-94. *520*

—. Franciscans. Indians. Indian-White Relations. New Mexico. Pueblo Indians. Rebellions. 1650-80. 1980. *398*

—. Immigrants. Puerto Ricans. Women. 1910-45. *1280*

League of United Latin American Citizens. American G.I. Forum. Mexican American Legal Defense and Education Fund. Pressure Groups. School integration. Texas. 1945-80. *981*

Lector (reader). Cubans. Florida (Tampa). Labor Disputes. Perez, Louis A., Jr. Personal narratives. Tobacco industry. ca 1925-35. *1243*

Legal Education. Indians. Medical education. New Mexico. 1960's-76. *972*

Legends. Alamo (battle). Historians. 19c. *453*

—. California. Murieta, Joaquín. Outlaws. 1850's. *556*

Legislation. Administration for the Development of Art and Culture. Bureaucracies. Musicians. New Progressive Party. Puerto Rico. 1980. *1284*

Leisure. California (East Los Angeles). Low-riders (automobiles). Social Customs. Youth. 1970's. *861*

Letters. Acadians. Colonial Government. Louisiana. Refugees. Spain. Ulloa, Antonio de. 1766-68. *178*

—. American Revolution. Bouligny, Francisco. Louisiana. Settlement. Spain. 1776-78. *200*

—. Annexation. Diplomacy. Eve, Joseph. Flood, George H. LaBranche, Alcée. Murphy, William S. Texas. 1837-43. *162*

—. Cahuilla Indians. California (Palm Springs region). Cocomaricopa Trail. Indians. Overland Journeys to the Pacific. Romero, José. ca 1823-24. *370*

—. Daily Life. Indians. Lummis, Charles. Smith, Joseph. Southwest. 1880's-1924. *544*

Lettuce. Agriculture. Boycotts. California. Chavez, Cesar. Grapes. International Brotherhood of Teamsters. Labor Unions and Organizations. United Farm Workers Union. 1962-74. *805*

Levine, Barry B. Centro de Estudios Puertorriqueños (History Task Force). Economic relations. Puerto Rico (review article). Sariola, Sakari. 1898-1970's. *1184*

Liberal Party. Andrade, Flores de. Immigration. Mexico. Personal narratives. Revolutionary Movements. Texas (El Paso). 1890-1911. *621*

—. Exiles. Mexico. Propaganda. Texas. Women. 1898-1910. *691*

Librarians. Castañeda, Carlos Eduardo. Colleges and Universities. Historiography. Texas, University of, Austin (Benson Latin American Collection). 1920-27. *603*

Libraries. 1960's-77. *847*

—. Bibliographies. Mexican Americans. 1960's-70's. *131*

—. California. Migrant Labor. 1970-80. *937*

—. New Mexico. 1598-1912. *98*

Liga Protectora Latina. Arizona. Benevolent organizations. 1914-40. *658*

Lilli Diamond Originals. California (Los Angeles). Immigration and Naturalization Service. Industrial Relations. International Ladies' Garment Workers' Union. Raids. 1976-77. *1027*

Linguistics. Bilingualism. Social Conditions. 1970-78. *942*

—. Grammar. Spanish language. 1976. *983*

Literacy. California (Los Angeles). Census. Education. Quantitative Methods. 1850. *596*

—. Texas (San Antonio). Whites. 1850-60. *540*

Literature. Acculturation. Immigration. Labor. 1830-1983. *443*

—. Anglo (character). Sanchez, Saul (review article). Villains. 1970's. *953*

—. Art. Bibliographies. Civil Rights. Mexican Americans. Southwest. 1936-73. *96*

—. Assimilation. Social Customs. Villareal, José Antonio (*Pocho*). 1959-76. *743*

—. Authors. 1974. *744*

—. Bibliographies. English Language. Puerto Rico. 1923-73. *80*

—. Bibliographies. History. Mexican Americans. Women. 1519-1976. *115*

—. California. Pachuco (term). Youth. 1940's-1960's. *904*

—. California. Stereotypes. 1850-1900. *553*

—. Chacón, Felipe Maximiliano. New Mexico. Newspapers. 1873-1922. *661*

—. Cities. Women. 1970's. *774*

—. Communist Party. Harlem Renaissance. Immigrants. New York City. West Indians. 1930's. *1301*

—. Culture. New Mexico. 1610-1983. *5*

—. Daily Life. Hinojosa, Rolando. Rivera, Tomás. Social Customs. Southwest. 1980. *756*

—. Elizando, Sergio. Gonzales, Thomas Rodolfo. 1970's. *742*

—. Films. Mass Media. Stereotypes. 20c. *446*

—. *Fotonovelas*. Values. Women. Working Class. 1976-80. *757*

—. Hinojosa, Rolando. 1976-80. *1009*

Livestock. Contracts, partido. Employment. New Mexico. 1905-11. *656*

Llana, Jerónimo de la. Maps. Marín del Valle, Francisco Antonio. New Mexico (Quarai, Tajique). 1659. 1759. *261*

Local government. California (Parlier). Models. Politics. 1971-73. *966*

—. Political Participation. Texas, South. 1971-83. *721*

Log structures. Architecture. New Mexico. 1756-1970's. *43*

Lopez, George. Catholic Church. Isidore the Husbandman, Saint. New Mexico (Córdova). Statues. Wood carving. ca 1070-1130. ca 1690-1980. *411*

—. Folk art. Lopez, José Dolores. New Mexico (Córdova). Santos. 20c. *412*

Lopez, José Dolores. Folk art. Lopez, George. New Mexico (Córdova). Santos. 20c. *412*

Lopez, Lorenzo. New Mexico (Las Vegas). Outlaws. Poets. Silva, Vicente. 1875-94. *561*

Louisiana. Acadians. Colonial Government. Letters. Refugees. Spain. Ulloa, Antonio de. 1766-68. *178*

—. Acosta Rodríquez, Antonio. Census. Colonial Government. Historiography. Spain. 1763-1803. 1976-80. *242*

—. American Revolution. Bouligny, Francisco. Letters. Settlement. Spain. 1776-78. *200*

—. Borders. Mexico. Puelles, José María de Jesús. Texas. 1512-1813. 1827-28. *230*

—. Bouligny, Francisco (report). Gálvez, Bernardo de. Immigration policy. Navarro, Martin (*Political Reflections*). Spain. 1776-83. *201*

—. Colonies. Hispaniola. Immigration. 1792-1804. *194*

—. Five Civilized Tribes. Fur Trade. Gálvez, Bernardo de. Indians. Maxent, Gilberto Antonio de. Spain. 1749-84. *382*

—. Fort Bute. Fort St. Gabriel. Great Britain. Military Occupation. Spain. 1768. *177*

—. France. Medicine (practice of). Pharmacy. Spain. 1717-1852. *203*

—. Indian-White Relations. Spain. Treaties. 1770-93. *264*

Louisiana (New Orleans). Ethnic Groups. Georgia (Atlanta). Labor. Texas (San Antonio). Women. 1930-40. *610*

—. Filibustering. *La Union*. Latin America. Newspapers. 1846-51. *328*

—. Hispaniola. Refugees. 1792-1804. *193*

Louisiana Territory. Colonialism. Culture. Florida. Spain. Texas. 1513-1803. *217*

Low-riders (automobiles). California (East Los Angeles). Leisure. Social Customs. Youth. 1970's. *861*

Lozano, Ignacio. Assimilation. California (Los Angeles). Exiles. Newspapers. *Opinión*. 1926-29. *660*

Lozano, José C. Folk medicine. Jaramillo, Pedrito. Texas (south). 19c. *511*

Lummis, Charles. Daily Life. Indians. Letters. Smith, Joseph. Southwest. 1880's-1924. *544*

Lyon, Eugene. Balseiro, José Agustín. Florida (review article). Menéndez de Avilés, Pedro. Spain. 1513-1977. *184*

M

Machismo (concept). Catholic Church. Ethnic Groups. Mexican Americans. Social Customs. Women. 1970's. *967*

Madero, Francisco. Mexico. Revolution. Reyes, Bernardo. Texas. 1910-12. *640*

Magee, Augustus W. Gutierrez de Lara, José Bernardo Maxmilliano. Independence Movements. Mexico. Republican Army of the North. Texas (San Antonio). 1811-15. *197*

Majolica pottery sherds. California. Excavations. Santa Barbara Presidio, Chapel. Spain. 1782-1850. *153*

Manitos. New Mexico. Politics. 1970-74. *816*

Manufactures. New Mexico, northern. Pottery. 17c-1930's. *351*

Manuscripts. Catholic Church. Design. Folk art. Iconography. New Mexico. 16c-17c. *233*

Map Drawing. Southwest. 16c-1980. *26*

Maps. Llana, Jerónimo de la. Marín del Valle, Francisco Antonio. New Mexico (Quarai, Tajique). 1659. 1759. *261*

Marcantonio, Vito. House of Representatives. New York. Puerto Ricans. Republican Party. 20c. *1196*

Marín del Valle, Francisco Antonio. Llana, Jerónimo de la. Maps. New Mexico (Quarai, Tajique). 1659. 1759. *261*

Marriage. Acculturation. California (Santa Clara County). Rites and Ceremonies. 1908-68. *421*

—. Antonia (Indian). Calusa Indians. Carlos (chief). Florida. Indian-White Relations. Menéndez de Avilés, Pedro. Politics. 1566-69. *327*
—. Attitudes. Generations. 1981-82. *910*
—. Blacks. Employment. Mothers. Whites. Women. 1970-84. *46*
—. Blacks. Interpersonal Relations. Whites. 1960-70. *792*
—. California (Los Angeles, Santa Barbara). Catholic Church. Mission Santa Barbara. Social Customs. 1786-1848. *298*
—. Catholic Church. Jaramillo, Cleofas M. New Mexico, northern. Social Customs. 1880-98. *547*
—. Cubans. 1957-74. *1059*
—. Fertility. Modernization. Puerto Rico. 1950-70. *1063*
—. Indian-White Relations. Inquisition. New Mexico. Plains Apache Indians. Romero, Diego. 1660-78. *260*
Marriage (mixed). Social Change. Texas (Pecos County). Whites. 1880-1978. *419*
Martí, José. City politics. Cubans. Florida (Jacksonville). Huah, José Alejandro. Independence Movements. 1836-1905. *1164*
—. Cubans. Exiles. Latin America. New York City. Reporters and Reporting. 1880-95. *1068*
—. Cubans. Florida (Key West). Labor. Tobacco Industry. 1891. *1170*
Martínez, Antonio José (report). Mexico. New Mexico. Territorial government. 1830-32. *383*
Martinez, Felix. Irrigation. New Mexico. Politics. Texas. 1877-1916. *598*
Martinez, Manuel. Intergovernmental Relations. Law. Mexico. New Mexico. Water. 1832. *205*
Marxism. California. Cultural identity. Political power. San Diego State University. 1965-74. *992*
—. Historiography. Puerto Rico. 19c-20c. *1203*
—. Immigration (illegal). Social policy. 1976. *749*
—. Social Classes. 1900-30. *607*
Mass media. Bibliographies. Mexican Americans. Periodicals. 1970's. *24*
—. Films. Literature. Stereotypes. 20c. *446*
—. Political Leadership. Texas (Austin). Whites. 1973. *877*
—. Spanish (language). 17c-1977. *44*
Massachusetts (Boston). Elections (mayoral). King, Mel. 1983. *1097*
Massachusetts (New Bedford). Personal Narratives. Puerto Ricans. Social Conditions. 1930-82. *1216*
Matamoros (colony). Blues. Folk Songs. Fugitive Slaves. Music. 19c-1940's. *458*
Matthews, Thomas. Americanization. Bhana, Surendra. Clark, Truman. Development. Politics. Puerto Rico (review article). 1917-76. *1261*
Maverick, Maury. Calleros, Cleofas. Federación de Sociedades Latinos-Americanos. McCammont, T. J. Powell, Alex K. Race Relations. Texas (El Paso). 1936. *627*
Maxent, Gilberto Antonio de. Five Civilized Tribes. Fur Trade. Gálvez, Bernardo de. Indians. Louisiana. Spain. 1749-84. *382*
McCammont, T. J. Calleros, Cleofas. Federación de Sociedades Latinos-Americanos. Maverick, Maury. Powell, Alex K. Race Relations. Texas (El Paso). 1936. *627*
McDermott, John Francis. Borderlands (review article). Jones, Oakah L., Jr. Mississippi Valley. Southwest. Spain. Weddle, Robert S. 1762-1804. 1973-74. *379*
McFarland, William. Arizona. Gándara, Francisco. Race Relations. Violence. Whites. 1872-73. *578*
McWilliams, Carey. California (Los Angeles). Personal narratives. Race Relations. 1940's-60's. *917*

Mead, Margaret (interview). Cultural identity. Economic conditions. Emigration. Puerto Rico. 1974. *1218*
—. National Self-image. Puerto Rico. Social Customs. 1975. *1323*
Measurements. Blacks. Mortality. Texas. Whites. 1980. *1008*
Mechicano Art Center. Art. California (East Los Angeles). Murals. 1970's. *759*
Medical Care. See also Health Care.
—. Behavior. Stereotypes. 1940's-70's. *797*
—. California. Women. 1977. *1004*
—. California (Los Angeles). Neighborhoods. Poor. 1970-79. *853*
—. Florida. Immigrants. Voluntary Associations. 19c-20c. *129*
—. Folk medicine. Historiography. Mexican Americans. 1894-20c. *100*
Medical Care (costs). California (Orange County). Whites. -1973. *1037*
Medical Education. California (San Diego). Colorado (Denver). Physicians. Texas (San Antonio). 1970-79. *980*
—. Indians. Legal Education. New Mexico. 1960's-76. *972*
Medicine (practice of). California. Cesarean operations. Franciscans. Missions and Missionaries. 1769-1833. *376*
—. France. Louisiana. Pharmacy. Spain. 1717-1852. *203*
Meier, Matt S. Bibliographies (review article). Rivera, Feliciano. 1974. *487*
Melgares, Facundo. Independence. New Mexico (Santa Fe). New Spain. 1822. *386*
Melville, Margarita B. DelCastillo, Adelaida R. Enriquez, Evangelina. Mexican Americans. Mirande, Alfredo. Research. Women (review article). 19c-20c. *135*
Memoirs. Authors. Jiménez, Juan Ramón. Nobel Prize. Palau de Nemes, Graciela. Puerto Rico (Ponce). Spain. 1930's-56. *1113*
—. Brown, Harold Palmer. Carranza family. Mexico. New Mexico (Columbus; attack). Photographs. Villa, Pancho. 1916. *612*
Men. Assimilation. Immigrants. Labor. 1960's-76. *733*
—. Blacks. California (Los Angeles County). Courts. Sentencing. Whites. Women. 1977-80. *839*
—. Blacks. Discrimination, Employment. Wages. Whites. 1980-81. *1029*
—. Blacks. Wages. Whites. 1979. *109*
—. Disability. Employment. English language. Wages. 1976. *705*
—. Discrimination. Income. Whites. 1976. *121*
—. Discrimination, employment. Economic Conditions. Productivity. 1960's-70's. *65*
—. Education. Language. Social Status. 1975-76. *119*
—. Ethnicity. Social Classes. Women. 1979. *1016*
—. Folklore. Vanishing hitchhiker (theme). Women. 1977. *892*
—. Immigrants. Income. Poverty. Self-perception. Working Class. 1978-79. *923*
—. Income. 1975-78. *732*
—. Intermarriage. Texas (San Antonio area). 1971-80. *1024*
—. Job satisfaction. Southwest. 1980. *848*
Mendez v. Westminster (California, 1946). California (Orange County). Public schools. Segregation (de jure, de facto). 1850-1970's. *690*
Mendinueta, Pedro Fermín de. Colonial Government. Land grants. New Mexico. Spain. 1767-79. *316*

Mendoza, Antonio de. Alvarado, Pedro de. Cabrillo, Juan Rodríguez. Colonial Government. Discovery and Exploration. New Spain. Printing press. 1515-52. *158*
Menéndez de Avilés, Pedro. Antonia (Indian). Calusa Indians. Carlos (chief). Florida. Indian-White Relations. Marriage. Politics. 1566-69. *327*
—. Balseiro, José Agustín. Florida (review article). Lyon, Eugene. Spain. 1513-1977. *184*
—. Commemorations. Explorers. Florida (St. Augustine). Spain. 1565. 1975. *310*
Mental Health Research Center. Bibliographies. Information storage and retrieval systems. 1971-79. *132*
Mental illness. Acculturation. Family. New York City. Puerto Ricans. Social Organization. 1950's-70's. *1271*
—. Cubans. Deportation. Refugees. 1980-83. *1162*
—. Immigration. Puerto Ricans. Social problems. 1493-1978. *1062*
—. Psychotherapy. Victimization. 1980. *108*
Mesoamerican Indians. Indian-White Relations. Pueblo Indians. Southwest. Spain. 1530-98. *329*
Methodist Church. Rio Grande Annual Conference. Southwest. 1874-1978. *457*
Methodology. Aliens, illegal. Interviews. 1975-81. *772*
—. Anthropology. Ecology. New Mexico (northern). Social organization. Trade. 17c-20c. *63*
—. Anthropology, Cultural. Economic Conditions. Puerto Rico. Steward, Julian H. *(People of Puerto Rico)*. 1956-77. *1311*
—. Anthropology, Cultural. Economic Development. Puerto Rico. Steward, Julian H. *(People of Puerto Rico)*. 1956-77. *1272*
—. Anthropology, Cultural. Ideology. Puerto Rico. Steward, Julian H. *(People of Puerto Rico)*. 1956-77. *1144*
—. Census. Population. Southwest. 1848-1900. *559*
—. Family. Mexican Americans. Social sciences. 1970's. *134*
—. Historiography. Mexican Americans. 1970-74. *38*
—. Mexican Americans. Politics. 1974. *10*
—. Research. Social Sciences. Southern California, University of. 1972. *776*
Metropolitan Areas. Blacks. Cubans. Discrimination, Housing. Mexicans. Prices. Puerto Ricans. Whites. 1975-76. *62*
—. Blacks. Income. Occupations. 1970. *808*
—. Blacks. Social Classes. Southwest. Whites. 1970. *790*
—. Fertility. Puerto Rico. 1950-70. *1289*
Mexia, José Antonio. Investments. Land. Mexico. Politics. Texas. 1823-39. *248*
Mexican American Legal Defense and Education Fund. American G.I. Forum. League of United Latin American Citizens. Pressure Groups. School integration. Texas. 1945-80. *981*
—. Courts. Interest groups. 1968-82. *941*
Mexican Americans. Agriculture. Indians. Irrigation. New Mexico. Pueblo Indians. 19c. *357*
—. American history. Colleges and Universities. History Teaching. Textbooks. 20c. *53*
—. Art. Bibliographies. Civil Rights. Literature. Southwest. 1936-73. *96*
—. Bibliographies. History. Literature. Women. 1519-1976. *115*
—. Bibliographies. Libraries. 1960's-70's. *131*
—. Bibliographies. Mass media. Periodicals. 1970's. *24*
—. Bibliographies. Social sciences. 20c. *101*
—. Bibliographies. Women. 1970-80. *64*
—. Borderlands (review article). Mexico. Social Conditions. ca 1600-1981. *41*

—. Catholic Church. Ethnic Groups. Machismo (concept). Social Customs. Women. 1970's. *967*
—. DelCastillo, Adelaida R. Enriquez, Evangelina. Melville, Margarita B. Mirande, Alfredo. Research. Women (review article). 19c-20c. *135*
—. Economic Conditions. Historiography. Labor. 1850-1976. *8*
—. Family. Methodology. Social sciences. 1970's. *134*
—. Folk medicine. Historiography. Medical care. 1894-20c. *100*
—. Historiography. 1960's. *87*
—. Historiography. 1970's. *45*
—. Historiography. 19c-20c. *20*
—. Historiography. Labor. Oral history. 1920's-30's. *127*
—. Historiography. Methodology. 1970-74. *38*
—. Historiography. Research. 19c-20c. *52*
—. Historiography. Social Classes. Women. 17c-20c. *4*
—. History Teaching. Interviews. Oral history. 1974. *37*
—. Methodology. Politics. 1974. *10*
—. Oral history. Research. ca 1930-78. *68*
—. Politics. Scholarship. Social conditions. 1974. *82*
Mexican Americans (review article). Camarillo, Albert. Cardoso, Lawrence A. Immigration. Reisler, Mark. ca 1848-1970. *112*
—. Camarillo, Albert. Historiography. 1848-1930. *106*
Mexican Labor in the United States (study). Interviews. Labor. National Endowment for the Humanities. Research. Taylor, Paul S. 1927-30. *646*
—. Labor. Research. Taylor, Paul S. 1926-34. *54*
Mexican Revolution. Arizona. Immigration. Refugees. 1910-11. *669*
Mexican War. Armies. Bounties. Land warrants. 1800-61. *309*
—. California. Daily Life. Diaries. Mormon Battalion. Social Customs. 1846-55. *601*
—. California. Kearny, Stephen Watts. San Pasqual (battle). 1846. *156*
—. California. Kearny, Stephen Watts. San Pasqual (battle). 1847. *253*
—. California. San Pasqual (battle). 1846-47. *252*
—. Commerce. Rio Grande. Texas (El Paso). 1821-48. *361*
—. Diplomacy. Guadalupe Hidalgo, Treaty of. Trist, Nicholas P. 1848. *517*
—. Guadalupe Hidalgo, Treaty of. 1846-48. *189*
—. Historiography. 1846-48. 1960's-79. *11*
—. Military Offenses. Texas rangers. 1846-48. *308*
Mexican War (review article). Antiwar sentiment. Expansionism. Pletcher, David M. Polk, James K. Schroeder, John H. 1830's-40's. *199*
Mexicans. Assimilation. Cubans. Exiles. Federal Policy. 1959-81. *138*
—. Blacks. Cubans. Discrimination, Housing. Metropolitan Areas. Prices. Puerto Ricans. Whites. 1975-76. *62*
—. Cities. Cubans. Puerto Ricans. Residential segregation. 1950's-70's. *69*
—. Cubans. Immigrants. Income. 1973-76. *92*
—. Cubans. Migration, internal. North Central States. Puerto Ricans. Social Conditions. Southwest. 1970. *32*
—. Folklore. Puerto Ricans. Theater. 1966-77. *60*
Mexico. Adolescents. Identity. Puerto Rico. USA. 1970's. *1159*
—. Agricultural Labor. Aliens, illegal. Attitudes. Bracero Program. Labor Unions and Organizations. 1943-74. *889*
—. Agricultural Labor. Berry pickers. California (El Monte). Foreign Relations. Japan. Strikes. 1933. *645*

—. Agriculture. Bracero program. President's Commission on Migratory Labor. Truman, Harry S. Workers, undocumented. 1950. *876*

—. Alamo (battle). Texas. 1836. *306*

—. Albuquerque, Duke of (Francisco Fernández de la Cueva Henríquez). Colonial Government. New Mexico. Politics. Social Problems. 1702-11. *318*

—. Aliens, illegal. Bracero Program. Immigration. Quota systems. 1960's-70's. *1007*

—. Aliens (illegal). Economic Conditions. USA. 1946-65. *807*

—. Aliens, illegal. Immigration. Statistics. 1978-79. *750*

—. Aliens, illegal. Research. 1930-76. *422*

—. Aliens, illegal. Workers, undocumented. 1930-77. *747*

—. Alvarez, Manuel. Commerce. Consular service. New Mexico (Santa Fe). 1818-47. *180*

—. Alvarez, Manuel. Diplomacy. New Mexico. Texas. Trading expeditions. 1841. *181*

—. Andrade, Flores de. Immigration. Liberal Party. Personal narratives. Revolutionary Movements. Texas (El Paso). 1890-1911. *621*

—. Anthropology. Borderlands studies. Sociology. Southwest. 20c. *114*

—. Anza, Juan Bautista de. Bicentennial Celebrations. California. Discovery and Exploration. Reenactments. 1775-76. 1975-76. *208*

—. Archival Catalogs and Inventories. California. 1535-1821. *72*

—. Arizona (Clifton-Morenci area). Copper Mines and Mining. Migrant Labor. Strikes. 1872-1903. *572*

—. Armies. California. Colonial Government. 1822-46. *257*

—. Armies. California (Los Angeles, San Diego). Presidios. Spain. 1770-94. *283*

—. Armijo, Manuel. New Mexico. Provincial Government. Texas. 1827-46. *371*

—. Ascensión, Antonio de la. California. Discovery and Exploration. Vizcaíno, Sebastian. Voyages. 1590-1737. *285*

—. Barreda, Gabino. Philosophy. Positivism. Values. 1860's-1982. *444*

—. Behavior. Cultural heritage. 16c-20c. *455*

—. Bibliographies. Southwest. 1821-45. *126*

—. Blacks. Carranza, Venustiano. Indians. Rebellions. Texas. Villa, Francisco. 1848-1920. *577*

—. Blacks. Press, black. Race Relations. 1890-1935. *681*

—. Border policy. Economic Conditions. Workers, undocumented. 1952-75. *739*

—. Borderlands. Diplomacy. Trade. 1858-1905. *516*

—. Borderlands (review article). Mexican Americans. Social Conditions. ca 1600-1981. *41*

—. Borderlands studies. Economic Conditions. Southwest. 1970's. *116*

—. Borderlands studies. Southwest. 1952-75. *113*

—. Borders. Folk Songs (review article). Paredes, Americo. Texas. 16c-20c. *474*

—. Borders. Foreign Relations (review article). Historiography. Southwest. 20c. *61*

—. Borders. Frontier and Pioneer Life. Race Relations. Southwest (review article). Weber, David J. 1821-46. *251*

—. Borders. Historiography. 1812-1975. *3*

—. Borders. Louisiana. Puelles, José María de Jesús. Texas. 1512-1813. 1827-28. *230*

—. Borders. Rebellions. Texas (Brownsville, Eagle Pass area). 1850-1900. *521*

—. Bracero program. Documents. 1944. *622*

—. Bracero program. Foreign Relations. Immigration. 1942-46. *642*

—. Brown, Harold Palmer. Carranza family. Memoirs. New Mexico (Columbus; attack). Photographs. Villa, Pancho. 1916. *612*

—. California. Colonization. Discovery and exploration. Spain. 1602-1769. *190*

—. California. Colonization. Population. Spain. 1760's-1840's. *222*

—. California. Franciscans. Missions and Missionaries. Southwest. Wheat growing. 1730's-70's. *335*

—. California. Immigration. Mineral resources. Settlement. 1683-1848. *231*

—. California. Indians. Missions and Missionaries. 1830's. *321*

—. California. Land tenure. Ranches. 1784-1846. *247*

—. California (Monterey). Great Britain. Jones, Thomas ap Catesby. Military Occupation. Navies. 1842. *218*

—. California (Monterey). Historical Sites and Parks. Landmarks. Spain. 1770-1849. *173*

—. California (Monterey). Spain. 1770-1849. *292*

—. California (San Diego). Colonial Government. Croix, Carlos Francisco de. Mission San Diego de Alcalá. Spain. 1760's-86. *160*

—. California, southern. Immigration. "Operation Wetback". Texas. 1950-74. *977*

—. Capitalism. Children. Labor. Women. Workers, undocumented. ca 1950-79. *833*

—. Carranza, Venustiano. Foreign Relations. Immigration. 1910-20. *674*

—. Carranza, Venustiano. Foreign Relations. Plan de San Diego. Race relations. Texas, south. 1915-16. *638*

—. Colonization. Muster rolls. New Mexico (Santa Fe). Páez Hurtado, Juan. 1695. 1978. *356*

—. Conspiracy. Foreign Relations. Revolutionary Movements. Reyes, Bernardo. State Politics. Texas. Trials. 1911-12. *639*

—. Deportation. Labor. Migration. 1920-75. *413*

—. Depressions. Migrant Labor. Obregón, Álvaro. Repatriation. 1920-23. *613*

—. Economic Conditions. Immigration. Labor. Social control. 1950's-70's. *865*

—. Economic Conditions. Workers, undocumented. 1972-73. *954*

—. El Paso-Juárez Conference. Foreign Relations. Punitive expeditions. Villa, Pancho. 1916. *637*

—. Emigration. 1900-70. *424*

—. Exiles. Liberal Party. Propaganda. Texas. Women. 1898-1910. *691*

—. Foreign Relations. Migrant labor. Texas. 1942-47. *659*

—. Garza, Catarino E. Newspapers. Texas. 1880-95. *525*

—. Gutierrez de Lara, José Bernardo Maxmilliano. Independence Movements. Magee, Augustus W. Republican Army of the North. Texas (San Antonio). 1811-15. *197*

—. Historiography. Southwest. 1821-54. *125*

—. Houston, Sam. Military. Revolution. Texas. 1835-36. *237*

—. Ideology. Philosophy. Positivism. Science. Social control. 1850-1984. *477*

—. Immigration. Law. Women. 1970's. *834*

—. Immigration. Law Enforcement. 1924-29. *644*

—. Immigration and Nationality Act (US, 1965; amended, 1976). USA. 1976. *3*

—. Imperialism. Migration. Sex Discrimination. Southwest. Women. Working class. 1850-1982. *428*

—. Independence, War of. Military Intelligence. Seguín, Juan Nepomuceno. Texas. 1830's-40's. *336*

—. Indian Wars. New Mexico. Trade regulation. Treaties. 1821-46. *372*

—. Indians. New Mexico (Estancia Basin). Salt. Spain. Trade. Prehistory-1840's. *265*

—. Intergovernmental Relations. Law. Martinez, Manuel. New Mexico. Water. 1832. *205*
—. Investments. Land. Mexia, José Antonio. Politics. Texas. 1823-39. *248*
—. Labor. Migration. Texas. 1960's-70's. *737*
—. Labor. USA. Workers, undocumented. 1970's. *955*
—. Labor. Workers, undocumented. 1973. *746*
—. Labor Unions and Organizations. Workers, Undocumented. 1867-1977. *407*
—. Land grants. New Mexico. San Antonio de las Huertas grant. Spain. 1765-1891. *348*
—. Madero, Francisco. Revolution. Reyes, Bernardo. Texas. 1910-12. *640*
—. Martínez, Antonio José (report). New Mexico. Territorial government. 1830-32. *383*
—. Migrant Labor. 1880-1980. *423*
—. Migrant Labor. Repatriation. Workers, undocumented. 1929-56. *636*
—. Migration. Missions and Missionaries. Southwest. 1867-1930. *416*
—. New Mexico. Revolution. Salazar, Jose Ines. Texas. ca 1910-18. *689*
—. Race Relations. Travel accounts. Western States. 1831-69. *571*
Mexico (Baja California). California (San Diego). Camino Real. Missions and Missionaries. 1697-1771. *187*
Mexico (Chihuahua, Sonora). Diaries. Fuente, Pedro José de la. Indian Wars. Military. New Mexico. Texas (El Paso). 1765. *192*
Mexico (Coahuila). Bandits. Big Bend region. Langhorne, George T. Punitive expeditions. Texas (Glenn Springs, Boquillas). 1915-16. *687*
Mexico (Guadalupe). Economic Development. Migrant Labor. 1977-78. *964*
Mexico (Loreto). California (San Diego). Camino Real. Serra Route. Trails. 1762-1975. *188*
Mexico (Mexico City). Apache Indians. Indians. Removals, forced. Southwest. Spain. 1729-1809. *300*
—. Archival Catalogs and Inventories. Historical Archive of the Secretary of Foreign Relations. 1900-39. *13*
Mexico (Michoacán). Migrant Labor. 1977-78. *963*
Mexico, northern. Arizona State Museum. Documentary Relations of the Southwest project. Indians. Southwest. Spain. 16c-1810. 1975-78. *322*
—. Defense Policy. Indian Wars. Southwest. Spain. 1759-88. *304*
—. Lancastrian system. Public Schools. Southwest. 1821-48. *373*
Mexico (Nuevo León). Catholic Church. Missions and Missionaries. Southwest. Verger y Suau, Rafael José. 1767-80's. *358*
Mexico (Nuevo Reyno de León). Assimilation. Jews. Texas. 16c-20c. *483*
Mexico (San Blas). California. Colonists. Hijar-Padres colony. 1834. *249*
Mexico (Sonora). Arizona (Nogales). Borders. Foreign relations. García, Jesús. 1893-96. *529*
—. California. Discrimination. Gold Rushes. Migration. 1848-56. *585*
—. New Mexico (Santa Fe). Roads. Spain. Trade. 17c-1850's. *345*
Mexico (Sonora; Caborca). Architecture. Arizona (Tucson). Churches. Mission Nuestra Señora de la Purísima Concepción del Caborca. Mission San Xavier del Bac. 1975. *228*
Mexico, west-central. California. Economic Conditions. Immigration, illegal. Labor. 1970's. *778*
Mexico (Yucatán). Colonization. Florida. Spain. 16c. *397*
Michigan. Minorities in Politics. Voting and Voting Behavior. 1960's-70's. *745*

Michigan (Detroit). California (Los Angeles). Europe. Family. Immigrants. Whites. 1850-80. *542*
Michigan, Lake. Immigration. Indiana (East Chicago; Indiana Harbor). Inland Steel Company. Social Conditions. 1919-32. *615*
Middle Classes. Assimilation. Socialization. Texas. 1976. *1013*
—. Cubans. Florida (Miami). Housing. Segregation. 1950-74. *1310*
—. Diego, José de. Independence Movements. Puerto Rico. 1867-1918. *1139*
—. Nationalism. Puerto Rico. 1920-70. *1147*
—. Political organizations. Texas. 1970's. *1014*
—. Public schools. School Integration. Texas. 1929-57. *680*
Middle East. Bibliographies. Educational policy. Energy crisis. Foreign Relations. National Autonomous University of Mexico (Faculty of Political and Social Sciences). Periodicals. Social Conditions. 1970-81. *7*
Midwest. Economic development. Migrant Labor. 1900-30. *685*
Migrant Labor. *See also* Agricultural Labor.
—. Agriculture. Documents. Economic Conditions. Social Conditions. Working conditions. 1942-45. *694*
—. Aliens (illegal). Oregon (Hood River Valley). Wages. 1978. *777*
—. Arizona (Clifton-Morenci area). Copper Mines and Mining. Mexico. Strikes. 1872-1903. *572*
—. Blacks. Farms. Jamaicans. New York. Social mobility. 1960's-70's. *1152*
—. Blacks. Florida. Jamaicans. 1980. *731*
—. California. Libraries. 1970-80. *937*
—. Carden, Georgiana. Compulsory Education. Elementary education. 1920's. *641*
—. Child Welfare. 1969-74. *766*
—. Colorado (San Luis Valley). 1973. *758*
—. Depressions. Mexico. Obregón, Álvaro. Repatriation. 1920-23. *613*
—. Economic Development. Mexico (Guadalupe). 1977-78. *964*
—. Economic development. Midwest. 1900-30. *685*
—. Economic structure. Education. 1970-80. *141*
—. Education. Social Problems. 1973. *905*
—. Elites. Political conditions. 1946-72. *57*
—. Fertility. Women. 1978. *111*
—. Foreign Relations. Mexico. Texas. 1942-47. *659*
—. Immigration. 1900-79. *406*
—. Immigration. 1950's-80. *712*
—. Immigration. North Central States. Social Conditions. 1919-76. *415*
—. Imports. Industrialization. 1940-77. *699*
—. Mexico. 1880-1980. *423*
—. Mexico. Repatriation. Workers, undocumented. 1929-56. *636*
—. Mexico (Michoacán). 1977-78. *963*
—. Photographic essays. Washington (Yakima Valley). 1974. *939*
Migration. Attitudes. California (San Diego). Workers, undocumented. 1984. *896*
—. Birth Rate. Census. Puerto Rico. 1965-70. *1262*
—. Bracero Program. Washington. 1940-50. *620*
—. California. Discrimination. Gold Rushes. Mexico (Sonora). 1848-56. *585*
—. Colonialism. Economic Structure. Puerto Ricans. 1900-80. *1090*
—. Colonies. Florida (St. Augustine). Quantitative methods. Spain. 1600-1800. *186*
—. Demography. Puerto Rico. Social Problems. 1960-75. *1176*
—. Deportation. Labor. Mexico. 1920-75. *413*
—. Educational achievement. -1973. *738*
—. Imperialism. Mexico. Sex Discrimination. Southwest. Women. Working class. 1850-1982. *428*

—. Industrialization. Politics. Puerto Rico. Working class. 1870's-1970's. *1108*

—. Labor. Mexico. Texas. 1960's-70's. *737*

—. Mexico. Missions and Missionaries. Southwest. 1867-1930. *416*

—. Political economy. Puerto Rico. Social Classes. 1898-1970's. *1135*

—. Puerto Rico. 1965-80. *1112*

—. Puerto Rico. Rural-Urban Studies. 1960-80. *1072*

—. Repatriation. Research. Taylor, Paul S. 1973. *858*

—. Social Conditions. Texas, south. Whites. 1850-1900. *527*

Migration, Internal. Agricultural Labor. New Mexico (North Central). Social Change. 1930-50. *888*

—. California (Monterey). Urban change. 1835-50. *246*

—. Change and Response, Theory of. Emigration. Fertility. Puerto Rico. 1940's-70. *1228*

—. Cubans. Mexicans. North Central States. Puerto Ricans. Social Conditions. Southwest. 1970. *32*

—. Economic Conditions. Models. Puerto Rico. 1935-40. *1092*

—. Labor. 1973-77. *84*

—. New Mexico (El Cerrito). Social Change. Values. 1939-56. *893*

Militancy. Ethnicity. Herrera, Juan José. Land grants. New Mexico (Las Vegas). Vigilantes. White Caps. 1887-94. *554*

—. High Schools. Students. -1973. *806*

Military. Diaries. Fuente, Pedro José de la. Indian Wars. Mexico (Chihuahua, Sonora). New Mexico. Texas (El Paso). 1765. *192*

—. Florida. Population. 1700-1820. *282*

—. Houston, Sam. Mexico. Revolution. Texas. 1835-36. *237*

—. Indians. Pueblo Indians. Social control. Spain. 1763-1821. *255*

—. New Mexico (Santa Fe). Presidial Company. Prices. 18c. *299*

—. Political economy. 1830-1980. *432*

—. Puerto Rico. 1898-1979. *1221*

Military Camps and Forts. Garita (fort). New Mexico (Santa Fe). Spain. 19c-1954. *206*

Military Finance. Archivo General de Indias. Colonial Government. New Mexico. Spain (Seville). Treasury. 1596-1683. *337*

Military Intelligence. Independence, War of. Mexico. Seguín, Juan Nepomuceno. Texas. 1830's-40's. *336*

Military Occupation. California (Monterey). Great Britain. Jones, Thomas ap Catesby. Mexico. Navies. 1842. *218*

—. Fort Bute. Fort St. Gabriel. Great Britain. Louisiana. Spain. 1768. *177*

Military Offenses. Mexican War. Texas rangers. 1846-48. *308*

Military Strategy. Anza, Juan Bautista de. Colonial Government. Concha, Fernando Simon Ignacio de la. Indians. New Mexico. Spain. 1787-93. *161*

Militia. Colonial Government. Croix, Teodoro de. New Spain (Nueva Vizcaya). 1776-83. *196*

Mills. Agricultural Production. Haciendas. Puerto Rico, southwestern. Sugar. 1902. *1306*

Mineral resources. California. Immigration. Mexico. Settlement. 1683-1848. *231*

Mines. Labor. South. Southwest. 1513-1846. *232*

Mining towns. Arizona, central. Cohabitation. Whites. 1863-73. *548*

Minnesota (St. Paul, lower west side). Community. 1914-65. *469*

Minorities. Annexation. 16c-20c. *103*

—. Attitudes. Texas (Houston). -1973. *779*

—. Capitalism. Economic Structure. Immigration. Labor. Latin Americans. ca 1950-70. *1290*

—. Civil rights movement. 1954-83. *22*

—. Colonization. Exploitation. Womack, John. 1841-1973. *447*

—. Puerto Ricans. 20c. *1089*

—. Racism. Reporters and Reporting. 1968-83. *118*

Minorities in Politics. Artists. Murals. 1970's. *791*

—. Government. Names (personal). Spanish language. 1973. *887*

—. Ideology. 1960's-70's. *968*

—. Michigan. Voting and Voting Behavior. 1960's-70's. *745*

—. Public Schools. Self-perception. Texas (southern). 1930's-69. *489*

Mirande, Alfredo. DelCastillo, Adelaida R. Enriquez, Evangelina. Melville, Margarita B. Mexican Americans. Research. Women (review article). 19c-20c. *135*

Mission Guevavi. Arizona (Nogales). Excavations. Jesuits. 18c. 1964-66. *333*

Mission La Purísima Concepción. California. Restorations. 1787-1973. *390*

Mission Nuestra Señora de la Purísima Concepción del Caborca. Architecture. Arizona (Tucson). Churches. Mexico (Sonora; Caborca). Mission San Xavier del Bac. 1975. *228*

Mission San Antonio de Padua. Agricultural Technology and Research. Assimilation. California. Indians. Salinan Indians. 1771-1832. 1976-79. *244*

—. Aqueducts. California Polytechnic State University, San Luis Obispo. Excavations. Spanish. 1776. 1979-81. *245*

—. California. Effigies. Pottery. 18c-19c. *214*

—. California (Monterey County). Firearms. Flintlocks. 18c. *391*

Mission San Carlo Borromeo. California. Franciscans. Serra, Junípero. 1784. *278*

Mission San Cayetano del Tumacacori. Arizona, southern. Mission San Xavier del Bac. Spain. 18c. 1979. *400*

Mission San Diego de Alcalá. California (San Diego). Colonial Government. Mexico. Spain. 1760's-86. *160*

—. California (San Diego). Franciscans. Jayme, Luís (death). Yuman Indians. 1775. *388*

Mission San Francisco Solano. California (Sonoma). Catholic Church. Indians. 1823-34. *176*

Mission San Juan Capistrano. Architecture. California. Franciscans. 1776-1976. *163*

—. California. Catholic Church. Serra, Junípero. 1775-76. *312*

Mission San Xavier del Bac. Animals, domestic. Arizona. Excavations. 17c-19c. 1974. *311*

—. Architecture. Arizona (Tucson). Churches. Mexico (Sonora; Caborca). Mission Nuestra Señora de la Purísima Concepción del Caborca. 1975. *228*

—. Arizona, southern. Mission San Cayetano del Tumacacori. Spain. 18c. 1979. *400*

Mission Santa Barbara. California (Los Angeles, Santa Barbara). Catholic Church. Marriage. Social Customs. 1786-1848. *298*

Missions and Missionaries. Adventists. Education. New Mexico (Sandoval). Spanish-American Seminary. 1928-53. *679*

—. Americanization. Protestant Churches. Puerto Rico. 1898-1917. *1239*

—. Architecture. Artisans. Churches. Texas (San Antonio). 18c. *338*

—. Arizona. Indians. Jesuits. Kino, Eusebio Francisco. Spain. 1680's-1711. *271*

—. Art. California. Catholic Church. Cultural myopia (Anglo-American). Scholasticism. 1740's-1976. *307*

—. Athapascan Indians. Indians. Indian-White Relations. New Mexico. Pueblo Indians. 1600-80. *220*

—. Bolton, Herbert Eugene. Borderlands studies. Catholic Church. Colonization. Historiography. Spain. 1917-79. *9*

—. California. Catholic Church. Economic conditions. Indians. 1803-21. *151*

—. California. Catholic Church. González Rubio, José. 1846-50. *566*

—. California. Catholic Church. Indians. Labor. 1775-1805. *152*

—. California. Catholic Church. Indian-White Relations. 1770's-1820's. *347*

—. California. Cesarean operations. Franciscans. Medicine (practice of). 1769-1833. *376*

—. California. Colonial Government. Discovery and Exploration. Settlement. Spain. 1691-1810. *262*

—. California. Conversion thesis. Cook, Sherburne Friend. Franciscans. Indians. ca 1790-1820's. 1943. *229*

—. California. Dominicans. Franciscans. Jesuits. Serra, Junípero. 1768-76. *287*

—. California. Durán, Narciso. Franciscans. Indians. Music. 1806-46. *224*

—. California. Durán, Narciso. Franciscans. Indians. Secularization. 1826-46. *305*

—. California. Excavations. Presidios. San Diego Presidio. Serra Museum. 1769-75. 1964-70's. *210*

—. California. Franciscans. Mexico. Southwest. Wheat growing. 1730's-70's. *335*

—. California. Indians. Mexico. 1830's. *321*

—. California. Presidios. 1769-84. *172*

—. California. Viticulture. 1697-1858. *389*

—. California (San Diego). Camino Real. Mexico (Baja California). 1697-1771. *187*

—. California (San Diego). Colonization. Indians. Spain. 1769-1834. *399*

—. Catholic Church. Coahuiltecan Indians. Indians. Texas (San Antonio). 1792. *277*

—. Catholic Church. Frontier and Pioneer Life. Southwest. Spain. 16c-18c. *164*

—. Catholic Church. Mexico (Nuevo León). Southwest. Verger y Suau, Rafael José. 1767-80's. *358*

—. Colonization. DeZorita, Alonso. Franciscans. Indians. Southwest. 1545-85. *378*

—. Documents. Episcopal Church, Protestant. Puerto Rico. 1870-1952. *1091*

—. Indian Wars. Pueblo Indians. Southwest. Spain. 1680. *314*

—. Indians. New Mexico. Secularization. Spain. 1767. *263*

—. Indian-White Relations. Pueblo Revolt (1680). Southwest. Spain. 1590-1680. *165*

—. Mexico. Migration. Southwest. 1867-1930. *416*

—. New Mexico (Quivira, Teguayo provinces). Posada, Alonso de. 1686-88. *374*

—. Presbyterian Church. Puerto Rico. 1899-1914. *1229*

Mississippi River. Explorers. Golden Cities myth. Northwest Passage myth. 1519-1679. *381*

Mississippi Valley. Borderlands (review article). Jones, Oakah L., Jr. McDermott, John Francis. Southwest. Spain. Weddle, Robert S. 1762-1804. 1973-74. *379*

Models. Assimilation. New York City. Puerto Ricans. Segregation, residential. 1960-70. *1274*

—. California (Parlier). Local government. Politics. 1971-73. *966*

—. Capital. Economic Development. Labor. Puerto Rico. 1945-70. *1222*

—. Econometrics. Puerto Rico. 1948-64. *1285*

—. Economic Conditions. Migration, internal. Puerto Rico. 1935-40. *1092*

—. Family. Stereotypes. 1968-74. *1012*

Modernism. National consciousness. Periodicals. Puerto Rico. *Revista de las Antillas.* 1913-18. *1130*

Modernization. California (Los Angeles). Family. Social change. 1850-80. *538*

—. Fertility. Marriage. Puerto Rico. 1950-70. *1063*

—. Population. Puerto Rico, western. Rural areas. 1940-70's. *1225*

Mormon Battalion. California. Daily Life. Diaries. Mexican War. Social Customs. 1846-55. *601*

Mortality. Blacks. California. Whites. 1969-71. *990*

—. Blacks. Measurements. Texas. Whites. 1980. *1008*

—. Indians. Infants. New Mexico. Whites. 1974-77. *971*

—. Infants. Prenatal care. Social Classes. Southwest. 1970. *793*

—. New York City. Puerto Ricans. 1969-71. *1276*

Mothers. Attitudes. New Mexico (Albuquerque). Sex roles. Women. 1960-83. *1050*

—. Blacks. Employment. Marriage. Whites. Women. 1970-84. *46*

Mothers, single. Blacks. Demography. Households. Puerto Ricans. Whites. 1970. *1119*

Mott, Thomas. California (Los Angeles). Daily Life. Sepúlveda y Ávila, María Ascensión. 1844-61. *600*

Moynihan, Daniel P. Assimilation. Glazer, Nathan. New York. Puerto Ricans (review article). 20c. *1265*

Multinational corporations. Labor movement. Neocolonialism. Puerto Rico. Self-determination. 1950's-70's. *1098*

Muñoz Marín, Luis. Art. Culture. Institute of Puerto Rican Culture. Puerto Rico. Romero Barceló, Carlos. 1948-55. *1277*

—. Economic Conditions. Independence. Interviews. Political issues. Puerto Rico. Social Conditions. 1948-64. *1186*

—. Elections. Funerals. New Progressive Party. Popular Democratic Party. Puerto Rico. 1980. *1215*

Murals. Art. California (East Los Angeles). Mechicano Art Center. 1970's. *759*

—. Art. California (East Los Angeles). Social Conditions. 1970-75. *872*

—. Art. California (East Los Angeles). Values. 1978. *1052*

—. Art. California (Los Angeles). Ethnicity. 1970's. *998*

—. Art. Culture. Ethnicity. 1960's-80. *714*

—. Artists. California (East Los Angeles, Boyle Heights). 1965-75. *860*

—. Artists. Minorities in Politics. 1970's. *791*

—. California. 1920's-80. *830*

—. California (San Diego; Barrio Logan). Community Participation in Politics. Parks. 1969-84. *767*

Murder. Carter, Jimmy. Cerro Maravilla scandal. Puerto Rico. Revolutionary Movements. Romero Barceló, Carlos. Statehood. 1978-80. *1288*

Murieta, Joaquín. California. Gold Rushes. Outlaws. ca 1848-53. *587*

—. California. Legends. Outlaws. 1850's. *556*

Murphy, William S. Annexation. Diplomacy. Eve, Joseph. Flood, George H. LaBranche, Alcée. Letters. Texas. 1837-43. *162*

Museum of New Mexico (Fred Harvey Collection). Horses. Museums. Southwest. Stable gear. 18c-20c. *1*

Museums. Horses. Museum of New Mexico (Fred Harvey Collection). Southwest. Stable gear. 18c-20c. *1*

Music. Blades, Rubén (interview). City life. Latin Americans. Panama. Salsa. 1974-84. *1088*

—. Blues. Folk Songs. Fugitive Slaves. Matamoros (colony). 19c-1940's. *458*

—. California. Durán, Narciso. Franciscans. Indians. Missions and Missionaries. 1806-46. *224*

—. Norteña (music). Photographs. Texas (San Antonio). 1930's-82. *688*

—. Puerto Rico. 1898-1910. *1141*

—. Texas. 1860's-1980. *473*

Music, religious. Catholic Church. 1962-75. *728*

Musical Academy of Puerto Rico. Gutiérrez y Espinosa, Felipe. Puerto Rico. 1871-1900. *1078*

Musicians. Administration for the Development of Art and Culture. Bureaucracies. Legislation. New Progressive Party. Puerto Rico. 1980. *1284*

—. Arizona (Tucson). Dancers. Popular Culture. 1892-1982. *682*

Muster rolls. Colonization. Mexico. New Mexico (Santa Fe). Páez Hurtado, Juan. 1695. 1978. *356*

Myths and Symbols. Americas (North and South). Colonization. Discovery and Exploration. Europe. Utopianism. 16c-18c. *225*

—. Discovery and Exploration. Settlement. Southwest. Spain. 16c-18c. *235*

N

Names, personal. *Con safos* (term). Graffiti. 1967-75. *838*

—. English language. Spanish language. Texas (El Paso). 1981. *769*

—. Government. Minorities in Politics. Spanish language. 1973. *887*

—. Slaves. Texas (Young County). 1856-65. *555*

National Autonomous University of Mexico (Faculty of Political and Social Sciences). Bibliographies. Educational policy. Energy crisis. Foreign Relations. Middle East. Periodicals. Social Conditions. 1970-81. *7*

National Characteristics. 1970's. *857*

—. Culture. Puerto Rico. Social Organization. 1930's-70's. *1258*

—. Discovery and Exploration. Ethnicity. Social Customs (review article). Urbansk, Edmund S. 17c-18c. *331*

—. Puerto Rico. 16c-1970's. *1206*

National Conference of Catholic Bishops ("Hispanic Presence: Challenge and Commitment"). Catholic Church. 1984. *81*

National consciousness. Modernism. Periodicals. Puerto Rico. *Revista de las Antillas*. 1913-18. *1130*

National development. Puerto Rico. 1830-1930's. *1256*

National Endowment for the Humanities. Interviews. Labor. *Mexican Labor in the United States* (study). Research. Taylor, Paul S. 1927-30. *646*

National Guard. Autonomy. Puerto Rico. 1898-1978. *1128*

National Labor Relations Board. Labor. *NLRB v. Apollo Tire Co.* (US, 1979). *NLRB v. Sure-Tan, Inc.* (US, 1978). Workers, undocumented. 1978-79. *1034*

National Self-image. Mead, Margaret (interview). Puerto Rico. Social Customs. 1975. *1323*

Nationalism. Campos, Albizu. Puerto Rico. 20c. *1205*

—. Latin America. Political Attitudes. Social Customs. 1848-1976. *480*

—. Middle classes. Puerto Rico. 1920-70. *1147*

Nationalism, cultural. Poetic consciousness. 1945-77. *1049*

Nationality. Citizenship. Courts. Race. 1846-97. *570*

Nativism. California. Gold Mines and Mining. Industrialization. 1845-70. *533*

—. California. Gold Rushes. 1848-53. *574*

—. Depressions. Discrimination. Indiana (Gary). Repatriation. 1920's-30's. *609*

—. Immigration. Periodicals. *Saturday Evening Post*. 1914-33. *662*

Naturalization. Cubans. Political Participation. Refugees. Voting and Voting Behavior. 1959-84. *1249*

—. Immigration. 1920-79. *435*

Navajo Indians. Arizona (Canyon de Chelly). Bones. Dogs. Indian Wars. Pictographs. Spain. 1750-1863. *202*

—. Blankets. Dye. Indians. New Mexico. Rugs. Spaniards. Weaving. 19c-1977. *353*

—. Diplomacy. Indians. New Mexico. Spain. 1770-90. *324*

—. Economic Conditions. Health services. Indians. New Mexico, northwestern. Population. Rural areas. Spaniards. 1971-78. *93*

—. Indian Wars. New Mexico. Spain. 1680-1720. *326*

—. Indians. New Mexico, northern. Pueblo Indians. Rio Grande Valley. Weaving. 15c-1979. *393*

—. Indian-White Relations. New Mexico. Peace. Spain. 1720-79. *325*

Navarro, Martin *(Political Reflections)*. Bouligny, Francisco (report). Gálvez, Bernardo de. Immigration policy. Louisiana. Spain. 1776-83. *201*

Navies. California (Monterey). Great Britain. Jones, Thomas ap Catesby. Mexico. Military Occupation. 1842. *218*

—. Civil-Military Relations. Foxardo (battle). Insubordination. Porter, David. Puerto Rico. 1823-25. *1087*

Nebraska. Political participation. -1973. *1043*

Nebraska (Omaha). Ethnic identity. Political participation. 1970's. *1042*

—. Social Organizations. 1956-77. *770*

Neighborhoods. Blacks. Florida (Miami). Population. Residential patterns. Whites. 1970-80. *1309*

—. California (Los Angeles). Catholic Church. Christmas. Posadas (celebrations). Rites and Ceremonies. 1975-80. *900*

—. California (Los Angeles). Medical care. Poor. 1970-79. *853*

—. Cities. Decisionmaking. Health centers. 1969-70. *854*

—. Cities. Race Relations. Western States. White flight. 1960's. *71*

Neocolonialism. Economic Conditions. Federal Aid to Education. Puerto Rico. Social Classes. 1970's. *1245*

—. Labor movement. Multinational corporations. Puerto Rico. Self-determination. 1950's-70's. *1098*

New Deal. Agricultural Labor Relations Act (California, 1975). California. Emergency Farm Labor Supply Program. Labor law. ca 1930-79. *434*

—. Deportation. Immigrants. Labor Unions and Organizations. 1930's. *618*

New Federalism. Economic Conditions. Federal Policy. Reagan, Ronald. Social Problems. 1980-83. *716*

New Jersey. Biculturalism. Bilingual education. Cubans. Puerto Ricans. 19c-20c. *1101*

—. Cubans. International Rescue Committee (Caribbean Relief Program). Refugees. Settlement. 1959-83. *1145*

New Mexico. Agriculture. Indians. Irrigation. Mexican Americans. Pueblo Indians. 19c. *357*

—. Albuquerque, Duke of (Francisco Fernández de la Cueva Henríquez). Colonial Government. Mexico. Politics. Social Problems. 1702-11. *318*

—. Alvarez, Manuel. Diplomacy. Mexico. Texas. Trading expeditions. 1841. *181*

—. Anaya, Toney. Elections. 1968-82. *1031*
—. Angel, Frank W. Corruption. Violence. Wallace, Lew. 1878. *591*
—. Anza, Juan Bautista de. Colonial Government. Concha, Fernando Simon Ignacio de la. Indians. Military Strategy. Spain. 1787-93. *161*
—. Apodaca, Jerry. Democratic Party. Elections (gubernatorial). Race Relations. 1974. *1032*
—. Architecture. Log structures. 1756-1970's. *43*
—. Archivo General de Indias. Colonial Government. Military Finance. Spain (Seville). Treasury. 1596-1683. *337*
—. Aristocracy. Colonial Government. New Spain. Settlement. 16c. *182*
—. Armijo, Manuel. Government. 1827-46. *274*
—. Armijo, Manuel. Kendall, George Wilkins. 1842-44. *275*
—. Armijo, Manuel. Mexico. Provincial Government. Texas. 1827-46. *371*
—. Arts and Crafts. Depressions. 1846-1930's. *505*
—. Assimilation. Social Customs. Villages. 1960's-79. *962*
—. Assimilation. Spain. 16c-19c. 1970's. *150*
—. Athapascan Indians. Indians. Indian-White Relations. Missions and Missionaries. Pueblo Indians. 1600-80. *220*
—. Atrisco grant. Land grants. New Spain. Pueblo Revolt (1680). 1680-1977. *454*
—. Attitudes. Diaries. Discrimination. Women. 1840's-50's. *593*
—. Attitudes. Identity. -1974. *919*
—. Attitudes. Spanish-American War. 1898-1900. *564*
—. Authors. Nichols, John. Social Conditions. Spaniards. 1841-1979. *499*
—. Authors. Racism. Stereotypes. 19c. *562*
—. Bibliographies. Land grants. 1851-1981. *85*
—. Bilingual education. Spanish language. 1968-78. *703*
—. Bilingualism. Newspapers. Spanish (language). 1834-1917. *569*
—. Blankets. Dye. Indians. Navajo Indians. Rugs. Spaniards. Weaving. 19c-1977. *353*
—. California. Colorado. Political representation. State Politics. ca 1850-1974. *464*
—. California. Demography. ca 1850. *568*
—. California (Monterey). Discovery and Exploration. Dominguez, Francisco Atanasio. Escalante, Silvestre Velez de. 1765-1805. *143*
—. Catholic Church. Colorado. Passion plays. Spain. 1830's-1978. *492*
—. Catholic Church. Design. Folk art. Iconography. Manuscripts. 16c-17c. *233*
—. Catholic Church. Feast days. 20c. *139*
—. Catholic Church. Fiestas. Rites and Ceremonies. Saints, patron. Villages. 1970's. *1036*
—. Catholic Church. Flagellants. Penitentes. 13c-20c. *878*
—. Catholic Church. Folk art. Santos. 1780-1900. *395*
—. Catholic Church. Penitentes. Social Customs. Villages. 19c-1978. *445*
—. Cattle Rustling. Comancheros. Hittson, John. Indians. Ranchers. 1872-73. *551*
—. Chacón, Felipe Maximiliano. Literature. Newspapers. 1873-1922. *661*
—. Chouteau, Auguste P. Demun, Julius. Indian-White Relations. Law. Trade. 1815-51. *375*
—. Cofradías (brotherhoods). Penitentes. Rio Grande Valley. ca 1770-1970. *404*
—. Colonial Government. Concha, Fernando Simon Ignacio de la. Indian-White Relations. Spain. 1787-93. *155*
—. Colonial Government. Documents. Spain. Vélez Cachupín, Thomas. ca 1754. *297*

—. Colonial Government. Frontier and Pioneer Life. Indian Wars. Pueblo Indians. Spain. Texas (El Paso). 1680-90. *219*
—. Colonial Government. Land grants. Mendinueta, Pedro Fermín de. Spain. 1767-79. *316*
—. Colonization. Indians. Land tenure. Social Organization. Spain. 1546-1692. *313*
—. Colonization. Land tenure. Spain. Whites. 16c-1974. *29*
—. Colonization. Latin America. Law. Spain. 15c-18c. *340*
—. Colorado. Folk art. Penitentes. 19c-20c. *503*
—. Commons. Land grants. Law. San Joaquín Grant. 1806-97. *531*
—. Contracts, partido. Employment. Livestock. 1905-11. *656*
—. Court of Private Land Claims. Embudo de Picuris grant. Land grants. 1725-1898. *430*
—. Culture. Literature. 1610-1983. *5*
—. Diaries. Fuente, Pedro José de la. Indian Wars. Mexico (Chihuahua, Sonora). Military. Texas (El Paso). 1765. *192*
—. Diplomacy. Indians. Navajo Indians. Spain. 1770-90. *324*
—. Discovery and Exploration. El Morro National Monument. Rock inscriptions. Spain. Prehistory-1620. *167*
—. Economic Conditions. Land tenure. Social Organization. Spaniards. Whites. 1846-91. *594*
—. Economic Structure. Villages. 18c-1978. *1039*
—. Equal opportunity. Public Employees. State government. Women. 1971-78. *819*
—. Ethnic Groups. Occupations. Population. Social Organization. 1790. *363*
—. Ethnicity. Social Classes. Teachers. Women. 1900-50. *649*
—. Folk art. Santos. 17c-19c. *15*
—. Folk Medicine. Indians. 19c-1930's. *408*
—. Folklore. Penitentes. Rites and Ceremonies. Social customs. 16c-20c. *472*
—. Food Industry. Ranches. Sheep Raising. Textile Industry. 1846-61. *589*
—. Franciscans. Indians. Indian-White Relations. Leadership. Pueblo Indians. Rebellions. 1650-80. 1980. *398*
—. Frontier and Pioneer Life. New Spain. 1598-1781. *294*
—. Frontier and Pioneer Life. Settlement. 17c-1810. *344*
—. Indian Wars. Mexico. Trade regulation. Treaties. 1821-46. *372*
—. Indian Wars. Navajo Indians. Spain. 1680-1720. *326*
—. Indian Wars. Our Lady of Macana (statue). Statues. 1598-1957. *179*
—. Indians. Infants. Mortality. Whites. 1974-77. *971*
—. Indians. Legal Education. Medical education. 1960's-76. *972*
—. Indians. Missions and Missionaries. Secularization. Spain. 1767. *263*
—. Indians. Political Participation. State politics. 1846-1976. *28*
—. Indians. Sheep raising. Weaving. Woolen Industry. 1540's-1860's. *166*
—. Indians. Toponymy. Whites. ca 1550-1982. *48*
—. Indian-White Relations. 17c-1978. *496*
—. Indian-White Relations. Inquisition. Marriage. Plains Apache Indians. Romero, Diego. 1660-78. *260*
—. Indian-White Relations. Navajo Indians. Peace. Spain. 1720-79. *325*
—. Intergovernmental Relations. Law. Martinez, Manuel. Mexico. Water. 1832. *205*
—. Intermarriage. Whites. 1846-1900. *563*
—. Irrigation. Martinez, Felix. Politics. Texas. 1877-1916. *598*

—. Land. Pino, Juan Estevan. Speculation. 1820-30. *234*
—. Land grants. Mexico. San Antonio de las Huertas grant. Spain. 1765-1891. *348*
—. Land grants. Ortiz y Alarid, Gasper. Roque Lovato Grant. 1785-1894. *532*
—. Land grants. Supreme Court (decisions). 1821-90. *579*
—. Law. Social Status. Women. 1821-46. *272*
—. Libraries. 1598-1912. *98*
—. Manitos. Politics. 1970-74. *816*
—. Martínez, Antonio José (report). Mexico. Territorial government. 1830-32. *383*
—. Mexico. Revolution. Salazar, Jose Ines. Texas. ca 1910-18. *689*
—. Otero, Miguel A. 1829-1901. *535*
—. Political participation. State Politics. Suffrage. Women. 1900-40. *648*
—. Settlement. Social Organization. Spain. 1790-1810. *256*
—. Social customs. 1850-1900. *506*
—. Texan-Santa Fe Expedition. Trade. 1841. *290*
—. Travel accounts. 1846-49. *518*
—. Travel accounts. Women. 1800-50. *266*
New Mexico (Albuquerque). Armijo, Salvador. Charities. Poor. 1874. *515*
—. Attitudes. Mothers. Sex roles. Women. 1960-83. *1050*
—. Colonial government. Cuervo y Valdes, Francisco. Spain. 1706-12. *343*
—. Daily Life. Labor. Social mobility. Trade. 1706-90. *330*
—. Economic growth. Urbanization. World War II. 1940-75. *920*
New Mexico (Colfax County, Uña de Gato grant). Land grants. 1870's. *590*
New Mexico (Columbus; attack). Brown, Harold Palmer. Carranza family. Memoirs. Mexico. Photographs. Villa, Pancho. 1916. *612*
New Mexico (Córdova). Catholic Church. Isidore the Husbandman, Saint. Lopez, George. Statues. Wood carving. ca 1070-1130. ca 1690-1980. *411*
—. Folk art. Lopez, George. Lopez, José Dolores. Santos. 20c. *412*
New Mexico (Corrales). Suburban Life. Whites. 1710-1970's. *417*
New Mexico, eastern. Cháves, Jesús (family). Daily life. Sheepherders. 1850's-1930's. *462*
New Mexico (El Cerrito). Migration, Internal. Social Change. Values. 1939-56. *893*
—. Population. 1939-80. *940*
New Mexico (El Rancho, Vadito). Indian-White Relations. Land Tenure. Pueblo Indians. Settlement. 17c-1970. *418*
New Mexico (Espanola Valley). Community Participation in Politics. Economic Development. Government. Indians. Water Supply. 1970's. *864*
New Mexico (Estancia Basin). Indians. Mexico. Salt. Spain. Trade. Prehistory-1840's. *265*
New Mexico (Guadalupita). Catholic Church. Folk medicine. Social Customs. Torres, Luisa. 1910's-70's. *497*
New Mexico Land and Livestock Company. Anton Chico grant. Land grants. Rivera, Manuel. Trials. 1822-1915. *334*
New Mexico (Las Trampas Grant). Federal government. Land grants. Swindles. 1859-1914. *526*
New Mexico (Las Vegas). Ethnicity. Herrera, Juan José. Land grants. Militancy. Vigilantes. White Caps. 1887-94. *554*
—. Land grants. Law. 1835-1902. *552*
—. Lopez, Lorenzo. Outlaws. Poets. Silva, Vicente. 1875-94. *561*
New Mexico (Manzano). *Gringo and Greaser.* Kusz, Charles L. Newspapers. 1883-84. *584*

New Mexico (North Central). Agricultural Labor. Migration, Internal. Social Change. 1930-50. *888*
—. Demography. Ecology. Economic Conditions. Social change. 1770-1970. *502*
New Mexico (northern). Anthropology. Ecology. Methodology. Social organization. Trade. 17c-20c. *63*
—. Bibliographies. Dialects. Espinosa, Aurelio M. Folklore. Spain. 1907-54. *31*
—. Catholic Church. Colorado, southern. Death Carts. Penitentes. 1860-90's. *586*
—. Catholic Church. Jaramillo, Cleofas M. Marriage. Social Customs. 1880-98. *547*
—. Indians. Navajo Indians. Pueblo Indians. Rio Grande Valley. Weaving. 15c-1979. *393*
—. Latin America. Social Organization. Spain. Villages. 16c-20c. *377*
—. Manufactures. Pottery. 17c-1930's. *351*
—. Rio Grande Valley. Weaving. 17c-20c. *352*
—. Social Organization. Villages. 16c-1978. *490*
New Mexico, northwestern. Economic Conditions. Health services. Indians. Navajo Indians. Population. Rural areas. Spaniards. 1971-78. *93*
New Mexico (Quarai, Tajique). Llana, Jerónimo de la. Maps. Marín del Valle, Francisco Antonio. 1659. 1759. *261*
New Mexico (Quivira, Teguayo provinces). Missions and Missionaries. Posada, Alonso de. 1686-88. *374*
New Mexico (Rio Grande Valley). Landownership. Pueblo Indian Grants, Northern. Spaniards. ca 1500's-1970's. *174*
New Mexico (Rio Puerco). Colonization. San Francisco (colony). 1866. *558*
New Mexico (Rio Puerco Valley). Farmers. Indians. Land (disputes). Whites. 19c-20c. *433*
New Mexico (Rito Colorado Valley). Excavations. Ranches. 1720-1846. *323*
New Mexico (Sandoval). Adventists. Education. Missions and Missionaries. Spanish-American Seminary. 1928-53. *679*
New Mexico (Santa Fe). Alvarez, Manuel. Commerce. Consular service. Mexico. 1818-47. *180*
—. Barceló, Gertrudis. Business. Elites. Gambling. Women. 1830's-40's. *273*
—. California (Monterey). Discovery and Exploration. Dominguez, Francisco Atanasio. Escalante, Silvestre Velez de. 1776-77. *169*
—. Catholic Church. Chapels. 1850's-70's. *346*
—. Colonization. Mexico. Muster rolls. Páez Hurtado, Juan. 1695. 1978. *356*
—. Discrimination, Employment. Family. Texas (San Antonio). 1860. *513*
—. Economic development. Ethnic Groups. Population. 1790-99. *146*
—. Excavations. Palace of Governors. 1609-1974. *350*
—. Garita (fort). Military Camps and Forts. Spain. 19c-1954. *206*
—. Independence. Melgares, Facundo. New Spain. 1822. *386*
—. Landholding. 1860-70. *514*
—. Mexico (Sonora). Roads. Spain. Trade. 17c-1850's. *345*
—. Military. Presidial Company. Prices. 18c. *299*
New Mexico (Santa Rita del Cobre). Copper Mines and Mining. 1800-25. *380*
New Mexico (Socorro). Baca, Elfego. Law Enforcement. 1865-1919. *580*
New Mexico (Tierra Amarilla). Architecture. Housing. Indians. *Jacal* (style). Spaniards. Wood. 8c-20c. *366*
New Mexico (Tome, Valencia). Anecdotes. Baca, Father. Easter Week. Frontier and Pioneer Life. Rites and Ceremonies. 1846. *209*

New Mexico (Torrance County). Superstition. Witchcraft. 1970's. *780*

New Mexico (Valles Caldera). Daily life. Sheepherders. ca 1875-1941. *582*

New Progressive Party. Administration for the Development of Art and Culture. Bureaucracies. Legislation. Musicians. Puerto Rico. 1980. *1284*

—. Elections. Funerals. Muñoz Marín, Luis. Popular Democratic Party. Puerto Rico. 1980. *1215*

New Rican Village. Arts. New York City. Puerto Ricans. 1960's-78. *1273*

New Spain. Alvarado, Pedro de. Cabrillo, Juan Rodríguez. Colonial Government. Discovery and Exploration. Mendoza, Antonio de. Printing press. 1515-52. *158*

—. Aristocracy. Colonial Government. New Mexico. Settlement. 16c. *182*

—. Atrisco grant. Land grants. New Mexico. Pueblo Revolt (1680). 1680-1977. *454*

—. Colonization. Indians. Policymaking. Settlement. Spain. 1750-1800. *149*

—. Frontier and Pioneer Life. New Mexico. 1598-1781. *294*

—. Independence. Melgares, Facundo. New Mexico (Santa Fe). 1822. *386*

—. Indians. Land. Southwest. Water rights. 1535-1810. *359*

New Spain (Nueva Vizcaya). Colonial Government. Croix, Teodoro de. Militia. 1776-83. *196*

New Spain (Sonora; Real de Arizonac). Arizona. Silver. 1736. *236*

New York. Assimilation. Glazer, Nathan. Moynihan, Daniel P. Puerto Ricans (review article). 20c. *1265*

—. Blacks. Farms. Jamaicans. Migrant Labor. Social mobility. 1960's-70's. *1152*

—. Education. Employment. Puerto Ricans. Women. 1960's. *1118*

—. Employment. Puerto Ricans. Women. 1920's-40's. *1188*

—. House of Representatives. Marcantonio, Vito. Puerto Ricans. Republican Party. 20c. *1196*

—. Identity. Puerto Ricans. -1974. *1266*

New York City. Acculturation. Family. Mental illness. Puerto Ricans. Social Organization. 1950's-70's. *1271*

—. Age. Education. Ethnicity. Family. Puerto Ricans. 1958-79. *1270*

—. Arts. New Rican Village. Puerto Ricans. 1960's-78. *1273*

—. Assimilation. Attitudes. Bilingualism. Puerto Ricans. Working class. 1979. *1073*

—. Assimilation. Models. Puerto Ricans. Segregation, residential. 1960-70. *1274*

—. Authors. Autobiographies. Blacks. Prisons. Puerto Ricans. Thomas, Piri. 1950-80. *1224*

—. Blacks. Economic Conditions. Immigration. Public Opinion. West Indies. 1965-79. *1099*

—. Blacks. England (London). Immigration. Social status. West Indians. 20c. *1153*

—. Blacks. Ethnic Groups. Social Change. 1960's-70's. *1230*

—. Blacks. Puerto Ricans. Voluntary associations. Whites. 1963-78. *1117*

—. Briski, Norman (interview). Exiles. Latin Americans. Theater. 1970's-82. *1096*

—. California (East Los Angeles). Immigrants (review article). Romo, Richard. Sanchez Korrol, Virginia E. 20c. *137*

—. Colombians. Dominicans. Employment. Family. Immigrants. Women. 1981. *1171*

—. Colombians. Dominicans. Social organizations. ca 1972-76. *1282*

—. Communist Party. Harlem Renaissance. Immigrants. Literature. West Indians. 1930's. *1301*

—. Cubans. Exiles. Latin America. Martí, José. Reporters and Reporting. 1880-95. *1068*

—. Cubans. Florida (Miami). Puerto Rico (San Juan). Social Classes. 1950-77. *1121*

—. Employment. Latin Americans. Women. 1970's. *1278*

—. Entrepreneurs. Garment industry. Immigrants. 1981-82. *1300*

—. Ethnicity. Politicization. Puerto Ricans. Social policy. 1955-75. *1175*

—. Florida (Dade County). 1960-80. *1150*

—. Mortality. Puerto Ricans. 1969-71. *1276*

—. Occupations. Puerto Ricans. Unemployment. 1970. *1168*

—. Race. Spanish language. West Indians. 1972. *1140*

New York City (Brooklyn; St. Ignatius Parish). Catholic Church. Charities. Immigration. 1945-81. *1294*

New York (Long Island). Barrios. Photographic essays. Puerto Ricans. Suburbs. 1981. *1275*

Newlands Act (US, 1902). Agricultural Labor. California, University of, Berkeley. Economics. Taylor, Paul S. 1895-1980. *494*

Newspapers. Assimilation. California (Los Angeles). Exiles. Lozano, Ignacio. *Opinión.* 1926-29. *660*

—. Attitudes. Blacks. Television. Texas (Lubbock). 1976. *1010*

—. Bilingualism. New Mexico. Spanish (language). 1834-1917. *569*

—. California (Los Angeles). *Heraldo De Mexico.* Immigrants. Press. 1916-20. *614*

—. Chacón, Felipe Maximiliano. Literature. New Mexico. 1873-1922. *661*

—. Deportation. Emigration. Reporters and Reporting. 1930-76. *420*

—. Filibustering. *La Union.* Latin America. Louisiana (New Orleans). 1846-51. *328*

—. Garza, Catarino E. Mexico. Texas. 1880-95. *525*

—. *Gringo and Greaser.* Kusz, Charles L. New Mexico (Manzano). 1883-84. *584*

—. Panama Canal. Political Campaigns (presidential). Reagan, Ronald. Treaties. 1976-80. *976*

—. Reporters and Reporting. 1970. *837*

Nichols, John. Authors. New Mexico. Social Conditions. Spaniards. 1841-1979. *499*

Nisei Farmers League. Agricultural labor. California (San Joaquin Valley). Japanese. United Farm Workers Union. 1971-77. *812*

—. California (San Joaquin Valley). Japanese. Labor Disputes. United Farm Workers Union. 1974-76. *811*

Nixon, Richard M. Grants. Political Campaigns (presidential). Revenue sharing. 1960-72. *23*

NLRB v. *Apollo Tire Co.* (US, 1979). Labor. National Labor Relations Board. *NLRB* v. *Sure-Tan, Inc.* (US, 1978). Workers, undocumented. 1978-79. *1034*

NLRB v. *Sure-Tan, Inc.* (US, 1978). Labor. National Labor Relations Board. *NLRB* v. *Apollo Tire Co.* (US, 1979). Workers, undocumented. 1978-79. *1034*

Nobel Prize. Authors. Jiménez, Juan Ramón. Memoirs. Palau de Nemes, Graciela. Puerto Rico (Ponce). Spain. 1930's-56. *1113*

Norteña (music). Music. Photographs. Texas (San Antonio). 1930's-82. *688*

North Carolina. Discovery and Exploration. Georgia. Salazar, Pedro de. Slave raids. South Carolina. Spain. 1514-16. *238*

North Central States. 1920's. *623*

—. Civil Rights. Labor Unions and Organizations. Social Organizations. 1900-76. *467*

—. Cubans. Mexicans. Migration, internal. Puerto Ricans. Social Conditions. Southwest. 1970. *32*

—. Discrimination. Labor Unions and Organizations. Steel workers. 1919-45. *677*
—. Geopolitics. Social Sciences. 1970-76. *755*
—. Immigration. Migrant Labor. Social Conditions. 1919-76. *415*
—. Income. 1970. *105*
Northwest Passage myth. Explorers. Golden Cities myth. Mississippi River. 1519-1679. *381*
Novels. Acosta, Oscar Zeta *(Autobiography of a Brown Buffalo)*. Ethnicity. Rivera, Tomás *(Y No Se Lo Tragó La Tierra)*. Villareal, José Antonia *(Pocho)*. 1970-79. *1054*
—. Puerto Rico. 20c. *1079*

O

Obregón, Álvaro. Depressions. Mexico. Migrant Labor. Repatriation. 1920-23. *613*
Occupational mobility. Asians. Blacks. Education. Ethnicity. Immigrants. 1965-70. *99*
—. California (Los Angeles). Geographic Mobility. 1918-28. *676*
—. Generations. 1979. *1002*
—. Generations. Social Mobility. 1979. *1003*
Occupations. Arizona (Tucson). California (Los Angeles). Property. Social Customs. 1775-1880. *543*
—. Bilingualism. Puerto Rico. 1970. *1066*
—. Blacks. Income. Metropolitan areas. 1970. *808*
—. Country Life. Economic Conditions. Family. Social Organization. Washington (Yakima Valley). 1971. *827*
—. Cubans. Education. Political Imprisonment. Refugees. 1973-80. *1077*
—. Education. Family. Fertility. Income. Puerto Ricans. 1969-70. *1325*
—. Education. Family. Income. 1969-70. *1057*
—. Ethnic Groups. New Mexico. Population. Social Organization. 1790. *363*
—. Family. Immigration. Social Classes. Women. 20c. *2*
—. New York City. Puerto Ricans. Unemployment. 1970. *1168*
O'Farrell, Jasper. California. Land grants. Surveying. 1844-46. *289*
Oil exploration. Puerto Rico. 1970's. *1291*
Old Southwest. Choctaw Indians. Indian-White Relations. Spain. Treaties. Villebeuvre, Juan de la. 1784-97. *241*
"Operation Wetback". California, southern. Immigration. Mexico. Texas. 1950-74. *977*
Opinión. Assimilation. California (Los Angeles). Exiles. Lozano, Ignacio. Newspapers. 1926-29. *660*
Oral history. Agricultural Labor. California Women Farmworkers Project. Women. 1870's-1970's. *73*
—. Historiography. Labor. Mexican Americans. 1920's-30's. *127*
—. History Teaching. Interviews. Mexican Americans. 1974. *37*
—. Mexican Americans. Research. ca 1930-78. *68*
Oregon. Employment. Immigration. 1900-70. *488*
—. Social Conditions. Washington. 1970-80. *1000*
Oregon (Hood River Valley). Aliens (illegal). Migrant Labor. Wages. 1978. *777*
Ortiz y Alarid, Gasper. Land grants. New Mexico. Roque Lovato Grant. 1785-1894. *532*
Otero, Miguel A. New Mexico. 1829-1901. *535*
Our Lady of Macana (statue). Indian Wars. New Mexico. Statues. 1598-1957. *179*
Outlaws. California. Gold Rushes. Murieta, Joaquín. ca 1848-53. *587*
—. California. Legends. Murieta, Joaquín. 1850's. *556*

—. Lopez, Lorenzo. New Mexico (Las Vegas). Poets. Silva, Vicente. 1875-94. *561*
Overland Journeys to the Pacific. Cahuilla Indians. California (Palm Springs region). Cocomaricopa Trail. Indians. Letters. Romero, José. ca 1823-24. *370*
Ownership. Business. Cubans. 1977. *1133*

P

P. K. Yonge Library of Florida History. Florida (Gainesville). Spain. Spanish Florida Borderlands Project. 1565-1821. 1977-78. *226*
P. K. Yonge Library of Florida History (guide). Borderlands. Colonies. Documents. Florida, University of, Gainesville. Spain. ca 1518-1821. *77*
Pachuco (term). California. Literature. Youth. 1940's-1960's. *904*
Pacific Coast. Canada. Scientific Expeditions. Spain. USA. 18c. *191*
Pacific Northwest. British Columbia. Columbia River. Discovery and Exploration. Heceta y Fontecha, Bruno de. Spain. 1775. *159*
—. Economic Conditions. 1960-79. *999*
Páez Hurtado, Juan. Colonization. Mexico. Muster rolls. New Mexico (Santa Fe). 1695. 1978. *356*
Palace of Governors. Excavations. New Mexico (Santa Fe). 1609-1974. *350*
Palau de Nemes, Graciela. Authors. Jiménez, Juan Ramón. Memoirs. Nobel Prize. Puerto Rico (Ponce). Spain. 1930's-56. *1113*
Palés Matos, Luis. Blacks. Poets. Puerto Rico. ca 1915-59. *1177*
Panama. Blades, Rubén (interview). City life. Latin Americans. Music. Salsa. 1974-84. *1088*
Panama Canal. Newspapers. Political Campaigns (presidential). Reagan, Ronald. Treaties. 1976-80. *976*
Paredes, Americo. Borders. Folk Songs (review article). Mexico. Texas. 16c-20c. *474*
Parents. Attitudes. Bilingual Education. Children. Curricula. 1960's-70's. *902*
Parks. California (San Diego; Barrio Logan). Community Participation in Politics. Murals. 1969-84. *767*
Passion plays. Catholic Church. Colorado. New Mexico. Spain. 1830's-1978. *492*
Peace. Indian-White Relations. Navajo Indians. New Mexico. Spain. 1720-79. *325*
Penitentes. Catholic Church. Colorado, southern. Death Carts. New Mexico, northern. 1860-90's. *586*
—. Catholic Church. Flagellants. New Mexico. 13c-20c. *878*
—. Catholic Church. New Mexico. Social Customs. Villages. 19c-1978. *445*
—. Cofradías (brotherhoods). New Mexico. Rio Grande Valley. ca 1770-1970. *404*
—. Colorado. Folk art. New Mexico. 19c-20c. *503*
—. Folklore. New Mexico. Rites and Ceremonies. Social customs. 16c-20c. *472*
Perez, Louis A., Jr. Cubans. Florida (Tampa). Labor Disputes. *Lector* (reader). Personal narratives. Tobacco industry. ca 1925-35. *1243*
Performing arts. Arts. Texas. 19c. *576*
Periodicals. Bibliographies. *Diario del Gobierno de la República Mexicana*. Texas. 1836-45. *75*
—. Bibliographies. Educational policy. Energy crisis. Foreign Relations. Middle East. National Autonomous University of Mexico (Faculty of Political and Social Sciences). Social Conditions. 1970-81. *7*
—. Bibliographies. Mass media. Mexican Americans. 1970's. *24*
—. Immigration. Nativism. *Saturday Evening Post*. 1914-33. *662*

—. Modernism. National consciousness. Puerto Rico. *Revista de las Antillas.* 1913-18. *1130*

Personal Narratives. Alamo (battle). DelaPeña, José Enrique. Santa Anna, Antonio Lopez de. Texas. 1836. *195*

—. Andrade, Flores de. Immigration. Liberal Party. Mexico. Revolutionary Movements. Texas (El Paso). 1890-1911. *621*

—. Archuleta, Eppie. Colorado (San Luis Valley). Folk art. Women. 1922-79. *460*

—. Attitudes. Discrimination. Family. Professions. Success. Women. 1980. *997*

—. Baca, Felipe. Colorado (Trinidad). 1862-74. *512*

—. Baptists. Costas, Orlando E. Ecumenism. 1980. *21*

—. Burgos, Julia de. Font Saldaña, Jorge. Lair, Clara. Poets. Puerto Rico. Ribera Chevremont, Evaristo. 20c. *1232*

—. California (Los Angeles). McWilliams, Carey. Race Relations. 1940's-60's. *917*

—. Cubans. Florida (Tampa). Labor Disputes. *Lector* (reader). Perez, Louis A., Jr. Tobacco industry. ca 1925-35. *1243*

—. Education. Rodriguez, Richard. 1950's-60's. *1053*

—. Massachusetts (New Bedford). Puerto Ricans. Social Conditions. 1930-82. *1216*

Pharmacy. France. Louisiana. Medicine (practice of). Spain. 1717-1852. *203*

Philosophy. Barreda, Gabino. Mexico. Positivism. Values. 1860's-1982. *444*

—. Ideology. Mexico. Positivism. Science. Social control. 1850-1984. *477*

Photographic essays. Barrios. New York (Long Island). Puerto Ricans. Suburbs. 1981. *1275*

—. Migrant labor. Washington (Yakima Valley). 1974. *939*

Photographs. Brown, Harold Palmer. Carranza family. Memoirs. Mexico. New Mexico (Columbus; attack). Villa, Pancho. 1916. *612*

—. Music. Norteña (music). Texas (San Antonio). 1930's-82. *688*

Photography, Journalistic. Daily Life. Smithers, W. D. Texas. 1910-60's. *471*

Physicians. California (San Diego). Colorado (Denver). Medical Education. Texas (San Antonio). 1970-79. *980*

Pico, Pío. California. Leadership. 1801-94. *520*

Pictographs. Arizona (Canyon de Chelly). Bones. Dogs. Indian Wars. Navajo Indians. Spain. 1750-1863. *202*

Pino, Juan Estevan. Land. New Mexico. Speculation. 1820-30. *234*

Pioneers. California (San Bernardino Valley; Agua Mansa). 1845-62. *597*

—. Indian-White Relations. Pueblo Indians. Southwest. Spaniards. 1492-1974. *55*

Plains Apache Indians. Indian-White Relations. Inquisition. Marriage. New Mexico. Romero, Diego. 1660-78. *260*

Plan de San Diego. Carranza, Venustiano. Foreign Relations. Mexico. Race relations. Texas, south. 1915-16. *638*

—. Rebellions. Texas (San Antonio). 1914-17. *655*

Plantations. Capital. Commodity exchange. Economic structure. Puerto Rico, southwest. Sugar cane. 1911. *1305*

—. Capitalism. Puerto Rico. Socialist Party. Sugar. Working Class. 19c-1976. *1255*

Plebiscites. Political status. Puerto Rico. Self-Determination. 1967. *1187*

Pletcher, David M. Antiwar sentiment. Expansionism. Mexican War (review article). Polk, James K. Schroeder, John H. 1830's-40's. *199*

Pocho (term). Acculturation. Social Status. Southwest. 1910's-40's. *657*

Poetic consciousness. Nationalism, cultural. 1945-77. *1049*

Poetry. 1970-73. *844*

—. Acculturation. Laviera, Tato *(La Carreta Made a U-Turn).* Puerto Ricans. 1979-80. *1151*

—. Labor. Popular culture. 1967-73. *952*

—. Political Protest. 1965-70's. *943*

—. Political Protest. Social Conditions. 1970's. *950*

—. Rhetoric. 1969-79. *991*

Poets. Blacks. Palés Matos, Luis. Puerto Rico. ca 1915-59. *1177*

—. Burgos, Julia de. Font Saldaña, Jorge. Lair, Clara. Personal Narratives. Puerto Rico. Ribera Chevremont, Evaristo. 20c. *1232*

—. Lopez, Lorenzo. New Mexico (Las Vegas). Outlaws. Silva, Vicente. 1875-94. *561*

Police. Attitudes. Barrios. California, southern. Civil Rights. Social Conditions. 1975. *927*

Policymaking. Colonization. Indians. New Spain. Settlement. Spain. 1750-1800. *149*

Political activism. Assimilation. Ethnicity. Institutions. Students. Texas (Corpus Christi, Crystal City). 1969-80. *753*

—. California. Chavez, Cesar. Rhetoric. Texas. Tijerina, Reies. 1960's-70's. *843*

—. California, Southern. Women. 1960-79. *785*

—. Gutiérrez, José Angel. Radicals and Radicalism. Rhetoric. Self-Determination. Texas (Crystal City). 1969-79. *868*

—. Gutiérrez, José Angel. Rhetoric. Self-Determination. 1979. *867*

Political attitudes. Blacks. Colorado (Denver). Voting and Voting Behavior. 1971. *897*

—. California. Children. Whites. -1973. *815*

—. Community control. Texas. 1971-77. *752*

—. Conservatism. Democratic Party. Elections. 1980. *1047*

—. Latin America. Nationalism. Social Customs. 1848-1976. *480*

—. Social programs. 1980-81. *34*

Political Campaigns (presidential). Grants. Nixon, Richard M. Revenue sharing. 1960-72. *23*

—. Newspapers. Panama Canal. Reagan, Ronald. Treaties. 1976-80. *976*

Political candidates. California (Los Angeles County). Congressional Districts (30th). Ethnicity. Race. Voting and Voting Behavior. 1982. *754*

Political change. Class struggle. Development. Ideology. Puerto Rico. 1940-78. *1238*

—. Cuba. Economic Conditions. Refugees. 1960-82. *1240*

Political conditions. Economic development. Imperialism. Puerto Rico. Social organization. 1900-72. *1131*

—. Elites. Migrant labor. 1946-72. *57*

Political consciousness. Discrimination. 1930-75. *486*

—. School boards. Texas (Crystal City). 1970. *841*

—. Self-identity. Students. Texas (Crystal City). 1973. *840*

Political Conventions. Elections. Puerto Rico. Rites and Ceremonies. 1968. *1257*

Political economy. Migration. Puerto Rico. Social Classes. 1898-1970's. *1135*

—. Military. 1830-1980. *432*

Political familialism. Discrimination. Sex roles. 1970-75. *719*

Political Imprisonment. Cubans. Education. Occupations. Refugees. 1973-80. *1077*

Political integration. Acculturation. Children. Texas (El Paso). 1978. *881*

—. Blacks. Kansas (Manhattan). 1971. *704*

Political issues. Economic Conditions. Independence. Interviews. Muñoz Marín, Luis. Puerto Rico. Social Conditions. 1948-64. *1186*

Political Leadership. Bossism. Puerto Ricans. 1935-73. *1269*

—. California (Los Angeles). World War II. 1941-45. *625*
—. Carter, Jimmy. Cubans. Federal Policy. Immigration. 1980. *1123*
—. Mass media. Texas (Austin). Whites. 1973. *877*
—. Puerto Rico (San Juan). Rincón, Felisa. Women. 1934-80. *1235*
Political machines. Race Relations. Social Change. Texas (Cameron County). Wells, James B. 1882-1920. *605*
Political organizations. Middle classes. Texas. 1970's. *1014*
Political Participation. 1967-82. *783*
—. Blacks. Ethnic groups. Whites. 1966-75. *707*
—. Blacks. Voting Rights Act (US, 1965; amended 1982). 1965-83. *83*
—. Canada. Puerto Rico. Voter registration. 1974-77. *1070*
—. Children. Japanese. Whites. 1970's. *1005*
—. Cubans. Naturalization. Refugees. Voting and Voting Behavior. 1959-84. *1249*
—. Ethnic identity. Nebraska (Omaha). 1970's. *1042*
—. Foreign Policy. Puerto Rico. Self-government. 1900-33. *1115*
—. Foreign Relations. 1970-82. *1033*
—. Indians. New Mexico. State politics. 1846-1976. *28*
—. Local government. Texas, South. 1971-83. *721*
—. Nebraska. -1973. *1043*
—. New Mexico. State Politics. Suffrage. Women. 1900-40. *648*
—. Primer Congreso Mexicanista (1911). Texas (Laredo). 1910-11. *654*
—. State Politics. Texas. -1973. *914*
Political Power. Apportionment. Congress. 1980-83. *123*
—. California. Cultural identity. Marxism. San Diego State University. 1965-74. *992*
—. California (San Diego). Californios. Upper Classes. 1846-60. *534*
—. Cubans. Education. Florida (Miami). Geographic mobility. Income. 1959-78. *1241*
—. Education. Labor. Southwest. 1848-1980. *635*
Political Protest. Ballads. "Corrido de Gregorio Cortez" (ballad). "Discriminación a un Martir" (ballad). Social change. Texas (Three River). 20c. *468*
—. California (East Los Angeles). Ethnic Groups. Social Change. 1968-74. *934*
—. Discrimination, Employment. World War II. Wyoming. 1941-45. *643*
—. Poetry. 1965-70's. *943*
—. Poetry. Social Conditions. 1970's. *950*
—. Social Change. Women. 1973-76. *709*
Political representation. California. Colorado. New Mexico. State Politics. ca 1850-1974. *464*
—. City Politics. Illinois (Chicago). Spaniards. Voting and Voting Behavior. 1975. *104*
—. Congress. Roll-call voting. 1972-80. *128*
Political repression. Puerto Rico. 1950's-79. *1158*
Political science. American Political Science Association. Colleges and Universities. Western states. 1970-74. *1058*
Political Socialization. California (Los Angeles). Chicano movement. Interviews. 1960's. *974*
—. Elites. 1978-80. *782*
Political status. Caribbean Studies Association (conference papers). Puerto Rico. 1976. *1106*
—. Economic development. Population growth. Puerto Rico. 1940-76. *1303*
—. Economic Structure. Puerto Rico. 1949-72. *1200*
—. Plebiscites. Puerto Rico. Self-Determination. 1967. *1187*
Political Systems. Bhana, Surendra (review article). Puerto Rico. 1936-68. 1975. *1293*

—. Foreign Policy. Public Opinion. Puerto Rico. 1970's. *1103*
—. Puerto Rico. 1900-75. *1116*
Politicization. Ethnicity. New York City. Puerto Ricans. Social policy. 1955-75. *1175*
Politics. 1846-1974. *459*
—. Albuquerque, Duke of (Francisco Fernández de la Cueva Henríquez). Colonial Government. Mexico. New Mexico. Social Problems. 1702-11. *318*
—. Americanization. Bhana, Surendra. Clark, Truman. Development. Matthews, Thomas. Puerto Rico (review article). 1917-76. *1261*
—. Antonia (Indian). Calusa Indians. Carlos (chief). Florida. Indian-White Relations. Marriage. Menéndez de Avilés, Pedro. 1566-69. *327*
—. Arizona. Copper industry. Labor Unions and Organizations. Racism. Working Class. 1900-20. *611*
—. Behavior. Bilingualism. 1970-75. *948*
—. California (Parlier). Local government. Models. 1971-73. *966*
—. Class struggle. Popular Democratic Party. Puerto Rico. 1930's. *1166*
—. Cuba. Cubans. 1959-81. *1322*
—. Cubans. Economic Conditions. Florida. Refugees. 1980-81. *1076*
—. Economic Conditions. Puerto Rico. 1975. *1292*
—. Economic Conditions. Southwest. Workers, undocumented. 1975-78. *740*
—. Employment. Illinois (Chicago Heights). Social Conditions. 1910-76. *436*
—. Identity. Puerto Rico. Social Customs. 1898-1980. *1220*
—. Industrialization. Migration. Puerto Rico. Working class. 1870's-1970's. *1108*
—. Investments. Land. Mexia, José Antonio. Mexico. Texas. 1823-39. *248*
—. Irrigation. Martinez, Felix. New Mexico. Texas. 1877-1916. *598*
—. Manitos. New Mexico. 1970-74. *816*
—. Methodology. Mexican Americans. 1974. *10*
—. Mexican Americans. Scholarship. Social conditions. 1974. *82*
Politics and Media. Cubans. *Diario Las Americas*. Florida (Miami). Journalism. Watergate scandal. 1970's. *1061*
Polk, James K. Antiwar sentiment. Expansionism. Mexican War (review article). Pletcher, David M. Schroeder, John H. 1830's-40's. *199*
Poor. *See also* Poverty.
—. Armijo, Salvador. Charities. New Mexico (Albuquerque). 1874. *515*
—. California (Los Angeles). Medical care. Neighborhoods. 1970-79. *853*
—. Family. Social Work. -1973. *960*
Popular Culture. Arizona (Tucson). Dancers. Musicians. 1892-1982. *682*
—. Attitudes. English language. Spanish language. Theater. 1970's. *1022*
—. Daily life. Immigrants. Latin Americans. West Indies. 1965-77. *12*
—. Ethnicity. Social Conditions. *Teatro Chicano*. Theater. 1965-79. *874*
—. Labor. Poetry. 1967-73. *952*
Popular Democratic Party. Class struggle. Politics. Puerto Rico. 1930's. *1166*
—. Elections. Funerals. Muñoz Marín, Luis. New Progressive Party. Puerto Rico. 1980. *1215*
Population. *See also* Demography.
—. 1970's. *735*
—. Agricultural Labor. Indians. Spain. Texas (El Paso). 1680-1784. *362*
—. Aliens, illegal. Immigration. Labor. 1970-80. *142*
—. Blacks. Employment. Race. Students. Whites. Youth. 1967-83. *133*

—. Blacks. Florida (Miami). Neighborhoods. Residential patterns. Whites. 1970-80. *1309*
—. California. Colonization. Mexico. Spain. 1760's-1840's. *222*
—. Census. 1970-78. *820*
—. Census. Florida (St. Augustine). 1786. *365*
—. Census. Methodology. Southwest. 1848-1900. *559*
—. Census. Quantitative Methods. 1960-70. *56*
—. Economic Conditions. Health services. Indians. Navajo Indians. New Mexico, northwestern. Rural areas. Spaniards. 1971-78. *93*
—. Economic development. Ethnic Groups. New Mexico (Santa Fe). 1790-99. *146*
—. Economic development. Puerto Rico. Unemployment. 1940's-70's. *1244*
—. Education. Income. Indiana (South Bend). Social Mobility. 1970-74. *798*
—. Ethnic Groups. New Mexico. Occupations. Social Organization. 1790. *363*
—. Ethnic Groups. Puerto Rico. 1940-70. *1297*
—. Florida. Military. 1700-1820. *282*
—. Immigration. Puerto Rico. 1800-30. *1208*
—. Modernization. Puerto Rico, western. Rural areas. 1940-70's. *1225*
—. New Mexico (El Cerrito). 1939-80. *940*
—. Puerto Rico (San Germán). Slavery. 1872. *1304*
—. Texas. 1887. *549*
—. Women. 1975. *1035*
Population control. Puerto Rico. Sterilization. Women. 1920-77. *1213*
Population (definition). Census. 1970-73. *851*
Population growth. Economic development. Political status. Puerto Rico. 1940-76. *1303*
Porter, David. Civil-Military Relations. Foxardo (battle). Insubordination. Navies. Puerto Rico. 1823-25. *1087*
Portolá, Gaspar de. California (San Diego area). Discovery and Exploration. Indians. South Carolina. 1769. *175*
Posada, Alonso de. Missions and Missionaries. New Mexico (Quivira, Teguayo provinces). 1686-88. *374*
Posadas (celebrations). California (Los Angeles). Catholic Church. Christmas. Neighborhoods. Rites and Ceremonies. 1975-80. *900*
Positivism. Barreda, Gabino. Mexico. Philosophy. Values. 1860's-1982. *444*
—. Ideology. Mexico. Philosophy. Science. Social control. 1850-1984. *477*
Pottery. California. Effigies. Mission San Antonio de Padua. 18c-19c. *214*
—. Manufactures. New Mexico, northern. 17c-1930's. *351*
Poverty. *See also* Poor.
—. Arizona (Phoenix). Public Welfare. 1870-1973. *475*
—. Borders. Cities. Daily Life. Social Conditions. 1945-77. *911*
—. Immigrants. Income. Men. Self-perception. Working Class. 1978-79. *923*
—. Puerto Ricans. Racism. 1898-1974. *1183*
—. Puerto Rico. 1970-77. *1143*
—. Southwest. 1970-73. *970*
—. Texas (El Paso). Women. 1880-1920. *626*
Powell, Alex K. Calleros, Cleofas. Federación de Sociedades Latinos-Americanos. Maverick, Maury. McCammont, T. J. Race Relations. Texas (El Paso). 1936. *627*
Power. Social reform. 1974. *969*
Power structure. Anthropology, Cultural. Puerto Rico. Steward, Julian H. (*People of Puerto Rico*). 1956-77. *1260*
Prenatal care. Infants. Mortality. Social Classes. Southwest. 1970. *793*
Presbyterian Church. Boycotts. Public schools. Segregation. Texas (San Angelo). 1910-15. *617*

—. Missions and Missionaries. Puerto Rico. 1899-1914. *1229*
—. Southwest. 1830-1977. *410*
Preservation. Florida. St. Augustine Restoration Foundation. 1977. *281*
President's Commission on Migratory Labor. Agriculture. Bracero program. Mexico. Truman, Harry S. Workers, undocumented. 1950. *876*
Presidial Company. Military. New Mexico (Santa Fe). Prices. 18c. *299*
Presidios. Armies. California (Los Angeles, San Diego). Mexico. Spain. 1770-94. *283*
—. California. Excavations. Missions and Missionaries. San Diego Presidio. Serra Museum. 1769-75. 1964-70's. *210*
—. California. Missions and Missionaries. 1769-84. *172*
—. Indian Wars. Southwest. Spain. 17c-18c. *212*
Press. 1970-79. *30*
—. California (Los Angeles). *Heraldo De Mexico*. Immigrants. Newspapers. 1916-20. *614*
—. Editors and Editing. Revolution. Southwest. 1911-17. *634*
Press, black. Blacks. Mexico. Race Relations. 1890-1935. *681*
Pressure Groups. American G.I. Forum. League of United Latin American Citizens. Mexican American Legal Defense and Education Fund. School integration. Texas. 1945-80. *981*
—. Asociación Nacional México-Americana. Civil Rights. 1949-54. *1021*
Prices. Blacks. Cubans. Discrimination, Housing. Metropolitan Areas. Mexicans. Puerto Ricans. Whites. 1975-76. *62*
—. Military. New Mexico (Santa Fe). Presidial Company. 18c. *299*
Primer Congreso Mexicanista (1911). Political participation. Texas (Laredo). 1910-11. *654*
Printing press. Alvarado, Pedro de. Cabrillo, Juan Rodríguez. Colonial Government. Discovery and Exploration. Mendoza, Antonio de. New Spain. 1515-52. *158*
Prisons. Authors. Autobiographies. Blacks. New York City. Puerto Ricans. Thomas, Piri. 1950-80. *1224*
Production. Capitalism. Developing nations. Puerto Rico. ca 1940-79. *1137*
Productivity. Discrimination, employment. Economic Conditions. Men. 1960's-70's. *65*
Professions. Attitudes. Discrimination. Family. Personal narratives. Success. Women. 1980. *997*
Project Fiesta. Anthropology, applied. Arizona, southern. Television, public. 1976. *794*
Propaganda. Exiles. Liberal Party. Mexico. Texas. Women. 1898-1910. *691*
Property. *See also* Land.
—. Arizona (Tucson). California (Los Angeles). Occupations. Social Customs. 1775-1880. *543*
Proposition 14 (1976). Agricultural Industry. California. Elections. Labor Unions and Organizations. United Farm Workers Union. 1976. *773*
—. Agriculture. California. Chavez, Cesar. Elections. United Farm Workers Union. 1975-76. *996*
Protestant Churches. Americanization. Missions and Missionaries. Puerto Rico. 1898-1917. *1239*
Protocol of Querétaro. Guadalupe Hidalgo, Treaty of. Land grants. Texas. Trist, Nicholas P. 1847-48. *560*
Proverbs. Bibliographies. 1913-80. *6*
—. California (Los Angeles area). Tradition. 1970's. *713*
—. Folklore. Spanish language. 20c. *465*
Provincial Government. Armijo, Manuel. Mexico. New Mexico. Texas. 1827-46. *371*
Psychotherapeutic processes. Cult practices. Puerto Rico. Social organization. 1975. *1189*

Psychotherapy. Mental Illness. Victimization. 1980.
108

Public Employees. Equal opportunity. New Mexico.
State government. Women. 1971-78. *819*

—. Southwest. 1973-78. *1040*

Public expenditures. Dominican Republic. Puerto
Rico. 1930-70. *1207*

Public health. California (Los Angeles). Infant
mortality. 1850-87. *537*

Public housing. Alazan-Apache Courts. Texas (San
Antonio). 1930-44. *693*

Public Opinion. Blacks. City government. Colorado
(Denver). Whites. 1974. *898*

—. Blacks. Economic Conditions. Immigration.
New York City. West Indies. 1965-79. *1099*

—. Discrimination. Ethnic Groups. Kansas (Dodge
City). 1900-84. *450*

—. Foreign Policy. Political Systems. Puerto Rico.
1970's. *1103*

—. Race relations. Whites. 1935-80. *50*

Public Policy. Aged. 1970-79. *795*

—. Aliens. Immigration. Labor. 1970's. *965*

—. Aliens, illegal. Congress. Economic conditions.
Immigration. 1978. *91*

—. Cities. Social problems. 1960's-83. *130*

—. Health. Workers, undocumented. 1975-82. *938*

—. Immigration. Labor. Workers, undocumented.
1950's-70's. *140*

—. Immigration. Workers, undocumented. 1970's.
835

Public Schools. Acculturation. Church Schools.
Texas (San Antonio). 1973. *882*

—. American G.I. Forum. School Integration.
Texas. 1948-57. *701*

—. Americanization. Employment. Immigration.
Industry. 1880-1930. *624*

—. Attitudes. Children. 1981. *973*

—. Bilingual education. 1968-76. *27*

—. Bilingual education. Puerto Rico. 1970's. *1104*

—. Boycotts. Presbyterian Church. Segregation.
Texas (San Angelo). 1910-15. *617*

—. California (Los Angeles). Curricula.
Educational reform. 1920's-30's. *631*

—. California (Orange County). *Mendez* v.
Westminster (California, 1946). Segregation (*de
jure, de facto*). 1850-1970's. *690*

—. California (Santa Ana). Segregation. 1913-48.
633

—. Lancastrian system. Mexico, northern.
Southwest. 1821-48. *373*

—. Middle Classes. School Integration. Texas.
1929-57. *680*

—. Minorities in Politics. Self-perception. Texas
(southern). 1930's-69. *489*

Public Schools (closures). *Angeles et al.* v. *Santa
Barbara School District et al.* (California,
1981). California (Santa Barbara). Children.
1981-83. *1025*

—. California (Santa Barbara). 1970's. *1026*

Public Welfare. Arizona (Phoenix). Poverty.
1870-1973. *475*

—. California (San Francisco Bay area). Refugees.
Resettlement. South Americans. 1973-79. *1169*

—. Spanish language. 1972. *717*

Pueblo Indian Grants, Northern. Landownership.
New Mexico (Rio Grande Valley). Spaniards.
ca 1500's-1970's. *174*

Pueblo Indians. Agriculture. Indians. Irrigation.
Mexican Americans. New Mexico. 19c. *357*

—. Athapascan Indians. Indians. Indian-White
Relations. Missions and Missionaries. New
Mexico. 1600-80. *220*

—. Colonial Government. Frontier and Pioneer
Life. Indian Wars. New Mexico. Spain. Texas
(El Paso). 1680-90. *219*

—. Franciscans. Indians. Indian-White Relations.
Leadership. New Mexico. Rebellions. 1650-80.
1980. *398*

—. Indian Wars. Missions and Missionaries.
Southwest. Spain. 1680. *314*

—. Indians. Military. Social control. Spain.
1763-1821. *255*

—. Indians. Navajo Indians. New Mexico,
northern. Rio Grande Valley. Weaving.
15c-1979. *393*

—. Indian-White Relations. Land Tenure. New
Mexico (El Rancho, Vadito). Settlement.
17c-1970. *418*

—. Indian-White Relations. Mesoamerican Indians.
Southwest. Spain. 1530-98. *329*

—. Indian-White Relations. Pioneers. Southwest.
Spaniards. 1492-1974. *55*

Pueblo Revolt (1680). Atrisco grant. Land grants.
New Mexico. New Spain. 1680-1977. *454*

—. Indian-White Relations. Missions and
Missionaries. Southwest. Spain. 1590-1680. *165*

Puelles, José María de Jesús. Borders. Louisiana.
Mexico. Texas. 1512-1813. 1827-28. *230*

Puerto Ricans. Acculturation. Economic Conditions.
Hawaii. Immigrants. 1900-02. *1287*

—. Acculturation. Family. Mental illness. New
York City. Social Organization. 1950's-70's.
1271

—. Acculturation. Immigrants. Interviews. 1982.
1134

—. Acculturation. Laviera, Tato (*La Carreta Made
a U-Turn*). Poetry. 1979-80. *1151*

—. Age. Education. Ethnicity. Family. New York
City. 1958-79. *1270*

—. Areíto, Grupo. Cubans. History Task Force.
Immigration. Johnson, Roberta Ann.
1960's-70's. *1226*

—. Arts. New Rican Village. New York City.
1960's-78. *1273*

—. Assimilation. Attitudes. 1975. *1264*

—. Assimilation. Attitudes. Bilingualism. New
York City. Working class. 1979. *1073*

—. Assimilation. Fertility. Social Status. 1969-77.
1120

—. Assimilation. Models. New York City.
Segregation, residential. 1960-70. *1274*

—. Authors. Autobiographies. Blacks. New York
City. Prisons. Thomas, Piri. 1950-80. *1224*

—. Barrios. New York (Long Island).
Photographic essays. Suburbs. 1981. *1275*

—. Bibliographies. 20c. *66*

—. Biculturalism. Bilingual education. Cubans.
New Jersey. 19c-20c. *1101*

—. Blacks. Cubans. Discrimination. Housing.
Metropolitan Areas. Mexicans. Prices. Whites.
1975-76. *62*

—. Blacks. Demography. Households. Mothers,
single. Whites. 1970. *1119*

—. Blacks. New York City. Voluntary associations.
Whites. 1963-78. *1117*

—. Bossism. Political Leadership. 1935-73. *1269*

—. Cities. Cubans. Mexicans. Residential
segregation. 1950's-70's. *69*

—. City Life. Cubans. Ethnicity. Folklore. Indiana
(East Chicago). 1976. *1161*

—. Colonialism. Economic Structure. Migration.
1900-80. *1090*

—. Cubans. Florida (Miami). Residential patterns.
1970's. *1060*

—. Cubans. Mexicans. Migration, internal. North
Central States. Social Conditions. Southwest.
1970. *32*

—. Education. Employment. New York. Women.
1960's. *1118*

—. Education. Family. Fertility. Income.
Occupations. 1969-70. *1325*

—. Emigration. Family. Social Organization.
1970-82. *1071*

—. Employment. New York. Women. 1920's-40's.
1188

—. Ethnic Groups (review article). Sowell, Thomas. 1898-1983. *1267*
—. Ethnicity. New York City. Politicization. Social policy. 1955-75. *1175*
—. Folklore. Mexicans. Theater. 1966-77. *60*
—. House of Representatives. Marcantonio, Vito. New York. Republican Party. 20c. *1196*
—. Identity. New York. -1974. *1266*
—. Illinois (Chicago). Residential patterns. Social conditions. 1920-70. *650*
—. Immigrants. Leadership. Women. 1910-45. *1280*
—. Immigration. Mental illness. Social problems. 1493-1978. *1062*
—. Labor. 1942-51. *1198*
—. Massachusetts (New Bedford). Personal Narratives. Social Conditions. 1930-82. *1216*
—. Minorities. 20c. *1089*
—. Mortality. New York City. 1969-71. *1276*
—. New York City. Occupations. Unemployment. 1970. *1168*
—. Poverty. Racism. 1898-1974. *1183*
Puerto Ricans (review article). Assimilation. Glazer, Nathan. Moynihan, Daniel P. New York. 20c. *1265*
Puerto Rico. 1493-1981. *1173*
—. Administration for the Development of Art and Culture. Bureaucracies. Legislation. Musicians. New Progressive Party. 1980. *1284*
—. Adolescents. Identity. Mexico. USA. 1970's. *1159*
—. Age. Economic conditions. Fertility. Social Status. Women. 1970. *1182*
—. Agriculture. Economic Conditions. Industrialization. 1960's-70's. *1126*
—. Agriculture. Economic Conditions. Social Organization. 1870-1930. *1083*
—. American Federation of Labor. Gompers, Samuel. Iglesias Pantín, Santiago. Labor Unions and Organizations. 1897-1920's. *1155*
—. American Revolution. International Trade. 1775-1854. *1210*
—. Americanization. Missions and Missionaries. Protestant Churches. 1898-1917. *1239*
—. Anthropologists. Hostos, Adolfo de (interview). 1974. *1179*
—. Anthropology. Steward, Julian H. *(People of Puerto Rico)*. 1956-77. *1223*
—. Anthropology, Cultural. Economic Conditions. Methodology. Steward, Julian H. *(People of Puerto Rico)*. 1956-77. *1311*
—. Anthropology, Cultural. Economic Development. Methodology. Steward, Julian H. *(People of Puerto Rico)*. 1956-77. *1272*
—. Anthropology, Cultural. Ideology. Methodology. Steward, Julian H. *(People of Puerto Rico)*. 1956-77. *1144*
—. Anthropology, Cultural. Imperialism. Steward, Julian H. *(People of Puerto Rico)*. 1956-77. *1299*
—. Anthropology, Cultural. Power structure. Steward, Julian H. *(People of Puerto Rico)*. 1956-77. *1260*
—. Archives. Spain. 1500-1975. *110*
—. Art. Culture. Institute of Puerto Rican Culture. Muñoz Marín, Luis. Romero Barceló, Carlos. 1948-55. *1277*
—. Attitudes. Blacks. 1950's-70's. *1219*
—. Autonomy. National Guard. 1898-1978. *1128*
—. Barceló, Carlos Romero. Elections (gubernatorial). Government. Hernández, Rafael. 1980. *1193*
—. Behavior. Drugs. High schools. Youth. 1970-80. *1263*
—. Bhana, Surendra (review article). Political Systems. 1936-68. 1975. *1293*
—. Bibliographies. English Language. Literature. 1923-73. *80*

—. Bilingual education. English language. Teaching. 1978. *1234*
—. Bilingual education. Public schools. 1970's. *1104*
—. Bilingualism. Occupations. 1970. *1066*
—. Birth Rate. Census. Migration. 1965-70. *1262*
—. Birth rate. Demography. 1974. *1296*
—. Blacks. Palés Matos, Luis. Poets. ca 1915-59. *1177*
—. Burgos, Julia de. Font Saldaña, Jorge. Lair, Clara. Personal Narratives. Poets. Ribera Chevremont, Evaristo. 20c. *1232*
—. Campos, Albizu. Independence Movements. 1910-65. *1247*
—. Campos, Albizu. Nationalism. 20c. *1205*
—. Canada. Political participation. Voter registration. 1974-77. *1070*
—. Capital. Economic Development. Labor. Models. 1945-70. *1222*
—. Capitalism. 1940's-70's. *1136*
—. Capitalism. Developing nations. Production. ca 1940-79. *1137*
—. Capitalism. Emigration. 1945-70. *1204*
—. Capitalism. Plantations. Socialist Party. Sugar. Working Class. 19c-1976. *1255*
—. Caribbean Studies Association (conference papers). Political status. 1976. *1106*
—. Carter, Jimmy. Cerro Maravilla scandal. Murder. Revolutionary Movements. Romero Barceló, Carlos. Statehood. 1978-80. *1288*
—. Catholic Church. Church and State. Law. ca 1863-1908. *1160*
—. Centers for Educational Services. Education, Experimental Methods. 1973-77. *1125*
—. Change and Response, Theory of. Emigration. Fertility. Migration, Internal. 1940's-70. *1228*
—. Chrisman, Robert. Independence. 1977. *1111*
—. Civil-Military Relations. Foxardo (battle). Insubordination. Navies. Porter, David. 1823-25. *1087*
—. Class consciousness. Latin America. Women. Working Class. 1959-75. *1279*
—. Class struggle. Development. Ideology. Political change. 1940-78. *1238*
—. Class struggle. Politics. Popular Democratic Party. 1930's. *1166*
—. Coalition Government. Economic Conditions. 1917-33. *1313*
—. Colonialism. Democracy. 1950-80. *1167*
—. Colonialism. Economic Conditions. Independence movements. 1898-1977. *1212*
—. Consumerism. Economic development. 1940-70. *1129*
—. Cubans. Exiles. 1959-73. *1081*
—. Cult practices. Psychotherapeutic processes. Social organization. 1975. *1189*
—. Cultural identity. Economic conditions. Emigration. Mead, Margaret (interview). 1974. *1218*
—. Culture. Institute of Puerto Rican Culture. Theater. 1955-80. *1211*
—. Culture. National Characteristics. Social Organization. 1930's-70's. *1258*
—. Demography. Migration. Social Problems. 1960-75. *1176*
—. Diego, José de. Independence Movements. Middle classes. 1867-1918. *1139*
—. Documents. Episcopal Church, Protestant. Missions and Missionaries. 1870-1952. *1091*
—. Dominican Republic. Public expenditures. 1930-70. *1207*
—. Dramatists. Women. 19c-1979. *1127*
—. Econometrics. Models. 1948-64. *1285*
—. Economic Conditions. 1946-81. *1107*
—. Economic Conditions. Federal Aid to Education. Neocolonialism. Social Classes. 1970's. *1245*

—. Economic conditions. Federal Government. 1898-1941. *1114*
—. Economic Conditions. Foreign Policy. 1982. *1178*
—. Economic Conditions. Government. Social classes. 1930-50. *1085*
—. Economic Conditions. Independence. Interviews. Muñoz Marín, Luis. Political issues. Social Conditions. 1948-64. *1186*
—. Economic Conditions. Migration, internal. Models. 1935-40. *1092*
—. Economic Conditions. Politics. 1975. *1292*
—. Economic Conditions. Rural Settlements. Social Organization. Standard of living. 1960-72. *1080*
—. Economic Development. 1940-81. *1281*
—. Economic development. 1950-74. *1110*
—. Economic development. Imperialism. Political conditions. Social organization. 1900-72. *1131*
—. Economic development. Income. Unemployment. 1959-70. *1201*
—. Economic development. Industrialization. 1960's-70's. *1102*
—. Economic development. Political status. Population growth. 1940-76. *1303*
—. Economic development. Population. Unemployment. 1940's-70's. *1244*
—. Economic growth. Education. Income distribution. 1950-76. *1199*
—. Economic Integration. Industrialization. International Trade. 1948-63. *1302*
—. Economic opportunity. Immigration. 1947-73. *1202*
—. Economic Structure. Political status. 1949-72. *1200*
—. Economics. Investments. USA. 1970's. *1315*
—. Education. 1940-77. *1084*
—. Education. Immigration. Unemployment. 1955-70. *1298*
—. Elections. Funerals. Muñoz Marín, Luis. New Progressive Party. Popular Democratic Party. 1980. *1215*
—. Elections. Political Conventions. Rites and Ceremonies. 1968. *1257*
—. Ethnic Groups. Population. 1940-70. *1297*
—. Federal Policy. 1898-1979. *1180*
—. Federal Policy. Self-government. Truman, Harry S. 1945-47. *1086*
—. Fertility. Marriage. Modernization. 1950-70. *1063*
—. Fertility. Metropolitan areas. 1950-70. *1289*
—. Food shortages. Unemployment. World War II. 1940-45. *1146*
—. Food stamp program. Income redistribution. 1974-75. *1065*
—. Foreign Policy. Industry. 1982. *1124*
—. Foreign Policy. Political Participation. Self-government. 1900-33. *1115*
—. Foreign Policy. Political Systems. Public Opinion. 1970's. *1103*
—. Foreign relations. Latin America. West Indies. 1975. *1105*
—. Gutiérrez y Espinosa, Felipe. Musical Academy of Puerto Rico. 1871-1900. *1078*
—. *Henrietta* (plantation). Sugar plantation. 1827-1918. *1236*
—. Historiography. Marxism. 19c-20c. *1203*
—. Hostos, Eugenio María de. Independence Movements. ca 1860-1903. *1174*
—. Identity. Politics. Social Customs. 1898-1980. *1220*
—. Immigration. 1909-77. *1321*
—. Immigration. Population. 1800-30. *1208*
—. Imperialism. 20c. *1094*
—. Income distribution. Labor. 1949-69. *1064*
—. Independence. 1940-75. *1185*
—. Independence Movements. 1898-1979. *1324*
—. Independence Movements. 1960-76. *1095*
—. Industrialization. 1940-70. *1142*

—. Industrialization. Migration. Politics. Working class. 1870's-1970's. *1108*
—. Industrialization. Surplus value. 1948-63. *1312*
—. Inflation. 1945-80. *1067*
—. International law. UN. 1950-73. *1172*
—. Labor movement. Multinational corporations. Neocolonialism. Self-determination. 1950's-70's. *1098*
—. Land distribution. Unemployment. 1970's. *1194*
—. Language. 1975. *1319*
—. Mead, Margaret (interview). National Self-image. Social Customs. 1975. *1323*
—. Middle classes. Nationalism. 1920-70. *1147*
—. Migration. 1965-80. *1112*
—. Migration. Political economy. Social Classes. 1898-1970's. *1135*
—. Migration. Rural-Urban Studies. 1960-80. *1072*
—. Military. 1898-1979. *1221*
—. Missions and Missionaries. Presbyterian Church. 1899-1914. *1229*
—. Modernism. National consciousness. Periodicals. *Revista de las Antillas*. 1913-18. *1130*
—. Music. 1898-1910. *1141*
—. National Characteristics. 16c-1970's. *1206*
—. National development. 1830-1930's. *1256*
—. Novels. 20c. *1079*
—. Oil exploration. 1970's. *1291*
—. Plebiscites. Political status. Self-Determination. 1967. *1187*
—. Political repression. 1950's-79. *1158*
—. Political Systems. 1900-75. *1116*
—. Population control. Sterilization. Women. 1920-77. *1213*
—. Poverty. 1970-77. *1143*
—. Race Relations. 1973. *1132*
—. Religion in the Public Schools. 1898-1979. *1197*
—. Research (review article). 19c-20c. 1979-80. *1138*
—. Santos. Wood carving. 1750-1975. *1122*
—. Sex discrimination. Values. Women. 1974. *1149*
—. Social Classes. 1980. *1156*
—. Spiritism. 1898-1970. *1093*
—. Theater. 1492-1979. *1246*
—. Theater. 1900-30. *1227*
—. Theater. 1939-79. *1209*
—. Values. 1981. *1181*
—. Violence. 1940-73. *1286*
Puerto Rico (Ponce). Authors. Jiménez, Juan Ramón. Memoirs. Nobel Prize. Palau de Nemes, Graciela. Spain. 1930's-56. *1113*
Puerto Rico (review article). 19c-1979. *1259*
—. Americanization. Bhana, Surendra. Clark, Truman. Development. Matthews, Thomas. Politics. 1917-76. *1261*
—. Centro de Estudios Puertoriqueños (History Task Force). Economic relations. Levine, Barry B. Sariola, Sakari. 1898-1970's. *1184*
Puerto Rico (San Germán). Population. Slavery. 1872. *1304*
Puerto Rico (San Juan). Cubans. Florida (Miami). New York City. Social Classes. 1950-77. *1121*
—. Political Leadership. Rincón, Felisa. Women. 1934-80. *1235*
—. Tapia Theater. Theater. 16c-1969. *1069*
Puerto Rico, southwestern. Agricultural Production. Haciendas. Mills. Sugar. 1902. *1306*
—. Capital. Commodity exchange. Economic structure. Plantations. Sugar cane. 1911. *1305*
Puerto Rico, western. Modernization. Population. Rural areas. 1940-70's. *1225*

Punitive expeditions. Bandits. Big Bend region.
Langhorne, George T. Mexico (Coahuila).
Texas (Glenn Springs, Boquillas). 1915-16. *687*
—. El Paso-Juárez Conference. Foreign Relations.
Mexico. Villa, Pancho. 1916. *637*
"Push/pull" hypothesis. Agricultural Labor. Aliens,
Illegal. Economic opportunity. Immigration.
1948-72. *866*

Q

Quantitative Methods. California (Los Angeles).
Census. Education. Literacy. 1850. *596*
—. Census. Population. 1960-70. *56*
—. Colonies. Florida (St. Augustine). Migration.
Spain. 1600-1800. *186*
—. Historiography. Research. Southwest.
Prehistory-20c. *42*
Quota systems. Aliens, illegal. Bracero Program.
Immigration. Mexico. 1960's-70's. *1007*

R

Race. Bilingual education. Ethnicity. Government.
1974-81. *89*
—. Blacks. Employment. Population. Students.
Whites. Youth. 1967-83. *133*
—. California (Los Angeles County). Congressional
Districts (30th). Ethnicity. Political candidates.
Voting and Voting Behavior. 1982. *754*
—. Citizenship. Courts. Nationality. 1846-97. *570*
—. New York City. Spanish language. West
Indians. 1972. *1140*
Race Relations. Apodaca, Jerry. Democratic Party.
Elections (gubernatorial). New Mexico. 1974.
1032
—. Arizona. Gándara, Francisco. McFarland,
William. Violence. Whites. 1872-73. *578*
—. Assimilation. Bilingual education. Blacks.
California (San Jose). School integration.
1950-79. *768*
—. Blacks. Civil-Military Relations. Discrimination.
Texas (Rio Grande City). Violence. Whites.
1899-1900. *524*
—. Blacks. Dating. Whites. 1978-79. *884*
—. Blacks. Mexico. Press, black. 1890-1935. *681*
—. Borders. Frontier and Pioneer Life. Mexico.
Southwest (review article). Weber, David J.
1821-46. *251*
—. California (Los Angeles). McWilliams, Carey.
Personal narratives. 1940's-60's. *917*
—. Calleros, Cleofas. Federación de Sociedades
Latinos-Americanos. Maverick, Maury.
McCammont, T. J. Powell, Alex K. Texas (El
Paso). 1936. *627*
—. Carranza, Venustiano. Foreign Relations.
Mexico. Plan de San Diego. Texas, south.
1915-16. *638*
—. Cities. Neighborhoods. Western States. White
flight. 1960's. *71*
—. Independence Movements. Tejanos. Texas.
Whites. 1822-36. *145*
—. Mexico. Travel accounts. Western States.
1831-69. *571*
—. Political machines. Social Change. Texas
(Cameron County). Wells, James B. 1882-1920.
605
—. Public opinion. Whites. 1935-80. *50*
—. Puerto Rico. 1973. *1132*
—. Texas. 19c. *557*
Racial Distance Indices. Colleges and Universities.
Ethnicity. Students. Texas (south). 1973. *741*
Racism. Arizona. Copper industry. Labor Unions
and Organizations. Politics. Working Class.
1900-20. *611*

—. Arizona (Tucson). California (Los Angeles).
Economic conditions. Social Conditions. Texas
(San Antonio). 1850-1900. *528*
—. Authors. New Mexico. Stereotypes. 19c. *562*
—. California (Los Angeles). Education. 1920-32.
632
—. Capitalism. 1845-1977. *491*
—. Federal Policy. Immigration. Labor. 1920's.
672
—. Films. Stereotypes. 1897-1917. *652*
—. Minorities. Reporters and Reporting. 1968-83.
118
—. Poverty. Puerto Ricans. 1898-1974. *1183*
—. Sterilization. Women. 20c. *425*
Radicals and Radicalism. Gutiérrez, José Angel.
Political activism. Rhetoric. Self-Determination.
Texas (Crystal City). 1969-79. *868*
Radio. KCOR, station. Spanish language. Texas
(San Antonio). 1928-74. *485*
Raids. California (Los Angeles). Immigration and
Naturalization Service. Industrial Relations.
International Ladies' Garment Workers' Union.
Lilli Diamond Originals. 1976-77. *1027*
Railroads. Bracero Program. Documents.
Employment. 1945. *695*
Ranchers. Cattle Rustling. Comancheros. Hittson,
John. Indians. New Mexico. 1872-73. *551*
Ranches. California. Land tenure. Mexico.
1784-1846. *247*
—. Cattle Raising. Frontier and Pioneer Life.
Southwest. Spain. 18c-19c. *303*
—. Excavations. New Mexico (Rito Colorado
Valley). 1720-1846. *323*
—. Food Industry. New Mexico. Sheep Raising.
Textile Industry. 1846-61. *589*
Ranching. Architecture. Texas, southern. 1750-1900.
332
—. Arizona. Cattle raising. 1853-1910. *510*
Rancho Camulos. California. delValle family.
Upper Classes. 1839-1938. *442*
Range wars. Coronado, Francisco Vásquez de.
Explorers. Sheep Raising. Southwest.
1540-1880's. *171*
Raza Unida Party. Texas. 1972-73. *951*
Reading. Blacks. California (Los Angeles).
Language. Whites. 1970's. *879*
Reagan, Ronald. Aliens, illegal. Carter, Jimmy.
1977-81. *49*
—. Economic Conditions. Federal Policy. New
Federalism. Social Problems. 1980-83. *716*
—. Newspapers. Panama Canal. Political
Campaigns (presidential). Treaties. 1976-80. *976*
Rebellions. Blacks. Carranza, Venustiano. Indians.
Mexico. Texas. Villa, Francisco. 1848-1920. *577*
—. Borders. Mexico. Texas (Brownsville, Eagle
Pass area). 1850-1900. *521*
—. Florida. Spain. Trials. 1795-98. *296*
—. Franciscans. Indians. Indian-White Relations.
Leadership. New Mexico. Pueblo Indians.
1650-80. 1980. *398*
—. Plan de San Diego. Texas (San Antonio).
1914-17. *655*
Recessions. Spaniards. Unemployment. 1974-75. *74*
Recreation. California (San Francisco). Social
Change. 1846-69. *573*
Redondo, José María. Arizona. Business. California.
Territorial Government. 1849-78. *592*
Reenactments. Anza, Juan Bautista de. Bicentennial
Celebrations. California. Discovery and
Exploration. Mexico. 1775-76. 1975-76. *208*
Reform. California (East Los Angeles). Catholic
Church. Economic Conditions. Social
Conditions. United Neighborhoods
Organization. 1960's-80. *945*
Refugees. Acadians. Colonial Government. Letters.
Louisiana. Spain. Ulloa, Antonio de. 1766-68.
178

—. Airplanes. Cuba. Deportation. Hijacking. International law. 1983. *1191*
—. Arizona. Immigration. Mexican Revolution. 1910-11. *669*
—. Assimilation. Cubans. 1980-83. *1320*
—. Assimilation. Cubans. Research. 1959-83. *1268*
—. Attitudes. Cubans. 1980. *1190*
—. Attitudes. Cubans. Working Conditions. 1970-81. *1148*
—. California (San Francisco Bay area). Public Welfare. Resettlement. South Americans. 1973-79. *1169*
—. Cuba. Economic Conditions. Political Change. 1960-82. *1240*
—. Cuba (Mariel). 1959-81. *1317*
—. Cubans. Deportation. Mental Illness. 1980-83. *1162*
—. Cubans. Economic Conditions. Florida. Politics. 1980-81. *1076*
—. Cubans. Education. Occupations. Political Imprisonment. 1973-80. *1077*
—. Cubans. Employment. Social Problems. 1982. *1316*
—. Cubans. Foreign Relations. 1980-82. *1233*
—. Cubans. International Rescue Committee (Caribbean Relief Program). New Jersey. Settlement. 1959-83. *1145*
—. Cubans. Naturalization. Political Participation. Voting and Voting Behavior. 1959-84. *1249*
—. Federal Policy. Resettlement. 1960-82. *136*
—. Hispaniola. Louisiana (New Orleans). 1792-1804. *193*
Rehabilitation. California (Los Angeles County). Drug abuse. Law Enforcement. Statistics. 1969-79. *906*
Reisler, Mark. Camarillo, Albert. Cardoso, Lawrence A. Immigration. Mexican Americans (review article). ca 1848-1970. *112*
Reisler, Mark (review article). Immigration. Labor. 1900-40. 1976. *628*
Religion. Behavior. Generations. Texas (San Antonio). 1981-82. *909*
Religion in the Public Schools. Puerto Rico. 1898-1979. *1197*
Religiosity. California (Los Angeles). Catholic Church. Fertility. Women. 1973. *979*
Relocation, forced. Barrios. Family. Housing. -1973. *1006*
Removals, forced. Apache Indians. Indians. Mexico (Mexico City). Southwest. Spain. 1729-1809. *300*
Repatriation. Depressions. Discrimination. Indiana (Gary). Nativism. 1920's-30's. *609*
—. Depressions. Indiana (East Chicago). 1919-33. *684*
—. Depressions. Mexico. Migrant Labor. Obregón, Álvaro. 1920-23. *613*
—. Hoover, Herbert C. 1930's. *651*
—. Mexico. Migrant Labor. Workers, undocumented. 1929-56. *636*
—. Migration. Research. Taylor, Paul S. 1973. *858*
Reporters and Reporting. Cubans. Exiles. Latin America. Martí, José. New York City. 1880-95. *1068*
—. Deportation. Emigration. Newspapers. 1930-76. *420*
—. Minorities. Racism. 1968-83. *118*
—. Newspapers. 1970. *837*
Republican Army of the North. Gutierrez de Lara, José Bernardo Maxmilliano. Independence Movements. Magee, Augustus W. Mexico. Texas (San Antonio). 1811-15. *197*
Republican Party. House of Representatives. Marcantonio, Vito. New York. Puerto Ricans. 20c. *1196*
Research. Aliens, illegal. 1975-77. *751*
—. Aliens, illegal. Mexico. 1930-76. *422*
—. Assimilation. Cubans. Refugees. 1959-83. *1268*

—. Daily life. Florida (St. Augustine). Spain. 1580. 1970's. *239*
—. DelCastillo, Adelaida R. Enriquez, Evangelina. Melville, Margarita B. Mexican Americans. Mirande, Alfredo. Women (review article). 19c-20c. *135*
—. Family. ca 1970-75. *925*
—. Historiography. Mexican Americans. 19c-20c. *52*
—. Historiography. Quantitative methods. Southwest. Prehistory-20c. *42*
—. Interviews. Labor. *Mexican Labor in the United States* (study). National Endowment for the Humanities. Taylor, Paul S. 1927-30. *646*
—. Labor. *Mexican Labor in the United States* (study). Taylor, Paul S. 1926-34. *54*
—. Methodology. Social Sciences. Southern California, University of. 1972. *776*
—. Mexican Americans. Oral history. ca 1930-78. *68*
—. Migration. Repatriation. Taylor, Paul S. 1973. *858*
Research (review article). Puerto Rico. 19c-20c. 1979-80. *1138*
Resettlement. California (San Francisco Bay area). Public Welfare. Refugees. South Americans. 1973-79. *1169*
—. Federal Policy. Refugees. 1960-82. *136*
Residence, prior. Discrimination, Employment. Immigration. 1973-74. *856*
Residential patterns. Blacks. Florida (Miami). Neighborhoods. Population. Whites. 1970-80. *1309*
—. California (Los Angeles). Gangs. Youth. 1980-83. *931*
—. Cubans. Florida (Miami). Puerto Ricans. 1970's. *1060*
—. Ethnicity. Fertility. 1969. *801*
—. Illinois (Chicago). Puerto Ricans. Social conditions. 1920-70. *650*
Residential segregation. Assimilation. Blacks. Social Status. Whites. 1960-70. *70*
—. Cities. Cubans. Mexicans. Puerto Ricans. 1950's-70's. *69*
Restorations. California. Mission La Purísima Concepción. 1787-1973. *390*
Revenue sharing. Grants. Nixon, Richard M. Political Campaigns (presidential). 1960-72. *23*
Revista Catolica. Catholic Church. Jesuits. Southwest. 1875-1962. *501*
Revista de las Antillas. Modernism. National consciousness. Periodicals. Puerto Rico. 1913-18. *1130*
Revolution. Acculturation. Attitudes. Cuba. Cubans. 1958-82. *1074*
—. Editors and Editing. Press. Southwest. 1911-17. *634*
—. Houston, Sam. Mexico. Military. Texas. 1835-36. *237*
—. Madero, Francisco. Mexico. Reyes, Bernardo. Texas. 1910-12. *640*
—. Mexico. New Mexico. Salazar, Jose Ines. Texas. ca 1910-18. *689*
Revolutionary Movements. Andrade, Flores de. Immigration. Liberal Party. Mexico. Personal narratives. Texas (El Paso). 1890-1911. *621*
—. Carter, Jimmy. Cerro Maravilla scandal. Murder. Puerto Rico. Romero Barceló, Carlos. Statehood. 1978-80. *1288*
—. Conspiracy. Foreign Relations. Mexico. Reyes, Bernardo. State Politics. Texas. Trials. 1911-12. *639*
—. Cubans. Florida (Key West). Spain. 1878-86. *1251*
Reyes, Bernardo. Conspiracy. Foreign Relations. Mexico. Revolutionary Movements. State Politics. Texas. Trials. 1911-12. *639*

—. Madero, Francisco. Mexico. Revolution. Texas. 1910-12. *640*
Rhetoric. California. Chavez, Cesar. Political activism. Texas. Tijerina, Reies. 1960's-70's. *843*
—. Gutiérrez, José Angel. Political activism. Radicals and Radicalism. Self-Determination. Texas (Crystal City). 1969-79. *868*
—. Gutiérrez, José Angel. Political activism. Self-Determination. 1979. *867*
—. Poetry. 1969-79. *991*
Ribera Chevremont, Evaristo. Burgos, Julia de. Font Saldaña, Jorge. Lair, Clara. Personal Narratives. Poets. Puerto Rico. 20c. *1232*
Rincón, Felisa. Political Leadership. Puerto Rico (San Juan). Women. 1934-80. *1235*
Rio Grande. Commerce. Mexican War. Texas (El Paso). 1821-48. *361*
Rio Grande Annual Conference. Methodist Church. Southwest. 1874-1978. *457*
Rio Grande Valley. Cofradías (brotherhoods). New Mexico. Penitentes. ca 1770-1970. *404*
—. Folk songs. Texas. 1860-1982. *466*
—. Indians. Navajo Indians. New Mexico, northern. Pueblo Indians. Weaving. 15c-1979. *393*
—. New Mexico, northern. Weaving. 17c-20c. *352*
Rites and Ceremonies. Acculturation. California (Santa Clara County). Marriage. 1908-68. *421*
—. Anecdotes. Baca, Father. Easter Week. Frontier and Pioneer Life. New Mexico (Tome, Valencia). 1846. *209*
—. California (Los Angeles). Catholic Church. Christmas. Neighborhoods. Posadas (celebrations). 1975-80. *900*
—. Catholic Church. Fiestas. New Mexico. Saints, patron. Villages. 1970's. *1036*
—. Elections. Political Conventions. Puerto Rico. 1968. *1257*
—. Folklore. New Mexico. Penitentes. Social customs. 16c-20c. *472*
Rivera, Feliciano. Bibliographies (review article). Meier, Matt S. 1974. *487*
Rivera, Manuel. Anton Chico grant. Land grants. New Mexico Land and Livestock Company. Trials. 1822-1915. *334*
Rivera, Tomás. Daily Life. Hinojosa, Rolando. Literature. Social Customs. Southwest. 1980. *756*
Rivera, Tomás *(Y No Se Lo Tragó La Tierra)*. Acosta, Oscar Zeta *(Autobiography of a Brown Buffalo)*. Ethnicity. Novels. Villareal, José Antonia *(Pocho)*. 1970-79. *1054*
Roads. Mexico (Sonora). New Mexico (Santa Fe). Spain. Trade. 17c-1850's. *345*
Rock inscriptions. Discovery and Exploration. El Morro National Monument. New Mexico. Spain. Prehistory-1620. *167*
Rodriguez, Richard. Education. Personal narratives. 1950's-60's. *1053*
Roll-call voting. Congress. Political representation. 1972-80. *128*
Romero Barceló, Carlos. Art. Culture. Institute of Puerto Rican Culture. Muñoz Marín, Luis. Puerto Rico. 1948-55. *1277*
—. Carter, Jimmy. Cerro Maravilla scandal. Murder. Puerto Rico. Revolutionary Movements. Statehood. 1978-80. *1288*
Romero, Diego. Indian-White Relations. Inquisition. Marriage. New Mexico. Plains Apache Indians. 1660-78. *260*
Romero, José. Cahuilla Indians. California (Palm Springs region). Cocomaricopa Trail. Indians. Letters. Overland Journeys to the Pacific. ca 1823-24. *370*
Romo, Richard. California (East Los Angeles). Immigrants (review article). New York City. Sanchez Korrol, Virginia E. 20c. *137*

Roque Lovato Grant. Land grants. New Mexico. Ortiz y Alarid, Gasper. 1785-1894. *532*
Rugs. Blankets. Dye. Indians. Navajo Indians. New Mexico. Spaniards. Weaving. 19c-1977. *353*
Rural areas. Economic Conditions. Health services. Indians. Navajo Indians. New Mexico, northwestern. Population. Spaniards. 1971-78. *93*
—. Identity. Social conditions. Texas. Youth. 1976. *924*
—. Modernization. Population. Puerto Rico, western. 1940-70's. *1225*
Rural Settlements. Economic Conditions. Puerto Rico. Social Organization. Standard of living. 1960-72. *1080*
Rural-Urban Studies. Migration. Puerto Rico. 1960-80. *1072*

S

St. Augustine Restoration Foundation. Florida. Preservation. 1977. *281*
Saints, patron. Catholic Church. Fiestas. New Mexico. Rites and Ceremonies. Villages. 1970's. *1036*
Salazar, Jose Ines. Mexico. New Mexico. Revolution. Texas. ca 1910-18. *689*
Salazar, Pedro de. Discovery and Exploration. Georgia. North Carolina. Slave raids. South Carolina. Spain. 1514-16. *238*
Salinan Indians. Agricultural Technology and Research. Assimilation. Indians. Mission San Antonio de Padua. 1771-1832. 1976-79. *244*
Salsa. Blades, Rubén (interview). City life. Latin Americans. Music. Panama. 1974-84. *1088*
Salt. Indians. Mexico. New Mexico (Estancia Basin). Spain. Trade. Prehistory-1840's. *265*
San Antonio de las Huertas grant. Land grants. Mexico. New Mexico. Spain. 1765-1891. *348*
San Diego Presidio. California. Excavations. Missions and Missionaries. Presidios. Serra Museum. 1769-75. 1964-70's. *210*
San Diego State College. California. Colleges and Universities. Student activism. Women. 1968-76. *852*
San Diego State University. California. Cultural identity. Marxism. Political power. 1965-74. *992*
San Francisco (colony). Colonization. New Mexico (Rio Puerco). 1866. *558*
San Joaquín Grant. Commons. Land grants. Law. New Mexico. 1806-97. *531*
San Pasqual (battle). California. Kearny, Stephen Watts. Mexican War. 1846. *156*
—. California. Kearny, Stephen Watts. Mexican War. 1847. *253*
—. California. Mexican War. 1846-47. *252*
Sanchez, George I. Bilingual education. Segregation. Southwest. 1930-70. *987*
Sanchez Korrol, Virginia E. California (East Los Angeles). Immigrants (review article). New York City. Romo, Richard. 20c. *137*
Sanchez, Saul (review article). Anglo (character). Literature. Villains. 1970's. *953*
Santa Anna, Antonio Lopez de. Alamo (battle). DelaPeña, José Enrique. Personal Narratives. Texas. 1836. *195*
Santa Barbara Presidio, Chapel. California. Excavations. Majolica pottery sherds. Spain. 1782-1850. *153*
Santa Elena (colony). Florida. Land. Settlement. Spain. 1560-87. *280*
Santa Fe Trail. Landmarks. 1806-80. *392*
Santos. *See also* Statues.
—. Catholic Church. Folk art. New Mexico. 1780-1900. *395*

—. Folk art. Lopez, George. Lopez, José Dolores. New Mexico (Córdova). 20c. *412*
—. Folk art. New Mexico. 17c-19c. *15*
—. Puerto Rico. Wood carving. 1750-1975. *1122*
Sariola, Sakari. Centro de Estudios Puertoriqueños (History Task Force). Economic relations. Levine, Barry B. Puerto Rico (review article). 1898-1970's. *1184*
Saturday Evening Post. Immigration. Nativism. Periodicals. 1914-33. *662*
Scholarship. Mexican Americans. Politics. Social conditions. 1974. *82*
Scholasticism. Art. California. Catholic Church. Cultural myopia (Anglo-American). Missions and Missionaries. 1740's-1976. *307*
Scholes, France V. Historiography. Southwest. 16c-20c. *97*
School boards. Arizona. Elections. Voting and Voting Behavior. 1972-74. *817*
—. Political consciousness. Texas (Crystal City). 1970. *841*
School integration. American G.I. Forum. League of United Latin American Citizens. Mexican American Legal Defense and Education Fund. Pressure Groups. Texas. 1945-80. *981*
—. American G.I. Forum. Public schools. Texas. 1948-57. *701*
—. Assimilation. Bilingual education. Blacks. California (San Jose). Race Relations. 1950-79. *768*
—. Middle Classes. Public schools. Texas. 1929-57. *680*
Schroeder, John H. Antiwar sentiment. Expansionism. Mexican War (review article). Pletcher, David M. Polk, James K. 1830's-40's. *199*
Science. Ideology. Mexico. Philosophy. Positivism. Social control. 1850-1984. *477*
Scientific Expeditions. Canada. Pacific Coast. Spain. USA. 18c. *191*
Secularization. California. Durán, Narciso. Franciscans. Indians. Missions and Missionaries. 1826-46. *305*
—. Indians. Missions and Missionaries. New Mexico. Spain. 1767. *263*
Segregation. Bilingual education. Sanchez, George I. Southwest. 1930-70. *987*
—. Boycotts. Presbyterian Church. Public schools. Texas (San Angelo). 1910-15. *617*
—. California (Santa Ana). Public schools. 1913-48. *633*
—. Cubans. Florida (Miami). Housing. Middle Classes. 1950-74. *1310*
Segregation (*de jure, de facto*). California (Orange County). *Mendez v. Westminster* (California, 1946). Public schools. 1850-1970's. *690*
Segregation, residential. Assimilation. Models. New York City. Puerto Ricans. 1960-70. *1274*
Seguín, Juan Nepomuceno. Independence, War of. Mexico. Military Intelligence. Texas. 1830's-40's. *336*
Self-concept. Adolescence. Blacks. California (Los Angeles). Whites. 1971. *863*
Self-Determination. Gutiérrez, José Angel. Political activism. Radicals and Radicalism. Rhetoric. Texas (Crystal City). 1969-79. *868*
—. Gutiérrez, José Angel. Political activism. Rhetoric. 1979. *867*
—. Labor movement. Multinational corporations. Neocolonialism. Puerto Rico. 1950's-70's. *1098*
—. Plebiscites. Political status. Puerto Rico. 1967. *1187*
Self-government. Federal Policy. Puerto Rico. Truman, Harry S. 1945-47. *1086*
—. Foreign Policy. Political Participation. Puerto Rico. 1900-33. *1115*
Self-identity. Political consciousness. Students. Texas (Crystal City). 1973. *840*

Self-image. Bilingual education. Students. 1975-77. *944*
Self-perception. Educational achievement. -1973. *799*
—. Immigrants. Income. Men. Poverty. Working Class. 1978-79. *923*
—. Minorities in Politics. Public Schools. Texas (southern). 1930's-69. *489*
Sentencing. Blacks. California (Los Angeles County). Courts. Men. Whites. Women. 1977-80. *839*
—. Blacks. Crime and Criminals. Discrimination. Southwest. Whites. 1976-77. *859*
Sepúlveda, Juan Ginés de. Americas (North and South). Indians. Slavery. ca 1550. *216*
Sepúlveda y Ávila, María Ascensión. California (Los Angeles). Daily Life. Mott, Thomas. 1844-61. *600*
Serra, Junípero. California. Catholic Church. Mission San Juan Capistrano. 1775-76. *312*
—. California. Dominicans. Franciscans. Jesuits. Missions and Missionaries. 1768-76. *287*
—. California. Franciscans. Mission San Carlo Borromeo. 1784. *278*
Serra Museum. California. Excavations. Missions and Missionaries. Presidios. San Diego Presidio. 1769-75. 1964-70's. *210*
Serra Route. California (San Diego). Camino Real. Mexico (Loreto). Trails. 1762-1975. *188*
Settlement. American Revolution. Bouligny, Francisco. Letters. Louisiana. Spain. 1776-78. *200*
—. Americas (North and South). Discovery and Exploration. LasCasas, Bartolomé de. 16c-17c. *276*
—. Aristocracy. Colonial Government. New Mexico. New Spain. 16c. *182*
—. Arizona (Tucson Basin). Ceramics. Excavations. 1690's-1856. *157*
—. California. 1769-96. *339*
—. California. Colonial Government. Discovery and Exploration. Missions and Missionaries. Spain. 1691-1810. *262*
—. California. Discovery and Exploration. Vizcaíno, Sebastian. 1602-32. *154*
—. California. Immigration. Mexico. Mineral resources. 1683-1848. *231*
—. Colonization. Indians. New Spain. Policymaking. Spain. 1750-1800. *149*
—. Cubans. International Rescue Committee (Caribbean Relief Program). New Jersey. Refugees. 1959-83. *1145*
—. Discovery and Exploration. Myths and Symbols. Southwest. Spain. 16c-18c. *235*
—. Florida. Land. Santa Elena (colony). Spain. 1560-87. *280*
—. Foreign Relations. Spain. Texas. Westward Movement. ca 1796-1819. *291*
—. Frontier and Pioneer Life. New Mexico. 17c-1810. *344*
—. Indian-White Relations. Land Tenure. New Mexico (El Rancho, Vadito). Pueblo Indians. 17c-1970. *418*
—. New Mexico. Social Organization. Spain. 1790-1810. *256*
Sex. English language. Family. Spanish language. 1970's. *697*
—. Folklore. Humor. Jokes. Women. 1970's. *761*
Sex Discrimination. Imperialism. Mexico. Migration. Southwest. Women. Working class. 1850-1982. *428*
—. Puerto Rico. Values. Women. 1974. *1149*
—. Southwest. Student movements. Women. 1960-72. *895*
Sex roles. Attitudes. Employment. Whites. Women. Youth. 1979. *88*
—. Attitudes. Mothers. New Mexico (Albuquerque). Women. 1960-83. *1050*

—. Blacks. Employment. Family. Income. Whites. 1982-83. *47*
—. Discrimination. Political familialism. 1970-75. *719*
Sheep Raising. Coronado, Francisco Vásquez de. Explorers. Range wars. Southwest. 1540-1880's. *171*
—. Food Industry. New Mexico. Ranches. Textile Industry. 1846-61. *589*
—. Indians. New Mexico. Weaving. Woolen Industry. 1540's-1860's. *166*
Sheep Shearers' Union. Strikes. Texas (west). 1934. *653*
Sheepherders. Cháves, Jesús (family). Daily life. New Mexico, eastern. 1850's-1930's. *462*
—. Daily life. New Mexico (Valles Caldera). ca 1875-1941. *582*
Shipbuilding. Cabrillo, Juan Rodríguez. California. Discovery and Exploration. 1532-42. *259*
Silva, Vicente. Lopez, Lorenzo. New Mexico (Las Vegas). Outlaws. Poets. 1875-94. *561*
Silver. Arizona. New Spain (Sonora; Real de Arizonac). 1736. *236*
Slave raids. Discovery and Exploration. Georgia. North Carolina. Salazar, Pedro de. South Carolina. Spain. 1514-16. *238*
Slavery. Americas (North and South). Indians. Sepúlveda, Juan Ginés de. Spain. ca 1550. *216*
—. Population. Puerto Rico (San Germán). 1872. *1304*
Slaves. Names (personal). Texas (Young County). 1856-65. *555*
"Sleepy Lagoon" trial. California (Los Angeles). Citizens Committee for the Defense of Mexican-American Youth. Trials. 1942-44. *616*
Smallpox. California (Monterey). Estrada, José. Europe. Jenner, Edward. Vaccination. 18c-1821. *301*
Smith, Joseph. Daily Life. Indians. Letters. Lummis, Charles. Southwest. 1880's-1924. *544*
Smithers, W. D. Daily Life. Photography, Journalistic. Texas. 1910-36's. *471*
Social Change. Agricultural Labor. Migration, Internal. New Mexico (North Central). 1930-50. *888*
—. Americanization. California (Santa Barbara). Urbanization. 1850-70's. *599*
—. Ballads. "Corrido de Gregorio Cortez" (ballad). "Discriminación a un Martir" (ballad). Political Protest. Texas (Three River). 20c. *468*
—. Blacks. Ethnic Groups. New York City. 1960's-70's. *1230*
—. California (East Los Angeles). Ethnic Groups. Political protest. 1968-74. *934*
—. California (East San Jose; Mayfair district). 1777-1975. *481*
—. California (Los Angeles). Family. Modernization. 1850-80. *538*
—. California (San Diego County). Californians, native. 1846-56. *546*
—. California (San Francisco). Recreation. 1846-69. *573*
—. Catholic Church. 1960's-82. *33*
—. Class consciousness. Ideology. Texas (San Antonio). 1930-40. *630*
—. Demography. Ecology. Economic Conditions. New Mexico (north central). 1770-1970. *502*
—. English language. 1976. *39*
—. Identity. Jokes. Texas. Whites. 1970's. *890*
—. Marriage (mixed). Texas (Pecos County). Whites. 1880-1978. *419*
—. Migration, Internal. New Mexico (El Cerrito). Values. 1939-56. *893*
—. Political machines. Race Relations. Texas (Cameron County). Wells, James B. 1882-1920. *605*
—. Political Protest. Women. 1973-76. *709*

Social Change (review article). California. Camarillo, Albert. Cities. Garcia, Mario T. Griswold del Castillo, Richard. Texas. 1848-1982. *508*
Social Classes. Blacks. Economic status. Ethnicity. Stress. Whites. 1974. *708*
—. Blacks. Metropolitan areas. Southwest. Whites. 1970. *790*
—. Californios. Virtue. Women. 1830-46. *268*
—. "Chicano" (term). 1911-78. *500*
—. Cubans. Exiles. 1959-74. *1248*
—. Cubans. Florida (Miami). New York City. Puerto Rico (San Juan). 1950-77. *1121*
—. Economic Conditions. Federal Aid to Education. Neocolonialism. Puerto Rico. 1970's. *1245*
—. Economic Conditions. Government. Puerto Rico. 1930-50. *1085*
—. Ethnicity. Men. Women. 1979. *1016*
—. Ethnicity. New Mexico. Teachers. Women. 1900-50. *649*
—. Family. Immigration. Occupations. Women. 20c. *2*
—. Historiography. Mexican Americans. Women. 17c-20c. *4*
—. Infants. Mortality. Prenatal care. Southwest. 1970. *793*
—. Marxism. 1900-30. *607*
—. Migration. Political economy. Puerto Rico. 1898-1970's. *1135*
—. Puerto Rico. 1980. *1156*
Social Conditions. Agriculture. Documents. Economic Conditions. Migrant Labor. Working conditions. 1942-45. *694*
—. Arizona (Tucson). California (Los Angeles). Economic conditions. Racism. Texas (San Antonio). 1850-1900. *528*
—. Art. California (East Los Angeles). Murals. 1970-75. *872*
—. Attitudes. Barrios. California, southern. Civil Rights. Police. 1975. *927*
—. Authors. New Mexico. Nichols, John. Spaniards. 1841-1979. *499*
—. Bibliographies. Educational policy. Energy crisis. Foreign Relations. Middle East. National Autonomous University of Mexico (Faculty of Political and Social Sciences). Periodicals. 1970-81. *7*
—. Bilingualism. Linguistics. 1970-78. *942*
—. Borderlands (review article). Mexican Americans. Mexico. ca 1600-1981. *41*
—. Borders. Cities. Daily Life. Poverty. 1945-77. *911*
—. California (East Los Angeles). Catholic Church. Economic Conditions. Reform. United Neighborhoods Organization. 1960's-80. *945*
—. Cubans. Mexicans. Migration, internal. North Central States. Puerto Ricans. Southwest. 1970. *32*
—. Drug abuse. Economic Conditions. Immigration. Inhalants. Youth. 1930-80. *429*
—. Economic Conditions. Independence. Interviews. Muñoz Marín, Luis. Political issues. Puerto Rico. 1948-64. *1186*
—. Employment. Illinois (Chicago Heights). Politics. 1910-76. *436*
—. Ethnicity. Popular culture. *Teatro Chicano*. Theater. 1965-79. *874*
—. Identity. Rural areas. Texas. Youth. 1976. *924*
—. Illinois (Chicago). Immigration. 1910's-20's. *678*
—. Illinois (Chicago). Puerto Ricans. Residential patterns. 1920-70. *650*
—. Immigration. Indiana (East Chicago; Indiana Harbor). Inland Steel Company. Michigan, Lake. 1919-32. *615*
—. Immigration. Migrant Labor. North Central States. 1919-76. *415*

—. Massachusetts (New Bedford). Personal Narratives. Puerto Ricans. 1930-82. *1216*
—. Mexican Americans. Politics. Scholarship. 1974. *82*
—. Migration. Texas, south. Whites. 1850-1900. *527*
—. Oregon. Washington. 1970-80. *1000*
—. Poetry. Political Protest. 1970's. *950*
Social consciousness. Theater, guerrilla. 1965-76. *788*
Social control. Economic Conditions. Immigration. Labor. Mexico. 1950's-70's. *865*
—. Ideology. Mexico. Philosophy. Positivism. Science. 1850-1984. *477*
—. Indians. Military. Pueblo Indians. Spain. 1763-1821. *255*
Social Customs. Acculturation. Cubans. Drug abuse. Immigration. Values. Youth. 1950-80. *1237*
—. Arizona (Tucson). California (Los Angeles). Occupations. Property. 1775-1880. *543*
—. Assimilation. Literature. Villareal, José Antonio (Pocho). 1959-76. *743*
—. Assimilation. New Mexico. Villages. 1960's-79. *962*
—. Borderlands. Southeastern States. Southwest. Spain. 1565-1976. *394*
—. California. Christmas. Spanish settlers. ca 1840-61. *293*
—. California. Daily Life. Diaries. Mexican War. Mormon Battalion. 1846-55. *601*
—. California. Dance. 1820's-50's. *341*
—. California (East Los Angeles). Leisure. Low-riders (automobiles). Youth. 1970's. *861*
—. California (Los Angeles, Santa Barbara). Catholic Church. Marriage. Mission Santa Barbara. 1786-1848. *298*
—. Californios. ca 1826-46. *183*
—. Catholic Church. Ethnic Groups. Machismo (concept). Mexican Americans. Women. 1970's. *967*
—. Catholic Church. Folk medicine. New Mexico (Guadalupita). Torres, Luisa. 1910's-70's. *497*
—. Catholic Church. Jaramillo, Cleofas M. Marriage. New Mexico, northern. 1880-98. *547*
—. Catholic Church. New Mexico. Penitentes. Villages. 19c-1978. *445*
—. Cuba. Florida (Dade County; Miami). Immigration. International Trade. Latin America. 1970's. *1314*
—. Cubans. Florida (Miami; Little Havana). 1959-80's. *1100*
—. Daily Life. Hinojosa, Rolando. Literature. Rivera, Tomás. Southwest. 1980. *756*
—. Discrimination. Humor. 1966-75. *891*
—. Florida (St. Augustine). Great Britain. Indians. Spain. 1700-83. *211*
—. Folklore. New Mexico. Penitentes. Rites and Ceremonies. 16c-20c. *472*
—. Food Industry. Values. Women. 1980. *784*
—. Frontier and Pioneer Life. Southwest. Spaniards. 18c. *254*
—. Identity. Politics. Puerto Rico. 1898-1980. *1220*
—. Latin America. Nationalism. Political Attitudes. 1848-1976. *480*
—. Mead, Margaret (interview). National Self-image. Puerto Rico. 1975. *1323*
—. New Mexico. 1850-1900. *506*
Social Customs (review article). Discovery and Exploration. Ethnicity. National Characteristics. Urbansk, Edmund S. 17c-18c. *331*
Social history. Historiography. Southwest. 20c. *470*
Social Mobility. Assimilation. 1945-80. *946*
—. Blacks. Farms. Jamaicans. Migrant Labor. New York. 1960's-70's. *1152*
—. Daily Life. Labor. New Mexico (Albuquerque). Trade. 1706-90. *330*

—. Education. Income. Indiana (South Bend). Population. 1970-74. *798*
—. Fertility. Integration. 1969. *907*
—. Generations. Occupational Mobility. 1979. *1003*
—. Labor. Workers, Undocumented. 1970-80. *720*
Social Organization. Acculturation. Family. Mental illness. New York City. Puerto Ricans. 1950's-70's. *1271*
—. Agriculture. Economic Conditions. Puerto Rico. 1870-1930. *1083*
—. Anthropology. Ecology. Methodology. New Mexico (northern). Trade. 17c-20c. *63*
—. Blacks. City Life. Economic Conditions. 1960-71. *994*
—. Civil-military relations. Daily life. Florida (St. Augustine). Spain. 1580. *279*
—. Colonization. Indians. Land tenure. New Mexico. Spain. 1546-1692. *313*
—. Country Life. Economic Conditions. Family. Occupations. Washington (Yakima Valley). 1971. *827*
—. Cult practices. Psychotherapeutic processes. Puerto Rico. 1975. *1189*
—. Culture. National Characteristics. Puerto Rico. 1930's-70's. *1258*
—. Czech Americans. Family. Labor. Land. Texas (Nueces County). 1880-1930. *608*
—. Economic Conditions. 1971-81. *932*
—. Economic Conditions. Land tenure. New Mexico. Spaniards. Whites. 1846-91. *594*
—. Economic Conditions. Puerto Rico. Rural Settlements. Standard of living. 1960-72. *1080*
—. Economic development. Imperialism. Political conditions. Puerto Rico. 1900-72. *1131*
—. Emigration. Family. Puerto Ricans. 1970-82. *1071*
—. Ethnic Groups. New Mexico. Occupations. Population. 1790. *363*
—. Ethnicity. Family. Whites. 1983. *875*
—. Ethnicity. Health. ca 1979. *706*
—. Latin America. New Mexico, northern. Spain. Villages. 16c-20c. *377*
—. New Mexico. Settlement. Spain. 1790-1810. *256*
—. New Mexico, northern. Villages. 16c-1978. *490*
Social Organizations. Civil Rights. Labor Unions and Organizations. North Central States. 1900-76. *467*
—. Colombians. Dominicans. New York City. ca 1972-76. *1282*
—. Nebraska (Omaha). 1956-77. *770*
Social Policy. Aged. California. Whites. 1978-82. *850*
—. Ethnicity. New York City. Politicization. Puerto Ricans. 1955-75. *1175*
—. Immigration (illegal). Marxism. 1976. *749*
Social Problems. Albuquerque, Duke of (Francisco Fernández de la Cueva Henríquez). Colonial Government. Mexico. New Mexico. Politics. 1702-11. *318*
—. Cities. Public policy. 1960's-83. *130*
—. Cubans. Employment. Refugees. 1982. *1316*
—. Demography. Migration. Puerto Rico. 1960-75. *1176*
—. Economic Conditions. Federal Policy. New Federalism. Reagan, Ronald. 1980-83. *716*
—. Education. Migrant labor. 1973. *905*
—. Immigration. Mental illness. Puerto Ricans. 1493-1978. *1062*
Social programs. Political attitudes. 1980-81. *34*
Social Psychology. Aliens, illegal. Attitudes. 1984. *722*
Social Reform. 1974. *903*
—. Ethnicity. 1960-80. *885*
—. Power. 1974. *969*
Social sciences. Bibliographies. Mexican Americans. 20c. *101*
—. Family. Methodology. Mexican Americans. 1970's. *134*

—. Geopolitics. North Central States. 1970-76. *755*
—. Methodology. Research. Southern California, University of. 1972. *776*
Social services. Employment. Workers, undocumented. 1975-79. *988*
Social Status. 19c-1973. *403*
—. Acculturation. Pocho (term). Southwest. 1910's-40's. *657*
—. Age. Economic conditions. Fertility. Puerto Rico. Women. 1970. *1182*
—. Assimilation. Blacks. Residential segregation. Whites. 1960-70. *70*
—. Assimilation. Family. Geographic mobility. Immigrants. 1890-1977. *1015*
—. Assimilation. Fertility. Puerto Ricans. 1969-77. *1120*
—. Blacks. Chinese Americans. Economic Conditions. Filipinos. Japanese. 1960-76. *51*
—. Blacks. England (London). Immigration. New York City. West Indians. 20c. *1153*
—. Discrimination. 1845-1980. *495*
—. Education. Language. Men. 1975-76. *119*
—. Job satisfaction. 1970's. *849*
—. Law. New Mexico. Women. 1821-46. *272*
—. Spanish language. Texas (El Paso). 1975. *929*
—. Texas. -1973. *916*
—. Texas (Lubbock). Values. 1974. *763*
Social Work. Family. Poor. -1973. *960*
Socialism. Labor Unions and Organizations. Texas. 1900-20. *692*
Socialist Party. Capitalism. Plantations. Puerto Rico. Sugar. Working Class. 19c-1976. *1255*
Socialization. Assimilation. Middle Classes. Texas. 1976. *1013*
—. Judges. Lawyers. Southwest. 1945-74. *947*
Sociology. 1981-82. *928*
—. Anthropology. Borderlands studies. Mexico. Southwest. 20c. *114*
Soldiers. California. 1769-1821. *267*
South. Labor. Mines. Southwest. 1513-1846. *232*
South Americans. California (San Francisco Bay area). Public Welfare. Refugees. Resettlement. 1973-79. *1169*
South Carolina. California (San Diego area). Discovery and Exploration. Indians. Portolá, Gaspar de. 1769. *175*
—. Discovery and Exploration. Georgia. North Carolina. Salazar, Pedro de. Slave raids. Spain. 1514-16. *238*
South Central and Gulf States. Blacks. Discovery and Exploration. Esteban. Florida. Spain. 1528-39. *302*
Southeastern States. Borderlands. Social customs. Southwest. Spain. 1565-1976. *394*
—. Colonization. Discovery and Exploration. Great Britain. Indian-White Relations. Spain. 1565-1685. *319*
Southern California, University of. Methodology. Research. Social Sciences. 1972. *776*
Southwest. Acculturation. Pocho (term). Social Status. 1910's-40's. *657*
—. Agricultural Labor. 1971-81. *862*
—. Agricultural labor. Bracero Program. Employment. Wages. 1954-77. *869*
—. Alienation. 20c. *476*
—. Anthropology. Borderlands studies. Mexico. Sociology. 20c. *114*
—. Apache Indians. Indians. Mexico (Mexico City). Removals, forced. Spain. 1729-1809. *300*
—. Arizona State Museum. Documentary Relations of the Southwest project. Indians. Mexico, northern. Spain. 16c-1810. 1975-78. *322*
—. Art. Bibliographies. Civil Rights. Literature. Mexican Americans. 1936-73. *96*
—. Bibliographies. Mexico. 1821-45. *126*
—. Bilingual Education. 1976. *984*
—. Bilingual education. Sanchez, George I. Segregation. 1930-70. *987*

—. Blacks. Crime and Criminals. Discrimination. Sentencing. Whites. 1976-77. *859*
—. Blacks. Employment. Whites. Women. 1950-70. *771*
—. Blacks. Metropolitan areas. Social Classes. Whites. 1970. *790*
—. Borderlands. Social customs. Southeastern States. Spain. 1565-1976. *394*
—. Borderlands (review article). Jones, Oakah L., Jr. McDermott, John Francis. Mississippi Valley. Spain. Weddle, Robert S. 1762-1804. 1973-74. *379*
—. Borderlands studies. Economic Conditions. Mexico. 1970's. *116*
—. Borderlands studies. Mexico. 1952-75. *113*
—. Borders. Foreign Relations (review article). Historiography. Mexico. 20c. *61*
—. California. Franciscans. Mexico. Missions and Missionaries. Wheat growing. 1730's-70's. *335*
—. Catholic Church. Clergy. 1821-46. *384*
—. Catholic Church. Frontier and Pioneer Life. Missions and Missionaries. Spain. 16c-18c. *164*
—. Catholic Church. Jesuits. *Revista Catolica.* 1875-1962. *501*
—. Catholic Church. Mexico (Nuevo León). Missions and Missionaries. Verger y Suau, Rafael José. 1767-80's. *358*
—. Cattle Raising. Frontier and Pioneer Life. Ranches. Spain. 18c-19c. *303*
—. Census. Methodology. Population. 1848-1900. *559*
—. Colonization. DeZorita, Alonso. Franciscans. Indians. Missions and Missionaries. 1545-85. *378*
—. Coronado expedition. Diaries. Explorers. Spain. 1540-42. *355*
—. Coronado, Francisco Vásquez de. Discovery and Exploration. 1540-42. *349*
—. Coronado, Francisco Vásquez de. Explorers. Range wars. Sheep Raising. 1540-1880's. *171*
—. Crusade for Justice. Gonzales, Rodolfo "Corky". 1966-72. *908*
—. Cubans. Mexicans. Migration, internal. North Central States. Puerto Ricans. Social Conditions. 1970. *32*
—. Culture. 1900. 1980. *507*
—. Daily Life. Hinojosa, Rolando. Literature. Rivera, Tomás. Social Customs. 1980. *756*
—. Daily Life. Indians. Letters. Lummis, Charles. Smith, Joseph. 1880's-1924. *544*
—. Defense Policy. Indian Wars. Mexico, northern. Spain. 1759-88. *304*
—. Dialects. Spanish language. 1976. *899*
—. Discovery and Exploration. 1776. *360*
—. Discovery and Exploration. Jesuits. Kino, Eusebio Francisco. 1645-1711. *258*
—. Discovery and Exploration. Myths and Symbols. Settlement. Spain. 16c-18c. *235*
—. Economic Conditions. Identity. 1900. *567*
—. Economic Conditions. Politics. Workers, undocumented. 1975-78. *740*
—. Economic Development. Working class. 1603-1900. *438*
—. Editors and Editing. Press. Revolution. 1911-17. *634*
—. Education. Labor. Political power. 1848-1980. *635*
—. English language. Illinois (Chicago). Spanish language. 1979. *710*
—. Fertility. 1970. *886*
—. Folk Medicine. Lead poisoning. 1983. *1018*
—. Frontier and Pioneer Life. Social Customs. Spaniards. 18c. *254*
—. Historiography. Mexico. 1821-54. *125*
—. Historiography. Quantitative methods. Research. Prehistory-20c. *42*
—. Historiography. Scholes, France V. 16c-20c. *97*
—. Historiography. Social history. 20c. *470*

—. Horses. Museum of New Mexico (Fred Harvey Collection). Museums. Stable gear. 18c-20c. *1*

—. Identity. 1598-1970's. *461*

—. Immigration. Income. Labor. Workers, undocumented. 1960-80. *828*

—. Immigration (illegal). Labor. Texas. 1821-1975. *493*

—. Imperialism. Mexico. Migration. Sex Discrimination. Women. Working class. 1850-1982. *428*

—. Indian Wars. Missions and Missionaries. Pueblo Indians. Spain. 1680. *314*

—. Indian Wars. Presidios. Spain. 17c-18c. *212*

—. Indians. Land. New Spain. Water rights. 1535-1810. *359*

—. Indian-White Relations. Mesoamerican Indians. Pueblo Indians. Spain. 1530-98. *329*

—. Indian-White Relations. Missions and Missionaries. Pueblo Revolt (1680). Spain. 1590-1680. *165*

—. Indian-White Relations. Pioneers. Pueblo Indians. Spaniards. 1492-1974. *55*

—. Infants. Mortality. Prenatal care. Social Classes. 1970. *793*

—. Intermarriage. 20c. *935*

—. Job satisfaction. Men. 1980. *848*

—. Judges. Lawyers. Socialization. 1945-74. *947*

—. Labor. 1896-1915. *522*

—. Labor. Mines. South. 1513-1846. *232*

—. Lancastrian system. Mexico, northern. Public Schools. 1821-48. *373*

—. Map Drawing. 16c-1980. *26*

—. Methodist Church. Rio Grande Annual Conference. 1874-1978. *457*

—. Mexico. Migration. Missions and Missionaries. 1867-1930. *416*

—. Poverty. 1970-73. *970*

—. Presbyterian Church. 1830-1977. *410*

—. Public Employees. 1973-78. *1040*

—. Sex Discrimination. Student movements. Women. 1960-72. *895*

—. Spain. 1540-1821. *385*

—. Stereotypes. Westward Movement. Women. 1846-1900. *565*

—. Stereotypes. Whites. 19c. *595*

Southwest (review article). Borders. Frontier and Pioneer Life. Mexico. Race Relations. Weber, David J. 1821-46. *251*

Sowell, Thomas. Ethnic Groups (review article). Puerto Ricans. 1898-1983. *1267*

Spain. Acadians. Colonial Government. Letters. Louisiana. Refugees. Ulloa, Antonio de. 1766-68. *178*

—. Acosta Rodríquez, Antonio. Census. Colonial Government. Historiography. Louisiana. 1763-1803. 1976-80. *242*

—. Agricultural Labor. Indians. Population. Texas (El Paso). 1680-1784. *362*

—. Alabama. Boucfouca, Treaty of. Choctaw Indians. Indian-White Relations. Villebeuvre, Juan de la. 1793. *243*

—. American Revolution. Bouligny, Francisco. Letters. Louisiana. Settlement. 1776-78. *200*

—. Americas (North and South). Colonization. Discovery and exploration. Vega, Lope de *(San Diego de Alcalá).* 17c-18c. *342*

—. Americas (North and South). Indians. Sepúlveda, Juan Ginés de. Slavery. ca 1550. *216*

—. Anza, Juan Bautista de. Colonial Government. Concha, Fernando Simon Ignacio de la. Indians. Military Strategy. New Mexico. 1787-93. *161*

—. Apache Indians. Indians. Mexico (Mexico City). Removals, forced. Southwest. 1729-1809. *300*

—. Archives. Puerto Rico. 1500-1975. *110*

—. Arizona. Indians. Jesuits. Kino, Eusebio Francisco. Missions and Missionaries. 1680's-1711. *271*

—. Arizona (Canyon de Chelly). Bones. Dogs. Indian Wars. Navajo Indians. Pictographs. 1750-1863. *202*

—. Arizona, southern. Mission San Cayetano del Tumacacori. Mission San Xavier del Bac. 18c. 1979. *400*

—. Arizona State Museum. Documentary Relations of the Southwest project. Indians. Mexico, northern. Southwest. 16c-1810. 1975-78. *322*

—. Armies. California (Los Angeles, San Diego). Mexico. Presidios. 1770-94. *283*

—. Armies. Indians. 1561-1886. *204*

—. Assimilation. New Mexico. 16c-19c. 1970's. *150*

—. Authors. Jiménez, Juan Ramón. Memoirs. Nobel Prize. Palau de Nemes, Graciela. Puerto Rico (Ponce). 1930's-56. *1113*

—. Ayala, Juan Manuel de. California (San Francisco Bay). Discovery and Exploration. Franciscans. Indians. 1775. *369*

—. Balseiro, José Agustín. Florida (review article). Lyon, Eugene. Menéndez de Avilés, Pedro. 1513-1977. *184*

—. Bibliographies. Dialects. Espinosa, Aurelio M. Folklore. New Mexico, northern. 1907-54. *31*

—. Bibliographies. Texas. 16c-20c. *76*

—. Blacks. Discovery and Exploration. Esteban. Florida. South Central and Gulf States. 1528-39. *302*

—. Bolton, Herbert Eugene. Borderlands studies. Catholic Church. Colonization. Historiography. Missions and Missionaries. 1917-79. *9*

—. Borderlands. Colonies. Documents. Florida, University of, Gainesville. P. K. Yonge Library of Florida History (guide). ca 1518-1821. *77*

—. Borderlands. Social customs. Southeastern States. Southwest. 1565-1976. *394*

—. Borderlands (review article). Jones, Oakah L., Jr. McDermott, John Francis. Mississippi Valley. Southwest. Weddle, Robert S. 1762-1804. 1973-74. *379*

—. Borders. Compromise of 1850. Texas Panhandle. 1819-50. *148*

—. Bouligny, Francisco (report). Gálvez, Bernardo de. Immigration policy. Louisiana. Navarro, Martin *(Political Reflections).* 1776-83. *201*

—. *Britain* (vessel). Confiscations. Foreign Relations. Great Britain. Texas (Matagorda Peninsula). 1769-70. *168*

—. British Columbia. Columbia River. Discovery and Exploration. Heceta y Fontecha, Bruno de. Pacific Northwest. 1775. *159*

—. California. Church and State. Colonization. Indians. 1775-1800. *221*

—. California. Colonial Government. Discovery and Exploration. Missions and Missionaries. Settlement. 1691-1810. *262*

—. California. Colonial Government. Foreign Policy. War. 1779-1818. *270*

—. California. Colonization. Discovery and exploration. Mexico. 1602-1769. *190*

—. California. Colonization. Mexico. Population. 1760's-1840's. *222*

—. California. Excavations. Majolica pottery sherds. Santa Barbara Presidio, Chapel. 1782-1850. *153*

—. California. Indian-White Relations. 1770's. *295*

—. California (Monterey). Historical Sites and Parks. Landmarks. Mexico. 1770-1849. *173*

—. California (Monterey). Mexico. 1770-1849. *292*

—. California (San Diego). Colonial Government. Croix, Carlos Francisco de. Mexico. Mission San Diego de Alcalá. 1760's-86. *160*

—. California (San Diego). Colonization. Indians. Missions and Missionaries. 1769-1834. *399*

—. California (San Francisco). Commerce. 1755-1822. *227*

—. California (Villa de Branciforte). Colonization. 1790's-1907. *223*

—. California (Villa de Branciforte). Colonization. ca 1790-1821. *317*

—. Canada. Pacific Coast. Scientific Expeditions. USA. 18c. *191*

—. Castañeda, Carlos Eduardo. Colonization. Historiography. Texas. 1693-1731. 1933-43. *144*

—. Catholic Church. Colorado. New Mexico. Passion plays. 1830's-1978. *492*

—. Catholic Church. Frontier and Pioneer Life. Missions and Missionaries. Southwest. 16c-18c. *164*

—. Cattle Raising. Frontier and Pioneer Life. Ranches. Southwest. 18c-19c. *303*

—. Census. Florida (Pensacola). 1784-1820. *364*

—. Choctaw Indians. Indian-White Relations. Old Southwest. Treaties. Villebeuvre, Juan de la. 1784-97. *241*

—. Cigar industry. Cuba. Florida (Tampa). General strikes. 1901-11. *1253*

—. Civil-military relations. Daily life. Florida (St. Augustine). Social organization. 1580. *279*

—. Colonial Government. Concha, Fernando Simon Ignacio de la. Indian-White Relations. New Mexico. 1787-93. *155*

—. Colonial government. Cuervo y Valdes, Francisco. New Mexico (Albuquerque). 1706-12. *343*

—. Colonial Government. Documents. New Mexico. Vélez Cachupín, Thomas. ca 1754. *297*

—. Colonial Government. Frontier and Pioneer Life. Indian Wars. New Mexico. Pueblo Indians. Texas (El Paso). 1680-90. *219*

—. Colonial Government. Land grants. Mendinueta, Pedro Fermín de. New Mexico. 1767-79. *316*

—. Colonialism. Culture. Florida. Louisiana Territory. Texas. 1513-1803. *217*

—. Colonies. Florida (St. Augustine). Migration. Quantitative methods. 1600-1800. *186*

—. Colonization. Discovery and Exploration. Great Britain. Indian-White Relations. Southeastern States. 1565-1685. *319*

—. Colonization. Florida. Mexico (Yucatán). 16c. *397*

—. Colonization. Indians. Land tenure. New Mexico. Social Organization. 1546-1692. *313*

—. Colonization. Indians. New Spain. Policymaking. Settlement. 1750-1800. *149*

—. Colonization. Land tenure. New Mexico. Whites. 16c-1974. *29*

—. Colonization. Latin America. Law. New Mexico. 15c-18c. *340*

—. Commemorations. Explorers. Florida (St. Augustine). Menéndez de Avilés, Pedro. 1565. 1975. *310*

—. Coronado expedition. Diaries. Explorers. Southwest. 1540-42. *355*

—. Cubans. Florida (Key West). Revolutionary Movements. 1878-86. *1251*

—. Daily life. Florida (St. Augustine). Research. 1580. 1970's. *239*

—. Defense Policy. Indian Wars. Mexico, northern. Southwest. 1759-88. *304*

—. Diplomacy. Indians. Navajo Indians. New Mexico. 1770-90. *324*

—. Discovery and Exploration. El Morro National Monument. New Mexico. Rock inscriptions. Prehistory-1620. *167*

—. Discovery and Exploration. Georgia. North Carolina. Salazar, Pedro de. Slave raids. South Carolina. 1514-16. *238*

—. Discovery and Exploration. Myths and Symbols. Settlement. Southwest. 16c-18c. *235*

—. Five Civilized Tribes. Fur Trade. Gálvez, Bernardo de. Indians. Louisiana. Maxent, Gilberto Antonio de. 1749-84. *382*

—. Florida. Fort Matanzas. 1565-1821. *147*

—. Florida. Indian-White Relations. *Visitas* (provincial tours). 1602-75. *320*

—. Florida. Land. Santa Elena (colony). Settlement. 1560-87. *280*

—. Florida. Rebellions. Trials. 1795-98. *296*

—. Florida (Gainesville). P. K. Yonge Library of Florida History. Spanish Florida Borderlands Project. 1565-1821. 1977-78. *226*

—. Florida (St. Augustine). Great Britain. Indians. Social Customs. Trade. 1700-83. *211*

—. Foreign Relations. Settlement. Texas. Westward Movement. ca 1796-1819. *291*

—. Fort Bute. Fort St. Gabriel. Great Britain. Louisiana. Military Occupation. 1768. *177*

—. France. Louisiana. Medicine (practice of). Pharmacy. 1717-1852. *203*

—. Garita (fort). Military Camps and Forts. New Mexico (Santa Fe). 19c-1954. *206*

—. Immigration. 17c-1975. *102*

—. Indian Wars. Missions and Missionaries. Pueblo Indians. Southwest. 1680. *314*

—. Indian Wars. Navajo Indians. New Mexico. 1680-1720. *326*

—. Indian Wars. Presidios. Southwest. 17c-18c. *212*

—. Indians. Mexico. New Mexico (Estancia Basin). Salt. Trade. Prehistory-1840's. *265*

—. Indians. Military. Pueblo Indians. Social control. 1763-1821. *255*

—. Indians. Missions and Missionaries. New Mexico. Secularization. 1767. *263*

—. Indian-White Relations. Louisiana. Treaties. 1770-93. *264*

—. Indian-White Relations. Mesoamerican Indians. Pueblo Indians. Southwest. 1530-98. *329*

—. Indian-White Relations. Missions and Missionaries. Pueblo Revolt (1680). Southwest. 1590-1680. *165*

—. Indian-White Relations. Navajo Indians. New Mexico. Peace. 1720-79. *325*

—. Land grants. Mexico. New Mexico. San Antonio de las Huertas grant. 1765-1891. *348*

—. Latin America. New Mexico, northern. Social Organization. Villages. 16c-20c. *377*

—. Mexico (Sonora). New Mexico (Santa Fe). Roads. Trade. 17c-1850's. *345*

—. New Mexico. Settlement. Social Organization. 1790-1810. *256*

—. Southwest. 1540-1821. *385*

Spain (Seville). Archivo General de Indias. Colonial Government. Military Finance. New Mexico. Treasury. 1596-1683. *337*

Spaniards. Architecture. Housing. Indians. *Jacal* (style). New Mexico (Tierra Amarilla). Wood. 8c-20c. *366*

—. Authors. New Mexico. Nichols, John. Social Conditions. 1841-1979. *499*

—. Blankets. Dye. Indians. Navajo Indians. New Mexico. Rugs. Weaving. 19c-1977. *353*

—. City Politics. Illinois (Chicago). Political representation. Voting and Voting Behavior. 1975. *104*

—. Economic Conditions. Health services. Indians. Navajo Indians. New Mexico, northwestern. Population. Rural areas. 1971-78. *93*

—. Economic Conditions. Land tenure. New Mexico. Social Organization. Whites. 1846-91. *594*

—. Frontier and Pioneer Life. Social Customs. Southwest. 18c. *254*

—. Indian-White Relations. Pioneers. Pueblo Indians. Southwest. 1492-1974. *55*

—. Landownership. New Mexico (Rio Grande Valley). Pueblo Indian Grants, Northern. ca 1500's-1970's. *174*
—. Recessions. Unemployment. 1974-75. *74*
Spanish. Aqueducts. California Polytechnic State University, San Luis Obispo. Excavations. Mission San Antonio de Padua. 1776. 1979-81. *245*
Spanish Florida Borderlands Project. Florida (Gainesville). P. K. Yonge Library of Florida History. Spain. 1565-1821. 1977-78. *226*
Spanish language. *See also* Bilingualism.
—. Adolescence. Bilingualism. Border towns. California. English language. 1970-79. *698*
—. Attitudes. English language. Popular Culture. Theater. 1970's. *1022*
—. Bilingual education. New Mexico. 1968-78. *703*
—. Bilingualism. New Mexico. Newspapers. 1834-1917. *569*
—. California. 18c-1979. *484*
—. California (Los Angeles). 1960's-70's. *894*
—. California (Los Angeles; Hollywood). Films. 1930-39. *670*
—. Dialects. 1974. *1023*
—. Dialects. Southwest. 1976. *899*
—. English language. Family. Sex. 1970's. *697*
—. English language. Illinois (Chicago). Southwest. 1979. *710*
—. English language. Names (personal). Texas (El Paso). 1981. *769*
—. Folklore. Proverbs. 20c. *465*
—. Government. Minorities in Politics. Names (personal). 1973. *887*
—. Grammar. Linguistics. 1976. *983*
—. KCOR, station. Radio. Texas (San Antonio). 1928-74. *485*
—. Mass media. 17c-1977. *44*
—. New York City. Race. West Indians. 1972. *1140*
—. Public Welfare. 1972. *717*
—. Social status. Texas (El Paso). 1975. *929*
Spanish settlers. California. Christmas. Social Customs. ca 1840-61. *293*
Spanish-American Seminary. Adventists. Education. Missions and Missionaries. New Mexico (Sandoval). 1928-53. *679*
Spanish-American War. Attitudes. New Mexico. 1898-1900. *564*
Speculation. Land. New Mexico. Pino, Juan Estevan. 1820-30. *234*
Speech. Bilingualism. Children. Texas (Austin; East Austin). 1974-80. *915*
Spiritism. Puerto Rico. 1898-1970. *1093*
Stable gear. Horses. Museum of New Mexico (Fred Harvey Collection). Museums. Southwest. 18c-20c. *1*
Standard of living. Economic Conditions. Puerto Rico. Rural Settlements. Social Organization. 1960-72. *1080*
State government. Equal opportunity. New Mexico. Public Employees. Women. 1971-78. *819*
State Politics. California. Colorado. New Mexico. Political representation. ca 1850-1974. *464*
—. Conspiracy. Foreign Relations. Mexico. Revolutionary Movements. Reyes, Bernardo. Texas. Trials. 1911-12. *639*
—. Indians. New Mexico. Political Participation. 1846-1976. *28*
—. New Mexico. Political participation. Suffrage. Women. 1900-40. *648*
—. Political participation. Texas. -1973. *914*
Statehood. Carter, Jimmy. Cerro Maravilla scandal. Murder. Puerto Rico. Revolutionary Movements. Romero Barceló, Carlos. 1978-80. *1288*
Statistics. Aliens, illegal. Immigration. Mexico. 1978-79. *750*
—. Aliens, illegal. Labor. 1968-80. *107*

—. California (Los Angeles County). Drug abuse. Law Enforcement. Rehabilitation. 1969-79. *906*
—. Deportation. Workers, undocumented. 1972-77. *762*
Statues. Catholic Church. Isidore the Husbandman, Saint. Lopez, George. New Mexico (Córdova). Wood carving. ca 1070-1130. ca 1690-1980. *411*
—. Indian Wars. New Mexico. Our Lady of Macana (statue). 1598-1957. *179*
Steel workers. Discrimination. Labor Unions and Organizations. North Central States. 1919-45. *677*
Steinbeck, John. Authors. Daily Life. 20c. *463*
Stereotypes. Aliens (illegal). Economic Conditions. 1930-76. *452*
—. Authors. New Mexico. Racism. 19c. *562*
—. Behavior. Medical care. 1940's-70's. *797*
—. California. Literature. 1850-1900. *553*
—. Educational Tests and Measurements. 1920-76. *401*
—. Family. Models. 1968-74. *1012*
—. Films. 1915-78. *504*
—. Films. Literature. Mass Media. 20c. *446*
—. Films. Racism. 1897-1917. *652*
—. Films. Television. 1960's-70's. *702*
—. Health care. -1973. *1038*
—. Southwest. Westward Movement. Women. 1846-1900. *565*
—. Southwest. Whites. 19c. *595*
Sterilization. California (Los Angeles). Women. 1970-78. *1028*
—. Population control. Puerto Rico. Women. 1920-77. *1213*
—. Racism. Women. 20c. *425*
Steward, Julian H. *(People of Puerto Rico)*. Anthropology. Puerto Rico. 1956-77. *1223*
—. Anthropology, Cultural. Economic Conditions. Methodology. Puerto Rico. 1956-77. *1311*
—. Anthropology, Cultural. Economic Development. Methodology. Puerto Rico. 1956-77. *1272*
—. Anthropology, Cultural. Ideology. Methodology. Puerto Rico. 1956-77. *1144*
—. Anthropology, Cultural. Imperialism. Puerto Rico. 1956-77. *1299*
—. Anthropology, Cultural. Power structure. Puerto Rico. 1956-77. *1260*
Stress. Acculturation. Women. Workers, undocumented. 1977. *918*
—. Blacks. Economic status. Ethnicity. Social Classes. Whites. 1974. *708*
Strikes. *See also* General Strikes.
—. Agricultural Labor. Berry pickers. California (El Monte). Foreign Relations. Japan. Mexico. 1933. *645*
—. Agricultural Labor. California. Chavez, Cesar. United Farm Workers Union. 1965-70. *723*
—. Agricultural Labor. California (Oxnard). Japanese-Mexican Labor Association. Sugar beets. Wages. 1902-03. *602*
—. Amalgamated Clothing Workers Union of America. Farah Manufacturing Company. Garment industry. Texas (El Paso). 1972-74. *800*
—. Arizona (Clifton-Morenci area). Copper Mines and Mining. Mexico. Migrant Labor. 1872-1903. *572*
—. California (Los Angeles). Garment Industry. International Ladies' Garment Workers' Union. Women. 1933. *619*
—. Farah Manufacturing Company. Texas (El Paso). Women. 1972-74. *775*
—. Labor Unions and Organizations. Texas. 1920-40. *666*
—. Sheep Shearers' Union. Texas (west). 1934. *653*
Student activism. California. Colleges and Universities. La Raza Unida Party. 1969-73. *933*

—. California. Colleges and Universities. San Diego State College. Women. 1968-76. *852*

Student movements. Sex Discrimination. Southwest. Women. 1960-72. *895*

Students. Assimilation. Ethnicity. Institutions. Political activism. Texas (Corpus Christi, Crystal City). 1969-80. *753*

—. Attitudes. Community Schools. Ethnic identity. 1974. *855*

—. Bilingual education. Self-image. 1975-77. *944*

—. Blacks. Employment. Population. Race. Whites. Youth. 1967-83. *133*

—. California. Higher education. Texas. 1970's. *787*

—. Colleges and Universities. Ethnicity. Racial Distance Indices. Texas (south). 1973. *741*

—. High Schools. Militancy. -1973. *806*

—. Political consciousness. Self-identity. Texas (Crystal City). 1973. *840*

Suburban Life. New Mexico (Corrales). Whites. 1710-1970's. *417*

Suburbs. Barrios. New York (Long Island). Photographic essays. Puerto Ricans. 1981. *1275*

Success. Attitudes. Discrimination. Family. Personal narratives. Professions. Women. 1980. *997*

Suffrage. New Mexico. Political participation. State Politics. Women. 1900-40. *648*

Sugar. Agricultural Production. Haciendas. Mills. Puerto Rico, southwestern. 1902. *1306*

—. Capitalism. Plantations. Puerto Rico. Socialist Party. Working Class. 19c-1976. *1255*

Sugar beets. Agricultural Labor. California (Oxnard). Japanese-Mexican Labor Association. Strikes. Wages. 1902-03. *602*

Sugar cane. Capital. Commodity exchange. Economic structure. Plantations. Puerto Rico, southwestern. 1911. *1305*

Sugar plantation. *Henrietta* (plantation). Puerto Rico. 1827-1918. *1236*

Superstition. New Mexico (Torrance County). Witchcraft. 1970's. *780*

Supreme Court (decisions). Land grants. New Mexico. 1821-90. *579*

Surplus value. Industrialization. Puerto Rico. 1948-63. *1312*

Surveying. California. Land grants. O'Farrell, Jasper. 1844-46. *289*

Swindles. Federal government. Land grants. New Mexico (Las Trampas Grant). 1859-1914. *526*

T

Tapia Theater. Puerto Rico (San Juan). Theater. 16c-1969. *1069*

Taylor, Paul S. Agricultural Labor. California, University of, Berkeley. Economics. Newlands Act (US, 1902). 1895-1980. *494*

—. Interviews. Labor. *Mexican Labor in the United States* (study). National Endowment for the Humanities. Research. 1927-30. *646*

—. Labor. *Mexican Labor in the United States* (study). Research. 1926-34. *54*

—. Migration. Repatriation. Research. 1973. *858*

Teachers. Cuba. Exiles. Florida. 1959-70. *1254*

—. Ethnicity. New Mexico. Social Classes. Women. 1900-50. *649*

Teaching. Bilingual education. English language. Puerto Rico. 1978. *1234*

Teatro Chicano. Ethnicity. Popular culture. Social Conditions. Theater. 1965-79. *874*

Teatro Nacional de Aztlán. California (Santa Barbara). Theater. 1979. *836*

Tejanos. Independence Movements. Race Relations. Texas. Whites. 1822-36. *145*

Television. Attitudes. Blacks. Newspapers. Texas (Lubbock). 1976. *1010*

—. Films. Stereotypes. 1960's-70's. *702*

Television, public. Anthropology, applied. Arizona, southern. Project Fiesta. 1976. *794*

Ten Years' War. Cuba. Exiles. Florida (Key West). Human Relations. Independence Movements. 1868-78. *1252*

Territorial Government. Arizona. Business. California. Redondo, José María. 1849-78. *592*

—. Martínez, Antonio José (report). Mexico. New Mexico. 1830-32. *383*

Texan-Santa Fe Expedition. New Mexico. Trade. 1841. *290*

Texas. Age. Blacks. Discrimination. Income. 1960-70. *926*

—. Alamo (battle). DelaPeña, José Enrique. Personal Narratives. Santa Anna, Antonio Lopez de. 1836. *195*

—. Alamo (battle). Mexico. 1836. *306*

—. Alvarez, Manuel. Diplomacy. Mexico. New Mexico. Trading expeditions. 1841. *181*

—. American G.I. Forum. League of United Latin American Citizens. Mexican American Legal Defense and Education Fund. Pressure Groups. School integration. 1945-80. *981*

—. American G.I. Forum. Public schools. School Integration. 1948-57. *701*

—. Annexation. Diplomacy. Eve, Joseph. Flood, George H. LaBranche, Alcée. Letters. Murphy, William S. 1837-43. *162*

—. Armijo, Manuel. Mexico. New Mexico. Provincial Government. 1827-46. *371*

—. Arts. Performing arts. 19c. *576*

—. Assimilation. Jews. Mexico (Nuevo Reyno de León). 16c-20c. *483*

—. Assimilation. Middle Classes. Socialization. 1976. *1013*

—. Bibliographies. *Diario del Gobierno de la República Mexicana.* Periodicals. 1836-45. *75*

—. Bibliographies. Spain. 16c-20c. *76*

—. Blacks. Carranza, Venustiano. Indians. Mexico. Rebellions. Villa, Francisco. 1848-1920. *577*

—. Blacks. City Government. Employment. Urbanization. 1973. *842*

—. Blacks. Measurements. Mortality. Whites. 1980. *1008*

—. Borders. Folk Songs (review article). Mexico. Paredes, Americo. 16c-20c. *474*

—. Borders. Louisiana. Mexico. Puelles, José María de Jesús. 1512-1813. 1827-28. *230*

—. California. Camarillo, Albert. Cities. Garcia, Mario T. Griswold del Castillo, Richard. Social Change (review article). 1848-1982. *508*

—. California. Chavez, Cesar. Political activism. Rhetoric. Tijerina, Reies. 1960's-70's. *843*

—. California. Higher education. Students. 1970's. *787*

—. California, southern. Immigration. Mexico. "Operation Wetback". 1950-74. *977*

—. Castañeda, Carlos Eduardo. Colonization. Historiography. Spain. 1693-1731. 1933-43. *144*

—. Castañeda, Carlos Eduardo. Historians. 1896-1927. *604*

—. Children. English language. Grammar. 1976. *832*

—. Colonialism. Culture. Florida. Louisiana Territory. Spain. 1513-1803. *217*

—. Community control. Political Attitudes. 1971-77. *752*

—. Conspiracy. Foreign Relations. Mexico. Revolutionary Movements. Reyes, Bernardo. State Politics. Trials. 1911-12. *639*

—. Daily Life. Photography, Journalistic. Smithers, W. D. 1910-60's. *471*

—. Exiles. Liberal Party. Mexico. Propaganda. Women. 1898-1910. *691*

—. Folk songs. Rio Grande Valley. 1860-1982. *466*

—. Foreign Relations. Mexico. Migrant labor. 1942-47. *659*

—. Foreign Relations. Settlement. Spain. Westward Movement. ca 1796-1819. *291*
—. Garza, Catarino E. Mexico. Newspapers. 1880-95. *525*
—. Guadalupe Hidalgo, Treaty of. Land grants. Protocol of Querétaro. Trist, Nicholas P. 1847-48. *560*
—. Houston, Sam. Mexico. Military. Revolution. 1835-36. *237*
—. Identity. Jokes. Social Change. Whites. 1970's. *890*
—. Identity. Rural areas. Social conditions. Youth. 1976. *924*
—. Immigration (illegal). Labor. Southwest. 1821-1975. *493*
—. Independence Movements. Race Relations. Tejanos. Whites. 1822-36. *145*
—. Independence, War of. Mexico. Military Intelligence. Seguín, Juan Nepomuceno. 1830's-40's. *336*
—. Investments. Land. Mexia, José Antonio. Mexico. Politics. 1823-39. *248*
—. Irrigation. Martinez, Felix. New Mexico. Politics. 1877-1916. *598*
—. Labor. Mexico. Migration. 1960's-70's. *737*
—. Labor Unions and Organizations. Socialism. 1900-20. *692*
—. Labor Unions and Organizations. Strikes. 1920-40. *666*
—. Labor Unions and Organizations. United Cannery, Agricultural, Packing and Allied Workers of America. 1935-50. *668*
—. Madero, Francisco. Mexico. Revolution. Reyes, Bernardo. 1910-12. *640*
—. Mexico. New Mexico. Revolution. Salazar, Jose Ines. ca 1910-18. *689*
—. Middle classes. Political organizations. 1970's. *1014*
—. Middle Classes. Public schools. School Integration. 1929-57. *680*
—. Music. 1860's-1980. *473*
—. Political participation. State Politics. -1973. *914*
—. Population. 1887. *549*
—. Race Relations. 19c. *557*
—. Raza Unida Party. 1972-73. *951*
—. Social Status. -1973. *916*
Texas (Austin). Blacks. Voluntary associations. Whites. 1969-70. *1046*
—. Catholic Church. Folk art. Home altars. 1970's. *1019*
—. Mass media. Political Leadership. Whites. 1973. *877*
Texas (Austin; East Austin). Bilingualism. Children. Speech. 1974-80. *915*
Texas (Brownsville, Eagle Pass area). Borders. Mexico. Rebellions. 1850-1900. *521*
Texas (Cameron County). Political machines. Race Relations. Social Change. Wells, James B. 1882-1920. *605*
Texas (Corpus Christi, Crystal City). Assimilation. Ethnicity. Institutions. Political activism. Students. 1969-80. *753*
Texas (Crystal City). Community control. Elections. 1910-75. *922*
—. Gutiérrez, José Angel. Political activism. Radicals and Radicalism. Rhetoric. Self-Determination. 1969-79. *868*
—. Political consciousness. School boards. 1970. *841*
—. Political consciousness. Self-identity. Students. 1973. *840*
Texas (El Paso). Acculturation. Children. Political integration. 1978. *881*
—. Agricultural Labor. Indians. Population. Spain. 1680-1784. *362*
—. Amalgamated Clothing Workers Union of America. Farah Manufacturing Company. Garment industry. Strikes. 1972-74. *800*

—. Andrade, Flores de. Immigration. Liberal Party. Mexico. Personal narratives. Revolutionary Movements. 1890-1911. *621*
—. Calleros, Cleofas. Federación de Sociedades Latinos-Americanos. Maverick, Maury. McCammont, T. J. Powell, Alex K. Race Relations. 1936. *627*
—. Colonial Government. Frontier and Pioneer Life. Indian Wars. New Mexico. Pueblo Indians. Spain. 1680-90. *219*
—. Commerce. Mexican War. Rio Grande. 1821-48. *361*
—. Diaries. Fuente, Pedro José de la. Indian Wars. Mexico (Chihuahua, Sonora). Military. New Mexico. 1765. *192*
—. Discrimination. Labor Unions and Organizations. 1880-1920. *629*
—. English language. Names (personal). Spanish language. 1981. *769*
—. Farah Manufacturing Company. Strikes. Women. 1972-74. *775*
—. Poverty. Women. 1880-1920. *626*
—. Social status. Spanish language. 1975. *929*
—. Voting and Voting behavior. 1972. *826*
Texas (Glenn Springs, Boquillas). Bandits. Big Bend region. Langhorne, George T. Mexico (Coahuila). Punitive expeditions. 1915-16. *687*
Texas (Houston). Attitudes. Minorities. -1973. *779*
Texas (Laredo). Political participation. Primer Congreso Mexicanista (1911). 1910-11. *654*
Texas (Los Almos). Folk Medicine. Jaramillo, Pedrito. 1881-1907. *509*
Texas (Lubbock). Attitudes. Blacks. Newspapers. Television. 1976. *1010*
—. Social Status. Values. 1974. *763*
Texas (Matagorda Peninsula). *Britain* (vessel). Confiscations. Foreign Relations. Great Britain. Spain. 1769-70. *168*
Texas (Nacogdoches). Alamo (battle). 1836. 1975. *367*
Texas (Nueces County). Czech Americans. Family. Labor. Land. Social Organization. 1880-1930. *608*
Texas Panhandle. Borders. Compromise of 1850. Spain. 1819-50. *148*
Texas (Pecos County). Frontier and Pioneer Life. Torres brothers. 1869-96. *575*
—. Marriage (mixed). Social Change. Whites. 1880-1978. *419*
Texas rangers. Mexican War. Military Offenses. 1846-48. *308*
Texas (Rio Grande City). Blacks. Civil-Military Relations. Discrimination. Race Relations. Violence. Whites. 1899-1900. *524*
Texas (San Angelo). Boycotts. Presbyterian Church. Public schools. Segregation. 1910-15. *617*
Texas (San Antonio). Acculturation. Church Schools. Public Schools. 1973. *882*
—. Alazan-Apache Courts. Public housing. 1930-44. *693*
—. Architecture. Artisans. Churches. Missions and Missionaries. 18c. *338*
—. Arizona (Tucson). California (Los Angeles). Economic conditions. Racism. Social Conditions. 1850-1900. *528*
—. Assimilation. Elementary Education. 1973. *883*
—. Assimilation. Ethnic identity. Intermarriage. Women. 1830-60. *530*
—. Behavior. Generations. Religion. 1981-82. *909*
—. California (San Diego). Colorado (Denver). Medical Education. Physicians. 1970-79. *980*
—. Catholic Church. Coahuiltecan Indians. Indians. Missions and Missionaries. 1792. *277*
—. Class consciousness. Ideology. Social Change. 1930-40. *630*
—. Desegregation. 1960-65. *829*
—. Discrimination, Employment. Family. New Mexico (Santa Fe). 1860. *513*

—. Ethnic Groups. Georgia (Atlanta). Labor. Louisiana (New Orleans). Women. 1930-40. *610*

—. Gutierrez de Lara, José Bernardo Maxmilliano. Independence Movements. Magee, Augustus W. Mexico. Republican Army of the North. 1811-15. *197*

—. KCOR, station. Radio. Spanish language. 1928-74. *485*

—. Literacy. Whites. 1850-60. *540*

—. Music. Norteña (music). Photographs. 1930's-82. *688*

—. Plan de San Diego. Rebellions. 1914-17. *655*

Texas (San Antonio area). Intermarriage. Men. 1971-80. *1024*

Texas, south. Carranza, Venustiano. Foreign Relations. Mexico. Plan de San Diego. Race relations. 1915-16. *638*

—. Colleges and Universities. Ethnicity. Racial Distance Indices. Students. 1973. *741*

—. Folk medicine. Jaramillo, Pedrito. Lozano, José C. 19c. *511*

—. Local government. Political Participation. 1971-83. *721*

—. Migration. Social Conditions. Whites. 1850-1900. *527*

—. Voting and Voting Behavior. 1956-78. *1048*

Texas, southern. Architecture. Ranching. 1750-1900. *332*

—. Catholic Church. 1836-1911. *550*

—. Minorities in Politics. Public Schools. Self-perception. 1930's-69. *489*

Texas (Three River). Ballads. "Corrido de Gregorio Cortez" (ballad). "Discriminación a un Martir" (ballad). Political Protest. Social change. 20c. *468*

Texas, University of, Austin (Benson Latin American Collection). Castañeda, Carlos Eduardo. Colleges and Universities. Historiography. Librarians. 1920-27. *603*

Texas, West. Education. Employment. Whites. 1860-1900. *588*

—. Sheep Shearers' Union. Strikes. 1934. *653*

Texas (Young County). Names (personal). Slaves. 1856-65. *555*

Textbooks. American history. 1975-80. *36*

—. American history. Colleges and Universities. History Teaching. Mexican Americans. 20c. *53*

Textile Industry. Food Industry. New Mexico. Ranches. Sheep Raising. 1846-61. *589*

Theater. Attitudes. English language. Popular Culture. Spanish language. 1970's. *1022*

—. Briski, Norman (interview). Exiles. Latin Americans. New York City. 1970's-82. *1096*

—. California (Santa Barbara). Teatro Nacional de Aztlán. 1979. *836*

—. Catholic Church. Indiana (East Chicago, Gary). 1920-76. *59*

—. Culture. Institute of Puerto Rican Culture. Puerto Rico. 1955-80. *1211*

—. Ethnicity. Popular culture. Social Conditions. *Teatro Chicano.* 1965-79. *874*

—. Folklore. Mexicans. Puerto Ricans. 1966-77. *60*

—. Puerto Rico. 1492-1979. *1246*

—. Puerto Rico. 1900-30. *1227*

—. Puerto Rico. 1939-79. *1209*

—. Puerto Rico (San Juan). Tapia Theater. 16c-1969. *1069*

Theater, guerrilla. Social consciousness. 1965-76. *788*

Thomas, Piri. Authors. Autobiographies. Blacks. New York City. Prisons. Puerto Ricans. 1950-80. *1224*

Tijerina, Reies. California. Chavez, Cesar. Political activism. Rhetoric. Texas. 1960's-70's. *843*

Tobacco Industry. Cubans. Florida (Key West). Labor. Martí, José. 1891. *1170*

—. Cubans. Florida (Tampa). Labor Disputes. *Lector* (reader). Perez, Louis A., Jr. Personal narratives. ca 1925-35. *1243*

Toponymy. California (Drake's Bay). Discovery and Exploration. Viscáino, Sebastian. 1602-03. *286*

—. California (Los Angeles). Croix, Teodoro de. 1769-82. *368*

—. Indians. New Mexico. Whites. ca 1550-1982. *48*

Torres brothers. Frontier and Pioneer Life. Texas (Pecos County). 1869-96. *575*

Torres, Luisa. Catholic Church. Folk medicine. New Mexico (Guadalupita). Social Customs. 1910's-70's. *497*

Trade. Anthropology. Ecology. Methodology. New Mexico (northern). Social organization. 17c-20c. *63*

—. Borderlands. Diplomacy. Mexico. 1858-1905. *516*

—. Chouteau, Auguste P. Demun, Julius. Indian-White Relations. Law. New Mexico. 1815-51. *375*

—. Daily Life. Labor. New Mexico (Albuquerque). Social mobility. 1706-90. *330*

—. Florida (St. Augustine). Great Britain. Indians. Social Customs. Spain. 1700-83. *211*

—. Indians. Mexico. New Mexico (Estancia Basin). Salt. Spain. Prehistory-1840's. *265*

—. Mexico (Sonora). New Mexico (Santa Fe). Roads. Spain. 17c-1850's. *345*

—. New Mexico. Texan-Santa Fe Expedition. 1841. *290*

Trade regulation. Indian Wars. Mexico. New Mexico. Treaties. 1821-46. *372*

Trading expeditions. Alvarez, Manuel. Diplomacy. Mexico. New Mexico. Texas. 1841. *181*

Tradition. California (Los Angeles area). Proverbs. 1970's. *713*

Trails. California (San Diego). Camino Real. Mexico (Loreto). Serra Route. 1762-1975. *188*

Travel accounts. Attitudes. Californios. Europeans. 1780's-1840's. *269*

—. Attitudes. Californios. Europeans. 1780's-1840's. *396*

—. Mexico. Race Relations. Western States. 1831-69. *571*

—. New Mexico. 1846-49. *518*

—. New Mexico. Women. 1800-50. *266*

Treasury. Archivo General de Indias. Colonial Government. Military Finance. New Mexico. Spain (Seville). 1596-1683. *337*

Treaties. Choctaw Indians. Indian-White Relations. Old Southwest. Spain. Villebeuvre, Juan de la. 1784-97. *241*

—. Indian Wars. Mexico. New Mexico. Trade regulation. 1821-46. *372*

—. Indian-White Relations. Louisiana. Spain. 1770-93. *264*

—. Newspapers. Panama Canal. Political Campaigns (presidential). Reagan, Ronald. 1976-80. *976*

Trials. Anton Chico grant. Land grants. New Mexico Land and Livestock Company. Rivera, Manuel. 1822-1915. *334*

—. California (Los Angeles). Citizens Committee for the Defense of Mexican-American Youth. "Sleepy Lagoon" trial. 1942-44. *616*

—. Conspiracy. Foreign Relations. Mexico. Revolutionary Movements. Reyes, Bernardo. State Politics. Texas. 1911-12. *639*

—. Florida. Rebellions. Spain. 1795-98. *296*

Trist, Nicholas P. Diplomacy. Guadalupe Hidalgo, Treaty of. Mexican War. 1848. *517*

—. Guadalupe Hidalgo, Treaty of. Land grants. Protocol of Querétaro. Texas. 1847-48. *560*

Truancy. Attitudes. California (Los Angeles). High schools. 1974-75. *845*
Truman, Harry S. Agriculture. Bracero program. Mexico. President's Commission on Migratory Labor. Workers, undocumented. 1950. *876*
—. Federal Policy. Puerto Rico. Self-government. 1945-47. *1086*

U

Ulloa, Antonio de. Acadians. Colonial Government. Letters. Louisiana. Refugees. Spain. 1766-68. *178*
UN. International law. Puerto Rico. 1950-73. *1172*
Unemployment. California (Los Angeles County). Davis, James J. Deportation. Depressions. 1931. *647*
—. Economic development. Income. Puerto Rico. 1959-70. *1201*
—. Economic development. Population. Puerto Rico. 1940's-70's. *1244*
—. Education. Immigration. Puerto Rico. 1955-70. *1298*
—. Food shortages. Puerto Rico. World War II. 1940-45. *1146*
—. Land distribution. Puerto Rico. 1970's. *1194*
—. New York City. Occupations. Puerto Ricans. 1970. *1168*
—. Recessions. Spaniards. 1974-75. *74*
—. Whites. 1970's. *822*
United Cannery, Agricultural, Packing and Allied Workers of America. Agricultural Labor. California. 1937-40. *667*
—. Labor Unions and Organizations. Texas. 1935-50. *668*
United Farm Workers Union. Agricultural Industry. California. Elections. Labor Unions and Organizations. Proposition 14 (1976). 1976. *773*
—. Agricultural Labor. California. 1960's-76. *810*
—. Agricultural Labor. California. Chavez, Cesar. Strikes. 1965-70. *723*
—. Agricultural labor. California (San Joaquin Valley). Japanese. Nisei Farmers League. 1971-77. *812*
—. Agriculture. Boycotts. California. Chavez, Cesar. Grapes. International Brotherhood of Teamsters. Labor Unions and Organizations. Lettuce. 1962-74. *805*
—. Agriculture. California. Chavez, Cesar. Elections. Proposition 14 (1976). 1975-76. *996*
—. California (San Joaquin Valley). Japanese. Labor Disputes. Nisei Farmers League. 1974-76. *811*
United Mexican American Students. California (Los Angeles). Youth Movements. 1967-69. *975*
United Neighborhoods Organization. California (East Los Angeles). Catholic Church. Economic Conditions. Reform. Social Conditions. 1960's-80. *945*
Upper Classes. California. delValle family. Rancho Camulos. 1839-1938. *442*
—. California (San Diego). Californios. Political power. 1846-60. *534*
Urban change. California (Monterey). Migration, Internal. 1835-50. *246*
Urbanization. Americanization. California (Santa Barbara). Social Change. 1850-70's. *599*
—. Blacks. City Government. Employment. Texas. 1973. *842*
—. Economic growth. New Mexico (Albuquerque). World War II. 1940-75. *920*
Urbansk, Edmund S. Discovery and Exploration. Ethnicity. National Characteristics. Social Customs (review article). 17c-18c. *331*
Utah. Acculturation. 1910-80. *451*

—. Curanderismo. Folk Medicine. 20c. *409*
Utah (San Juan County; Monticello). González, Ramon. 20c. *441*
Utopianism. Americas (North and South). Colonization. Discovery and Exploration. Europe. Myths and Symbols. 16c-18c. *225*

V

Vaccination. California (Monterey). Estrada, José. Europe. Jenner, Edward. Smallpox. 18c-1821. *301*
Values. Acculturation. Cubans. Drug abuse. Immigration. Social Customs. Youth. 1950-80. *1237*
—. Art. California (East Los Angeles). Murals. 1978. *1052*
—. Barreda, Gabino. Mexico. Philosophy. Positivism. 1860's-1982. *444*
—. Blacks. Child-rearing. Indians. 1979. *1045*
—. Food Industry. Social Customs. Women. 1980. *784*
—. Fotonovelas. Literature. Women. Working Class. 1976-80. *757*
—. Migration, Internal. New Mexico (El Cerrito). Social Change. 1939-56. *893*
—. Puerto Rico. 1981. *1181*
—. Puerto Rico. Sex discrimination. Women. 1974. *1149*
—. Social Status. Texas (Lubbock). 1974. *763*
Vanishing hitchhiker (theme). Folklore. Men. Women. 1977. *892*
Vega, Lope de *(San Diego de Alcalá)*. Americas (North and South). Colonization. Discovery and exploration. Spain. 17c-18c. *342*
Velasco, Carlos. Arizona (Tucson). Editors and Editing. El Fronterizo. Elites. 1865-1914. *536*
Vélez Cachupín, Thomas. Colonial Government. Documents. New Mexico. Spain. ca 1754. *297*
Verger y Suau, Rafael José. Catholic Church. Mexico (Nuevo León). Missions and Missionaries. Southwest. 1767-80's. *358*
Victimization. Mental Illness. Psychotherapy. 1980. *108*
Vigilantes. Ethnicity. Herrera, Juan José. Land grants. Militancy. New Mexico (Las Vegas). White Caps. 1887-94. *554*
Villa, Francisco. Blacks. Carranza, Venustiano. Indians. Mexico. Rebellions. Texas. 1848-1920. *577*
Villa, Pancho. Brown, Harold Palmer. Carranza family. Memoirs. Mexico. New Mexico (Columbus; attack). Photographs. 1916. *612*
—. El Paso-Juárez Conference. Foreign Relations. Mexico. Punitive expeditions. 1916. *637*
Villages. Assimilation. New Mexico. Social Customs. 1960's-79. *962*
—. Catholic Church. Fiestas. New Mexico. Rites and Ceremonies. Saints, patron. 1970's. *1036*
—. Catholic Church. New Mexico. Penitentes. Social Customs. 19c-1978. *445*
—. Economic Structure. New Mexico. 18c-1978. *1039*
—. Latin America. New Mexico, northern. Social Organization. Spain. 16c-20c. *377*
—. New Mexico, northern. Social Organization. 16c-1978. *490*
Villains. Anglo (character). Literature. Sanchez, Saul (review article). 1970's. *953*
Villanueva, Tino. Assimilation (review article). Calvo Buezas, Tomás. 19c-20c. *405*
Villareal, José Antonia *(Pocho)*. Acosta, Oscar Zeta *(Autobiography of a Brown Buffalo)*. Ethnicity. Novels. Rivera, Tomás *(Y No Se Lo Tragó La Tierra)*. 1970-79. *1054*
Villareal, José Antonio *(Pocho)*. Assimilation. Literature. Social Customs. 1959-76. *743*

Villebeuvre, Juan de la. Alabama. Boucfouca,
Treaty of. Choctaw Indians. Indian-White
Relations. Spain. 1793. *243*
—. Choctaw Indians. Indian-White Relations. Old
Southwest. Spain. Treaties. 1784-97. *241*
Violence. Angel, Frank W. Corruption. New
Mexico. Wallace, Lew. 1878. *591*
—. Arizona. Gándara, Francisco. McFarland,
William. Race Relations. Whites. 1872-73. *578*
—. Blacks. Civil-Military Relations. Discrimination.
Race Relations. Texas (Rio Grande City).
Whites. 1899-1900. *524*
—. Puerto Rico. 1940-73. *1286*
Virtue. Californios. Social Classes. Women.
1830-46. *268*
Visitas (provincial tours). Florida. Indian-White
Relations. Spain. 1602-75. *320*
Viticulture. California. Missions and Missionaries.
1697-1858. *389*
Vizcaíno, Sebastian. Ascensión, Antonio de la.
California. Discovery and Exploration. Mexico.
Voyages. 1590-1737. *285*
—. California. Discovery and Exploration.
1596-1627. *284*
—. California. Discovery and Exploration.
Settlement. 1602-32. *154*
—. California (Drake's Bay). Discovery
and Exploration. Toponymy. 1602-03.
286
Voluntary associations. Blacks. New York City.
Puerto Ricans. Whites. 1963-78. *1117*
—. Blacks. Texas (Austin). Whites. 1969-70. *1046*
—. Florida. Immigrants. Medical care. 19c-20c.
129
Voter registration. Canada. Political participation.
Puerto Rico. 1974-77. *1070*
Voting and Voting Behavior. Arizona. Elections.
School boards. 1972-74. *817*
—. Blacks. Colorado (Denver). Political attitudes.
1971. *897*
—. California (Los Angeles County). Congressional
Districts (30th). Ethnicity. Political candidates.
Race. 1982. *754*
—. City Politics. Illinois (Chicago). Political
representation. Spaniards. 1975. *104*
—. Cubans. Naturalization. Political Participation.
Refugees. 1959-84. *1249*
—. Michigan. Minorities in Politics. 1960's-70's.
745
—. Texas (El Paso). 1972. *826*
—. Texas, south. 1956-78. *1048*
Voting Rights Act (US, 1965; amended 1982).
Blacks. Political Participation. 1965-83. *83*
Voyages. Ascensión, Antonio de la. California.
Discovery and Exploration. Mexico. Vizcaíno,
Sebastian. 1590-1737. *285*

W

Wages. Agricultural labor. Bracero Program.
Employment. Southwest. 1954-77. *869*
—. Agricultural Labor. California (Oxnard).
Japanese-Mexican Labor Association. Strikes.
Sugar beets. 1902-03. *602*
—. Aliens (illegal). Migrant Labor. Oregon (Hood
River Valley). 1978. *777*
—. Blacks. Discrimination, Employment. Men.
Whites. 1980-81. *1029*
—. Blacks. Men. Whites. 1979. *109*
—. Blacks. Whites. 1976. *95*
—. Business Education. College graduates. Whites.
1972-80. *949*
—. Civil Service. Inequality. Whites. 1977. *1011*
—. College graduates. Discrimination. 1966-74. *961*
—. Disability. Employment. English language.
Men. 1976. *705*

Wallace, Lew. Angel, Frank W. Corruption. New
Mexico. Violence. 1878. *591*
War. California. Colonial Government. Foreign
Policy. Spain. 1779-1818. *270*
Washington. Bracero Program. Migration. 1940-50.
620
—. Oregon. Social Conditions. 1970-80. *1000*
Washington (Yakima Valley). Country Life.
Economic Conditions. Family. Occupations.
Social Organization. 1971. *827*
—. Migrant labor. Photographic essays. 1974. *939*
Water. Intergovernmental Relations. Law. Martinez,
Manuel. Mexico. New Mexico. 1832. *205*
Water rights. Indians. Land. New Spain.
Southwest. 1535-1810. *359*
Water Supply. Community Participation in Politics.
Economic Development. Government. Indians.
New Mexico (Espanola Valley). 1970's. *864*
Watergate scandal. Cubans. *Diario Las Americas*.
Florida (Miami). Journalism. Politics and
Media. 1970's. *1061*
Wealth. Bernal, Juan Pablo. Business. California.
Cattle Raising. Land disputes. 1822-78. *426*
Weaving. Blankets. Dye. Indians. Navajo Indians.
New Mexico. Rugs. Spaniards. 19c-1977. *353*
—. Indians. Navajo Indians. New Mexico,
northern. Pueblo Indians. Rio Grande Valley.
15c-1979. *393*
—. Indians. New Mexico. Sheep raising. Woolen
Industry. 1540's-1860's. *166*
—. New Mexico, northern. Rio Grande Valley.
17c-20c. *352*
Weber, David J. Borders. Frontier and Pioneer
Life. Mexico. Race Relations. Southwest
(review article). 1821-46. *251*
Weddle, Robert S. Borderlands (review article).
Jones, Oakah L., Jr. McDermott, John Francis.
Mississippi Valley. Southwest. Spain. 1762-1804.
1973-74. *379*
Wells, James B. Political machines. Race Relations.
Social Change. Texas (Cameron County).
1882-1920. *605*
West Florida. Education. 1781-1821. *240*
West Indians. Blacks. England (London).
Immigration. New York City. Social status.
20c. *1153*
—. Communist Party. Harlem Renaissance.
Immigrants. Literature. New York City. 1930's.
1301
—. Daily life. Immigrants. Latin Americans.
Popular culture. 1965-77. *12*
—. New York City. Race. Spanish language. 1972.
1140
West Indies. Assimilation. Blacks. Immigration.
1898-1979. *1195*
—. Blacks. Economic Conditions. Immigration.
New York City. Public Opinion. 1965-79. *1099*
—. Federal Policy. Foreign Relations. Immigration.
Latin America. 1924-79. *1217*
—. Foreign relations. Latin America. Puerto Rico.
1975. *1105*
—. Immigration. 1970's. *1075*
Western states. American Political Science
Association. Colleges and Universities. Political
science. 1970-74. *1058*
—. Blacks. Cowboys. Daily Life. Indians.
1860's-90's. *519*
—. Cities. Neighborhoods. Race Relations. White
flight. 1960's. *71*
—. Mexico. Race Relations. Travel accounts.
1831-69. *571*
Westward Movement. Foreign Relations.
Settlement. Spain. Texas. ca 1796-1819. *291*
—. Southwest. Stereotypes. Women. 1846-1900. *565*
Wheat growing. California. Franciscans. Mexico.
Missions and Missionaries. Southwest.
1730's-70's. *335*

White Caps. Ethnicity. Herrera, Juan José. Land grants. Militancy. New Mexico (Las Vegas). Vigilantes. 1887-94. *554*
White flight. Cities. Neighborhoods. Race Relations. Western States. 1960's. *71*
Whites. Adolescence. Blacks. California (Los Angeles). Self-concept. 1971. *863*
—. Aged. California. Social Policy. 1978-82. *850*
—. Arizona. Gándara, Francisco. McFarland, William. Race Relations. Violence. 1872-73. *578*
—. Arizona, central. Cohabitation. Mining towns. 1863-73. *548*
—. Assimilation. Blacks. Residential segregation. Social Status. 1960-70. *70*
—. Attitudes. Blacks. Earthquakes. 1977. *1020*
—. Attitudes. Employment. Sex roles. Women. Youth. 1979. *88*
—. Blacks. California. Mortality. 1969-71. *990*
—. Blacks. California (Los Angeles). Crime and Criminals. Judicial Administration. 1977-80. *1041*
—. Blacks. California (Los Angeles). Language. Reading. 1970's. *879*
—. Blacks. California (Los Angeles County). Courts. Men. Sentencing. Women. 1977-80. *839*
—. Blacks. City government. Colorado (Denver). Public Opinion. 1974. *898*
—. Blacks. Civil-Military Relations. Discrimination. Race Relations. Texas (Rio Grande City). Violence. 1899-1900. *524*
—. Blacks. Competition. Labor. 1976. *734*
—. Blacks. Crime and Criminals. Discrimination. Sentencing. Southwest. 1976-77. *859*
—. Blacks. Cubans. Discrimination, Housing. Metropolitan Areas. Mexicans. Prices. Puerto Ricans. 1975-76. *62*
—. Blacks. Dating. Race Relations. 1978-79. *884*
—. Blacks. Demography. Households. Mothers, single. Puerto Ricans. 1970. *1119*
—. Blacks. Discrimination, Employment. Men. Wages. 1980-81. *1029*
—. Blacks. Divorce. 1960-70. *809*
—. Blacks. Economic conditions. Wisconsin (Racine). 1960-71. *781*
—. Blacks. Economic status. Ethnicity. Social Classes. Stress. 1974. *708*
—. Blacks. Employment. Family. Income. Sex roles. 1982-83. *47*
—. Blacks. Employment. Marriage. Mothers. Women. 1970-84. *46*
—. Blacks. Employment. Population. Race. Students. Youth. 1967-83. *133*
—. Blacks. Employment. Southwest. Women. 1950-70. *771*
—. Blacks. Ethnic groups. Political participation. 1966-75. *707*
—. Blacks. Florida (Miami). Neighborhoods. Population. Residential patterns. 1970-80. *1309*
—. Blacks. Income. 1976. *94*
—. Blacks. Interpersonal Relations. Marriage. 1960-70. *792*
—. Blacks. Labor. Wisconsin (Racine). 1960-70. *995*
—. Blacks. Measurements. Mortality. Texas. 1980. *1008*
—. Blacks. Men. Wages. 1979. *109*
—. Blacks. Metropolitan areas. Social Classes. Southwest. 1970. *790*
—. Blacks. New York City. Puerto Ricans. Voluntary associations. 1963-78. *1117*
—. Blacks. Texas (Austin). Voluntary associations. 1969-70. *1046*
—. Blacks. Wages. 1976. *95*
—. Business Education. College graduates. Wages. 1972-80. *949*
—. California. Children. Political Attitudes. -1973. *815*
—. California (Los Angeles). Europe. Family. Immigrants. Michigan (Detroit). 1850-80. *542*
—. California (Orange County). Medical Care (costs). -1973. *1037*
—. Children. Japanese. Political participation. 1970's. *1005*
—. Civil Service. Inequality. Wages. 1977. *1011*
—. Colonization. Land Tenure. New Mexico. Spain. 16c-1974. *29*
—. Discrimination. Income. Men. 1976. *121*
—. Economic Conditions. Land tenure. New Mexico. Social Organization. Spaniards. 1846-91. *594*
—. Education. Employment. Texas, West. 1860-1900. *588*
—. Ethnicity. Family. Social Organization. 1983. *875*
—. Farmers. Indians. Land (disputes). New Mexico (Rio Puerco Valley). 19c-20c. *433*
—. Fertility. 1950-70. *736*
—. Identity. Jokes. Social Change. Texas. 1970's. *890*
—. Income. 1960. *958*
—. Independence Movements. Race Relations. Tejanos. Texas. 1822-36. *145*
—. Indians. Infants. Mortality. New Mexico. 1974-77. *971*
—. Indians. New Mexico. Toponymy. ca 1550-1982. *48*
—. Intermarriage. New Mexico. 1846-1900. *563*
—. Literacy. Texas (San Antonio). 1850-60. *540*
—. Marriage (mixed). Social Change. Texas (Pecos County). 1880-1978. *419*
—. Mass media. Political Leadership. Texas (Austin). 1973. *877*
—. Migration. Social Conditions. Texas, south. 1850-1900. *527*
—. New Mexico (Corrales). Suburban Life. 1710-1970's. *417*
—. Public opinion. Race relations. 1935-80. *50*
—. Southwest. Stereotypes. 19c. *595*
—. Unemployment. 1970's. *822*
Wisconsin (Racine). Attitudes. Blacks. Education. Immigration. 1974. *993*
—. Blacks. Economic conditions. Whites. 1960-71. *781*
—. Blacks. Labor. Whites. 1960-70. *995*
Wisconsin (Riverside). Assimilation. 1973-75. *1044*
Witchcraft. New Mexico (Torrance County). Superstition. 1970's. *780*
Womack, John. Colonization. Exploitation. Minorities. 1841-1973. *447*
Women. 1519-1979. *440*
—. Acculturation. Stress. Workers, undocumented. 1977. *918*
—. Age. Economic conditions. Fertility. Puerto Rico. Social Status. 1970. *1182*
—. Agricultural Labor. California Women Farmworkers Project. Oral history. 1870's-1970's. *73*
—. Archuleta, Eppie. Colorado (San Luis Valley). Folk art. Personal Narratives. 1922-79. *460*
—. Assimilation. Ethnic identity. Intermarriage. Texas (San Antonio). 1830-60. *530*
—. Attitudes. California (Los Angeles). Fertility. 1973-82. *978*
—. Attitudes. Diaries. Discrimination. New Mexico. 1840's-50's. *593*
—. Attitudes. Discrimination. Family. Personal narratives. Professions. Success. 1980. *997*
—. Attitudes. Employment. Sex roles. Whites. Youth. 1979. *88*
—. Attitudes. Mothers. New Mexico (Albuquerque). Sex roles. 1960-83. *1050*
—. Barceló, Gertrudis. Business. Elites. Gambling. New Mexico (Santa Fe). 1830's-40's. *273*
—. Bibliographies. History. Literature. Mexican Americans. 1519-1976. *115*

—. Bibliographies. Mexican Americans. 1970-80. *64*
—. Blacks. California (Los Angeles County). Courts. Men. Sentencing. Whites. 1977-80. *839*
—. Blacks. Employment. Marriage. Mothers. Whites. 1970-84. *46*
—. Blacks. Employment. Southwest. Whites. 1950-70. *771*
—. California. Colleges and Universities. San Diego State College. Student activism. 1968-76. *852*
—. California. Medical care. 1977. *1004*
—. California (Los Angeles). Catholic Church. Fertility. Religiosity. 1973. *979*
—. California (Los Angeles). Employment. Industry. Interviews. 1928. *686*
—. California (Los Angeles). Garment Industry. International Ladies' Garment Workers' Union. Strikes. 1933. *619*
—. California (Los Angeles). Garment Industry. Working Conditions. 1970-79. *986*
—. California (Los Angeles). International Ladies' Garment Workers' Union. Working Conditions. 1933-39. *664*
—. California (Los Angeles). Sterilization. 1970-78. *1028*
—. California (Santa Clara County). Electronics industry. Working conditions. 1970-79. *730*
—. California, Southern. Political Activism. 1960-79. *785*
—. Californios. Social Classes. Virtue. 1830-46. *268*
—. Capitalism. Children. Labor. Mexico. Workers, undocumented. ca 1950-79. *833*
—. Catholic Church. Ethnic Groups. Machismo (concept). Mexican Americans. Social Customs. 1970's. *967*
—. Cities. Literature. 1970's. *774*
—. Class consciousness. Latin America. Puerto Rico. Working Class. 1959-75. *1279*
—. Colombians. Dominicans. Employment. Family. Immigrants. New York City. 1981. *1171*
—. Discrimination, Employment. Working class. 1973-76. *982*
—. Dramatists. Puerto Rico. 19c-1979. *1127*
—. Education. Employment. Ethnicity. Family. 1970's. *1051*
—. Education. Employment. New York. Puerto Ricans. 1960's. *1118*
—. Education. Fertility. Generations. 1976. *725*
—. Employment. 1969-74. *715*
—. Employment. 1970-82. *16*
—. Employment. Latin Americans. New York City. 1970's. *1278*
—. Employment. New York. Puerto Ricans. 1920's-40's. *1188*
—. Equal opportunity. New Mexico. Public Employees. State government. 1971-78. *819*
—. Ethnic Groups. Georgia (Atlanta). Labor. Louisiana (New Orleans). Texas (San Antonio). 1930-40. *610*
—. Ethnicity. Men. Social Classes. 1979. *1016*
—. Ethnicity. New Mexico. Social Classes. Teachers. 1900-50. *649*
—. Exiles. Liberal Party. Mexico. Propaganda. Texas. 1898-1910. *691*
—. Family. 1977. *824*
—. Family. Immigration. Occupations. Social Classes. 20c. *2*
—. Farah Manufacturing Company. Strikes. Texas (El Paso). 1972-74. *775*
—. Fertility. Migrant Labor. 1978. *111*
—. Folklore. Humor. Jokes. Sex. 1970's. *761*
—. Folklore. Men. Vanishing hitchhiker (theme). 1977. *892*
—. Food Industry. Social Customs. Values. 1980. *784*
—. *Fotonovelas.* Literature. Values. Working Class. 1976-80. *757*

—. Historiography. Mexican Americans. Social Classes. 17c-20c. *4*
—. Immigrants. Leadership. Puerto Ricans. 1910-45. *1280*
—. Immigration. Labor. Mexico. 1970's. *834*
—. Imperialism. Mexico. Migration. Sex Discrimination. Southwest. Working class. 1850-1982. *428*
—. Law. New Mexico. Social Status. 1821-46. *272*
—. New Mexico. Political participation. State Politics. Suffrage. 1900-40. *648*
—. New Mexico. Travel accounts. 1800-50. *266*
—. Political Leadership. Puerto Rico (San Juan). Rincón, Felisa. 1934-80. *1235*
—. Political Protest. Social Change. 1973-76. *709*
—. Population. 1975. *1035*
—. Population control. Puerto Rico. Sterilization. 1920-77. *1213*
—. Poverty. Texas (El Paso). 1880-1920. *626*
—. Puerto Rico. Sex discrimination. Values. 1974. *1149*
—. Racism. Sterilization. 20c. *425*
—. Sex Discrimination. Southwest. Student movements. 1960-72. *895*
—. Southwest. Stereotypes. Westward Movement. 1846-1900. *565*
Women (review article). 16c-1980. *414*
—. DelCastillo, Adelaida R. Enriquez, Evangelina. Melville, Margarita B. Mexican Americans. Mirande, Alfredo. Research. 19c-20c. *135*
Wood. Architecture. Housing. Indians. *Jacal* (style). New Mexico (Tierra Amarilla). Spaniards. 8c-20c. *366*
Wood carving. Catholic Church. Isidore the Husbandman, Saint. Lopez, George. New Mexico (Córdova). Statues. ca 1070-1130. ca 1690-1980. *411*
—. Puerto Rico. Santos. 1750-1975. *1122*
Woolen Industry. Indians. New Mexico. Sheep raising. Weaving. 1540's-1860's. *166*
Workers, undocumented. *See also* Aliens, illegal.
—. 1910-75. *437*
—. 1978. *957*
—. Acculturation. Stress. Women. 1977. *918*
—. Agriculture. Bracero program. Mexico. President's Commission on Migratory Labor. Truman, Harry S. 1950. *876*
—. Aliens, illegal. Mexico. 1930-77. *747*
—. Attitudes. 1980-82. *921*
—. Attitudes. California (San Diego). Migration. 1984. *896*
—. Border policy. Economic Conditions. Mexico. 1952-75. *739*
—. California (Los Angeles). Labor. 1979. *718*
—. Capitalism. Children. Labor. Mexico. Women. ca 1950-79. *833*
—. Carter, Jimmy. 1977. *804*
—. Deportation. Statistics. 1972-77. *762*
—. Economic Conditions. Mexico. 1972-73. *954*
—. Economic Conditions. Politics. Southwest. 1975-78. *740*
—. Employment. Social services. 1975-79. *988*
—. Federal Policy. Immigration and Naturalization Service. 1966-76. *1001*
—. Geographic Mobility. 1978-79. *871*
—. Health. Public Policy. 1975-82. *938*
—. Immigrants. Labor. 1970's. *913*
—. Immigration. 1970's. *1056*
—. Immigration. 1975-82. *870*
—. Immigration. Income. Labor. Southwest. 1960-80. *828*
—. Immigration. Labor. Public policy. 1950's-70's. *140*
—. Immigration. Public Policy. 1970's. *835*
—. Labor. 20c. *748*
—. Labor. Mexico. 1973. *746*
—. Labor. Mexico. USA. 1970's. *955*

—. Labor. National Labor Relations Board. *NLRB v. Apollo Tire Co.* (US, 1979). *NLRB* v. *Sure-Tan, Inc.* (US, 1978). 1978-79. *1034*
—. Labor. Social mobility. 1970-80. *720*
—. Labor Unions and Organizations. Mexico. 1867-1977. *407*
—. Mexico. Migrant Labor. Repatriation. 1929-56. *636*
Working Class. Arizona. Copper industry. Labor Unions and Organizations. Politics. Racism. 1900-20. *611*
—. Assimilation. Attitudes. Bilingualism. New York City. Puerto Ricans. 1979. *1073*
—. California (Los Angeles). 1820-1920. *523*
—. Capitalism. Plantations. Puerto Rico. Socialist Party. Sugar. 19c-1976. *1255*
—. Class consciousness. Latin America. Puerto Rico. Women. 1959-75. *1279*
—. Discrimination, Employment. Women. 1973-76. *982*
—. Economic Development. Southwest. 1603-1900. *438*
—. *Fotonovelas.* Literature. Values. Women. 1976-80. *757*
—. Immigrants. Income. Men. Poverty. Self-perception. 1978-79. *923*
—. Imperialism. Mexico. Migration. Sex Discrimination. Southwest. Women. 1850-1982. *428*
—. Industrialization. Migration. Politics. Puerto Rico. 1870's-1970's. *1108*
Working conditions. Agriculture. Documents. Economic Conditions. Migrant Labor. Social Conditions. 1942-45. *694*
—. Attitudes. Cubans. Refugees. 1970-81. *1148*
—. California (Los Angeles). Garment Industry. Women. 1970-79. *986*
—. California (Los Angeles). International Ladies' Garment Workers' Union. Women. 1933-39. *664*
—. California (Santa Clara County). Electronics industry. Women. 1970-79. *730*
World War II. California (Los Angeles). Political Leadership. 1941-45. *625*

—. Discrimination, Employment. Political Protest. Wyoming. 1941-45. *643*
—. Economic growth. New Mexico (Albuquerque). Urbanization. 1940-75. *920*
—. Food shortages. Puerto Rico. Unemployment. 1940-45. *1146*
Wyoming. Discrimination, Employment. Political Protest. World War II. 1941-45. *643*
Wyoming (Lovell). Agricultural Labor. Beets. Great Western Sugar Company. Housing. 1916-54. *671*

Y

Youth. Acculturation. Cubans. Drug abuse. Immigration. Social Customs. Values. 1950-80. *1237*
—. Attitudes. Employment. Sex roles. Whites. Women. 1979. *88*
—. Behavior. Drugs. High schools. Puerto Rico. 1970-80. *1263*
—. Blacks. Employment. Population. Race. Students. Whites. 1967-83. *133*
—. California. Literature. Pachuco (term). 1940's-1960's. *904*
—. California (East Los Angeles). Leisure. Low-riders (automobiles). Social Customs. 1970's. *861*
—. California (Los Angeles). Gangs. Residential patterns. 1980-83. *931*
—. Drug abuse. Economic Conditions. Immigration. Inhalants. Social Conditions. 1930-80. *429*
—. Identity. Rural areas. Social conditions. Texas. 1976. *924*
Youth Movements. California (Los Angeles). United Mexican American Students. 1967-69. *975*
Yuma Indians. California. Catholic Church. Chapels. Indians. ca 1769-1840. *387*
Yuman Indians. California (San Diego). Franciscans. Jayme, Luís (death). Mission San Diego de Alcalá. 1775. *388*

AUTHOR INDEX

A

Aaron, William S. 696
Acredolo, Curt 849
Adams, Eleanor B. 143
Adams, Georgia B. 766
Agogino, George A. 509
Agoyo, Herman 398
Aguallo, Robert, Jr. 966
Aguirre, Adalberto, Jr. 401 697 698
Aguirre, B. E. 1059 1060 1061
Aguirre, Yjinio F. 510
Ahearn, Frederick L. 1062
Ahlborn, Richard E. 1
Alba, Francisco 699 700
Alba-Hernández, Francisco 402
Albuquerque, Klaus de 1063
Alcalay, Rina 2
Alexander, Charles S. 1225
Alger, Norman 696
Allsup, Carl 701 702
Almaguer, Tomás 602
Almaráz, Félix D., Jr. 3 144 145 603 604 703
Althoff, Phillip 704
Alvarez, Aldolfo J. 722
Alvarez, Rodolfo 403
Alvírez, David 851 958
Anders, Evan 605
Andic, Fuat M. 1064
Andic, Suphan 1065
Andreasen, Vera K. 883
Angel, Ronald 705 706
Angle, John 1066
Ansheles, Jill Louise 1301
Antunes, George 707 708
Apodaca, Maria Linda 4
Aponte, Juan B. 1067
Aragón, Janie Louise 146 404
Aragon de Valdez, Theresa 709
Arana, Luis Rafael 147
Arbuckle, H. C., III 511
Arce, Carlos H. 710 711
Archambeau, Ernest R. 148
Archer, Christon I. 149
Archibald, Robert 150 151 152
Ardura, Ernesto 1068
Arizpe, Lourdes 712
Armas, Isabel de 405
Armitage, Shelley 5
Arora, Shirley L. 6 713
Arreola, Daniel D. 714
Arriaga Weiss, David 7
Arrivi, Francisco 1069
Arroyo, Gilberto 1070
Arroyo, Laura E. 715
Arroyo, Luis Leobardo 8 38 606
Arthur, Don 153
Aschman, Homer 154
Ashmore, Harry S. 716
Ashton, Guy T. 1071 1072
Atkinson, Maxine P. 1000
Attinasi, John 1073 1151
August, Jack 155
Avila, Lorenzo 717
Azicri, Max 1074 1322

B

Babchuk, Nicholas 1046
Babín, María Teresa 1323
Baca, Facundo 512

Baca, Luis 512
Baca, Reynaldo 718
Baca Zinn, Maxine 719
Baca-Ramirez, Reynaldo 720
Bach, Jennifer B. 1317
Bach, Robert L. 92 406 407 956 1075 1076 1077 1248 1317
Bailey, David T. 513 514
Bain, Kenneth 721
Balderrama, Virginia 717
Ballard, Dave 156
Baloyra, Enrique A. 1322
Bannon, John Francis 9
Barnes, Mark R. 157
Barrera, Mario 10 607 933
Barrientos, Guido A. 722
Bartlett, Edward E. 93
Barton, Josef J. 608
Batchen, Lou Sage 408
Batista, Gustavo 1078
Batzer, Arild 723
Baxter, John O. 515
Bean, Frank D. 724 725 726 736 809 907 1295
Beauchamp, José J. 1079
Beerman, Eric 158 159 160
Belcher, John C. 1080
Belenchia, Joanne M. 727
Bell, Michael Davitt 1053
Bell, Samuel E. 516
Benavides, E. Ferol 409
Bender, Lynn Darrell 1081
Benes, Ronald J. 161
Benham, Priscilla 162
Benítez, Jaime 1324
Benjamin, Jules R. 1082
Benjamin, Thomas 11
Bensusan, Guy 728
Bentley, Sara 1055
Bergad, Laird W. 1083
Bernal, Ernest M., Jr. 729
Bernstein, Alan 730
Berríos Martínez, Rubén 1324
Berrocal, Luciano 1084 1085
Betten, Neil 609
Bewley, Fred W. 163
Bhana, Surendra 1086
Birkner, Michael 1087
Blackwelder, Julia Kirk 610
Blades, Rubén 1088
Blaut, J. M. 506
Blaut, James 1089
Blevins, Don 517
Bloom, John P. 518
Blount, Alma 731
Bolton, Herbert Eugene 164
Bonilla, Frank 1090 1107 1108
Booth, Karen Marshall 1091
Borjas, George J. 732 733 734
Boswell, Terry 611
Boswell, Thomas D. 735 1092
Bowden, Henry Warner 165
Bowen, Dorothy Boyd 166
Brackenridge, R. Douglas 410
Bradford, William Penn 1093
Bradshaw, Benjamin S. 736 737
Brandi, Gioia 497
Branson, Branley Allan 167
Bras, Juan Mari 1094 1095
Brasseaux, Carl A. 168
Brawner, Marlyn R. 738
Briggs, Charles L. 411 412
Briggs, Vernon M., Jr. 739 740
Briggs, Walter 169

Briski, Norman 1096
Brown, Frank 122
Brown, Harold Palmer 612
Brown, Robert L. 741
Bruce-Novoa, Juan 742 743 744
Brumgardt, John R. 170
Bruno, Melania 1097
Bruyn, Severyn T. 1098
Bryan, Dexter Edward 718 720
Bryce-Laporte, Roy S. 12 1099
Buehler, Marilyn H. 745
Bulger, Peggy A. 1100
Burke, Fred G. 1101
Burn, Henry Pelham 1102
Burroughs, Jean M. 171
Bush, Diane Mitsch 611
Bustamante, Jorge A. 413 746 747 748 749 750 751 762
Butruille, Susan G. 519
Buzan, Bert C. 752 753

C

Cabranes, José A. 1103
Cafferty, Pastora San Juan 1104
Cain, Bruce E. 754
Calderón Cruz, Angel 1105 1106
Campbell, Leon G. 172
Campos, Ricardo 1090 1107 1108
Candelaria, Cordelia 414
Cannon, Marian G. 520
Capen, Dorothy 173
Cardenas, Gilbert 415 755 1295
Cárdenas de Dwyer, Carlota 756
Cardoso, Lawrence A. 13 416 613
Carillo, Loretta 757
Carlson, Alvar W. 174 417 418 758
Carrico, Richard L. 175
Casal, Lourdes 1109
Case, Robert 521
Casillas, Mike 522
Castañeda, Carlos E. 622
Castel, Arnaud 1319
Castellanos, Leonard 759
Castillo, Leonel J. 760
Castillo, Pedro 523
Castro, Rafaela 761
Castro Arroyo, María de los Angeles 110
Cazares, Ralph B. 419
Chacón, Ramón D. 614
Chall, Jeanne 1053
Champlin, Brad 176
Chande, Roberto Ham 762
Chandler, Charles R. 763
Chandler, R. E. 168 177 178
Chapa, Jorge 850
Chappell, Bruce S. 77 226
Chavez, Angelico 179 506
Chavez, Cesar 764
Chavez, Mauro 765
Chavez, Thomas E. 180 181 398
Chavira, Ricardo 420
Chesnutis, Diane L. 1110
Cheyney, Arnold B. 766
Chipman, Donald 182
Chiswick, Barry R. 14
Choudhury, Parimal 1065
Chrisman, Robert 1111
Christian, Garna L. 524
Cintrón, Celia F. 1112

Cintrón García, Arturo 1113
Ciro, Sepulveda 615
Clark, Cal 819
Clark, Harry 183
Clark, Janet 819
Clark, Juan M. 1248 1318
Clark, Thomas R. 1114
Clark, Truman R. 1115
Clayton, Lawrence A. 184
Cleary, Paul D. 706
Cleland, Courtney B. 888
Clemens, Walter C., Jr. 1116
Cockcroft, Eva 767
Cockcroft, James D. 748
Cohen, Gaynor 768
Cohen, Steve Martin 1117
Coker, William S. 256
Cole, Thomas 909
Colgan, Susan 15
Collins, Marion 989
Coltharp, Lurline H. 769
Comer, John 770 1043
Contreras, Maria Alina 1121
Cook, Sherburne F. 421
Coomes, Charles S. 185
Cooney, Rosemary Santana 16
    88 771 1118 1119 1120 1121
    1270
Copeland, Earl, Jr. 1122
Copeland, Ronald 1123
Corbett, Theodore G. 186
Cordasco, Francesco 17 18 19
Cords, Nicholas 225
Cornelius, Wayne A. 422 423
    772
Corrada, Baltasar 1124
Corralejo, Jorge 773
Corwin, Arthur F. 20 424
Costas, Orlando E. 21
Costello, Julia 153
Cota-Cárdenas, Margarita 774
Coyle, Laurie 775
Crader, Kelly W. 1080
Crosby, Harry 187 188
Cruz, Ramón A. 1125
Cruz Báez, Angel David 1126
Cuellar, José B. 776
Cullen, Ruth M. 726 1182
Cuthbert, Richard W. 777
Cuthbertson, Gilbert M. 525
Cutter, Donald C. 189 190 191
Cypess, Sandra Messinger 1127

D

Dagodag, W. Tim 778
Daniel, James M. 192
Darragh, Shaun M. 1128
Daubon, Ramon 1129
Daudistel, Howard C. 859
Davidson, Chandler 779
Davis, Jacaleen 780
Davis, Lisa E. 1130
Davison, Victoria F. 781
Day, Mark 616
Days, Drew S., III 22
Debien, Gabriel 193 194
deBuys, William 526
DeLaGarza, Rodolfo 782 783
DelaIsla, José 23
DelaPeña, José Enrique 195
delaPeña Brown, M. H. 784
delaQuintana Oriol, Juan 102
delaTeja Angeles, Ileana 24
DeLaVina, Lynda Y. 949

DelCastillo, Adelaida R. 425 621
    664 691 730 775 785 852
    986 1027 1028 1035
DeLeon, Arnoldo 527 528 588
    617
Delgado, Gary 786
Delgado, James P. 426
Deloria, Vine, Jr. 25
DelosSantos, Alfredo G., Jr. 787
DeMoss, Virginia 427
Denis, Manuel Maldonado 1131
Depalo, William A., Jr. 196
Devereaux, Linda Ericson 197
Díaz Soler, Luis M. 1132
Díaz-Briquets, Sergio 1133
Díaz-Royo, Antonio T. 1134
Dickason, Olive Patricia 198
Dickey, Dan W. 688
Dietz, James L. 1135 1136 1137
    1138
Dilla Alfonso, Haroldo 1139
Dillon, Merton L. 199
Din, Gilbert C. 200 201
Dinwoodie, D. H. 618
Dix, Agnes S. 202
Dixon, Marlene 428
Dobson, John M. 529
Dodd, Horace L. 285
Domínguez, Virginia R. 1140
Donahue, Francis 788 789
Dornbusch, Sanford M. 796
Dowdall, George W. 790
Dower, Catherine 1141
Drescher, Tim 791
Duffy, John 203
Duggal, Ved P. 1142 1143
Duncan, Ronald J. 1144
Dunlay, Thomas W. 204
Durón, Clementina 619
Duty, Michael 26
Dworkin, A. Gary 429
Dysart, Jane 530

E

Eberstein, Isaac W. 792 793 809
Ebright, Malcolm 205 430 531
Edwards, J. R. 27
Ehrlich, Karen Lynn 431
Eiselein, E. B. 794
Ellis, Bruce T. 206 532
Ellis, Richard N. 28
Elsasser, Albert B. 207
Elstob, Winston 208
Engstrand, Iris Wilson 29
Epstein, Lee 941
Eribes, Richard A. 795 1040
Ericksen, Charles A. 30
Espinosa, Gilberto 209
Espinosa, J. Manuel 31
Espinosa, Judith M. 980
Espinosa, Rubén W. 796
Estevez, Guillermo A. 1145
Estrada, Leobardo F. 32 432
    851
Ezell, Paul 210

F

Fagan, Brian 153
Fairbanks, Charles H. 211
Farge, Emile J. 797
Farley, Ena L. 1146
Faught, Jim D. 798
Faulk, Odie B. 212
Feather, Adlai 213

Felice, Lawrence G. 799
Fenyo, Mario D. 1147
Ferguson, Bobbie 509
Ferguson, Catherine C. 214
Fernández, Celestino 796
Fernández, Frank 1323
Fernandez, Gaston A. 1148 1317
    1320
Fernández, José B. 215
Fernandez, Raul A. 833
Fernández Cintrón, Celia 1149
Fernández-Santamaría, José A.
    216
Fernandez-Shaw, Carlos M. 217
Finger, Bill 800
Finzsch, Norbert 533
Fischer, Nancy A. 801
Fitzpatrick, Joseph P. 33 1150
Flood, Lawrence G. 790
Flores, Juan 1151
Flores, Nancy de la Zerda 802
Flores, Ricardo 485
Florez, John 34
Fogel, Walter 140
Foley, Douglas E. 489
Foner, Nancy 1152 1153
Ford, Larry R. 803
Forest, M. Kathryn 848
Fradd, Sandra 1154
Fragomen, Austin T., Jr. 35 804
Freeman, Hal M. 717
Friedland, William H. 805
Friedlander, Judith 433
Frisbie, W. Parker 419 792 806
    807 808 809 935
Fritsch, Johann 810
Frost, Elsa Cecilia 413 438 523
Fugita, Stephen S. 811 812
Fulton, Tom 434

G

Gaitz, Charles M. 707 708 779
Galarza, Ernesto 622
Gallegos, Dennis 445
Galvin, Miles 1155
Gamarra, Eduardo A. 1316 1320
Gamboa, Erasmo 620
Gamio, Manuel 621 622
Gándara, Arturo 813
Gapp, Frank W. 218
García, Concepción 1254
Garcia, Eugene E. 814
Garcia, F. Chris 432 815 816
Garcia, Jesus 36
Garcia, John A. 435 817 818
Garcia, Jose Z. 819
Garcia, Juan R. 436 623
García, Mario T. 37 103 534
    624 625 626 627 628 629
Garcia, Philip 820 821 822 823
Garcia, Richard A. 630
Garcia, Robert 931
Garcia, Rupert 791
García Gómez, Alberto 437
Garcia-Bahne, Betty 824
García-Passalacqua, Juan M.
    1156
Garcia-Treto, Francisco O. 410
Gard, Elizabeth 304
Garner, Van Hastings 219 220
Garr, Daniel J. 221 222 223
Garrison, Vivian 1157
Garza, Rodolfo O. de la 825
Garza, Rudolph O. de la 826
Gaston, Mauricio 1097
Gautier Mayoral, Carmen 1158

Gecas, Viktor 827 1159
Geiger, Maynard 224
Gelpi Barrios, Juan 1160
George, Philip Brandt 1161
Gerking, Shelby D. 828
Gerster, Patrick 225
Getzler, Michael H. 226
Getzler-Eaton, Michael 77
Gil, Carlos B. 535
Gil, Rosa Maria 1162
Gilbert, Benjamin F. 227
Gilder, George 1163
Gillespie, Francis P. 1008
Godoy, Gustavo J. 1164
Goldberg, Robert A. 829
Goldman, Shifra M. 830
Gómez Martínez, Julián 1139
Gómez-Quiñones, Juan 38 438 439
Gonzales, Gilbert C. 631
Gonzales, Manuel G. 536
Gonzales, Ricardo T. 696
Gonzales, Sylvia 440 831
Gonzalez, Gilbert G. 632 633
González, Gustavo 832
Gonzalez, Isabel L. 1165
González, LaVerne 1055
Gonzalez, Martin 731
Gonzalez, Rosalinda M. 833 834
González, William H. 441
González Díaz, Emilio 1166 1167
Gordon, Chad 708
Goss, Robert C. 228
Gould, Sam 949
Graham, Otis L. 142 835 1056
Grandjeat, Yves-Charles 836
Gray, Lois S. 1168
Greenberg, Bradley S. 837
Grenier, Gilles 39
Grider, Sylvia Ann 838
Griffin, Ernst 803
Grijalva, Joshua 40
Griswold del Castillo, Richard 41 42 442 537 538 539 540 541 542 543 634
Gritzner, Charles 43
Gruhl, John 839 1041
Guagnano, Gregory A. 848 849
Guendelman, Sylvia R. 1169
Guerra, Carmen 1170
Guest, Francis F. 229
Gurak, Douglas T. 1171
Gutiérrez, Armando 467 635 840 841
Gutiérrez, Félix 44
Guzmán, Ralph 45 636

H

Habig, Marion A. 230 277
Haghe, Howard 46
Hale, Duane K. 231 232
Hall, E. Boyd 233
Hall, G. Emlen 234
Hall, Grace 842
Hall, Thomas D. 506
Hammerback, John C. 843 868
Hammond, George P. 235
Hancock, Joel 844
Hansen, Niles 507
Hardwick, Michael R. 390
Haro, Carlos M. 845 846
Haro, Robert P. 847
Harper, James W. 637
Harrington, Marie 544
Harris, Charles H., III 638 639

Haulman, Bruce E. 513 514
Hawkes, Glenn R. 848 849
Hayes-Bautista, David E. 850
Hayghe, Howard 47
Hector, Bruce J. 1172
Heine, Jorge 1173
Heizer, Robert 399
Helmick, Sandra A. 849
Henderson, Peter B. N. 640
Hendrick, Irving G. 641
Hennessy, Alistair 443
Henríquez Ureña, Camila 1174
Herbstein, Judith 1175
Hernández, Andrés R. 1109
Hernández, José 851 1176
Hernandez, Patrícia 852
Hernández Novás, Raúl 1177
Hernández Rodríguez, Rogelio 642
Hernández-Colón, Rafael 1178
Herrick, John M. 853
Herrick, Robert L. 48
Herring, Patricia Roche 236
Hershatter, Gail 775
Hessler, Richard M. 854
Hewitt, William L. 643
Hewlett, Sylvia Ann 49
Hibbing, John R. 128
Hill, Robert B. 50
Hirsch, Herbert 840 841 855
Hirschman, Charles 51 856
Hitsman, J. Mackay 237
Hoehn, Richard A. 857
Hoffman, Abraham 52 53 54 545 644 645 646 647 858
Hoffman, Paul E. 238 239
Hofstetter, C. Richard 896
Holmes, Jack D. L. 240 241 242 243
Holmes, Malcolm D. 859
Holscher, Louis M. 860
Holtz, Janicemarie Allard 861
Homberg, Joan J. 1268
Honig, Emily 775
Hoover, Robert L. 214 244 245
Hoppe, Sue Keir 910
Hopper, Robert 802
Horgan, Paul 55
Hornbeck, David 246 247
Hosch, Harmon M. 722
Hostos, Adolfo de 1179
Hout, Michael 1008
Howell, Frances Baseden 862
Howell, Gladys David 1054
Hoyt, Garry 1180
Hughes, Charles 546
Hughey, Kirk 584
Hurstfield, Jennifer 863
Hutchinson, C. Alan 248 249
Hutchison, Ray 56

I

Ives, Ronald L. 250

J

Jackson, Peter 1181
Jacobs, Sue-Ellen 864
Jaffe, A. J. 1182
James, Betsy 497
Jamison, W. Thomas 1055
Jenkins, J. Craig 57 865 866
Jenness, Doug 1183
Jennings, James 1184
Jensen, Carol 547

Jensen, Joan M. 648 649
Jensen, Richard J. 843 867 868
John, Elizabeth A. H. 251
John, Vera 58
Johns, Sally Cavell 252
Johnson, David R. 1046
Johnson, Kenneth M. 253
Johnson, Roberta Ann 1185 1186 1187
Johnson, Susan L. 548
Jones, Lamar B. 869
Jones, Oakah L., Jr. 254 255 256
Jones, Richard C. 870 871
Jones, Timothy C. 735
Jordan, Terry G. 549
Juárez, José Roberto 550

K

Kahn, David 872
Kane, Tim D. 873
Kanellos, Nicolás 59 60 874
Kapsis, Robert E. 1117
Karnig, Albert K. 1040
Kazlauskas, Edward John 132
Keefe, Susan Emley 875
Kells, Robert 257
Kelly, Annamaria 258
Kelly, María Patricia Fernández 61
Kelly, Philip 1033
Kelsey, Harry 259
Kenner, Charles L. 551
Kerr, Louise A. 650
Kessell, John L. 260 261 398
Kiecolt, K. Jill 1020
Kiewiet, D. Roderick 754
Killea, Lucy 262 399
Kinnaird, Lawrence 263 264
Kinnaird, Lucia B. 263
Kirstein, Peter N. 876
Kiser, George 651
Klor de Alva, Jorge 444
Knowlton, Clark S. 552
Korman, Frank 877
Korrol, Virginia Sánchez 1188
Koss, Joan D. 1189
Kozoll, Richard 93
Kraemer, Paul M. 265
Krauze, Enrique 413 438 523
Kritz, Mary M. 1171
Krivo, Lauren J. 62
Kutsche, Paul 63 445
Kutz, Jack 878

L

Lacy, James M. 266
LaGreca, Anthony J. 1060
Laguerre, Enrique A. 1323
Laine, Janice E. 879
Lajous, Roberta 880
Lake, Robert W. 1274
Lamare, James W. 881
Lamb, Blaine P. 652
Lampe, Philip E. 882 883 884 885
Langellier, John Phillip 267
Langum, David J. 268 269 270 396 553
Larson, Robert W. 554
Laughlin, Margaret A. 141
Lavender, David 271
Lecompte, Janet 272 273 274 275

Ledbetter, Barbara A. 555
Lee, Eun Sul 886
Lee, Hector H. 556
Lega, Leonor I. 1190
LeGardeur, René 193 194
Leich, Marian Nash 1191
Lemus, Frank C. 887
Lenoir, Claudia Kaiser 1096
Leon, Arnoldo de 557 653
Leonard, Olen E. 888
LeRiverend, Julio 276
Leutenegger, Benedict 230 277
Levenstein, Harvey 889
Levine, Barry B. 1192
Lidin, Harold 1193
Limón, José E. 446 654 890 891
892
Linares, Francisco Watlington
1194
Lindsay, Beverly 440
Lipsky, John M. 1319
Lloréns, Washington 1179
Loeb, Catherine 64
Loescher, Gilburt 1283
London, Clement B. G. 1195
Long, James E. 65
Long, John M. 1030
Long, Robert W. 285
Longoria, Mario D. 655
Loomis, Charles P. 893
Lopez, Adalberto 66 1196
Lopez, David 979
Lopez, David E. 894
López, Genevieve 906
Lopez, Larry 558 656
López, Manuel M. 1318
López, Sonia A. 895
López Yustos, Alfonso 1197
Lotchin, Roger W. 508
Loveman, Brian 896
Lovrich, Nicholas P., Jr. 897
898
Lozano, Anthony Girard 899
Lucas, Isidro 67
Lucker, William G. 722
Luebke, Frederick C. 608
Lummis, Keith 278
Lyon, Eugene 279 280
Lyson, Thomas A. 757

M

MacGregor-Villarreal, Mary 900
Macías, Reynaldo Flores 432
901 902
Macias, Ysidro Ramón 903
Mader, Paul D. 1063 1289
Madrid-Barela, Arturo 447 657
904
Mahood, Wayne 905
Maibaum, Matthew 906
Majka, Linda C. 448
Maldonado, Edwin 1198
Maldonado, Lionel 432 820
Maldonado, Rita M. 1199 1200
1201 1202
Maldonado-Denis, Manuel 1203
1204 1205 1206
Mann, Arthur J. 1064 1207
Manucy, Albert 281
Marazzi, Rosa 1208
Marchena Fernández, Juan 282
Marcum, John P. 801 907
Marenin, Otwin 897
Marin, Christine 908
Markides, Kyriakos S. 909 910
Márquez, Rosa Luisa 1209

Marrero, J. Edward 1210
Marshall, Wes 794
Martin, W. Allen 1308
Martinez, Arthur D. 449 450
Martinez, Elizabeth 428
Martínez, Gerónimo G. 750
Martínez, Iris 1211
Martínez, Oscar J. 68 559 911
Martinez, Reyes 472
Martínez, Rubén Berríos 1212
Martinez, Ruth E. 1263
Martinez, Vilma S. 912
Martinez Cruz, Rosa 115 824
895 982 1004
Mason, Bill 283
Mass, Bonnie 1213
Massey, Douglas S. 69 70 71
913 963 1214
Mathes, W. Michael 72 284 285
286 287
Mathews, Thomas 1215
Matter, Robert Allen 288
Mawn, Geoffrey P. 289 560
Mayer, Edward H. 451
Mazón, Mauricio 452
McBane, Margo 73
McBride, James D. 658
McCabe, Marsha 1216
McCain, Johnny M. 659
McCaughan, Ed 428
McCleskey, Clifton 914
McClure, Charles R. 290
McCoy, Terry L. 1217
McDivitt, Marilyn 1234
McDonald, Archie P. 291
McDowell, John H. 915
McGinty, Brian 292 293
McKay, Roberta V. 74
McKim, Judith L. 993 995
McLean, Malcolm D. 75 76
McLemore, S. Dale 916
McWatters, D. Lorne 77 226
McWilliams, Carey 78 917
McWilliams, Perry 453
Mead, Margaret 1218
Medeiros, Francine 660
Megenney, William W. 1219
Meinig, D. W. 506
Melville, Margarita B. 918
Méndez, José Luis 1220
Merrill, Bruce 914
Metzgar, Joseph V. 454 919 920
Metzler, William H. 455
Meyer, Doris L. 561 562 661
Meyer, Jean A. 456
Meyer, Larry L. 294 295
Meyer, Michael C. 413 438 523
Meyn, M. 1221
Miller, Darlis A. 563
Miller, David Harry 513
Miller, Janice Borton 296
Miller, Lawrence W. 921 1048
Miller, Michael V. 922 923 924
925
Miller, Robert Ryal 297
Min, Kyonghee 1119
Mindiola, Tatcho, Jr. 926
Mingo, John J. 1222
Mintz, Sidney 1223
Miranda, Gloria E. 298
Mirandé, Alfredo 927 928
Mirowsky, John 929
Mohl, Raymond A. 79 609 662
Mohr, Eugene V. 80 1224
Moles, Jerry A. 930
Monk, Janice J. 1225
Monroy, Douglas 663 664 665

Montemajor, Joaquin 787
Moore, Joan 931 946
Moorhead, Max L. 299 300
Mora, Magdalena 425 621 664
691 730 775 785 852 986
1027 1028 1035
Morales, Cecilio J., Jr. 81
Morales, Waltraud Queiser 1226
Morales del Valle, Zoraida 1297
1298
Morfi, Angelina 1227
Morrissey, Marietta 932
Moscoso, Margarita R. 1263
Moses, Robert J. 441
Mosher, W. D. 1228
Mount, Graeme S. 564 1229
Moynihan, Daniel Patrick 1230
Mozo, Rafael 1249
Mullan, Brendan P. 70
Muñoz, Carlos, Jr. 82 933 934
Murguia, Edward 419 935
Murray, Douglas L. 936
Mutti, John H. 828
Mutunhu, Tendai 302
Myres, Sandra L. 303 565

N

Naismith, Rachael 937
Nakadate, Neil 1054
Nalven, Joseph 938
Nanez, Alfredo 457
Napoli, Richard 1152
Narváez, Peter 458
Nasatir, Abraham P. 1231
Nash, Irwin 939
Navarro, Armando 459
Navarro García, Luis 304
Neggers, Gladys 1232
Neidert, Lisa 119 808
Neighbor, Howard D. 83
Nelson, Bardin H. 1013 1014
Nelson, Kathryn J. 460
Nelson, Verne E. 989 990
Nelson-Cisneros, Victor B. 666
667 668
Neri, Michael C. 305 566
Newman, Katherine D. 1323
Newman, Morris J. 84
Nichols, Nick 1233
Nobel, Barry 1234
Nofi, Albert A. 306
Nolan, James L. 307
Nostrand, Richard L. 461 506
507 567 568 940

O

Oates, Stephen B. 308
Oberly, James W. 309
O'Brien, David J. 811
O'Brien, Rita H. 310
O'Connor, Karen 941
Oczon, Annabelle M. 85 569
Okada, Yoshitaka 111
Olivas, Michael A. 86 1053
Oliveira, Annette 1235
Olsen, Stanley J. 311
Olson, James S. 87
O'Neill, Ynez Violé 312
Ornstein, Jacob 942
Oropeza, María Eugenia 880
Ortega, Adolfo 943
Ortega-DeSantis, Diana 462
Ortego, Philip D. 463
Ortiz, Alfonso 398

Ortiz, Florá Ida 944
Ortiz, Isidro D. 945
Ortiz, Roxanne Dunbar 313
Ortiz, Vilma 16 88 1270
Otheguy, Ricardo 89
Overman, Charles T. 1236

P

Pace, Anne 669
Pachon, Harry P. 946
Padilla, Felix M. 90
Padilla, Fernando V. 464 570 947
Padilla, Genaro M. 441
Page, J. Bryan 1237
Page, James K., Jr. 314
Pantojas García, Emilio 1238 1239
Paredes, Américo 465 466
Paredes, Raymund 315 571
Park, Joseph F. 572
Park, Roberta J. 573
Parker, Lourdes Travieso 1150
Parker, Robert A. 1088
Parra, Ricardo 467
Patrick, Elizabeth Nelson 316
Payne, Steven 317
Pearce, T. M. 318
Pearson, Fred Lamar, Jr. 319 320
Pedraza, Pedro, Jr. 1151
Pedraza-Bailey, Silvia 138 1240
Pena, Manuel H. 468
Peñalosa, Fernando 948
Penley, Larry E. 949
Percal, Raul Moncarz 1241
Perez, Arturo P. 950
Pérez, José G. 951
Pérez, Lisandro 138
Pérez, Louis A., Jr. 1242 1243
Perez de Jesús, Manuel 1244
Pérez Sala, Paulino 1319
Perrow, Charles 57
Peterson, Katherine Meyers 267
Peterson, Mark F. 1316
Peterson, Richard H. 574
Petrovich, Janice 1245
Petrow, Steven 731
Phillips, Diana Buder 753
Phillips, George Harwood 321
Pierce, Lorraine Esterly 469
Pilditch, Charles 1246
Pino, Frank 470 952
Pintó, Alfonso 670
Piore, Michael 91 140 142
Poiarkova, N. T. 1247
Pol, Louis G. 793
Polinard, Jerry L. 921
Polzer, Charles W. 322
Portales, Marco A. 953
Portes, Alejandro 92 954 955 956 957 1248 1249 1250 1318
Poston, Dudley L., Jr. 958
Poyo, Gerald E. 1251 1252
Pozzetta, George E. 1253
Primera, Joe C. 575
Provenzo, Eugene F., Jr. 1254
Puelles, José María de Jesús 230
Pullenza de Ortiz, Patricia 959
Pyle, David 471

Q

Quintana, Frances Leon 323
Quintero-Rivera, Angel G. 1255 1256

R

Rael, Juan B. 472
Ramirez, Carlos B. 464
Ramirez, Elizabeth C. 576
Ramírez, Rafael L. 1257 1258 1259 1260
Ramos, Reyes 960
Ranis, Peter 1261
Raymond, Richard D. 961
Redwine, Augustin 671
Reeve, Frank D. 324 325 326
Reich, Alice H. 962
Reichert, Joshua S. 963 964
Reid, Richard A. 93
Reilly, S. J. 1047
Reilly, Stephen Edward 327
Reilly, Tom 328
Reimers, Cordelia W. 94 95
Reinhardt, Karl J. 1055
Reisler, Mark 672 673
Reubens, Edwin P. 965
Reyna, José R. 473
Rice, G. Randolph 869
Richardson, Sister Jonathan 96
Richmond, Douglas W. 577 674
Riddell, Adaljiza Sosa 966 967
Riley, Carroll L. 329
Rindfuss, Ronald R. 1262
Rios, Victor 467
Ríos-Bustamante, Antonio José 97 330 506
Rivera, Julius 331
Rivera Quintero, Marcia 1149
Robe, Stanley L. 474
Roberts, Robert E. 886
Roberts, Shirley J. 475
Roberts, Virginia C. 578
Robinson, Warren C. 1129
Robinson, Willard B. 332
Robinson, William J. 333
Robles, Rafaela R. 1263
Rocard, Marcienne 476
Rocco, Raymond A. 477 968 969
Rochin, Refugio I. 970
Rock, Michael J. 334 579
Rock, Rosalind Z. 98
Rockett, Ian R. H. 99
Rodriguez, Clara 1264 1265 1266 1267
Rodríguez, J. 1221
Rodríguez, Jacobo 478
Rodriguez, Joe D. 1054
Rodriguez, Richard 1053
Roeder, Beatrice A. 100
Rogers, Richard G. 971 1008
Rogg, Eleanor 1268 1318
Rogler, Lloyd H. 1120 1269 1270 1271
Romero, Leo M. 972
Romo, Harriet 973
Romo, Ricardo 479 675 676
Rosales, Francisco A. 677 678
Roseberry, William 1272
Roseman, Marina 1273
Rosen, Gerald 974 975
Rosenberg, Terry Jean 1274 1275
Rosenwaike, Ira 1276
Ross, Catherine E. 929

Ross, Oliver D. 335
Ross, Steve 580
Rothenberg, Irene Fraser 480 976
Rott, Renate 101
Roucek, Joseph S. 102 977
Routté Gómez, Eneid 1277
Ruiz, Ramón Eduardo 103
Ruybalid, M. Keith 679

S

Sabagh, Georges 978 979
Sadler, Louis R. 638 639
Safa, Helen I. 1278 1279
Sainz Chávez, Luis 7
Salazar, Jaime G. 980
Salces, Luis M. 104
Saltzstein, Alan 842
San Miguel, Guadalupe, Jr. 680 981
Sanchez, Armand J. 481
Sánchez, Rosaura 115 482 824 895 982 983 984
Sánchez-Korrol, Virginia E. 1280
Santiago, Jaime 1281
Santos, Richard 105 336 483
Sapiens, Alexander 484
Saragoza, Alex M. 106
Sassen-Koob, Saskia 985 1282
Scanlan, John 1283
Scharf, Thomas L. 581
Schement, Jorge Reina 485
Schinek, Werner O. 850
Schlein, Lisa 986
Schlossman, Steven 987
Schmidt, Aurora 988
Schnabel, Kathleen 913 1214
Schoen, Robert 989 990
Scholes, France V. 337
Schroder, Edna 1120
Schuetz, Mardith 338
Schwartz, Francis 1284
Schwirian, Kent P. 1060
Scott, Judith 708
Scurlock, Dan 582
Sedano, Michael Victor 991
Segade, Gustavo V. 992
Sehgal, Ellen 107
Sena-Rivera, Jaime 108
Servín, Manuel P. 339 340 486
Sesnowitz, Michael 961
Shankman, Arnold 681
Shannon, Lyle W. 781 993 994 995
Shapiro, David 109
Sharma, M. Dutta 1285
Sharma, P. L. 1285
Shay, Anthony 341
Shearer, Derek 996
Sheridan, Thomas E. 583 682
Shields, Susan Walker 1011
Sifuentes, Roberto 683
Silkerstein, Fred B. 487
Silverman, David 651
Silverman, Joseph 342
Silvestrini de Pacheco, Blanca 110 1286
Simmons, Marc 343 344 345 398 506
Simon, Daniel T. 677 684
Simoniello, Katalina 997
Simson, Eve 998
Sinclair, John L. 346
Sizelove, Linda 347
Slatta, Richard W. 488 999 1000
Slesinger, Doris P. 111

Smallwood, James M. 516
Smardz, Zofia J. 1001
Smith, Andrew T. 63 348
Smith, Dean 349
Smith, Jeanne W. 848
Smith, Michael M. 685
Smith, Pamela 584
Smith, W. Elwood 489
Snipp, C. Matthew 1002 1003
Snow, Cordelia Thomas 350
Snow, David H. 323 351 490
Solis, Enrique, Jr. 787
Solís, Faustina 1004
Soto-Pérez, Héctor 491
Souza, Blase Camacho 1287
Sowell, Thomas 1057 1325
Spalding, Rose 112
Sperling, David 352
Spillman, Trish 353
Spohn, Cassia 839 1041
Standart, M. Colette 585
Steel, Thomas J. 492 586
Steffen, Jerome O. 513
Steiner, Stan 587
Steinman, Michael 1043
Stella, Tomás 1288
Stephen, Elizabeth H. 726
Stephens, Richard C. 429
Stevens, A. Jay 1005
Stevens, Joe B. 777
Stewart, Dennis 141
Stewart, Kenneth L. 527 528 588
Stinner, William F. 1063 1289
Stoddard, Ellwyn R. 113 114 493 1006 1007
Stoller, Marianne L. 354
Street, Richard Steven 494
Strout, Clevy Lloyd 355 356
Sullivan, Teresa A. 1008
Sunseri, Alvin R. 357 589
Surace, Samuel J. 495
Swadesh, Frances Leon 496
Sweeny, Judith 115
Swicegood, C. Gray 725 726
Szymanski, Albert 1290

T

Tafolla, Carmen 1009
Tan, Alexis S. 1010
Tanzer, Michael 1291
Tapia Méndez, Aureliano 358
Taylor, H. Darrel 374
Taylor, James R. 116
Taylor, Morris F. 590
Taylor, Patricia A. 1011
Taylor, Paul S. 686
Taylor, William B. 359
Teja Angeles, Ileana de la 7
Temply-Trujillo, Rita E. 1012
Teske, Raymond H. C., Jr. 1013 1014
Theisen, Lee Scott 591
Thernstrom, Abigail M. 117
Thomas, Darwin L. 1159
Thomas, Erwin K. 118
Thomas, Piri 1292
Thomas, Robert J. 805
Thompson, Bill 1218
Thompson, Mary Tittle 360
Tienda, Marta 119 120 121 1002 1003 1015 1016
Timmons, W. H. 361 362
Tjarks, Alicia V. 363

Tornero Tinajero, Pablo 364 365
Toro, Rafael de Jesús 1293
Torres, Esteban E. 1017
Torres, Luisa 497
Torrez, Robert J. 366
Tower, John 367
Trabold, Robert 1294
Trafzer, Clifford 592
Trafzer, Daniel 592
Travis, Paul 721
Treutlein, Theodore E. 368
Treviño, Jesús Salvador 498
Triplett, Timothy 1317
Trotter, Robert T., II 1018
Trudell, Clyde F. 369
Trulio, Beverly 593
Tucey, Mary 246
Turner, Justin G. 370
Turner, Kay F. 1019
Turner, Ralph H. 1020
Tyler, Daniel 371 372 373
Tyler, Ronnie C. 687
Tyler, S. Lyman 374

U

Ugalde, Antonio 1295
Ulibarri, George S. 375
Urrutia, Liliana 1021

V

Valdés, Guadalupe 1022
Valdes-Fallis, Guadalupe 1023
Valdez, Avelardo 923 1024
Valencia, Richard R. 1025 1026
Valenzuela, Nicholas 877
Valle, Rosemary Keupper 376
Valverde, Leonard A. 122
VanNess, John R. 63 377 594
VanOsdol, Scott 688
Vasquez-Calcarrada, Pablo B. 1080
Vaughan, David 782
Vázquez, José L. 1296
Vázquez, Mario F. 1027
Vázquez Calzada, José L. 1297 1298
Velázquez, René 1299
Velez-I., Carlos G. 1028
Venegas, Hernán 1170
Verdugo, Naomi Turner 1029
Verdugo, Richard R. 1029
Vialet, Joyce 107
Vigil, James Diego 931 1030
Vigil, Maurilio E. 123 1031 1032
Vigil, Ralph E. 378
Vigil, Ralph H. 379 499 689
Villalpando, Vic 1056
Villanueva, Tino 500
Villarreal, Roberto E. 1033
Vollmar, Edward R. 501

W

Wagner, Michael K. 1034
Wagner, Roland M. 481
Waldinger, Roger 1300
Waldman, Elizabeth 1035
Walker, Billy D. 380
Walter, John C. 1301
Wareing, J. 124
Warren, Alice E. Colón 1118

Warren, Nancy 398 1036
Watkins, T. H. 381
Watson, Thomas D. 382
Weaver, Jerry L. 1037 1038
Weber, David J. 125 126 164 191 212 235 303 304 344 383 384 385 386 395 396 508 595
Weber, Devra 127
Weber, Francis J. 387 388 389
Weber, Kenneth R. 502 1039
Weigert, Andrew J. 1159
Weigle, Martha 503
Weiss, Carol I. 1157
Weiss, Michael 596
Weisskoff, Richard 1302
Welch, Susan 128 839 1040 1041 1042 1043
Wells, Henry 1303
Wells, Miriam J. 1044
Wessman, James W. 1304 1305 1306
Westfall, Loy Glenn 129 1307
Whelan, Harold A. 597
White, Robert Rankin 598
Wilkinson, S. Kristina 390
Williams, Eric 1045
Williams, Herma B. 1045
Williams, J. Allen, Jr. 1046
Williams, Jack S. 391
Williams, James C. 599
Williams, Linda 504
Williams, Margaret Jean McClennan 392
Williams, P. M. 1047
Willie, Charles V. 1053
Wilson, Kax 393
Wilson, Kenneth L. 1308
Wilson, William Julius 130
Winegarden, Mary 73
Winsberg, Morton D. 1309 1310
Wittenburg, Mary Ste. Therese 600
Wolf, Eric R. 1311
Wolff, Edward 1302 1312
Wollenberg, Charles 690
Wong, Morrison G. 51
Woods, Richard D. 131
Worcester, Donald E. 394
Wrinkle, Robert D. 921 1048
Wroth, William 395 505

Y

Yanez, Elva Kocalis 132
Ybarra-Frausto, Tomás 1049
Young, Anne McDougall 133
Yurtinus, John F. 601

Z

Zamora, Emilio 691 692
Zapata, Carlos R. 1313
Zavella, Patricia 1050
Zelman, Donald L. 693
Zendegui, Guillermo de 1314
Zinn, Maxine Baca 134 135 1051
Zoraida Vázquez, Josefina 413 438 523
Zucker, Martin 1052
Zucker, Norman L. 136
Zunz, Olivier 137